ALSO BY KATHRYN HUGHES

George Eliot: The Last Victorian

George Eliot: Family History

The Victorian Governess

THE SHORT LIFE AND LONG TIMES OF

MRS. BEETON

Isabella Beeton née Mayson, aged nineteen,
in the iconic photograph
presented to the National Gallery.

THE SHORT LIFE AND LONG TIMES OF

MRS. BEETON

KATHRYN HUGHES

Alfred A. Knopf · New York · 2006

THIS IS A BORZOI BOOK
PUBLISHED BY ALFRED A. KNOPF

Copyright © 2005 by Kathryn Hughes

www.aaknopf.com

Originally published in Great Britain by Fourth Estate, an imprint of
HarperCollins Publishers, London, in 2005.

Library of Congress Cataloging-in-Publication Data

Hughes, Kathryn, [date].
The short life and long times of Mrs. Beeton / Kathryn Hughes.
p.   cm.
ISBN 0-307-26373-8
1. Beeton, Mrs. (Isabella Mary), 1836–1865. 2. Home economists—
Great Britain—Biography. 3. Home economics—England—History.
4. Cookery, English—History. I. Title.

TX140.B4H84 2006   640.92—dc22   [B]   2005044678

Manufactured in the United States of America
First American Edition

FOR MY PARENTS,

ANNE AND JOHN HUGHES

AGAIN, AGAIN

CONTENTS

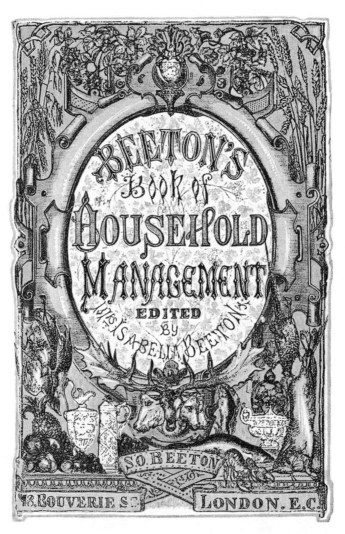

Title page of the Book of Household Management, *1861.*

ILLUSTRATIONS

The author and publishers would like to thank the following for kind permission to reproduce pictures. The National Portrait Gallery (1, 5, 6, 21), Camera Press Ltd. (2), Mary Rose Myrtle (3, 4, 12, 14, 15, 35), Mary Evans Picture Library (8, 11, 29, 30), The Tate (9), Bourne Hall Museum, Ewell (13, 17), Surrey History Service (17), Guildhall Library (19, 22), Joan Browne (34, 36, 37), Getty Images (16).

THE SHORT LIFE AND
LONG TIMES OF
MRS. BEETON

Newmarket, 21 July 1857

My Dear Mrs. Beeton

I see difficulties in your way as regards Publishing a Book on Cookery. Cookery is a Science that is only learnt by Long Experience and years of study which of course you have not had.

Yours v. sincerely

HENRIETTA ENGLISH

Grace [housekeeper] yesterday was looking out of the window at Cecil Beaton walking in the garden. I asked her if she knew who he was. When I told her it was Cecil Beaton, she said, "He's the cook, isn't he?" Not exactly, I replied, but a famous photographer. "But he cooks too," she said. I don't suppose Cecil can boil an egg. She is a goose.

JAMES LEES-MILNE, Diary, 7 July 1972

A TUB-LIKE LADY IN BLACK

ON BOXING DAY 1932 the National Portrait Gallery opened an exhibition of its new acquisitions to the public. There were twenty-three likenesses on display, all of which were to be added to the nation's permanent portrait collection of the great and the good. Cecil Rhodes, "South African Statesman, Imperialist and millionaire" was one of the new arrivals, as was the Marquis of Curzon, who had until recently been Conservative Foreign Secretary. By way of political balance there was also a portrait of James Keir Hardie, the first leader of the Labour Party in the House of Commons, and a replica of Winterhalter's magnificent portrait of the Duchess of Kent, Queen Victoria's mother. Oddly out of place amongst the confident new arrivals, all oily swirls, ermine and purposeful stares, was a small hand-tinted photograph of a young woman dressed in the fashion of nearly a hundred years ago. She had a heavy helmet of dark hair, a veritable fuss of brooch, handkerchief, neck chain and shawl, and the fixed expression of someone who has been told they must not move for fear of ruining everything. The caption beneath her announced that here was "Isabella Mary Mayson, Mrs. Beeton (1836–65)," journalist and author of the famous *Book of Household Management*.

By the time the first members of the public filed past the photograph of Mrs. Beeton on Boxing Day, her biographical details had already changed several times. Sir Mayson Beeton, who had presented the photograph of his mother to the nation nine months earlier, had insisted on an exhausting number of tweaks and fiddles to the outline of her life that would be held on record by the Gallery. Even so, Beeton was still disappointed when he attended the exhibition's private view a few days before Christmas. Particularly vexing was the way that the text beneath his mother's photograph described her as "a journalist." Beeton immediately fired off a letter to the curator G. K. Adams suggesting that the wording should be altered to "Wife of S O Beeton, editor-publisher, with whom she worked and with the help of whose editorial guidance and inspiration she wrote her famous BOOK OF HOUSEHOLD MANAGEMENT devoting to it 'four years of incessant labour' 1857–1861"—a huge amount of material to cram onto a little card. The reason Sir Mayson wanted this change, explained G. K. Adams wearily to his boss H. M. Hake, Director of the Gallery, was that "he said his father was an industrious publisher with a pioneer mind, who edited all his own publications, and but for him it is extremely unlikely that Mrs. Beeton would have done any writing at all."

Mayson Beeton, whose birth had been the occasion of his mother's death, was by now sixty-seven and getting particular in his ways. Even so, he had every reason to fuss over exactly how his parents were posthumously presented to the nation. Over the decades since their deaths Isabella and Samuel Beeton had all but disappeared from public consciousness. Beeton's *Book of Household Management* was in everyone's kitchen, of course, either as a newish wedding present or a handed-down heirloom to be consulted sporadically when you wanted to know how to get grease stains out of ribbons or the best way to make rice pudding. However, most people, if they bothered to think about Mrs. Beeton at all, assumed that she was a made-up person, a publisher's ploy rather than an actual woman who had once lived, cooked and kept house.

Part of the reason why so many Britons assumed that Mrs. Beeton must be a confection was the way she appeared to be able to refresh and update herself apparently at will. In the first major revision of her book in 1869, she included a new section on that latest bit of household technology, ice cream makers. By the 1880s she was puffing gas cookers. In 1906 she was setting the table with exactly the kind of fussy, luxurious detail that was just right for the newly lavish Edwardian period and during the inter-war period she was busy worrying about the effects on the middle-class household of the world-wide economic slump. Just as the fictional Betty Crocker was to be visually re-imagined by the Washburn Crosby Company (later named General Mills) throughout the twentieth century, first as a housewife, then as a career girl and most recently as a woman of indeterminate ethnic and social background so, on the other side of the Atlantic, Mrs. Beeton's text was tweaked to make her sound exactly right for each succeeding decade. Even though the tone of her voice remained the same—middle-aged, knowledgeable, tetchy about falling standards in modern housekeeping—the advice she gave was uncannily contemporary. This alone suggested that "Mrs. Beeton" must be nothing more than a convenient nom de plume behind which huddled a team of anonymous domestic science writers employed to keep the brand ever-green.

But now, here, in the deep mid-winter of 1932, came the incontrovertible evidence that, unlike Betty Crocker, Mrs. Beeton was a real, historic person who had indeed published the *Book of Household Management* in 1861 before dying just four years later at the age of only twenty-eight. Where Mrs. Beeton did, however, resemble Betty Crocker was the way in which her persona was embedded in that long tradition of printed housekeeping manuals in which a female authority—apparently a middle-aged domestically experienced woman—passed on her wisdom to readers who were presumed to be younger and less practised home-makers. As a result any U.S. reader coming to Mrs. Beeton's original *Book of Household Management* for the first time will find much that is familiar from near-contemporary American titles such as Lydia Maria Child's *American Frugal Housewife* or Julia McNair Wright's *The Complete Home*, through to the later Fanny Farmer's *The Boston Cooking School Book* and, ultimately, to Irma Rombauer's early twentieth century classic *The Joy of Cooking*.

While lacking the specifically religious or even moral slant of Child's or Wright's texts, Mrs. Beeton's main aim is nonetheless to coach the lower half of the new urban middle class in the idea that thrift and elegance, far from being mutually incompatible, are in fact soldered together. Thus the emphasis throughout the *Book of Household Management* is on avoiding the kind of splashy show which is not only financially ruinous but socially vulgar. Readers are instructed on exactly how many servants their annual income will allow, while recipes are carefully costed, and weekly menu plans designed to make the most of left-overs. While there are plenty of nods to high living—instructions on how to hire a footman or prepare a picnic for sixty people—the real heartland of Beeton's readership remains that of a modest family, struggling to keep up the newly genteel style of living required of the middle class on an income that is often actually not much higher than that of a skilled labouring man.

Grafted onto the kind of advice that would have been familiar to readers of Child or Wright—shop seasonally, keep rigorous accounts, never be tempted to over-dress—there is a strain of thought in the *Book of Household Management* that does not appear in U.S. advice books until the early years of the twentieth century. For Beeton's ideal household is also a scientific one, run according to the latest findings in biology, chemistry, physics and much more. Foods are analysed for their nutritional values, developments in canning are welcomed and the time-and-motion efficiencies of the factory are applied to making beds or bread.

This apparent precocity in comparison with American titles such as Maria Parloa's *Home Economics: A Guide to Household Management* (1898) or Marion Talbot's *The Modern Household* (1912) is explained, of course, by the fact that Britain's Industrial Revolution was all but complete by 1830 and its middle classes were far more urbanised by the mid-nineteenth century than the still-predominately agricultural America. The fact that Isabella Beeton was writing from a position fairly far along in the development of a capitalised economy also explains why she assumes that her readers are living in houses far removed from the places where men's work is carried on—the shop, factory or office. By the late 1850s British women from even the lower middle classes were exclusively confined to the domestic sphere, forbidden from engaging in profit-making activities on pain of irrevocably losing caste. It is for this reason that Beeton spends so much time trying to convince her readers to over-come their prejudices and accept that household management is a socially and economically crucial activity, as skilled and deserving of respect as any job carried out by men.

This mix of minute realism and softening fantasy evidently hit the right note with a whole swathe of the middle class households, since the *Book of Household Management* did very well right from the moment of its publication. It was reputed to have sold 60,000 copies in its first year (there is no way of knowing this is the case—Sam Beeton, like all mid-Victorian publishers, tended to inflate his sales figures) and by the time of Isabella's death in 1865 the figure touted was in the millions, although this almost certainly included sales of various abridgements such as *The Englishwoman's Everyday Cookery Book*. It was, however, in the years following Isabella Beeton's death that her masterwork really began to achieve the status and profitability of a legend. Each succeeding update, at first supervised by Sam and then by the publishers Ward, Lock, nudged *Mrs. Beeton* further into the limelight until by 1880 there was no-one to touch her. Rival publishers, naturally, attempted to bring out copycats, but *Mrs. Beeton*'s head start meant that there was never much chance of anyone catching up. By 1906, when the new edition of *Mrs. Beeton,* this time saturated with all the extravagance and vulgarity of the Edwardian age, hit the market, she was selling hundreds of thousands of copies every year. Many of these were destined to be carried away to the four quarters of Britain's vast Empire, where the name "Mrs. Beeton" became as swiftly embedded in the domestic culture of Australia, Canada and India as it did in the motherland itself. From this high point *Mrs. Beeton* sailed triumphantly onwards through the twentieth century, consolidating her name as a synonym for encyclopaedic domestic know-how, one that needed neither introduction nor explanation.

DURING THE TEN YEARS PRECEDING the gifting of his mother's photograph to the nation, Mayson Beeton had become obsessed with getting the presentation of Isabella and Sam Beeton just right. Only the previous year an article had appeared in the *Manchester Guardian* that managed to muddle Mrs. Beeton up with Eliza Acton, a cookery writer from a slightly earlier period. Beeton's inevitable letter pointing out the error was duly published, and from these small beginnings interest in the real identity and history of Mrs. Beeton had begun to bubble. In February 1932 Florence White, an authority on British food, had written a gushy piece in *The Times* entitled "The Real Mrs. Beeton" which drew on information provided by Sir Mayson to paint a picture of a "lovely girl" who enjoyed the advantages of "YOUTH, BEAUTY, AND BRAINS." Mrs. Beeton, it transpired, was a real person—albeit a rather two dimensional one—after all.

H. M. Hake had happened to read White's piece in *The Times* and was struck by her reference to the family owning "portraits" of Mrs. Beeton and wondered if there might be something suitable to hang in the NPG. The answer, when it came back, was disappointing. There was no portrait of Mrs. Beeton, just a black and white albumen print, taken by one of the first generation of High Street photographers, probably early in the early Summer of 1855 when she was nineteen years old. All the same, after a consultative meeting on the 7th April 1932 the trustees decided that they were prepared to accept, for the first time in their history, a photographic portrait to hang among their splendid oils and marble busts.

That the trustees of the National Portrait Gallery decided to hang Mrs.

Beeton on their walls at all says something about changing attitudes to the recent past. During the twenty-five years following the old Queen's death, the Victorians had seemed like the sort of people to run a mile from. Indeed, White's article in *The Times* had begun "Mrs. Beeton lived in the Victorian era, which, as every one under thirty knows, was dismally frumpish." It was lovely to be free of that mutton-chopped certainty, hideous building, starchy protocol and, of course, endless suet pudding. But as the years went by, what had once seemed oppressively close now became intriguingly quaint and people began to wonder about the names and faces that had formed the background chatter to their childhood. When Hake had written to the assistant editor of *The Times* asking to be put in contact with the Beeton family, he explained why he thought the time might be right for the NPG to acquire a portrait of Mrs. Beeton. "Recently we were bequeathed a portrait of Bradshaw, the originator of the Railway Guide, and I think that Mrs. Beeton is at least a parallel case."

Mayson Beeton would not have been pleased to hear Hake casually lumping his mother into a category of kitsch, brand-name Victorians. But then, he had never quite realised how lucky it was that some years previously Lytton Strachey, that arch pricker of Victorian pomposity, had abandoned his attempt to write a biography of Mrs. Beeton. Strachey had been apt to tell friends that he imagined Mrs. Beeton as "a small tub-like lady in black—rather severe of aspect, strongly resembling Queen Victoria," which sounds as if he was lining her up for the kind of robust debunking delivered to Florence Nightingale and others in his *Eminent Victorians* of 1918. In the end Strachey had given up on his plans to write about Mrs. Beeton because he could not find enough material, a continuing lack that explains why there have been so few biographies in total, and none at all since 1977.

Part of this absence is the result of the way that details about Mrs. Beeton's death—and hence her life—were suppressed almost from the moment she drew her last breath in 1865. In order to protect their investment in the growing *Mrs. Beeton* brand it made sense first for her widower Sam and then for Ward, Lock, the publishers who acquired his copyrights in 1866, to let readers think that the lady herself was alive, well and busy testing recipes to go into the endless editions of her monumental work that were beginning to proliferate in the marketplace. For by 1880, with cut-down versions of the original book such as *Mrs. Beeton's*

Shilling Cookery, Mrs. Beeton's Everyday Cookery and *Mrs. Beeton's Cottage Cookery* doing terrific business, *Mrs. Beeton* had become the kind of goose whose eggs were solid gold. The emphasis now was on keeping her alive for as long as possible.

On top of this intentional censorship, the circumstances of Mrs. Beeton's life had managed to keep her hidden from history. She was only twenty-eight when she died, which meant fewer letters written, fewer diaries kept and fewer photographs taken (the NPG picture is one of only two surviving adult portraits). After her death in 1865 the simmering tensions between her family, the Dorlings, and her widower flared into open warfare, and Sam broke off contact with her vast brood of siblings. This naturally stalled the flow of anecdotes, ephemera and memories about Isabella around her vast clan, and simultaneously created the conditions for rumour and innuendo to flourish, especially about what had actually happened during her nine year marriage. Brought up after Sam's death twelve years later by people who had never known Isabella, the two surviving children of the marriage, Mayson and his slightly elder brother Orchart, were left with only a small heap of fragments from which to reconstruct a mother they had never really met. There were forty or so love letters written between Sam and Isabella during their engagement in 1856, a couple of holiday diaries kept by Isabella from the 1860s, the increasingly iconic photograph now hanging in the NPG, and that was about it. In these circumstances, half-contrived and half-chance, Mrs. Beeton had slipped straight from life into myth.

So by 1932, and after decades of foggy indifference, the public was ready to be intrigued by the revelation that Mrs. Beeton, whose name they knew so well, had indeed been a living, breathing person. In a slow week for news, the presentation of the little photograph to the public had provoked a gratifying amount of press coverage, all of which Mayson Beeton hungrily collected for the slight family archive. One writer set the approving mood when he declared "Mrs. Beeton, it will be generally agreed, is the most famous English authoress who ever lived . . . Other popular authoresses . . . appear and disappear; but Mrs. Beeton has achieved the deathlessness of a classic as well as the circulation of a best-seller."

Other journalists followed this lead, waxing lyrical about a woman they had not bothered to think much about before, but were now happy to declare "the Confucius of the kitchen, the benefactress of a million homes." The man from the *Mirror* made a careful distinction between

Mrs. Beeton as an exponent of proper "womanly" ways as opposed to all the " 'feminists' in the NPG, the suffragette, the actress and the long-distance flyer." The *Evening News,* meanwhile, made the shrewd suggestion that part of this sudden interest in Mrs. Beeton might be the fact that she spoke from a by-gone world when "homes were homes, when cooks were cooks and above all when incomes were incomes and not illusory sums of money in uneasy transit from the pocket of trade and industry to that of the State." For by 1932, and with Britain mired in economic depression, political uncertainty and social unrest, it was easy to feel wistful for a time when middle-class households could afford to keep a full complement of domestic staff, none of whom would think of answering back.

The one point that all the commentators did agree upon was that the Mrs. Beeton who stared down at them from the walls of the National Portrait Gallery was light years away from the Queen Victoria look-alike that they, along with Mr. Strachey, had fondly imagined. The photograph was reproduced in countless newspaper articles, and even went on sale in August of 1933 as a postcard in the National Portrait Gallery's shop, where it quickly established itself as the third most popular portrait in the whole collection, after Rupert Brooke and Emma Hamilton. From being a virtually effaced person, "Mrs. Beeton" started to become one of the most widely recognised images circulating in British print culture.

There was something about the enigmatic young woman in the photograph that encouraged all kinds of speculations and projections. The critic from the *Daily Express* suggested that from Mrs. Beeton's body language it looked as if her cook had left the room a minute earlier (she didn't have one), while another referred to her as effortlessly "patrician," which she most certainly was not. The *Express* again mentioned "the firmness of the mouth" while someone else talked about her "gentle" face. The *Guardian* said it was reassuring to notice she was plump, while another paper mentioned her elegant slenderness. The *Mail,* in the strangest flight of fancy, suggested that "it is perhaps fortunate that she lived in a pre-Hollywood age, otherwise her undoubted charm might have borne her away on the wings of a contract."

FOUR YEARS LATER, and with the looming centenary of Mrs. Beeton's birth in 1836 provoking another wave of public interest, Mayson Beeton wrote an article entitled "How Mrs. Beeton wrote her famous book" for the *Daily Mail*, the paper for which he had worked as an administrator for so much of his career. The title was telling: Beeton's driving concern was to rescue his father's professional reputation from the long shadow cast by his mother's spectacular achievement. Its original name, after all, had been *Beeton's Book of Household Management* and there was no doubt about which Beeton was being referred to. Hence, in Mayson Beeton's re-telling of the story to *Daily Mail* readers, "Samuel Orchart Beeton was the successful young publisher who at the age of twenty-one took Fleet Street by storm" while Isabella was the "apt pupil" who gradually learned how to produce articles for his array of publications.

Such bias aside, a gratifyingly large number of letters arrived at High Lands, Beeton's Surrey villa, in response to the piece in the *Mail*. One was from an Old Marlburian who had been at school with Beeton over fifty years previously expressing mild surprise that "Curiously enough I never connected the book with you," voicing a common elision between the flesh-and-blood "Mrs. Beeton" and the one that was made out of one thousand pages of closely printed paper and handsome calf binding. An elderly gentleman wrote with fond memories of "messing" with Mrs. Beeton's recipes during his childhood in the '60s. A British woman wrote from Paris meanwhile to say that as a young bride her New Zealander husband had presented her with a "Mrs. Beeton" in recognition of the fact that his parents had relied on it during some tough years in a lonely sheep station.

To all of these correspondents Mayson Beeton dutifully responded. "Wrote a chatty letter" "replied with thanks" is regularly written in pencil across the top of incoming mail. To those who asked for it, he enclosed a copy of the National Portrait Gallery postcard. And, such being the good manners of the day, the recipients inevitably wrote back thanking him for his kindness and complimenting him on his mother's "beautiful," "charming," "kind," "sweet," "romantic" and, above all, "Victorian" face. To those correspondents who wrote offering photographs and recollections of his parents' extended families Beeton was especially warm, inviting them to "run down" to High Lands for a visit. For by now Beeton had decided that the time was right for him to write a proper "memoir" of his parents and he needed all the extra material he could scavenge if he was to produce something that would stretch to the length of at least a small book.

There was never any doubt in Beeton's mind about who was going to write the biography of his parents. Although the documentary evidence in his possession was, on his own admission, "scanty," he knew there were still plenty of awkward stories and embarrassing rumours about his parents' life at large that would need to be deftly despatched. These would need careful handling, and Beeton had no intention of letting an outsider clamber over the project, leaking secrets in the process. He had already had to deal with one particularly annoying young woman called Joan Adeney Easdale, who seemed determined to write a biography of Mrs. Beeton, with or without his approval. In the many letters Beeton fired off to radio producers and magazine editors in the mid-1930s urging them to have nothing to do with Miss Easdale's work, he always returns to the fact it is his parents' "<u>private family life</u>" (the underlining is his) that he is determined to protect from the impertinent and uncomprehending gaze of strangers.

With Miss Easdale's cautionary example in mind, Mayson Beeton dealt particularly firmly with the steady stream of lady writers who contacted him in the wake of the 1936 *Daily Mail* article asking for his blessing on their intention to put together a biography of his mother. To correspondents such as Winifred Valentine (Mrs.), Mrs. Sheriff Holt and Mary Stollard (Miss), Beeton wrote back stiffly, discouraging any hope that he might be about to turn his precious cache of material over to them. If they wished to publish a short biographical article on Mrs. Beeton in *The Woman's Magazine* or the *Lady* or *The Nursing Times* he would not stop them, but he asked that they submit a proof to him first. Quite sensibly they did not, which meant that Beeton was then able to work himself up into a delicious frenzy when their chatty, anodyne pieces finally appeared. "Full of Inaccuracies!" is scrawled across the top of pieces that, notwithstanding his contempt, have been pasted on to stiff card and carefully dated for posterity.

To those male, and on the whole better known, authors who wrote sounding Beeton out about the possibility of taking on his mother's biography, he tended to take a more gentlemanly tone. Responding to the professional biographer Osbert Burdett who had made contact in April 1936, Beeton explained that he was planning to do the job himself. In addition he also told Burdett what he does not seem to have told any of his lady correspondents, that he was going to be using a collaborator. Although Beeton had started his working life in magazine journalism, by the age of thirty-five he had shifted into management. It was years since he had done any writing and the *Daily Mail* piece had proved an arduous task. In any case, he was now seventy years old and needed someone to do the footslogging in the central London libraries that was increasingly beyond him.

What Beeton needed above all was someone who could be relied upon to be discreet. There were things in his parents' story that he was determined should not be put before the public, and he had to be certain that the person he worked with understood this. The chosen candidate also needed to realise that a key purpose of this "memoir" was to rescue Samuel Beeton's professional legacy from the long shadow cast over it by his wife's flukish achievement. Which is why Sir Mayson's choice of collaborator fell upon a young man who was actually related to him through his paternal, that is Beeton, line. Harford Montgomery Hyde was a thirty-year-old barrister and professional writer whose great-aunt had been married to Samuel Beeton's second cousin and whom Sir Mayson had known since he was a boy. Hyde had already published a couple of books since leaving Oxford where, like Beeton, he had been at Magdalen. But, most important of all, he had a reputation for a tenacious yet discreet approach to research: "Montgomery the Mole" would become his nickname in War-time intelligence "because I had the reputation of burrowing away among historical documents and discovering other people's secrets."

Through the late '30s Hyde went on "prospecting operations" for Sir Mayson, wading through administrative and legal records in Guildhall and Chancery to see if he could uncover any official information to supplement the family documents stored by Beeton in a series of japanned boxes at High Lands. No start, however, seems to have been made on the actual writing of the book and, just when things might really have got going, the War changed everything. Hyde went to the U.S. where he worked in counter-espionage, and Beeton shifted his focus from family matters to national ones. The last War had been his finest hour, with his work for the Finance Department of the Ministry of Munitions responsible for netting him a knighthood in 1920. That sort of active public role may have been beyond him now, but Beeton was still determined to be useful, and much of 1941 was spent arranging for his vast archive of antiquarian maps and topographical prints to be transferred to the Ministry of Works and Buildings, now temporarily housed in Oxfordshire. Even so, letters Beeton wrote at this time make it clear that he was still fully intending to write his parents' "memoir." However when Lady Beeton died two years later after fifty years of happy marriage, the old man found himself emotionally winded and suddenly frail. For the first time in his life he was ready to consider passing over the custodianship of his parents' reviving reputation to someone else.

Beeton's utterly misguided choice fell upon a young female writer called Nancy Spain. Spain was to become famous in the 1950s as one of Britain's first media personalities, writing punchy opinion pieces for middle-brow papers, and appearing on both radio and its skittish younger sister, television. Spain, a flamboyantly butch lesbian in an era that did not care to enquire too deeply into such matters, became an instantly recognisable crop-haired, trouser-wearing figure in middle Britain's landscape, until at the age of forty-six she died in a plane crash on the way to the Grand National with her female lover. All this was in the future, though, when, in 1945, Mayson Beeton asked the recently discharged WRNS officer down to High Lands. Spain had already had some success with her first book, a chatty recollection of her War-time Navy service called *Thank You Nelson.* More significantly, as far as Beeton was concerned, she had a blood connection with the family, although this time on his mother's side. Spain's grandmother, the recently deceased Lucy Smiles, had been one of Isabella Beeton's favourite half-sisters.

Given that one of the driving forces of Mayson Beeton's biographical ambitions had been to rescue his father's reputation from the slow drip of innuendo that had originated from his mother's family over the previous eighty years, it does seem odd that he should have blithely handed over the project to a Dorling descendant at this late stage. Even Spain was surprised, declaring later in her autobiography "To this day I don't know why he had picked me out of all the world." Perhaps a certain amount of contact between the Dorlings and the Beetons since the end of the Great War had made him believe that the rift was finally healed. Maybe Lucy Smiles' gently anodyne contributions to *The Times* and the *Star* in 1932 recalling her lovely elder half-sister and dynamic brother-in-law reassured him that this particular vertical line of his mother's family was benign to the Beetons. Perhaps Spain, at twenty-eight, seemed so young to the old man that it was impossible to believe that she would want to carry on a feud that had started nearly a century previously. Her mother had been at Roedean with Mayson Beeton's daughters and she herself had followed them there. Give or take her penchant for flannel trousers, she looked and sounded like one of the family. So Spain was duly invited to "run down" to High Lands, and work her way through Mayson Beeton's collection of his parents' love letters, Isabella's diaries and other ephemera which was now bulked out by all the articles that had appeared on Mrs. Beeton over the previous ten years.

What Beeton had missed entirely was that the wildly ambitious Spain was looking to make a splash. And since she was also an incorrigible spendthrift, she needed to make money too (not for nothing was her 1956 autobiography titled *Why I'm Not a Millionaire*). Spain was far less of a scholar than Hyde, and her writing on Mrs. Beeton is spattered with factual errors. Yet if Spain was sloppy over detail, she had a sharp nose for where the real drama of the Beeton story lay. Armed with a rich store of information from her late grandmother and a sole surviving great-aunt, she set about writing an account that managed to suggest, without exactly saying so, that Mrs. Beeton's homelife was not quite the model of well-regulated domesticity that the nation fondly imagined.

IN THE CIRCUMSTANCES it was probably lucky that Sir Mayson died before Spain's book appeared. Having grudgingly approved Spain's effort, the Beeton girls lost no time in putting pressure on Harford Montgomery Hyde, now finally free of war-time duties, to revive the biography on which he had been working with their father in the '30s. Four years later, *Mr. and Mrs. Beeton* duly appeared, bearing all the signs of being the book that Mayson Beeton would have wished to write, had he not run out of time. As if to emphasise that this really was the "authorised" version of the Beeton story, Hyde included the Preface that Sir Mayson had originally written for the book back in 1936 and also appended a biographical essay sketching out Sir Mayson's distinguished career. Whatever "Montgomery the Mole" had managed to find out about Mr. and Mrs. Beeton's "private family life" he was sufficiently loyal to his kinsman's memory not to reveal it.

And there the story might have ended, with two competing versions of the Beeton story, one originating from either side of the family, glaring at each other down the remaining decades of the twentieth century. On Mayson Beeton's death in 1947 the archive of letters and ephemera that had formed the nucleus of both biographies was left to his only grandchild Rodney Levick on condition that the young man incorporate the

Beeton family name into his. Levick, an eccentric man, lived in Budleigh Salterton, Devonshire, for the next fifty years on his grandfather's capital, writing periodically to the national newspapers to announce that he had devised a method of long-range weather forecasting far in advance of anything the Met Office could manage. He also took to riding his tricycle around Britain, dropping in unannounced on distant cousins from both the Beeton and Dorling sides and staying far too long. On returning to the home that he shared with his widowed mother Audrey Levick and a tribe of stuffed penguins (his father had been the surgeon on Scott's final Antarctic trek), Levick would dispatch tapes of classical music to his relieved hosts. Followed shortly, much to their astonishment, by an invoice.

From the late 1940s to the mid-1970s very few people beat a path to Budleigh Salterton to talk to the Levicks about Mrs. Beeton or try and coax access to the archive. The Victorians were under-going one of their periodic falls from favour. Increasing social and sexual post-War freedoms made them seem like the stuffy architects of everything that was now, finally, being swept away. The end of rationing had set the stage for Elizabeth David's lyrical advocacy of the fresh, sharp flavours of sunshiny Southern Europe. There was virtually no appetite for Mrs. Beeton, a woman whose very name seemed synonymous with roast beef, over-cooked vegetables and foggy winter evenings.

But by the early 1970s nostalgia was back in fashion. Laura Ashley was reworking Victorianism in a pretty print frock, *Upstairs, Downstairs* was on the television (and surely it was no coincidence that the cook was another Mrs. B—Mrs. Bridges), and there was the beginning of a revival of interest in the vernacular tastes of Great Britain (there was only so much packet paella that anyone could be expected to eat). A clever young woman at *Harpers & Queen* magazine, who combined the job of arts editor with an interest in food and cooking, had noticed the shift in mood. Moreover, she was intrigued by the little known fact that *The Queen* magazine, which was one half of *Harpers & Queen,* had been founded by Samuel Beeton in 1861 and counted none other than Mrs. Beeton as its first fashion editor. Searching around for a good subject for her first book, Sarah Freeman duly advertised in *The Times* in 1974 trawling for information about the Beeton archive.

The Levicks answered Freeman's advertisement and were doubtless delighted to find such an eligible person was once again interested in their family. Nonetheless, the elderly mother and son were not about to hand-over control of the Beeton legacy. Mrs. Freeman would be allowed to take away selected material to look at in batches, and these loans would be carefully logged in and out by Rodney, writing in pencil on Sir Mayson's original archive index. But in return she must undertake to skate over those parts of the story that were potentially embarrassing and which Nancy Spain had gone on to hint at even more strongly in a revised edition of her book published in 1956. As if to reinforce the fact that this is the version of Isabella Beeton's life that Sir Mayson had wished presented to the world, Freeman's book, which was published in 1977, comes with a baton-passing preface from none other than the now elderly Montgomery Hyde.

Nearly thirty years have passed since Freeman's book. History, if not exactly the Victorians, is once again in fashion. New technologies have revolutionised—the word really is not too strong—access to archival sources. There are fresh ways of thinking about the importance of book history (and this, as much as biography, is the discipline that presses most closely on Mrs. Beeton's story). Cooking and eating practices are no longer simply the concern of domestic science teachers but stand full square in our attempts to understand how people lived and traded a century or three ago. We know more than ever about what the Victorians wrote about their domestic lives, what they felt about them and, most importantly, the gap that lay between.

But it is not simply changing contexts that make Mrs. Beeton ripe for a new biography. In the late 1990s bits of the Mayson Beeton archive began to appear for sale in auction houses. It is difficult to track the exact pathways by which this material, once so closely guarded, came on to the market, but it seems to have been the consequence of the fact that Rodney Levick was now elderly, insane and in need of expensive residential accommodation. What can be said for certain is that by 2000, the year after Levick's death, the Mayson Beeton archive had been dispersed into several different hands. In 2002, after two years of sleuthing and negotiating, I managed to buy or borrow virtually all the important pieces of the archive and reassemble it once again. The important difference is that, this time, there are no restrictions on what may be done with the material.

As its title suggests, this book has attempted two distinct tasks. On the one hand it is a straightforward reconstruction of the known facts of

Mrs. Beeton's life. By going deep into the public archives, and working through registers and rate books, it has been possible to find out a great deal more about the girl who was born Isabella Mary Mayson in 1836 and who, by flukish chance, became one of the most famous women in history. What is more, as the first biographer who has had unfettered access to Beeton's letters and diaries, I hope I have managed to get closer than before to her interior life.

The second point of this book is to explore the way that, almost from the moment of her death at the age of twenty-eight in 1865, the idea of "Mrs. Beeton" became a potent commercial and cultural force. Detached from her mortal body, the ghostly Mrs. Beeton could be appropriated for a whole range of purposes. In the 140 years since she died she has been turned into the subject of a musical and several plays. She was once almost on Broadway. Over the last decade in Britain she has been used to sell every kind of foodstuff from Cornish pasties to strawberry jam. Every October images from her famous book are turned into best-selling Christmas cards. At time of writing you can take your pick from *Mrs. Beeton's Cookery in Colour, Tea with Mrs. Beeton* and *Mrs. Beeton's Healthy Eating* (although this is nothing compared with *Mrs. Beeton's Caribbean Cookery* and *Microwaving with Mrs. Beeton* from a couple of decades ago). The image of her face—that calm/stern/fat/thin face—has been worked into tea towels and stamped on table mats. You can even buy an apron adorned with Mrs. Beeton's likeness in which to wrap yourself like a second skin, in the hope perhaps that her qualities—whatever they might be exactly—will rub off. For if Mrs. Beeton is still to be remembered in another 150 years' time it will not be for writing the *Book of Household Management,* a book that surely very few people have read right through, but rather for holding up a mirror to our most intimate needs and desires. By representing "Home"—the place we go to be loved and fed—Mrs. Beeton has become part of the fabric of who we feel ourselves to be.

This desire to retreat to a safe space, a place outside the public and political order (or disorder), has never been so urgent than during the first few years of this new century. On both sides of the Atlantic the television schedules are saturated with programmes explaining how to tinker and freshen our experience of everyday living. There are whole channels showing how to make-over your sitting room, throw a dinner party, clear out your junk or re-do your garden. Just as the mid-Victorians imagined the middle-class home as a refuge from the perils of capitalism, with all its jostling competition and sudden threats, so 150 years later we have retreated from the terror of the world beyond our front door to a small pocket of space where we assume the consoling powers of gods.

Yet for all the mid-Victorians talked of "separate spheres," placing a firm boundary between the rowdy male world of getting and doing and the female domain of living and being, the trade between the two remained essential and brisk. From the 1850s a steady stream of goods designed to make a statement about the mistress's taste and the master's income passed over the threshold: carpets from China, crockery from Staffordshire and tableware from Sheffield might seem like nothing more than the embedded and invisible flotsam of private living, but they were also sending urgent messages concerning the household's income and status. And as more and more goods became available on the market, the choices the mistress made about how to furnish her house became increasingly crucial in determining not just its financial worth but something altogether more intangible—its style, its class.

This burden of choice—the worry about what your sofa says about you—remains an oppressive force in American and British middle-class culture today. Ironically, the range of manufactured goods available has become so over-whelming (and yet, in some essential way so same and safe) that we are currently seeing a revival of interest in craft skills. Consumers who could well afford to buy a quilt for their bed from the Ralph Lauren Homeware Collection are learning how to do patchwork. Martha Stewart, meanwhile, instructs a constituency made up of bankers and doctors as well as full-time homemakers how to make their own Christmas wreaths. All kinds of lost or degraded domestic skills—from knitting to fretwork, cooking to dress-making—are being re-discovered by a generation used to being able to order up anything it wants at the click of a computer mouse.

It is this hand-made world which was already on the point of disappearing in the late 1850s when Mrs. Beeton sat down to write her *Book of Household Management*. On the one hand Beeton was a firm advocate for the old ways, in which women used the skills and knowledge which had been passed down to them from their mothers and grandmothers to deal with everything from rice pudding to a chesty cough. Yet at the same time she was an alert and sympathetic greeter of the newly industrialised world, the one in which you no longer had to make your own bread if there was a quicker and cheaper option available on the market. And it is this tension between the old and the new, the then and the now of daily living, that makes Mrs. Beeton and her famous *Book* such a compelling subject for our closer scrutiny.

CHAPTER ONE

HEAVY, COLD AND WET SOIL

MRS. BEETON MAY HAVE come down to us as a shape-shifter, but her story starts in a settled enough place, at a time when most people still lived a minute from their parents, when men automatically followed their father's trade, when girls nearly always shared their Christian name with an aunt or cousin, and when it was not unusual to die in the bed in which you had been born. Thursby, in what was then called Cumberland, is a large village wedged between the Lakes and the Borders, flanked by the Pennines on one side and the Solway Firth on the other. It is not on the way to anywhere now, nor was it in the late eighteenth century, when the daily coaches between London and Carlisle were a distant rumble five miles to the northwest.

Most of the 240 inhabitants of Thursby owed their living to the "tolerably fertile" gravel and loam soil, which was parcelled up into a series of small mixed farms, owned by "statesmen" or independent yeomen who employed anything from two to twenty men. In 1786 Thursby got a new curate, John Mayson, grandfather to the future Mrs. Beeton. The curateship and the countryside taken together might suggest something rather smart, a gentleman vicar perhaps, with a private income, an MA from a minor Oxbridge college, and a passion for the flora of the Upper Lakes, the kind of man you find pottering in the background of so many of the people who made and changed the Victorian world. This, certainly, is the impression that Mrs. Beeton's family would conspire to create in years to come. When Isabella Beeton's marriage was announced in *The Times* in 1856, the fact that she was the granddaughter of the late Revd. John

Mayson of Cumberland was shoe-horned into the brief notice. Seventy years later when dealing with the National Portrait Gallery, Mayson Beeton insisted on having his mother's background blurb rewritten to include the important fact that her grandfather had been a man of the cloth.

But if anyone had bothered to look more closely they would have discovered that Revd. John Mayson was not quite the gentlemanly divine that you might suppose. He had been born in 1761 just outside Penrith to another John Mayson, a farmer who was obliged to rent his land from another man. As his Christian name suggests, John Mayson had the luck of being the oldest son, the one in whom the family's slight resources would be invested as a hedge against a chancy future (there were a couple of younger sisters who would need, somehow, to be taken care of). John would have gone to school locally and left around the age of fourteen, a superior kind of village boy.

The next clear sighting comes in 1785 when, at the age of twenty-four, Mayson was ordained as a deacon in the Church of England. The following year he became a fully fledged clergyman and was sent immediately as curate to St. Andrew's, Thursby. But this was hardly the beginning of a steady rise through the Church's hierarchy. Stuck for an extraordinary forty years at Thursby, it looked as if the Revd. John Mayson was destined to become the oldest curate in town. On two separate occasions he was passed over for the post of vicar, quite possibly because of his lack of formal education or social clout: St. Andrew's was a large parish with a fine church said to have been built by David I of Scotland—it needed a gentleman to run it. In 1805 the job went to a Joseph Pattison and then, on his death eight years later, to William Tomkyns Briggs, whose dynastically inflected name was buttressed with a Cambridge MA.

It wasn't until 1825 that Mayson's luck finally changed. At the age of sixty-four—retirement was not an option, except for a man of means—he was appointed vicar to the nearby parish of Great Orton, a substantial living worth perhaps £250 which brought with it the care of two hundred souls. Yet even this was not quite the opportunity that it might seem. The living was in the gift of Sir Wastal Briscoe, the lord of the manor who inhabited several hundred lush acres at nearby Crofton Hall. The previous incumbent of St. Giles had been Briscoe's brother and it was his intention that the living should pass eventually to one of his young grandsons who were being educated for the Church. Mayson, who probably already owed his appointment as curate at Thursby to Briscoe in the first place, was exactly the right candidate to caretake St. Giles until his patron wanted it back.

The life of a clergyman without polish, money or pull was not a particularly easy one. It was geared to pleasing the big house, to judging its moods and whims, and making sure you fitted its purpose. It was, though, enough to get married on, as long as you were careful in your choice of bride. Six years into the curateship at Thursby, John Mayson married a young woman whose name suggests that she had some ballast behind her. Isabella Trimble (or Tremel or Trumble—spelling was still an infant business and names changed with each entry in the parish register) was the daughter of a reasonably prosperous maltster, that is brewer. On his death in 1785 George Trimble divided his estate in the classic manner, with his eldest son inheriting the business along with Trimble's partner, while the younger brothers received "movable goods" in the form of wheat and cash. Isabella, the only girl, was a residual legatee, which gave her perhaps £80—not an enormous sum, but combined with the £100 that John inherited from his own father, just enough to marry on.

The first baby arrived in 1793, ten months after the wedding, as first babies mostly did in the nineteenth century. She was called Esther after John's mother. Three years later she was joined by yet another John Mayson and then, five years after that, by Benjamin, named biblically for his mother's youngest brother. The long spacing between the children, combined with the early evidence of fertility, suggests that there were probably other babies, born months too soon, some still and grey, others little more than bloody clots. These are the first of the many lost children that hover over the story of Mrs. Beeton, Benjamin Mayson's daughter, each one's failure to spark into life marking the moment when the future had to be imagined all over again.

Of the three Mayson children living, neither of the boys would see forty. John—perhaps originally destined for the Church, to be slipped into a place where Briscoe needed a caretaker or a willing plodder—died at the age of twenty-four "after a long and severe illness," according to a notice in the *Carlisle Journal,* and was buried at Thursby. The death of the elder son, that frail container of a family's best hopes, is always hard, but twenty years later John was followed to the grave by Benjamin, now living far away in London. It was time for another entry in the *Carlisle Journal:* "Suddenly, Mr. B. Mayson, linen factor, Milk Street, London, son of the Rev. John Mayson, aged 39 years."

In the early days, though, when the Mayson children were young and bonny, there was an almost pastoral feel to life at Thursby. Although he was only the curate, Mayson was able to live in the vicarage, a handsome building that would shore up anyone's sense of battered dignity. The diary of his fellow cleric Thomas Rumney of Watermillock tells of an Austenish existence of long tramps, impromptu tea parties and lovesick letter writing. In August 1803 Rumney walked six and a half hours to get to Thursby from his own parish, and then proceeded to conduct an epistolary courtship with one of John Mayson's sisters at the thumping cost of 11d a letter.

It was a small life, and it was never going to be enough to hold an energetic young man with neither property or business interests. While John, the eldest Mayson child, was kept close to the family by failing health, his brother Benjamin had other plans. Frustratingly, all record of Benjamin's early life has disappeared. Proving even more elusive than his daughter Isabella, Benjamin refuses to show up in school records, apprenticeship registers, or even, though we would hope not to find a clergyman's son here, in the local assizes. He may have received his education at nearby Wigton Grammar School, where Briscoe had pull. Or it is possible that he was sent to Green Row on the coast a few miles away, a forward-looking place which imparted a "modern" curriculum of maths and careful penmanship to young men who were destined for the counting house and the clerks' bench rather than an ivy-covered quad. Benjamin's grandsons, Isabella's boys, will get a gentleman's education at Marlborough, followed by the royal military academy at Sandhurst and Oxford. But those days are seventy years away. Benjamin Mayson, the second son of a poor curate, needed a grounding that would fit him to make his way in the brisk, new commercial world that was even now impinging on rural Cumberland.

In 1780 cotton processing had been introduced into the nearby village of Dalston from Manchester. The conditions were perfect: plenty of water power from the River Cardew and good communication links back down to Manchester, Liverpool, and beyond. By the time Benjamin was thinking about his future, there were three cotton mills and a large flax mill in Dalston, and the principal owners were, as luck would have it, old friends of his mother's family. All over the country neighbouring households like the Cowens and the Trimbles did business together, married one another's daughters, and blended their hard-won capital in carefully judged expansion plans. It is very likely that it was to the Cowens' Mill Ellers, on the edge of Dalston, that Benjamin was sent to serve his apprenticeship.

This, though, is a guess. Not for another eighteen years does Benjamin finally show up properly in the records. By 1831 he has moved to London and set up as a "Manchester Warehouseman"—a linen wholesaler who distributes cloth woven in the hot, damp sheds of the northwest to the fashionable drapers' shops of London. From the spring of 1834 he was living in classy Upper Baker Street, Marylebone, paying a sizable rent of £65 a year, and from 1831 he also had business premises across town at Clement's Court, in the shadow of St. Paul's. If Benjamin Mayson's daily commute of four miles sounds unconvincingly modern, it is worth bearing in mind that in 1829 a firm called Shillibeer's started a regular horse-drawn omnibus service between Paddington and the City. Londoners were becoming as used as everyone else to widening horizons and for Mayson, who had made the four-hundred-mile journey from Cumberland, the daily journey to the City must have seemed as nothing.

So by the age of thirty Benjamin Mayson could be said to be doing rather well for himself. He was a vicar's son and, though not quite a gentleman, was established in a gentlemanly line of business. Mayson, it is important to understand, was not a draper who stood behind a counter unrolling bolts of sprigged cotton for the approval of sharp-eyed housewives. He was a wholesaler, a merchant, a man who supplied the smarter kind of drapers with bulk orders and sealed deals with a handshake rather than a few warm coins. It was a profitable business. With the world getting dirtier and more polite at the same time, there was a hunger for fresh linen. No one with any self-respect wanted to be seen in a smutty shirt or streaky dress. The middle-class wardrobe was expanding and becoming more particular, good news for anyone who supplied the materials to make all those clean sleeves and dainty collars. And, as if that weren't enough bright fortune, Benjamin Mayson had arranged his private life carefully too. At an age when most men had already married, he was still a bachelor, having managed to avoid being jostled by loneliness or lust into a hasty match. He was, by anyone's reckoning, quite a catch.

Elizabeth Jerrom, the woman whom Benjamin Mayson would marry, was born on 24 May 1815, three weeks before the great victory at Waterloo. Her parents Isaac and Mary were domestic servants, working for one of the big houses around Marylebone, part of that feverish development of gracious squares that had been built towards the end of the last century to house the newer aristocracy during the "London" part of their wandering year. When the couple had married eleven months earlier at St. Martin-in-the-Fields, they had signed the register clearly, confident in themselves and their newly merged identity. The same, though, cannot be said of their witnesses. William Standage, Mary's father, has done his best but the sprawling scratch he makes in the register is indecipherable: underneath the parish clerk has been obliged—tactfully, crossly?—to write out his name properly, for the record. Mrs. Beeton is only twenty years away from people who would be happier signing themselves with a cross.

Elizabeth's mother, Mary Jerrom, the only one of Mrs. Beeton's grandparents who was to play a significant role in her life, had been born Mary Standage in 1794 in the ancient village of Westhampnett. Her father was a groom on the Duke of Richmond's estate at nearby Goodwood. William Standage had himself been born nine miles away, at Petworth where the huge Standage clan had for generations lived and worked with horses. But it was William who was the star of the stables. In 1792 he was headhunted by the horse-mad Duke of Richmond to work as a groom at Goodwood. Given that Mrs. Beeton would be so exact about what you should pay your groom, it is nice to be able to report that in 1792 her great-grandfather was getting £18 a year which, by 1807, had risen to £24, with extra allowances for clothing and travel.

The horse was God at Goodwood. When the 3rd Duke of Richmond inherited in 1756 his first thought was not to rebuild the unimpressive house but to commission the architect William Chambers to build a magnificent stable block as a kind of love song to the most important creatures in his life. Complete with Doric columns and a triumphal arch, the block was home to fifty-four lucky animals—hunters mainly, but from 1802 racers too. Family myth has it that it was William Standage who helped the Duke plot the track that would become one of the most important racecourses in the land.

Standage, who married a woman called Elizabeth, produced a string of daughters: first Mary, next Sarah and then Harriet. All three girls married men who worked with horses. This is not as odd as it might seem today. You can only marry someone you've already met, and a groom's daughter in the early nineteenth century met an awful lot of grooms. But none of the girls stayed in Sussex. Instead they followed the classic migratory pattern of their generation and poured into London, working first as servants in aristocratic mansions and then marrying men from the stables, men who knew or were known to their fathers. In time these men would set up as job masters or livery stable keepers, hiring themselves and their carriage out for a fee, doing for several families what they had formerly done for just one. By the end of the nineteenth century, you could still find the grandsons of these people working as omnibus and cab drivers, transporting restless crowds of shopgirls, clerks and housewives around a teeming central London.

Sometime around 1812 Mary came to London to work as a servant, and two years later she married twenty-eight-year-old Isaac Jerrom. By the time their first baby Elizabeth—named for Mary's mother—came to be christened the following year, Isaac and Mary "Jurrum," as the parish clerk would have it, were living in Marylebone and gave their occupation as "servants." Two years later, with the arrival of their new baby William, they are still describing themselves in the same unembarrassed way, tucked in amongst a dense urban parish swarming with labourers, gentlemen, shopkeepers, artists, clerks, peers, diplomats, musicians, and, of course, an army of domestic staff responsible for keeping this huge social beast trundling forward.

John Jerrom, Isaac's father, who had probably migrated from Hampshire to London as a young man, now ran a livery stables in Marylebone. By 1820 Isaac starts to appear in the Marylebone rate books on his own account, running a stables just around the corner in Wyndham Mews, a newly built series of stables on the Portman Estate. Livery stables supplied carriages and drivers to those households who did not keep their own groom and horse. Most of the mansions in Marylebone had no need for this service since they were well able to make their own arrangements. Indeed, the status of a family was intimately tied up with the show it made in the streets, as it trotted around town in a carriage bearing its own insignia, driven by a couple of tall and handsome grooms. But there were households—often headed by women—who were happy to use freelance carriage services as and when they needed them. William Tayler, a footman in a Marylebone house in 1837, was edgy about the fact that his household, headed by a widow, used the services of a "jobber." He knew exactly what it implied about the status of a household in which he was the only resident male servant.

Isaac and Mary Jerrom, released from personal service, did well at business. The world was changing, people were on the move as never

Elizabeth Jerrom, Isabella Beeton's mother, aged sixteen in 1831.

before, and there was only so far a pair of sturdy legs could take you. As well as catering for the horseless mansions of Marylebone, Isaac provided a taxi service for its less exalted residents, ferrying them around the rapidly extending city. In a classic combination, his wife Mary ran a lodging house, offering bed and board to all those bewildered new arrivals to London. Little by little Isaac rented adjoining properties in Wyndham Mews. In 1826, his high-water mark, the Jerroms were operating out of four separate properties—numbers 1, 4, 5, and 10.

We do not really know what Isaac and Mary's daughter was like as a young girl. There are family stories of her as a beauty, but then family stories nearly always assign someone to play that role. Certainly a watercolour of her at sixteen shows a very pretty girl. The fact that the Jerroms could afford to have her painted and framed suggests the good fortune of being the only child in a working-class family—baby William has disappeared, leaving all the resources concentrated on pretty Bessie. The way she is painted Elizabeth Jerrom could be the daughter of one of the big houses around Marylebone: the sloping shoulders, the little head with the elaborately worked hair, the snub features all suggest a dainty miss rather than a girl who has grown up with the stink and clatter of livery nags directly under her bedroom window. This class-shifting will be a theme in Elizabeth's life over the next thirty years, as she moves from mews, to warehouse, to townhouse and, finally, to a suburban mansion with over a dozen servants and her own busy programme of balls and At Homes.

Girls who are as pretty as princesses attract all kinds of courtship stories, and Elizabeth Jerrom was no exception. Indeed, the tale that was handed down about her was so potent that it was still being rehashed in newspapers a hundred years later. The story, impossible to confirm, begins with one of Mrs. Jerrom's lodgers, a young printer called Henry Dorling. Dorling's father was a printer in Epsom who produced the running cards for the Derby. Mrs. Jerrom's father had been a key groom at

Elizabeth Dorling, née Jerrom,
in prosperous middle age.

Goodwood. The courses were only thirty miles from each other, and were connected by a network of owners and grooms who continuously passed between the two. Names, tips, gossip, information would have been exchanged along the way, so that when William Dorling was looking for respectable people with whom his son could lodge during his vulnerable bachelor years in London, he naturally thought of the Jerroms.

The story runs that Henry Dorling and Elizabeth Jerrom fell in love but her parents refused to countenance an engagement. Instead they favoured the suit of the gentlemanly wholesaler Mr. Mayson. Mayson was an established businessman with a residence in Marylebone and a warehouse in the city. What is more, he was a vicar's son, which to country people (which is what the Jerroms still were) meant a great deal.

The dates, however, do not work. The records show that a good nine months before Benjamin Mayson and Elizabeth Jerrom became man and wife Henry Dorling had already married a London girl called Emily Clarke. The fact that Dorling asked Benjamin Mayson to stand godson to his first child and named the boy "Henry Mayson Dorling," also tends to argue against any kind of love triangle. If there was any rivalry at 1 Wyndham Mews it must have been of a very mild variety. As far as we know Elizabeth Jerrom never looked back on 2 May 1835 when she walked up the aisle with Benjamin Mayson.

The Maysons' first child was born on 14 March 1836 at the end of the snowiest winter that anyone could remember. She was fifteen months too early to be a Victorian. The Maysons were shrewd with their naming strategies, careful to tie the child to the wealthier side of the family. The baby was called Isabella after her Mayson grandmother, the brewer's daughter, and Mary . . . after whom exactly? Possibly after her other grandmother, Mrs. Jerrom, the groom's daughter, but also, perhaps, after her father's grandmother. "Mary" was one of those handily common names that provided cover for a multitude of dynastic ambitions.

Shortly after Isabella's birth the little family of three moved from Marylebone to Benjamin's business premises which were situated at the heart of the textile business in the City of London. In the early nineteenth century the short streets that run north from Cheapside towards Guild-hall were lined with warehouses storing fabric of every kind. In addition to "Manchester" goods of linen and cotton, there were "Nottingham warehouses" stocked with lace, as well as other businesses specializing in silk products from Coventry and Derbyshire or woollens from Yorkshire. Within a few hundred yards you could find all the new mass-produced fabrics of the industrial age, funnelled down from their place of production and disgorged into the chief marketplace of the country, indeed of the whole world.

The City of London was still a residential area in the 1830s. Ware-housemen, in particular, liked to live close to their capital, setting up home on the top floor of their premises, which also provided lodgings for clerks and apprentices. Mayson's first warehouse was in Clement's Court, a narrow cul-de-sac which ran off the west side of Milk Street, where the fine houses had gradually been taken over by textiles. Every corner of the warehouse would have been stacked high with bales of fabric: an eye-witness from twenty years later talks of the clerk in a large Cheapside warehouse "piling up innumerable packages in forms that would exhaust the devices of solid geometry." During most of the year Mayson would have dealt in linen, "Scotch Derry," and perhaps "linsey-woolsey," but during the summer months there would have been lighter mousselines, georgettes, and silks. One corner of the warehouse might well have been set aside for crapes and "kindred vestments of woe," styled and textured to denote every phase of mourning. Samples of the new season's fabrics were sent out to valued customers in March and then again in September.

As baby Isabella crawled, then toddled, among the giant fabric pillars she would have absorbed the smells and textures of the trade, the sharp tang of Manchester cotton, the powdery feel of velvet, the flutter of muslin. In twenty-five years' time, as editress of the *Englishwoman's Domestic Magazine,* she will become expert at evaluating and describing the new season's materials. Her writing is terse and expert, shot through not with the approximating gush of a Lady of Fashion but with the understanding of someone who has grown up feeling fabric between her fingers. Here she advises her readers on the styles for July 1860:

SHAWLS, of any and every material, are worn; some are made of black Grenadine, square, and with a binding of black or violet glacé all round, two inches in width, and of crossway silk; others are of the same material as the dress (some barèges being made wide for this purpose), and bound in the same manner, or have a ribbon laid on with a narrow straw trimming on each edge. A great many muslins are also made to match the dresses, the border being the same as that on the flounces. Shawls of white muslin, with embroidered borders, are very dressy and stylish, also those of plain white muslin, bound with black velvet.

Two years later, and with civil war in America cutting Lancashire and Cumberland off from their vital cotton supplies, Isabella mounted a relief effort to sustain the textiles industries' starving workers. Old clothes, boots, bedding but above all money were to be sent to Mrs. Beeton care of the *Englishwoman's Domestic Magazine* in readiness for their dispersal among the cottages of northwest England. Even now, sixty years after Benjamin Mayson had first struck out from the damp, close sheds along the River Ribble, his eldest daughter still understood the way that cotton worked—and what happened when it didn't.

Mayson prospered in the City. By 1836 he has moved out of Clement's Court and onto Milk Street itself, buying substantial premises at number 24, an investment that brings with it the right to vote. Legend has always had it that Isabella was born here, in Milk Street, which would have made her a cockney, since the Bow Bells ring out from a few hundred yards away on Cheapside. Indeed, Nancy Spain actually has Isabella christened at St. Mary-le-Bow, the result of a common enough confusion with Mary-le-bone, in a glorious christening gown covered with a pattern of ears of wheat which Spain maintains was still doing service within her family seventy years later. The story cannot be confirmed although, even allowing for Spain's mixture of exaggeration and elision, it makes a kind of sense. If Benjamin Mayson knew anything, it was how to pick a piece of cloth that would last.

While Isabella was neither cockney nor Victorian, her brother and sisters were. Just as she turned two she was joined by Elizabeth Anne, always known as Bessie. In September 1839 came yet another John Mayson, followed by Esther, named for her Cumberland aunt, in February 1841. All were christened in St. Lawrence Jewry, which stands a couple of hundred yards away in the forecourt of the Guildhall. The first three Maysons were all said to be pretty, Esther less so, but this may be

*Isabella Beeton in a rarely-seen version
of the National Portrait Gallery photograph
that shows her as she really was,
with light auburn hair.*

Isabella, Bessie, Esther and John Mayson
painted as unlikely cherubs in 1848.
Isabella is farthest left.

because a riding accident in her twenties left her with a blinded eye. Later photographs of the Maysons are not much help when it comes to working out their colouring. The iconic National Portrait Gallery portrait shows Isabella with very dark, almost black hair. However, Marjorie Killby, Mayson Beeton's eldest daughter and a keen photographer, always maintained that this was inaccurate, the fault of the rudimentary technology of the time. Drawing on family intelligence, Killby insisted instead that Isabella had "light reddish auburn hair" and even set about making a new print of the photograph in order to show her grandmother in her true colours, as a strawberry blonde. By way of confirmation, a watercolour of the four Mayson children from around 1848 shows them all as redheads but with Isabella a shade or two fairer than the rest.

It is harder to work out how the Maysons sounded. A great-niece going to visit her maiden aunts Bessie and Esther in genteel Kensington in the 1920s remembered them with cockney accents that struck her, a colonel's granddaughter, as decidedly comic. In this incident, recorded in

Sarah Freeman's biography in 1977, Rosemary Fellowes explains away her great-aunts' dropped aitches and their use of "ain't" as a fashionable affectation from their youth. But the fact is that by the time Edwardians were using cockney to sound smart, the Misses Mayson were already in their eighth decade. The way they spoke had been picked up much earlier, during the 1840s and before English accents had become codified according to class. From their father they might have got some flat vowels, and from their mother and neighbours they would have heard the kind of cockneyfied speech in which "w"s were still doing service for "v"s. Boarding school in Germany would have added another complicating layer. Whatever the exact sound eventually arrived at, we can be fairly safe in saying that Mrs. Beeton and her sisters did not speak like ladies.

The birth of Esther, the youngest Mayson child, in February 1841 must have been bittersweet. Seven months earlier Benjamin had died at the age of only thirty-nine. The notice inserted by his father in the *Carlisle Journal* suggests that the death was sudden: certainly there is no suggestion that he was suffering from the kind of degenerative illness that had made his brother linger for so long. The death certificate, a recent innovation, part of the new Victorians' desire to count, clarify, and mark their hectically expanding population, says "Apoplexy." This sounds sudden and convulsive, until you realize that in the 1840s it stood for many things: alcoholism, syphilis, epilepsy as well as the more obvious heart attack or stroke. It is "apoplexy" that will kill Benjamin's son, the baby John, only thirty years later.

Death may have been everywhere in early Victorian England, but to find yourself pregnant with your fourth child and suddenly responsible for a highly capitalized business was unlucky by any standard. Although her widowed mother Mary Jerrom was helping with the domestic side of life at Milk Street, Elizabeth Mayson soon buckled under her burden. The only solution, a common enough one, was to farm out the two elder children to relatives. Isabella, still only five years old, was sent like a parcel to the other end of the country to lodge with her clergyman grandfather at Great Orton. The census entry for 1841 gives a bleak snapshot of what she found there. Apart from the seventy-nine-year-old John Mayson, himself recently widowed, the thatched vicarage was home to one thirty-year-old servant, Sarah Robinson. For a little girl four hundred miles from home, Great Orton must have seemed the strangest place to be. Instead of the companionable man-made bustle of Cheapside, there were

country noises: shivering trees, rumbling carts, and endless fields of caw-
ing sheep. In place of scurrying clerks and warehousemen there was a single shoemaker, schoolmaster, and blacksmith. It got dark early, stayed
colder longer, and the food, coaxed from the "heavy cold and wet soil,"
tasted different. The bread was made of barley, black and sour ("Everybody knows that it is wheat flour which yields the best bread," noted
Isabella pointedly twenty years later in the *Book of Household Management*). Oatmeal, meanwhile, turned up at virtually every meal. There was
porridge for breakfast, and maybe crowdy—oatmeal steeped in beef marrow—for midday dinner. Ginger, which came all the way from China,
made cake and biscuits burn in your mouth. As if that weren't enough
strangeness for five-year-old Isabella, there were the voices too, speaking
in a language to strain her understanding. Just why Bessie, two years
younger, was not sent with her as a consoling companion in exile is a
mystery.

Even with two fewer people to worry about, life was not easy for Elizabeth Mayson. Still only twenty-five, she now ran the business in her own
name—the trade directories describe her as a "warehouseman." In the
1840s it was not unusual for widows to take over this way, and the directories show many heading up pubs, livery stables, and every kind of shop
from baker to jeweller. Elizabeth had grown up among the artisans and
tradesmen of Marylebone, watching women like her mother working
alongside husbands and brothers as book-keepers, shop assistants, and
storeroom supervisors. The 1841 census shows her employing one young
maidservant and an older man called Robert Mitchell who was originally
from Sussex. Mitchell's father had worked alongside various Standages
in the stables at Petworth House and his presence in Milk Street is a
reminder of how, in the first half of the nineteenth century, rural communities had a habit of reconstituting themselves at the very heart of commercial and industrial landscapes. Elizabeth Mayson may have been
operating out of one of the busiest streets in London, but when it came to
investing her precious trust she relied on a network that had been forged
sixty years earlier and in a different place entirely.

There remains some mystery about Elizabeth's finances during her
widowhood. Benjamin had not left a will, and ten days after his death
she was granted administration as his "relict." His estate amounted to
£8,000, a small fortune. However, much of this must have been tied up in
stock and Benjamin doubtless left a fair number of outstanding debts to

his suppliers that needed to be paid before arriving at any real sense of his legacy. For how else can one explain the fact that only two years later Elizabeth, now reunited with Isabella and Bessie, is writing a begging letter to her father-in-law in Great Orton? From John Mayson's reply it transpires that warehousing has not been kind to Elizabeth: quite possibly the drapers to whom she tried to sell her cloth were not happy dealing with a young woman. Certainly it looks as if she was thinking of switching to another trade, perhaps lodging house keeping like her mother. We will never know the precise nature of Elizabeth's problems, since the letter to her father-in-law has been lost. Here, though, is the Revd. Mayson's reply:

My dear Bessie

I am sorry the business you entered upon did not answer your expectations. Of the one you are going to begin I can form no opinion, as I am totally ignorant about it. You say you have seen a House which might answer your purpose. You do not mention the Rent, but I understand the first Quarter's Rent is to be paid in advance, and if the rent be high you will observe another Quarter's Rent will soon be due. Do you suppose you will be able to meet it at the time, as he requires a Qr. in advance? I am afraid he will be a sharp landlord.

You say you want a little money. I think I can advance you 50£, if that will do. Since last Christmas I have had a great deal to do. As I was not able to do any Duty, I was obliged to engage a curate. I think I shall never be able to attend the Church again to do Duty. If 50£ will be of any service to you, after you receive it you must send me a Note, as I wish at my Decease to have something made up for your children, and the above 50£ was part of it. I intended to make you an allowance yearly. But if I do too much there will be less afterwards. I assure you I am anxious to save something for my little grandchildren. I have my curate to pay quarterly. I do not wish you to sell your house, and also not to lay out your money extravagantly. I hope to hear that you are doing well. Carefulness will do a great deal.

I am sorry to say I do not improve much, I cannot leave Home. I do not enjoy Company. I am best when alone. I was glad to hear that you and the little ones were well. Make my love to Isabella and Bessy. The other 2 do not know me. They are very well at Thursby. I have not seen them lately except Anne who was at our House yesterday. I have not had

much of Anne's Company lately. I want to know when Esther was born.
I have forgot. Write soon.

 With kind regards I subscribe myself,

 Yours sincerely,

JOHN MAYSON

To Elizabeth, a crisp young woman who had grown up watching her
parents run an expanding business, it must be galling to be told by a
querulous elderly clergyman that rent comes due every quarter. Likewise
the reminder that "carefulness will go a great deal." Mayson's fussiness
over his post-mortem financial plans is odd, too, when you consider that,
on his death three years later, it turned out that he had not got round to
making a will. His substantial estate of £1,500 passed automatically to
Esther Burtholme, his only living child, an already prosperous farmer's
wife. The little cockney grandchildren, about whom the Revd. Mayson
said he cared so much, got nothing.

Perhaps, though, by the time of his death Mayson felt that Elizabeth's
fortunes had shifted sufficiently for him not to bother. For it is now that
the stalled courtship story reaches its happy ending. The bare facts are
these: only eight months after writing that letter to her father-in-law, we
find Elizabeth getting married again. Her husband is Henry Dorling, the
young printer who had lodged in her mother's boarding house all those
years ago. This means that the two young families must have stayed in
touch: godparenting in the nineteenth century was a serious business, and
it is highly unlikely that Benjamin Mayson, a clergyman's son, would
have let his relationship with young Henry Mayson Dorling lapse. So
Elizabeth would have been quite aware that Dorling's wife had died giving birth to her fourth child, only a few months before she had lost her
own Benjamin. The early biographers see in this symmetry—both Henry
and Elizabeth recently widowed, both with four children apiece—a lovely
coincidence, a chance to make the fairy story come out right. But the fact
is that this second marriage was as cool as a business deal. Elizabeth
needed a husband to rescue her from life as a "warehouseman," and
Henry a mother for his children.

In the spring of 1843 Elizabeth and Henry headed north to Great
Orton, so that John Mayson could meet the man who was going to
replace his late son. On 24 March the couple headed over the border to
Gretna where they were married by John Linton the hotel keeper who

doubled as "priest." There was a hearty wedding breakfast washed down with ale, whisky, and gin.

Did John Mayson, a clergyman of the Church of England, approve of this, the nineteenth-century equivalent of getting married in a Las Vegas wedding chapel? Probably not. Perhaps, too, Elizabeth and Henry had surprised themselves by their skittishness, the last time in their lives that they displayed such impulsive behaviour. Or perhaps the fact that Elizabeth was already pregnant made them rush: baby Charlotte would be born only seven and a half months later. Whatever the reason, the very next day Henry Dorling returned to London and applied for a licence to marry "Elizabeth Mayson, widow" in the old-fashioned way. On 27 March they did the whole thing all over again and walked up the aisle at St. Mary's Islington, the parish where Elizabeth was temporarily living. And then shortly afterwards, gathering up her four children and her mother, the newly minted Mrs. Dorling headed off to her second husband's family home in Epsom, to the place that would become the shape, the sight, and the sound of Mrs. Beeton's childhood.

INTERLUDE

"The Free, Fair Homes of England"
Caption to the Frontispiece of the
Book of Household Management

YOU DO NOT HAVE TO GET VERY FAR into the *Book of Household Management* (*BOHM*) to realize that one of its main preoccupations is the loss of Eden. The Frontispiece is an exquisitely coloured plate that shows an extended family group from the early nineteenth century, clustered around the door of a tiled cottage at harvest time. The men are plump John Bulls, prosperous in gaiters. The principal female figure is serving them beer which, judging from the golden haze in the middle distance, she has brewed from her own grain. In the foreground ducks dabble, hens peck and cows drowse under a tree, while a bulldog keeps a beady watch on the men gathering hay on the horizon. The caption underneath explains that this scene represents "The Free Fair Homes of England," a line from the Romantic poet Felicia Hemans. In other words, here is a time before industrialization scarred the land, cut a generation of town dwellers from its gentle rhythms, and replaced convivial kin groups with edgy strangers.

You just know that Mrs. Beeton would love to step into that picture. The *Book of Household Management* is saturated with a longing for an agrarian world that has already slipped into extinction but just might, by some enormous effort of will, be brought back into being. So, in her instructions for making a syllabub Mrs. Beeton suggests mixing up some

39

"The Free, Fair Homes of England": The Frontispiece to the
Book of Household Management *shows an idealized pastoral scene
that had little to do with Mrs. Beeton's own life experience,
or that of her readers.*

sugar and nutmeg and then simply squirting the milk from the cow's udder straight into the bowl. (For those unlucky readers who do not have their own cow immediately to hand Beeton suggests substituting a milk-filled jug poured from a great height to produce the required froth.)

Throughout the *BOHM* animals destined for the table are described in their natural habitat with such lulling, lyrical grace that you seem to find yourself watching them from the corner of a hot, summer meadow. Here, for instance, is Beeton describing the eating habits of a sheep: "indolently and luxuriously [the sheep] chews his cud with closed eyes and blissful satisfaction, only rising when his delicious repast is ended to proceed silently and without emotion to repeat the pleasing process of laying in more provender, and then returning to his dreamy siesta to renew the delightful task of rumination." Elsewhere Beeton's text is scattered with drawings that reinforce the unforced bounty of nature. Pigs snuffle in well-kept sties (no nasty urban courtyard here), a landrail hares through the undergrowth, while deer bound through what looks like heather with the Scottish Highlands peaking in the background. The illustration heading up the chapter on vegetables is a cornucopia of cabbage, onions, and leeks, seeming for all the world like something that has just been plucked from the soil in time for the Harvest Festival supper.

Such soft-focus rural fantasy was only possible because Mrs. Beeton, like most of her readers, was actually a sharp-edged daughter of the industrial age. Her guidelines for domestic bliss have less to do with the farmhouse than the factory. Briskly she divides the working day into segments and allots each household member from the mistress to the scullery maid a precise set of tasks that read like a time and motion study. (There is no point in housemaids starting work until 7 a.m. in the winter, for instance, since rising any earlier will be a waste of candle.) The labour is specialized, repetitive, and, more often than not, mechanized. Kitchen equipment is described and illustrated as if it were an industrial plant; the laundry maid's duties make her sound like the head boilerman on a steamship.

So, too, for all that Mrs. Beeton gestures dewy-eyed to the days of "auld lang syne" when households produced their own butter, eggs, bread, and wine, she spends much of her time urging short cuts on her readers. Commercially bottled sauces and pickles get a cautious welcome (they're probably not as good as home-made, she admits, but at least they don't cost any more). And when it comes to baking Beeton is ambivalent about whether you should even bother to do it yourself. The illustration to "General Observations on Bread, Biscuits and Cakes" may show an artful pyramid of rustic-looking loaves, with a windmill grinding in the background, yet a few pages later Mrs. Beeton dedicates several enthusiastic paragraphs to a newly patented system for mass-producing aerated bread. During this process "the dough is mixed in a great iron ball, inside which is a system of paddles . . . then the common atmospheric air is pumped out, and the pure gas turned on." It was from these unappetizing beginnings that the Aerated Bread Company or ABC would emerge to become a commercial giant of the nineteenth and twentieth centuries, providing white sliced loaf, as smooth and tasteless as sponge, to the nation.

None of this makes Mrs. Beeton's rusticism phoney, although her vision of agrarian Britain is quaintly out of date, lacking any mention of intensive farming methods, high seasonal unemployment, and endemic poverty among the rural working class. But what Beeton shared with some of the most persuasive voices of her age was the nagging feeling that all the good things about modern urban living—heat on demand, sauces that came out the same every time, a dripping pan furnished with its own stand—arrived at a cost. But what that cost was exactly, and whether it was too high a price to pay for convenience, safety, and comfort was something that she hardly had time to consider. Whirling not so much like a dervish as a cog in a particularly intricate machine, she pressed on in a blur of activity, determined to finish her 1,112 pages in record time. "The Free, Fair Homes of England" remained a lovely, compensating dream.

CHAPTER TWO

CHABLIS TO OYSTERS

ALTHOUGH EPSOM LIES only fourteen miles from the City of London as the crow flies, it could not have been farther from the cluttered streets and close courts in which Isabella Mayson had spent most of the first seven years of her life. Positioned on a ridge in the North Downs, the town manages to be both flat and high at the same time. In the seventeenth and eighteenth centuries it enjoyed an extended spell as a restorative spa, when its indigenous salts were said to work wonders on jaded digestions. Samuel Pepys took the waters there a couple of times, finding it funny to watch as his fellow sippers rushed for the bushes, caught short by the salts' laxative effect. But by the opening of the nineteenth century, the fashionably liverish had moved on to Cheltenham and Bath, leaving Epsom to its devices as a quiet market town that turned, once a year, into Gomorrah. Dickens got the scale of the transformation, writing in 1851 that for most days of the year Epsom was virtually dead but how "On the three hundred and sixty fifth, or Derby Day, a population surges and rolls, and scrambles through the place, that may be counted in millions."

For a few short days during the summer race meeting, well-mannered Epsom became the destination of every swell, Guards officer, dwarf, clerk, tart, orange-seller, thimble rigger, prize-fighter, crook, and lady of fashion in the country. Ruskin called the Derby the "English carnival" and from the breaking hours on the day itself—usually in June—a spirit of excitement and misrule began to bubble far away in London. In Clapham, Mitcham, and Tooting, not to mention Belgravia, Hyde Park, and Knightsbridge people commandeered every phaeton, gig, barouche, four-in-hand, brake, tilbury, and donkey cart for the short journey south. Alongside the shambling caravan of race-goers trundled dusty sellers of every kind of snack, novelty, and stimulant, all shouting and shoving in their attempt to turn a copper, honest or otherwise. Every public house along the route was packed with Derby-goers in various stages of tipsiness and with only a passing interest in racing. Some indeed never got further than the Swan at Clapham or the Cock at Sutton, and Dickens reckoned that most returned from the day unable to remember the name of the winning horse, let alone its jockey. As the chaotic column of humanity approached the Surrey Downs the sheer press of numbers caused it to stall. A seven- or eight-mile backup was not unknown and it could take a whole hour to clear the final three miles. Local hawkers took advantage of this pooling throng to press upon it anything from a racing card to pigeon pie, lemonade to a second-hand umbrella. The mood could turn merry, but seldom sour. As the *Illustrated London News* advised Derby-goers briskly: "if things are thrown at you, just throw them back."

From 1837, if you were modern-minded, you could make the journey from London by train. The London-Brighton line took you as far as the quaintly named Stoat's Nest, from where it was a seven-mile tramp to the Downs. Next year came the welcome news that a rival line, the London and South-Western, was to run special Derby Day excursion trains on their Southampton line. But such was the press at Nine Elms in south London, the result of thousands of people trying to pile onto eight meagre trains, that the police were called in to disperse the increasingly desperate crowd. Even then, the train only went as far as Surbiton, which was still a good five miles from the course. It was not for nearly another decade that a line was built all the way to Epsom.

Once the crowds were disgorged—in 1843, the year that Isabella arrived in Epsom, it was reckoned that 127,500 extra souls poured into the town for the Derby—the party continued, helped along by liberal supplies from the temporary beer and spirit stalls. Up on the Hill, the large bank rising at the edge of the racetrack, there was a temporary funfair with swings, roundabouts, Italian hurdy-gurdy players, and acrobats who insisted on twisting themselves into impossible shapes. Winding among the crowd you could see jaunty perennial eccentrics like "Sir" John Bennett, a prosperous jeweller from Cheapside who resembled a

A contemporary cartoon showing the different experiences of travelling to the Derby by train for first-, second- and third- class passengers.

beery Father Christmas and would drink anyone's health while ambling along on his cob. Others, who liked to think themselves fashionable, bought cheap German articulated wooden dolls and crammed them around the brims of their hats—an odd craze that no one could satisfactorily explain.

This gaggle of humanity was augmented by a fair number of gypsies, who had gathered the previous weekend on the racecourse for "Show Out Sunday," their annual meeting of the clans. Fortunes were told, palms crossed with silver, and heather thrust under reluctant noses. The place was a petty criminal's paradise: in the squawk and clatter it was child's play to pick a pocket or sneak off with someone else's lunch. Prostitutes worked swiftly and unobtrusively, card sharps blended back into the crowd at a moment's notice. A temporary magistrates' court was set up in the Grandstand to deal with all the extra business, and additional policing was, by tradition, partly paid for by the winner of that year's Derby. During race week the manager of the Epsom branch of the London and County Bank kept a loaded rifle with a fixed bayonet close by his desk while Baron de Tessier, one of the local grandees and Steward to the Course, hired extra police protection for his family. Still it felt like a losing battle: right-minded burghers could only fume over the rude interruption of their lives. Unless, of course, they happened to be publicans, shopkeepers or pie makers, in which case they hiked their prices and pasted on a welcoming smile.

Artists loved the Derby, although not necessarily for its horses, which they tended to paint as little rocking creatures whose hooves never quite contacted the ground. It was the crowds they came to see. Over the years, Millais, Degas, "Phiz," Doré, and Géricault would all take their turn at trying to get the spirit of the place down on paper. George Cruikshank did a brilliant six-foot cartoon strip called "The Road to the Derby," showing every aspect of human and horsey life on the long trail down from London. But the most successful execution came from William Frith. His *Derby Day* of 1858 (the not very inspirational title was suggested by Isabella's step-father, Henry Dorling) is a wide-screen panorama of the crowd on the Hill, consisting of ninety distinct figures. Carefully composed in his London studio in a series of artful triangles, it depicts smocked countrymen, sinister gypsies, tipsy ladies, flushed punters, a sly thimble rigger, and a hungry child acrobat who watches in disbelief as a top-hatted footman unpacks a feast (the child model, hired from the circus, proved to be a menace in the studio—somersaulting into props and teasing the little Friths about their posh manners).

Derby Day was so hugely popular when it was shown at the Royal Academy that it had to be protected by a policeman and an iron railing in order to stop the admiring crowds pitching forward. On the stately world tour that followed, the painting attracted huge attention wherever it went. Since Frith was known to have been paid a whopping £1,500, *Derby Day* naturally spawned a whole host of flattering copy-cats. The best of these, the much engraved *At Epsom Races,* 1863 by Alfred Hunt, rearranges the tipsy ladies, adds an urchin and some shady tradesmen in an attempt to recreate that same sense of fluxy human life.

What drew artists to Epsom was the fact that the racetrack was a place where the lowest and the highest met, a space outside the normal social order. Or as the *Illustrated London News* put it: "there is a sort of magic in the words Epsom Races, which arouses the hopes, recollections, antic-ipations, and sympathies of hundreds and thousands of people of all classes of society." Essentially a rich man's hobby, the track had been dominated for decades by aristocrats who travelled around the country from course to course. They were shadowed by their grooms who, in the days before horseboxes and trains, were responsible for riding the pre-cious beasts from Goodwood to Ascot to Doncaster in preparation for the next meeting. Behind the grooms trailed a job-lot of racing "types"—

W. P. Frith's famous Derby Day *of 1858 shows every kind of race-goer from acrobat to pick-pocket, footman to prostitute.*

47

bookies, gypsies, hucksters of every kind. Periodically this odd caravan trundled into well-regulated market towns, took over the taverns and local manors, tumbled the servant girls, cheeked the policemen and made an almighty mess, departing before anyone could be quite sure exactly what they had seen and heard.

Corruption was woven into the weft of the sport of kings, only adding to its seedy glamour. Horses were nobbled, trainers coshed, jockeys squared, fortunes won and lost, all under the shadiest of circumstances. Epsom in the 1840s was especially rich in this kind of rottenness. In 1844 the Derby was won by a horse called Running Rein, who turned out to be a four-year-old named Maccabeus (the Derby was strictly for three-year-olds). The deception had been managed by painting the animal's legs with hair dye bought from Rossi's, a smart barber's shop in Regent Street. There was nothing new about the trick. With record-keeping so hit-and-miss, it was simple to lie about a horse's age or even do a straight swap. The case of Running Rein, however, was referred to the Jockey Club. The publicity attending the sorry business only served to show half-delighted middle-class newspaper readers what they had always suspected: that racing was run by decadent toffs and their rackety hangers-on whose glory days could not pass too soon.

The, by now, infamous hair dye had been traced to Rossi's by Lord George Bentinck, the "Napoleon of the Turf," and the whole incident investigated initially by his protégé Henry Dorling, the Clerk of the Course at Epsom, who swiftly declared Orlando, the horse second past the finishing post, to be the official Derby winner. Over his lengthy tenure it was Dorling's great achievement to bring to Epsom his own bourgeois brand of probity, order and storming profit. His *Sporting Life* obituary recalled admiringly how "promptitude and regularity were the order of the day in all . . . [his] business arrangements," although the fact that the newspaper had once been managed by his son may account for some of the fulsome tone. Even so there could be no denying that by the 1850s Dorling had managed to make a substantial change in the racecourse's culture, turning it from a discredited and slightly sleazy club for aristocrats and chancers into virtually a family business, complete with programmes, ledgers, and a tidy moral climate. The sort of thing that Queen Victoria, had she deigned to return after her damp squib of a visit in 1840, might actually quite have liked.

This process of cleaning up and sorting out had been started by Henry

Dorling's father, William, who had arrived in the town in 1821. Family legend has him riding over the Downs from Bexhill, where he worked as a printer, and seeing Epsom spread beneath him as if it were the Promised Land. Deciding that his destiny lay there, Dorling returned to Bexhill, scooped up his wife, six children, and printing press and retraced his steps over the county border into Surrey. More practically—and the Dorlings were nothing if not practical—William had spotted that Epsom, a town full of business and bustle, did not have a resident press. Moving there would assure him brisk custom from every auctioneer, estate agent, parish officer, butcher, baker, and candlestick maker in the place. In addition, he would continue as he had in Bexhill to combine his printing business with a circulating library and general store. For as well as lending you the latest novel, William Dorling could sell you a shaving cake, a set of Reeves paints or a packet of Epsom Salts, hire you a piano, supply you with fine-

William Dorling, Isabella Beeton's
step-grandfather, who founded the famous
Dorling racing dynasty of Epsom which lasted
for a 150 years.

quality tea from the London Tea Company or a copy of Watts's *Psalms and Hymns* and insure your property through the Kent Fire Office. And then, when you did eventually die, it was Dorling's job as registrar to record the fact, along with the happier news of any births and marriages that occurred within the town. In fact there was not much you could do in Epsom without running into William Dorling.

If Epsom was basically a one-horse town for most of the year, for a single week every summer it was inundated with the very finest examples of the species. For a man as canny as William Dorling, the obvious next step was to insinuate himself into the racing culture. In 1826 he started printing "Dorling's Genuine Card List," colloquially known as "Dorling's Correct Card"—a list of the runners and riders for each race. It sounds a simple thing, hardly a product on which you could found a fortune and a business dynasty, but in a world as chaotic and cliquey as racing, accurate information was at a premium. The Correct Card, put together from knowledge Dorling gleaned as he walked the Heath early every morning chatting to trainers, grooms and jockeys, was a way of communicating intelligence that would otherwise lie scattered and obscured to the ordinary race-goer. Indeed, as the *Illustrated London News* reported during Derby week of 1859: "half of the myriad who flock to the Downs on the Derby Day would know nothing of the names of the horses, the weights and colours of the riders, were it not for Dorling's card, printed feverishly through the night in the printing shed next to the family house and sold the next morning by hoarse vendors posted at every likely point."

As William's eldest son, Henry Dorling gradually took over the running of the business. His appointment as Clerk of the Course in 1839 was a recognition of the family's growing involvement in Epsom's chief industry. But there was only so much that the position allowed him to do in the way of cleaning up the moral slurry that was keeping respectable people away. To have real influence, to pull Epsom together so that it was a smoothly integrated operation, Dorling would need to take control of the Grandstand too. When it had opened in 1830 the Grandstand had been the town's pride and joy. Designed by William Trendall to house five thousand spectators, it had cost just under £14,000 to build, a sum raised by a mixture of mortgage and shares. The imposing building—all Doric columns, raked seating and gracious balconies—was designed to combine the conveniences of a hotel with the practicalities of a head office. According to the *Morning Chronicle*, which puffed the grand opening on its front

page of 12 April 1830, the Grandstand incorporated a "convenient betting room, saloon, balcony, roof, refreshment and separate retiring rooms
for ladies." And in case any readers of the *Morning Chronicle* were still
doubtful that Epsom racecourse really was the kind of place for people
like them to linger, they were assured that "The whole arrangement will
be under the direction of the Committee, who are resolved that the
strictest order shall be preserved."

From the moment that the Grandstand had first been mooted back in
1824, the Dorlings had been eyeing it hungrily. William Dorling had been
canny enough to buy some of the opening stock, and by 1845 Henry was
the single biggest shareholder. Early on, in 1830, William suggested that
he might put the prices of entry on the bottom of Dorling's Correct Card,
a stealthy way of identifying the name of Dorling with that of the Grandstand. Although the Grandstand Association initially rejected the idea, by
the time of next year's Derby the prices are firmly ensconced at the bottom of the card, where they would remain for over a century. William
Dorling's hunch about Epsom's promise had paid off after all.

But by the 1840s, and despite all that "strictest order" promised by the

Epsom Grandstand on Derby Day, 1830s.

committee, the Grandstand was not quite the golden goose that it had once seemed. Its early glamour and promise had leaked away and it was no longer turning a profit. Now that people came to think about it properly, it was not actually very well placed, being parallel to the course and unable to offer more than a partial glimpse of the race. The majority of visitors, everyone from Guards officers to clerks, preferred to follow the action from the Hill, the large high bank which offered a much better view of the entire proceedings. Having finished their Fortnum and Mason picnic (Fortnum and Mason so dominated the feasting on the Hill that Dickens declared that if he were ever to own a horse he would call it after London's most famous grocery store), they simply stepped up onto their hampers in order to see the race. Unless a Derby-goer was actually inside the Grandstand—and increasingly there was no reason why he would wish to be—then not a penny did he pay.

In 1845 Henry Dorling became the principal leaseholder of the Grandstand, thanks to Bentinck's strenuous string-pulling at the Jockey Club. This meant that Dorling was now in complete charge of all aspects of racing at Epsom. But in order to deliver the 5 per cent annual return he had promised the Grandstand Association on its capital, he would need to make substantial changes to the way things were done. So he came up with a series of proposals designed to make racing more interesting for the spectators, especially those who had paid for a place in the Grandstand. Horses were now to be saddled in front of the stand itself, where punters could look over their fancy (this already worked a treat at Goodwood and Ascot). And to make the proceedings more intelligible for those who were not already initiates, Dorling instituted a telegraph board for exhibiting the numbers of riders and winners. Races were now to start bang on time (Dorling would have to pay a fine to the Jockey Club if they did not) and deliberate "false starts" by jockeys anxious to unsettle their competitors were to be punished. And, not before time one might think, Dorling put up railings to prevent the crowds surging onto the course to get a better view. Finally, and most controversially, he laid out a new course—the Low Level—which incorporated a steep climb over four furlongs to provide extra drama for the watchers in the Grandstand.

The fact that these changes were designed for the convenience of investors rather than devotees of the turf was not lost on Dorling's critics. For every person who benefited from his innovations—the Grandstand shareholders, Bentinck, Dorling himself—there was someone ready to carp. Different interest groups put their complaints in different ways. The *Pictorial Times* of 1846, for instance, suggested that as a result of Dorling's tenure of the Grandstand (only one year old at that point) "the character of its visitors was perhaps less aristocratic than of old; but a more fashionable display we have never met in this spacious and, as now ordered, most convenient edifice." In other words, the punters were common but at least the event was running like clockwork.

Within Epsom itself the opprobrium was more personal. By the end of his life Dorling had become a rich man and, according to one maligner, strode around "as if all Epsom belonged to him." The obituary in which this unattributed quote appeared went on to add, in the interests of balance, that under Dorling's reign there had been "no entrance fees, no fees for weighing, no deductions" nor the hundred other fiddles by which clerks of racecourses around the country attempted to siphon off extra income. In other words: Dorling was sharp, but he was straight. Other carpers couched their objections to his dominance by attacking the new Low Level Course which, while it might provide excitement for the Grandstanders, was actually downright dangerous for the horses and jockeys. But, no matter how the comments were dressed up, the real animus was that Henry Dorling was simply getting too rich and too powerful.

The bickering rumbled on through the 1860s and 1870s, pulling in other players along the way. There were constant disputes, some of which actually came to court, over who had right of way, who was due ground rent, who was entitled to erect a temporary stand. The overall impression that comes through the records of Epsom racecourse is that of a bad-tempered turf war, a contest between ancient vested rights and newer commercial interests. Everyone, it seemed, wanted a slice of the pie on the Downs.

By the time Charles Dickens visited Epsom in 1851 to describe Derby Day to

Henry Dorling,
Isabella's step-father, master of all
he surveyed in Epsom.

the readers of his magazine *Household Words,* Henry Dorling was sufficiently secure in his small, if squabbling, kingdom to be a legitimate target of Dickens's pricking prose:

> A railway takes us, in less than an hour, from London Bridge to the capital of the racing world, close to the abode of the Great Man who is—need we add!—the Clerk of Epsom Course. It is, necessarily, one of the best houses in the place, being—honour to literature—a flourishing bookseller's shop. We are presented to the official. He kindly conducts to the Downs . . . We are preparing to ascend [the Grand Stand] when we hear the familiar sound of the printing machine. Are we deceived? O, no! The Grand Stand is like the Kingdom of China—self-supporting, self-sustaining. It scorns foreign aid; even to the printing of the Racing Lists. This is the source of the innumerable cards with which hawkers persecute the sporting world on its way to the Derby, from the Elephant and Castle to the Grand Stand. "Dorling's list, Dorling's correct list!" with the names of the horses, and colours of the riders!

But there were limits even to Dorling's ascendancy. No amount of cosy cooperation with Lord George Bentinck—Bentinck lent him £5,000 and Dorling responded by giving his third son the strangely hybrid moniker William George Bentinck Dorling—was going to turn Dorling into anything more than a useful ledger man as far as the aristocrats of the Jockey Club were concerned. Dorling, a small-town printer, had made a lucky fortune from Epsom racecourse and that, as far as the toffs were concerned, was that. One family anecdote has Henry complaining to his new wife Elizabeth that being Clerk of the Course was not a gentleman's job. She was supposed to have replied, "You are a gentleman, Henry, and you have made it so." But both of them knew that, actually, it wasn't true.

The new home to which the just-turned-seven Isabella Mayson arrived in the spring of 1843 was simply William Dorling's High Street print shop. But by the time Dickens visited Epsom eight years later she had moved with her jumble of full, step- and half-siblings into one of the most imposing residences in the town. Ormond House, built as a speculative venture in 1839, stood, white and square, at the eastern end of the High Street, usefully placed both for driving the two miles up to the racecourse and for keeping a careful eye over the town's goings-on. A shed adjacent to the building housed the library and, initially, the printing business too.

For all that Dickens described Dorling in 1851 as a "great man" with a house to match, the census of that year tells a more modest tale. Ten years earlier, just before Elizabeth Mayson and her little cockney brood had arrived in Epsom, there were two servants at the Dorling's High Street premises to cope with William, Henry and the four motherless Dorling children. By 1851, though, there is just one sixteen-year-old maid to look after the entire household which includes fifteen-year-old "Isabella Mason" [sic], and a permanent lodger called James Woodruff, a coach proprietor. Whatever Epsom gossips might have said, it was not until the 1860s that Dorling really began to live like a man with money.

The emotional layout of the newly blended Mayson-Dorling household is harder to gauge. Initially there were eight children under eight crammed into the house. The four children on each side matched each other fairly neatly in age, with Henry Mayson Dorling just the oldest at eight, followed by Isabella Mayson, a year younger. At the outset of the marriage Henry Dorling had promised that "his four little Maysons were to be treated exactly the same as his four little Dorlings" and, in material terms, this certainly does seem to have been the case. There were no Cinderellas at Ormond House. The Mayson girls received the same educa-

Ormond House, with Dorling's stationers,
library and print works housed to the side.

tion as their Dorling step-sisters and, as soon as he was old enough, John Mayson was integrated into the growing Dorling business empire along with Henry's own sons. On Henry's death in 1873 his two surviving step-children, Bessie and Esther, were left £3,000 each, a sum that allowed them to live independently for the rest of their very long lives.

The new Mr. and Mrs. Dorling quickly went about adding to their family. Charlotte's birth, an intriguing seven and a half months after their marriage, was followed by another twelve children in all, culminating with Horace, born in 1862 when Elizabeth was forty-seven. In total the couple had twenty-one children between them, a huge family even by early Victorian standards. People didn't say anything to their faces, but there must have been smirking about this astonishing productivity which Henry, a touchy man, did not find funny. By 1859, thirteen-year-old Alfred Dorling was clearly feeling embarrassed by his parents' spectacular fertility, perhaps because it offered such obvious evidence of the fact that they still enjoyed a vigorous sex life. As a joke, perhaps one whose implications he did not wholly understand, the boy sent his papa a condom anonymously through the post. Henry Dorling was not amused: condoms were the preserve of men who used prostitutes and were trying to avoid venereal disease, not of a paterfamilias who wished to limit the size of his brood. In effect, Alfred Dorling was calling his mother a tart and his father a trick. His punishment was to be sent to join the Merchant Navy where presumably he learned all about condoms and a great deal more. That Alfred drowned in Sydney harbour three years later is no one's fault. And yet, given the way that family anecdotes get compressed in their endless retelling, it is hard to avoid the impression that it was Henry's awkwardness over his sexual appetite that was responsible for the death of his teenage son.

What was seven-year-old Isabella like, as she packed up her toys in the City of London, and prepared to move to Epsom? Over the previous three years, she had lost her father, been sent to live on the other side of the country with an old man she didn't know, acquired a new papa and was now being moved from her home in Cheapside to a grassy market town. She had also acquired four step-siblings and was now obliged to share her mother with a series of exhausting new babies who arrived almost yearly. The one thing she would have picked up from the tired and distracted adults who bustled round her was that there was no time and space in this hard-pressed world for the small worries and anxious needs of one little

56

*Alfred Dorling, who anonymously sent his
prolific father a condom in the post.*

girl. The best thing she could do—for herself and other people—was to become a very good child, one who could be guaranteed never to make extra work for the grown-ups. And so it was that in order to distance herself from the chorus of tears, tantrums, dripping noses and dirty nappies that surrounded her in a noisy, leaking fug, little Isabella Mayson became a tiny adult herself, self-contained, brisk, useful. A sketch executed by Elizabeth Dorling in 1848 shows the entire family, at this point consisting of thirteen children, gathered in a jostling group. Elizabeth, who puts herself in the picture, is in a black dress and white cap and is nursing the latest baby, Lucy. Henry, dishevelled and standing slightly apart, gazes wild-eyed on the sketchy crew of small dependants as if contemplating how on earth he will cope. The only other figure who is properly inked in is Isabella, who stands immediately behind Elizabeth. She is wearing a black dress and white cap identical to her mother's, with the same centre-parted hairstyle. In her arms she holds a wriggling toddler on whom her watchful gaze is fixed. She is twelve, going on twenty-five.

Cartoon showing the thirteen-strong
Mayson-Dorling clan in 1848. Twelve-year-old Isabella
is standing behind her mother, care-taking a toddler.

Soon Isabella's nannying duties were expanded even further. As the clutch of children increased, it soon became clear that Ormond House could not hold the growing Dorling brood. The noise alone was unbearable: one day Henry Dorling, disturbed by the din, stuck his head around his study door and demanded to know what was going on. "That, Henry," Elizabeth is reported to have said, "is your children and my children fighting our children." The solution, though, was close at hand. The Grandstand was not needed for all but a few days a year. It would provide the perfect place to store extra children, those who were old enough to leave their mother but not yet sufficiently independent to be sent away to school. In this satellite nursery, housed in a building that resembled a stranded ocean liner on a sea of green, the little Dorlings would be watched over by Granny Jerrom and sensible, grown-up Isabella.

The fact that Isabella Beeton spent part of her youth in the Epsom Grandstand has insinuated itself into her mythology, until the idea has become quite fixed that she spent years at a time up there, running a kind of spooky orphanage. This, as commentators have been quick to point out, could not be in greater contrast to the cosy intimate atmosphere that Mrs. Beeton urges her readers to create for their own families: "It ought, therefore, to enter into the domestic policy of every parent, to make her children feel that home is the happiest place in the world; that to imbue them with this delicious home-feeling is one of the choicest gifts a parent can bestow." What has been missed, though, in the rush to point out the discrepancy between Mrs. Beeton's advice and her personal experience, is the fact that in the first half of the nineteenth century it was entirely usual for tradesmen to shunt their families round in this way. Grocers, drapers, and chemists all used their premises flexibly, sometimes raising an entire family over the shop, and at others sending some of the children to live in other buildings associated with the business. The Dorlings' decision to use the Grandstand as an annexe to Ormond House may seem odd to us now, but to their Epsom neighbours it was simply the way things were done. No more peculiar than the fact that the now elderly William Dorling had moved out of the High Street premises and gone to live with his daughter at the post office in the High Street. People were more portable than buildings.

The second point about Isabella's creepy kingdom on top of the hill is that there is no way of telling how often and for how long she was up on the Downs. For at least two years of her teens she was away at boarding school, first in London and then Heidelberg, and so unavailable for Grandstand duties. Once she returned home for good, probably in 1854, her letters make clear that, far from being marooned for weeks at a time, she moved constantly between Ormond House and the Downs. For instance, in a letter that she writes to her fiancé Sam Beeton in February 1856 she explains that she and her stepsister Jane have just got back from the Grandstand where they "have been doing the charitable to Granny. Poor old lady, she complained sadly it was so dull in the evening sitting all alone, so we posted up there to gossip with her." Another time she mentions that she has been up at the Grandstand all day "and of course have not sat down all day," yet makes it clear that she is now writing from the relative calm of Ormond House. When the Grandstand was needed for a race meeting, it was Isabella who was responsible for "transporting that living cargo of children" to alternative accommodation, usually a house at 72 Marine Parade in Brighton, close to the racecourse where Dorling also held the position of clerk. Far from being in permanent exile, Isabella Mayson was a body in a perpetual state of motion.

Still, whether or not Isabella was in attendance at any particular moment, it remains the case that the Grandstand made a strange kindergarten. A huge barn of a building—fifty yards long and twenty yards wide, and designed to hold five thousand people—it was now home to perhaps no more than six little children and their minders. It has been suggested that the closest analogy would be that of living in a boarding school during the holidays. But there was an important difference. The Grandstand had never been built with children in mind. It was designed for adults and adult activity—betting, drinking, flirting, parading, coming up before the makeshift magistrate. On the one hand the world of the Dorlings and the world of Epsom racecourse were soldered together to the point where one had become a synonym for the other: or, as the *Illustrated London News* would put it in a few years' time: "What cold punch is to turtle, mustard to roast beef, ice to Cliquot champagne, Chablis to oysters, that is Mr. Dorling to the Derby." Yet, at the same time, there were occasions when those two worlds, the world of the bourgeois family and that of the seedy racetrack were a very awkward fit. It was this paradox that poor little Alfred Dorling, acquiring his fatal condom from among the "racy" characters who hung around the Downs, had failed to understand.

Certainly we can say that the scale of the place was grand, designed to see and be seen in. As such it was a public theatre, something that older, aristocratic members of the racing fraternity found hard to grasp. The Duchess of Richmond of Goodwood wrote to Dorling about this time grandly informing him: "The Duchess of Richmond would *prefer* a portion of the Grand Stand railed off, if she could have it to *Herself*." But there was little chance of the Duchess, even with her Goodwood credentials, getting her way. The point about the Grandstand was that it belonged to the modern world and, as such, was a democratic space to which anyone could buy the right to enter. There was a huge pillared hall, a thirty-yard-long saloon, four refreshment rooms, and a series of committee rooms. In 1840 when Queen Victoria had made her second and final visit to Epsom, £200 had been spent on getting the Grandstand's wallpaper and carpets up to scratch, with the result that the Dorling children, quite literally, lived in a place that was fit for a queen. Eighteen years later when Prince Albert made a return visit, this time with his future son-in-law the German Crown Prince Frederick, the papers reported that on the receiving room wall was "the Royal Coat of Arms, executed in needlepoint by the Misses Dorling." The nursery, then, was a curiously public and even ceremonial space inside which the children were expected to eat and sleep while leaving as little trace as possible of their small lives. At night they lay on truckle beds that could be folded up during the day. Whenever Henry Dorling needed to show a visiting dignitary around they could be herded into another room. At a moment's notice all evidence of their existence could be made to disappear.

Particularly intriguing about the Grandstand set-up is the fact that the future Mrs. Beeton spent formative stretches of her young life next to a commercial kitchen that catered to thousands at a time. Much has been made of Mrs. Beeton's picnic plans for forty people, or her dinner party menus for eighteen. Perhaps the fact that she lived on a Brobdingnagian scale—the eldest girl in a family of twenty-one and an amateur nursery maid in a space designed for thousands—explains the ease with which she

Epsom Grandstand from the rear.

came to think in large numbers. For this reason Dickens' description of the Grandstand kitchens working at full pelt for the Derby is worth quoting in full.

> To furnish the refreshment-saloon, the Grand Stand has in store two thousand four hundred tumblers, one thousand two hundred wine-glasses, three thousand plates and dishes, and several of the most elegant vases we have seen out of the Glass Palace, decorated with artificial flowers. An exciting odour of cookery meets us in our descent. Rows of spits are turning rows of joints before blazing walls of fire. Cooks are trussing fowls; confectioners are making jellies; kitchen-maids are plucking pigeons; huge crates of boiled tongues are being garnished on dishes. One hundred and thirty legs of lamb, sixty-five saddles of lamb, and one hundred shoulders of lamb; in short, a whole flock of sixty-five lambs, have to be roasted, and dished and garnished, by the Derby Day. Twenty rounds of beef, four hundred lobsters, one hundred and fifty tongues, twenty fillets of veal, one hundred sirloins of beef, five hundred spring chickens, three hundred and fifty pigeon pies; a countless number of quartern loaves, and an incredible quantity of ham have to be cut up into sandwiches; eight hundred eggs have got to be boiled for the pigeon-pies and salads. The forests of lettuce, the acres of cress, and beds of radishes, which will have to be chopped up; the gallons of "dressing" that will have to be poured out and converted into salads for the insatiable Derby Day, will be best understood by a memorandum from the chief of that department to the *chef-de-cuisine*, which happened, accidentally, to fall under our notice: "Pray don't forget a large tub and a birch-broom for mixing the salad!"

We do not know if some of the Grandstand rooms were permanently out of bounds to the children, but certainly Amy Dorling, born in 1859 and still going strong during the Second World War, remembered playing tag around the huge public rooms, which must have echoed strangely to tiny thudding feet and shrill screams. The children might have turned feral were it not for the fact that Henry Dorling now ran his printing business from the Grandstand (yet more evidence of the fudging of interests which so alarmed hostile commentators) and visited almost daily. And then, of course, there was Granny Jerrom, that solid constant in this story who nonetheless left virtually no trace in the formal records. All we have to make her real is a family anecdote, and a recently discovered photograph.

First, the anecdote. Nancy Spain has the old lady sitting tight on top of the box in which the first year's takings of the Grandstand under Henry Dorling's regime were stored. In the story, according to Spain, Mrs. Jerrom is knitting furiously. The image neatly sums up the qualities of a whole generation of pre-Victorian women. Money is crucial, far from vulgar, but needs to be watched carefully if it is not to disappear into thin air. There is no shame in guarding it with your life, or at least with your sturdy body weight. But knitting is important too. This is not the fancy needlework that will come to define a whole new generation of young "genteel" middle-class women, certainly not the royal coat of arms executed a few years later by her granddaughters "the Misses Dorling." Instead, Mrs. Jerrom is engaged in a serviceable craft that will clothe a family, save expenditure, and eke out an income. And, what is more, there is no shame to be seen doing it.

Then there is the photograph, lately discovered among a box of prints taken by the Epsom photographer Cuthbert John Hopkins. During the 1860s every worthy burgher and his lady seem to have passed through Mr. Hopkins's studio in their best bib and tucker, ready to be captured for posterity by this promising new process. There is also a picture of sixty-eight-year-old Mrs. Jerrom, probably taken in 1862, wearing a solid black dress and white cap, the standard garb of a widow. Her mouth is slightly ajar, as if surprised by the flash of Mr. Hopkins's magic box. She is a neat, serviceable little woman. Perhaps because she only had two pregnancies to Elizabeth's seventeen she has kept her figure in a way that her dropsical daughter never managed.

Mrs. Jerrom's image is in sharp contrast with that of three of her grandchildren, who were photographed during the same session: Bessie and Esther Mayson and Amy Dorling. Both the Mayson girls are fashionably dressed, smooth-haired, and look straight into the camera with the confidence of eligible young women who have no worries about the old-maidism that lies ahead (they are only twenty-four and twenty-one and, while Bessie is probably the prettiest, Esther has that striking auburn hair and slender figure that people will still be noticing when she is in her eighties). The other granddaughter photographed is Amy Dorling, who at

Esther Mayson, Isabella's youngest sister,
and her grandmother, Mary Jerrom, photographed around 1862.

three years old is a spoiled lolling brat with ringlets and a challenging look, as if she knows she is a rich man's daughter entitled to anything she wants, including the photographer's patience. The Mayson girls and Amy, although divided by twenty years, are both of a generation that understands the camera's eye and can meet it on its own terms. Mrs. Jerrom, by contrast, looks suspiciously over the shoulder of the photographer and into the distance, to a time before a machine could capture your soul.

ISABELLA MAYSON'S education was patchy, but no more so than virtually every other girl of her class and time. She was sent for a while to a school in Islington, chosen more for its familiarity and convenience than anything else, since it was directly opposite 14 Duncan Terrace, where Elizabeth Mayson and her little brood were living just prior to their move to Epsom. Until 1844, 1 Colebrooke Row had housed a boys' school, but in that year it started to cater for girls under the watchful eyes of Miss Lucy and Miss Mary Richardson. Five years later the school was taken over by two sisters from Hackney, with the delightfully Austenish names of Sarah and Fanny Woodhouse. The 1851 census shows them with five pupils, four of whom were either Maysons (Bessie and Esther) or Dorlings (Mary and Charlotte).

If this sounds cottagey and amateurish, it is only a fair measure of how small private boarding schools operated during the early Victorian period. Quite unlike the public and high schools of a later date, these little commercial enterprises, headed by a clergyman or a couple of spinster sisters, were flighty affairs, quite capable of closing down or changing hands at a moment's notice when, say, a particular family decided to withdraw its patronage. The quality of the education the pupils received varied wildly, dependent entirely on the skills and abilities of the person who happened to be in charge at any moment. At 1 Colebrooke Row it is most likely that Isabella was taught to read and write, sew and perhaps speak a little French. She almost certainly learned to draw and paint, since the Misses Richardson's brother, a portrait painter, ran his studio from the same address. The fact that Isabella's younger sisters, step-sister, and half-sister were sent to the same establishment—though under different management—suggests that the Dorlings, who knew a good bargain when they saw one, thought that they were getting value for money.

However, to their credit, the Dorlings wanted more than a just-so education for their girls. "Boarding school misses" were becoming an increasingly visible—and mockable—part of the social landscape. Social commentators saw them as part of that whole process whereby the rising commercial middle classes were trying to turn their girls into what they fondly imagined were ladies. Farmers, always the particular butt of critics' complaints, were said to be sending their daughters to pretentious boarding schools for a year or two where they picked up a little French and piano and felt themselves, once home, too grand to help with the domestic chores. The accusation could be extended to include every chief clerk, wealthy grocer, and small-time solicitor who was now busy trying to scramble up the social ladder by turning his daughters into something very different from their mothers. Instead of moulding gracious and accomplished ladies, so the argument ran, these cheap boarding schools were churning out silly girls with ideas above their stations. It was a stereotype that a young publisher and editor called Samuel Beeton was, at this very moment, spoofing in his new magazine the *Englishwoman's Domestic Magazine* (*EDM*): "the young lady's peculiar talents consisted in dress and fancy-work, with some interludes of novel-reading and playing fantasias on the piano (in company), and, as we were forced to admit on seeing her with some of her particular friends, in a great faculty of talking and laughing about nothing."

The Dorlings wanted something better for their girls, and they decided to send them abroad to school in Heidelberg, the small historic town in southwest Germany. In no way a "finishing school" (the concept had no purchase in Germany), the Heidels' establishment had started as a day school in the late 1830s, providing a rigorous syllabus for the daughters of well-to-do local people. However, by 1850, the forty-year-old head-mistress Miss Auguste Heidel was actively seeking British girls as boarders for her school, which occupied a series of premises in the picturesque heart of the city. Every year, in late spring, Miss Heidel visited London, took rooms in the City and invited prospective parents to deposit their daughters with her for immediate passage to Germany. These invitations took the form of announcements in *The Times* and the *Athenaeum*:

GERMAN EDUCATION,—Miss HEIDEL'S ESTABLISHMENT, Heidelberg—Miss Heidel will remain in London a short time longer, and will take charge of any YOUNG LADIES intended to be placed in her seminary. She may be spoken with, between the hours of 3 and 4 o'clock every day, Monday excepted, at Mr. Young's, Walbrook

The school timetable from 1837—fifteen years before Isabella travelled to Heidelberg—still survives. Dance, music, and domestic economy had no part in the syllabus. Instead the curriculum centred on French and German, which was taught to the younger girls by Miss Charlotte Heidel and to the more advanced by Miss Auguste. Charlotte also taught "logical thinking," natural history and mathematics. Karl Heidel, their brother and a university graduate, was in charge of history and geography. Miss Louisa, another sister, taught needlework and German to the little ones. Calligraphy and mathematics were the preserve of a visiting master, Herr Rau, who normally worked at the rigorous Höheren Bürgerschule. Teaching started at 8 a.m. and did not finish until 5 p.m.

Isabella probably entered the school in the summer of 1851, when she was fifteen and a half. It is most likely that she was accompanied by her step-sister Jane Dorling who was virtually the same age. In the following years the slightly younger Bessie and Esther Mayson and Mary Dorling would also attend the Heidel Institute, as well as a family of girls called

Beeton, who had been the Maysons' neighbours in Milk Street. This decision of friends and neighbours to send their daughters to the same school on the other side of Europe might seem quaint to modern eyes, but it made sense. Girls who already knew each other made good travelling companions and congenial schoolfellows. If ladies' boarding schools were all about creating a home-from-home atmosphere, then what could be more natural for people who already liked each other to use the same institution? And, given that the journey to Heidelberg took a couple of days either way, sharing chaperonage represented a significant saving of time and money.

It was this tradition of sending whole clutches of sisters, friends and neighbours to the same school that gave these boarding schools a family feel. While the Heidels' regime was rigorous by English standards, a sweetly sisterly atmosphere prevailed among the young ladies who attended. In letters which the younger Beeton and Mayson girls sent to the now married Isabella in 1857 to congratulate her on her twenty-first birthday we hear how "On Shrove Tuesday we girls got up a Mask Ball, and invited the governesses . . . to join us. . . . Miss Louisa was perfectly enchanted with our costumes." Another governess, who has recently married, sends her "best love" to Isabella. Writing three years later—in German—to Isabella, Miss Auguste Heidel sends her congratulations to "your dear parents" on the birth of a new baby boy "of whose arrival my dear Bessie has just informed me."

Quite what the young British women who attended the Heidel Institute did when they were not busy learning arithmetic and French is not entirely clear. The city was dominated by the ruins of Heidelberg Castle, a tumbledown thirteenth- to seventeenth-century palace that had done so much to spark Goethe and his contemporaries into Romantic reveries at the beginning of the century. By the time the rather stolid Mayson, Dorling, and Beeton girls got there in the 1850s, the castle had become one of those key stop-offs in the burgeoning European tourist industry. When Sam Beeton visited his half-sisters Helen and Polly at school in 1856 he felt obliged to visit "the renowned ruin of Germany" first before sweeping the girls off to the Prince Carl café where they stuffed themselves with honey and chocolate. Doubtless on Sundays the young ladies from the Heidel Institute plodded up to the castle, drank lemonade bought from a vendor, and looked over the spectacular but by now wearingly familiar view of the wooded River Neckar. Perhaps they blushed when students from the renowned university strayed too near and wondered hopefully whether there was a forgotten prince somewhere in the ruins who might rescue them from intermediate German and composition.

By the summer of 1854, eighteen-year-old Isabella was back home in Epsom and ready for the role of "daughter at home," that odd period between school and marriage which might last for a few months or a lifetime. She was, without doubt, a superior model of the species. She had learned French and German at the Heidels' from native speakers and heard the languages spoken in a constant babble from dawn until dusk. She was also musical: all young ladies could bang out a waltz on the piano, but Isabella was lucky enough to be both genuinely talented and to have parents who were prepared to nurture that gift. Henry Dorling could himself play several instruments and was happy to pay for his stepdaughter to take lessons with Julius Benedict. Benedict, the son of a rich Jewish banker from Stuttgart, was by the 1850s a highly visible force in British musical theatre. Coaching young ladies at the piano was the way he paid the rent. Benedict's sessions with the promising Miss Mayson required her to make a weekly trip up to town to his rooms in Manchester Square, which happened to be virtually next door to where Isaac and Mary Jerrom had once run their stables and lodging house.

As Isabella stepped into Manchester Square each week for her lesson with Benedict she was herself a kind of pattern of what was happening to the middle classes during this first slice of Victoria's reign. As a child she had lived over the shop, in rooms above her father's City warehouse. As a teenager she had lived inside the shop, spending days in the Grandstand at Epsom, providing labour which the Dorlings could not afford to pay for on the market (a wealthier family would have had nurses and nursemaids and, more obviously, a bigger house). But at fifteen, as the stepdaughter of an increasingly wealthy man, Isabella had been sent off to Germany to acquire a good education, something more than the usual veneer that the lower middle classes were busy painting over their daughters.

What the Dorlings almost certainly didn't account for was the fact that Isabella would return from her stay in Germany with a keen interest in baking. While the Heidels' school was academically rigorous, it was firmly rooted in a German cultural tradition that saw no tension between women being both learned and domestic. George Eliot, the British novelist who arrived to spend some months in Weimar just as Isabella was getting ready to leave Heidelberg, put this very un-English model of culti-vated, practical femininity at the heart of her fictional universe. In *Middlemarch,* for instance, it is Mrs. Garth and her daughter Mary who most obviously win the author's approval, with their ability to bake and teach their children Latin virtually in parallel. So while the Heidel sisters con-centrated on teaching Isabella German, French and composition, they also initiated her into the pastry-making in which southwest Germany specialized.

Isabella had clearly caught the baking bug in Heidelberg, for on returning home to Epsom in 1854 she asked for lessons in pastry-making from the local baker William Barnard. The only reason she was allowed to go was because making cakes, and fancy cakes at that, was a thing apart from the general drudge of cookery. Isabella was not being

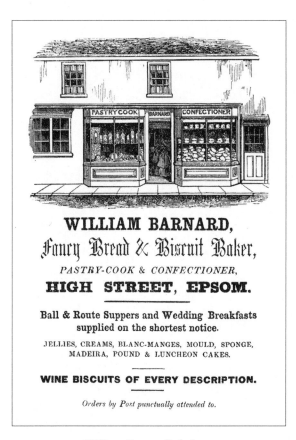

William Barnard's bakery,
where Isabella took lessons in pastry-making.

despatched to learn how to peel potatoes or cook stew, but was participating in the one branch of cookery that gentlewomen had traditionally
practised, at least during the earlier part of the previous century. Even so,
the Dorlings were sufficiently jumpy about the social implications to
worry whether they were doing the right thing. Nearly a hundred years
later Isabella's sessions at Barnard's were still being recalled by her
younger half-sisters as "ultra modern and not quite nice."

INTERLUDE

Cherishing, then, in her breast the respected utterances of the good and the great, let the mistress of every house rise to the responsibility of its management.

ISABELLA BEETON,
Book of Household Management

EVERYONE IN MRS. BEETON'S imaginary household is rising, moving upwards, heading *somewhere*. The servants are busy working their way through the ranks (if there are no chances of promotion where they are, says Beeton, they will shift sideways to a smarter household). The mistress, meanwhile, isn't simply getting up early for the sake of it, but in order to manage her household more efficiently, keeping a hawk-eye out for wasted time or money. Embedded in Beeton's text is the assumption that this household is an aspirational one, busy edging itself into a style of living that currently lies just out of reach.

In order to achieve that lifestyle—an extra housemaid, a second footman—the income of the household will need to rise too, and Mrs. Beeton thoughtfully provides a table showing what each jump of £200 or so will give you. So although the head of the household remains mainly off stage in the *Book of Household Management*, his economic efforts remain absolutely crucial to the whole enterprise. He, too, is busy improving his position in the workplace so that his wife can run a better-staffed home, and his servants can in turn push for promotion.

Since everyone in Beeton's household is busy helping themselves (in all senses) it is a nice coincidence that 1859, the year that the *Book of House-hold Management* first started appearing in parts, is also the year that Samuel Smiles published his iconic *Self-Help*. These days more referred to than read, *Self-Help* consists of thirteen chapters with stirring titles such as "Application and Perseverance" and "Energy and Courage" in which lower-middle-class men are urged to emulate the educational and social trajectories of such titans as Robert Peel, James Watt, or Josiah Wedgwood. The message of Smiles' book, repeated over and over again as if in an attempt at self-hypnosis, is that in the new industrial age pedigree and birth no longer make a gentleman. What matters now are thrift, hard work, and temperance. Properly pursued—and perseverance is everything here—these qualities won't simply make you pleasant, civilized and cultured, they will also make you rich: "energy enables a man to force his way through irksome drudgery and dry details, and carries him onward and upward in every station in life." Rich enough, in fact, to afford the cook, upper housemaid, nursemaid, under-housemaid and manservant that Mrs. Beeton envisages for the household whose income is "About £1,000 a year."

But *Self-Help* and Beeton's *Book of Household Management* are bound together by more than a shared publication date and a driving concern with social advancement. The Smiles family happened to be very good friends of the Dorlings. Although Samuel Smiles was a Scotsman who had worked as both a doctor and a newspaper editor in Leeds, by 1854 he was settled in Blackheath where he was employed as a railway executive, writing his books on the side. The two families were initially intimate in south London where both households were known for their generous hospitality. This intimacy continued after Henry and Elizabeth Dorling's deaths in the early 1870s when six of the unmarried Dorling and Mayson girls moved to Kensington, just around the corner from where the Smiles were now living in style in Pembroke Gardens. In April 1874 Lucy Dorling, the little half-sister who had always been closest to Isabella, walked up the aisle with Willy Smiles, Samuel Smiles' second eldest son.

And there the story might have ended, with the neat coming together of the two families that between them produced the founding texts of mid-Victorian social aspiration. But there is a final, chilling coda, which suggests just what happened when *Self-Help* and *Household Manage-*

ment blended a little too enthusiastically. Lucy and the tyrannical Willy, who ran the Belfast Rope Works, produced eleven children. The story goes that in order to encourage early rising, perseverance and so on in his brood, Willy insisted that every morning there would be only ten boiled eggs provided for the children's breakfast. The last one down, the sluga-bed, went hungry.

CHAPTER THREE

PAPER WITHOUT END

AT 39 MILK STREET, on the opposite side of the road and a little further up from Benjamin Mayson's warehouse, stood the Dolphin public house. It was on the corner with, in fact virtually part of, Honey Lane Market. In its original, medieval incarnation, the market had been at the centre of the brewing industry, the place where local beer makers, the forerunners of the Victorian giants Charrington and Whitbread, went to get their mead. At some point Honey Lane had turned into a general food market with a hundred stalls, and then, in 1787, it had been developed into a parade of thirty-six lock-up shops. Now, in 1835, two years before Benjamin Mayson brought his new bride Elizabeth and baby Isabella to live in Milk Street, the market had been knocked down to make way for the new City of London Boys' School, which promised to provide a modern, liberal education for the sons of commercial or trading men to fit them for the brisk new world that everyone agreed was on its way.

The evolution of Honey Lane Market is a timely reminder that until well into the nineteenth century the City of London was as much a place of manufacture, retail and residence as it was the hub of the nation's finances. To the outsider who happened to stray too far along its narrow, crooked streets it was as closed and as inscrutable as any village. Everywhere you looked in the square mile around St. Paul's you could see ordinary, everyday needs pressing on the landscape. Long before Lancashire cotton had taken over Milk Street, it was the place where you went for your dairy produce. Wood Street, which ran parallel and was now the epicentre of the textile trade, had once been thick with trees and the source of cheap and easy kindling. Just over the road, on the other side of Cheapside, were the self-explanatory Bread Street and Friday, that is Fish, Street. All these were now given over to the ubiquitous "Manchester warehouses," wholesaling operations that functioned as a funnel between the textile factories of the northwest, bulked out by cheaper imports from India, and the luxury drapery stores of the West End. A hundred yards to the east was Grocers' Hall Court and just beyond that was Old Jewry where the Jews who had come over with Norman William had settled to live and trade. Now, in a pale copy of its original self, it was the place you went if you wanted to pawn your jewellery, get a valuation, or simply have your watch set to rights.

From the beginning of the eighteenth century the pace of change picked up as men and women from the countryside poured into the City, bringing their skills as carpenters, printers, carriage builders, sign painters, butchers, glue boilers, farriers, nail makers—everything, in short, that a community needed to thrive in a pre-industrial age. On top of this, the large financial institutions that had settled in the area a hundred years earlier were beginning to expand as Britain became the money capital of the world. Threadneedle Street, home of the Bank of England, was both the heart of the financial district and the place where prostitutes queued patiently, like cabs. From there it was a short walk to the Stock Exchange, Royal Exchange, the Baltic and Lloyd's coffee houses, not to mention the offices of bill brokers, merchant bankers, and private bankers. Yet even in the middle of the nineteenth century many of these smaller "houses" were still family businesses, handed down from father to son with occasional injections of capital from a lucky marriage. Right up to the middle of Victoria's reign the City of London continued to be a place where the public and private, professional and personal sides of life were pursued from the same streets, often, indeed, from the same set of rooms.

At the heart of these overlapping worlds stood the public house. The "pub" was built as a house, looked like a house, and in this early period was indistinguishable from the family homes on either side of it. Yet it was public, in the sense that anyone might enter from the streets and use its domestic facilities—food, chairs, fire, silent companionship or lively conversation—for the price of a drink. It stank, of course, as all public places did, from a mixture of its clients' private smells and a few extra of its own: old food, flat beer, dead mice, linen that never quite got dry. The Dolphin, just like an ordinary domestic house, had its own aura that you would recognize as instantly as that of your child's or lover's. The plans for the pub do not survive, but this kind of place usually had five separate rooms on the ground floor, including a public parlour, taproom, kitchen, and the publican's private parlour. There was no bar as such; beer (not spirits, which needed a separate licence) was brought to the customers by waitresses and potboys. The effect was simply as if you had popped into someone else's sitting room to be offered refreshment by the mistress of the house, or her maid. Often these people felt as familiar as your own.

The Dolphin, like all pubs in the first half of the nineteenth century, doubled as a community hall, council chambers, coroner's court, labour exchange, betting shop, canteen, and park bench. It would not be until the 1840s that the temperance do-gooders would manage to forge the link in people's minds between social respectability and total abstinence from drink. In fact until that time, which coincided with the first steps in public sanitary reform, drinking alcohol was a great deal safer than risking the local water. It was for that reason that when Milk Street tradesmen like Mr. Chamberlain at number 36, a lone leather worker in a sea of cotton, came to take their lunch at the Dolphin every day, they washed it

The junction of Cheapside and Milk Street. The Dolphin pub is next door to the impressive-looking City of London School.

down with several glasses of port before tottering back for the afternoon's work. And in a world before town halls and committee rooms— the very setting in which Mr. Chamberlain's own son, the Liberal politician Joseph, would eventually make his mark in faraway Birmingham—many political organizations, charities, chapters, friendly societies and trades associations including, oddly, the fledgling temperance societies, would choose to hold their meetings in the snug surroundings of a public house rather than trying to pile into someone's inadequate lodgings.

From 1808 the Dolphin was run by Samuel Beeton, a Stowmarket man who was part of his generation's tramp from the Suffolk countryside into the capital. Born in 1774 into a family of builders, Beeton had broken with tradition by becoming a tailor. Arriving in London in the closing years of the century he settled at a number of addresses around Smithfield Market, the centre of the skinning, cobbling, and clothing trades. The market at the time was a smoking, bloody tangle of streets where life was nasty, brutal and short, at least for the livestock. Cattle and sheep were herded up from the country before being slaughtered, dismantled, and sold on in bits. The best meat went to the butchers, the bones to the glue makers, the hides to the cobblers and tailors who had settled in surrounding Clerkenwell.

It might seem lazy to use Dickens to describe the streets that Beeton knew, but there is no one else who does London—stinking, noisy, elemental London—quite so well. Here, then, is the master's description from *Oliver Twist*, as Bill Sikes drags Oliver through Smithfield on their way to commit a burglary:

> It was market-morning. The ground was covered, nearly ankle-deep, with filth and mire; a thick steam, perpetually rising from the reeking bodies of the cattle, and mingling with the fog, which seemed to rest upon the chimney-tops, hung heavily above. All the pens in the centre of the large area, and as many temporary pens as could be crowded into the vacant space, were filled with sheep; tied up to posts by the gutter side were long lines of beasts and oxen, three or four deep. Countrymen, butchers, drovers, hawkers, boys, thieves, idlers, and vagabonds of every low grade, were mingled together in a mass; the whistling of drovers, the barking dogs, the bellowing and plunging of the oxen, the bleating of sheep, the grunting and squeaking of pigs, the cries of hawkers, the shouts, oaths, and quarrelling on all sides; the ringing of bells

and roar of voices, that issued from every public-house; the crowding, pushing, driving, beating, whooping and yelling; the hideous and discordant din that resounded from every corner of the market; and the unwashed, unshaven, squalid, and dirty figures constantly running to and fro, and bursting in and out of the throng; rendered it a stunning and bewildering scene, which quite confounded the senses.

Samuel Beeton lived right at the heart of all this driving, beating, whooping chaos. By 1803 he was keeping a pub, the Globe, in the aptly named Cow Lane, which led straight off the marketplace and most likely catered mainly for his former colleagues, the tailors. His first daughter—by now he was married to Lucy Elsden, a Suffolk girl—was christened at nearby St. Sepulchre, the church from where "the bells of Old Bailey" rang out twelve times on the eve of an execution at adjoining Newgate. Perhaps the child, Ann Thomason (Thomasin had been Samuel's mother's name), found this doomy world too hard to bear: born in May 1807, she left it soon afterwards. Her siblings, by contrast, were patterned on what would soon emerge as the Beeton template: robust, canny, pragmatic. All seven survived into thriving middle age.

Beeton's shift from tailoring to the hospitality business played straight to his natural strengths. He was outgoing, clubbable, the sort of man who joined organizations and rose through them by being pleasant, useful, good to have around. In October 1803, and already working as a "victualler," he paid to become a member of the Pattenmakers' Guild. Pattens, those strap-on platforms that raised the wearer's everyday shoes above the dead cats, horse shit and other debris of the metropolitan streets, might seem exactly the right thing for filthy Smithfield. But, in fact, pattens and their makers had been in decline for some time. The guild clung to existence by exploiting the fact that it was one of the cheapest to join, and so provided an economical way into City of London politics for those who might otherwise find it too rich for their pockets. You did not need to know how to make wooden clogs in order to belong, although plenty of its members, like Beeton himself, had once belonged to the allied tailoring trade.

By 1808, and with the arrival of their second daughter, Lucy, the Beetons had moved to the Dolphin in Milk Street. Samuel may not have been born to the life of a City worthy, but he lost no time in catching up. In

1813 he was elected to the Common Council for the ward of Cripplegate Within (you had to be a guild member to qualify—the Pattenmakers had come in useful) and proved both popular and effective. Fifteen years on and he was still getting the highest number of votes for re-election. The Common Council, part of the arcane City of London government, was a mixture of the powerful and the picturesque. Seen from the outside the 234 council men were pompous and reactionary, clinging to ancient rights of administration in a way that blocked London from getting the city-wide police force or sewerage system it so desperately needed. The council men, however, saw themselves as defenders against creeping bureaucracy and standardization, proud advocates of an ancient and honourable independence. The minutes for Cripplegate Ward during the period Beeton served show the council men setting the rates, choosing the beadle, worrying about street security, congratulating the alderman on his recent baronetcy and, in the manner of ponderous uncles, sending their thoughts on various topics to His Majesty. The Beetons clearly felt themselves intimately implicated in the life of the royal family: two of Samuel's grandchildren would be christened "Victoria" and "Edward Albert."

Beeton was also active within his adopted trade. He served on the Committee of the Society of Licensed Victuallers, becoming their chairman in 1821. This meant attending the meetings every week on Monday at 5 p.m., either in the Fleet Street office of the publicans' daily paper, the *Morning Advertiser*, or at Kennington Lane at the Licensed Victuallers' School which, despite its name, was more orphanage than academy. At the end of his presidency, Beeton was presented with a snuffbox, the early-nineteenth-century equivalent of the carriage clock, in recognition of his "exemplary conduct, strict integrity and unceasing perseverance."

As the nineteenth century, with its new opportunities for personal advancement, got under way Beeton's steady climb up the twin ladders of respectability and wealth provided a model for the rest of his extended family. The first of his generation to leave the countryside for London, he became a beacon, pattern, and support for those who followed in his wake. There was Benjamin, his much younger brother, who arrived in London around 1809 and set up in Marylebone as a farrier, and may well have been an acquaintance of the jobmaster Isaac Jerrom. Samuel's nephew Robert, meanwhile, made the journey from Suffolk ten years later and also went into the pub-keeping business, initially in Spitalfields and then in St. Pancras, borrowing money from his uncle to buy the substantial Yorkshire Grey. By the time he died in 1836 Samuel Beeton had built up a tidy estate, consisting not only of the Dolphin itself, but property carefully husbanded both in London and back home in Suffolk. For a man who had started out as a tramping tailor, it was a glorious finish.

The child who matters to this story is, fittingly, the eldest son of Samuel's eldest son. First, the son. Samuel Powell Beeton—named after a fellow member of the Society of Licensed Victuallers—was born in 1804, Samuel and Lucy's first child. He was not christened until July 1812, when he was taken to St. Lawrence Jewry with his new baby brother, Robert Francis. The intervening girls—the frail Ann Thomason and Lucy—had been baptized in the usual way, as babies. This suggests two things. First, that Samuel Powell was obviously robust, so there was no need to whisk him off to the church in case he died before being formally accepted as one of God's own. Second, that the Beetons were not religious people. They christened a child because it seemed frail, or because a nagging vicar told them they should, not out of any urgent personal need. To be a Beeton was to live squarely on the earth, planted in the here and now.

Samuel Powell did what first sons should and modelled himself on his father. In 1827 he joined the Pattenmakers, this time by patrimony rather than purchase, and from 1838 he was a member of the Common Council for Cripplegate Ward. He was prominent in City politics, to the point where he felt it necessary in January 1835 to write to *The Times* to explain that he was emphatically *not* the Beeton who had signed the Conservative address to His Majesty (his affiliation was Liberal). It was assumed that Samuel Powell would eventually take over from his father at the Dolphin. But until that moment came in 1834, he filled the years as a Manchester warehouseman, trading out of Watling Street, a stone's throw away from Milk Street on the other side of Cheapside. In 1830 Samuel Powell married Helen Orchart, the daughter of a well-to-do baker from adjacent Wood Street. The Beetons' first child, Samuel Orchart, was born on 2 March 1831 at 81 Watling Street and christened at All Hallows Bread Street, a church traditionally connected with the brewing trade.

As early as the 1830s Londoners were dreaming of getting out and getting away, partially retracing the journey that their fathers had made from the countryside a generation earlier. The City was getting used up, stale, filthy. In 1800 you could swim in the Thames on a hot summer's day. By 1830 a gulp of river water would make you very ill indeed. The graveyards were so overstocked that a heavy downpour regularly uncovered the dead who were supposed to be sleeping peacefully. The streets were hung around with a greasy fug that followed you wherever you went, sticking to your clothes and working its way deep into your skin. In the circumstances, Samuel Powell and his wife, being modern kind of people, decamped to Camberwell, a short walk over London Bridge, to an area that still passed for country. It was there, south of the river, that the Beetons had a second son, a child who until now has slipped through the records, perhaps because the parish clerk at Camberwell was particularly careless, or hard of hearing. For William Beeton, born September 1832, is recorded as the son of "Samuel Power Beeton" and his wife "Eleanor." William must have died, because no other mention is made of him. He probably took his mother with him, for Helen Beeton—this time going by her correct name—was buried only eight weeks later. Family tradition always had it that Helen died of TB, which she bequeathed to her firstborn, Samuel Orchart. In the days before death certificates it is impossible to be certain, but it looks as if Helen Orchart was a victim of that other nineteenth-century common-or-garden tragedy, the woman who died as a result of childbirth.

Samuel Powell lost no time in doing what all sensible widowers with young children were advised to do and went looking for a new wife. Eliza Douse, the daughter of a local warehouseman, was working for people out in Romford when she and Samuel got married in 1834. On becoming mistress of the Dolphin two years later, Eliza quickly ensured that her sisters Mary and Sophia were provided for by getting them jobs and lodgings in the pub. If Helen, the first Mrs. Beeton, had been a delicate merchant's daughter, too weak for a world of bad fogs and babies, her successor Eliza proved to be a sturdy workhorse. She produced seven children, all of whom survived into adulthood and, following Samuel Powell's early death in 1854, continued to run the pub on her own before making a second marriage three years later.

Life as a Beeton was typical of the way that the families of the trading classes organized themselves in the early nineteenth century. Every member of the family, including the women, was expected to contribute something to the family enterprise whether it was a dowry (in the case of Helen Orchart) or labour, as in the case of her successor Eliza. If an extra pair of hands was needed at the Dolphin they were supplied from the extended family, as was the case with the Douse sisters. If there was no one immediately available, then a cousin might be imported from the home county. Thus Maria Brown, a cousin from Suffolk, was brought in to help in various Beeton enterprises. She shuttled between Marylebone and Milk Street until, in an equally likely move, she married Thomas Beeton, Samuel Powell's youngest brother who lodged at the Dolphin.

Marriage alliances were used to strengthen business connections in a way that seems cold to modern eyes. Thus Thomas Orchart, the baker from Wood Street, had a financial stake in the Dolphin before marrying his only daughter to his business partner's eldest son. Samuel Powell, in the years before taking over the pub from his father, worked as a warehouseman in partnership with Henry Minchener who was married to his younger sister Lucy. In the next generation down, their children—first cousins Jessie Beeton and Alfred Minchener—married. Samuel Powell's best friend, a warehouseman called George Perkes, had a son called Fred who married his second daughter Victoria. Meanwhile Samuel Powell's second son Sidney was given the middle name of "Perkes" as a token of respect and friendship. The man you did business with was the man whose name your son bore and whose daughter married your younger brother.

Old women were not exempt from responsibility to the family enterprise. Just as Mary Jerrom spent her long years of widowhood running a nursery on the Epsom Downs for the overspill of children from Ormond House, so Lucy Beeton looked after the eldest Dolphin children. In this case, though, her satellite nursery was far away in Suffolk. In 1836 the newly widowed Lucy returned to her native Hadleigh, where her elder brother Isaac was one of the chief tradesmen. Along with Lucy came her five-year-old grandson, Samuel Orchart. With the boy's mother dead and his step-mother busy creating a new family with his father, the Dolphin was overflowing. Family tradition puts a more benign spin upon it, saying that it was for the benefit of little Sam's precarious lungs (the ones he was supposed, for reasons that seem increasingly unlikely, to have inherited from his mother) that he was shuffled off to the country to live with his grandmother. This is fine in principle, except that by 1841 he had been joined by his younger half-sister Eliza whose lungs, as far as we know, were clear as a bell.

The other reason why it is unlikely that Sam was sent to stay with his grandmother for the sake of his health was that life in Hadleigh was hardly a pastoral idyll. Stuck in a dip between two hills, drainage was always a problem (after a storm it was possible to sail down the High Street), and the brewery near Lucy's house discharged its effluent into the open gutter. What's more, the town was a byword for viciousness and street crime: arson, sheep stealing, horse theft, house breaking and "malicious slaying and cutting and wounding" were all everyday hazards to be avoided by right-minded citizens, who were constantly agitating for extra policing. And yet, there can be no doubt that little Sam and his half-sister Eliza lived well in Hadleigh. Their grandmother had been left with a comfortable annuity of £140, her house in the High Street was substantial and her brother, Isaac, a wealthy maltster, had pull. And then, there was eighteen-year-old Aunt Carrie who acted as nursemaid, at least when she was not busy courting a local gentleman farmer called Robert Kersey. All the same, it was ten hours by coach back to the Dolphin.

We know as little about Samuel Beeton's childhood as we do about Isabella Mayson's. Sometime before the age of ten he was sent to a boarding school just outside Brentwood in Essex, midway between Hadleigh and London. Pilgrim's Hall Academy—also known as Brentwood Academy—had been set up in 1839 to educate the sons of the very middling classes. These kinds of boys' small private schools, very different from the ancient foundations such as Eton or Winchester, were as ephemeral as their female equivalents. Indeed, Pilgrim's Hall managed to last only thirteen years as a school, before reverting once again to a private residence. Although the advertisement that appeared in the *Illustrated London News* in 1843 promises prospective parents that pupils would be prepared for the universities as well as "the Naval and Military Colleges," it seems unlikely that any of them really did continue on to Oxford or Cambridge or make it into the Guards. Instead, most of the fifty-three pupils were, like young Samuel, destined for apprenticeships or posts in their fathers' businesses: tellingly, the 1841 census shows no boy at the school over the age of fifteen. Rather than ivy-covered quads and ancient towers, Pilgrim's Hall was a higgledy-piggledy domestic house from the Regency period which had been chopped and changed to make it a suitable place to house and school sixty or so boys as cheaply as possible (the house still stands but these days it caters for, on average, seven residents).

The fact that Pilgrim's Hall Academy was started by one Cornelius

Zurhort who employed Jules Doucerain as an assistant master suggests that the school concentrated on a modern syllabus of living rather than dead languages. And even once the school passed to a young Englishman, Alexander Watson from St. Pancras, in 1843, the stress on modern languages remained, with the employment of another Frenchman, Louis Morell. Clearly, though, the school prided itself on developing the whole boy, rather than merely helping him to slot into a world where he might be called upon to stammer a few words of business French. The *Illustrated London News* advertisement promises that the pupils' "religious, moral, and social habits and gentlemanly demeanour are watched with parental solicitude" and, indeed, as early as 1839 a gallery had been built in the local church for the very purpose of accommodating the shuffling, coughing Pilgrim's Hall boys as they trooped in every Sunday morning.

Samuel Orchart was quick and knowing, bright rather than scholarly. Like his future bride he had a flair for languages, winning a copy of *Une Histoire de Napoléon le Grand* for his work in French. Extrapolating from his adult personality we can assume that he was boisterous, involved, fun as a friend, cheeky with the teachers. Working back from the letters that he wrote to his own sons when they were at prep school in the mid 1870s we can guess that the young Sam was always bursting with enthusiasm for "the last new thing," whether it was comets, cricket scores, spring swimming, close-run class positions, or clever chess games. Clearly keen on literature—his father gave him a complete Shakespeare when he was twelve, and Samuel Powell was not the kind of man to waste his money on an empty gesture—there was, nonetheless, no question of the boy going on to university.

But a career as a publican was not quite right either, despite the fact that as the eldest son Samuel Orchart stood to inherit a thriving business. In the end none of Samuel Powell's three sons chose to run the Dolphin. That was the problem with social mobility, you left yourself behind. There was, though, a kind of possible compromise, one that allowed Sam to follow his literary bent without taking him too far from his social or geographic roots. He had grown up a few hundred yards from Fleet Street and its continuation, the Strand, which had for two centuries been the centre of the publishing trade. Now, in the 1840s, as the demand for printed material of all kinds exploded, it seemed as if everyone who set foot in the area was in some way connected with print. Inky-fingered apprentices hurried through the streets at all hours and from the open doors of taverns around Temple Bar you could see solitary young men poring over late-night proofs while gulping down a chop. Up and down Fleet Street new-fangled rotary presses were clanking through the night, producing newspapers, magazines, and books, books, books. In Paternoster Row—an alley off St. Paul's, a hop, skip, and a jump from Milk Street—booksellers and publishers so dominated the landscape that, among those in the know, "the Row" had become shorthand for the whole Republic of English Letters.

In any case, as the son and grandson of a publican Sam was already part of the newspaper trade. Pubs were frequently the only house in the street to take a daily paper, and many did a brisk trade in hiring it out at 1d an hour. In addition, the Society of Licensed Victuallers produced the *Morning Advertiser,* which, at that time, was the nation's only daily newspaper apart from *The Times.* It was to the *Advertiser's* offices at 27 Fleet Street that the original Samuel Beeton had headed every Monday afternoon during the early years of the century for the Victuallers' committee meetings. Even more importantly, the publicans' paper delivered a healthy profit to the society, which was regularly divvied up among the members. So as far as the Beetons were concerned, a man who went into print would never go hungry.

Sam does not seem to have served a formal apprenticeship, the kind where you were bound at fourteen to a single master and graduated as a journeyman in the appropriate livery company seven years later. That system, based on a medieval way of doing things, had long been winding down. The printing industry, exploding in the 1840s, appeared so modern that it seemed increasingly irrelevant to enter your lad's name on the rolls at Stationers' Hall, and pay for the privilege. The vested interests, of course, were worried at this new chaotic way of doing things, in which boys learned their trade with one firm for a few years before hiring themselves out as adult workers, well before their twenty-first birthdays.

It was, in any case, not to a printer that Sam was set to learn his trade, but to a paper merchant. The main cluster of London's paper merchants was on Lower Thames Street, situated handily on the river to receive supplies from the paper mills in estuarine Kent. New technologies meant that paper could now be made out of cheap wood pulp rather than expensive rags, with the result that barges bearing bales of paper were starting to appear almost daily in the bowels of the City. Since Lower Thames Street was only a few hundred yards from Milk Street, Sam almost certainly came back from Suffolk to live at the Dolphin in 1845, the year he turned fourteen. That Sam's was not a formal apprenticeship is confirmed by the fact that in 1851, one year short of the twenty-first birthday that would have ended any contractual arrangement, he gives his employment to the census enumerator as a "Traveller" in a wholesale stationery firm. Always in a hurry, it would be hard to imagine Sam Beeton serving out his time as a "lad" when he knew himself to be a man, and one with places to go.

Working in a paper office may sound peripheral to the explosion in the knowledge industry, but actually it was one of the best groundings for life as a magazine editor and book publisher. Young men higher up the social scale—not university graduates, but the sons of men with more cash and clout—went into junior jobs on the staff of publishers or newspapers. Here they may have learned about the editorial side of things, but they were often left ignorant of the pounds, shillings, and pence of the business. Sam, by contrast, with his less gentlemanly training, got to grips with how the product worked from the bottom up. Whether you were publishing high literature or low farce, ladies' fashions or children's Bible stories, elevating texts or smutty jokes, you needed what Sam, in a letter written fifteen years later when he was a fully fledged publisher, would describe triumphantly as "paper without end."

This is not to suggest that this latter phase of Sam's education was confined to counting reams, hefting quires and sucking fingers made sore from paper cuts. Being a stationery seller took you into other people's offices and it was here Sam made friends with a group of young men working in adjacent trades. There was Frederick Greenwood, a print setter who had probably been apprenticed to a firm in nearby New Fetter Lane but, after only a year, found himself engaged as a publisher's reader. Greenwood would become Beeton's right-hand man for nearly a decade, before striking out on a glittering career as an editor on his own account. He had an equally talented though more mercurial younger brother, James, who would go on to be one of the first investigative journalists of his day and who would publish much of his work under the imprint of S. O. Beeton. Then there was James Wade, who may have served an apprenticeship in the same firm as Frederick Greenwood and would print many of Beeton's publications, especially the initial volumes of the ground-breaking *Englishwoman's Domestic Magazine.*

Whether your first job was in a paper merchant's or a printing house, the work was hard, taking up to twelve hours a day and a good part of Saturday. But that did not stop these vigorous young men getting together in the evening. These were exciting times and it was impossible for them not to feel that they had been set upon the earth at just the right moment. In an interview towards the end of his life Greenwood maintained, "It was worth while being born in the early 'thirties' in order 'to feel every day a difference so much to the good.' " Coming into the world around the time of the Great Reform Act, these boys had lived through the three big Chartist uprisings, witnessed the repeal of the Corn Laws and seen the beginnings of legislation that would go to create the modern state (hence Greenwood, who remembered from his early working days the sight of shoeless boys wandering around St. Paul's, maintaining that things really were getting better every day). Now as they came into manhood these young men insisted on seeing signs all around them that the world—or their world—was moving forward. After the rigours of the "hungry forties" Britain was entering a golden age of prosperity, a sunny upland where it was possible to believe that hard work, material wellbeing and intellectual progress walked hand in hand.

More specifically, these young men had seen at first hand just how the social and political changes of the last few years had been lobbied, debated, modified, and publicized through the burgeoning culture of printed news. Greenwood paying to read a paper every morning from nine to ten, or Sam popping into the Dolphin for the latest edition of the *Morning Advertiser* were part of a new generation of people who expected to get their information quickly and accurately, rather than picking up third-hand gossip days later around the village pump. On top of this, these young men had seen their changing world refracted in the bold new fiction that was pouring off the presses. *Mary Barton, Wuthering Heights* and *Jane Eyre* all burst upon the world during the hectic decade that coincided with their apprenticeships. Nor was it just the content of these books—rough, even raw—that was new. The way they were produced, in cheap cardboard formats, sometimes serialized in magazines, or available in multiple volumes from Mr. Mudie's lending library in New Oxford Street or Mr. Smith's railway stands, announced a revolution in reading habits. No wonder that, years later, when writing to his elder son at prep school, a boy who had never known what it was not to have any text he wanted immediately to hand, Sam counselled sadly "you do not read books enough."

There were other excitements, too, of a more immediate nature. It was now that Sam Beeton and Frederick Greenwood discovered sex and spent their lives dealing with its consequences. At the time Greenwood was living in lodgings off the Goswell Road, away from his parental home in west London. In June 1850, at the age of only twenty he married Catherine Darby. Although the marriage was not of the shotgun variety—the first baby wasn't born until a decorous eighteen months later—it was miserable, ending in separation and a series of minders for the increasingly alcoholic and depressed Mrs. Greenwood (when visitors came round for tea she promptly hid the cups under the cushions on the grounds that she didn't want company). But in one way Greenwood was lucky. Early marriage did for him what a growing band of moralists maintained it would, providing him with a prophylactic against disease, drink, and restlessness.

Greenwood's friend Sam Beeton was not so fortunate. Just what happened during his crucial years of young adulthood has been obscured by embarrassment and smoothed over with awkward tact. Nancy Spain, no fan of Sam, quotes from a conversation he had in later life. Strolling through London, Sam was supposed to have pointed out "the window he used to climb out at night" as a lad, adding wistfully that "he began life too soon." Spain does not source the quotation and it would be easy to dismiss the whole anecdote were it not for the odd fact that H. Montgomery Hyde, who researched his biography independently of Spain, evidently had access to this same conversation. Hyde has the young man "confessing" that he contrived to have "quite a gay time" in his youth, before going on to point out the infamous window.

The language that both Spain and Hyde ascribe to Sam speaks volumes. Climbing out of a window immediately suggests something illicit, something which the boy did not wish his father, step-mother and gaggle of half-sisters and step-aunts to know about. "Beginning life too soon" makes no sense, either, unless it refers to street life—drink, cards, whores (boys of Sam's class were used to the idea that their working lives began at fourteen). Also telling is Hyde's detail about Sam referring to having had a "gay time"—"gay" being the standard code word designating commercial heterosexual sex. ("Fanny, how long have you been gay?" asks one prostitute of another in a cartoon of the time.)

Once Sam had scrambled out of the Dolphin window it was only a ten-minute saunter to the Strand, that no-man's-land between the City and the West End which had long been synonymous with prostitution. What was mostly a male space during the day—all those print shops, stationers and booksellers—turned at night into something altogether more assorted. From the nearby taverns and theatres poured groups of young men in varying states of cheeriness, while from the rabbit warren of courts and alleys came women who needed to make some money, quickly and without fuss. (Brothels were never a British thing, and most prostitutes worked the streets as freelance operators.) The young men who used the women's services were not necessarily bad, certainly not the rakes or sadists or degenerates of our contemporary fantasies. In fact, if anything, they were probably the prudent ones, determined to delay marriage until they were thirty or so and had saved up a little nest egg. So when the coldness and loneliness of celibacy became too much, it was these careful creatures of capitalism who "spent"—the polite term for male orgasm—5 shillings on a dreary fumble which, if Sam is anything to go by, they shuddered to recall years later. In this early part of Victoria's reign, before the social reformer Josephine Butler started to provide a woman's perspective on the situation, there were plenty of sensible people who believed that prostitution was the price you paid for keeping young middle-class men focused, productive and mostly continent during their vital teens and twenties.

The man whom Sam accused of initiating him into the city's night life was Charles Henry Clarke, a bookbinder ten years older than himself. Recently Clarke and his partner, Frederick Salisbury, had branched out from simply printing and binding books for other publishers to producing them themselves, mostly reissuing existing texts (British copyright at this point was a messy, floutable business). It was this expanding side of the business that particularly attracted Sam, who wanted to be a proper publisher rather than simply a paper man. Armed with some capital, possibly from his mother's estate, and a burning sense of destiny, Sam joined Salisbury and Clarke as a partner around the time of his twenty-first birthday in the spring of 1852 with the intention of building a publishing empire to cater for the reading needs of the rising lower middle classes, the very people from whom he had sprung. Newly confident, flush with a little surplus cash, literate but not literary, comprising everyone from elderly women who had come up from the country, through their bustling tradesmen sons to their sharp, knowing granddaughters, these were the people whom Samuel was gearing up to supply with every kind of reading material imaginable, as well as some that had yet to be thought of.

And, for a while, he was flukishly successful. During those last few months of Sam's informal apprenticeship, Harriet Beecher Stowe's *Uncle Tom's Cabin* had been doing huge and surprising business in her native America. Since there was no copyright agreement with the States—in fact there would be none until 1891—a whole slew of British publishers immediately scented the possibility of making a profit simply by reprinting the book and adding their own title page and cover. One of these was Henry Vizetelly, a brilliant but permanently under-capitalized publisher and engraver who made an arrangement with Clarke and Salisbury to split the costs of publishing 2,500 copies of the book to sell at 2s 6d. Initially *Uncle Tom's Cabin* made little impact in Britain, but a swift decision to bring out a 1s edition paid speedy dividends. By July 1852 it was selling at the rate of 1,000 copies a week.

Using the extra capital that Sam had brought into the firm, he and Clarke now set about exploiting this sensational demand for Mrs. Stowe's sentimental novel about life among black slaves in the southern states of America. Seventeen printing presses and four hundred people were pulled into service in order to bring out as many new editions of *Uncle Tom* as anyone could think of—anything from a weekly 1d serial, through a 1s railway edition to a luxury version with "forty superb illustrations" for 7s 6d. This was a new way of thinking about books. Instead of a stable entity, fixed between a standard set of covers, Beeton's *Uncle Tom's Cabin* was a spectacularly malleable artefact, one that could be repackaged and re-presented to different markets an almost infinite number of times.

Inevitably this feeding frenzy attracted other British publishers—seventeen in fact—who lost no time in producing their own editions of Mrs. Stowe's unlikely hit, often simply reprinting Clarke and Beeton's text and adding their own title page. What many of them had missed, though, was the fact that some of these Clarke, Beeton editions contained significant additions to the original American text, comprising a new Introduction and explanatory chapter headings written by Frederick Greenwood. By unwittingly reproducing these, publishers such as Frederick Warne were infringing Clarke and Beeton's British copyright. As a result of this greedy mistake, Clarke and Beeton were in an extraordinarily strong position, able to insist that the pirated stock was handed over to them, whereupon they simply reissued it under their own name. *Uncle Tom* probably achieved the greatest short-term sale of any book published in Britain in the nineteenth century, and the firm of Clarke and Beeton walked away with a very large slice of the stupendous profits. For a young man venturing into the marketplace for the first time, the omens must have seemed stunning.

Fired by his spectacular good fortune, Sam was determined to get first dibs on Mrs. Stowe's follow-up book. And so late in that delirious summer of 1852 he took the extraordinary step of tearing off to the States to beard the middle-aged minister's wife in her Massachusetts lair. Initially she refused to see him, then relented and almost immediately wished she had not. The young man's opening gambit, of presenting her with the electrotype plates from the luxury British edition, was sadly misjudged. Included among these was a cover illustration comprising a highly eroticized whipping scene, exactly the kind of thing that Mrs. Stowe had taken pains to avoid. "There is not one scene of bodily torture *described* in the book—they are *purposely* omitted," she explained reprovingly to him in a later letter, probably wondering whether this brash young Englishman had really got the point of her work at all.

Next Sam tried cash, offering Mrs. Stowe a payment of £500. If he thought that she would roll over in gratitude, then he could not have been more mistaken. For all that she liked to present herself as an unworldly minister's wife, Mrs. Stowe had a surprising grasp of the pounds, shillings and pence of authorship. It had not escaped her sharp attention that Sam, together with other British firms, had harvested from her work "profits . . . which I know have not been inconsiderable." In the end she accepted the £500, together with a further £250, but not before making it quite clear in a letter to Sam that this did not constitute any kind of payment, promise, or obligation.

As if to emphasize to Sam that he was not quite the uniquely coming man he thought himself to be, the Fates conspired that as he left Mrs. Stowe after his first interview, he bumped into another British publisher walking up her drive. Sampson Low had crossed the Atlantic for exactly the same purpose, to coax Mrs. Stowe into giving him an early advantage in publishing the sequel to *Uncle Tom*. In the end Mrs. Stowe agreed to furnish both Beeton and Low, together with another British publisher,

Thomas Bosworth, with advance pages of her next work, *The Key to Uncle Tom's Cabin*. As it turned out, this shared arrangement was lucky, since it meant that each of the firms got to bear only one third of the colossal losses. *The Key* turned out to be a dreary affair, nothing more than a collection of the documentary sources on which the novel had been based. The fact that Mrs. Stowe insisted beforehand that "My Key will be stronger than the Cabin," suggests how little she understood—and, perhaps, cared about—the reasons for her phenomenal popular success.

It says something about Sam's character that, right from the start, there were people who were delighted to see him take this tumble. Vizetelly, the man who had first brought *Uncle Tom* to Clarke but who had missed out on the staggering profits from the subsequent editions, was particularly thrilled at the loss that Sam was now taking with *The Key*. When Vizetelly, who was ten years older than Beeton and already recognized as a noisy talent in Fleet Street, had approached the lad at the end of the summer of 1852 to ask about his share of the profit, he was sent away with a flea in his ear and an abiding dislike of the cocky upstart. Decades later, writing his puffily self-serving autobiography, Vizetelly was still gloating over the fact that "With a daring confidence, that staggered most sober-minded people, the deluded trio, Clarke, Beeton, and Salisbury, printed a first edition of fifty thousand copies, I think it was, the bulk of which eventually went to the trunk makers, while the mushroom firm was obliged to go into speedy liquidation."

Vizetelly's claim that Clarke, Beeton went into immediate liquidation looks like wishful thinking. Certainly there is no formal record of them being forced to close down. Nor is it true, as earlier Beeton biographers have maintained, that it was at this point that Beeton ditched Clarke and went into business on his own. Right up until 1855 Clarke and Beeton were printing some books and magazines under their joint names while also continuing to work separately. It was not until 1857 that the break finally came, with characteristic (for Sam) bad temper. In February of that year *Beeton v. Clarke* was heard before Lord Campbell. Both parties had hired QCs, which hardly came cheap, to argue over whether Clarke, who was now operating independently out of Paternoster Row, owed Beeton £181. The wrangle dated back to the mad days of summer 1852 when, during their scrappy coming to terms over the profits of *Uncle Tom*, the firm of Clarke, Beeton and Salisbury had bought from Henry Vizetelly his profitable imprint "Readable Books." Now that the relationship between Clarke and Beeton had dramatically soured, they were bickering like estranged lovers over small sums of money. The jury found for Sam, one of the few occasions in his long litigious career when he would emerge vindicated.

Typically, Sam made huge cultural capital from the *Uncle Tom* affair. Not only did he manage to win Mrs. Stowe round by his charismatic presence for long enough to extract introductions to several American intellectuals, including her brother Revd. H. W. Beecher of Brooklyn, Wendell Holmes, and Longfellow, he also talked up his relationship with the celebrity authoress thereafter, managing to imply that she was anxiously watching over the affairs of Clarke, Beeton from the other side of the Atlantic. The Preface to the sixth edition of *Uncle Tom*, published this time by "Clarke & Co, Foreign Booksellers," shows just how far he was prepared to go:

> In presenting this Edition to the British public the Publishers, equally on behalf of the Authoress and themselves, beg to render their acknowledgements of the sympathy and success the work has met with in England. . . . Our Editions are the *real* "Author's Editions"; we are in direct negotiation with Mrs. Stowe; and we confidently hope that when accounts are made up we shall be in a position to award that talented lady a sum not inferior in amount to her receipts in America.

Thereafter, Sam would tie his own name to Mrs. Stowe's in the public's mind wherever possible. Thus, years later, in *Beeton's Dictionary of Universal Information,* he could not resist retelling the story of how he had crossed the Atlantic in the late summer of 1852 to present Mrs. Stowe with a voluntary payment of £500. The fact that he had first tried to get away with giving her some printers' plates that he no longer needed and she particularly disliked was, typically enough, never mentioned.

INTERLUDE

We are so sorry to say that the preserved meats are sometimes carelessly prepared, and, though the statement seems incredible, sometimes adulterated.

ISABELLA BEETON,
Book of Household Management

MAKING SURE THAT THE FOOD that came to table was pure was something of an obsession with Mrs. Beeton. Now that the average household was dependent not on the farmer but the greengrocer and baker for its provisions, the opportunities for contamination were legion. A series of investigations carried out by the *Lancet* between 1851 and 1854 had revealed to a horrified nation that a whole range of its staple foods were routinely watered down, bulked out, tinted up and, by a whole series of sleights of hand, turned into something that they were not. Every single one of forty-nine random samples of bread examined by the *Lancet* were found to contain alum; the milk turned out to have water added in amounts ranging from 10 to 50 per cent; and of twenty-nine tins of coffee examined, twenty-eight were adulterated with chicory, mangel-wurzel, and acorn, while a typical sample of tea contained up to half its own weight in iron filings.

The reasons for this terrible state of affairs are various, but mainly come down to the voracious conditions in which retailers were operating in Mrs. Beeton's day. Bread, for instance, was frequently sold below the cost of flour, which meant that the baker had to find some way of bulking out his loaves in order to avoid making a loss. Likewise, milk was bought wholesale for 3d a quart and retailed at 4d. So by adding just 10 per cent of water the tradesman reaped 40 per cent extra profit.

Popularized versions of the *Lancet*'s findings appeared throughout the press, creating a climate of fearful protest throughout the 1850s. Disappointingly, the resultant 1860 Adulteration of Foods Act turned out to be a toothless tiger, and responsibility for cleaning up Britain's food was left in the hands of various voluntary groups, as well as to the manufacturers themselves. In 1855 Mr. Thomas Blackwell of Crosse and Blackwell explained to a Select Committee that his firm had recently given up the habit of coppering pickles and fruits and artificially colouring sauces, despite consumers initially being disgruntled to discover that pickles were actually brown not green and that anchovies were not naturally a nice bright red. It was not until 1872 that Britain got an effective Adulteration of Food, Drinks and Drugs Act.

During the years when Isabella Beeton first started contributing to Sam's *Englishwoman's Domestic Magazine* anxieties about food adulteration were running high. Readers write in wanting to know how to spot if their bread has been compounded with chalk and are in turn advised on gadgets they can buy to check whether their milk has been watered down. In the *Book of Household Management* itself the fear initially appears more muted, although hovering over the text you can still discern a continuing worry that the meat that is about to come to table may be off; that vegetables are apt to rot in the containers in which they are stored, thereby becoming "impregnated with poisonous particles"; and that the tin that lines saucepans may well be adulterated with lead, "a pernicious practice, which in every article connected with the cooking and preparation of food, cannot be too severely reprobated."

In other words, Mrs. Beeton's imaginary household is in constant danger of being poisoned. What makes it all so frightening is the fact that this is an invisible threat, impossible to detect by the inexpert eye or hand. Here is a neat metaphor for how the middle-class household was beginning to think about itself in the middle of the nineteenth century. The earlier extended household consisting of apprentices, clerks, lodgers, and shopmen (remember the examples of the widowed wholesaler Elizabeth Mayson in Milk Street or the Dolphin with its sisters and cousins and aunts) had now slimmed itself down so that it was more recognizably a nuclear family. This made the boundary between the household and the world beyond the front door clearer, which in turn made the possibility of any breach doubly terrifying. Hence Mrs. Beeton's constant alertness to the danger represented by apparently harmless objects such as saucepans and vegetables that could be smuggled into the family hearth to do their corrupting work.

This is the reason why Beeton gave such a rhapsodic welcome to the introduction of mechanically preserved food. To her tinned meat and fish were not, as they might be to us, a second best option, something for the campsite or the bank holiday. For Mrs. Beeton the canning of food represents the privileged opportunity to be in complete control of its purity from farm to fork.

> At Leith, in the neighbourhood of Edinburgh, at Aberdeen, at Bordeaux, at Marseilles, and in many parts of Germany, establishments of enormous magnitude exist, in which soup, vegetables, and viands of every description are prepared, in such a manner that they retain their freshness for years.

You get the feeling that if only it were possible, Mrs. Beeton would make the household safe by putting it in a tin, soldering the covers and exposing it to boiling water for three hours. That she is forced to acknowledge that adulteration, "amazing to say," can take place even before the tinning process begins, so contaminating the whole food chain, shows that—alas—it is never possible to turn an Englishman's home into a moated castle, no matter how hard you might try.

✳

CHAPTER FOUR

THE ENTIRE MANAGEMENT
OF ME

 ISABELLA MAYSON AND SAMUEL BEETON had
been in and out of each other's lives from well
before they were born, five years apart, in the early
springs of 1831 and 1836. The Mayson-Dorling
clan may not have been related to the Beetons by
blood or marriage, but they did belong to that category of people, defined
by personal history, geography, commerce, and affinity, that went by the
name of "kith." Both Samuel Powell Beeton and Benjamin Mayson had
been Manchester warehousemen. Their wives had arrived in Milk Street
at exactly the same time and both proceeded to give birth to a tribe of
girls and the occasional boy. Eliza and Victoria Beeton were almost
exactly the same ages as Isabella and Bessie Mayson and it was only natural for the little girls to troop across the road to play together among the
barrels or the bales. This intimate daily contact stopped in 1843 when the
Maysons were whisked away to begin a new life with the Dorlings in
Epsom. However, the friendship between the two families must have
remained strong, since a few years later all the girls—Maysons, Dorlings,
and Beetons—were sent, in batches, to Miss Heidel's in Heidelberg.

There are other reasons for thinking that contact between the two families continued even once they had ceased being neighbours. Samuel Powell Beeton was a keen racing man and had turned the Dolphin into
something of a sporting pub. Raising a large prize purse was, as Henry
Dorling was fast discovering in his job as Clerk of the Course at Epsom,
a perpetual challenge. Beeton's canny solution in 1846 was to post subscription lists in the Dolphin and other busy City pubs, with the result

that the new Epsom two-mile handicap was known from the outset as "The Publican's Derby" (part of the money raised went to the Licensed Victuallers' School). Nor did Beeton's connection with Dorling stop there. In the early 1850s he was regularly racing his own horses at various of the lesser Epsom meetings. One final point of contact: although William Dorling had set up as a printer in Bexhill all those years ago, he was actually an Ipswich man. For at least the last hundred years Dorlings and Beetons had lived and worked alongside each other in Suffolk.

So from the very moment they were old enough to register such things, Isabella and Sam would have been aware of each other's existence through the networks of chat and mutual interest that bound their families together, the female members particularly. They may well have met as small children on those occasions when Sam came back to Milk Street from his grandmother's house in Hadleigh to visit the Dolphin. They almost certainly encountered each other in the late 1840s and early 1850s when Samuel Powell Beeton was a regular fixture at the Epsom racetrack. In a world where you married the boy next door, or at least the boy in the next street, who also happened to be the son of your father's business partner and a school friend of your brother, Sam was pretty much marked out for Isabella. It didn't feel like that, of course. Arranged marriages were out of fashion, even for the aristocracy, and among young, middle-class people love matches were the order of the day. But while she probably believed that she was following her heart, Isabella was actually revealing herself as a creature of her time and place.

Since we will never know the moment they actually met, it is worth considering just what made Isabella Mary Mayson and Samuel Orchart Beeton give each other a second, third, and fourth glance. It is easy to imagine what she saw in him. He was sufficiently like her step-father, whom she called "Father," to feel familiar, part of the kith network that held her world together. Sam talked of deadlines and printing presses, proofs, boards and first copies just arrived, using a language that had been the background clatter of her childhood. But he was sufficiently different from Henry to seem exciting too. Even in twenty years' time Sam Beeton was never going to be a mutton-chopped paterfamilias, rigid with respectability and self-regard. The excitement of the streets hung around him like the smoke from his habitual cigars. His particular pleasures included prize-fights, ratting contests, and, although Isabella probably didn't know this, prostitutes. (Two thirds of the way through their courtship, according to Sam, she teased him about "what you are pleased to call my roving nature," but it is impossible to know exactly what she meant by it.) He was both of her class and yet not quite. Although she had been at school with his sisters—one of the key indicators of a young man's suitability as a husband—there was still a cockneyism about him that was thrilling, especially since she had been brought up by people keen to forget that sort of thing in their own backgrounds. He was that delicious thing, a familiar stranger, a buried subtext.

To Isabella, a girl who had learned to deal with her emotional needs by displacing them onto other people (all those infant tantrums and wet nappies to be calmly coped with), Sam offered thrilling access to her own occluded interior life. His intense emotionality, conveyed both in person and in the many letters he wrote to her at this time, unlocked an answering response in her. Over the length of the year's courtship we can watch as Isabella evolves from a self-contained and defensive girl into an expansive and loving young woman. Thus while her first surviving letters to her fiancé are curt and cautious—"My dearest Sam . . . Yours most affectionately, Isabella Mayson"—only six months later they are racing with spontaneous affection, "My own darling Sam, . . . Yours with all love's devotion BELLA MAYSON." A latish letter, written on 1 June just six weeks before the wedding, shows Bella taking flight into a candour and rapture that would have been impossible to predict only a few months earlier:

> My dearly beloved Sam,
>
> I take advantage of this after dinner opportunity to enjoy myself and have a small chat with you on paper although I have really nothing to say, and looking at it in a mercenary point of view my letter will not be worth the postage. I am so continually thinking of you that it seems to do me a vast amount of good even to do a little black and white business, knowing very well that a few lines of nonsense are always acceptable to a certain mutable gentleman be they ever so short or stupid . . .
>
> You cannot imagine how I have missed you, and have been wishing all day that I were a bird that I might fly away and be at rest with you, my own precious one.

If Sam set Bella soaring, then she grounded him. Her phlegmatic caution and emotional steadiness provided the much needed anchor for his volatility and frighteningly labile moods. In a letter written towards the end of their engagement in which Sam starts off by reporting that he is "horribly blue" he ends, four pages later, "I'm better now than when I began this letter—talking with you, even in this way and at this distance always makes me feel very jolly." At the beginning of June 1856, a few weeks before the wedding and worried to distraction by the sluggish launch of his new magazine, the *Boy's Own Journal,* Sam explains beseechingly that "I can think and work and do so much better and so much more when I can see and feel that it is not for myself, (about whom I care nothing) I am labouring, but for her whom I so ardently prize, and so lovingly cherish in my inmost heart—my own Bella!" Isabella was the isle of sanity that Sam created outside himself, his superego, his conscience, his place of safety.

And then there was the fact that Sam Beeton was that rare thing, a Victorian man who liked and respected women as much as he loved them. Brought up by his grandmother and surrounded by a clutch of younger half-sisters, he wanted a genuinely companionate marriage, one based on affinity rather than rigid role-play. In Isabella he had found his perfect match, although he could not yet know how profitable that match would become. If he had the flair and the imagination, she had the caution and dogged determination. If he had the manic energy of the possessed, she had the sticking power of an ambitious clerk. At the end of May 1856 and following a colossal row that nearly derailed their engagement altogether, Sam is genuinely disturbed by Isabella's self-abnegating promise that very soon he would have the "entire management" of her. Puzzled, offended even, he writes back: "*I* don't desire, I assure you, to *manage* you—*you* can do that quite well yourself," before proceeding to pay admiring tribute to her "most excellent abilities." It was those abilities—including her capacity to "manage" both herself and other people—that would be the making of them both.

Sam's family was delighted by the news of the engagement, which was formally hatched around the time of the 1855 summer meeting. Eliza Beeton, who had always been extremely fond of her step-son, went out of her way to contrive occasions by which the young people could be alone together during the twelve bumpy months of their engagement. With the sudden loss of her husband just nine months earlier, this young love affair was a happy distraction. Sam's sisters, too, were thrilled that the girl they had known as a classmate was now to become a member of their family.

Eighteen months after the wedding Nelly Beeton, still languishing at school in Heidelberg, was tickled pink to be able to sign her letter "Your affectionate *sister-in-law*."

Bella's family, though, was not so sure. Since she was only nineteen, Sam would first have had to ask her step-father for permission to propose. Quite why Henry agreed to his step-daughter marrying a man he evidently disliked and soon came to loathe remains a mystery. Perhaps the fact that within nine months of her wedding Isabella would turn twenty-one made him think that there was little point in trying to delay the inevitable. Elizabeth Dorling, meanwhile, was in no position to warn against an early marriage: when she had walked up the aisle with Isabella's father in 1835, she too had been barely twenty.

However Sam's formal relationship with the Dorlings actually began, it soon developed into a war of attrition that would end, ten years later, with a rupture between the two families that would take a hundred years and several generations to heal. Right from the start the older Dorling and Mayson girls lined up against Sam. Jane Dorling, just a year younger than Isabella, was edgy about the way that she was getting left behind in the marriage race. Her strenuous attempts to woo a certain Mr. Wood by singing him German songs were coming to nothing just at the moment when Isabella and Sam were putting the final touches to their wedding plans. Jane responded by taking out her frustration on the happy couple. In a letter written in the middle of June Sam talks ruefully about Jane's "little sharp ways" and hopes that Mr. Wood succumbs soon since "fellow feeling makes us wondrous kind." (In fact it would be another five years before Jane would get married, and not to the resistant Mr. Wood.)

Bessie and Esther, meanwhile, were jealous right from the start, resenting Sam for taking their eldest sister away so soon. The smaller girls Charlotte and Lucy were besotted with Sam at this point, but soon changed their minds once they were old enough to understand the hints and gossip that trickled down from their sisters. In fact, there was only one person in Epsom who was unambiguously thrilled by the news of the engagement and she didn't count. Tucked away in the Grandstand, Granny Jerrom could not stop talking about the joys and wonders of "dear Sam."

Put simply, Henry Dorling did not think that Samuel Orchart Beeton was good enough for his eldest step-daughter, whom he regarded as his own flesh and blood. Beneath this judgement lay a fair degree of self-loathing. Sam, like Henry, was an energetic eldest son who had started out in printing before quickly spotting the potential in adjacent pursuits (racing in Henry's case, book publishing in Sam's). Both men were sharp, bright, keen self-publicists who knew how to make money. This meant they should have liked one another, were it not for the fact that the prime dynamic of the rising middle classes involved not looking back. Henry had not worked hard, improved his situation, and spent all that money on turning his eldest step-daughter into a lady in order for her to marry a man who seemed and sounded like himself. His own two eldest girls, Isabella's near contemporaries Jane and Mary, would eventually marry a lawyer and doctor respectively. A son-in-law belonging to one of the gentlemanly professions was the kind of return Henry expected on his investment, and it looked as though Bella was going to throw it—herself—away.

And then there was Sam's rackety family. His sisters, who went to school with the Dorling girls in Heidelberg, were nice enough, but there was something raffish about the male members of the Beeton clan. Throughout the period various Beetons had a nasty habit of popping up in the Law Court reports. There is Thomas Beeton, Sam's uncle and lodger at the Dolphin, who in 1834 is charged with making impertinent remarks to women in the street. In the next generation down things were no more promising. Sam's younger half-brother Edward Albert would, while still in his teens, be charged with insurance fraud, go bankrupt, flee the country, and eventually serve eighteen months' hard labour. A quick flick through *The Times* shows other members of the extended Beeton tribe regularly coming up on charges of arson, careless driving, and a clutch of other minor but unpleasant crimes. Significantly, one of the few times a Dorling is mentioned in the newspaper in a less than benign tone is in 1864 when Sam Beeton went into partnership with Isabella's step-brother Edward Dorling and managed to drag him into a bad-tempered property dispute that ended, typically, in court. Whichever way you looked at it, the Beetons were not the kind of people you would rush to call family.

So Henry and Sam embarked upon an uneasy Oedipal relationship in which the elder man could never resist a dig at the younger, and the younger could never quite throw off his need to impress and surpass the elder. During the end part of 1855 Sam, nearly always writing from his hectic office in Bouverie Street, just off Fleet Street, had been sending his letters to Isabella in envelopes that were stamped with the logo of his newest venture, the *Boy's Own Journal,* a companion weekly title to the well-established monthly *Boy's Own Magazine.* Henry hated this vulgarism—he was already worried that the smarter part of Epsom did not consider him quite a gentleman—and insisted that it stop forthwith. In a letter of 3 January 1856 Isabella writes to Sam nervously: "I hope you will not be offended with me for sending you a few envelopes. Father said this morning he supposed your passion for advertising was such that you could not resist sending those stamped affairs." This, surely, was rather rich coming from a man who had worked hard to make sure that the name "Dorling" appeared on every poster, pamphlet, and local newspaper circulating in Epsom.

Still, Sam continued to yearn for Dorling's approval while pretending that he did not. In June 1856 he nonchalantly sends Isabella a copy of the brand-new *Boy's Own Journal* hot off the press so that she could "show the guv'nor so that it may receive his approbation or thunders." In the run-up to the spring races in 1856 he dutifully intones, "I hope your father will have a good meeting next week," before making sure that he isn't available to watch Henry play the Great Man of Epsom. Sam is careful, too, to feign an unconvincing indifference to the whole horsey world. In a postscript to a letter of 10 April 1856, written a week later, Isabella explains, "I would have sent you a return List but I know you don't care about racing."

It was not even as if, by way of compensation for his rough edges, Sam was a wealthy man. Henry Dorling, whose fondness for money-making was beginning to attract jealous talk, would have noticed the way in which the small fortune Sam had made from the lucky strike of *Uncle Tom* had been frittered away in the debacle of *The Key.* And then there was the unfortunate fact that while Sam's magazines, the *Englishwoman's Domestic Magazine* and the *Boy's Own Magazine,* appeared to be selling well, this was partly because their publisher was giving away a huge number of loyalty prizes in the form of glitzy trinkets—watches, bracelets, penknives and even pianos. If Dorling was worried that he might be handing over his girl to a man with no money, then the events of February 1856 only confirmed his worst suspicions. For it was now that Sam got himself into some kind of muddle with his lottery arrangements, which meant that he forfeited a colossal £200 a year, about half his annual income. This must have led to some very heated discussions in the drawing room of Ormond House, for by the middle of the month Isabella is writing consolingly to her fiancé, "I am sorry to hear you are not likely to get out of your Lottery mess nicely. . . . However, I don't believe things will be so bad as many people try to make out; as long as you have a head on your shoulders I think you will manage to scrape a living together somehow," which hardly sounds like a vote of confidence.

The tensions between the Dorling and Beeton clans would deepen with each year of the nine-year marriage as Sam's recklessness and cockneyism became more and more apparent. In the early summer of 1855, however, the full extent of these pains lay far in the future, as the newly engaged Isabella and Sam delightedly contemplated each other and the life they would make together. Two images from this time, one of each of them, have come down to us (none has ever been found of them together). The first of these is the iconic photograph of Isabella that now belongs to the National Portrait Gallery. Taken in the London studios of Maull and Polybank, probably at their Cheapside branch, it shows a solemn, solid girl weighed down by the visual signifiers of early Victorian ladyhood. First there is the poker-straight, heavy hair wound into a plaited coronet, so big and tight that it looks as if she is wearing a particularly unbecoming hat (minute inspection reveals that a sturdy chenille net is keeping the whole thing steady). Then there is the dress, made locally in Epsom out of a length of silk given to her by Ralph Sherwood, the Epsom trainer, in celebration of the fact that his horse Wild Dayrell had won the highly dramatic Derby of that year. Patterned with broad bands of colour, pinched into horizontal tucks, and decorated with fussy buttons, the whole thing looks as if it would be better suited to a sofa. The effect is finished with full lace sleeves and collar, a silk shawl edged with heraldic-looking velvet scutcheons, a faceted glass brooch and a fancy wristwatch. As a final touch Isabella clutches at a voluminous handkerchief with one hand while with the other she points to her ample bust. She is twenty years old, trussed up like a fussy matron, entirely innocent of the flair that she would display in a few years' time as fashion editor of the *Englishwoman's Domestic Magazine.* A photograph taken of her when she was about twenty-four shows her from this later period, which was how her sisters always chose to remember her: slender, elegant, emphatically unpatterned, with just one striking row of jet beads and not a brooch or handkerchief in sight.

The surviving image of Sam from 1853, two years before the engage-

*An elegant Isabella in 1860, the year that
she began to write about Parisian fashion for the*
Englishwoman's Domestic Magazine.

ment, is a head and shoulders chalk drawing by Julian Portch, a well-known artist who had sketched many young men in Sam's circle. In the sketch, Portch presents Sam as a romantic hero. His face is long, his eyes large and lingering, his mouth pronounced and sensuous (although we must beware of crude face-mapping—all the Beetons had that mouth and some of them, the women especially, lived blameless lives). The hair is wavy and longish, the necktie soft, large, and careless. This is a young man who likes to think of himself as a rebel, impatient with the ponderous respectability of his elders (significantly he has no beard). If Shelley had been reborn as a Cheapside publican's son he might have looked a lot like Sam Beeton. A second photograph, taken when Sam was twenty-nine, shows little change. There is a light beard and moustache now (he had problems growing a full one), but the general effect is the same. The

*Sam, left, at the age of twenty-three. Six years later, right,
little about his appearance has changed.*

clothes are self-consciously "bohemian," and the necktie appears to be identical to the one from his youth—casual and imprecise. While Isabella has matured, Sam has contrived to stand still.

During the year of their engagement Isabella continued to live with her family in Epsom while Sam was in London. Around 1853 he had moved into offices in Bouverie Street, a hop, skip, and jump from 148 Fleet Street, where Charles Clarke was still running the printing side of the business. Sam mainly lodged at the Dolphin, although he frequently spent nights away at the homes of various members of his extended clan around north London. During the first six months of the engagement, until the close of 1855, the arrangement seems to have been that Sam would come down to Epsom every Sunday on the train, the standard pattern for dutiful sons and prospective sons-in-law. In addition there would be weekly rendezvous in London when Isabella went up to Manchester Square for her piano lesson and returned back to London Bridge station via the Dolphin. No letters have come down from this first half of the engagement, which suggests that few needed to be written. Isabella and Sam were seeing each other a couple of times a week, and their thoughts, wishes, needs and tiffs could be saved up and played out in person, either in London or Epsom.

But by the end of six months' worth of Sunday lunches with the chilly Dorlings, Sam had reached breaking point. Working, as always, like a maniac, he knew that he could not bear another half year's worth of lost and disagreeable weekends. It may even be that he was beginning to wonder whether he could go through with the marriage at all. For it was becoming painfully clear that Isabella, still only nineteen, was utterly under the thumb of her parents, parents who were unable to disguise the fact that they didn't really like him. Henry and Elizabeth quizzed Isabella constantly about the relationship: "I trust you will not have been much tortured with many catechizings?" asks Sam nervously in late April. They also continued to drop hints about Sam's unsuitability to the extent that, only a couple of months before the wedding, we find Sam consoling Isabella over the "many cutting speeches" that she has recently been forced to endure: "I fear that you are made very miserable oftentimes on my poor account." In addition, the Dorlings made sarcastic comments about the frequency with which the couple wrote to each other, and made sure to pass on disagreeable gossip about Sam that they knew was bound to hurt. Isabella, in turn, became pliant to the point of imbecility in her parents' presence. Marriage should, in theory, have resolved this unpleasant state of affairs—when a woman left her father's home for her husband's she was supposed to switch allegiance—but what if the Dorlings continued to be a daily dogmatic presence in their eldest daughter's life? It didn't bear thinking about. In a state of imminent collapse, coughing compulsively, looking "queer" and sunk in "the miserables," Sam did something quite unheard of for him and went on holiday. Taking refuge with various Beetons in Suffolk and Cambridgeshire, he refused to budge until he had formulated a strategy for dealing with the second half of what had by now become a kind of purgatory.

The first two surviving letters that Isabella wrote to Sam come from the closing days of 1855, just before he left for Suffolk, and give a flavour of their relationship during the first half of the engagement. Writing to Sam on Boxing Day Isabella laments the fact that she has been tied up with domestic duties—mopping up after her poorly half-siblings Walter, Frank and Lucy in the Grandstand—rather than flirting with her husband-to-be: "I cannot say I spent a happy Christmas day, *you* can well guess the reason and besides that Frank being so poorly, we were not in spirits to enjoy ourselves." Still, there is something to look forward to: Sam has suggested coming down to Epsom that very evening to escort her up to London to see Jenny Lind in concert. For many a young Victorian woman a trip to hear the Swedish Nightingale—in this case for the second time—might seem like a sort of polite bore. Isabella, though, is genuinely musical and therefore genuinely thrilled: "I do not know how to thank you enough for your kind invitation, the more delightful because so unexpected."

The next letter, again from Isabella to Sam, is written a few days later, on New Year's Eve. Still in role as mother hen to a brood of sickly siblings, Isabella is inclined to fuss over her fiancé: "I was very glad to hear your cold was so much better, only mind and take proper care of yourself, as you promised me you would, for I certainly was terribly afraid you were going to be seriously ill when I left you on Friday night." Next she makes sure to let Sam know how well she got on with his taciturn Uncle Thomas on her last brief visit to the Dolphin after the Lind concert: "seldom has he been so agreeable to me before." Then comes the pang of realization that, despite the fact that their lives are soon to be united, they are at present running on divergent tracks. Sam is about to set off for his holiday in East Anglia while she is obliged to stay in Epsom and continue on the same round of dreary duties and doubtful pleasures. Particularly grim is the thought of having to attend a looming New Year's dinner party—"that terrible ordeal"—given by the middle-aged solicitor Mr. White: "I am very sorry you will not be able to go," writes Isabella ruefully, although as it turned out the meal was followed by "a good dance . . . which exactly suited me." Isabella's brother John, by contrast, will be celebrating New Year with Sam's sisters at a black-tie party held by some cousins of the Beetons in Mile End. Penned up in a world of provincial domesticity, the only thing Isabella can think to do is ask Sam: "When do you start for Suffolk? I should like to know because then I can fancy what you are doing."

The next letters in the sequence are, even now, 150 years later, painful to read. Isabella, unaware that Sam might be embarking on anything other than a short break of a few days, makes excited plans for a romantic reunion, which she believes will come any day now. Sam, meanwhile, stays pointedly entrenched in East Anglia, deliberately missing each deadline that she sets for their next meeting, which has the effect of sending her frantic with frustration. On 3 January, only a couple of days after Sam has left for Suffolk, Isabella is already writing to say that she had hoped that he would be home by next Saturday as "I intended writing to invite you to join our family circle . . . as we are going to the Stand to keep Christmas now the small ones are recovered," apparently unaware that a room full of other people's children is hardly the sort of thing to tempt a young man about town. Sam, though, has evidently already written to explain that he has extended his stay in East Anglia, so instead Isabella floats the idea of meeting on the 11th, after her next piano lesson. "It will then be a fortnight since I have seen you. Absence &c &c &c. I don't know whether you have found that out. I for one have." But Sam, clearly, does not feel Absence &c &c &c quite as urgently, since he writes back explaining that, sadly, he still won't be home by the 11th.

Here was the signal for Isabella to swing into action. She wanted Sam back, and she wanted him back now. In her letter of 8 January she is careful to let him know what he has been missing: "We spent a very merry evening at the Stand on Saturday. I was very sorry you were not present, for I am sure you would have enjoyed yourself," apparently unaware how unlikely this was. Having spent a couple of routine sentences saying how pleased she was to hear that Sam was feeling better, she launches into her plan.

> Now for business. Will you be so kind to arrange your affairs, so that you will be home by Monday night or Tuesday morning as we are going to have a few friends to dinner and you are to be one of the dozen if you can manage to be home by then. I hope you will not disappoint me because you know very well these formal *feeds* I abominate, and if you come of course it will be much pleasanter for me. I am the only one of the girls going to dine with them, so pray do not leave me to sit three or four hours with some old man I do not care a straw about.

After a few more limp courtesies, Isabella signs off before adding what Sam would come to know and joke about as the crucial postscript, the one in which the real purpose of her letter was revealed: "Let me have a letter soon telling me how you have been amusing yourself, and bear in mind Tuesday, Jany 15th."

Notwithstanding the peremptory postscript, Sam's response was to send a note explaining that, alas, he was not coming home until Thursday evening and so would be obliged to miss the Dorlings' dinner party. This made Isabella redouble her efforts. Determined to get Sam down to Epsom by hook or by crook, she contrived to get the dinner party set back a couple of days. What was the point of having a fiancé, if you never got to show him off?

My dear Sam,

You say you intend returning home on Thursday evening, but as our dinner party is put off till *that* day perhaps you will have the kindness to favour us with your company. One day I am sure cannot make much difference to you, and besides you have had such a nice long holiday you will be quite ready to come home by that time. Mama sends her kind regards and says she cannot hear of a refusal, and the girls say they are quite sure you would not think of refusing now you have been pressed so much.

I cannot tell you how disappointed I was in reading in your last letter that you were not coming home so soon as I expected. We do not dine till 6 o.c. so I beg *once* more that you will come, and if you do not I shall begin to think you are a little bit unkind . . . Hoping you will not refuse my *first* request, with love of the very best quality,

Believe me, dearest Sam,

Yours devotedly,

ISABELLA

I hope you will reach your journey's end safely and that I shall see you on Thursday. I think I shall feel desperate if you refuse to come.

Whether or not Sam did finally make it to Epsom in time for dinner at six o'clock sharp on Thursday the 17th is unclear. Certainly the atmosphere between the young couple remained watchful for the next few weeks. Over the next five months Sam would contrive to have as little contact with the Dorlings as possible. Isabella must be enticed up to London, or possibly to Brighton, a town that she considered an "earthly paradise" and which they both visited regularly. And wherever possible his easy-going step-mother rather than her hawk-eyed mama should be pressed into service as chaperone. It was now, too, that Sam made a decision about where they were to live once they were married. Two months after returning from Suffolk he took a lease on a house in Pinner, a village well to the north of London. A southerly suburb like Croydon or Beckenham would have been the obvious place for the young couple to settle: both were a short shift from Epsom yet also a mere half-hour from Fleet

Street and the Dolphin. Instead Sam pointedly chose a place that was about as far away from the Dorlings as it was practically possible to be.

All this made perfect sense, but unfortunately Sam did not feel able to share his ponderings and strategies with Isabella. They were not yet on terms where they could giggle together over her ghastly parents and tribe of gossipy, jealous sisters. Instead Isabella was left floundering, trying to make sense of Sam's sudden departures and constant evasions which, inevitably, she interpreted as insults to herself. No longer able to count on meeting at least once a week or even once a fortnight, the young couple now fell back on the mail to keep their relationship ticking over, if not exactly moving forward. Isabella addressed her letters to Sam at the Dolphin because, she said, she did not want people in the office, especially Sam's brother Edward, opening them and knowing their business.

This arrangement allowed for plenty of delay, confusion, and resentment since Sam had neither the time nor, quite probably, the inclination, to bob and weave through half a mile of heavy traffic every hour or so to see whether any communication had arrived for him at home. As a result he habitually got Bella's letters late and wrote fewer in reply than she thought he should. Equally suspicious is the way that Sam seems to be unreachable on those weekends when he is busy out of town getting their new house ready: "They do not seem to be particularly quick in postal arrangements at Pinner, for I did not receive your note till this morning. How do you account for it?" All the same, the Victorian post was a marvel—communications sent from Ormond House in the morning arrived only a few hours later at the Dolphin.

What emerges from the letters that Sam and Isabella wrote to each other during these intense, miserable five months was just how different were the lives of a single man and single woman at mid-century. Sam's existence is busy, crammed with people, surprises, obligations, calamities, and sudden dashes here, there, and everywhere. It is a life lived in public spaces, on the streets, in parks. "I have been exceedingly busy all the week,—was at Covent Garden on Monday, Dalston on Tuesday, and Holloway on Wednesday, and to-night I go again to . . . Manor House." He works late on Saturday and now usually most of Sunday too. His letters to his fiancée have to be written in snatched moments during a bursting day.

Isabella is busy too, but with domestic duties and social obligations that leave her plenty of mental energy to dream and fret. There are the hated "formal feeds" with middle-aged neighbours such as Mr. White and Mr. Sherwood, a notecase to make for Uncle Edward (Henry's brother), fittings with the dressmaker and, of course, the tribe of "children on the hill" to be supervised and soothed and periodically transported into Epsom or down to Brighton. Significantly, Isabella's piano playing—always remembered sentimentally by her sisters as the bedrock of her life—was often shunted aside when pressing domestic duties intervened. During Christmas week of 1855 with the younger children struck down with heavy colds, Isabella is unable to find a moment to practise and so cancels her lesson with Benedict since "it would be useless to come up." Indeed, references to trips to Benedict peter out over the course of the engagement, just at the point when mentions of new clothes, furniture and window blinds increase. Just what Julius Benedict—fast on his way to becoming Sir Julius for his services to music—thought about Miss Mayson's growing disinclination to concentrate on her art in favour of her coming nuptials goes unrecorded.

Isabella's life, then, may have been frenetic but it was small, mundane. In her letters to Sam, she apologizes constantly for not having any news—"it is rather a scarce article in Epsom"—and worries that when Sam's sisters Lizzie and Viccie come to stay in the country in late January there is nothing for them to do except take long, muddy walks and fiddle with embroidery. Isabella tries hard to empathize with Sam's situation—the thousand letters a day spilling into his office, the crazy schedule of deadlines, and worries about spiralling costs—but it is quite apparent that she has no concept of the pressure he is under. When he fails to spend a Sunday with her she sulks, when he arrives late or leaves early she cannot resist a sly dig in her next letter. So in mid-April she signs herself "Your loving and affectionate deserted one," while on 3 May she grumbles, "It is needless to say how disappointed I am that you are not coming down this evening, rather hard lines. . . ." She wants his health to improve but only because it means that he will be able to spend more time with her. Without enough to think about, Isabella turns her searching intelligence onto her relationship with Sam. Letter after letter finds her mulling over their last encounter, looking for meaning in a throwaway phrase, worrying that he is angry with her when he is probably simply tired: "I imagine you are cross with me and don't care so much about me." There are rows and reconciliations, accusations and apologies, most of them the result of the fact that this is, increasingly, a relationship that exists mainly on paper.

And yet, there is nothing out of control about Isabella's letters. They are neatly written, crossed in order to save the postage; about half of them are dated in full. Initially her letters are cautious and impersonal, confined to practicalities, descriptions of dull days with the children in the Grandstand, detailed arrangements for the next longed-for rendezvous. Isabella knows, though, that she sounds closed and stiff and struggles to find a voice more appropriate for what is supposed to be a letter to her lover. And yet the moment she lets down her guard, the insecurities come rushing out—worries that Sam does not love her enough, that she appears aloof, that she is untidy, even that she is fat—and she finds herself writing letters that surprise and embarrass her by their neediness. It is then that she backtracks sharply, begging Sam to take no notice of her "nonsense," or "scribble," maintaining, "I do not really know what I have said," and urging him to "burn this as soon as perused" in case—her nightmare—other people find out that she is "*soft.*" (Sam, thankfully, did not follow this instruction and her letters were found in his coat pocket when he died.)

Sam's letters are quite different. They are carelessly written and hardly ever dated beyond "Friday afternoon" or "Tuesday morning" and their punctuation consists mostly of dashes. Like the editorial voice he employs in his magazines, especially in the *Englishwoman's Domestic Magazine,* Sam's style tends to be verbose, overblown. Times change, and so do prose styles. It is Isabella's letters—reminiscent of the crisp, clear voice of the *BOHM*—that have lasted best. Sam's prolixity, his fanciful diversions, his self-conscious "literariness" make him sound, to our ears, like a true Victorian. Nothing can ever be said simply. Asking Isabella to meet him next Saturday at Anerley Bridge station turns into: "Thus, then, fair maid, do I beseech thee to name the hour at which I shall meet thee at the ancient tryst of Anerley on the Jews' next Sabbath Day." Or, describing to her how he spent last Sunday in the country at Pinner: "I commenced the day badly, I fear, for I was *violating* the Sabbath by *violetting* in the fields and woods, this morning." He can never be feeling low, but must always be "horribly blue, wretchedly cobalt, disagreeably desolate." No wonder that Isabella drops hints about the length of his letters, refers ironically to "your large catalogue of words" and asks him outright to avoid any "namby pamby nonsense."

The five months that followed Sam's return from Suffolk and Cambridge were inevitably turbulent as Isabella tried to fathom how she was meant to behave in a situation that had changed without her really knowing why. Her first letter after Sam's return is written in a white-hot fury, at least if the lack of a date and frostily formal "Ever yours, ISABELLA MAYSON" is anything to go by. She wastes no time getting to the point: "My dear Sam" (previously he has been "dearest") "Your sisters have kindly invited me to come up with them on Friday to the Concert [this time to see Opertz], but as you said nothing about it on Sunday to *me*, I thought I would write and ascertain your intentions on the subject." She then proceeds to tick him off, obliquely, about the indecent haste with which he scampered away from Epsom the last time she saw him: "You went off in such a hurry the other morning, I have scarcely recovered the shock yet. Your reason for doing I suppose was business." Then the imperious postscript that Sam would come to dread: "I shall expect a note by return of post, so please don't disappoint."

This sounds like the Riot Act and Sam sensibly responds immediately with a letter that, unusually for him, is dated, perhaps because he wants to prove to Isabella that he really has attended to her the first chance he has got. He gets straight to the point, making it clear that the reason for his tentativeness over making plans for the opera is entirely due to her parents' coldness towards him: "the suggestions of your most humble and loving servant have been latterly so unfortunately received that I have not had the courage to utter my notions with respect to your going anywhere or doing anything." He is careful to explain, too, why he has not written before: "I did not get your letter till 10 o'c last night, or I would have posted me to you before this."

Yet Sam was not so biddable that he was going to be shamed, nagged, or bullied into abandoning the strategy he had devised for making the last few months of the engagement bearable. He is sure enough of himself, and sure enough of Isabella, to risk weeks of escalating tension as he repeatedly tries to dodge his prospective in-laws. On 31 January he turns down yet another invitation from the hospitable Epsom lawyer Mr. White and, while pronouncing himself "very vexed" at not being able to attend, seems unworried by the thought of Isabella having a good time with other men: "you will enjoy yourself, very much, I hope, and find some good [dance] partners," which is hardly the sort of thing any girl wants to hear from the man who is supposed to be in love with her. What Sam really wants is to be alone with Isabella and he drops constant hints to that effect. For instance, if, on her next London visit, she could arrange things so that there was time "to go for a short walk with me," he would be "very glad."

Three weeks later and the couple are on better terms, with Isabella more bewildered than resentful about Sam's reluctance to visit Epsom: "Anyone would think our house was some Ogre's Castle, you want so much pressing to come down. I am sure we are not so very formidable." Another month on and Sam has been restored, finally, to "My dearest Sam." Just for once it is Isabella who is obliged to put distance between them. During the coming weekend the Grandstand is needed for the spring race meeting with the result that Ormond House will be crammed with a "living cargo" of small Dorlings. Ever resourceful, though, she has come up with a contingency plan: perhaps he could come down on the first train on Sunday morning instead? Having not heard from him for a week she is feeling "desolate" and begs him to write: "Please don't call me silly, it is a fact, and facts are stubborn things."

Sam's reply is loaded with the usual ambivalence: "If I can rise early enough tomorrow morning, I will come down by the early train, but don't *quite expect* me, as in the case of a snooze and a turn around I shall be a lost man." Deep in the middle of an *EDM* promotion and busy launching the brand-new *Boy's Own Journal*, Sam is currently drowning in a "huge and dreary desert of notepaper and Envelopes." And yet, he hints, if there were a chance of seeing Bella on her own, the correspondence could magically be left to its own devices. In fact, this time it is Sam who has a plan: his step-mother is going to spend a few days at Brighton with a friend. Could Bella not "steal away from Surrey to its sister county, Sussex, for a few days, or even one?"

In the end, of course, Sam did not get to Epsom during the spring meeting week. At least this time he sent Isabella a note on Sunday morning to warn her, for which she thanked him profusely—"if you had not done so I would have expected you all day"—and sent as a telling postscript "*1000000 kisses.*" Still, that doesn't stop her immediately wanting to plan ahead for next weekend, and she demands to know "your arrangements for Sunday." Unable to stand the thought of a trip to Epsom, it was now that Sam seems to have resorted to lying. He told Isabella that Mr. Hagarty, a friend of his late father's, was dining at the Dolphin, and he couldn't really get out of it. For Isabella this resulted in a dreary day, one of the quietest Epsom Sundays she had ever known, and she writes to tell Sam that she wished Mr. Hagarty "were at the bottom of the Red Sea today instead of at Milk St., for then *he* would not have deprived me of the pleasure of your company."

But in fact Mr. Hagarty was not dining that Sunday at the Dolphin, and Sam, mindful of the way that news and gossip flew back and forth between the Mayson, Dorling and Beeton girls, knew that he had to cover himself. At nine o'clock that night (a guilty conscience perhaps making him put the hour on his letter) he sat down and wrote a letter of explanation to Isabella:

> First of all, by some misunderstanding, Mr. Hagarty didn't dine with us to-day and consequently I had not even the satisfaction of being able to say unto myself—Well, if you *would have* preferred being with *Bella*, still you are doing your duty in paying all the respect you can unto a good fellow, and most valued friend of your Father's—you see I couldn't even gammon myself with that small specific, so I ate my dinner with the best grace possible, *potted* everybody, was surly to all, and escaped to my den in Bouverie—have written a multitude of people on different matters, looked at Ledgers, Cash books, Cheque books, etc., and, after all this dreadful wickedness, complete the scene by annoying you.

Sam had given a suspiciously full account of his Sunday, but it was probably enough to convince Bella, who never seems quite to have understood the depths of his aversion to Ormond House. Her parents, though, were not so trusting. Henry and Elizabeth Dorling were increasingly critical of the way in which Sam was leading a life that was insultingly independent of his fiancée, the woman with whom he was supposed to be getting ready to share his life. Four days after the Mr. Hagarty Sunday, Henry and Elizabeth made a point of telling Isabella that they had discovered that Sam had recently invited friends to the house in Pinner and had a tea party without bothering to ask her, or, indeed, even mentioning it to her. "Naughty boy to thus forget your nearest and I hope dearest friend," Isabella starts her next letter with gritted gaiety. And, indeed, she had every reason to be piqued: this was *their* house, after all, and the fact that Sam had borrowed a proper tea service showed that it was no hugger-mugger affair, unfit for ladies. From here Isabella lurches back into her usual refrain, which sounds much nearer her real feelings: "You are sadly tiring my patience; consider it is ten days since I saw you. Anyone would think you lived in Londonderry instead of London, you are so very sparing of your company."

Late April finds the courting couple happier again, enjoying what will be the calm before the final big storm. Indeed, by 23 April Sam is in a positively flowery mood, perhaps because as the wedding nears he knows this ghastly regime cannot go on for ever: "Oh—what I would not resign to see you now for just one short half-hour? That sweet, short preface that I have read and studied during the past few days—what a joyous volume does it not foretell?—a book of bliss, with many pages to smile and be glad over." All the same, he still manages to get in a sly dig at Henry's famous stinginess: next Saturday is the last Saturday that Bella's season ticket is valid for the Great Exhibition, and surely for that reason alone she will be granted permission to visit it with him? Bella gets her parents to agree, but immediately worries that Sam will do his usual trick of not appearing, or else spoil the day by being spectacularly unpunctual. Written firmly across the top of her next letter is the stern warning: "Do not be too late for the train to-morrow."

Whether or not Sam turned up on time, the trip to the Crystal Palace, on 26 April, went well, perhaps too well. Mrs. Dorling was, of course, ever present as chaperone, and the Crystal Palace would have been full of crowds and bustle. Still, the occasion seems to have unlocked an intensity of feeling in Bella that was both wonderful and alarming (only the previous day she had written, "Do not be too sanguine, dear Sam, do not look forward to too much happiness for fear of being disappointed in *me*"). At any rate, very soon after their outing they had a row, a terrible one. It is difficult to work out the exact sequence of events, since some of the letters have gone missing, perhaps because someone considered them too painful to retain. What we do know is that during the last few days of April Sam was too busy to write a letter to Isabella and that she paid him back by deliberately cutting off contact. Always uncertain of getting her emotional needs met, Isabella did her usual thing and simply ceased presenting them, withdrawing into the self-contained competence where she felt most comfortable. Unsurprisingly, when she does eventually deign to write on 2 May it is simply to ask Sam stiffly to bring down some embroidery that was being professionally cleaned in London. She also pointedly reminds him of his promise to arrive on the 6:15 from London, "so if you do not make your appearance you will have much to answer for," although she does soften it with an emollient "Goodbye with much love and many kisses." It looks as though it is to this letter that Sam replied with a sharp little note, the tartest he ever wrote: "As I think you will have so much to do, and your house be so pressingly full, I shall not have the pleasure of seeing you next Saturday and am Yours most affectionately S. O. Beeton."

Panicked by a tone that she has not heard before, perhaps terrified that he was going to break off the engagement altogether, Isabella immediately responds with an abject apology. Writing probably on 3 May she is contrite, aware that she has been beastly.

I know I have been a very cruel, cold and neglectful naughty girl for not having written to you for so many days and cannot sufficiently reproach myself for the sad omission . . . What a contrast is my frigid disposition to your generous, warm-hearted dear self; it often strikes me, but you know I cannot help it, it is my nature . . . You have guessed my weak point, for if there is one thing more than others I detest, [it] is to be chafed in that quiet manner as you did in the note I received this morning . . . Now my darling I must say good bye, hoping you will freely pardon this my first offence (at least I hope so), with much love, Believe me, my dearest boy,

Yours penitently and most lovingly,
ISABELLA MAYSON

Pray don't write any more cutting letters as you did yesterday, or I don't know what will be the consequence.

Isabella's apology apparently did the trick and from this point the correspondence resumed its normal rate, although lingering tensions about the way that Bella allows her parents to dominate her continue to prevent an entirely easy exchange. On 26 May, and still cogitating on the subject, Isabella sat down in an attempt to explain her position to Sam:

My own darling Sam

As I have here two or three little matters in your note of yesterday which rather puzzled me, I thought I must write and ask an explanation; very stupid of me you will say, as I am going to see you on Wednesday morning, no doubt you will think I could just as well have *my say* then as trouble you with one of my unintelligible epistles. In the first place in what way does Bella *sometimes now* pain Sam just a little? Why does he not wish to be near her? Secondly; what right has he to conjure up in his fertile imagination any such nasty things as rough corners to smooth down, when there is one who loves him better and more fondly than ever one being did another on *this* earth at least. Oh Sam I think it is so wrong of you to fancy such dreadful things. You also say you don't think I shall be able to guide myself when I am left to my own exertions. I must certainly say I have always looked up to, and respected, both parents and perhaps been *too* mindful of what they say (I mean respecting certain matters), but then in a very short time you will have the entire management of me and I can assure you that you will find in me a most docile and willing pupil. Pray don't imagine when I am yours—that things will continue the same way as they are now. God forbid. Better would it be to put an end to this matter altogether if we thought there was the slightest possibility of *that,* so pray don't tremble for our future happiness. Look at things in a more rosy point of view, and I have no doubt with the love *I am sure* there is existing between us we shall get on as merrily as crickets, with only an occasional sharp point to soften down, and not many, as you fancy . . . Good night, my precious pet, may angels guard and watch over you and give you pleasant dreams, not *drab* colours, and accept the fondest and most sincere love of,

Your devoted,

BELLA MAYSON

Burn this as soon as perused.

Either in response to this letter or a slightly earlier lost one, Sam acknowledges with obvious relief that Isabella does, finally, seem able to see that her relationship with her parents would need to change once they were married if either of them were to have a chance of being happy.

Bouverie
Tuesday aftn

My dearest Bella,

I was most delighted with your kindest of notes, so considerably better than *some* sharp keel'd cutters that have sailed thro' the post to the Milk St. Haven.

You're a dear little brick, and blessed must have been the earth of which you were baked. I could not find the slightest spec of a fault in any one of your remarks, for there exists no one more mindful of the respect and love due to a parent than your cavaliero, who is now writing to you . . .

Well, my own loved one, you have made me so much happier and more comfortable to-day as I see you write so firmly, yet so prettily, upon that dreaded subject of interference, that I now do quite hope that matters will not remain as they *now* are . . .

I have written you this, with many people in and out of the Office so if anything is particularly absurd, consider it not there.

But even this newfound understanding between the couple was not enough to stop Sam indulging in his old trick of dodging the Dorlings. In the middle of June, with Epsom taken over by the Derby, Granny Jerrom had escorted the children down to Brighton, to stay at the Dorling family house at 72 Marine Parade. On Friday the 13th, Isabella and her parents are due to join them, and Isabella writes hopefully to Sam suggesting that he might come down for the night. Sam, as ever, cries off, citing the excuse of work: "You are a very good, kind girl to invite me to Brighton, and I hope you won't think me a barbarian for not coming, but I have so many things to do which I can do on Sunday alone."

For some reason Isabella insisted on believing that there was still a chance of a Brighton rendezvous. Even after six months of Sam not turning up whenever her parents were present, she chose to hope that he might, which means that she chose to be permanently disappointed. By Monday, and back home in Epsom, Isabella sat down to write a letter to her elusive fiancé that is a model of wounded narcissism.

My very dear Sam,

I have just returned from Brighton and hasten to write you a few lines just to give you a short account of my trip to Brighton.

In the first place I was very much disappointed at your not coming on Saturday evening. I waited and looked out anxiously for you but no Sam did I see to gladden my eyes. Naughty and very cruel of you to serve me so . . . After dinner . . . I and Bessie walked about the Parade till long after the train was due expecting you every moment . . . We shall not be in Town till Thursday when I hope to see you. Could you not run down to-morrow evening to see me. I am quite sure you could if you liked. It seems such an age since I have spoken to you and I can assure you I quite long for a quiet little chat with my old man, my dear darling *venerable*. I want to ask so many things about I don't know what. I shall expect to see you to-morrow evening, so goodbye till then. Accept my fondest love and believe me my dearest.

Yours ever lovingly

BELLA MAYSON

I was sorry to hear the journal had not answered your expectations, you have had scarcely time to judge yet. You must give it three or four weeks trial before you begin to despond.

Adieu

Isabella's postscript—a hurried note to show that she is not entirely caught up in her own needs—refers to the fact that the *Boy's Own Journal* which Sam had been busy launching over the past few weeks was not doing well and, indeed, would soon fail. Her blithe advice not to worry, to take the long view, betrays a lack of any real interest in Sam's business affairs. From the minute amount of attention she gives the *Boy's Own Journal* in her letters you would hardly guess that its genesis had run parallel to their engagement, nor that its aim—to provide cheap but original printed material for working-class boys—was one that lay particularly close to Sam's heart. So in the circumstances Sam's reply to his fiancée's letter the very next day is extraordinarily generous. He starts by telling her something that he knows she will love to hear—that while spending the weekend in Pinner he has done nothing but think of her: "the moon is electro-typing at this moment with its beautiful silvery light all around, and I instinctively am walking with you on Brighton Pier." From here, though, he can't resist launching a final sally at her parents, in the process betraying his real reason for failing to appear at Marine Parade. "Have Father and Mamma been using you to-day as of old monarchs used the man who stood behind their chair, ornamented with cap and bells—to wit—to trot him out, and then laugh at his stepping?"

But just at the point when Sam might be tipping over into giving offence—fiancés at mid century are not supposed to liken their future in-laws to medieval tyrants—he remembers the delightful fact that the wedding really is now drawing near: "3 Sundays more, and then the Holidays, as school-phrase has it." The ghastliness of the past six months is almost over. There will be no more dodging the Dorlings. Indeed, there will be no more seeing the Dorlings, since Pinner is a good thirty miles from Epsom. Sam's letter ends with a swell of joy and thanksgiving that he is about to marry the girl whom, despite the terrible "wear and tear of the past few months," he truly loves.

None can tell how grateful I feel and am to the "Great Good," for having brought me thus near to a point of earthly felicity, which, twelve little months ago, I dared not have hoped for. May He bless and protect you, my own dearest one, and make us happy, and contented in each other's true and ardent love. Je t'embrasse de tout mon Coeur.

Yours, in all things,

S. O. BEETON

INTERLUDE

Hot suppers are now very little in request, as people now generally dine at an hour which precludes the possibility of requiring supper; at all events, not one of a substantial kind.

ISABELLA BEETON,
Book of Household Management

THROUGHOUT THE *Book of Household Management* Mrs. Beeton stays pointedly vague on every meal apart from dinner. Breakfast, lunch, and supper are all despatched in a couple of paragraphs, and afternoon tea never gets a mention. Nothing peculiar, though, should be read into Beeton's haziness. During the nineteenth century the gastronomic shape of the day was changing so fast that it was almost impossible to be definite about who was eating what when.

Over the previous 150 years dinner had become a movable feast, leaving the lesser meals to be added and subtracted around this shifting main event. At the beginning of the eighteenth century you might sit down to dine as early as noon in Scotland and the north where daylight was at a premium, although in fashionable, that is artificial, London 2 p.m. was the more usual time. By the 1780s the quality were now eating as late as 5 p.m. although working people stuck to 1 p.m., opening the way for the class-marking difference of "lunch" and "dinner." But whether you took your main meal at noon or six or sometime in between, one thing was certain: by mid-evening you were starting to feel hungry again. This was where supper came in: a light meal, often a cold collation (bread and dripping for the workers), which ensured you went to bed drowsily replete.

But by the time Mrs. Beeton was writing in 1861 the shape of the day had once again been bent out of shape. Middle-class men now left the house for their place of work early in the morning, not arriving home until 6 p.m. Dinner was correspondingly shifted back to take account of the wanderers' return. The result, as Mrs. Beeton notes, was that there was no longer much call for supper at 9 p.m. since most people, except the neurotically greedy, were still perfectly full from dinner.

There was, however, one context in which supper remained important. If your dining room was small and your budget tight, then inviting a large group to what Mrs. Beeton calls a "standing supper" started to look like an attractive alternative to a more formal dinner party. At a standing supper people helped themselves from dishes such as "sandwiches, lobster and oyster patties, sausage rolls, meat rolls, lobster salad, dishes of fowls, the latter *all cut up*," which certainly saved on servants. What's more, the custom of displaying all the dishes at once made you look like a more generous host than if one course followed another as was usual with a more formal dinner.

Dinner's slow shunt backwards inevitably ended up having an effect on the other end of the day too. With men now needing to be at their place of work across town for 9 a.m., the first meal of the day moved forwards to 8 a.m. And instead of the bread, tea, coffee, and possibly chocolate of the eighteenth century, what Mrs. Beeton described as "that comfortable meal called breakfast" was now turning into something more substantial. Despite her studied refusal to list "a long bill of cold fare" for breakfast, Beeton does go on to suggest the following hot items: mackerel, herring, haddock, mutton chops, bacon and eggs, muffins, toast, marmalade and butter. Here are the origins of the meal that will become the Edwardian country house breakfast of popular fantasy.

With the two meals of the day now stretched nearly twelve hours apart, that left an awful lot of time to be got through on an emptying stomach. Lunch had made a sketchy appearance during the eighteenth century, but now started to become a permanent event in the timetable of the mid-Victorian household. It was still a scrappy business, though, and Mrs. Beeton deigns to give it only one short paragraph and a brief description along the lines of "The remains of cold joints, nicely garnished, a few sweets, or a little hashed meat, poultry or game, are the usual articles placed on the table for luncheon." It was, after all, a lady's meal, quite likely to be taken in the nursery where little stomachs could not be expected to last more than two hours or so without a snack. Middle-class men continued to work on heroically without a midday break, hating the way that lunch interrupted concentration and gobbled up time. Meanwhile, servants, like the rest of the working class, continued to take their main meal, their "dinner," in the middle of the day, usually half an hour or so after their mistress had finished her "lunch."

CHAPTER FIVE

CROCKERY AND CARPETS

 IN THE LAST FEVERISH WEEKS before the wedding, issues of chaperonage became more, rather than less, intense. Eliza Beeton, as moral guardian of a young man rather than a young woman, was naturally laxer, happy to find ways in which the couple could be alone together. In early May she suggested that Isabella should come up to London to view the fireworks staged to mark the end of the Crimean War. She would love to have asked all the Dorlings, Sam explained unconvincingly, but there were simply too many of them to parade around the streets. Despite his offer to escort his fiancée back down to Epsom immediately the display was over, the plan was firmly vetoed from Ormond House.

The Dorlings, as guardians of their eldest girl's reputation, were naturally stricter about the circumstances under which the couple could meet. Six weeks before the wedding Isabella is thrilled to be able to tell Sam that she has obtained a major concession: "I have asked and obtained permission to spend a very happy evening with you on Thursday, although your dear Mother is not at home." In fact, the Dorlings had every reason to be watchful. As the wedding day drew nearer the young couple were allowing themselves an increasing degree of sexual intimacy. Following what must have been a particularly intense moment *à deux,* Sam writes wildly to Isabella: "I was traitor to my own notions through the exercise of a power: the intensity of which is almost fearful to contemplate. My only means of being saved is by keeping you *in company*—solus, I am powerless, vanquished, and in future I intend to surrender at discretion, (or

indiscretion, possibly) without affecting a combat." In a later letter, after
another of their rare meetings alone, he declares that he is still "in a state
of electricity," suggesting the afterglow of a delicious physical convulsion. During the last week of May Isabella and Sam slept for one night
under the same roof, probably at the Dolphin. This physical proximity
sent Sam into raptures. Writing probably on 27 May he declares:

> I have been (and am) most happy since the morning of Friday last—the
> remembrance of your society for so many sweet hours on Thursday
> Eveng, and the charm of your company on Friday morng, still dwell
> with me most pleasantly, albeit I was so rude as to wake you so gently—
> I really am quite astonished at my temerity . . . I wish at this moment I
> could breathe into your ears, closely and caressingly, all the fond hopes
> I feel for your dear welfare . . .

Far from being offended by all this ear nibbling, Isabella was enjoying
her first experience of adult sexuality. When it comes to taking the lead,
though, she is still sufficiently a girl of her time and class to worry about
going too far, if only on paper. So she closes her letter of 1 June with a
daring yet coy "I am looking forward with great pleasure to that evening
at the Opera, that is to say if we go by ourselves; rather a bold expression
for a maiden of twenty." On another occasion when she fantasizes about
shutting herself up with Sam in a cupboard in their new Pinner home she
checks herself immediately for seeming a "very rude girl." As the wedding approaches her letters flip-flop between unguarded expressions of
sexual need followed by clumsy retreats and denials. It is not until a mere
three weeks before the big day that Isabella allows herself, finally, a statement of unqualified desire: "The time is fast approaching my precious
pet, for our affair."

Sam and Isabella used a code word for their stolen pats, kisses, hugs
and squeezes. Whenever they wanted to refer to the state of feeling
swoony, they described themselves as "cabified," presumably because
these moments took place most often in the privacy of a hansom cab, on
the journey home from the opera, or on the way to London Bridge station. Alone and forlorn in Brighton only a month before the wedding,
Isabella writes to Sam that the beautiful twilight is making her all "*cabified* and nonsensical and I am sure if you were near me I should feel
inclined to hug you to pieces." Sam brings himself up short in one letter

when he is in danger of becoming too aroused: "*I am getting into Cabs again*—am I not, darling?"

Reading again these sweetheart exchanges, it is easy to forget the full facts of the matter. Far from being an uncertain demi-virgin, electrified by the flash of an ankle, Sam was a young man who had enjoyed all the usual pleasures of city living. During a trip made to Paris a few months earlier he had crammed his way into a Lenten Ball at the Opéra to stand for an hour gawping at "les dames, all masked, and many in the most outra-geous costumes," clearly relishing "the intensity of the light, the heat of the crush room, and the loudness of the music, with the excitement of the dancers." Isabella's purity, the fact that she represented the remnants of a more innocent way of life, was an integral part of her appeal, as it was to so many early Victorian men who had been pushed by delayed marriage into a sexual life that consisted of picking up strangers in the Strand. In an odd sentence, written three weeks before their wedding, Sam talks of longing to get his new bride back to "our quiet home at Pinner . . . and commence in right good earnest a settled life, for which after all my wan-derings and vagaries I yearn immensely." Apart from his single trip to Massachusetts to see Mrs. Stowe four years earlier, there is no record of Sam straying much further from Milk Street than Heidelberg. These "wanderings and vagaries" were of an entirely different order.

But it would be wrong, too, to see Isabella as an innocent lamb led to the slaughter. Clearly she enjoyed the idea of her fiancé as a sexual man, attractive and attracted to other women. In the letter that he writes describing the sexual excitement of the masked ball in Paris, Sam ends with a deliberately sheepish, "hope you won't think me, dear Bella, a naughty boy for going." But the fact is that if Sam really thought that Isabella would have minded him playing *flâneur*, staring at all that gleam-ing cleavage, he would simply not have mentioned it.

It was in another letter, written at the end of May, that Sam dropped a bombshell, provoking a final row in what had already been a remarkably bad-tempered engagement. Slipped in among prattle about new toilet tables and wedding invitations, Sam artlessly asks, "Now, my dearest, are yr parents going to Germany this year? if they are not I really don't see how I can avoid going there myself with Mrs. B. You are aware of my notions of duty on this point." What Sam is actually announcing is that his step-mother will be accompanying them on their honeymoon, and adds, for prissy good measure, that he considers it his bounden duty to escort her round Europe. Given that Sam had spent the last six months lecturing Isabella on the way that she put herself too much at her parents' beck and call, this was more than a little rich. Even a compromise plan—that Sam and Isabella should honeymoon alone together but immediately afterwards he would escort Mrs. Beeton to Heidelberg—found no favour with Isabella who responded with great firmness and, just for once, no embarrassment about the fierceness of her desire.

> My notions on the subject are that it would be very disagreeable to have a third party with us on our journey, and that it would be wrong and very unkind of you to leave me so soon after—. You say it is a matter of duty. Do you think it would be dutiful to me, to go away so soon looking at it in that point. You ought certainly to consider me first in that respect because after a man marries he is supposed to look first to his better or worse half as the case may be.

In the end a compromise was reached. Sam and Isabella would spend most of their honeymoon alone. Only towards the end would they meet Mrs. Beeton and Eliza in Paris and continue in a foursome to Heidelberg to visit Esther Mayson, Mary Dorling, Helen and Mary Ann Beeton, all of whom would miss the wedding.

What becomes apparent during these tense final weeks of the engagement is the different way in which Sam and Isabella met stress. Sam, who had been far the jauntier of the two during the chaotic but open-ended period of February to June, now did what he always did when he felt boxed in and escaped into ill health. Isabella, by contrast, who had found the ambiguities and ambivalences of spring and early summer hard to handle, came into her own once she was presented with a well-defined set of challenges. Lists, schedules, and deadlines didn't simply make her feel secure, they energized her, turning her sharp and crisp. From being the clinging, dependent partner in the relationship, she became the calm, cool voice of common sense. Increasingly wise to the way that Sam used his physical state as a way of controlling situations that didn't suit him (she hadn't yet forgotten the ghastliness of his January flight to Suffolk), she handles him with a gentle firmness that shows she is not prepared to let him spoil her big day. "Before finishing this [letter] I must give you a little piece of advice that is for the next three weeks to take things quietly, and not fume and fret yourself about trifles. You will find it much better for yourself and me also. Now Goodbye, my darling, you have my sincerest wish for recovery."

Middle-class weddings in the mid-nineteenth century were not necessarily fancy affairs. Indeed sometimes they involved nothing more than the happy couple going off quietly in their best clothes to church, witnessed only by their close family. At this point in the century marriage, like Christmas, still meant more as a sacrament than a secular jamboree. It was the Dorlings who were determined to make a splash, staging an event that would mark just how far they had come since William trundled into town with his printing press nearly forty years earlier. Isabella was the first of the new generation to marry, and it was the perfect occasion to put on a show. For the marriage of Miss Mayson to Mr. Beeton, St. Martin's parish church would be packed with guests, the bride would be luminous in white, there would be a procession of eight matching bridesmaids and the wedding breakfast, held in the Grandstand, would be fit for a queen, or at least for a passing duchess.

If the idea of a wedding as a kind of spectacle seems very contemporary, there are some details about the Beeton wedding that seem strange to modern eyes. The fact, for instance, that the final date was not fixed until a month before it actually took place on Thursday, 10 July. Odd, too, is the way that Isabella did not bother to confirm the date to Sam until after the invitations had already been sent out. This, though, still left plenty of time for the familiar jostling, squabbles, and fallings-out. The first major blow-up, which was between Henry Dorling and his younger brother Edward and sister-in-law Eliza, had started as long ago as May. The roots of the row are unclear, although it looks as though it might have had something to do with the issue of how many Dorlings were to go to London to see the Crimean fireworks. The end result was that Eliza, "Aunt Edward," refused to attend the wedding. Just to stir things up a little further, Eliza dropped in on Sam at his Bouverie Street office (she was a devoted reader of his *Englishwoman's Domestic Magazine*) to elaborate on her reasons for turning down the invitation and, as Sam reported to Isabella, "to beg that neither you or I should consider in any degree that it was a slight to us." Here was a rare and golden opportunity for Sam to lay into a Dorling, and he lost no time in piling on the moral relish: "Oh! how much happier would the dwellers in this world be if they thought a little more of others, and a little less of self."

Isabella, loyal to her parents as always, wrote back to Sam on 3 June calling Aunt Edward "so very stupid" (Eliza was, after all, only a Dorling by marriage) and promising: "I must tell you the other side of the question when I see you." Isabella, in turn, was not above taking every chance to make digs at Sam's clan. On 20 June she is careful to tell him that his friend Fred Perkes has promised to reply to the invitation in "a very dirty scrawl in pencil," while the offhand Uncle Tom Beeton has managed to accept for the 8th rather than the 10th. But there are genuine worries too: two days later Isabella is writing to tell Sam that his Aunt and Uncle Kersey from Hadleigh "have refused our invitation on account of poor Mr. Kersey's health." This, for Sam, is a genuine loss since Aunt Kersey, otherwise known as Aunt Carrie, had been his nursemaid during the Suffolk stretch of his childhood. Nothing, though, can dampen the complacent spirits of a young and popular bride: "I regret it much but I suppose we must put up with the disappointment," chirps Isabella. "All our friends invited have accepted; our numbers bid fair to be very strong."

Work had started on Isabella's trousseau at the beginning of May. As was the custom, the bride and her sisters had been involved in the actual making of some of the items and on the 8th Isabella writes to tell Sam about her marathon sessions with the visiting seamstress: "Yesterday and to-day I have been sitting a great deal with Miss Findley, and scarcely seem to have an idea beyond a needle and thread. There is one thing to be said if you feel at all dull she amuses you much with all sorts of poetry, as well as tales in prose which by the way are not of the most delicate nature." It is most likely that racy Miss Findley herself made the dress, which would have cost anything up to £20 (£5 or so for the fabric, another £4 on whalebone, tape, hooks, edging, and lace and with a further £12 going on accessories—shawls, bonnet, mantle and so forth). There is some confusion as to the exact contributions of the various Mayson and Dorling girls. Charlotte Dorling, writing in 1918, remembered each of them contributing a different tier to the skirt of the dress itself. Her younger sister Lucy, however, insisted in old age that it was the stiff flounced petticoat underneath to which each girl had added her own unique design. Either way, this domestic effort was supplemented by shop-bought goods.

During Derby week, when Isabella and Bessie were supervising the children in Brighton, they took advantage of being among bigger and different shops to go scouting for clothes "for the small children to appear at our wedding in something more than usual" (in other words, to kit out those children who were not to be bridesmaids in something that would look suitably smart). Even Sam, as the groom, found himself dragged that summer into interminable conversations about dresses and millinery. One Sunday in late May he writes to Isabella: "Have dined at the Dolphin to-day, passing a most quiet day . . . talk being mostly on Epsom subjects, and of July performances: An inspection of the green flounced dresses of the girls [his sisters], their bonnets, and the Missus' [Mrs. Beeton's] dress for the occasion."

The last few days before the wedding passed in a whirr of short, imperative notes, hectic errands, interspersed for Isabella with long patches of dreamy boredom. On 22 June she confides to Sam that during church that morning, "instead of listening to the sound of the Gospel and profiting thereby, I have been giving my imagination full play . . . I am so very sorry you are not here to-day. I seem quite lost without you. Don't you think I shall have a deal to answer for, I mean thinking so much about you now, always saying to myself, I wonder what Sam is doing and what he is thinking about, &c. &c. &c."

Isabella Mary Mayson and Samuel Orchart Beeton were married on Thursday, 10 July at St. Martin's parish church by Revd. Benjamin Bock-ett. Our main witness for the day is eight-year-old Lucy Dorling who, as an old lady in Belfast eighty years later, wrote a piece recalling the happy event for the *Star* newspaper. Isabella wore white silk, which had been fashionable ever since the Queen had worn it to marry her Albert in 1840. On her head was a bonnet trimmed with flowers, probably the ever popular orange blossom, rather than a new-fangled veil.

No fewer than eight girls followed the bride up the aisle, ranging in age from nineteen to six. They were Bessie Mayson, and Jane, Charlotte, Helen, and Lucy Dorling, and Eliza, Victoria, and Jessie Beeton. It was considered too expensive to bring Esther Mayson, Isabella's other full sister, back from Heidelberg and she was obliged to make do with a piece of the duplicate wedding cake from Gunter's, along with her step-sister Mary Dorling and her brand-new sisters-in-law Helen and Mary Ann Beeton. The older Beeton bridesmaids wore pale green and the Mayson-Dorlings wore mauve, each with three tiered skirts. It was this, more than anything, that marked this out as a showy wedding: at this point in the century most bridesmaids simply turned up at the church in their Sunday best. The girls' bonnets echoed that of the bride and were decorated with flowers resting on the hair in front. The two little ones, six-year-old Jessie

Beeton and eight-year-old Lucy Dorling, wore embroidered white muslin, with straw hats and beige boots which pinched so tightly that they gave Lucy her first corn.

There are no clues as to what Sam wore, but as a man with a clutch of half-sisters and more than a passing interest in his own image, it is likely that he made a stab at looking right. *Minister's Gazette of Fashion* for 1861, aiming at a slightly smarter constituency than the Beeton-Mayson wedding, suggested that the bridegroom should aim to blend in with the other gentlemen attending the ceremony. A frock coat of blue, claret, or mulberry was probably the thing, set off with a waistcoat of white quilting. Trousers, meanwhile, were of pale drab or lavender doeskin.

After the service the happy couple, wedding party and guests trundled the two miles up the hill from the church to the Grandstand, where the breakfast was to be held. And it really was a breakfast, since the law demanded that all weddings take place in the morning. Lucy Dorling remembered "how picturesque the guests looked out on the course in front—the big skirts and fringed parasols." By holding his daughter's reception in the commercial premises with which he was associated, Henry Dorling was once again demonstrating his fatal lack of gentility. To the fastidious mind it was almost as if he were using his daughter's wedding as an advertising opportunity. And yet who could blame him? The Grandstand kitchens were accustomed to catering for thousands during race meetings, and it would be a surprise if they were not able to rise magnificently to the task of providing a wedding meal for seventy or so. Certainly his trade connections allowed Henry Dorling to provide champagne of extremely good quality—probably the Moët et Chandon that was habitually served at the Grandstand. The menu for that day has not come down to us, but perhaps it was not so very different from that suggested by the brand-new Mrs. Beeton in her *Book of Household Management* only a few years later.

At this point in the century wedding presents were contributed by the family only and not expected from the rest of the guests. The gifts would have been sent on in advance to the Grandstand so that they could be displayed on tables in one of the reception rooms set aside for the purpose. The most heartfelt present came from little Lucy who had spent months making a mat for her sister's new house in Pinner: "very pretty it looks; I think you will be very pleased with it," Isabella had loyally enthused to Sam. The most spectacular came from Henry Dorling in the form of a

Tongue.

Ribs of Lamb.

Two Roast Fowls.

Mayonnaise of Salmon.

Dish of Lobster, cut up.

Veal-and-Ham Pie.

Charlotte Russe à la Vanille.

Lobster Salad.

Epergne, with Flowers.

Lobster Salad.

Savoy Cake.

Mayonnaise of Trout.

Tongue, garnished.

Boiled Fowls and Béchamel Sauce.

Collared Eel.

Pigeon Pie.

Dish of Lobster, cut up.

Ham.

Raised Pie.

Two Roast Fowls.

Shoulder of Lamb, stuffed.

Mayonnaise of Salmon.

Lobster Salad.

Dish of Lobster, cut up.

Larded Capon.

Lobster Salad.

Epergne, with Flowers.

Boar's Head.

Pigeon Pie.

Mayonnaise of Trout.

Tongue.

Boiled Fowls and Béchamel Sauce.

Lobster Salad.

Raised Pie.

Ham, decorated.

Pigeon Pie.

Shoulder of Lamb, stuffed.

Dish of Lobster, cut up.

Two Roast Fowls.

Mayonnaise of Salmon.

Dish of Lobster, cut up.

Savoy Cake.

Lobster Salad.

Epergne, with Flowers.

Lobster Salad.

Charlotte Russe à la Vanille.

Veal and Ham Pie.

Mayonnaise of Trout.

Tongue, garnished.

Boiled Fowls and Béchamel Sauce.

Dish of Lobster, cut up.

Collared Eel.

(Left margin, top to bottom:) 3 Compôtes of Fruit. 3 Blancmanges, to be placed down the table. 4 Blancmanges, to be placed down the table. 3 Dishes of Small Pastry. 3 Fruit Tarts. 3 English Pines.

(Left margin, lower:) 20 Small Dishes of various Summer Fruits. 3 Fruit Tarts. 3 Cheesecakes. 4 Jellies, to be placed down the table. 4 Jellies, to be placed down the table. 3 Dishes of Small Pastry.

(Right margin, top:) 20 Small Dishes of various Summer Fruits. 3 Cheesecakes. 3 Fruit Tarts. 4 Blancmanges, to be placed down the table.

(Right margin, lower:) 3 Compôtes of Fruit. 4 Jellies, to be placed down the table. 3 Dishes of Small Pastry. 3 English Pines.

Bill of fare for a July wedding, ball, or christening, for seventy or eighty guests, as suggested by Mrs. Beeton in the Book of Household Management, *1861.*

white piano. It was an interesting choice, angled so obviously towards Isabella rather than Sam. Henry and Isabella had always bonded over their shared love of music and the fact that the piano was white marked it out as a lady's instrument. One of the more modest gifts was a toast rack from William Dorling, and the accompanying note in his old man's hand still survives: "Though trifling in value I can venture to say there is not one of your numerous friends can be more sincere in wishing you and Mr. Beeton all the happiness and prosperity this world can afford. I am, My Dear Isabella, Your affectionate Step-Grandfather W. Dorling." William Dorling died shortly afterwards, his name still packing a sufficient punch for the news to make several of the national sporting papers.

After an hour or two at the table, Isabella would have slipped out to one of the Grandstand rooms set aside for the purpose and changed into her going-away outfit. Then she and Sam climbed into the waiting carriage that was to take them the nine miles to Reigate train station. From Reigate the new Mr. and Mrs. Beeton travelled by train to Folkestone and then crossed the Channel to begin married life together.

SAMUEL BEETON WOULD NOT have been allowed to marry Isabella Mayson had he not been able to provide her with a proper "establishment." This didn't mean that he had to buy her a house—only 10 per cent of the population owned their homes at this time—but he did need to be able to afford the rent on a suitable property and to fit it out from scratch. It was these prohibitive costs that accounted for so many middle-class men leaving it late to marry. At mid-century, the average age of a groom was almost thirty. Sam, by being in a position to set up home at only twenty-four, was a lucky (that is, a comparatively wealthy) man.

Pinner, where Sam had rented a house from early 1856, was a village thirteen miles to the northwest of London. The opening of a station there in 1844 on the London–Birmingham line had changed the place radically, making it ripe for development as one of London's earliest suburbs. It took only forty minutes to get into Euston Square, just right for the new generation of middle-class men who wanted to raise their families away from the racket and fevers of London (1858 would be the year of the Great Stink, when even parliamentarians were obliged to go about their business with handkerchiefs clamped to their noses). In fact, recent historical research suggests that these first Victorian suburbs were far from being dreamy Edens: shoddy building, poor drainage, and an inadequate infrastructure often meant that within a few years they had become little more than slums. Nonetheless at this early stage everyone, including the Beeton family still residing in the shadow of St. Paul's, saw this move to the quasi-country as a delightfully healthy one. Writing from Heidelberg in 1857, Helen Beeton tells Isabella that she thinks it is "very gesund" for her brother Sam to work in his Pinner garden, "much better than sitting reading a newspaper or smoking a cigar in that smoky London."

Sam had taken out a lease on a house in the brand-new Woodridings Estate built along and behind a stretch of the Uxbridge Road, about a hundred yards from Pinner station, which is today called Hatch End. Woodridings had been heavily advertised in *The Times* during the closing months of 1855 by Richard Field, the surveyor responsible for developing the estate, and the plans had been available to view at his offices in Coleman Street, just round the corner from the Dolphin. This new way of living—*rus in urbe* or perhaps *urbe in rus*—was still unusual, which is why Field produced an elaborate brochure designed to sell the concept to Londoners considering moving out of town. Having assured his readers that love of the countryside was "a universal passion" amongst all right-thinking Englishmen, Field—or someone hired to produce persuasive prose on his behalf—went on to set out the reasons why living at Pinner, and Woodridings specifically, would provide the best of both worlds.

The first advantage of moving out to Woodridings, said the blurb, was the high chance of avoiding cholera, "which leaves unscathed many a rural district." In fact, this was spectacularly untrue of Pinner, where the majority of houses emptied their sewage into the sluggish Pinn and high summer was always a stinking business. Still, to prove his point Field goes on to inform potential Pinnerites that the natives are spectacularly long-lived, with the oldest inhabitant of the parish graveyard having died at 118. And yet, says Field, anxiously anticipating his wavering audience's objections, there is no danger that living in Pinner means that you will be left out of the loop. Rather, "The Morning Papers are supplied to the regular Traveller, who sits at ease in his First Class Carriage and reads the Times, and comes to Business primed with all the News of the previous night, and is literally beforehand of the Cit[y worker], who has slept in town all night and knows nothing." As a final incentive, anyone who takes out a lease on a Woodridings property will be entitled to a free first-class season ticket to London.

Field also takes care to address the prospective Woodridings mistress. She is assured that tradesmen from nearby Watford and Bushey make daily deliveries and that, thanks to the excellent pasture nearby, the local dairy produce is first rate. The prospectus also makes much of the fact that, by ancient statute, Harrow School provides free education to any boy born in the area, a fantastic bonus that is worth £200 a year. The extraordinary fact that leasing a £50 house on the Woodridings Estate entitled you to educate your boys for free at Lord Byron's alma mater was, inevitably, too good to last for long. By 1868 the loophole in Harrow's statutes had been closed for good.

Houses on the brand-new Woodridings Estate all came in pairs, in a series of semi-detached blocks which meant that, at first sight, each house appeared to be twice its actual size, an apt metaphor for the desires of the rather middling classes who lived in them. There were fifty houses in all, together with a public house called the Railway Hotel. Most of the houses were in the Italian style favoured by the great west London estates in Bayswater and Belgravia. Each block was carefully distinct to preserve the sense that these were homes for the discerning gentry rather than jerry-built hutches for lower-ranking professional men. There was Wellington Villas, which, as the name suggests, were sturdy, martial, and looked like homes fit for heroes. Oak Villas were Gothic and cottagey, although Cambridge Villas, far from resembling some ancient seat of learning, looked boxy and sensible. Chandos Villas, where the Beetons

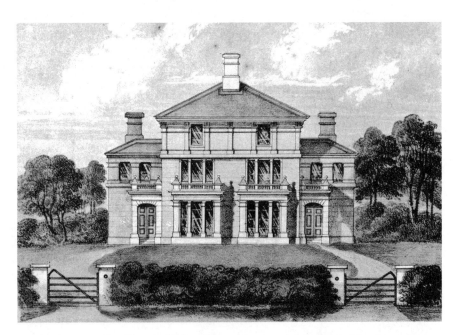

Numbers 1 and 2 Chandos Villas, Pinner. It was while living in Number 2 from 1856 to 1862 that Isabella wrote her Book of Household Management.

were to live, was one of the cheapest buildings on the estate, nondescript, flat-fronted townhouses fifty feet wide built of red brick that Isabella immediately set about covering with quick-growing creeper. There were, according to Field's specifications, a lobby and entrance hall, dining room sixteen feet square, drawing room seventeen feet by fifteen feet, five large bedrooms, two water closets and "domestic offices." Like the other houses on the estate, 2 Chandos Villas had piped water and oil lighting.

The 1861 census gives some idea of the kind of people who became the Beetons' neighbours. On the night the census was taken thirty of the fifty houses were inhabited. Twenty-five of these were headed by professional people—barristers, surgeons, clergymen. There were also superior clerks—administrators who worked in the Admiralty, the India Office, and War Office. In the *BOHM*, published in a single volume the same year that the census was taken, Mrs. Beeton advises that house rental should represent about one eighth of a family's annual income. According to this calculation, this means that the inhabitants of Woodridings earned between £400 and £600. Certainly they were not carriage people, for only four or five stables were provided on the entire estate (it is probably no coincidence that it was around now that fly driving became a new occupation in Pinner). The majority of the households employed three servants, a cook, housemaid, and nurse, while six houses had only one servant and two employed an ample five.

As was the custom, Sam had started getting 2 Chandos Villas ready several months before the wedding. The idea was that the house would be in a suitable state for the couple to move into on return from their honeymoon in August. Isabella, as the future mistress, was naturally to be consulted on everything. Yet given Pinner's distance from Epsom and the problems of chaperonage, most of her input had to be conveyed by letter. It was Sam's job, as a young man able to move freely between the Dolphin and Pinner, to direct operations on the ground, overseeing gardeners and workmen and supervising the delivery of furniture and household goods from London stores. Isabella had never had any doubts that finding and setting up a new home was going to be an anxious, exhausting business. Writing the opening pages of the *BOHM* only a year later she announces, as if from weary experience: "Many mistresses have experienced the horrors of house-hunting, and it is well known that 'three removes are as good (or bad, rather) as a fire.' " Sam, inevitably, was more optimistic about the whole process, but even he was obliged to admit after a few months that the task had proved harder than he had expected: "You truly said—I didn't know what I had to do, and I certainly didn't, for what with pots and potatoes and Gravel and Carpets, and Crockery and Creepers, Grates and Greens, Fenders and Scrapers and other him's and her's it certainly keeps a fellow well up to the mark."

Despite pretending to grumble, it is quite clear that Sam enjoyed this rehearsal for domesticity. Right from the start he was able to use 2 Chandos Villas as his personal playground, camping out there at weekends and inviting his friends down for impromptu adventures. Isabella's upset in mid-April at learning that Sam had held a tea party without asking her spoke volumes about the different experiences of a young man and a young woman setting up their first home. Sam is able to start a relationship with the place immediately, possessing and inhabiting it and making it his own. Isabella, by contrast, can only visit 2 Chandos Villas with a chaperone and, while she has a say in fitting it out, all her purchasing decisions must be overseen by an older and more experienced woman, either her own mother or her future mother-in-law.

Sam first started going up regularly to Pinner in the second week of April: the free season ticket that came with the house gave him unrestricted first-class travel to and from town. There is no disguising his young man's glee at being able to camp out with his best friend Fred Perkes, a young warehouseman who lived around the corner from the Dolphin in Wood Street:

Fred P. went down with me last night, and we "made out," as the Yankees say, tolerably . . . Our bachelor bedroom is quite comfy—the bed and bedstead are capital, and the chest of drawers, complete with toilet cover, with my old Buffalo rug before the fireplace, and a washing stand, borrowed from Mrs. Scott [the gardener's wife] constitute the furniture—I had forgotten,—the sheet nailed in front of the window, so as not to expose us too much to Mrs. Browne's [who lived at No. 1 Chandos Villas] ken—We took down Coffee, and Sugar and Sausages, and had a good tea last night, and a first rate breakfast this morning . . .

The first challenge was to construct a garden out of what was still a building site. In early April Sam reports that two gardeners have started levelling the ground and digging the borders. A week later Isabella, writing from Epsom, offers her thoughts on planting: "You wished to know my favourite seeds; I have no partiality for anything in particular but Mignonnette, and I think that would look best planted at the edge of the Border; however, please yourself and you please me, my dear. Honeysuckle, Jasmine, Clematis, Canaryanthus are all very pretty creepers. The first named grows very quickly and soon covers a place, and that I think is very desirable at Pinner." Sam duly ordered these seeds, added some standard roses and scoured the sky hopefully for signs of rain. By the end of June he and Mr. Scott the gardener had contrived a fine path made out of brick dust and a "rather primitive hotbed for a vegetable Marrow plant."

When it came to the house itself, however, Isabella's desires were more easily accommodated. Storage was a particular preoccupation, and she wanted to add two big cupboards to the basic design of the house, one in the cellar and one in the passage. Finding it hard to picture exactly what she had in mind, Sam asks her around 23 April to "oblige me with a Crayon sketch" that he could show the carpenter. Isabella, mindful of Sam's shaky grasp of detail, immediately spots the scope for misunderstanding: "I fancy I could draw a plan for shelves in that cupboard you were speaking of, but as it would be absolutely necessary for me to be on the spot to explain the said plan, I think I had better bring it up with me to-morrow."

By late May much of the work had been completed. The kitchen had long been painted and the grate "is properly fixed, so as to be useful in case of much fire being required for our 'petit dinners.' " In one of the reception rooms Sam has settled on a fireplace, despite anxieties about his capacity to choose: "I've no doubt I shall make a terrible mess over this and other matters." The carpenter has departed, having completed an enormous cupboard in the passage that means "there'll be room for 4 people to sleep, if we're hard up for beds." Decorative paper, all the way from Paris, is now hanging on the walls. The house reeks of fresh paint, but this is hardly a problem, reports Sam, because the sashes and frames of the windows are letting in "a very large amount of the chilly exterior atmosphere—and the doors are usually all wide open." This sounds worrying, especially the bit about the windows letting in air even when closed. But, in fact, only a year or so later Isabella will be extolling the importance of gaping windows in the *Book of Household Management*: "In a general way, enough of the air is admitted by the cracks round the doors and windows; but if this be not the case, the chimney will smoke."

Doors, though, are a different matter entirely: "Cold air should never be admitted under the doors, or at the bottom of a room, unless it be close to the fire or stove; for it will flow along the floor towards the fireplace, and thus leave the foul air in the upper part of the room, unpurified, cooling, at the same time, unpleasantly and injuriously the feet and legs of the inmates."

If Isabella was fairly sanguine about rattling and chilly windows, she was positively hawkish about drains. In the *Book of Household Management* she makes it clear that the issue of water supply and removal is nothing less than a matter of life and death: "It has been proved in an endless number of cases, that bad or defective drainage is as certain to damage health as the taking of poisons." The supply of safe water was equally important: "No caution can be too great to see that it is pure and good, as well as plentiful; for knowing, as we do, that not a single part of our daily food is prepared without it, the importance of its influence on the health of the inmates of a house cannot be over-rated." She was also positively messianic about the taking of baths: "Cold or tepid baths should be employed every morning unless, on account of illness or other circumstances, they should be deemed objectionable." We know that both Isabella and Sam were enthusiastic takers of cold morning dips before breakfast, which makes it odd that they had chosen a house in which no proper bathroom had been installed. There were two plumbed-in lavatories at 2 Chandos Villas, but ablutions would have had to be performed in a free-standing tub, filled and emptied by the luckless maid. It was not until surprisingly late, June in fact, that Isabella announced that she intended to have a proper bath with running water. This is a complicated business, explains Sam, and involves installing an extra cistern so that "water can be laid on upstairs, on 1st floor." However, when it came to keeping clothes rather than bodies clean the young Mrs. Beeton followed the general custom of the day and put out the household's washing to a local laundress.

Choosing goods and furniture for the house was more easily managed, since Isabella could make her decisions in London stores and have the items delivered to Pinner independently. By some cosmic act of serendipity, Sam and Mrs. Dorling had each settled on Messrs. Green in Baker Street as the best place from which to buy furniture: Mrs. Dorling particularly liked the fact that it was *very reasonable.* Sam arranged initially that Isabella could buy £120 worth of goods from the shop, to which he later added a further £200: "what a rash, reckless character I am, am I not?" he crowed triumphantly, to which the answer is "actually no." Given the size of both the house and Sam's probable income (between £400 and £500), advice manuals for the period reckoned he should be spending about £585 on setting up home, the expectation being that all those chairs, forks, and candle snuffers would last for life.

There could, however, be no question of Isabella picking out the items for her future home unsupervised. Even Sam takes it for granted that she will need to be accompanied to the shops by an older, more experienced woman. Towards the end of May he asks:

> Will you come up on Thursday, and choose the Bedstead, Furniture, and Kitchen Utensils? My Mother is going to Oxford, so if you think well, will you ask your Mamma if she will come with you to assist your selection . . . Your Toilet table, I have ordered and by the end of the Week I hope some of the goods and chattels—SIB [engraved for Samuel and Isabella Beeton] will be in Chandos Villa. I have so much on my hands after to-morrow week [with the launch of the *Boy's Own Journal*] that I should feel very grateful if your Mamma and you would assist in putting the finishing stroke on the furnishing details in conjunction with the Milk St. division.

One of these finishing strokes involved stocking the larder with non-perishable goods, ready for the happy couple's return from honeymoon in early August.

One household item that caused more letters to fly back and forth between Epsom and Pinner was the Venetian blinds. In mid-April Isabella explains that her mama recommends that Sam buys them from a man called Smith whose shop is somewhere between the City Road and the Angel, Islington "as he has made them twice for her, so you see she speaks from experience." As for the colours, Isabella has no hesitation in asking for green "as it looks more subdued in the summer and much warmer than that in the winter." When it comes to the trimmings, Isabella declares in mid-June in a voice that beautifully anticipates the *Book of Household Management*: "White cords and tassels I think are most suitable for the country. . . ." This letter crosses with a decidedly more histrionic one from Sam, who is losing his fight with home furnishings: "These blinds, Oh! these blinds, I can't get along with them at all."

By the end of June, and with barely three weeks to go before the wedding, Isabella was eager to put the finishing touches to the house. "Now you are better I am going to ask you a question about the rest of the furniture. I did not like to worry you on Wednesday evening as you seemed so poorly. When shall I come up to finish, because as you well know there are several things to do yet? You can write and let me know what time will suit you best." What is immediately apparent is the shift of tone in Isabella's voice when she is dealing with practical matters. In those letters to Sam that touch on their relationship she is tentative, resentful, needy. Writing to him about plumbing, blinds, and garden paths she is brisk and knowledgeable, assuming leadership and waiting with barely disguised impatience for him to catch up. The loving, patting and petting that brought so much reassurance in the middle phase of the engagement now becomes nothing more than a distraction, a point that is not lost on Sam who, in a jokey letter in late April, has Isabella declaring, "Sam, I wish you would leave me alone, and allow me to continue my preparations in peace and quietude!"

This shifting dynamic is nowhere clearer than in Sam and Isabella's exchanges about domestic servants. During his camping-out days Sam had made do with Mrs. Scott—wife of the gardener—for the "rough cleaning." Isabella, though, has firm ideas about the kind of people she wants working for her. In an undated letter Sam tells Isabella how well Mrs. Scott is managing with the cleaning and then, anticipating Isabella's reaction to the implications of his remark, quickly rushes to neutralize its power: "now, my dear girl, don't get in a fume and think I'm suggesting her for a continuance." Earlier biographers have always assumed that the Beetons had three servants, since this was the qualifying mark of the comfortably off middle classes. And certainly, according to the *Book of Household Management,* which Isabella would begin writing in a year's time, a family on £500 would expect to employ a cook, housemaid, and nursemaid. However, since Sam's income may have been a little under this, and since there was no need for a nursemaid just yet, one scenario was that they followed her suggestions for a family on £300 and started with a cook and housemaid. And yet, evidence from other sources flatly contradicts this. Little Lucy Dorling, who went to stay at Chandos Villas in 1858, remembers there being two maids and a visiting gardener, quite possibly Mr. Scott. And in 1861, when Sam was said to be at the height of his prosperity, the census reveals that the Beetons' staff consisted of only twenty-one-year-old nursemaid Mary Lawrence and twenty-nine-year-old housemaid Anne Green. This opens up the distinct possibility that Isabella Beeton never actually employed a professional cook (certainly most middle-class newly-weds would not have been able to afford such a luxury). Thus the much vaunted "testing" of all the recipes in the *BOHM* were carried out either by herself alone, or with the help of a general servant with no particular kitchen skills.

There has, naturally, been much speculation about what Mrs. Beeton's kitchen looked like. In the *BOHM* she maintained that there were five golden requirements: first, the kitchen should be large and roomy; second, it should be light; third, it should be easy to get to from the rest of the house; fourth, it should be sufficiently remote so that you couldn't detect cooking smells from the drawing room; and fifth, it needed to be near the water and fuel supplies. There is no way of knowing whether the kitchen at Chandos Villas fulfilled all these requirements but, given that it was a new house built from scratch, it would be unlikely if it did not honour most of them and it is impossible to believe that Bella and her mama had not given the place, or at the very least the plans, a thorough examination before advising Sam to take the lease.

When it comes to Mrs. Beeton's stove, however, we can venture more than a guess. In the *BOHM,* her normally even and disinterested prose breaks down into something approaching personal rapture at the point when she is obliged to advise on the matter of cooking equipment. The Leamington Kitchen Stove, she declares resoundingly, "is said to surpass any other range in use" and, by way of verification, she lists the Leamington's recent achievements: "it took a first-class prize and medal in the Great Exhibition of 1851, and was also exhibited, with all the recent improvements, at the Dublin Exhibition in 1853." She is precise, too, about the reasons for its success:

It has a hot plate, which is well calculated for an ironing stove, and on which as many vessels as will stand upon it, may be kept boiling . . . it has a perfectly ventilated and spacious wrought-iron roaster, with movable shelves, draw-out stand, double dripping-pan and meat-stand. The roaster can be converted into an oven by closing the valves, when bread and pastry can be baked in it in a superior manner. It also has a large iron boiler with brass tap and steam-pipe, round and square gridirons for chops and steaks, ash-pan, open fire for roasting, and a set of ornamental coverings with plate-warmer attached.

A clue to Mrs. Beeton's passion for the Leamington is found in the last sentence of her puff: "they are supplied by Messrs. Richard & John Slack, 336, Strand, London." Messrs. Slacks' business premises were only a few hundred yards away from Sam's Bouverie Street Office. What is more, they were heavy advertisers in the *Englishwoman's Domestic Magazine* and also in the *BOHM* when it first appeared in pamphlet form. Isabella Beeton's plug for the Leamington was probably rather

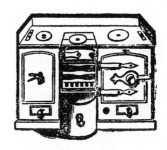

The Leamington Kitchener, which Isabella puffed heavily in the Book of Household Management *and which may have been installed at 2 Chandos Villas.*

more than a favour for a business neighbour of her husband. For four pages later in the *BOHM,* instead of giving her own rundown of what you needed to kit out a kitchen, Mrs. Beeton abdicates all responsibility by simply cutting and pasting the relevant section from the Slacks' catalogue before reminding readers once again of their address in the Strand. This was almost certainly paid for by the Slacks. Another possibility is that a Leamington Kitchener was supplied free to Chandos Villas on the understanding that the Slacks would receive plenty of "editorial support" across the range of S. O. Beeton's publications.

If that sounds improbably modern, it is worth considering the odd appearance of an advertisement from A. Green and Co. of 25 Baker Street on the inside back cover of the June 1856 edition of the *Boy's Own Magazine.* It would be hard to imagine a more inappropriate place for a "General and Furnishing and Upholstery Warehouse" to spend money advertising its wares. Were the pubescent boys who read *Boy's Own Magazine* really in the market for a "Solid Walnut or Rosewood Chair, price £1 1s"? The strange appearance, for one issue only, of such a prominent advertisement for the company that Sam Beeton was in the process of paying to equip his new home suggests that some kind of deal had been done. Perhaps in return for giving A. Green and Co. the back cover of his magazine *gratis* Sam was able to extract some extra goods from them. Might that lie behind his sudden announcement at the end of April that he has arranged for Isabella to have an extra £200 worth of furniture from Green? Whatever the precise nature of the deal, it is clear from a careful reading of Sam's magazines, both the editorial and the advertisements, that he consistently did favours for individuals or companies who were in a position to return the compliment, either by supplying gifts for his loyalty lotteries or taking large sections of expensive advertising space. There was nothing corrupt about this. Print was a commodity, like anything else, to be exchanged in return for a free cooker or a cheap set of rosewood chairs.

Sam and Bella moved into 2 Chandos Villas on 2 August, having finished what Sam described as their three-week "race" on the Continent. Our only account of the honeymoon comes in a letter that Sam wrote two weeks into the holiday to his friend Frederick Weaklin, whose wedding present had been a set of Murray's guidebooks to southwest France. These, Sam assures him, have been "of immense service" and he proceeds to give his friend an account of their travels. After Paris Sam and Isabella had moved on to Tours where they stopped a few days at the Hôtel de l'Univers. From there it was on to Bordeaux, which Sam pronounced "the finest Commercial City I have ever seen." Doubtless he was speaking with the expert eye of a man who had given his late father's occupation on the wedding certificate as "wine merchant" rather than publican. From there to Arcachon with which he declares himself "much amused." Part of the pleasure is the absence of "J. B.s" or John Bulls, in other words British tourists. Next it is on to Bayonne and Biarritz which Sam describes as being "so a propos for my business"—presumably referring to his ongoing efforts to get English-language booksellers on the Continent to stock his publications—that he decided to stay there for four days. Sam finishes his letter to Weaklin, sweetly, with expanded family business: "You will see by the date that we have now reached Orleans en route for Paris, where I have to meet my Mother and Sister to take them with *my wife* (I hardly am used to this word yet) to see our four sisters (2 of ours and 2 of Mrs. B's) who are en pensionnat at Heidelberg."

Sam's letter to Weaklin is full of a young man's excited sense that life is opening up, or perhaps beginning all over again. This is the first time that he and Isabella have been able to be alone together properly, and the experience has evidently been delightful. Any lingering worries that they were not, after all, suited have melted away, never to return. The fact that the marriage would last only nine years makes the letter particularly poignant, or at least that is how it must have seemed to Weaklin when he happened to stumble upon it again by chance in October 1877. Sam had died a bare six months earlier, and Weaklin, with his tidy lawyer's mind, felt that the place for this letter, with its recollection of much happier times, was back with the family. So, on 10 October, the fifty-five-year-old bachelor sat down to write to Thomas Beeton, Sam's surviving uncle, the one whom Isabella had always found such a grouch.

> 14, Clement's Inn,
> London, W.C. Oct. 10, '81
>
> Dear Mr. Beeton,
> Clearing out a box of old letters and papers yesterday, two or three of "S.O.B.'s" turned up, one of which I see was written to me during his Honey-moon tour—twenty-one Yrs ago! since when I have never dropped upon it until I read it again yesterday.
> This tour of his to the South of France on the occasion referred to was selected by him partly, if not indeed wholly, on my suggestion & recommendation, I having had a very delightful trip over the same ground the year before, with a friend . . .
> These letters being now to me of no further interest, it occurred to me that his eldest Son might like to possess a letter of his father's written so long ago and under the circumstances which *the Orleans* letter was written: but as to this you may do with them as you please.
> I Remain
> Dear Mr. Beeton
> Yours very truly
> FREDK WEAKLIN

INTERLUDE

A noble dish is a turkey, roast or boiled. A Christmas dinner, with the middle classes of this empire, would scarcely be a Christmas dinner without its turkey; and we can hardly imagine an object of greater envy than is presented by a respected portly paterfamilias carving, at the season devoted to good cheer and genial charity, his own fat turkey, and carving it well.

ISABELLA BEETON,
Book of Household Management

HERE, IN A NUTSHELL, or a turkey carcass, is Mrs. Beeton's vision of the fitness of things. She writes emphatically, explicitly for the middle classes, the rulers not just of the country but "this empire," which will soon pretty much mean the whole world. Foppish aristocrats who might have chosen exotic game from their estates rather than turkey from the butcher have no place at this particular table. Nor, at the other end of the social scale, is there any room for those who opt for the more workaday goose, which is half the price of turkey. Their job, instead, is to stand and watch, noses pressed to the window, exhibiting the "envy" that validates this little scene as the distillation of all that is great about Britain.

Writing seventeen years after Dickens' *A Christmas Carol* and twenty years after Prince Albert arrived in Britain with his yuletide habits, Mrs. Beeton's Christmas is clearly of the new-fangled codified kind, the sort we have come to know as "Victorian." In her rendering turkey has become the only option for the table, presumably to be followed by recipe 1328 for Christmas Plum Pudding which, to cement its importance in the scheme of things, gets its own colour illustration. The stress on the paterfamilias *carving* the bird nods towards the continuing sense, stressed by Lord Chesterfield, that you could always tell a gentleman by the grace and style with which he apportioned a roast. Finally, that Dickensian phrase "good cheer and genial charity" denotes a holiday from normal class and economic relationships and so softens the "envy" felt by everyone who is banished from Mrs. Beeton's Christmas table.

So far so sentimental. But read on a little further and you will see that Beeton's own investment in her festive sketch is only glancingly concerned with Christmas carolling. Having soldered class and empire together in the second sentence (it is the middle, that is professional, classes who run Britain and Co. around the world), she proceeds to provide a masterclass in those skills required for building bridges, subduing the natives, and balancing the books. And she does it all with a turkey.

> The only art [of carving] consists . . . in getting from the breast as many fine slices as possible; and all must have remarked the very great difference in the large number of people whom a good carver will find slices for, and the comparatively few that a bad carver will succeed in serving . . . the carver should commence cutting slices close to the wing, from 2 to 3, and then proceed upwards towards the ridge of the breastbone: this is not the usual plan, but, in practice, will be found the best.

So carving the roast becomes an object lesson in managing and deploying your resources. But it is also a parable about who does (and eats) what in the middle-class household. For Mrs. Beeton continues:

> The breast is the only part which is looked on as fine in a turkey, the legs being very seldom cut off and eaten at table: they are usually removed to the kitchen, where they are taken off, as here marked, to appear only in a form which seems to have a special attraction at a bachelor's suppertable—we mean devilled: served in this way, they are especially liked and relished.

Note the fudging of functions belonging to people and the spaces they inhabit. The turkey is "removed to the kitchen" where the legs "are taken off." No mention of the housemaid who whisked it away down the stairs, nor the kitchen maid who performed the amputation. And then look who get these waste products—bachelors, those yet-to-be patresfamilias who must practise domesticity in their digs until they are of an age and status to be elevated to a family dinner table of their own. And, tellingly, it is only these young bucks who can stand to have their meat "devilled," that is spiced to the point where it becomes too hot for anyone else to handle. In the safer confines of the paterfamilias' house, the one that everyone envies, it is the breast—plump, sweet, maternal—that gets devoured.

CHAPTER SIX

A MOST AGREEABLE MÉLANGE

ISABELLA WAS PROBABLY DELIGHTED, and not a little scared, at the ease with which she got pregnant. By late August, only one month after stepping through the door as mistress of 2 Chandos Villas, all the signs were there. Did this mean that she was doomed to follow her mother's spectacular example and produce seventeen babies, swelling each year until she resembled some enormous ship in full sail? And what about poor cousin Anne Burtholme, who had died during Isabella's honeymoon, yet another casualty of childbirth?

It was better than staying a spinster, of course, that ghastly fate that had come to preoccupy young British women as the effects of the demographic shifts of the previous decades played themselves out, leaving about 20 per cent without any hope of marriage. The terror of being left an "old maid" was something that especially preoccupied readers of the *Englishwoman's Domestic Magazine* and they wrote to its agony column, "Cupid's Letter Bag," asking how to avoid it at all costs. Sam, as part of a larger response throughout all sections of the magazine, was careful to run pieces that celebrated the unsung virtues of all those extra cousins and aunts who had no household of their own but helped other people's run more smoothly. And, indeed, there is something to be said for the example of Bessie and Esther Mayson who as prosperous old maids stayed close to the Dorling mother ship, managing to live to an impressive ninety. On their parents' deaths in the early 1870s they went to live with their younger Dorling half-sisters in a big house in Kensington. When the last of these girls eventually married, the Misses Mayson moved into a nearby flat on their own. They helped out with children's parties when they felt like it, went to dances and dinners, and, in Bessie's case at least, pursued a passion for fashionable dressing that bordered on the eccentric. By the 1920s, when life was almost done, some of the more prolific Dorling sisters began to wonder whether Bessie and Esther hadn't had the best deal after all. "I feel now that a large family is a terrible anxiety," wrote Jane Dorling White, mother of eleven, to her half-sister Lucy Dorling Smiles, mother of another eleven, on the occasion of the latter's eightieth birthday, "you cannot help taking part in all their doings grandchildren and all."

As Isabella got used to the idea of being a wife and mother, she also had to come to terms with the fact that she had not the slightest idea how her new husband spent his days. During the twelve months of their bumpy courtship she had pretended to be interested in Sam's work but more often than not ended up sounding like a petulant miss who sulks because her young man is always at the horrid office when he should be paying court to her in Mama's drawing room. Every time Isabella tried to do what a good fiancée should, and provide counsel and support in her letters to Sam, she comes across as spectacularly silly. And yet the curious fact remains that within nine months of becoming Mrs. Beeton, Isabella would be working as a journalist. Within a year she would start compiling the *Book of Household Management,* the huge domestic bible that would make her name live for ever. By 1860 she would be co-editing one of the century's most important women's magazines as well as helping to launch another. For the last four years of her short life she would be a full-time London magazine publisher. Never a slouch in her maiden days, Isabella started to live and work at her new husband's hectic speed. The making of Mrs. Beeton must go down as one of the most spectacular transformation scenes in Victorian domestic history.

She did it because she had no choice. While still single and longing to see her elusive fiancé more than once a fortnight, Isabella had fantasized about how marriage would mean that they could always be together. "I have been thinking how nice it will be at Pinner with the only being I at this moment care for on earth; how kind you will be to poor little me, and how you will say sometimes, 'I don't think I shall go to town this morning but stay and have a quiet day in the country,'" she writes a bare three weeks before the wedding. But within days of getting back to Pinner from honeymoon and watching Sam settle into his routine, it quickly became clear that these stolen days of nest building were never going to happen. Habitually rising at six, Sam took a cold bath in the first-floor modern bathroom before catching an early train up to Euston, not returning until late in the evening. By this time the hour for dinner had long since passed and it was Isabella's forlorn task to make sure that there was always something kept warm for the wanderer's return. Once, when Sam missed the last train home, he was said to have walked the whole way back from Fleet Street to Pinner, a distance of about twelve miles. It is not absolutely impossible—in his courtship days he had certainly talked to Isabella of walking to the office after a night spent at Manor House, a suburb four miles north of the City of London. But whether or not Sam really did choose to tramp home through the night, the anecdote was carefully preserved by the Dorlings, who liked the way it confirmed Sam as a reckless show-off and, most of all, inconsiderate of poor Bella.

The source for the story about Sam's long march home originates with Lucy Dorling, who went to stay with her sister and new brother-in-law two years into their marriage, when she was ten. Brown-haired and sharp-featured, Lucy was the Dorling half-sister who most closely resembled Isabella and who, in later years, took to tending the latter's reputation in public. In 1932 she wrote a long article for the *Star* in which she recalled for readers her memories of this trip to Pinner in 1858. Some things about life at 2 Chandos Villas, Lucy had to admit, were lovely. She enjoyed being fussed over (supper came on a tray in bed, complete with fresh flowers) and it certainly made a difference from the Grandstand where you had to put your bed away before the day could begin. She was shocked, though, by the way that Isabella no longer went to church. The Dorlings were conspicuously observant: when they moved a few years later to a big house in a scattered parish on the outskirts of Croydon they immediately raised a subscription to build a new chapel. Sundays chez Beeton, by contrast, were spent rambling through the countryside surrounding Pinner, sometimes walking over to Harrow, during which Sam would direct the conversations. But Sam's constant absence and occasional loud presence intrigued ten-year-old Lucy, who declared him "the most selfish man she had ever met," a casual phrase that passed down through the Dorling line until it became lodged at the heart of their angry chatter.

Yet in that first autumn of 1856 the question was still unanswered in

Isabella's mind: What was it that Sam actually did all day? Initially he specialized in reprinting American books, continuing to take advantage of the fact that there was no copyright agreement between the two countries. Minor works from Longfellow, Poe, and of course Mrs. Stowe figured strongly, although there was also work from Robert Southey, the poet laureate, and other British authors. Original work, meanwhile, could be funnelled into the "Literature for the Rail" series which was nothing if not eclectic: setting off on the train to Exeter or Birmingham you could choose between *Select Scenes from Shakespeare* and *How to Get Money.*

Few of the books cost more than 2s, and usually they went for half that price. Beeton, Clarke, and Salisbury—together with a new generation of publishers such as Routledge, Macmillan, and Warne—were marketing themselves directly towards the bottom half of the middle classes, the kind of people to whom a shilling made a difference. With the industrialization of the British economy, the small freeholders and domestic craftsmen of the early nineteenth century were gradually being replaced by an army of lower-middle-class clerks, draughtsmen, engineers, and teachers. These people were ravenous for information about the new and complex world that was unfolding around them. With Lord Brougham famously declaring in the wake of the 1832 Reform Act that "the schoolmaster was abroad," the new Queen's reign was turning into an age of heroic self-education. There was a huge demand for books that explained everything from how to classify ammonites to the basics of shorthand, the rudiments of Latin to the periodic table. Books were no longer symbols of an achieved and cultivated mind, they were the tools you used to get to the next place in your social journey. And they were fun, too. Reading for pleasure was on the rise, especially among women, who had always been the biggest consumers of novels and were now spending less and less time helping their husbands and brothers in the family business.

Magazines were part of this new print-based mass culture too, and the proof was in the large number of new titles angled at niche readerships that were coming onto the market from the late 1830s. It was here that Sam was to show his real talent and flair, producing periodicals that, while not as original as has sometimes been suggested, were among the most innovative and influential of the nineteenth century. In this part of the business he worked more independently of Clarke, mostly producing magazines under the name "Samuel O. Beeton" which, from February

1856, settled into its final form of "S. O. Beeton." A few years later the firm of S. O. Beeton would adopt a beehive as its logo. Bees were industrious, as was S. O. Beeton. They produced honey, and he had grown up next door to Honey Lane. Most cleverly of all, if you put equal stress on both syllables of his surname you got something that sounded like "Beetown" which was, in turn, as good a definition of a beehive as you were likely to get.

Unfortunately, there are no surviving business records from Sam's various incarnations as printer and publisher, so it is impossible to know how many people he employed. What is clear, however, is that during these early years, before Isabella became his business partner, Sam relied heavily on Frederick Greenwood. From his mid-teens Greenwood had been producing copy for a huge range of periodicals, including the innovative *Illustrated London News* and the upmarket *New Monthly Belle Assemblée,* and so was able to bring invaluable experience to the fledgling company's first magazine launch, the *Englishwoman's Domestic Magazine.*

The *Englishwoman's Domestic Magazine,* which was launched in May 1852 and ran for twenty-five years, was the publication that most surely shaped the magazines we read today. But if you were to pick up a copy of the *EDM* from the 1850s you would initially find it hard to see why. The type is tightly packed in two dense columns; there are few illustrations and of course no photographs at all. The subject matter, too, seems rather worthy, more reminiscent of a textbook than a magazine designed to be read at leisure (did women in the 1850s really look forward to putting their feet up after a busy day to read "Women of the Old Testament" or "The Harvesting of Cotton"?). But look more closely and you will find within the pages of the *EDM* elements that are entirely familiar from our own weekly magazines and mid-market monthlies. There is a problem page, tips on fashion and beauty, instructions on how to make your own clothes, an essay competition, advice on gardening and pets, and a system of loyalty rewards: save up your tokens from

The logo of the publishing firm of S. O. Beeton, built around the activities of the industrious honey bee.

twelve consecutive issues and you get the chance to enter a draw and win anything from a gift voucher to a piano. Yet the single most modern and distinctive thing about the *EDM* is the way that it puts the reader's experience of herself at its very heart. Lurking beneath the endless articles on keeping chaffinches in cages and Hindu wedding customs, the real subject of Samuel Beeton's magazine is always "what does it mean to be a woman?" followed closely by "how could I do it better?"

To see what innovations were truly Sam's and which elements of the women's magazine format he inherited and tweaked, you have to look at what had gone before. The previous generation of ladies' magazines had been slightly stiff, like an awkward visitor in the drawing room who refuses to stay for a second cup of tea. And yet most of the ingredients that Sam was to finesse in the *EDM* were already conspicuously present in the long-established *Lady's Magazine,* the *Ladies' Museum* and *La Belle Assemblée* as well as the more recent *Ladies' Companion.* First, there was the careful avoidance of anything that might qualify as "news," which would have made the magazine liable to newspaper tax and therefore prohibitively expensive. Then there was the promiscuous mix of genres—fiction, biography, readers' letters—delivered in a wide variety of authorial voices from chatty, through schoolmasterly to confidential.

Typically a magazine would open with a biographical essay on a distinguished woman. Famous women authors were particularly popular subjects, perhaps because they represented a viable fantasy of creative fulfilment and economic independence to the magazines' readers. Fiction tended to be serialized and run over several issues, although complete short stories were also included. Historical settings were popular, and courtship plots often centred on a perceived discrepancy in class or "station" between the lovers that was always resolved improbably in the last instalment. On occasion magazines ran fiction by well-known writers: for instance in 1819 the *Lady's Magazine* serialized Miss Mitford's *Our Village,* a happy arrangement that boosted the fortunes of both parties. There were, in addition, rudimentary problem pages, to which readers could write with their love tangles.

The *Ladies' Museum, Lady's Magazine* and *Lady's Cabinet* were, as their names insist, aimed at "ladies"; the cover price of at least 1s filtered out all but the reasonably well-to-do. In those slots that directly address the reader or imply the kind of life she led, it is always assumed that she is the mistress of a substantial household. Indeed one magazine, the

Ladies' Companion, dedicated a regular monthly column to dealing with servants (what to feed them, how much to pay, what to do when they answered back). Likewise, when the readers of *La Belle Assemblée* were promised a cookery series, it was quickly explained that this would not deal with "the lower, more practical part of cookery," but with "the ornament of the table and the general management of the family."

The tone and content of the smaller, regular slots in the ladies' magazines reinforced the sense that their readers enjoyed a great deal of leisure time which they were obliged to fill with conspicuously unprofitable activities. To this end these magazines carry reviews of concerts, plays, suggestions for showy embroidery (nothing practical like making a new collar for your second-best dress), sheet music, and notices of books which are pitched distinctly higher than the pulpy fare serialized throughout the magazines themselves. A large part of these magazines' appeal was the way they presented the reader with a flattering portrait of herself as stylish and cultured. For instance in 1823 the slightly newer *La Belle Assemblée* decided to run a series of pieces written in French on the grounds that "the French language being now familiar to almost every person of education we feel persuaded that the readers of *La Belle Assemblée* will approve of our occasionally presenting them with extracts from the travels of a young French nobleman." Even if your foreign languages were not up to scratch, you could always leave the magazine lying around in the drawing room.

And yet there are plenty of signs that the "ladies" who bought these magazines, the forerunners of our own "glossies," were not quite the passive consumers of culture that some parts of the editorial liked to imply. Readers of the *Ladies' Monthly Museum* and the *Lady's Cabinet* were continually exhorted to send in their contributions, not just to the obvious slots such as the problem pages and readers' letters, but to the main body of the magazine. Fiction, biography, translations, the ever-popular poetry, and what we now call "think pieces," were all supplied at a furious rate by eager reader-writers. The work was not paid, which suggests that what drove the contributors was the need to speak to a world beyond the drawing room. In addition the magazines ran essay competitions, frequently setting titles that asked the reader to reflect upon the state of contemporary womanhood, including that perennial favourite "On the Comparative Merits of Domestic and Scholastic Education for Females."

Yet by 1832 these ladies' magazines were struggling to maintain viable circulations. The times were changing, and their brand of refined gentility no longer seemed to speak clearly or confidently to the post–Reform Act age in which a new kind of female reader was emerging. The solution was to merge titles that, in any case, were finding it harder and harder to sound distinct. In 1832 the *Ladies' Monthly Museum,* now re-named the *Ladies' Museum,* joined with the *Lady's Magazine* before merging in 1838 with *La Belle Assemblée,* in which awkward hybrid form it limped on until 1847.

Now the focus shifted to providing magazines for the opposite end of the market. With the infamous "taxes on knowledge"—duties on paper and print that had made production prohibitively expensive—beginning to ease from 1836, it was increasingly viable to produce magazines that sold at 1d or 2d and aimed for a mass circulation. Some of these titles were explicitly designed with an educative, moralizing purpose in mind: for instance, Charles Knight of the Society for the Diffusion of Useful Knowledge produced the *Penny Magazine* in an attempt to keep the respectable working man educated, entertained and away from vice. The following decade, the 1840s, saw a proliferation of titles intended for a slightly higher class, the kind of households whose breadwinners did the clerical, technical, and supervisory jobs that had not existed a generation earlier. To this end a new slew of periodicals including the *Family Friend* and the *Family Economist* combined resolutely "useful" instruction with easily digested fiction (these people worked hard, they deserved some dream time). For those a little lower down the social scale, there were publications such as the *Family Herald* and the *London Journal* which, for a remarkable 1d a week, included a higher proportion of even more fantastic fiction.

Strictly speaking these publications were not aimed specifically at women, but were designed for the whole family: the magazine format was ideal for catering to a variety of readers living at the same address yet whose interests differed according to age and gender. Yet, at the heart of magazines like the *Family Friend,* launched in 1849 at 2d a month, you were left in no doubt that at the heart of this reading community there was a woman who was almost certainly a wife and mother. This woman could not be more different from the lady reader of the earlier part of the century. She made her family's clothes as well as her own, and looked forward to the patterns printed in the magazine. Since the female reader of the *Family Friend* most emphatically did not employ a cook (at best she might have one harassed maid-of-all-work), she was always on the lookout for fool-proof recipes that had been recommended by other readers. In the Preface to the 1852 quarterly volume the owner and editor Robert K. Philp exhorted: "He hopes that every one having a tried and approved Recipe will forward it for the general good of our 'Family,' always stating it has been tested, and giving particulars as simply and concisely as possible."

Sam Beeton's genius was to take elements from these two publishing strands, the ladies' magazines and the family magazines, and meld them into something that hit the right note for 1852. If the times had changed radically between the 1820s when the ladies' magazines were flourishing and the 1840s when the new generation of family magazines were launched, they had changed again by the century's halfway mark. The economic gloom and social unrest of the "hungry forties" were now fading into memory and the country's mood was lifting into something approaching optimism. With Chartism definitively trounced in 1848 it looked as if Britain had pulled through that dangerous year without following Europe into revolution, demonstrating once again its enviable brand of social and political cohesion. Economically, too, the country was doing well. The price of many basic commodities began to fall, allowing respectable working people a little money to play with. The Great Exhibition of 1851, housed in Paxton's sparkling glass palace at Hyde Park, gave a taste of what those spare shillings, carefully hoarded, might one day buy.

And yet the crowds who flocked to Hyde Park and who later, like Sam and Isabella, used their season tickets at the new site at Sydenham, were not always smiling stupidly, awash with pleasurable awe at the sense of being Fortune's favoured children. No matter how many beautiful figurines were produced by Wedgwood's factories or puddles of molten steel in South Wales, there was no avoiding the evidence that bad things continued to happen to nice people. In 1854 forty years of peace were broken when Britain sent troops to the Crimea to take part in a bloody argument in which it had no real stake. That autumn the newspapers were full of the magnificent cack-handedness of the Charge of the Light Brigade and, later, the hellish conditions in Scutari, the hospital camp to which the wounded were ferried from the battle front.

And then the uncomfortable fact was that, while the country as a whole might be prospering, individual citizens were as likely as ever to find themselves beating off the bailiffs. Small local banks were still capable of going under, bringing down whole communities and family networks overnight. Life assurance was in its infancy, and the unexpected loss of a father, husband, or brother could plunge an affluent household into a poverty that was not even shabbily genteel (it was these sudden switches in fortune that provided the starting point for so much of the fiction that was serialized in the magazines of the 1840s and 1850s).

All these pressures meant that while Britain appeared to be entering a golden period of economic prosperity and political stability, for a huge section of its population, and particularly middle-class women, life was far from certain. People who had been born over a stable were moving upwards (we have seen the radical transformation of Elizabeth Jerrom into one of the first ladies of Epsom) and those who grew up in a comfortable rectory were on their way down (the annual reports of the Governesses' Benevolent Institution are full of just such sudden falls from grace). Meanwhile, the new Victorian morality, buttressed by more than a little Evangelical righteousness, was insisting that virtuous women of all classes should derive their power and satisfaction from running a moral home that offered a haven from the competitive economics of the outside world. Yet, with new luxury goods available, and the material side of life speeding up, it was also increasingly the case that you were what you bought, or at least owned. Many of the tensions that had been there in the old-style ladies' magazines—between woman as luxury item and angel in the house—were being felt by a new generation of women, one that had moved far from its social and geographic roots and was no longer sure about where to turn for clues on how to live.

If all this sounds contradictory then that's because it was. The genius of the magazine format—today, as much as then—is the way it is able to represent a whole range of conflicting anxieties, wishes, desires, and solutions while always managing to stop just short of fatal incoherence. Sam Beeton inherited from the earlier generation of ladies' magazines an editorial voice that was able to talk in various registers. So, while in the practical parts of the *EDM* the reader is assumed to be a sensible woman of modest means who would never blow her housekeeping money on fripperies, only a few pages later she is being advised what the ladies of Paris are wearing this year. In the editor's Preface that appeared at the front of each yearly volume as it was bound, the reader is congratulated on her patriotism (especially during the Crimean War) and her ability to run an efficient, happy home. Yet in "Cupid's Letter Bag" and its later incarnation, the "Conversazione," she is teased for her empty-headed chasing after men. This unevenness allowed Sam, who grew more radical as he grew older, to smuggle in pieces that would have seemed dangerous if they were allowed to stand on their own, or were surrounded by similar articles, as they were in the overtly feminist *English Woman's Journal*. In Sam's magazine a piece explaining why the divorce laws should be liberalized to allow women to escape from wretched marriages could be juxtaposed with a fluffy stretch of fiction celebrating the self-sacrificing heroine who manages to save her husband—in fact a viscount in disguise—from a life of gambling and degradation.

During the first five years of its existence, before Isabella started writing for the *EDM*, it was, by modern standards, a dull thing. And yet, right from the start, the *Englishwoman's Domestic Magazine* clearly knew exactly what it was about. The editor's Introduction to the very first issue has a sureness to it that is remarkable for its confidence, especially from a boy of twenty-one.

Under the emphatic title "Our Address," Sam declaims: "If there is one thing of which an Englishman has just reason to be proud, it is of the moral and domestic character of his countrywomen," before going on to explain that:

> THE ENGLISHWOMAN'S DOMESTIC MAGAZINE will doubtless be found an encouraging friend to those of our countrywomen already initiated in the secret of making "home happy"; and to the uninitiated, who, sometimes from carelessness, but oftener from the want of a guiding monitor, have failed in this great particular, we shall offer hints and advice by which they may overcome every difficulty, and acquire the art of rendering their efforts successful and their homes attractive.

For the Frontispiece of the magazine, Sam had commissioned Julian Portch, whose work could already be seen to great effect in the *Illustrated London News*, to produce a visual representation of what the *Englishwoman's Domestic Magazine* stood for. Portch, who was clearly influenced by the busy and explicit Frontispiece of the *Family Friend*, places a bust of the young Queen Victoria—the greatest living Englishwoman—at the top of his design for the new magazine. Immediately beneath is a sketch of Windsor Castle, with the Union Jack flying, a reminder that the Queen is also a domestic Englishwoman, whose moral power derives as much from her traditional female responsibilities as wife and mother as it does from her extraordinary constitutional position. On either side, and a little below Victoria, are two female classical figures in Grecian-style dress. One holds a quill pen and leans against some books, while the other is holding a palette and brush. Artists they may be, and creatures from an ancient age, but they are both looking with loving reverence towards the figure of the Queen. Perhaps to nullify any suggestion of

Frontispiece to the Englishwoman's Domestic Magazine, *designed by the artist Julian Portch.*

paganism, the painting of Windsor Castle is held up by two plumply Christian cherubs.

Next come two classical columns, on which are inscribed the subjects in which the *EDM* intends to instruct and entertain its readers. The lists read "cookery, household pets, toilette, sick nurse, dress, amusements" and "fashion, embroidery, fruit and flower garden, wisdom, wit, poetry." The columns lead the eye downwards to a group of five young women in contemporary British dress, busy with the activities listed immediately above their heads. One girl is surrounded by dogs, rabbits, goldfish, a parrot, and some kind of small animal in a wheeled cage. Another, who has an open sewing box lying at her feet, is preoccupied with embroidery stretched on a frame. And then, directly beneath the Queen and Windsor Castle, is a cluster of three girls busy reading a copy of what is presumably the *Englishwoman's Domestic Magazine*, reinforcing the link between Englishness, femininity, and the love of home that binds women of all classes. The girls are elegantly but not showily dressed, pursuing their various activities out of an inward, authentic need rather than any desire of being seen. Drawn without any reference to the interiors they would normally inhabit, we are left with no clues as to whether they might or might not count as "ladies."

Significantly enough, the very first article ever to appear in the *EDM* was on the subject of female education, that perennial favourite of women's magazines, which was really a covert way of debating what was becoming known as "the woman question" without appearing too radical. The anonymous piece—could it really have been written by Sam or is it the work, as custom usually demanded, of an older woman writer?—takes the familiar line that "ornamental" education turns girls silly, if not downright immoral, making them quite useless for the discipline of marriage: "it must be the aim of a sound system of education to cultivate those sterling qualities which will make a good wife, instead of imparting that superficial polish which only gives the *appearances* of one." Languages and music, says the writer, are pleasant accomplishments, but they do not lie at the heart of what young women—and the men they are to marry—really need. The emphasis should be on absorbing knowledge from first principles, rather than sticking it on to produce a thing of shreds and patches. "Cookery," for instance, "is more a matter of common-sense than most people imagine; and a slight tincture of chemical knowledge is very useful to those who practise it, so as to enable them to simplify by generalisation, and to deviate successfully from ordinary modes, as new circumstances arise to render such a course expedient." Likewise, knowing how to do the weekly wash properly, make clothes, care for furniture, economize on heat and ensure effective ventilation builds the kind of systematic knowledge that can always be applied to new circumstances as they arise. In a refrain that will come to lodge at the very heart of the *EDM*'s philosophy, the writer concludes that by these means "a love of order and cleanliness and neatness should be so grafted upon . . . [a woman's] nature by habit that her home, *however high or humble,* shall never be deficient in these qualities."

It is important, though sometimes difficult, when reading pieces like "Family Portraits," to remember that Sam, and eventually Isabella too, were not presiding over a reactionary publication, bent on returning women barefoot to the kitchen. On the contrary, the magazine frequently ran articles suggesting that those women who needed to should have access to properly paid and respectable jobs. But the key phrase here was "women who needed to." The *EDM,* in common with the most radical feminist thinking of the time, assumed that a woman's first and proper desire was always to marry, have children, and run a happy home. It was only because it was becoming clear that this was not going to be possible for a sizable minority, that it made sense to set up a system whereby single women could also enjoy the benefits of a comfortable home life, paid for by the fruits of their labour. Training young women to be teachers, hospital nurses, secretaries, tailors, engravers, watchmakers, jewellers, and upholsterers would release the entire sex from a humiliating dependency on men's favour. What the magazine hated more than anything was the kind of faux femininity that turned its nose up at hard work: "To be feminine, it is no more necessary that a woman should be idle or listless, or waste her time in frivolous occupations, than that a man, to become manly, should spend his life in perpetual brawls."

Over the next few years, Sam included many articles supporting various new initiatives to change the legal and social status of women. At the end of 1855, for instance, he ran a piece suggesting bringing back the stocks for men who beat up their wives, and the following year, in the very month that the Beetons married, the magazine welcomed the loosening up of the divorce laws, on the trenchant grounds that "The plea that we have no right to start on the journey of married life with the slightest idea that any eruption of disagreement *may* take place, is a mawkish sen-

timentality, unworthy of a second consideration." That same year the
EDM was equally positive about a petition to parliament which marked
the first step in what would culminate in the Married Women's Property
Acts, arguing that it was ridiculous that a woman should not have the
right to her own earnings and that, equally, it was unfair that a man
should be held responsible for the debts his wife had accrued before her
marriage. In case this seemed like worryingly radical stuff, Sam was
always careful to neutralize any suggestion that any of it represented a
slippery slide towards systematic reform. A thoughtful piece in May
1856, yet again on the subject of women's education, ends with the sen-
tentious, and slightly unconvincing, "Neither need we ever fear that, in
equalising the education of the sexes and conducting it on the same principles, we shall ever overturn that moral supremacy which the Maker and
Upholder of all things has committed into the hands of men."

A safer way of circling around the central topic of what it meant to be
a woman was to displace the discussion over time and space. A central
tactic of the *EDM* was to focus on domestic life and habits in previous
centuries or in other countries. In the first few issues the magazine ran
pieces on Spartan wedding laws, "A Jewish Wedding in the East," "The
Women of Ancient Greece," and "Manners and Domestic Arrangements
in Lapland." Biographical essays on achieving women were another
way of dealing with the issue of what woman was and what she might
be. Writers such as Hannah More and Harriet Beecher Stowe continued
to be popular subjects, although they were increasingly joined by social
activists such as Elizabeth Garrett Anderson, Florence Nightingale and
Elizabeth Fry. Whatever the exact shape of their lives and achievement,
these women's professional success is always represented as an amplifica-
tion of their essential female nature—a desire to share their knowledge
with their sisters, or relieve suffering—rather than the result of any personal ambition.

Just like the earlier generation of ladies' magazines, the *EDM* encouraged its readers to think of themselves as writers too, and urged them to
send their contributions to the editor at his Bouverie Street office. Not
only was this a cheap way of filling thirty-two pages each month, but it
tied the reader into buying the publication regularly, in order to see
whether the editor had "noticed" her piece. To neutralize any suspicion
that this arrangement was pursued because it was cheap, Sam, in his persona as world-weary man of letters, went out of his way to give the

impression that it was he who was performing a service for his "friends" rather than the other way round. In only the second issue of the magazine, he writes his half-joking "Rules for Correspondents," which place the readers firmly in the client position:

> Never write on both sides of a sheet. Always keep a copy of your article, which is apt to get mislaid among the haystack of an editor's manuscripts. Never send an article unfinished, or say you have scrawled it off hastily and left it full of imperfections. Never require the editor to read your article at once, and say whether he will publish it or not, but give him a reasonable time to consider it. Never imagine because he writes a sorry hand himself he is partial to that sort of chirography. Write plainly if possible—write decipherably anyhow; or pray don't write at all.

In December 1852, sensing the strength of his "friends' " desire for self-expression, Sam introduced the monthly essay competition. Initially he set topics that were pegged to events of the day, such as "The Funeral of the Duke of Wellington" (readers who had not been present were advised to read the newspaper reports and use their imagination), or "Christmas Day Customs in England." There was to be one outright winner each month who received a "magnificently printed volume," probably some Clarke and Beeton production that happened to be lying around the office, and two "honourable mentions" who were sent certificates. As time went by the topics slipped towards that familiar subject that was never far from the magazine's heart, namely the reader herself. "The Attributes of a Fair Lady," "The Rights of Women," "The Unselfish Love of Women Contrasted with the Exacting Selfishness of Man" were all set as subjects, in different guises, over and over again. Occasionally Sam was not above varying the tone with the potentially risqué "Do Married Rakes Make the Best Husbands?"

Another way of participating in the magazine was to send a letter to Cupid, who presided over the agony column. With characters such as "The Busy Body" or "The Old Woman" from the ladies' magazines in mind, Sam followed the convention of presenting Cupid/Mr. Editor (they were acknowledged as being the same person) as "old and steady" in contrast to his dizzy correspondents. What is new about the *EDM*'s problem page, though, is the practice of either printing the original letter of enquiry in full, or incorporating lengthy quotations from it into Cupid's answers, so that the readers' voices are distinctly heard (how heavily they were edited or even invented remains, of course, another matter). The problems that vexed *EDM* readers seem strikingly modern and mostly concern the riddle that is man. Lavinia Clotida, writing all the way from Copenhagen, has a typical puzzle:

> A young man whom I love, and who used, when he lived in the same town, to be very kind to me, will now, when he occasionally comes, pass me in the street without looking or speaking. What should I do?

To which Mr. Cupid briskly replies:

> Forget him as soon as possible.

Other problems include fiancés who refuse to dance, husbands who stay out too late too often, jealous sisters, long-gone first loves, a very religious boyfriend who doesn't want to "make love," queries about whether love potions work, and whether or not young single men and women really can be "just good friends." On this last point Mr. Cupid, who in his real life as S. O. Beeton had been brought up among women, was decidedly clear: frank and easy friendship between young men and women is an admirable idea and leads, where appropriate, to companionate marriage.

If the *EDM* reader was neither a natural essay writer nor a romantic casualty, there were still ways in which she could become part of the community of reader-writers and see herself, even if only pseudonymously, in print. There were plenty of slots to which she could address practical questions, such as how to get a stuck stopper out of a bottle or a good recipe for Rice Cake. Readers were also encouraged to send in their own tried and tested domestic tips and embroidery patterns. For, just as the *Family Friend* had worked to create a virtual family of readers in the 1840s, so the *EDM* positioned itself as a kind of proxy mother, a repository of all kinds of wisdom from how to get mildew out of underclothes to how to avoid chilblains in winter or neutralize the bite of a viper.

Alongside those parts of the magazine that functioned as a place to exchange information there were more formal slots where professional contributors handed down advice. There was a column on keeping pets, and another on managing your garden. "Things Worth Knowing," meanwhile, was a wonderful lucky dip that told you how to do everything from gilding wood to curing the diseases of horses to cooking carrots (it takes two hours). The emphasis, as elsewhere in the magazine, is always on saving money, as suggested by the slightly unconvincing recipe for making sugar out of sawdust.

But perhaps the single slot that stands most exactly at the heart of the *Englishwoman's Domestic Magazine* is "The Work Table," which was lifted straight from the *Family Friend*. "Work" was the standard word used to describe the craft activities in which all women were expected to participate—anything from embroidery to sewing on buttons. Its use here, however, underlines the seriousness of traditional female skills when performed in the context of the *EDM*. Thanks to the highly precise descriptions and patterns provided each month, readers could learn to make all kinds of useful household articles from a gentleman's purse to a child's collar to endless pairs of slippers. Diagrams to explain both the cutting out of the fabric and the pattern for the embroidery were printed in the magazine and proved so popular that, by the third year of the magazine, there was a free supplement consisting of "twelve original fancy-work patterns." This was a huge success, as Sam rushed to tell Isabella in a letter of 25 April 1856: "more than 1000 Volumes ordered to-day, quite 'supple-endid' isn't it?"

But for all the *EDM* readers were exhorted to stay home and stay humble, there is everywhere in the magazine a sense of them encountering a new world, a place of sociability and refinement that they have not quite met before. Luckily, the Editor of the *EDM* was on hand to smooth the way. In December 1853 he was able to explain to Caroline Alberta from Glamorganshire that "When a gentleman asks a lady to take wine with him, she should merely bow in acquiescence, and sip her wine when he drinks his." In another issue A.K. is told: "The name of the younger sister by whom you are accompanied should be written on the card, and the corner is only turned down in case of a mutual friend of both families calling with you." Answers to tricky French pronunciations are frequently provided, and there are endless pieces instructing readers on everything from the plots of operas, through the rules of chess, to the correct way to dance the polka.

It wasn't all instructional: fiction accounted for about a quarter of the magazine. Those novels and short stories that were sourced from Britain—whether or not written specifically for the magazine—tended to reinforce the central argument of the *EDM*, namely that what matters is inner worth rather than material show. One of the first serials in the magazine was "Millicent Harvey, or Genius Can Never Be Depressed" which tells the story of a quiet governess whose ladylike ways are nonetheless recognized by those of good breeding around her. At the end of an almost endless number of trials and tribulations Millicent is rewarded with the hand of a viscount, and so the inner world of moral value and the external one of social rank are neatly made to come together on the final page.

Nowhere, though, is the true nature of the *EDM* reader more clearly revealed than in her reaction to what was Sam's greatest innovation: the loyalty lottery. For all she was supposed to be content with simple things—a much cherished rag rug made by her mother as opposed to something smart from China—it is quite clear that what the *EDM* reader really loved were bright, shiny things that came from shops but were even nicer when they were free. The system worked like this. Each copy of the magazine came with a numbered ticket attached on which there was space to write your name and address. Once you had twelve tickets from a year's worth of consecutive magazines you sent them off to Bouverie Street whereupon your name was entered into the lucky draw. The scheme proved so successful at boosting sales that Sam extended it to customers who bought a whole bound volume's worth of issues retrospectively each April. The prizes varied slightly each year, but the best one ever offered was indubitably a piano "worth 60 guineas," that much maligned symbol of gentility for which small-time clerks and farmers' daughters were said by conservative commentators, including sometimes the *EDM,* to be quite desperate. And, indeed, a sketch of the *EDM* piano shows a cheap-looking specimen, over-decorated with swirls and curls. The minor prizes varied from year to year but usually included gold watches, gold chains, and anything up to 250 gift vouchers redeemable at a number of shops that sold perfume, fancy items, and household goods.

It is not exaggerating to say that the prizes caused a storm of excitement. In a letter to Sam in April 1856 Isabella reports that her Aunt Eliza, Henry Dorling's sister-in-law from Ipswich, "fancies like the rest of the Englishwomen she is going to have the Piano" and has enthusiastically placed an order for four previous volumes of the magazine in order to better her chances. Other readers, baffled by the mechanisms of the lottery, bombarded Bouverie Street with doubts and questions. They fretted because the copy of the magazine they had just bought did not seem to have a voucher, or they sent the vouchers in one by one instead of waiting until the end of the volume, or they got suspicious that the draw would never actually be made, or they complained that men should not be allowed to win the ladies' watches. In the end, because there were so many queries about how the scheme worked, Sam was obliged to issue a Prospectus that explained the details once and for all. For years afterwards, however, he was still having to reassure suspicious readers that formal receipts for all the prizes could be viewed on demand at the office.

All the prizes came from traders who advertised in the magazine (the advertisement tax had been repealed in 1852) and were local to Beeton's Bouverie Street office. We know from Isabella's comments about Sam's "Lottery mess" in February 1856 that a fair amount of financial negotiation was involved in obtaining this volume of prizes cheaply, and it seems likely that suppliers agreed upon a reduced price in return for discounted advertising or free editorial support. Indeed, read carefully, the whole of the *EDM* can seem like one long product placement. Clarke and Beeton books were reviewed far too often for it to be mere coincidence, and in 1855 when the *Boy's Own Magazine* was launched it was puffed constantly, presumably on the assumption that *EDM* readers must have magazine-reading brothers and sons. In "The Work Table," meanwhile, readers are repeatedly told exactly which number silk thread they will need to get from Messrs. Evans of Derby in order to complete the pattern best, and it seems likely that Messrs. Evans paid for the privilege of being delivered such a choice bit of business.

This editorial mix of the down-to-earth and the highfalutin, the domestic and the exotic, worked wonderfully well. There is no accurate way of telling how many copies of the *EDM* were sold, and we have to rely on Sam's probably inflated claims made each year in his Introduction to the bound volume. At the end of the second year he announced a circulation of 25,000 and by the time that Isabella started writing for it, this figure had sped upwards to 50,000. By 1860, when the *EDM* was relaunched as a luxury product and Isabella came on board as "editress," Sam was claiming 60,000 copies sold. Perhaps the surest indicator of the magazine's success was the fact that, in 1856, it got a copycat rival in the shape of the lacklustre *Ladies' Treasury*.

Certainly the provincial press were quick to spot that the *EDM* was a genuinely innovative publication directed at a new constituency. By early 1855, when the magazine had been running nearly three years, it had garnered very favourable reviews from the *Birmingham Mercury,* the *Doncaster Gazette,* the *Welshman,* the *Portsmouth Guardian,* the *Exeter Flying Post,* the *Halifax Courier,* the *Clifton Chronicle* and the *Ipswich Express.* The *London Atlas* declared the *EDM* to be "one of the most pleasing and best conducted of the cheap monthlies," while the *Durham Chronicle* announced it "a most agreeable mélange of literary and domestic information."

And yet despite these optimistic pointers, by 1856 the magazine was already showing signs of strain. By October of that year several of the regular domestic slots had petered out. The "Cooking, Pickling and Preserving" column had originally been rather good, arranging a list of ingredients in season and providing clear and highly detailed recipes. In time, though, its organization had broken down and reverted to the usual woolly format that passed for cookery advice in magazines. For instance, by 1856, instructions for making kedgeree were perfunctory to the point of mystifying: "Any fish that has been previously dressed, one teacupful of boiled rice, one ounce of butter, one teaspoonful of mustard, two soft-boiled eggs, a little salt and cayenne pepper. Mix the ingredients, and serve hot. The quantities may be varied according to the quantity of fish used." The wonderfully catholic "Things Worth Knowing" column had also shrunk to the point where it disappeared for months at a time.

The fact that it was six months before these slots were revived by Isabella suggests that it had never been part of any grand plan that she should write for her husband's magazine. This is also supported by the fact that she didn't start to produce copy until mid-March 1857, by which time she was just weeks away from giving birth, which hardly suggests a well thought out handover. What seems, rather, to have happened is that Sam had let matters slide for several months (women journalists were a rarity, and finding someone who could produce monthly copy on domestic matters was harder than it sounds) before either he, or Isabella, or both realized that the solution was right under their noses. Isabella had been running a home for a full six months by now. In addition, she had been translating fiction from French and German for the magazine, which meant that she was beginning to get a feel for the way the publication worked. Her natural writing style, as evidenced in those courtship letters, was terse and to the point. She would become the new cookery writer of the *Englishwoman's Domestic Magazine.* In addition to the "Cooking, Pickling and Preserving" columns, she would write a new section, called simply "The Nursery." All those dreary days spent wiping up sick and snot in the Grandstand had come in useful after all.

Isabella's baby was born during the last week of May. The fact that the child's details were never registered, even by the normally efficient Isabella, suggests how frantic both she and Sam now were with magazine business. Congratulations and presents poured in from both their vast families. Eliza Stagg, Sam's aunt, wrote to ask what Bella would like for the little boy. Perhaps a little cap? No one would have mentioned it, but they would all have been thinking: how nice the baby came so soon, how lovely it was a boy. This, surely, would be the beginning of a dynasty. The child was to be called Samuel Orchart Beeton.

Amid all the excitement there are hints, here and there, that not everything was quite as it should be. Bulletins about the new mother's ailing health—and possibly the baby's too—sped around the gossipy networks that linked Epsom, Suffolk, and the City of London. One family friend, Mrs. Henrietta English, wrote from Newmarket on 21 July, clearly annoyed that Isabella, with uncharacteristic sluggishness, had only just got round to acknowledging the congratulations she had sent a whole two months earlier. Clearly someone soon told Mrs. English the reason for Isabella's tardiness, for two weeks later she is writing in a much more amenable way:

> I am glad to hear the Baby is progressing and doing well. But I do not hear so favourable an account of yourself, however. I hope you will improve as you get stronger. You must Eat well and drink well. I should think Porter or Stout would give you strength and be very beneficial to you.

Mrs. English, whose husband Robert was an old racing connection of the Dorlings, also suggested that a break in Newmarket might do the little family good. At this point she does not seem to have been suggesting that the Beetons stay with her. She had only just finished playing hostess to Isabella's teenage step-sister and half-brother Mary and William Dorling, who were probably the source of her updated intelligence on the mother's and baby's health. Suffolk was awash with Dorlings and Beetons, and Sam and Isabella seem originally to have planned staying with members of their extended clans. However, the next thing we hear, the Beeton family are at Warren Villa, the Englishes' house on the side of the Newmarket racing flats.

The next few days were ghastly. The baby sickened, seemed to rally, and then on 25 August he died, aged just three months. The cause remains a puzzle. The death certificate says that the child had "Diarrhoea several days and Cholera for 12 Hours certified." Cholera, though, looks extremely unlikely, since there were no cases reported that year in Newmarket, nor would there be for several more. The two early Beeton biographers, Hyde and Spain, stay vague, speculating about draughty carriages and easterly winds, although interestingly Hyde refers to the baby having a "relapse" in Newmarket, suggesting that the child had been ailing well before he left Pinner. Clearly, though, death had not seemed inevitable when the child began his last crisis. Several days into the illness when Robert English was obliged to leave Newmarket on business, little Samuel had seemed to be rallying: "I really felt every hope and I may say almost certain of a speedy recovery," English wrote hopelessly in his letter of condolence. Sarah Freeman insists, on no discernible grounds, that the cause of death was croup, a horrible disease in which the child's windpipe closes up and the infant suffocates.

In fact the diagnosis that fits best is "congenital" or, more accurately, prenatal syphilis. Babies who develop the disease in the womb of their infected mothers are weak and sickly and typically die during the first few months of life, displaying the symptoms of vomiting and diarrhoea that were noted on the death certificate. This would make sense of some odd language that Sam used when recalling, towards the end of his life, his rackety bachelor days. Along with the anecdote about climbing out of the window at the Dolphin and having had a "gay time," Sam accused his business partner Charles Henry Clarke of having "tried to poison him and caused his first illness." Victorians habitually described venereal disease as a "poison"—in part because the lingering nausea and lassitude that came with both syphilis and gonorrhoea made the patient feel as if he had ingested something toxic. But even more telling is the fact that Sam links his "poisoning" with what he describes as "his first illness." Syphilis typically starts with an initial burst of symptoms—a chancre followed by weeks of low fever, a rash, sore throat, a general debility—before going underground for several years, even decades. During this latent phase the patient is symptom-free, leading to the assumption of a spontaneous cure.

If and when the symptoms return with a vengeance many years later in the ghastly tertiary stage it feels to the sufferer as if an entirely new disease has been contracted.

Syphilis may have been endemic in Victorian England (in 1846 it was reckoned that half of all the outpatients at St. Bartholomew's just around the corner from the Dolphin were suffering from it), but it was particularly concentrated among middle-class men, those prudent creatures of capitalism who were most likely to pick up the pox when the pressures of celibacy became too intense. Whether they quite understood what those dreary commercial encounters in the Haymarket, Piccadilly or The Strand had cost them is unclear. Those who plucked up courage to see a doctor might be told that they were lucky: the symptoms were already disappearing, which meant that they had been spared the full horrors of the disease (and, indeed, the doctors were not entirely wrong here—up to two thirds of people who were initially infected never progressed to the tertiary stage). Other medics might warn the worried young man that he was probably still infectious, and should leave it a couple of years before marrying to avoid passing the disease on to the young lady, the one for whom he had been saving so hard. (This was disastrous, since the patient was actually infectious for up to five years.) Others still recommended mercury pills, horrible little blue chips of poison that left the patient slobber-mouthed and pig sick, probably wondering whether attempting a cure was even worth it.

Assuming that Sam was infected around the summer of 1852, when he first went into business with Clarke, he would still have been contagious in the summer of 1856 when he first slept with Isabella. Neither Isabella nor Sam would have noted any signs of infection in her, since the initial chancre is often undetectable in women, making its appearance deep inside the vagina. Any soreness from this original site of infection could be put down to the body adjusting to regular sex. In any case, the usual telltale signs of a first syphilitic episode—shivering, lassitude, joint pain— may not actually have been apparent in Isabella. Pregnancy offers protection against symptoms, although this benign effect terminates abruptly with childbirth, leaving new mothers feeling worse than anyone can quite account for. And we know, certainly, that Isabella's health was giving particular concern to her family in the first few weeks following the birth, the only time in her generally robust life that she is on record as being unwell.

Isabella's subsequent medical history also strongly suggests that she was one of the thousands of unfortunate young Victorian brides who were infected with syphilis on their honeymoon. Dorling family stories abound that it was during this early part of her marriage that Bella experienced a string of miscarriages before a second living baby was finally born in June 1859. This is a classic pattern: syphilitic women have no trouble conceiving but, during the first five years following infection, they produce miscarried and stillborn foetuses that tend, distressingly, to be bloated and peeling blobs. If a child *does* survive, it is for only a few sickly, miserable months.

There is other evidence, too, that little Samuel was ailing right from the start of his short life, and did not simply become ill and die as a result of an unlucky infection picked up in Newmarket. The fact that Isabella's cookery column and "Things Worth Knowing" did not appear in the August issue of the magazine has always been used to show how badly upset she was by her baby's death. But the child did not die until 25 August, and Isabella's copy for that month's issue would have had to be written by about 13 July (we know this from the deadlines that Sam used to set for the essay competition). So it seems that it was during July, only six weeks after the birth, that the crisis both in the baby's health and in his mother's was at its height. This, too, would make sense of Montgomery Hyde referring to the baby having a "relapse" in Newmarket, and also of the remark about the baby "progressing well" in the letter of 9 August from Mrs. English.

Little Samuel Orchart Beeton was buried in the local parish of All Saints in Newmarket. The notes of condolence came pouring in from the very people who only three months earlier had been writing with excited enquiries about caps. Now Eliza Stagg felt so "sorry you have been from home when the sad event occurred." Viccie Perkes, just married to Sam's old friend from Wood Street, Fred Perkes, "delayed writing . . . until you were settled again." Aunt Caroline Kersey, herself newly widowed, wrote from Suffolk: "How trying for you to be away from home, I feel for you in this respect," and in a P.S.: "Do try, dear Bella, to compose yourself for the sake of your own health," suggesting once again that the normally robust Isabella Beeton was, for the first time in her strong life, the cause of concern among her extended family. But the chances are that Bella did not need to be told to pull herself together. Babies died, it happened. If

Sam had any inkling as to the cause, he probably said nothing. Neither of the Beetons was silly enough to blame the east wind in Newmarket or any strange atmosphere at Warren Villa. Seven years later, and now deeply devoted to the pleasures of the racetrack, Sam was once again staying with the widowed Robert English. From there he wrote a letter to Isabella, full of publishing talk and excited gossip about horseflesh. Right at the end, though, Sam manages to slow down long enough to tell Isabella sadly: "slept in the room last night—it made my heart ache—you may know—where our first little chappy went away from us."

INTERLUDE

GENERAL OBSERVATIONS ON QUADRUPEDS
The General Characteristics of the Mammalia have been frequently noticed. The bodies of nearly the whole species are covered with hair, a kind of clothing which is both soft and warm,
little liable to injury, and bestowed in proportion to the necessities
of the animal and the nature of the climate it inhabits.

ISABELLA BEETON,
Book of Household Management

ALL THIS IS BY WAY OF Mrs. Beeton's introduction to beef—how to turn
it into a nice Baked Beef-Steak Pudding or serve it up cold with oysters. It
is hard to believe that a hard-pressed housewife thumbing through the
Book of Household Management for inspiration about Sunday's leftovers
would really bother to plough through seven pages of such numbing
pseudo-science before alighting, thankfully, on the recipe she was after.

But Mrs. Beeton was writing at the fag end of nearly a century of science, during which ways of understanding the natural world had been
turned upside down. In 1859, the same year that the *Book of Household
Management* had started appearing in parts, Darwin finally published his
Origin of Species, which argued for the spontaneous adaptation of animal species to their environment over generations. You can see the influence of this way of thinking everywhere in the *Book of Household
Management.* Beeton places animals and vegetables in an elaborate rank-
ing according to their hooves, mammary glands, seed-scattering mecha-

*One of the many animal illustrations in the
BOHM that manages, disconcertingly, to be both
anatomically exact and romantically pastoral.*

nisms, and reproductive habits. Meanwhile, in her opening remarks on
"Fishes" she explains that they "form the fourth class in the system of
Linnaeus, and are described as having long under-jaws, eggs without
white, organs of sense, fins for supporters, bodies covered with concave
scales, gills to supply the place of lungs for respiration, and water for the
natural element of their existence."

But it isn't just in the pantry that Beeton insists on following Darwin
and the scientific writers who preceded him. Her account of the household's human inhabitants also owes much to his example of marshalling
the raw stuff of life into a set of observable hierarchies. From the mistress
at the top to the scullery maid at the bottom, everyone has their place,
their price, their specialist function. And, just like Darwin, Beeton sees
signs of adaptation everywhere: in a small house the parlour maid does
the work of the second footman, in a large one the housekeeper takes on
the function of the mistress. The household is evolving, becoming more
efficient, busy adapting to its changing circumstances.

The chances are that the average reader of the *Book of Household
Management* would hardly have noticed any of this as she thumbed
through pages spattered with intricate biological diagrams on her way to

a recipe for "Vicarage Pudding" (flour, suet, ginger, and raisins). What she *might* have asked herself, though, is where is God in all this? For Mrs. Beeton's implicit assumption that the natural world has evolved over centuries left little space for a divine creator who built the whole thing in seven days. As worried as Darwin himself about giving offence to the millions of Britons who continued to believe in the literal truth of the Bible, Genesis especially, Mrs. Beeton was forced to tread carefully. And so her elaborate description of the fish's place in the Linnaean system is followed by a clumsy attempt to harmonize the scientist's and the theologian's world view. Turning from her microscope to her Bible, she explains nervously that fish are "wonderful to all who look through Nature up to Nature's God, and consider, with due humility, yet exalted admiration, the sublime variety, beauty, power, and grandeur of His productions, as manifested in the Creation."

Whether this was an accurate account of Isabella Beeton's personal beliefs or simply a tactful fudge is hard to say. After she got married in Epsom parish church in July 1856 there is no record of her ever again attending an Anglican service. And yet during her holidays and working trips abroad she always made a point of popping in to the local Roman Catholic church to watch while Mass was sung, or attending a local Quaker meeting. This, combined with Sam's references at times of great stress or happiness to a "Supreme Being," suggests that the Beetons were typical of a growing swathe of curious, intelligent, middle-class people in the 1860s. The Anglicanism in which they had been raised no longer felt like the only or natural way to think about life on earth. Other denominations and even other religions increasingly seemed to offer an equally appropriate path to the Supreme Being. Developments in science, in particular, suggested that there were still more things in heaven and earth to be discovered than had yet to be dreamt of. In the meantime, however, there was absolutely no point in losing readers by coming out and saying so.

✳

CHAPTER SEVEN

DINE WE MUST

 IT WAS NOT MERELY an ill-fated search for health and spirits that had taken Sam, Isabella and the first little Samuel Orchart to Newmarket in late August of 1857. Whenever the Beetons travelled they did so with a purpose, and that purpose nearly always involved business: even their honeymoon had been organized to allow Sam to do a little bookselling on the side. The point of this particular trip was to make contact with Mrs. English, whom the Beetons hoped had something to contribute to the next stage of what was fast becoming their joint enterprise.

When Isabella had begun writing the "Cookery, Pickling and Preserving" slot for the *EDM* back in March, it looks as though she and Sam already envisaged that the columns would be the starting point for a full-length cookery and household management book. Sam was beginning to add a new kind of title to his publication list. Instead of simply reprinting books that were out of copyright, he was starting to compile and co-write a series of huge encyclopaedic reference tomes. At this very moment, for instance, he was embarking on the project that would finish up as *Beeton's Dictionary of Universal Information* and appear the year after *Beeton's Book of Household Management*. In the *Dictionary*, co-written with John Sherer, you would be able to learn about everything from General Aa who protected his native Holland against Philip II of Spain to Zywiec, which was apparently a town in Austrian Poland. In time there would be *Beeton's Book of Birds*, *Beeton's Historian*, *Beeton's Book of Songs*—titles that would typify the totalizing, categorizing culture that drove the early Victorians and which Sam Beeton would come to exploit so successfully. Indeed, it is worth remembering that *Beeton's Book of Household Management,* which seems to us both monumental and unique, was simply one of a series of pragmatically conceived books, any of which might have caught on in that same spectacular way. If history had gone differently, then it could have been a well-thumbed copy of *Beeton's Book of Birds* rather than *Beeton's Book of Household Management* that stood full square on the nation's bookshelves.

The problem was that Isabella didn't know the first thing about cookery, and while the *EDM* experience would doubtless prove useful, especially once readers responded to requests to send in their own tried and tested recipes, it was going to need a great deal of extra material before she would have enough for a book. Enter Henrietta English, a middle-aged Frenchwoman whose relationship with food included both the macabre fact that she was rumoured to have survived the 1830 Revolution in Paris by eating rats and that she knew some of the best cooks working in the great homes of England.

In 1835 Henrietta Mary Pourtois had married Robert English, a footman who had once worked and travelled in the household of George IV but was now in service in Chelsea. This meant she knew all about grand kitchens and the people who ran them (there were no restaurants in Britain at this point—the best chefs pursued their art in the households of dukes, princes, and ambassadors). She had worked alongside her husband in at least one large British household and seems to have had entrées into several others. Certainly by 1857, and living on Newmarket land owned by the Dukes of Rutland, Mrs. English had an insider's knowledge of their ancestral home, Belvoir Castle. She was a friend and fan of the cook there, the thirty-four-year-old Joseph Orpwood, who presided over what was, in Mrs. English's brisk opinion, the best run kitchen in the country. She also knew Lord Wilton's cook, the celebrated Monsieur Rotival of Heaton Hall near Manchester, and another woman, Mrs. Munn, who had worked for an unspecified admiral and was, by Mrs. English's reckoning, "one of Our Best Woman Cooks." The stress on gender was important here: in the great houses the chefs were men and usually French (Mr. Orpwood of Belvoir was an honourable exception) while in the homes of the gentry they were known as "cooks" and were usually British and female.

In that first letter of 18 July, in which Isabella belatedly responded to

Mrs. English's congratulations on the birth of her baby, she mentions that she is thinking of writing a cookery book and sounds Mrs. English out for ideas about how to proceed. Mrs. English, already peeved by Isabella's slackness over social niceties, loses no time in telling the much younger woman what she thinks of her plan to set herself up as an authority on a subject about which she knows nothing. On 21 July Mrs. English sat down to give Isabella a piece of her mind, albeit in her distinctly mangled adopted tongue.

My Dear Mrs. Beeton—Yours of the 18 received

I thought you dead as Emma [her daughter, Caroline Emma, always known as Emma] wrote to say by my wish 2 months since relative to yourself and baby. But to which you never answer.

As regards yours of the 18 I see difficulties in your way as regards publishing a Book on Cookery. Cookery is a Science that is only learnt by Long Experience and years of study which of course you have not had. Therefore my advice would be compile a book from receipts from a Variety of the Best Books published on Cookery and Heaven knows there is a great variety for you to choose from. One of our best Woman Cooks who is now retired recently told me one of the Best and Most Useful books is

SIMPSON'S COOKERY
REVISED AND MODERNISED

Published by Baldwin and Craddock, Longman and Co. and other Publishers. She is good authority for I consider her one of the best woman cooks in England. She is now retired and living near you at East Barnet. I had her and Husband Lately on a visit with me and showed her several books I had but she Preferred Simpson's.

And is your *intended* book meant for the Larger or the Higher Classes or the Middle Class? The latter is one I should recommend you. I enclose you 12 Rules for General Guidance if you Approve of them . . .

Yours v. sincerely

H ENGLISH

What makes Mrs. English's breathless letter important (the penmanship was as scrappy as the grammar) is the way it reveals the misconceptions that dogged the *BOHM* from its very beginning. Right from the start Isabella was advised to get her "receipts" by filleting them from existing cookery books. She was to be an editor rather than an author, a status that is acknowledged on the cover of the book: what is usually known as *Mrs. Beeton's Book of Household Management* was originally *Beeton's Book of Household Management, edited by Mrs. Isabella Beeton.* Copyright issues were vague, the provenance of any recipe being particularly hard to track, and Mrs. English's blithe suggestion that Isabella simply lift other people's recipes reflects the way that cookery books had been put together from time immemorial (although whether Mrs. English intended her young friend to pilfer without acknowledging her sources remains a moot point).

Also crucial is the fact that Mrs. Beeton's own social contacts, "the large private circle" that she mentions in her Preface to the *BOHM* as supplying her with recipes, are drawn mainly from below rather than above stairs. The Beeton and the Dorling clans may have been busy rising in the world, but their roots were firmly in the upper echelons of the servant classes. They knew, and were on visiting terms, with butlers, housekeepers, and grooms and not with the dukes and society ladies who employed them. The social mobility of the Englishes is typical of the people who inhabited the Beetons' world. When Robert and Henrietta went to baptize Emma in the Anglican Church of St. Peter's, Pimlico, in 1835 they were almost certainly working as servants. By 1871 the newly widowed Robert is describing himself to the census enumerator as "Butler (retired)," although a surviving painting of his house by Emma shows the kind of handsome habitation you might expect of a prosperous farmer. By the time of his death twelve years later, Robert English has become, quite simply, a "gentleman." It was this kind of gentleman—one whose father had been a coachmaker rather than a clergyman—who made up the world from which the *Book of Household Management* emerged.

Most importantly, Mrs. English's letter articulates the continuing confusion about exactly who the *Book of Household Management* was meant for. Was it addressing middle-class housewives keen to know about what went on in "the best circles"? Or was it, like several classic cookery titles from the previous century, aimed at working men and women keen to rise in aristocratic service? Mrs. English is herself clearly confused, at one moment urging Isabella to write for the middle classes and yet pressing on her material and contacts that refer to the luxury dining practices of those at the very top of the social tree. The Simpson book that English recommends to Isabella as a model was written by the former chef to the Marquis of Buckingham and includes handy bills of fare, such as the one for 10 July, which consists of no less than thirty-eight separate dishes. The people she nags Isabella and Sam to meet are similarly unsuitable for their purpose. Mr. Orpwood may well have been "very minute and very cleanly in the kitchen," to use Mrs. English's odd franglais phrase, but there would have been little point in the Beetons pestering him, as Mrs. English suggested, for the rules of the kitchen at Belvoir Castle, since they were unlikely to be of much use in a semi-detached in Didsbury.

Sam and Isabella took up Mrs. English's invitation to stay at Warren Villa at the end of August. Perhaps they hoped that once they explained their intentions in detail Mrs. English would begin to understand just what was required. For, in fairness, she did eventually turn out to be of some use. Early in the correspondence with Isabella she had enclosed a recipe for Portable Soup (stock cubes) from M. Rotival, Lord Wilton's celebrated cook, delivered with the kind of snappy epigram that Mrs. Beeton would soon come to make her very own: "You will find the Stockpot is the great secret of the kitchen," declared Mrs. English, for once sounding completely at ease in her adopted tongue. "Without it nothing can be done, *with it everything* can be done."

Stock cubes—quick, easy, convenient as long as you were the sort of person who planned ahead—were exactly the sort of thing that Mrs. Beeton thought her readers should know about. She had made it clear right from her very first excursion into print, in the April issue of the *EDM*, that her guiding philosophy was about finding the most economical—in both time and money—way to run a family kitchen. And in this at least she was writing from some experience. When Sam had announced halfway through their engagement that he looked likely to lose a substantial £200 a year as a result of his "Lottery mess," Isabella knew exactly what would need to be done: "You must smoke one or two cigars less a day, and I must economise as much as possible."

All the same, Isabella was not about to confide to the readers of her *EDM* cookery column that she too had a husband whose income was not all that it might be. Instead, she adopts the standard voice of the female advice giver familiar from countless conduct books and magazine columns down the decades: middle-aged, knowledgeable, tetchy about the falling standards of modern womanhood. Thus Isabella's very first appearance in print begins:

To Wives and Housekeepers

THE AFFECTATION OF FASHION

It is the fashion now-a-days of many ladies to ignore their husbands' pecuniary affairs; they profess ignorance of money matters, and encourage themselves in the idea that *their* wishes at least must be gratified—with the rest they have nothing to do. Now the affectation of this is bad enough, but nothing can be worse than the actual practice—many a ruined house, many a bankruptcy and insolvency springs out of it—many a domestic circle is broken up, and the pride which caused the ruin is humbled to dust as a reward . . .

The fear that spendthrift women were driving their families to ruin had been a standard tack in conservative social commentary ever since people had first thought about telling other people how to live. If the middle classes had been "rising" since the dawn of time, their women had been accused of extravagance for almost as long. More recently, writers including William Cobbett and Thomas Carlyle were agreed that much of the economic uncertainty of the early part of the century could be put down to the daughters of farmers and clerks choosing to blow the household budget on pianos, carriages, and yards of silk ribbon (international trade conditions and poor harvests evidently having nothing to do with it). What is interesting here, then, is not so much what Isabella says as how she says it. She adopts a rhetorical voice that allows her to create an imagined audience, which she then proceeds to address by name, "Wives and Housekeepers." Previously the *EDM*'s "Cookery, Pickling and Preserving" columns had been presented without preamble, pitching straight in with the first recipe. But by personalizing the format Isabella was also pulling the cookery column into the very heart of the magazine's project, that of helping middle-class women value themselves as "domestic women" rather than second-rate ladies. Whereas previously the only recognizable individual voice in the magazine had been "the editor" (in fact a blend of Sam and Frederick Greenwood), now there was the counterbalance of an equally identifiable, albeit anonymous, female presence.

The second paragraph of the April column begins with the very first Mrs. Beeton aphorism on record—"A daily supply is a daily waste"—and proceeds to set out the advantages to the housekeeper of pre-planning and bulk purchase.

> the running to and fro from the street-door to the chandler's shop; the purchase of an ounce of this thing, or a quarter of a pound of that, is an error. Your grocery, candles, soap . . . should be obtained regularly in quantities from respectable traders; potatoes should come in a sack . . . apples by the bushel . . . and not only may you have many pleasant additions to your dinner table by adopting a system of wholesale purchase, but you will, upon the whole, have more and pay less; be free of the worry of sending out continually for small supplies, and have at hand a stock to meet emergencies.

Again, there was nothing new about this advice to middle-class women to reconnect with the thrifty housekeeping practices of an earlier and less convenient age, one in which neighbourhood shops were few and far between. Nor was there anything particularly striking about the first set of recipes that Mrs. Beeton then proceeded to place before the public. Continuing the example of her immediate predecessor on the *EDM* she presents a hotchpotch of dishes—Pungent Salads, How to Dress a Dried Haddock, Instantaneous Beef Tea, How to Cook Haricot Beans and A Good Sponge Cake—making no attempt to return to the genuinely innovative "Things in Season" that had been practised by the magazine's first cookery correspondent.

All this suggests a rhetorically confident if not especially innovative start for Mrs. Beeton's cookery writing career. So it was a shame that Isabella sabotaged her authoritative persona almost immediately by making an elementary and embarrassing mistake. In the recipe for A Good Sponge Cake, which appears in her very first column, she forgot to mention how much flour was needed. Ignominiously, she was obliged to print an erratum in the next issue of the magazine, informing perplexed readers that the amount required was "the weight of four or five eggs."

With the baby dead and autumn passing miserably with no sign of a viable new pregnancy, it was now that Isabella began in earnest on the *BOHM*. It is not possible at this distance to reconstruct her working patterns in detail. However, the internal evidence from the parallel texts she was engaged with at this time suggests that the most intense part of the research and writing of the *BOHM* was carried out between the death of her first baby and the birth of the second in June 1859, a period of just under two years. Before the book was published as a monumental tome in the autumn of 1861 it first appeared in parts, with the initial forty-eight-page installment arriving on the market on 1 November 1859, five months after the second Samuel Orchart Beeton had been born. It was a canny way of spreading the costs for both parties: instead of forking out 7s 6d all in one lump, the careful reader could assemble the book over two years for a modest 3d a month. In this way Sam managed to spread his costs too, ending up with a flexible text that could be repackaged in as many ways as anyone could think of.

It is a testimony to the way in which the *BOHM* seemed so much a part of the fabric of the *EDM* that several modern scholars have mistakenly suggested that it appeared initially as a supplement to the magazine, whereas in fact it always had a completely distinct identity. What may have confused them was the way that Sam heavily promoted the *BOHM* within the *EDM,* making it seem as if the two publications were somehow formally joined. From this advertising copy it is apparent that initially the part work *BOHM* was conceived in only "fifteen to eighteen" installments. It was not until the spring of 1861 when the book was three quarters written that it became clear that it would stretch to twenty-four parts. This confirms that Isabella was still busy working on the second half of the book when the first half was already appearing on the bookstands.

As well as compiling the colossal *BOHM*, Isabella was obliged to continue filing her monthly copy for the "Cookery" and "Things Worth Knowing" columns (the third column, "the Nursery," seems to have disappeared, perhaps because of the painful emptiness of the nursery at 2 Chandos Villas). However, once Isabella started working properly on her book in the autumn of 1857, her contributions on household and cookery tips to the *EDM* became sketchy and rushed, a disappointing sequel to her flourishing opening letter to the Wives and Housekeepers of England. All her energies now went into the intellectually more satisfying task of building a totalizing and self-contained system of household management. From now on the *EDM* would have to make do with whatever scraps Mrs. Beeton happened to have left over. The very last cookery column Isabella ever wrote, in April 1860, is in fact only a half-column of hastily assembled random recipes, including Solid Custard, Cowslip Wine and Plum Cake.

The *BOHM,* then, is emphatically not a repository of one woman's expertise and experience in the kitchen. It was conceived and executed as simply one more clever publishing idea from the firm of S. O. Beeton. Although Isabella had agreed to undertake the mammoth project while little Sam was still alive, the fact that after August 1857 she had long, empty days to fill allowed her to bring an energy and commitment to it that no one could have anticipated. There is no evidence that Isabella was interested in cooking, and every sign that, once the great labour of compiling the book was over, she was never more than a dutiful and perfunctory presence in the kitchen. What excited her was the challenge of bringing order to the chaos and provisionality of the middle-class household—at least on paper. She liked making lists, tables, rules much more than she cared about Victoria sponge or the best way to get stains out of silk.

So it is for this reason that the single surviving anecdote presenting Mrs. Beeton as an accomplished cook needs to be treated with caution. In the mid-twentieth century Frederick Greenwood's centenarian niece recalled hearing a story about how a group of Sam's friends used to grumble that their wives could not cook as well as Mrs. Beeton, with the result that "at the next gathering at the house of Mrs. Beeton, she dished up a shocking meal in order to teach men not to criticize their wives." What raises warning bells here is that no other source has Isabella and Sam engaging in the kind of dinner party culture suggested by the anecdote. Work-driven, emotionally self-contained and still socializing at this point within her vast clan, Isabella confined her voluntary excursions into the kitchen to making sure that Sam's supper was left on the hotplate when he arrived home late from town. Like so many eager-to-please witnesses from the mid-twentieth century who had once spoken to someone who had once met the increasingly legendary Mrs. Beeton, Greenwood's niece seems to have been tweaking her stories to make them come out the way she thought posterity wanted.

The case for the prosecution, one that has been gathering force over the last forty years, is that Mrs. Beeton was a plagiarist who copied down other people's recipes and passed them off as her own, thus perpetuating one of the great British swindles of all time. Behind that authoritative, all-knowing voice was simply a frightened girl with scissors and paste. Elizabeth David was one of the first people to alert readers to the fact that Beeton was not a cook but a journalist and a light-fingered one to boot. In a series of articles written in the mid-twentieth century David suggested that much of what was good about Beeton's work was a straight steal from Eliza Acton's slightly earlier *Modern Cookery for Private Families*. David, who was a genuine fan of Acton's work, could not help setting up a moral hierarchy whereby Acton was a proper cook, original and engaged, while Beeton was nothing more than a heavy-handed and duplicitous hack. "How was it then that this peerless writer came to be superseded by imitators so limited in experience, and in capacity of expression so inferior?" wailed David, in a 1968 essay on Acton, making it pretty clear which particular imitator she had in mind.

But although it is true to say that there is no sentence in the *Book of Household Management* that isn't a tweak or copy of someone else's work, it is quite wrong to suggest that Eliza Acton was the chief victim of Mrs. Beeton's light-fingeredness. "Heaven knows, there is a great variety [of cookery books] for you to choose from," Mrs. English had declared when suggesting that her young friend simply follow the usual practice of copying other people's recipes, and Isabella seems to have taken her at her word, surrounding herself with the most successful cookery books of the previous hundred years. From these earlier authorities Isabella took not just recipes, but erudition, practical experience, anecdotes, tone, their take on everything from how many people you should have at a dinner table to the Romans' attitude to turnips. By working in this way the Beetons were anticipating a trend from the second half of the century whereby cookery books were often written by publishers' wives. Publishers needed cheap (or, better still, free) copy and, from their incestuous dens in Paternoster Row or the Strand, they had convenient access to the most popular books already on the market.

This does not mean that Isabella's task was easy, or that she was being defensive or misleading when she spoke wearily in the Preface of her "four years of incessant labour." For by pillaging so widely she was faced with the difficult task of blending material that had been written with very distinct readerships in mind. English cookery writing over the previous hundred years fell into two loosish camps. First came the books written by chefs, often Frenchmen, who had worked in the kitchens of Britain's grandest households and aimed to share their expertise with other professionals. The Prince Regent and his gang of brothers may have been hopeless in many ways, but they certainly knew how to eat. One of the happier effects of the French Revolution had been a sudden emigration of talent from the recently shut-down *hôtels particuliers*. The Prince of Wales, in whose household Robert English later worked, employed the legendary Antonin Carême, a Parisian whose specialty was producing pâtisserie that resembled something else—a cathedral, a pineapple, a peacock. Having come to the kitchens of the Brighton Pavilion by way of the Napoleonic and Restoration courts, Carême had gone into print in 1815 with his monumental *Le Pâtissier royal parisien*. This was aimed at fellow chefs who wanted to know the secrets of Carême's sublime babas, madeleines, flans and Pithiviers. His second cookery book, *Le Maître d'hôtel français* (there were also two on his first love, architecture, which naturally didn't sell), was published in 1822 and combined below-stairs insight with an ambitious attempt to codify the bewildering number of dishes that made up what was increasingly known as *haute cuisine*. It is a testimony to his selling power that Isabella Beeton included his "Nesselrode Pudding (a fashionable iced pudding—Carême's recipe)" in her book, Carême's name functioning as a kind of shorthand for elegant luxury.

The Duke of York, meanwhile, employed Louis Eustache Ude, another Frenchman who had previously worked for the unfortunate but well-fed Louis XVI. Ude's single book, *The French Cook*, published in 1813, is an attempt to explain to his ploddy and unappreciative adoptive British masters just how sublime the art of cookery can be. Ude's particular ire is reserved for those bluff John Bulls who expect miracles from their chefs yet continue to treat them as jumped-up servants. None of Ude's campaigning agenda particularly concerned Isabella, who was interested only in using *The French Cook* as a rummage bag for suitable recipes. In the *Book of Household Management* she deploys Ude just as she deploys other sources—that is, by occasionally acknowledging a major borrowing while letting three or four others pass without comment. Thus she sensibly acknowledges that her recipe for Boudin à la Reine is "M. Ude's recipe" (not of the cherry variety), just as she also makes it clear that she is basing her recipe for French Puff-Paste on his. However, having thrown in the great man's name she feels no obligation to strain for accuracy, happy instead to put a loose paraphrase of his original text into quotation marks and pass it off as an exact transcription. Other recipes of Ude—

such as that for Pastry Ramakins, to serve with the Cheese Course—pass verbatim into the *BOHM* without comment.

The third great court chef who unwittingly contributed recipes to *Beeton's Book of Household Management* was Charles Elmé Francatelli, a British-born Italian who rose through Carême's kitchen to become maître d'hôtel to Queen Victoria in 1841. Previous biographers have maintained that Mrs. Beeton never borrowed from Francatelli, wary of the fact that his books were so nearly contemporaries of hers. However, Francatelli's recipe for Boiled Whiting in the earlier book provides a clear basis for Beeton's version—the phrasing is too close to be a coincidence—as does his rendering of Haricots à la Maître d'Hôtel (Beeton gives her dish exactly the same title but fails to hint as to who this particular "maître d'hôtel" might be).

The fourth great kitchen that is plundered to provide material for *Beeton's Book of Household Management* is that of the Marquis of Buckingham. Despite Mrs. English's failure to understand just what the Beetons were about, her suggestion that Isabella take a look at *Simpson's Cookery,* written by the Marquis's chef, proved to be profitable. Isabella lifts several of her recipes straight from *Simpson's,* often not bothering to change a word at all. Thus her Soup à La Reine is a straight steal ending with, "Note—all white soups should be warmed in a vessel placed in another of boiling water," while Simpson has, "NB All white soups should be warmed by putting the soup pot into hot water." Her recipe for stewed oysters follows his exactly, even down to his advice to use a wooden spoon and avoid over-boiling.

But if Mrs. Beeton's relationships with Carême, Ude, Francatelli, and Simpson were glancing, the same can hardly be said for her wholesale pilferings from Alexis Benoît Soyer. Although the Frenchman Soyer had started in England as a court cook, working for another of George's piggy brothers, by 1837 he had moved to the Reform, one of the new generation of gentlemen's clubs which aimed to give its members the kind of gastronomic experience they anticipated in the homes of their smarter friends. The club's kitchens, designed by the technologically minded Soyer himself, were state-of-the-art and attracted a daily flood of sightseers, larger than the queue that snaked around Madame Tussaud's. From his gas-powered kingdom Soyer served up meals that everyone, but especially he, agreed were legendary: a breakfast for two thousand people on the day that Queen Victoria was crowned, a luxurious banquet in honour of

Ibraham Pasha in 1846. By the time of this last triumph the *Globe* newspaper was openly floating the possibility that M. Soyer, rather than Sir Robert Peel or Lord John Russell, might properly be considered "the man of his age."

This was exactly the kind of public recognition that Soyer went out of his way to court. Part showman, part artist (he married a painter and slept with a ballet dancer) and part fraud, Soyer was too desperate for attention to stick to doing one thing for very long. The next decade saw him running soup kitchens on an industrial scale and shipping out to the Crimea at his own expense to show Her Majesty's troops how to get the best from their rations. His reward was exhaustion and a spate of nasty fevers, quite possibly exacerbated by his fondness for drink. Soyer died in 1858, a year before *Beeton's Book of Household Management* started appearing in monthly parts.

Mrs. Beeton's borrowings from Soyer come mainly from *The Modern Housewife* and the *Pantropheon,* just two out of his total of six books. *The Modern Housewife* (1849) is closest in scope to the *Book of Household Management*. Written in an epistolary form, and using the familiar conceit of a conversation between an older woman and an inexperienced bride, *The Modern Housewife* is aimed squarely at the middle-class woman who runs her household with the minimum of staff. The recipes are economical, reliable, a gift for Isabella who was aiming at exactly the same market. Perhaps because of this obvious similarity between the two books Isabella was careful to honour her debt to *The Modern Housewife*. Thus her instructions for making Puff-Paste and Beef Tea are both ascribed to "Soyer" (he is so famous he needs no other name) although, true to form, she tweaks the recipes and improves their presentation.

But it was from a very different publication that Isabella took most of her Soyer material. Perhaps she felt entitled to lift whole paragraphs of the *Pantropheon* on the grounds that Soyer had himself stolen the book from someone else. Written originally in French by Adolphe Duhart-Fauvet, Soyer seems to have promised that this work on "the history of food and its preparation in ancient times" would appear in English under Duhart-Fauvet's name, with himself credited as translator (this alone should have raised alarm bells—Soyer was barely literate in either language). However, when the book was eventually published in London in 1853 the only name that appeared on the front was that of Alexis Soyer.

The *Pantropheon* is a strange book, one of the many part-historical part-anthropological studies on the subject of food that appeared in the thirty years following the startling success of the genre-busting *La Physiologie du Goût* by the French lawyer turned gourmand Brillat-Savarin. The 469-page *Pantropheon* contains vanishingly few recipes, but offers instead a sweeping survey of food custom and lore from ancient times to something approaching the present day. The haphazard collection of facts and figures, often backed up by important-sounding sources (Seneca, Homer, the Prophets) was perfect for Isabella's purposes. By thumbing through the *Pantropheon* with a pencil and notebook at the ready, she could find definitive-sounding but ultimately unverifiable information about when humans started to eat meat, what Horace thought about peacocks, and why the Countess of Beunchlingen squandered a fortune on her favourite delicacy, eelpout livers. In Soyer/Duhart-Fauvet's text all eras of history exist in a kind of synchronicitous present and all named authorities are treated as if they were handing down eternal verities. It was an approach to knowledge—reverential yet utterly uninterested in provenance—that exactly mimicked the Beetons' own, as witnessed by this early advertisement that appeared in the *EDM*.

A new and important feature, which, it is felt, will form an invaluable part of BEETON'S BOOK OF HOUSEHOLD MANAGEMENT, is the history, description, properties, and uses, of every article directly or indirectly connected with the Household. Thus, if in a recipe for a Christmas plum-pudding, are named the various ingredients of raisins, currants, candied oranges and lemon-peel, sugar, citron, bitter almonds and brandy, BEETON'S BOOK OF HOUSEHOLD MANAGEMENT will give ample information on questions such as these:—
Where are Raisins grown, and how are they dried?—In what Countries do Currants flourish most, and what Process do they undergo in order to be made suitable for the English market?—How are Candied Orange and Lemon-peel manufactured, and what are the characteristics of the growth of the Orange and Lemon-trees? . . . What enters into the manufacture of Brandy, and what are the names of the principal places it comes from?—Do we distil any in this country? &c

Depending on your own intellectual confidence, the end result was either terribly clever or the sort of thing constructed by a particularly conscientious schoolgirl.

Presumably it was because the *Pantropheon* dealt with information that was already in the public domain that Isabella felt no need to disguise her many borrowings from it. As with Ude, she adopts the strategy of selectively crediting Soyer as her source, followed by whole paragraphs that have been lifted from him without comment. Beeton's paraphrases remain so close to the original text that no one (and especially, had he lived, Soyer) could be in any doubt about where she had got her material. For instance, on the subject of pickles, the *Pantropheon* maintains:

> The Greeks and Romans esteemed highly their pickles: these consisted of flowers, herbs, roots, and vegetables, preserved in vinegar, and which kept a long time in cylindrical vases with wide mouths. They were prepared with the greatest care; and these plants were often macerated in oil, brine, and vinegar, with which they were impregnated drop by drop. Meat, also, cut in very small pieces, was treated in the same manner.

In Beeton's book this becomes:

> PICKLES—The ancient Greeks and Romans held their pickles in high estimation. They consisted of flowers, herbs, roots, and vegetables, preserved in vinegar, which were kept, for a long time, in cylindrical vases with wide mouths. Their cooks prepared pickles with the greatest care, and the various ingredients were macerated in oil, brine, and vinegar, with which they were often impregnated drop by drop. Meat, also, after having been cut into very small pieces, was treated in the same manner.

This is one of the more blatant examples of Beeton's borrowing from the *Pantropheon*. Her more typical modus operandi was to mix up a chunk of Soyer with material drawn from an entirely different source to create a kind of hybrid text which, once put through the Beeton blender, comes out sounding British, contemporary and full of brisk common sense.

For instance, on the subject of eating fish, the *Pantropheon* declares:

> [Among the Romans] the love of fish became a real mania: turbots excited a *furore* of admiration—the *muroena Helena* was worshipped.
>
> Hortensius, the orator, actually wept over the death of the one he had fed with his own hands; the daughter of Drusus ornamented hers with

golden rings; each had a name, and would come with speed when it heard the voice of the master, whose happiness depended on his fish.

In Beeton's tauter and tarter text this becomes:

The love of fish among the ancient Romans rose to a real mania . . . Hortensius, the orator, wept over the death of a turbot which he had fed with his own hands; and the daughter of Drusus ornamented one that she had, with rings of gold. These were, surely, instances of misplaced affection; but there is no accounting for tastes. It was but the other day we read in "The Times" of a wealthy *living* hermit, who delights in the companionship of rats!

Why did Isabella Beeton, writing a cookery book for the inhabitants of Pinner, Beckenham, Edgbaston, and Harwich, go out of her way to absorb work produced by professional French chefs working for the upper ten thousand? Glamour, certainly, had something to do with Beeton's determination to use and deploy their work. Serving up green beans "à la Maître d'Hôtel" or merely reading about Carême's Nesselrode Pudding gave the wife of a solicitor, draper, or even stationmaster the sense that she was participating, vicariously, in "the best circles." Armed with *Mrs. Beeton,* she knew what was what and, more importantly, who was who.

And yet, Mrs. Beeton was far from being an uncritical sycophant, a mere status snaffler. In only the second paragraph of her "Introduction to Cookery" she declares that one of her main intentions is to get rid of the mysterious vagueness that still clings to recipe writing, especially that which appears in the more courtly cookery books: "Accordingly, what is known only to him [i.e. the chef], will, in these pages, be made known to others. In them all those indecisive terms expressed as a bit of this, some of that, a small piece of that, and a handful of the other, shall never be made use of, but all quantities be precisely and explicitly stated." From here Mrs. Beeton proceeds to define exactly how much is meant by a tablespoon, dessert spoon, teaspoon, and drop.

Beeton is determined, then, to harness the glamour of high-end cookery to her project while simultaneously showing that there is nothing much to it. Armed with the proper tools and clear instructions—the fundamental ingredients of middle-class expertise in a whole range of activities from Christian worship to building bridges—anyone can learn to turn out soufflés and Haricots Verts à la Maître d'Hôtel. As Isabella Beeton makes clear in an address immediately preceding her very first recipe, even a novice cook can, by following her instructions carefully, produce a "repast for any number of persons." The *BOHM* is not simply a reference book, it is a manual of instruction.

Beeton's insistence on demystifying the practices of professional chefs and relocating them in the middle-class domestic kitchen was nothing new. It stood at the heart of another tradition in British cookery writing, and the one on which she chiefly drew. The typical author in this second camp was always British and usually female. Like Carême et al., she had often worked as a professional cook in Britain, but always in the homes of the lesser aristocracy and gentry. Her entry into the book-writing business usually had an explicitly commercial motivation: either she had a business to puff or she needed to generate income. The demand for cookery books had been as buoyant in the eighteenth century as it was in the nineteenth, and writing one allowed you to make a modest income without having to leave the kitchen, or at least the house. It was for these reasons, or ones very like them, that Hannah Glasse, Elizabeth Raffald, Maria Rundell, and Eliza Acton—all of whose recipes ended up in the *Book of Household Management*—first launched themselves into print.

The Art of Cookery, Made Plain and Easy by Hannah Glasse was not simply one of the most successful cookery books of the eighteenth century, it was one of the most successful books full stop. Appearing first in 1746, it remained in print until 1843, only fourteen years before Isabella Beeton started work on her own book. The illegitimate daughter of a gentleman, Glasse had spent some time in service with the Earl of Donegal, though in exactly what capacity is not clear. *The Art of Cookery* was written in London when she was desperately trying to support her family (there were several children and a husband who was not a natural businessman). Published in the old-fashioned way by subscription, which meant that patrons contributed to the production costs in advance and in return saw their name printed proudly at the front of the book, Hannah Glasse's *The Art of Cookery* was a product designed to make money.

Scholars of the eighteenth-century cookery book have worked out that Glasse borrowed 342 of her 972 receipts from earlier texts, most particularly from the 1743 edition of *The Lady's Companion* by Hannah Woolley. If this seems shocking, there is a kind of natural justice in the fact that

Glasse, in her turn, was heavily plagiarized throughout the second half of the eighteenth century. In any case, as with Isabella Beeton a hundred years later, Glasse's reworkings of earlier recipes led to clearer, more practical formats. Her adoption of a detailed index at the back of her book, allowing readers to locate quickly the dish they were after, was a real innovation, and one that became a standard fixture.

The Art of Cookery initially appeared anonymously, described only as being "By A Lady." The opening address, together with the 5s cover price, made it clear that the author envisaged her book being bought by other "ladies"—that is middle-class mistresses—who would either hand the book over to their cook or, to avoid kitchen spills, copy out individual recipes before passing them on. However the transmission exactly occurred, Glasse explains that she has taken care to write in plain, simple English using homely terms: instead of "lardoons," she points out proudly, she refers to little bits of bacon. She also takes a robustly sceptical attitude to the current fashion among the Whig aristocracy for fancy foreign dishes, declaring, "if Gentlemen will have *French* Cooks, they must pay for *French* Tricks." Glasse's job, as she sees it, is to turn junior and general servants into good, honest British cooks. "I dare say, that every Servant who can but read will be capable of making a tollerable good Cook, and those who have the least Notion of Cookery can't miss of being very good ones." *The Art of Cookery* was an early example of what publishers now call a "crossover" title, appealing to more than one audience. In addition to its primary imagined readership—the middle-class mistress with staff to instruct—it might also be bought by ambitious servants keen to improve their skills (there was a cloth-bound version which sold for 1s) or by middle-class housewives obliged to do their own cooking and uncertain where to start.

Glasse's decision to angle her book towards the servants' hall turned out to be a canny one, judging by the way it was duplicated by most of her important successors. Only twenty years later when Elizabeth Raffald published *The Experienced English Housekeeper,* she felt no need to make much of the fact that she too was writing in as plain a style as possible "so as to be understood by the meanest capacity." Like Glasse, Elizabeth Raffald belongs to that tradition of English female cookery writers who had once worked as senior servants and now aimed to share their experience for a profit. After fifteen years in domestic service, Raffald joined the staff of Arley Hall, Cheshire, as housekeeper in early 1748. Her job required her to market for the entire household, as well as produce those items that were traditionally the responsibility of the housekeeper: cakes, wine, pickles, and preserves. Marrying the head gardener meant leaving domestic service, and in 1763 the new Mr. and Mrs. Raffald moved to Manchester where Elizabeth opened a shop specializing in the confectionery, baked products, and "made dishes" that were so much part of North Country tradition. An advertisement for the shop from this time mentions sweetmeats, mushroom ketchup, potted meats, and the inevitable "portable soups." With several daughters and a husband partial to drink, Mrs. Raffald needed to maximize her income. Always at ease in print culture (she would later compile the first trade directory for her part of Manchester), in 1769 she set about codifying her recipes and arranged to have them published by subscription. The book was an immediate success, and an expanded edition appeared two years later (there would be thirty-three in all).

Mrs. Raffald makes it clear in her opening address "To The Reader" just what kind of cookery book this is going to be. She insists that there will be none of the usual light-fingered borrowing from earlier printed sources. And indeed, to ensure that no pirated versions of her work were put in circulation, Raffald doggedly signed the front page of every copy. She stresses that her receipts "are wrote from my own experience" and double-checked with a sharp eye for ambiguities or slips, "every sheet carefully perused as it came from the press." If anyone requires proof that the author is no opportunistic hack, but a busy, professional cook, they are welcome to visit her shop and see the finished made-up goods. Raffald followed Glasse in angling her book towards two distinct markets. Her opening address to her former employer, the Honourable Lady Elizabeth Warburton, gives a genteel spin to the whole enterprise, and plants the careful claim that many ladies have urged her to publish just such a book "for the instruction of their housekeepers." At the same time she has written in clear and simple English so that her work may be "of use to young persons who are willing to improve themselves." Despite the book's title, Raffald makes it clear in her Introduction that her repertoire goes far beyond the pickles, preserves, cakes, and wines that are the usual domain of the housekeeper. Experience tells her that there is a demand among servants for instruction in the more basic branches of cookery, and for that reason she has included sections on "Soup," "Fish," "Roasting" and "Boiling."

Thanks to her lessons at Barnard's, the Epsom bakers, Beeton's slightly practised eye evidently registered that Raffald knew what she was doing in the matter of confectionery, cake making, and preserving, with the result that many of Raffald's instructions in this department of cookery go virtually unchanged into the *Book of Household Management*. Elsewhere Beeton adopts her usual strategy of amplifying a pilfered recipe with material drawn from an entirely different source, so that the borrowings become harder to spot. For instance, the basis of the *BOHM*'s recipe for Pickled Cucumbers is clearly Mrs. Raffald's To Pickle Cucumbers a Second Way. Yet Beeton uses the fact that Raffald suggests using "long pepper" in her recipe as an occasion for including in her own text a detailed footnote explaining the geographical origins of long pepper, even though her version of the recipe makes no mention of this particular ingredient. The effect on Beeton's reader, presented with a detailed description and the natural history of an item that doesn't appear in any of her recipes, must have been anything from jarring to downright mystifying.

Many of Mrs. Raffald's more elaborate recipes did not find their way into the *Book of Household Management*. Not only was it just too fiddly to make Cribbage Cards in Flummery or Gilded Fish in Jelly, but the fashion for such sugary metamorphoses had long passed by the time Mrs. Beeton came to be writing in the 1850s. All the same, whenever Beeton came across one of Raffald's recipes that spoke to her readership, she included it in her own text, making few alterations in the process. Beeton's recipe for Rich Bride or Christening Cake is a clear lift from Raffald, who specialized in producing just such items to mark the rites of passage among the smarter families of Manchester. Perhaps it was also in deference to the trickiness of producing these kinds of fancy artefacts that Mrs. Beeton was happy to suggest that housewives might prefer to buy them ready-made. She was all for rediscovering lost or degraded domestic skills, but not when there was a Raffald's or Barnard's on hand to provide an alternative. Of macaroons she firmly declares, "We have given a recipe for making these cakes, but we think it almost or quite as economical to purchase such articles as these at a good confectioner's."

Mrs. Beeton took even more recipes from Raffald's successor, Maria Rundell, author of the book whose title eventually settled into *A New System of Domestic Cookery*. Rundell breaks the mould of English female cookery writers of this time by not being a professional servant.

Rather, she was the widow of a prosperous surgeon and wrote her book at the age of sixty for the instruction of her married daughters (she wished, she said, that something similar had been available to her when she first started keeping house). Both Glasse and Raffald had emphasized the need for economy in the kitchen, especially in contrast to the wasteful ways of French chefs, but Rundell took this a stage further. Anticipating Mrs. Beeton by fifty years, Rundell yoked together the ideas of economy, elegance, and domestic know-how. In her Preface she laments the fact that it is now not considered genteel for young ladies to be skilled in keeping house. Instead, she argues for busy, useful women who find nothing shameful in being, and being seen to be, active, engaged, and prudent housewives. Her book, crucially, is not designed to be passed on to the servants' hall, but is intended to be read carefully by young mistresses who are obliged to involve themselves closely in the daily running of their households.

Of all the books that preceded the *Book of Household Management,* Rundell's comes closest in scope and tone to Beeton's own. Just like Beeton, Rundell cherishes the "ordinary, every day things" and is anxious that her readers should not, in their rush to gentility, forget how to produce "fine melted butter, good toast and water, or well made coffee!" Her book is full of thrifty vernacular recipes such as To Force Hog's Ears or Cockle Ketchup so it is hardly a surprise to find that the very first paragraph of the *Book of Household Management* consists of a reworking of Mrs. Rundell's introductory remarks. Rundell, whose discourse shows signs of being inflected by the Evangelical revival of the early nineteenth century, declares, under the heading of "The Mistress of the House": "Happy the man who call [*sic*] her his wife, Blessed are the children who call her mother." The usually Godless Beeton, in turn, opens her book with a direct quotation from Proverbs, declaring of this same angel in the house, otherwise known as "The Mistress": "Her children rise up, and call her blessed; her husband also, and he praiseth her."

Having made a detour into the Bible, Beeton then gets down to what she does best, that is lifting and tweaking other people's recipes. Rundell is the source for about a dozen of Beeton's dishes, mainly sweets but also at least one soup. Probably working from the 1854 edition of *Domestic Cookery,* Beeton clearly took Rundell's "Observations on Making and Baking Cakes" as the basis for her "Hints Respecting the Making and Baking of Cakes." For instance, Rundell advises that "Currants should be very nicely washed, dried in a cloth, and then set before the fire. If damp they will make cakes or puddings heavy." In Beeton this becomes: "Currants should be nicely washed, picked, dried in a cloth . . . then be laid on a dish before the fire, to become thoroughly dry; as, if added damp to the other ingredients, cakes will be liable to be heavy." When it comes to actual recipes Beeton continues with this practice of paraphrase combined with some rearrangement of syntactical order.

When Rundell's book finally slipped out of print in the mid-1850s, it was because another cookery book had eclipsed it. Eliza Acton's *Modern Cookery for Private Families,* which first appeared in 1844, had a distinctly modern feel, not least because of its radical innovations in layout and organization that would, in time, be carelessly credited to the legendary Mrs. Beeton. Acton, who was born in 1799, is important because she provides the link between those female cookery writers who were professional or expert housekeepers (Glasse, Raffald, Rundell) and Isabella Beeton, who came to the topic as a journalist with little prior interest in the subject matter. Acton could not quite be described as a hack, but like Beeton she does not seem to have had much experience in the kitchen prior to the writing of her book. Her main passion was producing poetry, and she had already had one volume of verse published by 1826. It was with a view to getting more of her work in print that she approached the London publisher Longman in the late 1830s. Longman explained that poetry didn't sell but cookbooks did. If Miss Acton wanted to continue as a professional author she should forget about verse and try her hand at a collection of recipes.

It is quite possible that Longman never expected the middle-aged poetess to take his words to heart. However, Acton returned to the home she now shared with her mother in Tonbridge and spent the next few years collecting and testing recipes. What makes her book so delightful, the confirmed favourite of Elizabeth David, Delia Smith, and thousands of amateur cooks, is her prose style which is clear, fresh, unafraid without being over-emphatic. A sly wit pokes through in her recipes for Printer's Pudding (all rich milk, sugar and nutmeg) and her Poor Author's Pudding (thin suet). She is also wry about what happens when things go wrong: marmalade boiled up too quickly, for instance, will turn into "a strange sort of compound, for which it is difficult to find a name. . . ." But the single thing that distinguishes Acton as an innovator is her sometime habit of listing ingredients and cooking times separately at the end of the recipe, instead of burying them in the running copy as was the normal practice. Beeton's much vaunted introduction of the modern recipe format, with the ingredients listed first, turns out to consist of simple inversion of Acton's genuinely innovative format. (In any case, as we shall see, Beeton was not necessarily the first person to do this.) What is more, to Elizabeth David's critical eye, Beeton's decision to put the ingredients at the beginning rather than the end of the recipe demonstrates her lack of kitchen flair. Real cooks read all the way through the recipe first to get the feel of the thing, by which time they need to know precise measurements. Book cooks begin by marshalling all their ingredients at the beginning before setting out on a literal route march through the recipe.

Right from the start readers spotted that Acton's book was the real thing, a labour of love by someone who had come to understand food. *Fraser's Magazine* declared that the section on sauces placed Acton "in the class of Vatel, Carême, Ude and other great professors . . . the whole chapter should be *studied*." Studied was one thing, copied quite another. Acton, naturally, started to find it irritating when barely disguised versions of her recipes started popping up in other people's publications. By the time of the second edition of her book in 1856 she was declaring: "At the risk of appearing extremely egotistical, I have appended 'Author's Receipt' and 'Author's Original Receipt' to many of the contents of the following pages . . . in consequence of the unscrupulous manner in which large portions of my volume have been appropriated."

This warning shot was not enough to make Isabella Beeton steer clear of Acton's book altogether. Rather, it simply made her stealthier in her rewriting of Acton's material. Acknowledging only two borrowings, Beeton nonetheless used *Modern Cookery* for about a third of her soup recipes, a quarter of her fish dishes, and many other preparations besides. However, she went out of her way to alter the formulations so that no one—and especially not the hawk-eyed Miss Acton, had she lived—could point an accusing finger.

There are two books concerned with food, cooking and dining on which Beeton heavily relied, yet which fit into neither of the major strands of English food writing discussed so far. William Kitchiner's *The Cook's Oracle* is *sui generis,* a crotchety and unique creation which emerged not from a particular strand in British cooking or publishing history, but out of the determined fancies of one man. Although Kitchiner liked to let people think he was a doctor who chose not to practise, in fact he was simply a man of independent means with a library stuffed with medical books. His most famous book, *The Cook's Oracle* published in 1817, is an eccentric, informative treatise on how to eat. Kitchiner makes no effort to conceal his contempt for the cookbook genre—he lists the 200 or so that he claims to have read, condemning them all as scissor-and-paste jobs. He, by contrast, has worked with several cooks (Kitchiner is too much a gentleman actually to descend to the kitchen) to devise entirely new dishes which have been set before the august Committee of Taste, a group of his friends that convened at his rooms in Marylebone just around the corner from Isaac Jerrom's stables. By introducing this element of connoisseurship into his discourse Kitchiner manages to turn what is actually rather an ordinary scenario—a "doctor" inviting his friends round for dinner to try out some new dishes—into an epicurean taste trial. The mystique that surrounded Kitchiner's dinners was notable enough to have been recorded by some of the participants: guests were invited for 5 p.m. precisely and the doors were locked against late-comers. Each dish was accompanied by a disquisition from the "doctor" as to the item's cost, nutritional value and novelties of taste and presentation. Guests were given less alcohol than they might have hoped for and were expected to leave at bang on eleven o'clock.

William Kitchiner's approach to food, then, was not simply about aesthetics. As a "doctor" he was vitally interested in the nutritional value of what he ate. *The Cook's Oracle,* indeed, could be said to be an attempt to discover the first principles of pleasurable yet healthy eating. For, as Kitchiner declared in his opening section: "the *energy of our* BRAINS is *sadly dependent on the behaviour of our* BOWELS—those who say 'Tis no matter what we eat or what we drink,—may as well say, 'Tis no matter whether we eat, or whether we drink." Given Kitchiner's off-putting emphases (there are few sentences that are not spattered with italics or capitals), it is grimly pleasurable to learn that he died at the age of forty-nine, having failed in his boast to demonstrate that good diet prolonged life beyond its usual span.

Beeton never acknowledges Kitchiner as one of her sources, probably because his book was still in print when she started on her own. Still, that doesn't stop her leaning heavily on him. Her instructions for poaching an egg and boiling a ham are lifted straight from *The Cook's Oracle,* as are recipes for Potato Snow and Stewed Oysters. More generally, but perhaps more important, is what Beeton took from Kitchiner in terms of aims, tone, and organization. Kitchiner, for all his epicurean fancy, positioned himself as a bourgeois with sensible, British tastes rather than fancy foreign ones. It was probably in *Cook's Oracle* that Beeton first saw the connection made between vagueness of expression in recipes and exclusive kitchen practice. Kitchiner also described himself consistently as the "editor" of his book rather than its author and it may be that this gave the Beetons the idea for their own face-saving formula. He also stressed seasonality, insisting that the cheapest produce, since it was also the freshest, was necessarily the best. To this end Kitchiner included tables to help the debutante housekeeper know when was the right time to buy anything from artichokes to turnips, rump or heels, green geese or wild pigeons.

But the single most important thing that Beeton got from Kitchiner was attack. Kitchiner's voice may be cranky but it is confident and declamatory, able to deliver complex information in a series of polished but informative aphorisms. He hopes, for instance, that his receipts will be "as easily understood in the Kitchen as He trusts they will be relished in the Dining Room." Likewise he believes that "to *prevent* Diseases,—is surely a more advantageous Art to Mankind, than to *cure* them." And, on the subject of economy: "It has been his aim, to render Food acceptable to the Palate,—without being expensive to the Purse, or offensive to the Stomach—nourishing without being inflammatory, and savoury without being surfeiting,—constantly endeavouring to hold the balance even between the agreeable and the wholesome—the Epicure and the Economist." Kitchiner speaks with the confidence of an educated man of independent means and strong opinions, one who is sufficiently sure of being understood not to need pages of circumlocution. It is this crisp *de haut en bas* delivery that Isabella Beeton ventriloquizes so memorably in the *Book of Household Management,* allowing her to sound like a matron of fifty with years of housekeeping experience rather than a newly married girl of twenty-one.

While Soyer's *Pantropheon* had given Mrs. Beeton what she needed to look clever, it was to another book entirely that she turned in order to seem wise. *La Physiologie du Goût* had been published in France in 1825 and was a brilliant genre-hopping meditation by a provincial magistrate on his first love—food. Neither a cook nor professional writer, Brillat-Savarin's slim volume is an eccentric notebook of musings, anecdotes, hard science, and gentle humour. The setting is *haut bourgeois* rather than courtly, and the emphasis is on sensual domestic pleasure rather than brittle public display. (One of lifelong bachelor Brillat-Savarin's major preoccupations is proving that women who like their food are warm and eager lovers.) Since the Brillat-Savarin text was so well known, and had been translated into English by 1854, Beeton was sensible about acknowledging a good percentage of her borrowings from it. For instance, she makes it clear that the famous anecdote about the Croat soldiers cooking raw steak under their saddles and the sad story of the anorectic girl who died from drinking too much vinegar come from Brillat-Savarin. On other occasions, however, she adopts her more usual strategy of acknowledging an occasional borrowing from her source before slipping in several passages without comment. For instance she follows "Brillat-Savarin's Recipe for Roast Pheasant" a page later with his detailed instructions on how to tell when pheasant meat is ready to cook without making it clear that she is not writing from her own experience. Another time, in the retelling of Brillat-Savarin's famous declaration that a meal without cheese is like a woman with only one eye, the Frenchman has been demoted to "a celebrated gourmand"; and in other cases—when, for example, Beeton lifts Brillat-Savarin's history of the sugar industry in France—he is not referred to at all.

All the careful forensics in the world, however, will not convey just what it was that Beeton got from Brillat-Savarin. Splicing his anecdotes, wit, and philosophy into her text gave it an extra dimension, throwing a kind of epistemological grandeur over what is essentially a collection of recipes aimed at the hard-pressed British housewife. For instance, in the introductory section to "On Dinners and Dining," Beeton harnesses Brillat-Savarin's unshakable conviction that food culture lies at the heart of developing civilization—functions, indeed, as a kind of litmus test for it. And so, setting her tin-lined saucepans and menu plans to one side for a moment, Isabella Beeton declares, "The nation which knows how to dine has learnt the leading lesson of progress," sounding for all the world like a French gentleman of the post-Revolutionary era rather than a young Victorian girl constructing a cookery book from other people's recipes. After proceeding to make a characteristic detour into eating scenes from the works of Byron, Milton, Keats, and Tennyson and a quick pit stop at the dining rooms of William III and General Napier, Beeton emerges at the end of the fourth paragraph of "On Dinners and Dining" with a sentence so resounding that it feels as if it ought to be wrapped in quotation marks and credited to Jean-Anthelme Brillat-

Savarin, a gentleman judge speaking from his gourmandizing home town of Belley near Lyons: "Dine we must, and we may as well dine elegantly as well as wholesomely." But the words, and their sentiment, remain Isabella Beeton's own, some of the very few to appear in the *Book of Household Management*.

There is, finally, one more major source for *Beeton's Book of Household Management*. Thomas Webster's *Encyclopaedia of Domestic Economy* is a vast 1,264-page work (250 pages more than Beeton) that treats the whole business of running a home as a kind of industrial engineering project. This approach makes sense from a man who trained as an architect and became the clerk of works at the Royal Institution, before taking up a new chair in Geology at University College, London. Published in the same year and by the same publisher as Acton's *Modern Cookery,* Webster's book covers everything from how to plan your drains through the varieties of butter found in Britain to the processes involved in calico printing (should you wish, presumably, to try it for yourself). Webster's *Encyclopaedia* sums up exactly the enquiring, universalizing, scientific spirit of the early Victorians. It assumes that everything is knowable, if only you take the trouble to learn (cooks, says Webster in his Introduction, have as much need to master chemistry as any man of science).

The domestic chapters were not written by Webster himself but by "the late Mrs. Parkes" and it is from this section of the book that Beeton does most of her scavenging. Indeed, at times Beeton's thefts are so large that one wonders whether it was because she knew that both Webster and Parkes were dead by the time the *Encyclopaedia* was published in 1844 that she felt safe in making so little attempt to disguise what she was doing. Even then, one wonders why Longman, Webster's publisher and near neighbour of S. O. Beeton, not to mention the publishers of Acton, did not raise the alarm. Perhaps, ultimately, it says something about the way these huge books, issued initially in parts, were actually read. Designed to be dipped into rather than scrutinized, Webster's *Encyclopaedia* and *Beeton's Book of Household Management* were so capacious that only a line-by-line comparison would throw up suspicious similarities. Life, really, was too short, especially when the person most likely to complain, Thomas Webster, had been dead for fifteen years.

But by doing what Longman presumably failed to do, one finds evidence of Beeton's borrowings from the *Encyclopaedia* coming sharply into focus. Plotting these plagiarisms is not simply a gleeful exercise in revealing Mrs. Beeton's feet of clay. It also allows us to look through the text of the *Book of Household Management* at mid-Victorian society in a more knowing way. For instance, the various qualities ascribed to the *Book of Household Management* often turn out to be imprints left from the texts from which it was pieced together. Commentators have always made much of the way that Beeton opens her remarks on "Arrangement and Economy of the Kitchen" with a quotation from Count Rumford before launching into a description of the domestic kitchen that makes it sound like an industrial space, complete with diagrams of various stoves. In fact, the quotation from Rumford and the five-point plan for kitchen design—light, ventilation, and so forth—are taken directly from Webster, who tells us in his Preface that he had been "intimately acquainted with Count Rumford," who introduced him to "the principles relating to Domestic Economy, for which he was so deservedly celebrated." Knowing that Beeton copied her information from Webster does not, of course, invalidate the suggestion that she conceived of the domestic household— and encouraged her readers to think of it—as a well-oiled machine from the new industrial age. But the fact that she found material she approved of in a book that had been written fifteen years before her own does suggest that she was following rather than setting dominant trends in conceptualizing the mid-Victorian family home.

Likewise Beeton's much vaunted innovation in giving costings for her recipes turns out to be more complicated than it once seemed. Mrs. Parkes, who contributed the recipe chapters to Webster's *Encyclopaedia*, gives a detailed breakdown of the cost of each of her menu plans, although she does not divide it by the number of diners to give a per capita figure as Beeton does. Moreover, on many occasions Parkes also lists her ingredients at the beginning of each recipe. Thus the claim that Beeton was the first person to invert Acton's layout begins to look shaky too.

In her Preface Isabella went out of her way to explain: "For the matter of the recipes, I am indebted, in some measure to many correspondents of the 'Englishwoman's Domestic Magazine' who have obligingly placed at my disposal their formulae for many original preparations." And, indeed, this became a crucial part of the book's mythology, leading perhaps to the mistaken assumption that the book was initially issued as a supplement to the magazine. In fact, internal evidence from the two publications suggests that, despite the strenuous requests for material in the editor's letter, only a handful of recipes sent in by readers found their way into the

BOHM. Anyone who has ever worked on a newspaper or magazine will have a strong suspicion why this might be. Readers, while well-meaning, tend to send in information that is incomplete, illegible, vague, or baffling. In the end it was easier for Isabella to work from printed sources than from stray bits of paper.

This is not to suggest that the *Book of Household Management* superseded that older tradition of women writing down recipes and circulating them among their friends and relatives. For those many middle-class women still living near their families, the practice of learning cookery by example from an older servant or from a manuscript book compiled by an aunt continued right through the nineteenth century. But, as Sam's experience of deciphering his readers' contributions to the *EDM* showed, there was nothing more baffling than trying to enter a stranger's world through a scrap of handwritten text. In the case of a recipe, you would have to be familiar not only with the author's handwriting, but with her thought patterns, her habits, and even her saucepans.

In her Preface Isabella also thanked the "large private Circle" that had furnished her with recipes. So far it has been possible to identify only three friends who contributed to her book. There was Baroness de Tessier of Epsom who supplied the distinctly thrifty Baroness Pudding which initially appeared in the *EDM* before transferring to the *BOHM*. There was a man called Vulliamy who was said to have contributed the recipe for Soup à la Solferino. And, finally, there were Auguste and Louisa Heidel, who in September 1860 responded to Isabella's urgent request for some recipes by sending her a cookery book of German dishes, making the interesting point in their covering letter that it would be far easier for Bella to work from a printed source than from their scrappy handwritten notes.

The question that still remains, though, is whether Isabella Beeton really did do as she was supposed to and test every dish before allowing it into the book. In the promotional material that appeared in the *EDM* it was certainly always claimed that "no recipe will be given which has not been tried or tested either by the Editress herself or by her confidential friends and correspondents." Family anecdote also liked to stress the fact that Isabella's mantra during preparation for the *BOHM* was that "nothing must go into the book untried," perhaps because it elevated her from mere kitchen drudge to laboratory technician and even connoisseur. The source of this story is Lucy Dorling, whose 1858 visit to Pinner fell within the most intense phase of research on the book. Lucy remembered one day being handed a curranty biscuit by her half-sister and finding it absolutely delicious. But the biscuit, apparently, was supposed to have been a cake. "This won't do at all," was Isabella Beeton's damning verdict.

While Lucy's recollection of the failed cake may well be accurate, it is difficult to believe that Isabella Beeton really did test every recipe before giving it a place in her book. Given that there are two thousand recipes in all and that the cookery writing was wrapped up by the end of 1860, Isabella would have had to cook two separate dishes a day over the thirty-eight months from August 1857 to December 1860. Also telling is the fact that Isabella was happy to copy dishes from Eliza Acton even when the latter made it clear that she had not herself tried them. Thus a recipe for Broiled Partridge is described by Miss Acton as having been passed on to her by people who had enjoyed the dish at a weekend house party. Beeton simply inserts the recipe into her own text without comment. Likewise Acton scrupulously explains that she hasn't actually tried Carême's Nesselrode Pudding but has made an assumption that, given its pedigree, it must be fine. Beeton simply copies out the recipe, without indicating that it has come via Acton rather than directly from Carême.

What all this suggests is that Isabella made a series of ad hoc judgements about which recipes to test and which to take on trust. If something came from a well-respected source such as Acton, or Glasse, or Ude, then it was simply reformatted into the standard Beeton template and allowed to go into the book untried. If something seemed more chancy, perhaps because it was a compound of two recipes, then Isabella rehearsed it herself at home. Despite the impression that the advertising blurb for the *BOHM* would give over the next twenty years, it remains highly unlikely that Mrs. Beeton really did test every recipe in the *BOHM* from Apple Soup to Toast Sandwiches.

INTERLUDE

USEFUL SOUP FOR BENEVOLENT PURPOSES

Ingredients—An ox-cheek, any pieces of trimmings of beef, which may be bought very cheaply (say 4 lbs), a few bones, any pot-liquor the larder may furnish, ¼ peck of onions, 6 leeks, a large bunch of herbs, ½ lb of celery (the outside pieces, or green tops, do very well); ½ lb of carrots, ½ lb of turnips, ½ lb of coarse brown sugar, ½ a pint of beer, 4 lbs of common rice, or pearl barley; ½ lb of salt, 1 oz of black pepper, a few raspings, 10 gallons of water. Time—6½ hours. Average cost, 1½d per quart.

Note—The above recipe was used in the winter of 1858 by the Editress, who made, each week, in her copper, 8 or 9 gallons of this soup, for distribution amongst about a dozen families of the village near which she lives.

ISABELLA BEETON,
Book of Household Management

WE KNOW THAT THE OUTLINE OF Mrs. Beeton's anecdote about serving soup to the poor in 1858 is accurate, since Lucy Dorling also mentioned it when she wrote to *The Times* in 1932 recalling the visit she made to Pinner that winter as a ten-year-old. Over the previous fifteen years dishing up soup to the poor had become a national pastime, ever since Alexis Soyer, chef at the Reform Club, had travelled to Dublin in a blaze of publicity to feed the victims of the 1845–46 potato famine. Soyer, however, managed to fill empty stomachs even more cheaply than Mrs. Beeton.

Whereas her brew cost 6d a gallon, the Frenchman's Turnip and Barley Water came in at 3½d for the same volume.

The real point about giving soup to the poor, though, was not so much to get hot food inside them cheaply, as it was to teach them a lesson. Traditionally the working class had given sloppy or liquid meals a wide berth, on the sensible grounds that they lacked the cooking facilities to make them, not to mention the crockery and cutlery to eat them with. Bread, by contrast, could be bought ready-made, wrapped in a handkerchief and held in the fingers.

What was worse, from the middle-class philanthropist's point of view, was that the working class lacked the prudence, patience, and foresight that it took to make soup in the first place. Soup was a moral food, the emblematic product of the well-run middle-class kitchen in which everyday ingredients were slowly transformed through skill and knowledge into something that served both body and soul. And for a few weeks at least, the poor of Pinner who clustered around the back door of 2 Chandos Villas were given a taste of how fine their lives might be if they could only muster the capacity for the delayed gratification and forward planning required to become efficient soup makers. Contemporary analysis of Mrs. Beeton's charity soup suggests that an average serving would provide a very substantial 454 calories. Three servings a day, and you had just about enough fuel to carry you through until better times returned.

But soup wasn't simply moral and useful, it was, declares Mrs. Beeton, parroting what her friend Mrs. English had told her, the starting point for all "excellence in cookery." So important, indeed, does Mrs. Beeton believe the process of distilling the essence of meat and vegetables into liquid form to be that she devotes eight whole pages to its general principles. The idea is to keep a pot bubbling away for six hours on the stove into which you put a slice of beef, mutton, and veal and a clutch of mainly root vegetables and add water at the rate of a quart for every pound of meat. And since Mrs. Beeton is a modern woman who knows all about the work of the German scientist Von Liebig, she explains that it is also crucial to include broken animal bones from which the rich, wholesome marrow will gradually be extracted. (Liebig's investigations led, in a roundabout way, to the development of the commercial product Marmite which, while vegetarian, derives its name from *marmite*, the French word for a stockpot.)

Once the scum has been skimmed and the stock allowed to cool you have, says Mrs. Beeton, the starting point for an almost infinite number of soups, from Almond Soup (needs a beef and mutton stock), via Giblet Soup (needs shin of beef and mutton shank) to Hare Soup (needs lean beef and ham). Every one of her ninety-six Bills of Fare includes at least one soup in the opening course.

There was, however, one recipe for soup that departed from this model of distilling humble, healthy ingredients into a nutritionally and morally rich compost. Newly fashionable Turtle Soup, explains Beeton, is now served annually at the Lord Mayor's Banquet every November and, should you wish to make it yourself, she includes instructions "founded on M. Ude's recipe." But the first line, surely, would be enough to put anyone off: "to make this soup with less difficulty, cut off the head of the turtle the preceding day." From here Beeton takes us on a squeamish route march that involves boiling off the beast's shell and then making an accompaniment out of calf's udder. So it should come as no surprise that by the end of this exhausting operation, Beeton suggests that it might be simpler, after all, to buy tinned green turtle fat in "hermetically sealed cannisters" for 7s 6d "from which 6 good quarts of soup may be made." Just occasionally, it seemed, soup worked better as fast food.

❊

CHAPTER EIGHT

THE ALPHA AND THE OMEGA

EXACTLY WHAT PEOPLE do when they read a book remains pretty much a mystery. Do they start at the beginning and work through steadily to the end? Do they skip, reread, or scribble in the margins? Do they copy bits out and circulate them to their friends or do they do what Victorians are popularly supposed to have done, and read passages out to each other in the evening around a companionable fire? Until we have a more fully developed history of reading, as opposed to writing, it remains impossible to know just what effect any particular publication has on the people who buy, borrow or otherwise get access to a particular text.

One day this kind of work will be done for the *Book of Household Management*. Perhaps more than any other kind of text, cookery books bear the imprint of their users, with busy readers altering and adapting them to their particular needs. The copy of *Simpson's* held in the British Library, for instance, includes a handwritten index of favourite recipes added by a previous owner, keen to be able to locate favourite pages easily. To understand how the *Book of Household Management* was originally read will mean painstakingly going through each extant copy of the first edition, looking for those places where the pages are bowed out through constant reading, or stuck together with gobs of pastry left by busy working hands. You would have to notice the places where someone had altered the recipe to make it work better, and see if any page corners had been turned down to mark a favourite place. It would mean scanning kitchen notebooks to see whether recipes from the book had been copied out, and looking through letters from mothers to daughters and sisters to cousins to see if bits and pieces drawn from the Beeton book were circulated as precious family lore, reversing that usual traffic from manuscript to printed text.

Until the time when this work can be done—it is enormously labour intensive and expensive—we will have to use our imagination to understand what it might have been like when the *Book of Household Management* first appeared before the public in November 1859. In its very first incarnation it was hardly impressive—a series of forty-eight-page pamphlets with drab buff covers. Each installment ended *in media res,* regardless of whether it was the natural moment to take a break. In this way Sam avoided the expense of resetting the type when he came to release the text as a single volume in 1861. The effect for the reader, though, must have been odd. For instance, in November 1859, the housewife who was following Mrs. Beeton's recipe for Baked Apple Pudding (Very Good) would have been left hanging with "bake in a moderate oven for an hour, and cover," before having to wait a whole month to discover how the sentence ended. (In fact, it was "when served, with sifted loaf sugar.") Quite apart from the annoyance factor, this practice of producing the book in illogical fragments had the interesting effect of breaking up the monumental text that was the *Book of Household Management* and turning it into something slight, provisional, and tentative.

In the absence of any clues as to how the first edition of the single volume *Beeton's Book of Household Management* was used, consumed, and deployed in ordinary British homes, we will have to take (or make) an imaginary reader. Mary Price lives in the upper end of the Holloway Road, towards Archway. She is married to an engineer, thirty-four-year-old George, who is employed by the London & Birmingham Railway Company. Mary is twenty-six and has a four-year-old son, little Georgie, and three-year-old Matilda, known as Mattie. Mary's life is very different from her mother's who, confusingly, was christened Mary Ann but goes by the customary shortening of Polly. Mary, strictly speaking, is "Mary Ann" too but, disliking the bumpkin associations of the name, shortened it to its present form on the day she started boarding school. Polly, Mary's mother, was born in 1812 in Saffron Walden, the daughter of a blacksmith. In 1834 she married the town's draper whose shop provided sprigged cotton, stout linen, and serviceable serge to the local households of farmers, busy artisans, and the occasional gentleman (Essex soil is so good that it tends to produce prosperous fruit-growing yeomen rather than threadbare squires). During the years 1835–50, Polly Unwin ran a household that, in addition to her husband and four little girls, included an apprentice and a shopman. As well as providing these two young men (later there were three) with board and lodging, Polly acted as their laundress, sick nurse, and surrogate mother.

Sharing the workload with Polly was Old Nanna, the family servant, who evolved over the twenty years she spent in the Unwin household from nursemaid to maid-of-all-work to cook, depending on what needed doing most at any particular moment. For ten years, when the house was at its noisiest and busiest with babies, there was a series of extra maids, whey-faced little girls of no more than fourteen who helped Nanna and Polly with the endless loop of cooking and cleaning.

But that was only part of Polly Unwin's responsibilities. For most of that time she also organized the stockroom, kept the accounts and helped in the shop. There is a story of how Polly got so busy one day, serving customers and supervising the shopmen, that she tucked the youngest baby into one of the deep drawers and forgot where she had put her. What a fuss there was, and what crying with relief when little Eliza made her presence felt with a long wail! Mary flushes when she thinks of this story, or at least when she thinks of it being told to new people, which Mama will insist on doing. She hates the way it makes her people look pinched and mean. It is *years* since Mama served in the shop, although it is true that latterly she worked in the back room, out of view, making up the haberdashery orders. These days the widowed Mrs. Unwin is quite the lady, tucked away in a snug little house on the other side of Saffron Walden with a maid in uniform to wait on her. Nanna, by contrast, always wore her own clothes, a black stuff gown in winter and a cotton one in summer. A third dress, her Sunday best, was the one she was buried in two years ago.

Mary is quite the lady too. By the time she was fourteen the business was flourishing; Papa had expanded into haberdashery and also added an agency for Indian tea. So in 1849 Mary was sent away for two years to a boarding school in Colchester, to be followed by her younger sisters at yearly intervals. Mary's life at the Misses Russell was filled with piano playing, painting and French, as well as the cold Sunday morning and evening walk to service (although Mary's family used to be chapel people, they were quite happy for her to attend the local parish church with the other young ladies). Now those days seem to belong to another life, one that Mary is no longer certain ever existed. For instance, she always tells people how much she loves music, but the truth is that she has barely touched the piano that came as a wedding present five years ago. Instead, it stands in the corner of the parlour at 2 Fairbridge Road, a boxy upright on top of which the household's flotsam and jetsam collects in drifts. Harriet, the maid, complains in that sly, provoking way of hers that the "pianer" is nothing but a dust trap. But Mary, equally determined, thinks how nicely it fills out the corner of the room.

Married life, then, has not turned out quite the way Mary expected. Everyone is agreed that George is a good man but she had expected, oh, something more. The year before she met him there had been a young solicitor, very gentlemanly, but he married a Miss Phipps while on a visit to Harrogate and nothing more was ever said. And so, at twenty-two, with her mother getting anxious and her younger sisters restless, Mary accepted an offer from George Price. It was a very quick engagement, thought by some to be not quite nice and by others sweetly romantic (at twenty-two Mary was actually young to be getting married, but she had been thinking of nothing else for ten years). Papa made enquiries and learned that George was a steady young man and likely to progress in his profession which, after all, is a coming one. The world will always need engineers. With his £200 a year salary and her settlement of £50 a year there was just enough to marry on. Mama said that when she married Mary's father in 1834 they had scarcely two pennies to rub together. You have to cut your coat to suit your cloth.

But sometimes Mary isn't really quite so sure about coats and cloth and all the bother of making them suit. She thinks back to those years that came after school and wonders now why she felt so anxious to start this new life, the life of a married woman. Back then she did not have to worry about snuffling children, silent husbands, or nursemaids who stare too long at bakers' boys. By the time she was sixteen, back from school and living the life of a young lady at home, the Unwins had a girl to help Nanna in the kitchen as well as another maid. All Mary had to do, really, was please herself. She carried on with daily piano practice and also with sketching the wide fenny sky. Indeed, Papa used to joke that he felt cold just looking at her paintings, but still he hung them proudly on the wall. There were walks into town, and visits to Aunt Matilda in Birmingham, who never had any children of her own and liked Mary to keep her company for several weeks every year. And then, during the summer of 1856, there was that fateful journey to Chelmsford to stay with Jane Price, a friend from her schooldays. Jane had a brother, George, a handsome fellow, who blushed whenever Mary's glance happened to fall upon him. By the end of her visit they had an understanding and, just two months later, they were formally engaged. Mary loved George, of course she did. But more than that, she loved the chance of moving to London and having an establishment of her own.

But this proper life, the life of a married woman, has proved far more trying than Mary ever imagined. Her attempts at running the little household at 2 Fairbridge Road have not always gone well and George has been spending more and more of his evenings in town. Once, in that hateful period after Mattie was born and she felt so tired all the time, George came home at six o'clock to find her only half dressed, the baby still in night clothes, and the supper two hours away from the table. The next three nights in a row George dined with some of the fellows from work at a tavern near Euston station where you can get a chop supper for 6d. Afterwards he came home with a queer flushed look on his face and pressed his wet mouth against hers.

When Mary first saw the advertisement for the *BOHM* in the *Englishwoman's Domestic Magazine* it immediately lodged in her mind: "A New and Practical Work Adapted for every family and one that will save money every day and last a life-time" sounded exactly what she needed. Mama had tried to teach her when she was young, but Mary would wriggle and sigh until she was told sharply to go and play. She wishes, now, that she had stayed to watch and learn. There is the matter of the accounts for instance. Each year Mama bought an account book from the stationers, one with neatly ruled columns and lines, in which you could write down everything you had ordered from the butcher or fishmonger, and the amount you had agreed to pay. When Mary was young, this figure work of Mama's had seemed natural, as much a part of daily life as the bales of Belfast linen or the cards of Coventry ribbon, but by the time she was at school it seemed illiberal. Mary was quite sure that her friends' mothers didn't spend an hour every Saturday afternoon frowning and peering at rows of pencil marks. Now that she is the mistress of her own household, though, Mary can see the point. When the bills from the tradesmen come at the end of the quarter it really is vexing how they are always higher than she reckoned on. Asking Harriet is no help, since she simply stares straight ahead like a foolish thing and mutters that she really "couldn't say" whether the butcher sent chops on the fourteenth.

Harriet is the Prices' maid-of-all-work. Along with Sarah the nurse-maid it is her labour that keeps the household at 2 Fairbridge Road ticking over. The Prices fall into a crack between the two lowest income categories in Mrs. Beeton's servant-employing taxonomy. At £150 or £200 a year, Beeton says that a family should be able to manage "a maid-of-all-work (and girl occasionally)." At £300 a year the same family will be permanently able to afford a maid-of-all-work and nursemaid, just like the real Mrs. Beeton of 2 Chandos Villas. The Prices' income is around £250 a year, which means that they are struggling to find the annual wage (paid quarterly in arrears) of £12 for Harriet and £9 for Sarah. Wages are higher in London than they are in the country, and servants exploit the fact that the labour market is tipped in their favour. Harriet is always making meaningful comments to Mary about friends of hers who left their place because they couldn't stand their missus and walked straight into another situation, "no trouble at all." Trouble for whom? Mary thinks wearily, not able to meet Harriet's daring stare.

On the bad days, which are becoming more frequent now, Mary dreams of being in command of an income of £500 a year (Aunt Matilda is strongly tipped to be remembering her favourite niece in her will; Mary thinks of all those trips to Birmingham as an investment). At £500 a year the Prices would be able to employ that prized symbol of middle-class status, a cook. In fact, sometimes Mary goes even further and closes her eyes and imagines what it would be like to belong in Mrs. Beeton's top category, where the household income is over £1,000. If George were a society doctor or a rich City man there would be a cook, an upper housemaid, an under-housemaid, nursemaid and, last but far from least, that greatest trophy of all, a manservant. Mary's shoulders soften slightly as she imagines living in a household that runs like a well-oiled machine, requiring of its mistress only the occasional touch on the tiller. There would be invisible patters on the stairs (the back stairs, naturally; this imaginary house would have one set for the servants and another for the family), quiet thuds as beds are efficiently patted down and remade, carefully lowered voices caught as the parlour is turned out before breakfast. The front door opens magically as if by itself, and everywhere there are respectful, downcast eyes. Mary would see these servants—their names and faces are smudgy in her imagination—as she glides past on her way to a dinner party, or a picnic, or a concert, or a dozen other engagements that require her to wear long gloves, and a dress of deep green silk with large velvet sleeves. She would smile and nod, happy to acknowledge her obligations to the people whose physical hard work guarantee her own comfortable progress through life. Oh yes, with an income of £1,000 a year Mary Price knows she could be the very model of a mistress.

All mistresses, whatever their means, are advised by Mrs. Beeton that, after an early breakfast, they should make "a round of the kitchen and other offices, to see that all are in order, and that the morning's work has been properly performed by various domestics," by which she means that the main living rooms have been swept out, the fires laid and the beds made. Then that odd little note in smaller type: "In those establishments where there is a housekeeper, it will not be so necessary for the mistress, personally, to perform the above-named duties." For a moment, Mary imagines herself graciously walking around "the offices" (at 2 Fairbridge Road these consist of the kitchen and the scullery and it takes only a dozen goodish strides to get right across), serenely answering a question from the upper housemaid as to whether the parlour chairs should be moved to avoid the harsh afternoon sun or else, perhaps, unlocking the storeroom to dole out the soap that the scullery maid has requested. Or maybe Mary belongs in that elite paragraph of small print, mistress of an establishment where a housekeeper is employed as a shadow monarch in the kingdom below stairs. In which case, Mary thinks, she would simply retire to her parlour after breakfast, write letters and wait for the house-keeper—a crisp, bustling little body with a notebook and eye glasses—to arrive and sketch in the day's proceedings, enquiring politely whether madam would care to make any adjustments.

In fact, what actually happens after breakfast in 2 Fairbridge Road is that Sarah clumps down the front (and only) stairs with the lagging children, ready to march them along the dull stretch of the Holloway Road for an hour's fresh—that is damp, sooty—air. With the front door slammed accusingly shut (what is the accusation, though? Simply, per-haps, that no one at 2 Fairbridge Road is quite living the life they think they should), Mary goes down to see Harriet in the kitchen to talk about tonight's dinner. Harriet has washed up the breakfast things (*her* dream is to have a scullery maid to do these chores and perhaps, while she's at it, a kitchen maid to boss and scold). The moment Mary walks into the kitchen she can tell that Harriet is in a temper. By now she is an expert reader of the younger girl's moods, and that hot flush of colour over her neck says that something is amiss. And, indeed, it soon turns out that Harriet has just had words with the fishmonger's boy who has delivered stale turbot, with dull eyes and gasping mouth. Harriet says she wouldn't like to risk it, and could missus go down to Harris's and set them right? Mary, secretly, thinks she would be happy to risk the turbot since the thought of putting on her bonnet, going down to the fishmonger and remonstrating with him under the mocking eyes of the shopmen is just too much. But all she says is "yes, indeed" and tries to sound as if she is positively spoiling for a fight with Mr. Harris.

After this initial soothing and settling of the household, Mrs. Beeton is clear about what should happen next: "Unless the means of the mistress be very circumscribed, and she be obliged to devote a great deal of her time to the making of her children's clothes and other economical pursuits, it is right that she should give some time to the pleasures of literature, the innocent delights of the garden, and to the improvement of any special abilities for music, painting, and other elegant arts, which she may, happily, possess."

Mary has tried, she truly has, to make clothes for little Georgie. She did needlework at the Misses Russell, the fancy kind, and from her workbox flowed an endless stream of slippers for Papa, spectacle cases for Mama and, on one occasion, a pretty set of trimmed napkins for Aunt Matilda. So, naturally, Mary feels that she ought to be able to manage some of the simpler patterns for children's apparel that she sees so often in the *Englishwoman's Domestic Magazine* which one of her sisters sends on to her at irregular intervals. But when she tried that sweet little cape for Georgie last year it came out all bunched on one side, with the left shoulder distinctly higher than the right. What's more Georgie, who has taken a dislike to this lopsided article, says it makes him itch and now every time Mary goes to put it on him he twists and cries and, one terrible time, held his breath until his little face turned blue. These days Mary relies on Mama, who has always been so clever with her needle, to make the children's clothes and send them by carrier.

So with no sewing tasks to occupy her, Mary is free to try what Mrs. Beeton describes as "the innocent delights of the garden." During her two years at school Mary was taught botany by the younger Miss Russell, who praised her for her carefully hatched drawings of *Wachendorfia, Bifora officinalis,* and *Noisettiana* and once burst into spontaneous applause when she saw her *Muscosa multiplex*. But it is real plants that concern Mary now. Venn, the gardener, comes in only once a week and they cannot afford a boy. So it is up to Mary to keep things shipshape. As well as banks of flowers—so difficult to coax to maturity in the soot-choked garden (the railway line passes only a mile or so away)—Mary also grows vegetables for the kitchen, yet remains shy about harvesting them. Venn, a fierce old man of fifty, seems to think that she should ask his permission before pulling up the potatoes and onions. So instead they tend to stay there, softening and spotting until past their prime. It takes Mary an hour and a half to clear the hothouse marrow bed of weeds, by which time there isn't any chance for the "music, painting, and other elegant arts" that Mrs. Beeton suggests. So this morning, as with every other morning for the last couple of years, the piano stays closed and the dried-out paints remain stowed away in the boxroom where they have languished for the past three years.

While lunch is the main meal of the day for most of the inhabitants at 2 Fairbridge Road, for Mary it is a rushed and sketchy snack. Mrs. Beeton suggests that a joint be sent up to the mistress first and then on to the nursery, but she obviously hasn't been to 2 Fairbridge Road. What actually happens is this. At 12 noon Harriet divides up some chicken into three substantial portions. One portion is minced and shared between the children, who eat in the nursery under Sarah's superintendence. At about 12:30 Mary goes up to see the children and help Sarah settle them down for their nap. If there is any food left over, Mary takes a forkful before Sarah whisks the plates down to the kitchen, where Harriet has set out a substantial dinner for the two of them: chicken together with cold roast potatoes and rice pudding from Mary and George's dinner last night. There is, then, always something of a battle over lunch, with Sarah hovering around the remains of the children's meal, anxious to be done with it so that she can descend for her own dinner, and Mary, famished, watching as the food disappears before she has had a chance to help herself.

At 2 p.m. Mary pops out to Harris's, blushes and stutters while she explains that the turbot just won't do, and returns with a damp, chilly package in her basket at which Harriet merely prods suspiciously. Thank heavens there is now a chance to leave the house properly. For on Tuesday and Thursday afternoons Mary makes what are confusingly known as Morning Calls. She has a new dress that she would like to wear. It is a joint effort between the dressmaker Miss Finch, who has done the cutting, fitting, and "making up," and Mary, who has used her skills in fancy needlework to add the trim on the sleeves and make the collar. The material is a deep brown silk of a very superior quality—how much Papa, the draper, would like it if he were still alive, taking a pinch between his thumb and forefinger and looking carefully at the flow and fall of the thing. The pattern comes from the *EDM* and the fashion notes are written, though Mary does not know this, by Mrs. Beeton who describes the dress as "made of plain brown silk, trimmed with brown velvet and black buttons. The bows at the neck and wrists, and the waistband, are in black velvet, embroidered with gold, and finished off by a very narrow black edging. Embroidered collar, and puffed under sleeves with a cuff, formed of Valenciennes lace and insertion."

The problem is that the dress may actually be too showy for this time of day. But it is a whole year since Mary has had anything new and she would love to wear it, enjoying the swish of it, the sloping shoulders, the way it swerves into her waist before flaring out over her crinoline. She is planning to call upon her fashionable neighbour Mrs. Jones this afternoon. Mr. Jones does very well as the London agent for a Sheffield cutlery company, and Mrs. Jones signals this success by wearing his fortune on her back. Mrs. Jones prides herself on keeping up with the Paris fashions—a new monthly magazine called the *Queen* provides her with the last word on what is happening in the *ateliers*—and never seems to balk at the cost of three or four new gowns every single year. So Mary would naturally love to present Mrs. Jones, who if truth be told is rather stout and florid, with the sight of herself in the new brown silk wonder. But Mary has been reading Mrs. Beeton and Mrs. Beeton says of morning calls: "as a general rule, it may be said, both in reference to this and all other occasions, it is better to be under-dressed than over-dressed." Mrs. Jones, now Mary comes to think of it, is not quite ladylike. Mary is ladylike, Mary will wear her second best silk, a slub grey. As she leaves the house she catches Harriet staring at her muted ensemble. Pity and triumph burn in the maid's eyes. When Harriet goes out on her day off it is always in her very best frock, the singing colour of sapphire.

Mary sets off on the five-minute walk to Mrs. Jones's house. The Prices are a long way off being able to keep a carriage (carriages are up there in dreamland, along with liveried footmen with nicely turned calves in silk stockings). Ideally Mary should be accompanied by a maid to shield her from the squalors of the street—horse shit, dead cats, the bold, assessing stares of delivery boys—but the thought of suggesting to an incredulous Harriet that she leave her labours in the kitchen to act as chaperone is too absurd to contemplate. "What, to walk with you, mum? As far as the corner with Marlborough Road?" So Mary sets off alone. During her walk she keeps her eyes directly in front of her and ponders the strangeness of morning calls. Her mother, she is pretty certain, never made or received one in her life. With six sisters and two brothers all living around Saffron Walden there was no time, and no need. The children of this extended tribe ran in and out of each other's houses, and at high days and holidays there was always a throng of people sitting down to table. It was not until Mary went away to school in Colchester that she thought about making friends with people whom she didn't call cousin.

Tuesday is Mrs. Jones's customary day for receiving visitors. But the maid who answers the door tells Mary that her "missus is not at 'ome." Mary has doubts about this since, as she was approaching the house, she swore she saw a twitch of the curtain from the upstairs parlour. What is more, the maidservant—Bessy, Betty?—turned pink and would not meet her gaze. But Mary is too ladylike to give any sign that she has noticed anything amiss. As Mrs. Beeton rightly says, "The form of words, 'Not at home,' may be understood in different senses, but the only courteous way is to receive them as being perfectly true. You may imagine that the lady of the house is really at home, and that she would make an exception in your favour, or you may think that your acquaintance is not desired; but, in either case, not the slightest word is to escape you, which would suggest, on your part, such an impression."

So Mary leaves her card—"Mrs. George Price"—and turns around to retrace her steps. Actually, to tell the truth, Mary is relieved not to find Mrs. Jones "at home." For today is a red letter day. Two couples will be coming to dinner at Fairbridge Road this evening, though not the Joneses who already have a prior engagement. Or at least they say they do. Mary finds entertaining a terrible worry: it puts Harriet in a dreadful mood and the children are always so naughty. Mary read somewhere, probably in the *Englishwoman's Domestic Magazine,* that someone of the Prices' sort should entertain three times a year, but three times as long has gone by since Mary last invited people to dinner. It makes her anxious, George is always bad-tempered and she hates the feeling that her guests are scrutinizing her home. But this is her duty and her obligation, just as it is George's to go to the office every day and Sarah's to sleep in a truckle bed in the nursery.

Mary's mother did not go in for dinner parties. Instead, Polly Unwin was known for keeping "a good table" which meant that when friends, usually family, called there was always something delicious in the pantry ready for any extra mouths. Mary, by contrast, has been obliged to consult household manuals several weeks in advance in order to decide what to give her guests. This time, after much discussion with Harriet, Mary has decided to attempt Mrs. Beeton's Bill of Fare for six persons (February). She won't follow the plan to the letter, since Harriet says she can't do the Fricasseed Rabbit that Mrs. Beeton suggests as an entrée and George can't abide Tartlets of Greengage Jam. So they will substitute pork cutlets instead and Mary will buy some of the desserts ready-made from the baker. This is how the menu will go.

FIRST COURSE
Spring Soup
Boiled Turbot and Lobster Sauce

ENTRÉESS
Pork Cutlets
Oyster Patties

SECOND COURSE
Boiled Round of Beef and Marrow-bones
Roast Chicken, Garnished with Water-cresses and Rolled Bacon
Vegetables

THIRD COURSE
Cheesecakes, Lemon Cream, Plum Pudding, Rhubarb Tart
Dessert

George has agreed that Harriet can have extra help for the day, although secretly he doesn't really see why she needs it. His mother always managed perfectly well, but then she had a cook, a proper one, with a kitchen maid to help her. Anyway, he has agreed that Mary may hire fourteen-year-old Susan, Sarah's sister, to help Harriet in the kitchen or, more accurately, in the scullery (the washing-up will need to be done as the evening goes along since the Prices' dinner service will not stretch to accommodate even three courses, consisting as they do of so many different dishes). The cheesecakes and lemon creams have been ordered from the baker's, Graham's, and are now sitting in the larder alongside the rhubarb tart that Harriet made yesterday. Instead of marrow pudding suggested by Mrs. Beeton, there will be plum pudding. There is one left over from Christmas six weeks ago which Mary's mother made and brought with her when she came to stay in December.

Even with these cuts and conveniences, there is still an awful lot to do. Mary has arranged that the moment the children go off to sleep at 6 p.m. Sarah will come down from the nursery and offer reinforcement in the kitchen. But it is still only 3 p.m., which leaves Harriet pretty much single-handed (little Susan can be trusted to peel vegetables, but that is about all). So Mary herself will have to help. Having changed into her oldest dress, she ties on a large apron at the waist (she is not going to lower herself to Harriet's level and wear one with a bib), and tries to give the impression that she knows what she is doing. The stock for the spring soup—a rich mix of poultry, veal knuckle, ham, and onions—has been simmering since before lunch. So, too, on a corner of the range is one of the second courses, a round of beef, which will be boiled for about four hours until it is tender. Lying in the fish kettle, just covered in water, is the troublesome, tiresome turbot. Mary gives the soup stock a quick stir before setting about making the lobster sauce to go with the fish. This means melting some butter, adding cream and anchovy sauce as well as the little pearls of spawn and then setting it in a *bain marie* where it will keep warm without overcooking and losing its distinctive red colour. Nearer dinner time Harriet will add squares of hen lobster.

The oyster patties, thank heavens, are simpler. Harriet made the puff-paste patties this morning. But now two dozen oysters need to be opened, bearded, and divided into threes. Mary is not going to do this since it is almost certain that she will cut herself in the process and cannot afford to sit down at dinner with hands scarred with signs of hard work. The operation requires too much strength and skill for little Susan, so Harriet gets to work with a stubby oyster knife. Mary meanwhile makes the butter and flour sauce and, once more, puts it to stand in the *bain marie* until the moment when the oysters will be added, just two minutes before serving.

When that is done Harriet turns her attention to the chicken that is going to be one of the second courses. Although it was plucked at

Illustration for the "Bain Marie" from the Book of Household Management.

the butcher's, it still needs to be trussed. This means cutting off the head and claws, and dipping the legs in boiling water before scraping them clean. A skewer goes through the bird from one side to the other and then the legs are tied together with a trussing needle. Harriet despatches all this matter-of-factly and then places a piece of buttered paper over the bird and puts it back in the larder where it will stay until 6:30 p.m., when it will need to go into the oven. Little Susan, meanwhile, sits in the corner, peeling the potatoes, carrots, and turnips and cutting the broccoli into neat pieces, occasionally glancing up at her elders with saucer eyes.

By now it is 5:30 p.m. and there is nothing more that Mary can do. The pork cutlets, spring soup, and turbot cannot be cooked until the last hour before dinner, which will be served at the fashionably late time of 7:30. In half an hour Sarah will be liberated from the nursery and able to help in the final crucial ninety minutes when different dishes will be placed on specific parts of the range, according to how much heat is needed (it is an inexact science, and chances are that some items will go to table a little singed, while others will be distinctly tepid). So Mary goes up to lay the table in the dining room. This dinner party will be served more in the French than Russian style, which means that lots of dishes will be crammed onto the table and the guests will help each other. Harriet, aided by Sarah, and both wearing their best dresses, will be on hand to take away the plates and hand things round. The Prices have neither the staff nor the crockery to manage the more fashionable practice of having each person served their meal separately by a servant. For this reason, too, there will be no space for any table decorations, except for a vase of fresh flowers that Mary now places in the middle of the table. Then she lights the oil lamps, lays the table for six, and takes a last, careful look at the dining room before going upstairs to dress. The new brown silk will have an outing, after all.

The dinner has cost just under £2, about half a week's salary for George Price. The whole evening has strained the little household to the point of collapse. Mary has mounted a kind of performance, a piece of theatre that gestures towards a way of living that is not really hers. Over the next week the inhabitants of 2 Fairbridge Road will be living off the remains from the feast. The boiled beef will come back as stew, the chicken will be minced and sent up to the nursery for four days in a row. The vegetable peelings will be sold to the pig man who comes round twice a week to collect them, and the profit split between Harriet and Mary (although Harriet has found a way of keeping more than half). The plum pudding will return and return until George declares himself sick of the sight of it. All the same, he has to agree that the dinner was a triumph, and his Mary has done him proud.

THE PRECEDING ACCOUNT of one harried day in the life of Mary Price is fictional. Even a preliminary reading should suggest that too much of everything—information, activity, explanation—has been crammed into the space of a few short hours in order to produce an account of a "typical" lower-middle-class household in the early 1860s. The result is over-determined, too relentlessly emblematic, as if each person or event comes embedded in a dense network of secondary reading. Real life, including the real life of mid-Victorians, is a mix of the programmed and the random. Would Mary really have made a morning call on the very day that she was nervously embarking upon a dinner party? What are the chances of Harriet intercepting her on her way out, providing the perfect opportunity to explain how maidservants were well known for dressing flashily on their days off? Naming the snooty neighbours the Joneses and their maid Betty smacks of cliché, and setting the whole thing near the Holloway Road nudges rather obviously at references to the Pooters thirty years later. The business of who opens the oysters is a sly nod to the fact that Dora, David Copperfield's hopeless child-wife, didn't even realize that such a task was necessary. The fishmonger was obliging in choosing that particular day to deliver stale turbot and, since this is February, it is quite likely that one of the children would actually have spent the day being wheezily ill upstairs rather than dawdling down the Holloway Road with Sarah the nursemaid.

Still, the point is that Mary and her stressful day are no more fictional than the domestic scenario that Mrs. Beeton presents to her readers in the *Book of Household Management*. For at the heart of Beeton's account of the well-run home is an imaginary household that has been constructed from wage tables, conduct books, servants' manuals, and wishful thinking rather than described from direct personal experience. It is a household belonging to someone on £1,000 a year who can afford a staff of at least five, each of whose specialized duties are carefully set out in the section on "Domestic Servants." It is the household of a lucky barrister or a baronet, certainly not that of a magazine publisher or even the Clerk of the Epsom racetrack. It is also, tacitly, a household presided over by a mistress who is married and a mother, whereas in real life, as we have seen from the examples of the Mayson, Beeton, and Dorling families, many mid-Victorian households were actually a jumble of step-parents, half-siblings and even paying guests.

This is not, of course, the only household described in the *BOHM*. The table near the beginning of the book showing how many servants can be afforded on five different income bands starts with those on £150 who can manage no more help than a single maid-of-all-work. And at many points in her run-through of the mistress's duties Beeton makes a detour into the households of the less well-off (that point, for instance, about mistresses who are obliged to spend the hours after breakfast making their children's clothes). The fact, too, that the sections on the mistress, the housekeeper, and the cook appear together at the front of the book, with the rest of the servants shuffled together at the back, suggests that Isabella Beeton was perfectly aware that her book was most likely to be read in households where one woman combined the duties of the first three. The fact that recipes are arranged according to ingredients (fish, beef) rather than in courses also suggests that the book was designed to be used by the woman doing the cooking, rather than the one drawing up the menu plans. Or, as was most likely of all, the woman who did both.

What is more, in the sections towards the back of the book that set out the duties of the specialized servants, Mrs. Beeton includes plenty of swaps, substitutions, and special pleadings. For instance, the lengthy section on the housemaid includes the qualifying phrases "where there is only a cook and housemaid kept," "kitchen-maid where one is kept," "where no footman waits," and proceeds to adjust the details of the housemaid's routine accordingly. Likewise, under the cook's duties Beeton explains, "when circumstances render it necessary, the cook engages to perform the whole work of the kitchen, and, in some places, a portion of the house-work also," while under those of the footman, she explains,

"Where a valet is not kept, a portion of his duties falls to the footman's share." Embedded within the *BOHM* are the building blocks for a whole series of parallel households, each ready to be assembled by the reader to match her own particular circumstance. If the book were being written today, it would work wonderfully as hypertext.

At the other end of the social spectrum, Beeton includes information that refers to the smartest social circles. Her table on servants' wages includes no fewer than twenty-six different functionaries, ranging from the House Steward at the top to the Scullery Maid at the bottom. Any household that contained this many staff would be paying £700 a year in wages, indicating an income of roughly ten times that amount. But it is hard to imagine someone in this league anxiously flicking through Mrs. Beeton's book for hints on how to deal with the second footman. Likewise, some of the menu plans towards the end of the book—Bill of Game Fare for 30 Persons, A Ball Supper for 60 Persons—are drawn from a fantasy world of fine dining far beyond the means of the vast majority of Beeton's readers, who were unlikely to be roaming the grouse moors with the Duke of Rutland or performing a minuet with the Countess of Warwick. These tantalizing vignettes of aristocratic life functioned as a kind of sweetening fantasy, leavening the relentless routine of carpet cleaning and "plain family suppers for 6" which comprised the real beating heart of the *Book of Household Management.*

In order for the book to work the reader needed to be able to find the information she wanted within seconds. This was where the "Analytical Index" came in. Previous commentators have suggested that Mrs. Beeton was the first person to include a comprehensive index at the front, rather than the back, of her book. In fact, the enterprising R. K. Philp, editor of *Family Friend,* had already led the way in 1855 with his *The Practical Housewife,* a fact which suggests strongly that the Beetons kept a close eye on everything Philp did, before attempting to go one better. At twenty-six pages long, the *BOHM*'s index is fabulously detailed and exhaustively cross-referenced. Thus "Almond, the" is followed by twelve subheadings including "Bitter," "Pudding, baked," and "Uses of the Sweet," and each has a paragraph rather than a page number for even closer identification. But that isn't all. "Almond" is also a side heading under "Soup," "Pudding," and "Cake." What is more, all recipes are arranged alphabetically within each section, with "Oysters" followed by "Perch," followed by

"Pike" in the fish section. Once a reader had got the hang of this, she simply had to turn to the relevant section and skim through alphabetically to reach the recipe that she wanted.

The index did not simply cover the recipe section of the book. All the household segments are included, and key information is once again listed under the different relevant sections, so there is no chance of missing something simply because you are not looking in the obvious place. "Plate-cleaning" is listed both as a subcategory of "Housemaid" and separately as a category in its own right between "Plaice" and "Plover." Likewise "Hooping-cough" is listed as a side heading under "Nurse" and also between "Honeycake" and "Horse."

As with the cookery section, Isabella Beeton lifted her material on household management from a variety of sources, each of which had been written with a slightly different audience in mind. Books advising women how to run their homes had been available from the earliest days of print culture and, as the example of Philp's *The Practical Housewife* shows, were continuing to flourish in the 1850s. Often linked to concerns about moral conduct, these books roamed over all aspects of a middle-class woman's life. Hannah Woolley's *The Gentlewoman's Companion* of 1673, for instance, was written in the wake of the Restoration and includes advice on such ticklish matters as urging your daughter not to wear beauty spots and black patches, how to avoid "wanton Songs, and idle Ballads" and "An Introduction to Physick and Chyrurgery." As this last example suggests, in the seventeenth century household books often doubled as cookery books and medical manuals, the most obvious bridge between the two domains coming in the form of recipes, or receipts. In the days before proprietary brands, the kitchen was not just the place where foodstuffs were processed, but also the laboratory where cough syrup, furniture polish, and even soap were made. Hannah Woolley's book moves seamlessly between a recipe "for one hurt with Gun-powder" to one for "Cherries Preserved."

By the time Hannah Glasse, who copied many of Woolley's recipes, and her successor Elizabeth Raffald were writing in the mid-eighteenth century, cookery books had been shorn of much of their moralizing tone. Both Glasse and Raffald were clear in their own minds that they were producing recipe books pure and simple, even if those recipes were drawn as much from the housekeeper's stillroom as from the cook's kitchen. Thus Glasse includes a section on making wines, and another on distilling, as well as attaching "A Certain Cure for the Bite of a Mad Dog." Raffald, meanwhile, follows Glasse with a chapter on distilling and also includes a whole section on "Table Decorations," albeit of the strictly edible kind (how, for instance, to model a hen's nest out of jelly and sago).

By the end of the eighteenth century a new moralizing discourse was creeping back into the presentation of cookery books, placing them once again in a wider context of household management. Successive waves of Evangelicalism had turned the spotlight on the importance of the well-run home as the starting point for a more general spiritual rearmament. One particularly conservative strand within this new moralizing tendency was the rural economy books which appeared from the beginning of the nineteenth century urging housewives to return to the old ways of curing hams and brewing that were falling out of use in the new factory age. The best known of these was by the political journalist William Cobbett, whose *Cottage Economy* of 1822 went through seventeen editions. Although Cobbett's rhetoric was grounded in his deeply felt pessimism about the social and political consequences of industrialization, there are scattered clues that his commitment to rural culture had put down even deeper roots in his psyche. In one peculiar passage he fantasizes about how he would always prefer to kiss the honest sweat of a busy baking housewife, rather than "lick the plaster from the cheek of a duchess." Such erotic kinks aside, Cobbett's nostalgia for a time when there was a more personal connection to the land was inherited by the *Book of Household Management,* written as it was for the first generation of middle-class women who were more likely to buy their ham ready-cured from the butcher than go through the whole complicated process of smoking it themselves.

Cobbett's most obvious successor allowed little that was erotic to creep into her bracing advice to rural housewives. *Cottage Comforts,* published three years later in 1825, was the work of Esther Hewlett Copley, who was determined to improve the lives of the working people whom she met in the course of her work as a Sunday School teacher. Copley's way, however, eschewed Cobbett's thunder in favour of gentle hints on cooking, furnishing, and rational recreation. A decade later she turned her attention to the middle-class housewife, in *The Housekeeper's Guide: or, A plain and practical system of domestic cookery,* which emphasized the moral duty of the middle-class mistress in keeping her expenditure in check by brushing up her arithmetic rather than her conversational Italian.

By the 1830s and 1840s much of the piety that infused Copley's texts had fallen away. Writers such as Sarah Stickney Ellis, author of the immensely popular *Wives of England* and *Daughters of England,* now promoted a more amenable, secularized morality in which the domestic sphere remained the natural theatre for female virtue but was no longer its only possible location. As part of this more relaxed attitude to the world beyond the front door, there emerged a thriving subgenre of instruction manuals that instructed young women, and sometimes men, on the correct way to make and receive morning calls, write a letter of condolence, or hail a passing bishop. By the first decade of Victoria's reign matters of etiquette—a word derived from the French word referring to the entrance "ticket" that one needed to attend a smart public event—were becoming increasingly pressing. As the population multiplied and relocated to towns and cities, middle-class life became fractured and anonymous. Instead of neighbours, there were people you met at dinner parties; colleagues replaced cousins as the main fixture in day-to-day life. In a world where you no longer automatically knew where someone came from, nor where they were going, it made sense to adopt a set of standardized procedures that allowed strangers to mix smoothly.

The older etiquette manuals, often written anonymously "by a member of the nobility," tended to imply that there was an unchanging set of social rules which, once mastered, provided a permanent key to polite circles. In fact, the exact opposite was true, as a more realistic generation of writers in the 1830s were increasingly happy to acknowledge: Charles Day, writing in his role of "Agogos," explained: "Of the Etiquette of a dinner party, it is extremely difficult to say anything, because fashions are continually changing, even at the best tables; and what is considered the height of good taste one year, is declared vulgar the next." Nonetheless, Day clearly had a pretty realistic idea about the kind of person he was addressing, for he felt it necessary to explain to his readers that knives should never go anywhere near mouths.

By the 1850s the etiquette books coming onto the market had shaken off any residual worry that they were corrupting the social order by showing the hoi polloi how to infiltrate the best circles. Books such as J. H. Walsh's *A Manual of Domestic Economy,* which includes a section on "modern manners," are matter-of-fact about giving the aspiring middle classes what they need to rub along in life (how long to leave it before visiting a friend's new baby, whether you need to provide refreshments for unexpected callers) without pretending to offer them an introduction to court circles. Isabella Beeton likewise displays little embarrassment about the task she has set herself, that of telling her reader how to perform the role of mistress in the modest middle-class home. For all her talk of house stewards and balls for sixty Beeton doesn't include tables of precedence or rules about writing letters to dukes. Aimed at a generation of women who were facing the intricacies of dinner parties and morning calls for the first time, Mrs. Beeton provides a full and frank run-down on what to wear when visiting a bereaved neighbour, how to reply to a dinner invitation and when to remove your white kid gloves in the course of the evening. This information is available to anyone who can muster the price of the book, just as the Epsom Grandstand is open to anyone who can pay for an entry ticket.

Only occasionally is there a hint that at the very edges of the middle classes there may be some women who will never get the hang of gloves. Under the heading "Duties of the Maid-of-all-Work" Beeton refers to the "small tradesman's wife" who is most likely to be this unlucky girl's mistress. Unlucky because, as Beeton points out, "although the class contains among them many excellent, kind-hearted women, it also contains some very rough specimens of the feminine gender. . . ." It was not just knowing when to take off your kid gloves that mattered, but the fact of owning them in the first place. For the first time in history, ordinary women of modest means were experiencing the privileges and burdens of consumer choice. By the 1850s your purchasing decisions about everything from blinds to paintings, pork chops to lavatory handles mattered in a way that they had not quite mattered before. Choosing one table meant rejecting another, opting for Staffordshire pottery implied that you thought it superior to Worcester. What you owned sent a message not simply about how much money you had at your disposal, but that infinitely trickier matter of your taste, which was, in turn, an indicator of your class or breeding. Advice writers were emphatic that "ladies" were instinctively elegant while *parvenues* tended to over-egg things with one frill too many.

This pressure on a middle-class woman to create and manage a well-stocked domestic interior was all the more intense now that she was increasingly unlikely to be engaged in other kinds of activities that contributed to the status of her household. Over the period from 1841 to 1914 the greatest change in women's occupations was the rising incidence of housewifery as the sole activity for married women. In 1851, one in four married women (with husbands alive) was employed. By 1911, the figure had dropped to one in ten. Mary Price's mother belonged to the last generation of British women to feel no shame at being seen contributing to the family enterprise, although even she had spent the final few years out of sight, invisibly making up the orders in the back room.

Over the past twenty years historians have debated the degree to which this mid-Victorian doctrine of "separate spheres," in which women presided over the home while men slayed dragons in the marketplace, represented a sharp break with what had gone before. Some have argued, for instance, that as early as the seventeenth century middle-class women were being encouraged to concentrate their energies on domestic work and disengage with active labour in the marketplace. Others have pointed out that this domestic work was still nonetheless economically significant, in the sense that its end products were the butter, cheese, cloth, and even wine that would otherwise have had to have been bought on the open market.

Whatever the exact speed and nature of the changes, it is still fair to say that by the middle decades of Victoria's reign the lives of middle-class women were significantly different from those that had gone before. Compared with her mother or grandmother, a *BOHM* reader was more likely to live in a town than the countryside, her day punctuated by encounters with people whom she hardly knew. She would own (or, until the Married Woman's Property Act of 1882, her husband would own) more manufactured goods and enjoy a wider choice of furnishings, kitchen equipment, styles of furniture, clothing, and foodstuffs than her mother could have dreamt of. Yet there would be new stresses and strains in her life. Her surroundings would be dirtier, mainly thanks to the widespread adoption of coal for fuel, and all those extra ornaments, carpets, and pianos attracted layers of dust. And finally, to make matters even more complicated, she was under a growing requirement not to be seen to be doing any kind of useful labour, which included housework and even childcare.

This was how things were meant to be. In fact, there is plenty of evidence to suggest that this ideology of separate spheres, which confined middle-class women to a non-productive home life, was lived out in a much fuzzier way. The domestic space was always as much an imaginary as an actual place, and its boundaries were constantly being tested and renegotiated as individual women found themselves unable or unwilling to live within its unbending walls. The instruction, for instance, that no middle-class lady would involve herself in housework or childcare was quite impossible to follow for all but perhaps 5 per cent of the population. The reality was that most households muddled along with a maid-of-all-work and a great deal of input from "the lady of the house," who was pretty much a full-time domestic worker. As the income of the household increased, a second servant, usually a nursemaid, would be added to its personnel. It was only once a very substantial annual income of £500 had been reached that sufficient servants could be employed to allow their mistress to become that thing she was supposed to have been all along, a lady of leisure.

Isabella Beeton was hardly the first person to have noticed this discrepancy between the theory and practice of mid-Victorian women's lives. Magazines, including the *Englishwoman's Domestic Magazine,* had for several years been running advice pieces that spoke straight to the heart of the problem (and it *was* a problem, the commentators all agreed). Often these articles were presented in the form of a serial story, with a fancily educated young matron getting into trouble with her housekeeping and turning to an older family member or friend for practical tips. The most successful examples of these domestic economy narratives were spun off into full-length books by Eliza Warren, a contributor to the *Ladies' Treasury* magazine who in 1864 produced *How I Managed my House on Two Hundred Pounds a Year,* soon to be followed by *My Lady-Help, and What She Taught Me.* One book that Mrs. Warren never wrote, but perhaps should have, was "How I Turned to Authorship in Order to Pay Someone Else to Do My Domestic Work for Me."

Leaving R. K. Philp's much smaller *The Practical Housewife* to one side, *Beeton's Book of Household Management* was the first full-length manual to help readers negotiate the strong contradictory currents that operated on women in the lower half of the middle class. It did this in two distinct ways. First, by allowing these tensions to coexist peaceably side by side (the book's large and capacious nature made this possible). Second, by overlaying them with a new discourse of domestic "management" that went a long way towards obscuring older tensions to do with class and gentility. The first of these effects was unintentional, the result of Isabella's usual method of filching material from earlier books written with very different audiences in mind. The second was a more self-conscious attempt to provide middle-class women with an approach to their daily lives that matched the one increasingly expected from men. Old trades such as engineering and medicine were in the process of professionalizing themselves, setting qualifying exams to restrict access to those who could show they had mastered a particular body of knowledge. Lower down the social scale, punctuality and efficiency were qualities that the bank clerk and factory foreman were bringing to their work in this newly mechanized age. Indeed, through the possession and deployment of such skills a man from a humble background might rise in the world, his professional accomplishments wiping away any lingering worries about his flat vowels or clumsy way with a knife. The science of household management, as formulated by Mrs. Beeton, offered women from the same modest backgrounds the opportunity to feel a sense of mastery as they presided over a household that ran like clockwork.

Isabella Beeton realized what historians have not always quite understood: the Victorian middle-class home, far from being removed from the public sphere, was intimately connected with it. All those purchases of fans, pianos, and carpets drove the economy forward just as surely as the factory and workshop clattering far into the night. What is more, in the late 1850s, when the book was being written, the working classes were still as likely to receive their training for life within the middle-class home as they were down a mine or out in the fields. Managing your servants properly was not just about creating a harmonious environment in which to live, it also meant creating the kind of disciplined, deferential workforce which Britain needed if it was to maintain its position as the world's premier nation. Domestic life may have been geographically removed from the streets, shops, warehouses, and factories of industrial production and commercial traffic, but psychically, socially and even economically it was wedded to the world beyond the front door.

Beeton's Preface opens with that famous sigh: "I must frankly own, that if I had known, beforehand, that this book would have cost me the labour which it has, I should never have been courageous enough to commence it." Some commentators have taken this literally, using it as evidence of Beeton's peculiar conscientiousness. In fact, the lament is a standard one, which had appeared at the beginning of household and cookery books from the seventeenth century, presumably as a way of neutralizing any suspicion that the writer had embraced authorship as a way of evading the domestic duties that she is busy urging on her readers. Beeton's "four years' incessant labour" is presented as a gift arising spontaneously out of concern for her countrywomen's housekeeping, rather than as what it actually was—a shrewd investment of time and energy in a product aimed at a new niche market.

Perhaps, too, this is the reason why one particular myth about the book's genesis was allowed to flourish. Dorling folklore has Isabella, during those early months of married life at Pinner, searching for a housekeeping guide and asking in despair, possibly of one of her sisters, "why has no one written a book—a *good* book for brides? To help them learn these things?" before deciding to do so herself. This doesn't ring true. The marketplace already had a good selection of housekeeping manuals, a fact of which Sam would be only too aware. An altogether more likely scenario would be Isabella casting around for such a book, asking Sam whether he knew of a good one, and together the sharp young couple discussing whether there was a gap in the market for another.

The Beetons, however, were careful to nurture the myth that Mrs. Beeton was writing out of the goodness of her heart, sorrowing over the low standards of housekeeping among British women. These shoddy levels, explains Mrs. Beeton firmly in her Preface, are the reason why so many married men prefer to spend their evenings "at their clubs, well-ordered taverns, and dining-houses" instead of where they should be, snug in their well-serviced homes. Nicola Humble, in her excellent Introduction to a recent, abridged edition of the *BOHM*, suggests that here is the real reason that Isabella Beeton wrote her book: "It is no exaggeration to say that Isabella Beeton's preoccupation with getting her husband to spend more time at home was in no small part responsible for the new cult of domesticity that was to play such a major role in mid-Victorian life."

The problem with this hypothesis is that there is no evidence that Isabella's housekeeping was ever a bone of contention in her marriage, let alone that she ever managed to stop Sam spending so much time at work. A far more likely explanation, given what we know of Isabella's usual methodology, is that she simply paraphrased Hannah Woolley, who urged her readers in 1673: "And let what-ever you provide be so neatly and cleanly drest, that his fare, though ordinary, may engage his appetite, and disingage his fancy from Taverns, which many are compell'd to make use of by reason of the continual and daily dissatisfactions they find at home." Variations on Woolley's theme can be heard echoing loudly through household management books down the centuries. Keeping your husband close to home by offering him delicious food, virtually invisible children, and a warm bed had been the standard formula for domestic bliss peddled in household management books almost since the genre began.

More novel altogether is Beeton's next sentence, in which she famously describes the mistress as "The Commander of an Army" whose organizational skills and exemplary efficiency provide the leading example for her well-drilled domestic staff. In the 1850s the prevailing model for the middle-class wife and mother was "The Angel in the House," an almost incarnate creature of total virtue whose power lay in her capacity to influence and inspire rather than draw up plans and bark orders. In the space of this single sentence Mrs. Beeton provided a new way for the hard-pushed middle-class woman, one who had neither the emotional nor the financial resources to imitate an angel, to think about her life. Instead of being a failed member of the heavenly host—with three bawling children and one witless girl to help, it was hard to cultivate the required serenity—the lower-middle-class woman could feel a sense of accomplishment as she rolled up her sleeves and endeavoured to bring order and method to the chaos that was always in danger of engulfing her.

Yet the moment she had written these two sentences Isabella seems to have realized their potential to unsettle and even offend. For no sooner has she elevated her reader to the rank of commander than she immediately makes it clear that the power that goes with the position is to be channelled exclusively into the domestic sphere: "Of all those acquirements, which more particularly belong to the feminine character, there are none which take a higher rank, in our estimation, than such as enter into a knowledge of household duties; for on those are perpetually dependent the happiness, comfort, and well-being of a family." To further neutralize any suggestion that she is urging her readers on to a dangerous independence, Beeton then pitches straight into a quotation from "the author of The Vicar of Wakefield" (Oliver Goldsmith), who intones: "The modest virgin, the prudent wife, and the careful matron, are much more serviceable in life than petticoated philosophers, blustering heroines, or virago queens." Or lady commanders, presumably.

Having relocated her reader back where she belongs, in a domestic role untainted by the impulse towards power or control, Beeton then sets out a system for household management that virtually turns the private household into a small and efficient factory. Early rising, cleanliness, frugality, and not wasting your time chatting with women friends were all qualities that had been routinely urged on the reader of household manuals since the seventeenth century. For Beeton to include them in her book was to do no more than acknowledge the conventions of the genre. What was different, though, was the way she sustained and developed these precepts into something approaching a system of rational domestic "science." The tables showing how many servants could be afforded on a particular income, the detailed line drawings and explanatory notes on various types of stoves, the insistence on saving money by bulk purchase, the explanation that it was a waste of coal and candle for the housemaid to get up before seven in the winter, all proceed from a view of the household as an integrated mechanism, run on sound commercial principles rather than the inspiration or love of an angel in the house.

To hammer the message home, Beeton concludes her section on the duties of the mistress with a rousing reminder of the strategic significance of her role: "She ought always to remember that she is the first and the last, the Alpha and the Omega in the government of her establishment. . . . She is, therefore, a person of far more importance in a community than she usually thinks she is."

Having done the daring thing of raising the dignity of housework to that of any rational occupation carried on by men—railway clerking, land agenting, shopkeeping—Beeton then does what she always does when feeling nervous about her own authority and takes refuge in a qualifying quotation, in this case from "the pious prelate Jeremy Taylor." Taylor, true to form, likes his ladies to exert their power through influence rather than command: "A good wife is Heaven's last best gift to man,—his angel and minister of graces innumerable,—his gem of many virtues,—his casket of jewels—her voice is sweet music, her smiles his brightest day;—her kiss, the guardian of his innocence;—her arms, the pale of his safety, the balm of his health, the balsam of his life;—her industry, his surest wealth;—her economy, his safest steward." By adopting a seesaw pattern of authorial assertion, followed immediately by a muffling quotation from "a great man," Beeton manages to set out a radical model of domestic femininity without frightening the horses.

Domestic frugality is returned to in paragraph 15 (Beeton's practice of numbering each of the book's paragraphs boosts the sense that the reader is being presented with a set of definitive rules, rather than a series of observations loosely embedded in running copy). She follows the example of her immediate predecessors by urging her readers to make use of a pre-printed account book (Mrs. Rundell even tells you where you can buy one) in which every expenditure is written down: "then, at the end of the month, let these various payments be ranged under their specific heads of Butcher, Baker, &c; and thus will be seen the proportions paid to each tradesman, and any one month's expenses may be contrasted with another." Beeton is clear, as Kitchiner and Rundell have been before her, that "In Marketing . . . the best articles are the cheapest." If a young bride is unsure as to how to pick the right items, "a little practice and experience will soon teach her who are the best tradespeople to deal with, and what are the best provisions to buy." By using her growing expertise in the marketing process Beeton's mistress adds capital value to the family enterprise, just as her mother and grandmother before her. The significant difference is that Beeton's mistress needs a book not only to tell her how to do it, but to reassure her that it is an entirely proper thing for her to do.

From here Beeton proceeds to the business of hiring, firing, and keeping servants. The disproportionate amount of space she dedicates to the subject suggests that she assumes that she is writing for families who are new to this defining aspect of middle-class life. And even if Beeton's reader had grown up in a household where there were servants, she would be only too well aware how vexed the whole business was becoming. With more and more families requiring at least one maid, and other kinds of employment opening up to the working classes, the market was decisively tipped in the servant's favour, especially in London. In this culture of quick turnover it was unlikely that you would know anything about the girl who you were considering having to live in your house. Hence Beeton's insistence on the importance of asking for a personal recommendation, and the equally important duty of the householder not to fake a good "character" for a maidservant merely because it was the quickest way of getting rid of her. This advice was pretty much universal in the household manuals at the time, but it does look as though Beeton took her lead specifically from *The Complete Servant* by Sarah and Samuel Adams. This book was purported to have been written by a married couple who had risen in service and who, like Glasse and Raffald before them, were aiming to advise both employers and employees on how to promote a more harmonious domestic environment.

In the next section, which explains how to deal with morning calls and dinner parties, Beeton follows the technique that she uses in the cookery sections of her book and simply copies out information from earlier texts. Her source here is a book called *Domestic Duties* by Mrs. Parkes, which was written in 1824. This was the same "late Mrs. Parkes" who had contributed the household sections in Webster's *Encyclopaedia* of 1844. The fact that Beeton's source material for this part of her book was thirty-five years old by the time she came to use it verbatim is particularly striking. As we have seen, most commentators agreed that the rules of social engagement were changing fast, to match the modernization of public and collective life. Yet here was Beeton using information that had been written in the wake of the Regency. The reason why her readers were not jolted by any obvious anachronism is because, as the century progressed, ideas about etiquette were collapsing into definitions of behaviour that were more concerned with the inner, moral life than the outer worldly one. Thus being interested in other people, sensitive to their feelings and tactful about their failings became as important as knowing exactly what "rsvp" stood for. (Having said that, Beeton still feels the need to explain to any of her readers who may not know.)

Whatever the exact reason that Mrs. Parkes's advice managed to sound apt and fresh, Beeton was clearly happy with the effect. Her borrowings from Parkes are so extended that, once again, one wonders whether the fact that the lady was safely dead accounts for the fact that Beeton felt no worries about appropriating her words. Here is Mrs. Parkes on how to behave during social calls: "Morning visits should not be long. In this species of intercourse, the manners should be easy and cheerful, and the subjects of conversation such as may be easily terminated." In Mrs. Beeton's rendering this becomes: "During these visits, the manners should be easy and cheerful, and the subjects of conversation such as may be readily terminated." In fact, Beeton clearly feels so unsure herself about what is supposed to go on during a morning call that she relies entirely on Mrs. Parkes. Thus Mrs. Parkes explains that "the occupations of drawing, music and reading, should be suspended on the entrance of morning visitors. But if a lady be engaged with light needlework, and none other is appropriate in the drawing-room[,] it promotes ease, and [it] is not inconsistent with good breeding to continue it during conversation; particularly if the visit be protracted or the visitors be gentlemen." In Beeton's rendering this becomes: "the occupations of drawing, music or reading should be suspended on the entrance of morning visitors. If a lady, however, be engaged with light needlework, and none other is appropriate in the drawing-room, it may not be, under some circumstances, inconsistent with good breeding to quietly continue it during conversation, particularly if the visit be protracted, or the visitors be gentlemen."

Significantly, Beeton's insecurity extends even into the dining room, that domain in which popular imagination has always assumed her to be supremely at ease. Mrs. Parkes advises: "When Dinner is announced, the gentleman of the house selects the lady most distinguished by rank, or respectable by age; or the one who is the greatest stranger in the party, to lead to the dining room, where he places her by himself. If her husband be of the party, he takes the lady of the house to her place at table, and seats himself beside her." In Beeton's version this becomes: "Dinner being announced, the host offers his arm to, and places on his right hand at the dinner-table, the lady to whom he desires to pay most respect, either on account of her age, position, or from her being the greatest stranger in the party. If this lady be married and her husband present, the latter takes the hostess to her place at table, and seats himself at her right hand."

But just when one has Beeton down as a hack, a sewer together of other people's bits and pieces, a paragraph appears that reconnects the reader to a sense that there is a living, breathing individual behind the text who has direct experience of the dilemmas described. Paragraph 34, sandwiched between brisk instructions for sending out invitations and Mrs. Parkes's rehashed rules of precedence for dinner, seems to talk directly to the anxious reader who is waiting for the curtain to go up on her big performance. "The Half-Hour before Dinner has always been considered as the great ordeal through which the mistress, in giving a dinner-party, will either pass with flying colours, or, lose many of her laurels. The anxiety to receive her guests,—her hope that all will be present in due time,—her trust in the skill of her cook, and the attention of the other domestics, all tend to make these few minutes a trying time." But if the reader is expecting any sisterly confidences as to how these tricky moments are handled at 2 Chandos Villas, she is about to be disappointed. Instead of reassuring the hostess that she, too, gets anxious before a dinner party, Mrs. Beeton merely advises her to "display no kind of agitation, but show her tact in suggesting light and cheerful subjects of conversation, which will be much aided by the introduction of any particular new book, curiosity of art, or article of vertu, which may pleasantly engage the attention of the company."

Having dealt with the duties of the mistress, Mrs. Beeton now turns to the housekeeper, a rare creature found only in the most magnificent households where the lady of the house is hardly involved in its day-to-day running. These duties, as Beeton describes them, divide pretty much between those that in reality would be absorbed into the work of the reader/mistress herself (keeping an account book, checking the linen) and those that are relevant only to an aristocratic great house (the production of ice cream, desserts and cordials in the stillroom). And, indeed, as Beeton herself admits in small print, this busy stillroom is itself something of a nostalgic fantasy, belonging to what she vaguely designates as the days of "auld lang syne" (in fact the seventeenth century) when the great country houses of England were virtually self-sufficient.

It is at this point, only twenty-four pages into the *BOHM*, that the section on household advice is abruptly interrupted by the cookery section, which then proceeds to run over the next nine hundred pages. It is only in Chapter XLI, "Domestic Servants," that we return once again to household matters and a detailed description of the duties of the remaining servants. Why did Beeton arrange the book in this oddly broken way? A more obvious organization would be to move from the section on the housekeeper to a description of the cook's duties and then seamlessly into Chapter XLI and from there to the present end of the book, to be followed by the cookery section. In this way all the household personnel from the mistress to the monthly nurse would be marshalled in descending rank at the front of the book, to be followed by the specialized chapters on "Rearing Children," "The Doctor," and "Legal Memoranda." Only at this point, after the end of the present Chapter XLIV, would it make sense to begin the cookery section. According to this reordering the book would consist of two distinct parts, the housekeeping and general information sections, followed by the food section (marketing information, recipes, dinner plans).

We know that, until March 1861, Sam and Isabella had no clear idea about how long the book was going to be. However, from the advertising blurb that he wrote, Sam clearly believed that it was the cookery section of the book, and the recipes in particular, that were going to be the main selling point. It made sound commercial sense to move the cookery section to the front of the book so that this part appeared early on in the serialization and would benefit from the initial burst of publicity. In fact, it was as early as the first issue in November 1859 that the first parts of the cookery section appeared, quite possibly timed to take advantage of the fact that high-spending and big-eating Christmas was approaching.

Chapter XLI, which deals with the duties of different kinds of specialist servants, from butler to under-nursemaid, are lifted from a variety of sources, including the Adamses' and Mrs. Parkes's books. As a result Beeton's tone swoops between several registers. Her opening remarks are very much in the serious, caring mistress mode, taking issue with the tendency of "Society"—that is fashionable aristocratic circles together with the nouveaux riches who long to join them—to speak snobbishly about servants as if they were "the greatest plague in life." These silly, careless people complain that "domestics no longer know their place; that the introduction of cheap silks and cottons . . . have removed the landmarks between the mistress and her maid." Such employers have only themselves to blame: their over-attention to superficial appearances, which includes employing footmen on the sole basis of their height and the shape of their calves, means they have set the tone for a shallow household based on affectation and appearance rather than solid social bonds. Instead Beeton posits the example of a moral, happy home where servants are treated "like reasonable beings" and in return reward their employers with years of sustained and loyal service.

The real point about Beeton's section on the duties of the footman and the housemaid is that it allows her to follow the Adamses' very useful plan of including recipes for home-made products from pomade to boot polish together with detailed instructions on how to carry out basic tasks (cleaning a water jug without breaking it, lighting a fire). At times Beeton unconsciously betrays the fact that she knows perfectly well that she is being read by the person who will actually carry out the task, rather than by the supervising mistress or housekeeper. Thus she periodically slips from the third person into a direct imperative, as when she declares "fill [the decanters] about two thirds with hot but not boiling water" or "mix as much hartshorn powder as will be required, into a thick paste, with cold water or spirits of wine." One alternative explanation could be that Beeton is imagining herself being read by the footman or housemaid who was to carry out the task. But this is unlikely since servants learned from practice and example rather than book reading. It is far more likely that Beeton imagined herself being read by someone like Mary Price, thumbing through the *BOHM* for tips on how to clean her wedding china without chipping it.

At times Beeton's carelessness about continuity of tone and address reaches baffling proportions. The section on "The Coachhouse and Stables" not only sounds as if it has been written by a man, but includes an anecdote that begins, "The writer was once employed to purchase a horse for a country friend" and goes on to tell an elaborate story of equine know-how that only makes sense if the speaker is male. Any reader still under the impression that Mrs. Isabella Beeton penned every word that went into her book would surely have been brought up short by the thought of their lady editor hanging round stables discussing horsey form (in fact, as chance would have it, this was something that the Epsom Isabella might conceivably have done, but the point is that, in this instance, she almost certainly didn't). Likewise under the duties of the footman the writer breaks off to tell an anecdote whereby "he" was misannounced by a careless footman and found himself being briefed by a solicitor on the opposing side of a legal case in which he was currently involved. Taken together these anecdotes suggest strongly that it was Sam, who loved both horses and litigation, who wrote the section on the stables. The fact that no attempt was made to smooth over the odd shifts in register suggests that the book was put together at great speed and carelessness. Even though the errors must have been spotted when the book appeared in serial form, it was not thought necessary to go to the extra expense of resetting the print for the single-volume version. Nor was there any point in including them in the list of errata: the only mistakes that are acknowledged concern the recipes.

One section that we can be fairly certain Isabella Beeton did write was the one on nursing an invalid, which, following her usual plan, she included under a description of the duties of the sick-nurse. In most of the households for which Mrs. Beeton was writing, looking after an ill member of the family fell on the mistress of the household (public hospitals were still places of dirt and destitution). Beeton had already followed the earlier example of Mrs. Rundell, among others, of including a whole chapter on "Invalid Cookery," which turned out to be an unappetizing affair of barley gruel, baked beef tea, eel broth, and stewed rabbits in milk. Now she turned her attention to the daily disciplines required to nurse an acutely or chronically ill person within the bosom of the family.

This was an area of which Isabella had little or no experience, so she turned to the most obvious source material available to her, Florence Nightingale's *Notes on Nursing*. Published at the same time as the early installments of the *BOHM* first appeared on the bookstands, Miss Nightingale's book had been written in the wake of her Crimean experience. In perhaps the most blatant borrowing of the whole *BOHM,* Beeton lifts whole sections from Nightingale's manual, while mentioning it by name just once, under the section concerned with the nursemaid. Instead, she throws in an occasional "Miss Nightingale says" to cover herself against any charge of plagiarism. Trotting briskly through the main issues, Beeton (or rather Nightingale) warns against closed windows, stagnant slop pails, and, the worst sin of all, whispering about the patient just within his earshot.

The three remaining chapters—"On the Rearing of Children," "General Medicine," and "Legal Advice"—were, according to Mrs. Beeton in her Preface, "contributed by gentlemen full entitled to confidence; those on medical subjects by an experienced surgeon, and the legal matter by a solicitor." In fact, the doctor had not even written his chapters specifically for the *BOHM*. Rather they had originally appeared as a series of regular articles within the *EDM* and had simply been run together to make two decent-length chapters.

What stands out about these final three chapters is the contrast they make with what has gone before. In one's mounting incredulity at the amount of prose that Beeton simply stole from other sources, it is easy to lose sight of just how skilfully she deployed her purloined material. For compared with the meandering and confusing style of the doctor, Beeton's sentence structure starts to seem like a model of clarity and impact. It would, for example, be impossible to imagine her producing the following sentence from "On the Rearing of Children":

> We turn to the foetor and darkness that, in some obscure court, attend the robust brood who, coated in dirt, and with mud and refuse for playthings, live and thrive, and grow into manhood, and, in contrast to the pale face and flabby flesh of the aristocratic child, exhibit strength, vigour, and well-developed frames, and our belief in the potency of the life-giving elements of air, light, and cleanliness receives a shock that, at first sight, would appear fatal to the implied benefits of these, in reality, all-sufficient attributes of health and life.

Mrs. Beeton could have said the same thing—isn't it odd how working-class children, with all their disadvantages, can still manage to thrive?—in half the space.

The lawyer's chapter is about half the length of the doctor's preceding two. The emphasis is again on explaining those parts of professional lore that are most likely to impinge on lay people. House purchase, rental agreements, and will-making are all explained in detail, but the most interesting paragraphs are those that spell out clearly what rights a woman has in relation to a deserting or abusive spouse. Since the legal chapter, like those written by the doctor, consists of a series of the magazine's columns simply run together, it reflects the same tone: broadly supportive of women's economic and social rights but stopping short of any radical declarations that might upset a general readership. Oddly, though, the lawyer tends to assume a mainly male audience, which only adds to the multivocal effect of this last part of the book.

Before one dismisses the *BOHM* as a ragbag of other people's material which, by some stroke of collective amnesia, managed to go down in history as an original and authoritatively voiced piece of work, it is worth considering just what Isabella Beeton achieved. For although there is scarcely a line in the book that can be said to belong to her, still she did something unique with the material that she borrowed. She turned it into that thing most beloved by the mid-Victorians, a *system* which, if properly applied, would produce a guaranteed result—in this case domestic well-being. For the vast majority of middle-class women who had no choice but to do some of their own housework, here was a text that validated their activities. Instead of feeling embarrassed or diminished at having to count the pennies and keep a close eye on the servant (and there probably was only one) the Beeton reader could feel that she was engaged in work that was, in its own way, as skilled and as vital as that performed by her husband. She was, as Mrs. Beeton had so wisely remarked, "a person of far more importance in a community than she usually thinks she is."

INTERLUDE

Note—Dinners à la Russe are scarcely suitable for small establishments; a large number of servants being required to carve; and to
help the guests; besides there being a necessity for more plates,
dishes, knives, forks, and spoons, than are usually to be found in
any other than a very large establishment.

ISABELLA BEETON,
Book of Household Management

AT THE BEGINNING OF the nineteenth century the standard way of
arranging a formal dinner—known as Service à la Française—went like
this. Each of the three courses consisted of a set of different dishes, both
sweet and savoury, that were placed on the table from which people
helped themselves and each other. Ideally, everything was arranged with
textbook symmetry, with a spine of big dishes down the centre and, in
Beeton's own words, "the spaces filled up with the smaller dishes, fruit,
and flowers, taking care that the flavours and colours contrast nicely, and
that no two dishes of a sort come together." When one course ended, the
servants cleared the dishes and the next course was laid out with equally
elaborate attention to detail.

The effect was spectacular and it meant, as the hostess, that you got to
show off the look, if not the taste, of your food to its best advantage. A
dish of lobster provided visual balance for a Veal and Ham Pie, a Charlotte Russe à la Vanille nodded across the table to its opposite number, a
Savoy Cake. But there was a distinct downside too. Since guests weren't

1887.—DINNER FOR 18 PERSONS.

First Course.

Stewed Eels.	Mock Turtle Soup, removed by Cod's Head and Shoulders. Vase of Flowers. Clear Oxtail Soup, removed by Fried Filleted Soles.	Red Mullet.

Entrées.

Ragoût of Lobster.	Riz de Veau aux Tomates. Vase of Flowers. Poulet à la Marengo.	Cotelettes de Porc à la Robert.

Second Course.

Boiled Turkey and Celery Sauce.	Roast Turkey. Pigeon Pie. Vase of Flowers. Tongue, garnished. Saddle of Mutton.	Boiled Ham.

Third Course.

Charlotte à la Parisienne.		Pheasants, removed by Plum-pudding. Jelly. Vase of Flowers. Jelly. Snipes, removed by Pommes à la Condé.		Apricot-Jam Tartlets.
	Cream.		Cream.	
Mince Pies.				Maids of Honour.

Dinner laid out for Service à la Française, in which many dishes are placed on the table at once and diners help themselves and each other.

allowed into the dining room until the table was set up, it meant that the food was already cold by the time the meal started. And even once seated you couldn't be sure of getting the dish you wanted, since you were entirely dependent on negotiating with your neighbours to stretch and pass and lean. And the waste was criminal. Up to half of everything got thrown away.

Naturally, it didn't take long for the middle classes to tweak the format to suit themselves and their dining tables, which tended on the whole not to resemble something that had been salvaged from Versailles. According to the new, hybrid custom, all the food for each course continued to be present on the table, but with the difference that the hostess served the soup and the host carved the joint before passing round individual plates. However, when it came to getting your hands on the entrées (side dishes such as Fricasseed Chicken or Curried Rabbit) or the third course (delicacies including, oddly, both game and fruit creams), it was still every man and woman for themselves.

Well before the middle of the nineteenth century the smart money had moved on to Service à la Russe, which had only the vaguest connection with what actually went on in the dining rooms of St. Petersburg. According to this system the courses were rationalized into more coherent groupings (a typically Victorian strategy) and the carving was done by a servant at the sideboard. Instead of the dishes themselves providing the visual pleasure, the table was decorated, in Beeton's words, with "flowers and plants in fancy flowerpots down the middle." The guests were happy because they got their dinner hot, but the strain for the hostess was huge. Each individual dish now got more attention, that is scrutiny, from the guests. What's more, you needed a tribe of servants, hired for the night if that's all you could manage, to make sure that every diner had exactly what they wanted (even passing the salt to your neighbour was now frowned on). Trickiest of all: you needed double or even treble the usual amount of crockery and cutlery to cope with the seemingly endless roll call of courses.

This is the reason why, anachronistically for 1861, Mrs. Beeton gave all but two of her eighty-one dinner plans in the manner of Service à la Française, even though she had a clear preference for the more "enjoyable" Service à la Russe. She understood her readers' houses and knew the way their minds worked. Service à la Russe was all very well, but it required the diner to have a very sure grasp of etiquette, something that Beeton realized was not necessarily the case with the constituency she was addressing. What's more, the mistress might find her dinner table, cutlery and even housemaids all shown up as inadequate, setting the scene for an evening of ritual humiliation. In the circumstances Mrs. Beeton believed that what would work best was the old-fashioned, companionable, hit-and-miss, cold-to-table, help-your-neighbours Service à la Française, or at least its English variation. Despite the danger of looking dowdy, Mrs. Beeton let real life win.

❋

CHAPTER NINE

PERFECT FASHION AND ELEGANCE

IN 1859, THE YEAR THAT ISABELLA turned twenty-three and Sam twenty-eight, the Beetons appear all at once crisper, clearer, and finally in full colour. Their talk is suddenly familiar—a chatter of train times, restaurant meals, hiring nannies, window shopping—and their dilemmas—stubborn officials, lost purses, creepy colleagues, watching the pennies—make them seem real. Instead of loopy love letters there is brisk and purposeful talk. In place of a highly charged courtship there is a marriage and business partnership that works. And, finally, instead of pinched monochrome, there is drenching colour.

In the early summer of 1859 Isabella gave birth to another boy, another Samuel Orchart. The two years since she had last been viably pregnant were, according to family whispers, punctuated by miscarriages. This symptomatic pattern fits with what is known of syphilitic mothers during the first few years following infection. For this reason—and also because of that dreadful early loss of the first little Samuel Orchart—this child's arrival was greeted with what sounds, even at this distance, like slightly hysterical joy. Cards and presents poured in to 2 Chandos Villas.

That year was a turning point for Isabella in other ways too. By the time of the baby's birth on 3 June she had broken the back of her labours on the *BOHM* and only a few months later Sam was announcing the publication of the first forty-eight-page installment. Even by the usual hyperbolic standards of S. O. Beeton, the *BOHM* was given a huge puff in the Christmas number of the *EDM,* which carried a special four-page insert in shrieking yellow. After a lengthy description of the book, which included the usual promise that everything had been personally tested by Mrs. Beeton, the Prospectus (the technical name for such a document) went on to announce the by now familiar system of sweeteners. If you managed to get 250 of your friends to take out a subscription to the *BOHM* then you received a ten-guinea gold watch from the grateful publisher. Fifty subscribers netted you a gold pencil case and, for those who enrolled twenty-five names, there was a choice between a silver pencil case and a silk umbrella. Even if you managed to find only ten subscribers, you were still the lucky recipient of "A Beautiful Steel Engraving."

It was at this point that Isabella must have undergone some kind of internal transformation, a shift in self-perception. For there is simply no other way to explain what happened next. With the back of the work on the *BOHM* broken and a baby in her arms, this would have been the obvious moment for the young Mrs. Beeton to take a step back into the anonymous domesticity of 2 Chandos Villas. She could have spent the next two years serving out her time on the *BOHM*, copying out the chapters on servants from other people's books, and playing with lovely little Samuel Orchart. The dark days of childlessness were over, the *BOHM* had served its purpose as a substitute and salve. Now might be the appropriate moment to start living a life like that of her step-sister Jane, who was about to marry the compulsively sociable Epsom solicitor George White, move into one of the handsomest houses in Epsom, and give birth to eleven strapping children.

But Isabella did not do that. Instead of stepping away from the firm of S. O. Beeton she plunged further in. From being a printer's wife who helped out by providing free copy for her husband's publications, Isabella now became a full-time journalist, editor and publisher in her own right. By the time the *EDM* was relaunched in a new and luxurious format in May 1860, Isabella was installed as "The Editress" alongside Sam who remained "The Editor." Instead of making piecemeal contributions from home, Isabella started to accompany Sam on his daily journey to the office, which made her a virtually unique sight in the smoky, clubbable, and overwhelmingly male first-class carriage of the early morning commuter train. Nor was "Editress" a sinecure or mere term of convenience. Isabella's remit at the magazine was vastly expanded, for as well as continuing to work on the cookery and household content, she was now in charge of the radically overhauled fashion coverage.

Isabella took on this new role because it suited her and because Sam needed her as never before. The "house" (as it was known) of S. O. Beeton was undergoing a rapid expansion. It had recently started to publish two successful part works—*Beeton's Book of Household Management* and *Beeton's Dictionary of Universal Information*—both of which in time would become high-selling single volumes. Other part works were in preparation, and Sam was also picking up once more on the book publishing side of his operation, producing both original and classic fiction. In addition he was getting ready to relaunch the two periodicals that had made his name, the *Boy's Own Magazine* and the *English-woman's Domestic Magazine,* as luxury products. Finally, as if this weren't enough upheaval, he was on the move again. From 1 June 1860 S. O. Beeton would be operating out of 248 Strand, three hundred yards or so further west from the old addresses in Fleet Street and Bouverie Street. Splashed across the exterior of the handsome building were the words "BOY'S OWN MAGAZINE" and "THE ENGLISH-WOMAN'S DOMESTIC MAGAZINE." What Henry Dorling had once sneeringly referred to as the young man's "passion for advertising" had reached new heights.

This shift away from the artisanal print sheds of the City towards the shops and consumer culture of the West End was highly significant. The Beetons, just like the British middle classes to whose desires they so expertly catered, were feeling flush. By the early 1860s the domestic landscape was furnished with more goods than ever before. Different spaces, activities, and even times of the day now required a growing number of props and markers. The table that looked right in the kitchen was wrong in the parlour, the dress that carried you through a morning at home needed changing by the time it came to making afternoon calls. Eating fish called for fish knives, photographs needed frames. Everyday items—anything from collars to pie dishes—were replaced not because they had worn out but because something more fashionable had appeared on the market. And increasingly that market was not the local haberdasher's or the dressmaker in the next town, but nothing less than the world itself. London was no longer a distant dream that you might never realize in the course of a long lifetime. It was, instead, the place you looked to for news, gossip, inspiration for what to wear and how to be. Life had never been so good, so busy, or quite so baffling.

Against this new, highly detailed backdrop the existing *English-*

woman's Domestic Magazine was beginning to look dowdy. Its main fashion feature, the "Practical Dress Instructor," was genuinely innovative, but its format of a no-nonsense description of an item of clothing followed by a scaled-down pattern showing how to lay out the pieces on the fabric was hardly chic. "Mlle. Roche's Fashion Notes," a later addition, tried hard but sounded pedestrian and parochial (despite her promising name there was little sense that Mlle. Roche spent much time trend spotting on the boulevards). If the magazine was to work as well in the 1860s as it had during its first decade then it needed to graft a new sense of style and luxe onto its continuing heartland of domestic know-how and making do.

The boldest way to achieve this was to look to Paris, which was home to high fashion—not simply to women like the Empress Eugénie who embodied it, but to the *ateliers* that produced it and to the premium magazines that disseminated intelligence about it around the world. One of the best of these publications was *Le Moniteur de la Mode,* which ran parallel texts in both French and English and was read as far away as America. The key selling point of *Le Moniteur* was the stunning colour plates, produced each month by top graphic artists, including the prince of them all, Jules David. David had started as a book illustrator, and he brought some of that sense of narrative and place to his fashion plates. In his drawings, which have since become classics of their kind, groups of plump-faced young women gossip at balls, stroll along promenades, and dally in parks. Each of them wears an exquisite outfit, made up of several layers of dress, jacket, and shawl and carefully accessorized with parasols, hats, and the occasional over-dressed child looking like a stuffed sofa. But it is the elaborate backgrounds that most surely mark these out as the work of David. His ladies either linger in the dining room and the boudoir, or else they step out smartly at Longchamps or Auteuil. Sometimes they are visiting the Alps, other times it is the Riviera. The mood is expensive, aspirational, just the right side of daunting.

The fashions that *Le Moniteur de la Mode* showcased could not be bought from a shop or couturier, even in Paris. They needed to be made up, either by a local dressmaker or, if she were ambitiously handy, by the reader herself. To this end, each issue of the magazine carried a full-size paper pattern folded into the magazine which, when smoothed out, would provide a template from which to cut the pieces that were stitched together to produce the final outfit. This was quite different from the

EDM's "Practical Dress Instructor," which simply sketched out a minia-ture diagram of pattern placement from which the reader was obliged to produce her own template. It was this combination of beautiful artwork and free dressmaking patterns that accounted for the fact that, by the time it found its way across the Channel and into London stationers, *Le Moniteur de la Mode* sold for a sky-high 3s 6d.

For some time now Sam and Isabella had cast knowledgeable and cov-etous eyes on *Le Moniteur.* Glamorous fashion plates had been seen before in British magazines, but they had belonged to the older genera-tion of shilling ladies' magazines, the kind of publications that had petered out under the mid-century success of the more workaday tup-penny magazines. Times, though, had changed and now it seemed only right to harness some of that upscale chic to a relaunched *EDM*. The cul-tural fit between the two magazines was high, for *Le Moniteur,* like the *EDM,* was a family affair. The owner was Adolphe Goubaud, who over-saw the artwork, the fashion copy was written by his wife, and in time the magazine would be taken over by their son Abel who also produced some of the increasingly luscious fashion plates. Over the next few years the Beetons and the Goubauds would become not only firm friends but part-ners in a pattern business run out of an office virtually next door to 248 Strand. At this point, though, the relationship was tentative, formal. After a brief correspondence with M. Goubaud in March 1860, Sam and Isabella arranged to visit Paris to explore whether some kind of reciprocal deal could be struck between their respective publications.

Part of the reason why the Beetons suddenly take a step towards us around this time is that Isabella kept a diary of this Parisian trip that still survives. It is written down in a tiny maroon leather engagement diary, which originally came with a little pencil. All the entries are written in soft lead, which means that they are beginning to smudge. Ever matter-of-fact, Isabella fills the pygmy pages with dates, places, faces, and the cost of everything, in the process showing herself to be a skilled narrator of her own life. Ridiculous strangers and travel mishaps are described along-side business meetings and contractual letters. She has a quick eye for character, knows how to shape a story. But anyone hoping to wrench psy-chological insights from this dove-grey script will be disappointed. This is an engagement diary after all, the place where personal life meets public obligation and the crucial crossing points get duly noted. It is not a jour-nal, a repository for Isabella's deepest wishes or private thoughts.

The very first entry in the diary reminds us just what dynamos the Beetons were. The night before setting out to France on 7 March they had stayed with the Swaintons, old friends of Sam's clan who lived in Watling Street, the very place where he had been born almost exactly twenty-nine years earlier. An exhilarating night at the Lyceum, where they saw *School for Scandal* and *The Forty Thieves,* was followed by a very late supper and bed at three o'clock. Rising a mere three and a half hours later, Isabella and Sam probably walked to nearby London Bridge station where they caught the boat train. With no intention of sleeping on the journey to Folkestone, Isabella busies herself observing the other people in their second-class carriage: "Travelling companions a french gentleman who had been in the habit of travelling for 30 years; had been all over the continent of Europe; square face, wore an Inverness cape. No. 2. A lonely French female who was returning to her *patrie;* for a frenchwoman very quiet indeed. No. 3, A sleek Doctor with a white beard and moustaches; somewhat seedy as to outer garments but of a very intelligent turn of mind."

Once this oddly assorted crew reached Folkestone and embarked for Boulogne, Isabella's mind was forced onto other matters. "Weather very rough," she records grimly. "People said we had a very good passage, very difficult to agree with the general opinion as I was very ill." On finally reaching the safe haven of the French coast it immediately became clear that something was wrong with the Beetons' passport. Sam's paperwork could always be counted on to go awry and Isabella, probably still sour-mouthed and swimmy from the crossing, was obliged to kick her heels in a local pâtisserie while things got sorted out. Supper that night was a tense affair. In the dining room of Boulogne's Hôtel de la Gare Sam got into a row with three Frenchmen on a point of detail about which port Louis-Philippe, the late King of France, had arrived at to start his exile in Britain.

The long evening train trip in a second-class carriage from Boulogne to Paris via Amiens was not made any shorter by the "sleek Doctor," who turned out to be called Levinson, battening on Sam and insisting on talking to (or at) him on literary matters all the way to their destination. Isabella was clearly put out: "can't be bothered with that sort of thing," she noted tersely and concentrated instead on the other passengers who included "an oldish, crabby-faced woman in a brown blanket, [who] couldn't speak a word of French" and "frenchmen, who managed to sleep the whole of the journey." Looking out of the window while Sam and Dr. Levinson chatted and the Frenchmen snored, Isabella was "very much struck by the appearance of the signal women who looked so cold in the snow; wore black hats like sailors."

By the time they steamed into the Gare du Nord it was midnight, and all the *fiacres* were gone. Instead Sam and Isabella were obliged to squeeze into a packed omnibus: "got possession of 2 seats, I thought the vehicle was quite full, but were obliged to cram in a very stout english lady with a huge crinoline. Stowed her among [us] all right, but the question arose, 'Where was her husband to go[']. One proposed he should lie down in the middle with his legs out of window [*sic*], another that he should sit in his wife's lap, but he saw the impossibility of this proceeding & jumped up outside." Arriving at the Hôtel de Rivoli, Sam and Isabella had a quick snack of bread and pale ale before falling into bed "quite tired out with our long journey." As well they might: they had been travelling for eighteen hours solid on only three hours' sleep.

The next morning, a cold and snowy one, it soon became apparent that Sam's organizational skills had once again let them down. On the previous night he had left a big box of books at the Gare du Nord—probably Beeton publications intended for distribution through French booksellers—which he now went back to collect. But when he returned with Isabella the station officials told them that there was something wrong with the paperwork. The books would have to stay put until after the weekend, when the Beetons would need to go to the Ministère de l'Intérieur and pay 5 francs. Much to her credit Isabella seems never to have got angry with Sam about his chaotic administration, which must surely have driven her tidy mind to distraction. Instead the jaunty young couple simply switched plans and "jumped into an omnibus" and went on to see Mr. Fowler, the English bookseller in Palais-Royal who would be responsible for forwarding the material from *Le Moniteur* every month. From there it was on to nearby 92 rue Richelieu where they "had an interview with Mr. Goubo [*sic*] respecting the fashion plates." (For all Isabella's much vaunted proficiency in French she seems to have had a hard time spelling Goubaud's name.) They then took a cab, which Isabella noted carefully cost 2 francs, to see a Mr. Meyer, to whom they had letters of introduction from their engraver at the *EDM*, Mr. Woods. Meyer seems to have been involved in the production of the dressmaking patterns that were enclosed in *Le Moniteur* and which the Beetons hoped could now be distributed to *EDM* readers. Dinner followed at the Restaurant de Paris, Palais-Royal, where Mr. Fowler had pre-ordered a meal of soup, sweet-breads, Poulet aux Cressons, Sole à la Normandie and Charlotte aux Pommes.

After all the trouble Fowler had gone to, it would be nice to report that Isabella was appreciative. But in fact, she notes only that the meal was "tolerably nice." The Beetons, like most British people of their class and generation, were distinctly wary of French cuisine, and they stuck as far as possible to their familiar way of eating. Breakfast was always a large plate of meat and eggs, followed by bouillon for lunch and then a full din-ner, usually of chicken with a pudding that featured apple in some form or other, at 5:30 p.m. This, of course, was the reverse of the French pat-tern, which involved a light breakfast, large lunch, and then late light sup-per. As a result of their insistence on dining so early Sam and Isabella often found themselves eating in solitary splendour in the hotel's coffee room, the dining room staying firmly closed for at least another hour.

The next day, Saturday, 10 March, passed in a blur of meetings. By the afternoon the Beetons are back with "Mr. Goubo" [*sic*] and have made an arrangement with him regarding the fashion plates. The Beetons' profit margins were clearly paper thin, and the whole arrangement with *Le Moniteur* was possible only because of a recent Anglo-French trade agreement that had dramatically lowered the excise on commerce between the two countries. Back at the hotel the Beetons had an appointment with a custom house officer who presented them with the piece of paper they needed to claim their box of books from the Ministère de l'Intérieur on Monday. After a "very nice little dinner," including a bottle of Saint-Julien, the indefatigable couple set off again to Mr. Fowler's "to make arrangements about sending off the box of fashion plates every month." From there they went to another associate, a sinister-looking man called Mr. Gowland whom Sam was convinced was going to hit him on the back of the head at any moment. Isabella, however, liked Gowland's wife (pos-sibly because she was British; Meyer's French wife, by contrast, was dis-missed as "fat and dirty") with whom she had a long conversation about employing a French *bonne* or nursery maid.

Baby Samuel had been left at home in Pinner, which suggests that, at the age of nine months, he was now fully weaned and ready to be looked after by someone other than his mother. The fact that Isabella was consid-ering employing a French girl to do that job suggests two things. First, that she and Sam continued to put a high price on the ability to speak European languages and wanted to make sure that their own children enjoyed every opportunity to learn French. Second, that neither of them was much bothered by handing their child over to a Roman Catholic, something that would have worried the vast majority of British parents at that time.

That very afternoon Isabella had interviewed a nice French girl at the hotel who had seemed like she might do. However Mrs. Gowland was quick to put her off and "nearly upset all notions of French nursemaids as she gave them all such a bad character." This, though, was not enough to make Isabella give up the idea altogether. A couple of days later, the search for a French nursemaid resumed. A girl came up to Isabella's hotel room and "wished to know whether I would engage her." Following her own advice in the *BOHM,* Isabella went to have "an interview" with the girl's present employer, an American woman staying in the hotel: "Told me the girl was very respectable & kind to her children, but could not do so much in the way of needlework as she had represented to me." This is the last we ever hear of Isabella's plans to hire a French nursemaid. Just over a year later, the 1861 census shows her employing Mary Lawrence, a local girl, to look after little Samuel Orchart.

The next day was a Sunday, and the Beetons followed their usual substantial breakfast by going to watch Mass being said at the Madeleine. Isabella managed to tear herself away from the sight of a funeral going on in another part of the church to notice that everything looked rather dingy. (Allying Catholicism with a spiritual and literal grubbiness was a standard defensive Protestant strategy.) From the Madeleine the Beetons walked into the Place de la Concorde and up the Champs-Elysées, spotting just how many new houses had been built since they had spent their honeymoon there nearly four years earlier. After lunch, Isabella "sat down & wrote from Sam's dictation the agreement for Monsieur Goubaud." Tea with Mr. Fowler was followed by bed at eleven o'clock for Isabella while Sam stayed up and finished "his prospectus"—presumably for the new-look luxury *Englishwoman's Domestic Magazine.*

The next afternoon, at the Ministère de l'Intérieur in St.-Germain, the Beetons paid 5 francs to liberate their books. Then back to M. Goubaud's "to see coloured patterns for bonnets." Isabella was frank, but realistic about what she saw: "Did not like them much, but as there is little time must content ourselves with them for the first month." She cheered up, however, for long enough to note that supper at the Hôtel Palais-Royal consisted of a "beautiful dinner for 2 francs, wine included." The next day of their stay, Tuesday, Sam made a tour of various booksellers while Isabella went to 92 rue Richelieu "to tell Monsieur Goubaud about the slipper pattern." Then she went to the studio in rue St. Anne and "saw the girls colouring the various fashion plates."

At this point Isabella's account of the Paris trip peters out. But skip to the back of the little diary and you will find a series of important sums jotted down in her hand. Clearly she is trying to work out whether the whole enterprise of importing French fashion plates for the new-look *EDM* can be made to turn a profit. Carefully she adds up the costs of the paper, the plates, the patterns, and the editing before coming to the conclusion at the bottom of the page that "12000 just pays." They would need to sell twelve thousand copies each month to make the thing work. Given that the circulation of the *EDM* was running at a steady sixty thousand (or at least that is what Sam noisily claimed in public), this might look like a very mild gamble. But at this point Sam and Isabella had no idea whether the new-look luxury *EDM* would prove as popular as its more modest predecessor.

What Isabella's Paris diary shows, even at this distance, is a young couple of extraordinary energy. Never taking a cab or even the bus when they could walk, the Beetons managed to tramp at least three miles a day, often in extremely wintery conditions. Unsurprisingly, they like and need their food, tucking away two substantial meals a day, although managing on only bouillon at lunchtime. Isabella clearly enjoys alcohol, since she mentions with relish the pale ale that the waiter provided them with on their first late night in town, and she is always delighted when a bottle of good wine is included in the cost of their meal. She also considers herself, and is considered by others, to be an equal partner in the firm of S. O. Beeton. On those occasions when she and Sam separate, she is quite happy to carry out business on her own, confidently inspecting the studios where the plates will be made (although she does note that the gentleman in charge offers to send her back to the hotel in his carriage—presumably not something he would have done for Sam). Being without a chaperone seems not to have fazed Isabella at all. When she returns to the hotel and discovers that Sam is not yet there, she simply walks about the boulevards until he appears. What's more, the sums at the back of the diary suggest that it is she who is in charge of the business's finances. In the awful years that lay ahead for the house of S. O. Beeton, everyone agreed that if only Isabella with her careful little rows of figures had still been alive, things might have turned out very differently.

The effect of the Paris trip was immediately visible in the first issue of the new-look *EDM,* which appeared six weeks after the Beetons' return, on 1 May 1860. The magazine is much thicker and slightly larger, the result of the British government repealing the final "tax on knowledge," the heavy paper duty. Isabella's cookery column, already fitful by the end of the old series, was now reduced to a "Bill of Fare," which simply told you each month what meat and vegetables were in season. Occasionally there would be recipes but these, it was made clear, had simply been plucked from what was now, significantly, known as *Mrs. Beeton's Book of Household Management.*

For what really mattered in the new-look *EDM* was not cookery but fashion. Each issue contains a plate from *Le Moniteur,* which is re-captioned: "The Fashions—Expressly designed and prepared for the Englishwoman's Magazine." The illustrations, often by David, show two or three anatomically impossible young women dressed in the latest fashions, and function both as a piece of visual pleasure, and as a how-to primer for those who wanted to achieve the effects for themselves. Near

One of the fashion plates for the new-look Englishwoman's Domestic Magazine, *which have since become collectible classics.*

the end of each issue, Isabella provides a detailed description of the clothes worn by the figures in the plate along the lines of:

> One of the prettiest [dresses] we have seen, intended for the spring season, had nine narrow flounces scarcely exceeding a nail in width. Just over the highest flounce, a row of buttons begins and runs up to the top. The body is plain and the waist short. The sleeves, wide, with an elbow, form a band just below the bend of the arm. A narrow frill is put on the revers. These sleeves are always accompanied by large puffed muslin undersleeves.

This level of detail did not, naturally, make for scintillating copy, but was doubtless read with great attention by dressmakers, both amateur and professional, who were trying to recreate the effect.

From this point readers had a choice. Those who bought the shilling version of the magazine received its greatest innovation of all: "A large separate sheet (equal to thirty-two pages) on which is printed a number of Original, Practical, and Beautiful Designs for all kinds of Ladies' Work, and of the exact size for working." In other words, free paper dressmaking patterns from which you might make anything from a new bodice to a child's overcoat, a spring bonnet to a lady's mantle. In a particularly extravagant gesture in May 1861, each magazine came with a piece of cambric, stamped in ink, from which you could construct your own "Mary Stuart night or morning cap" (these were apparently all the rage). Those who bought the 6d version of the magazine still had the option of sending off for the patterns at an extra charge.

For those who preferred to read about fashion rather than make it, the *EDM* offered the more discursive feature, "The Fashions," which Isabella worked up each month from the briefing notes supplied by Mme. Goubaud. Although unsigned, "The Fashions" appeared, at least initially, to be written by a lady of high Parisian society who could count on being asked to all the best places. For instance, Isabella's October 1860 piece begins:

> We must describe the toilets of two young sisters, whose appearance attracted great attention at a recent fete in Paris. They wore piqué dresses, braided in black at the bottom; long jackets, braided in the same manner, came to the top of the braiding on the skirt. Their bonnets were

of white tulle, trimmed with black velvet primroses with gold centres, and a bandeau inside to match.

Over time, as Isabella became more confident in her ability to read the fashion of the streets for herself, she seems to have relied less and less on Mme. Goubaud's briefings. Rather than describing what was happening on the boulevards, she is increasingly happy to talk about the ladies she has seen walking down Regent Street, or at the Crystal Palace in Sydenham. And instead of simply reporting what she has seen, she is prepared to intervene with criticism and warning: "Many ladies seem to think that their dress is in perfect fashion and elegance if only it be entirely composed of blue, green, mauve, or any other colour, no matter what the difference in the shades may be; and yet this is one of the greatest mistakes that can be made." Or again, on turned-back cuffs: "This is not very graceful, and it has already been suggested, with much sense, that such a style of sleeve could not be thought of for dresses of a light, transparent fabric." For those readers who craved even more fashion advice, the *EDM* now published extra supplements twice a year, which could be bought for 6d.

So in only four years, the stern Isabella Beeton who had warned

A fashion plate by Jules David showing readers of the Englishwoman's Domestic Magazine *the sort of thing they should be aiming at for evening wear.*

"Wives and Housekeepers of Britain" about the wastefulness of running to and from the chandler's every day had transformed herself into an elegant lady of fashion who accepted with an indulgent shrug that her readers love to shop. In June 1862 she opens "The Fashions" with the trilling "Certain it is that we do not live in an economical age; and perhaps husbands are more indulgent and lenient than of yore to their wives' little foibles and weaknesses in their love of finery; and, as ladies will dress, and must have their garments fashionably made, we will proceed to describe a few very pretty things we noticed in our walk westward." This new, positively luxurious, Mrs. Beeton is happy to puff the products of M. Rimmel of 96 Strand, or the silks of Messrs. Debenham and Freebody. Readers are advised on the cleverest Christmas gifts and encouraged to follow the French and give New Year presents too. Gone is the atmosphere of retirement and thrift. Instead, Mrs. Beeton is happy to lead her readers out into a world of expense, sociability, and display.

And yet, as always, the magazine format allowed several voices to exist side by side, catering for readers who one month might feel extravagant and the next need to tighten their belts. As the historian Margaret Beetham has pointed out, the patterns provided by the Beetons brilliantly papered over any tensions between the "old" *EDM* woman of the original series—domestic, thrifty, English—and the "new" one—social, fashionable, international. By making up the clothes herself, or with the help of a local dressmaker, the new *EDM* woman could absolve herself of any suggestion that she had strayed too far from her earlier identity. Advertisements and articles endorsing the new sewing machines were run throughout the 1860s in the magazine and served to remind the reader that her transformation into a lady of fashion remained rooted in traditional domestic skills, albeit ones that had been brought up to date by the new technology.

In addition to the patterns offered free with the magazine there were also extra dressmaking services for the less confident. Those who preferred to have their patterns already cut and tacked need only send the appropriate amount of money in stamps to Mme. Goubaud, care of Mr. Beeton, always remembering to give their waist and shoulder size. This service proved to be one of the more lasting legacies of the Beeton enterprise. Although the timeline remains smudgy, it is clear that Sam himself eventually took over the London agency for the Goubauds and that he and an associate called Charles Weldon carried on with the pattern-making side of the business out of an office in Bedford Street, Covent Garden, eventually employing his half-sister Mary Ann (one of those Heidelberg girls) as the manageress. By the 1890s Sam and Isabella's youngest son Mayson was producing another magazine, *Hearth and Home*, from Bedford Street, and the pattern side of the business seems to have devolved entirely onto Charles Weldon. "Weldon's" became a staple of the domestic magazine and paper pattern industry until well into the 1950s.

Dressmaking patterns for home use were new to Britain so, while *EDM* readers were excited by their possibilities, they were frequently baffled by them too. A few weeks after the pattern service started, Sam, in his incarnation as "Editor," described one particular letter of complaint sent in by a reader called Sophia Anderson, who was convinced that a jacket pattern had no armhole.

> Commotion in the office of the *Englishwoman* . . . the Editor and his staff looking like so many monuments of despair. Recovering himself, however, our chief bravely put the bomb in his pocket (with other most kind and compensatory letters, be it gratefully said), and delivered it to the Editress . . . Undismayed, but evidently hurt at the ingratitude of Sophia and her friends, she calmly traced the pattern on to some whitey-brown paper: first pinned it together, and then tacked it, showing us triumphantly a little boy's jacket in paper, with armhole, sleeve, and cuff, as complete as possible. So when SOPHIA ANDERSON "would like to know how it would be possible," &c, she has only to write . . .

Thankfully, most of the *EDM*'s readers proved to be handier than Sophia Anderson. The provincial press, certainly, rushed to congratulate the magazine on its originality and "ingenuity" in introducing dressmaking patterns into the editorial mix. Favourable comment came in from the *Illustrated Times*, the *Illustrated News of the World*, the *Civil Service Gazette*, the *Sunday Times*, the *News of the World*, the *Weekly Times*, *Penny Newsman* and the *Universal News*. These comments were, naturally enough, saved up, set in print and incorporated into future puffs and notices.

All the same, even the new *EDM*, with its beefed-up fashion coverage and greater attention to the latest books, concerts, court, and metropolitan goings-on, still left a gap in the periodical market. A year after its unveiling, the Beetons launched another magazine, the only one of theirs that is still running today. The *Queen*, which went through various incarnations until it eventually became *Harpers & Queen*, was a sophisticated weekly "illustrated Journal and Review" costing 6d and aimed at well-to-do upper-middle-class women.

The decision to tie the publication's identity to the reigning monarch (a photograph of Victoria by the photographer Mayall was given away with the first issue) set in play a whole series of possibilities as to who a typical subscriber might be. Clearly, like the Queen herself, the *Queen* reader was a woman whose main priority was her family: "when we write for woman we write for home," intoned the first sentence of the first issue. But, as with Her Majesty, the *Queen* reader employed servants, which allowed her to pursue important duties and pleasures beyond the domestic sphere. (The fact that Victoria was about to go deep into mourning would inevitably complicate the picture.) Thus it was feminine but *public* interests that lay at the heart of the *Queen's* constituency: society news, cultural gossip, fashion, but also an emerging concern for social issues and women's expanding employment and education opportunities.

Frederick Greenwood was appointed to run the new magazine, and the success he made of it during those first few months went a long way towards cementing his reputation beyond the house of S. O. Beeton. Isabella, meanwhile, was in charge of the needlework and fashion features. Each week a fashion plate by Jules David or one of the other *Le Moniteur* artists was available as a supplement, and there was also a page of needlework designs.

That autumn of 1861 must have been ferociously busy. For as well as the launch of the *Queen*, there was also the publication of the single-volume *BOHM* to attend to. The book received the usual Beeton promotional treatment, which meant being assiduously plugged across its sibling publications. In the September 1861 issue of *Boy's Own Magazine*, a trio of brothers who write in asking what they should give their sister as a wedding present are told: "Well, my boys, we do not see why we should not say Mrs. Beeton's Household Management, which will be ready, handsomely and strongly bound in cloth, on 1st October next, price 7/6d—post free."

Although *Management*, as Isabella and Sam familiarly called it, sold extremely well—Sam claimed that sixty thousand volumes had shifted in the first year—it was not the kind of book that looked likely to attract much notice in the serious press. It was a woman's book in several senses, concerned with the ephemera of domestic life, and hardly seemed to merit sustained critical attention. And yet, there are signs that only six months after publication the book was starting to attract glances from important publications, that is publications edited and written by men. The *Saturday Review*, interestingly, immediately understood the book's intentions in terms of demographics, although its claim that the section of the population under discussion lived in a household employing three female servants and a boy was wildly inflationary. On 1 March 1862 the anonymous reviewer commented:

It is not in its highest aspects that English cookery is deficient. It is on that vast level of society which has only three female servants and a boy that the pinch of starvation presses. It is in those moderate households where good cookery is theoretically appreciated and never experienced, that we want a Gastronomic Regenerator. And for a really valuable repertory of hints on all sorts of household matters, we recommend Mrs. Beeton with few misgivings.

Three months later the *BOHM* came to the notice of that most prestigious of periodicals, the *Athenaeum*. The unlikeliness of this is explained by the fact that the anonymous reviewer was, in fact, Geraldine Jewsbury, one of the handful of serious women journalists of the time. Jewsbury wanted to write—or more probably was asked to write—what would today be called a "round-up" piece on the flood of new cookery and household titles that were coming onto the market. As was the custom of the day, Jewsbury's article was more like a discursive essay than a sustained examination of the books under review. Yet from her opening paragraph it is clear that household management was a subject on which she had thought deeply, and that those thoughts happened to chime nicely with those of Mrs. Beeton. Thus Jewsbury declares: "a woman who has not judgement, firmness, forethought and general good sense cannot manage her house prudently or comfortably, no matter what amount of money she may have at her command . . . it is not money, but management, that is the great requisite." After virtually ventriloquizing Isabella like this, it is disappointing that Jewsbury did not spend much time actually discussing her book. All the same, she did report the highly favourable verdict of a cook to whom she claimed to have shown *Man-*

agement: "I consider it an excellent work; it is full of useful information about everything, which is quite delightful, and I should say anyone ought to learn to cook from it who never tried before." By contrast, Charles Francatelli's book of cookery for the working classes, which was the main title under review, attracted Miss Jewsbury's sharp disdain for the way in which it was so blithely ignorant of the actual "manners, customs and prejudices of the class he addresses."

More extended and thoughtful praise for Mrs. Beeton's work also arrived in the unlikely form of a letter from Harriet Martineau. Isabella must have sent the veteran journalist a copy of the book and Miss Martineau, with her typical scrupulosity, wrote from her cottage in the Lake District to let her know exactly what she thought of it. Martineau, who was not inclined to gush, produced what amounted to a fan letter.

> [Your book] has given me a great deal of pleasure; and my niece, who relieves me of housekeeping, declares the book to be very valuable indeed in the cookery parts. To us it seems new to state the cost of the dishes, and in the last degree useful. . . . The specifications of the servants are excellent too.

Stopping only to explain that she disliked the medical chapter because she was a homeopath and considered such orthodoxy "very dangerous," Miss Martineau concluded with a rousing "In nineteen-twentieths of the book, I think we may delight and rejoice; and I heartily wish you the joy of it." Since Miss Martineau had herself published on domestic matters, even writing a pseudonymous series of guides for domestic servants, this was praise indeed.

Despite such powerful support from two of the most important female critics of the day, there was still no obvious reason why the *BOHM* should sell. True, its range and voice had not quite been seen before but then, as now, awareness of such things takes time to build to a critical mass. In fact, the secret of the book's success lay not so much in the superiority of its content, as in the imaginative way it was marketed. By 1863 it was becoming apparent that it was the recipes that were the real selling point of *Management,* so Sam lost no time in putting them in a book of their own, entitled *The Englishwoman's Cookery Book* and selling for just 1s. Isabella's Preface makes it clear that this book, with its utilitarian black and white illustrations, is aimed at a different readership from that of the 7s 6d *Book of Household Management.*

> To help Plain Cooks and Maids-of-all-Works to a knowledge of some of their duties, and to assist them in the important task of dressing and serving daily food, I have printed the following Recipes, along with some directions and hints as to the Arrangement and Economy of the Kitchen. The recipes are taken from my book on Household Management, and I hope both mistress and maid will find some of the information serviceable. I have sought to make all the directions plain and practical, eschewing everything that was not likely to be useful and was not to the point.
>
> IB
>
> January 1863

Two years later a second abridged version of the recipes appeared, this time entitled the *Dictionary of Everyday Cookery* and packaged as the first in a new series called "Beeton's All About It." Isabella's Preface, one of the last things she ever wrote, is especially interesting for the way that it represents the decision to publish this new edition in terms of pricing and, by implication, demographics. This, quite explicitly, is to be a version of her book for the "middling sort."

> Many wishes have been expressed to the Authoress of the "Book of Household Management" that a volume of Recipes in Cookery should be written which could be sold at a price somewhere between the seven-and-sixpenny "Household Management" and the Shilling Cookery Book. Accordingly Mrs. Beeton has prepared a Collection of Recipes, and of other Practical Information concerning the Dressing and Serving of Family Fare, which, when completed, will be published, in serviceable binding, at the price of Three Shillings and Sixpence.

Given the sheer press of things to do, it is surprising to find the Beetons taking time for one of their rare holidays in the summer of 1860. Family gossip maintained that the usually robust Isabella was in need of recuperation, which suggests that she may once again have been going through a sad string of miscarriages. There was to be an unaccountably long five years between getting pregnant with Samuel Orchart the second and giving birth to the next baby at the very end of 1863. However, true to form, the four weeks that the Beetons spent touring Ireland, Wales, and northwest England had very little of the gentle convalescence about them. Instead their time away was punctuated by trips to the post office to collect parcels from London, writing magazine copy, visiting booksellers, and generally cramming in as much work as possible while still remaining, technically, on holiday. As was the custom of the day, thirteen-month-old Samuel was left at home with his nurse.

Isabella kept an account of this holiday, recorded in the same little pocket diary in which she had made notes about the earlier Paris excursion. From Dublin the Beetons set out early for the inland tourist resort of Killarney and checked into the Railway Hotel, which still stands today as the Great Southern Hotel. As its name suggests, the hotel had been built in the early 1850s by the Great Southern and Western Railway Company, which had also been responsible for building the train line between the capital and Killarney. It is a measure of how commercially developed the whole area had become that the company refused to allow porters and drivers from rival hotels onto the platform to meet the tourist trains from Dublin. Still, Isabella's first impression of the establishment was highly favourable: "Very large hotel indeed with very comfortable accommodation for ladies. Nice drawing-room and coffee room." Had they wished, the Beetons could also have taken advantage of a Turkish bath and "an airing room."

From the 1820s the glacier-raked landscape of southwest Ireland had been strenuously developed as a tourist resort by resident grandees, including the Kenmare and Herbert families. By the time the Beetons visited the area in 1860 they were part of a huge March–October influx of visitors from both Britain and continental Europe, drawn by the possibility of seeing a patch of unspoiled Wordsworthian heaven, not to mention the chance of following in royal footsteps: the Prince of Wales himself had paid a brief visit only two years previously. As well as three large inland lakes, rich in fish and fowl, Killarney offered a range of spectacular mountains, culminating in the high point of Mangerton, the frothy Torc waterfall, the Gap of Dunloe with its spectacular echoes, as well as the man-made attractions of Muckross Abbey, Ross Castle, and Kate Kearney's cottage. A ready supply of picturesque locals happy to gibber about headless horsemen guided earnest and energetic ladies and gentlemen up hills and down dales, creating for them a fantasy Ireland of good-hearted whimsy. The recent famine of the late 1840s, together with the associated bother of violent republicanism, had been written out of this charming picture, perhaps because local inhabitants knew that their chances of surviving any future potato blight depended on keeping the tourists coming back.

So the Killarney that the Beetons visited in the summer of 1860 was a neatly packaged experience. There were hotels everywhere (Isabella herself was fussed that the Lake Hotel might have been a better choice on account of the view but on the whole was happy with the more luxurious Railway Hotel), jaunting cars available for hire on every corner, barefoot girls selling everything from mittens to whiskey, and guidebooks telling you in what order you should visit the sights. It is more than likely that the Beetons were travelling on an excursion ticket, which provided seamless rail and sea transport from Euston together with the option of breaking their journey as many times as they liked during one calendar month. In a few years' time Julius Benedict, Isabella's former piano teacher, would write an opera based on a local legend, the Colleen Bawn, and only twelve months after the Beetons' visit, Queen Victoria would enjoy a well-publicized four-day stay. Killarney was starting to resemble London-by-the-Lakes.

When set against accounts from other visitors to the region around this time, Isabella's experiences follow a fairly standard pattern. Certainly, on that first evening she found herself reacting to all the stock images: "Walked to Ross Castle & had our first peep at the lakes of Killarney. Very much delighted with the Castle, magnificent ruins covered with the most lovely ivy. . . . Ascended the Tower, from there had a lovely view of the surrounding country." The next day was the Beetons' fourth wedding anniversary: "how time slips away," noted Isabella, a remark that gains extra pathos from the knowledge that she was already halfway through her marriage. The Beetons celebrated by going again to Ross Castle and taking a boat to Innisfallen island, "walked about there, & sat for about ½ hour on the ledge of a rock overhanging the lake & admired the scenery," and heard about the local ghostly legends from the garrulous boatmen.

The Beetons approached the Killarney experience with the kind of attack that they brought to everything else in their lives. Up early the next day, they hired a boat at Ross Castle and rowed directly to the spectacular middle and upper lakes where they landed and walked to the Gap of Dunloe. Here they were pestered by barefoot girls selling goat's milk

(Isabella seems not to have realized that this was heavily spiked with hooch). Then, as now, the Gap of Dunloe was a tourist bottleneck, with groups of visitors pooling around the place, whooping and clapping in order to provoke the famous echo. Local women, dressed up in rings and shawls, danced in a way that was supposed to be authentic but struck Isabella as "very peculiar." Still, altogether, this was "one of the pleasant-est days" of the trip.

Two days later, an ominous Friday 13th, the weather had turned rainy. There were a "heap of letters from London" (it took only twenty-four hours to get post from the capital to Killarney) so they "stayed in all morning & attended to business. Sam with his Conversazione [the letters section of the *EDM* that had replaced "Cupid"] & I with the fashions, &c." Mindful of her own clambering and boating experiences of the past week, Isabella decided to dedicate her August column to advising readers on what to wear when "seeking health and pleasure by the seaside, [or] making excursions into the country."

> DRESSES of any soft, dust-colour washing silk are very cool and pleas-ant to wear; also those of Holland and linen, braided down the front and sides and round the sleeves. Any light material, a mixture of silk and wool, is also suitable, with a CLOAK of the same; both the skirt of the dress and the cloak should be bound with some dark shade of glacé.

Some days later, the weather having turned a corner, the Beetons hired a pony and a young guide called Pat to ascend Mangerton Mountain, tak-ing it in turns to walk and ride. From the top there was a superb view of Kenmare Bay, Dingle Bay and the Corm Mountains. In her diary account, written retrospectively, Isabella slips at this point into the present tense: "Now we come to something far grander & more Majestic than anything we have as yet seen. The horse's glen [Horses' Glen], a series of rough, rugged mountains with a dark stream at the bottom." If it had been any-one else, one would put the odd shift of tense down to rapture at the moment of recollection. Given that it is Isabella Beeton, what seems alto-gether more likely is that she is jotting down some notes that could be worked up into a travel piece for the *Englishwoman's Domestic Maga-zine* once she was back in London. In the world of Beeton, there was no point in wasting anything, including a view.

Wednesday, 18 July was the most picturesque so far, and included the obligatory fishing expedition (the lakes were so rich that it was virtually impossible to come home empty handed). With Pat again as their guide, the Beetons hired a boat and "Succeeded in catching 6 Perch between us," whereupon they rowed to Cors Island, kindled a fire and cooked the fish. The following day was dedicated to business. Sam was busy reading proofs of the *Boy's Own Magazine,* while Isabella went out and booked two seats on the public coach to Glengariff before returning to the hotel to write letters. This was to be their final night. "After dinner walked to Ross Castle, to bid a wistful farewell to the Lakes. This was the first & last place visited at Killarney," wrote Isabella, already sounding nostalgic. The Beetons had been whisked around what amounted to a mid-Victorian theme park and yet, like most contemporary visitors, still managed to come away feeling that they had touched the authentic Ireland.

After Isabella and Sam visit Cork, Queenstown, and Dublin, the diary ceases with a few remarks about the dirtiness of their last destination, Chester. However, at the back of the book, Isabella has neatly noted down everything that she and Sam had had to eat and drink during seven of the days that they had spent at Killarney. Thus under Tuesday, 10 July, her wedding anniversary, she has written: "2 breakfasts, Cold ham & boiled eggs. 2 dinners, Bottled Beer, Soda & sherry." This list spans 9 July, their first night in Killarney, until the 16th. No prices have been attached, and it remains unclear just why Isabella would have wanted to note down everything she ate for a space of a week. The fact that each entry has been firmly scored through suggests that she may have been tallying her records with her receipts, which fits with what we know of her businesslike mind. What these jottings do definitively reveal, however, is that like most travelling Victorians who could afford it, Isabella and Sam drank alcohol rather than risk the local water. Nearly every day they opted for beer and sometimes a pint of sherry, yet never refer to feeling tipsy or longing for a lie-down.

Sam and Isabella returned to a business that was expanding at a giddying speed. Just like the *EDM,* in 1863 the *Boy's Own Magazine* would be dusted down and given a new suit of splendid clothes, consisting of more pages and, in time, coloured plates. From its very start in 1855, when it had been a dull octavo publication in black and white, the *Boy's Own Magazine* had been Sam's pet project. More than anything he had wanted to transform the kind of reading matter on offer to British boys. Before the *Boy's Own Magazine,* young men between the ages of ten and twenty had been obliged to swallow sanctimonious pap, the type of thing that Sam characterized as "goody two shoes." The *Boy's Own Magazine* was, in its own way, pretty didactic, but it did manage to bury its message in stirring articles about crocodile hunting, "poor boys who became Great Men," and the possibilities of making your own magic lantern slides. Authors of the stature of Captain Mayne Reid, Tom Hood, and, of course, James Greenwood produced tales of suitably moral derring-do. The magazine also appealed to young men's enduring love of bright, shiny gadgets: collect enough vouchers and you were entered into a lottery for penknives, pencil cases, and silver lever watches.

The *Boy's Own Magazine* had been a success from the start. By October 1858 it had taken over its nearest rival, the drearily named *Youth's Instructor,* and by the end of its first series in 1862, it was claiming to sell forty thousand copies each month. But this was still not enough for Sam. More than anything he wanted to reach deep into the layers of the working class and produce reading matter for poor boys—then, as now, the single demographic group that most worried commentators—that would entertain, educate and, while he would probably not have seen it in this way, co-opt them as respectable citizens. But as we have seen, his first effort, the penny weekly the *Boy's Own Journal,* folded within a year of its 1856 debut. Nothing daunted, Sam kept trying and in January 1863 he launched the *Boy's Penny Magazine,* on the grounds that the newly expensive *Boy's Own Magazine* would be beyond the pockets of "a great number of Boys." But even in this format, the project refused to take fire. After only a year the *Boy's Penny Magazine* was turned into the *Boy's Monthly Magazine* at double the price of 2d, in effect becoming the publication that the *Boy's Own Magazine* had been before its move upmarket in 1863. In this new format it limped on for another four years.

If working-class boys refused to become avid Beeton readers, the same was not true of their slightly better-off peers. What would today be called the *"Boy's Own* brand," based around the market leader *Boy's Own Magazine,* went from strength to strength. In 1861 Sam launched the *Boy's Own Library,* consisting of novels issued in 6d monthly installments which sold as 5s single volumes. The first stories to appear under the new imprint, such as *Wild Sports of the World* by James Greenwood, had already been serialized in the magazine, but in time Sam would commission new work specifically for the Library, the advertising puff proclaiming: "They have all been prepared by Mr. Beeton with a view to their fitness in manly tone and handsome appearance for presents for Youth, amongst whom they enjoy an unrivalled degree of popularity." A sample of titles—*Wild Sports of the World* was soon joined by *Curiosities of Savage Life* and *The World's Explorers*—gives an idea of the kind of things that went down well with British boys living on the cusp of empire. The books were written by employees such as John Tillotson, who also helped edit the magazine, and freelance associates such as James Greenwood, who lived by their pen on the open market.

It was this part of the Beetons' publishing empire that caught the attention of a critic from the *Morning Herald* who, on 26 January 1863, proceeded to offer a fulsome tribute to S. O. Beeton and all who sailed in her. This panegyric was reprinted later the same day in the *Evening Standard*. As well as the *EDM,* the reviewer was especially taken with the Greenwood part work *Wild Sports,* applauding it as "not only enthralling but . . . instructive in a very high degree . . . The monthly coloured frontispieces are veritable works of art." The rest of the review went on wordily, drawing the reader's attention to the high circulation of all the Beeton magazines and referring to the man himself as "a publisher who in enterprise and judgement is one of the first in the kingdom." The *Boy's Own Magazine* is puffed as "a perfect marvel for the money," while the *Boy's Penny Magazine* is described as "even better than its bigger and dearer brother." In conclusion Sam is congratulated on "doing a great work in our national education," a compliment that would have thrilled him. The *Book of Household Management* never gets a mention.

Before one follows Sarah Freeman, Nancy Spain, and H. Montgomery Hyde in using this *Herald* piece as evidence that by the beginning of 1863 the Beeton name was spontaneously being heard in all the right places, it is worth taking a closer look at its provenance. The *Morning Herald* and the *Evening Standard* were versions of the same paper, printed at different times of the day. So the fact that the *Herald* piece was recycled in the *Standard* is evidence of nothing more than the internal workings of the newspaper company. Even more significant is the fact that the *Evening Standard* was owned and edited by James Johnstone, who turns out to have been the father-in-law of Sam's cousin, Edmund Beeton. Edmund's father Robert Beeton was the young man who had followed his Uncle Samuel from Suffolk to London all those years ago and had borrowed money in order to set up the Yorkshire Grey in St. Pancras. In later life

Robert always maintained that he owed his uncle a great debt. That debt, it seems, was finally paid off fifty years later when Robert's son arranged for Uncle Sam's grandson to get a puff in his new father-in-law's paper.

According to the early biographers, this review in the *Herald* sparked off a whole sheaf of other papers into "noticing" the house of S. O. Beeton. But a closer look at the details again suggests that this was not quite the spontaneous and disinterested compliment that it might at first have seemed. The *Weekly Dispatch,* which carried a flattering assessment of Beeton's work, was a paper that Sam already had strong links with and which he would be editing outright in a few years' time. The *Illustrated Times,* meanwhile, boasted both the Greenwood brothers among its regular contributors. The *Literary Times* sounds smart, but lasted for only nine weeks. Finally the *Penny Illustrated Paper* was, as its title implies, aimed at the same class of people whom Sam was chasing with his own penny publications. Perhaps this similarity explains why its critic concluded with the heartfelt comment that Mr. Beeton must surely have "a higher motive than mere money-making."

None of this is to deny that the Beeton name was beginning to circulate. But it was among a relatively closed and familiar network of friends of friends. What Sam really needed now was attention from the big national presses. The problem was that critics from more prestigious titles were unlikely to be quite so kind or understanding about the little bits of sloppiness that marked so many of Beeton's publications. On 13 March 1862, for instance, *The Times* gave a generally welcome reception to the *Dictionary of Universal Information,* but couldn't help noticing that it "is not free from blunders" and pointed out a case where a "celebrated Frenchman, the author of a Latin romance, is described as the son of an English monk of the same name who appears from the work itself to have died 32 years before the subject of the memoir was born." Another of Sam's prestige publications, the *Illustrated Family Bible* published initially in twenty-four 2s parts and then as a single volume, likewise raised adverse comment, this time from the previously encouraging *Athenaeum.* Although the text and illustrations by artists of the calibre of Schnorer were admired, it was the commentaries that appeared to be shoddy and shallow, the work of someone who didn't quite understand the provenance of his information. Or, in the words of Samuel Davidson, the *Athenaeum*'s specialist on biblical matters, "The editor, a man of much learning, has displayed little taste or judgement in the accumulation of materials. No *system* of selection appears. Hence they are a medley of good and bad—the latter, unfortunately, prevailing." The editor, in fact, was a man called Dr. Kitto. All the same, it would be hard to think of anyone to whom Davidson's words applied more closely than Samuel Orchart Beeton himself.

The fact that Mrs. Beeton's *Book of Household Management* was still not the first—or even the fifth or tenth—work that got mentioned when public commentators turned their gaze onto the house of S. O. Beeton may be surprising to us, but we need to try to think ourselves back into the year 1863. The economy was beginning to slow and would soon stall. In towns and cities around the country, working-class men were agitating for the right to vote alongside their middle-class masters. Already the mood was turning militant and in only a few years' time a mass meeting at Hyde Park in support of an extension to the suffrage would end with the iron railings being pulled down. All this only added to the gloomy feeling that, in the words of the Conservative politician Lord Derby, to give working-class men the vote would be a colossal "leap in the dark" which might end either in revolution or, as was the heartfelt hope, a strengthened sense of national cohesion.

For this reason it had never felt so important to shine a light into that dark in order to investigate the health and temper of that part of the population that would soon comprise the electoral majority in most of Britain's towns. One way of doing this was to look at the magazines that these people liked to read, which of course included the *Boy's Own* brand. And so it was, with an almost audible sigh of relief, that reviewers were happy to report back that they felt entirely reassured by what they had found. All those articles on crocodile hunting, boys who became great men and making your own fireworks suggested that what respectable lads from modest backgrounds wanted was to feel part of what might be termed the national project—manly, resourceful, and probably Protestant. If, in a few years' time, these boys got the vote there was absolutely no reason to think that they would immediately be ushering in the new and deadly peril of socialism. When the reporter from the *Morning Herald* congratulated S. O. Beeton on his "great work in our national education," what he really meant was its political stability.

Against this sense of urgency, it is no wonder that Mrs. Beeton's *Book of Household Management* frequently failed to fight its way to the front of reviewers' consciousness. And yet, there are signs that another constituency, closer than reviewers to the desires and demands of readers, was taking notice of Isabella's achievement. From as early as 1860 rival publishers began to bring out their own versions of her book. Starting as a slow trickle at first, and then broadening into a river, came titles that unashamedly attempt to speak to the same audience as Mrs. Beeton. J. H. Walsh's *British Housekeeper's Book* of 1859 was followed the next year by R. K. Philp's *Family Save-All* (this was only fair since the Beetons had almost certainly got the idea for the *BOHM* from Philp's *The Practical Housewife*). In 1862 came *Domestic Hints to Young Mothers* by the wonderfully named Martha Careful and the anonymous *Book of the Household*, while 1863 saw Barbara Hutton's *Monday Morning*, which was followed by the first of Mrs. Warren's immensely popular domestic narratives, *How I Managed My House*. For the remainder of the 1860s the various cut-down editions that Isabella and Sam, and then Sam alone, brought forth from the *BOHM* ran alongside a slew of new titles along similar lines, culminating perhaps with the most obvious straight steal in 1868, *Cassell's Household Guide*, to which Sam responded by bringing out a "revised and corrected" edition of Mrs. Beeton's book, claiming that the original had already sold an extraordinary 178,000 copies. In an increasingly crowded and chronically copycat market where one book looked and sounded a lot like another, it is perhaps easy to see why reviewers did not consistently notice *Beeton's Book of Household Management* more than any other title. But readers did, and it was on this groundswell of recognition that Mrs. Beeton had managed to produce something better than her rivals, that the fortunes of the book began, slowly but surely, to be made.

INTERLUDE

Setting his coarse feeding and slovenly habits out of the question, there is no domestic animal so profitable or so useful to man as the much-maligned pig, or any that yields him a more varied or more luxurious repast. The prolific powers of the pig are extraordinary, even under the restraint of domestication; but when left to run wild in favourable situations, as in the islands of the South Pacific, the result, in a few years, from two animals put on shore and left undisturbed, is truly surprising; for they breed so fast, and have such numerous litters, that unless killed off in vast numbers both for the use of the inhabitants and as fresh provisions for ships' crews, they would degenerate into vermin.

ISABELLA BEETON,
Book of Household Management

NATURE, IN MRS. BEETON'S VIEW, may be bountiful, but it is also extremely dangerous. Turn your back for a moment, and civilization will be overrun, crowded out, reduced to the level of beasts. And it isn't just pigs that will take over if they get the chance. In the chapter on fish Mrs. Beeton tells the story of a sailor in ancient times who fell overboard and within minutes was nibbled to death by a huge shoal of mackerel.

For Mrs. Beeton, civilized society measures its achievements by its ability to subdue and transform such natural chaos: "A nation which knows how to dine has learned the leading lesson of progress. It imposes both the will and skill to reduce to order and surround with idealisms and

Illustration from the Book of Household Management
that hints at how frighteningly prolific the natural world could be.

graces the more material conditions of human existence." So dining well isn't simply a pleasure, it is a civilizing duty, part of the obligation of those who have access to culture to take it to places where nature might otherwise run amok.

This might seem doubly apt for a book that was soon to become one of those talismanic gifts that a young matron packed in her trunk as she set off for India. But that transforming, civilizing function of the British middle-class household was required nearer to home too. Pigs were, after all, domestic animals, the one bit of livestock that a cottager was likely to have apart from a few chickens. This made them doubly threatening because, just like fish, they seemed so harmless, so much a part of the landscape.

Switch the phrase "working class" for "pigs" and you have a fair snapshot of where bourgeois anxieties lay at the beginning of the 1860s. The working class appeared to be multiplying at an alarming rate, while the size of middle-class families was starting to fall. Statistical projections suggested that this urban scum would grow and grow until checked by the illness and disease that would inevitably follow from overcrowding. If the urban working classes got the vote—as the male half did in 1867—

they would, in effect, be running the country. Here, in all their unlovely squalor, were the pigs/people who would soon become the masters.

There was one possible way of modifying the situation, though. Just as a pig could be brought into civilization, kept in a clean stye, fattened up and killed at the appropriate moment and turned into delicious bacon or sizzling sausages, so the same sort of transformational magic might be worked on the proletariat. If individuals were taken into the middle-class household, trained as servants, inculcated with all those polite little points of behaviour, then they too could be made useful—and harmless. For it was indeed the case that during this period country girls who went into service were in the habit of returning to their native villages furnished with the dainty ways that allowed them to marry well, so spreading the civilizing mission of the middle classes even further down the social scale.

And yet, from Beeton's point of view, this process of transforming rough, frighteningly fecund country people into manageable petits bourgeois was always on the point of falling through. Despite her general remarks on servants which recommend treating them with kindness, the more detailed chapters that follow show them as, at best, children and at worst not fully human. Beeton tells the story of one footman who used to comment loudly on his mistress's hand at cards, and of another who nudged his master and asked loudly why he hadn't bothered to offer any wine to the lady in the green dress. More barbaric is a story from Scotland's feudal times that has servants murdering their laird. Elsewhere, Beeton portrays servants listening at doors and reading private letters, a set of popular prejudices that would result, by the 1900s, in the decline of domestic staff in the households of the urban middle class. Making purses out of sows' ears turned out to be harder than anyone would have thought possible.

CHAPTER TEN

HER HAND HAS LOST ITS CUNNING

THE TAG OF "TRAGEDY" is habitually used to describe situations that are not in fact tragic, but simply sad. But in the case of what happened next to Isabella Beeton it is hard to think of a more apt way of characterizing the years from 1863 to 1866 when health, money, and eventually life itself drained away, leaving others to profit from her spectacular misfortune. Most crucially, the seeds of this horrible destruction were sown by Sam himself who managed to wreck the very things—work, family—that meant the most.

First comes the hubris, which Sam Beeton had in spades. His behaviour had always been jaunty but from 1861 it becomes positively reckless. As we have seen, in 1860 he had anticipated the final repeal of the paper tax by a year, which resulted in the loss of at least £1,000 in extra production costs. A more cautious businessman would have waited until the new legislation was signed and sealed at Westminster, but at least Sam's preemptive strike allowed the Beeton publications to get a lead in the new era of luxury magazines. It also meant, though, that he was soon in financial difficulties. After only six months he was forced to sell his flagship magazine, the *Queen*, the project that most signified his and Isabella's attempt to inhabit the newly glossy world of Victorian consumerism. The buyer was Edward Cox, a barrister and well-funded publisher who ran his own stable of magazines from an office a few doors further down the Strand and who, together with his partner Wyman, had been responsible for printing the magazine from its promising beginning.

There is no way that the sale of the *Queen* in April 1862 can be finessed to make it seem anything but a humiliation. For Isabella, this was the only magazine with which she had been involved from the start, and came closest to being the kind of thing that she might have read herself if she hadn't been involved in the business. For Sam, it marked the end of his professional relationship with Frederick Greenwood, the most talented journalist ever to work for the house of S. O. Beeton. When Cox took over the *Queen* he immediately appointed one of his own people—a woman—as editor, which meant that Greenwood was left without a job. Whether Greenwood's and Sam's personal friendship was put under strain is not clear, but the fact remains that after ten years' service Greenwood now left to pursue a highly successful career with other publishers, most especially with George Smith. Smith was everything that Sam might have been but was not. A shrewd businessman as well as a deep lover of literature, by the time he was in early middle age Smith had sufficient capital to tempt the best writers to his flagship publication, the *Cornhill.* Thackeray had been its editor and Eliot, Gaskell, Trollope, and Browning contributed to its prestigious pages. With Thackeray's sudden death in 1863, Smith put Greenwood in as his successor, where the young man acquitted himself marvellously. Two years later they together launched the daily evening paper the *Pall Mall Gazette,* which quickly established itself as a central fixture in metropolitan political and literary life. When Greenwood died in 1909 there was a *Times* obituary describing him as "a maker of history," warm anecdotes from respectful colleagues and, in time, a biography. Sam, by contrast, would pass from the world virtually unnoticed.

The handover of the *Queen* to its new owners was conducted with characteristic carelessness. In June 1862 Sam found himself up in court on a charge that had arisen simply because he had not bothered to notify the engraver Meason who had supplied some woodblocks to the *Queen* that he was no longer liable for the magazine's bills. The judge asked the court pointedly: "had not the defendant allowed the plaintiff to consider that he was responsible?" and the jury, taking the hint, found for Meason.

This chaos, which extended into every area of Sam's life, soon spilled into Isabella's too. The census shows the Beeton family snugly intact at 2 Chandos Villas on 8 April 1861. But only a year later the household has been disbanded. The early biographers are nervous about the reasons behind this sudden departure. Sarah Freeman has a complicated explanation involving the Beetons being so busy with their work that they overlooked the fact that the lease on 2 Chandos Villas was going to run out in the autumn of 1862. Since the couple, according to Freeman, now "wanted to buy their own house rather than continuing to rent," they did not go straight into another house but moved temporarily to the offices in the Strand and lived over the shop.

There are several problems with Freeman's account. First, Sam had initially taken out a lease on the Pinner house in the spring of 1856, which makes it impossible for the contract to expire in the autumn. Second, leases on domestic properties usually ran for seven years—certainly this seems to have been the length of the free season ticket which had come with 2 Chandos Villas—which would mean that it was due to end in spring 1863. Third, Sam and Isabella, like 90 per cent of mid-Victorians, had no intention of buying a house. Nearly everyone rented, regardless of their age or stage in life. What actually seems to have happened is that Sam and Isabella quit Pinner in the spring of 1862, a full year before the lease on the house was up. This was an odd turn of events, and usually only happened when a tenant suddenly found himself unable to meet the rent. With this in mind, the decision to move into the Strand looks more like a desperate attempt to save money than an administrative stopgap.

The offices of S. O. Beeton. Isabella lived here from 1862 to 1864,
during which time she gave birth to her third baby.

This becomes even more likely with the discovery that the Beetons actually stayed there for two years, rather than the few months implied by
both Freeman and Nancy Spain or the few weeks suggested by H. Montgomery Hyde.

At this distance it is hard to recapture just how radical the Beetons' decision to live over the shop would have seemed to their family and friends.
The Dorlings especially were appalled at the thought of Isabella camping
out among boxes of books and piles of ledgers. A slip of paper survives
from a slightly earlier time when they must have made a visit to 2 Chandos
Villas. Written in the form of a spoof entry in a guest-house register, the
text reads: "Hotel Beeton, Woodridings. Mr. and Mrs. Dorling of Epsom
arrived here on the 18th left 20th. Attendance good, cookery etc. ditto."
These days, though, the Dorlings were unlikely to play the same charming
game in relation to 248 Strand, a house which shouted its commercial
associations to every passer-by. True, its position on the main highway
running east–west through London gave one a sense of being at the heart
of things (in 1863 Lucy Dorling was delighted to be able to stand at the
window and cheer as Princess Alexandra, the Prince of Wales's bride, made
her stately entrance into the country). But living on the city's pulse brought
problems too: take just a few steps back from 248 Strand and you would
have been confronted with some of the poorest and filthiest courts and
alleys to be found in London. The place was a slum, as different as it was
possible to be from the greenery and good manners of Pinner.

So in the circumstances you can see why the Dorlings would have been
horrified. Elizabeth Dorling may have given birth to her eldest daughter
in a room at the top of her husband's warehouse only a few hundred
yards away, but that did not mean she wanted the same thing for that
baby when she grew up. Henry Dorling may have profited from the practical help of both his wives as he built up his Epsom printing business, but
that did not mean he thought Sam Beeton should expect the same contribution from his eldest step-daughter. The vast Mayson-Dorling clan may
have slept, eaten, and played in the Epsom Grandstand, but that did not
mean that, nearly a decade on, anyone thought it was desirable to mix up
commercial and domestic life quite so promiscuously. Times change, families reinvent themselves, and what seemed sensible in one generation
becomes eccentric and undignified in the next. It was bad enough that
Isabella had lost her status as a lady by going to work in her husband's
business, but now she was signalling to the world that there was not

much to choose between her and a shopkeeper's wife, up at dawn to sweep the front step and polish the counter.

The change in Sam and Isabella's style of living was even more startling when compared with the reverse fortune of the Dorlings. While the Beeton clan had remained fairly steady in its ways—Eliza still running the Dolphin with the help of her new husband, the girls mostly making matches with local warehousemen—the Dorlings had been going up in the world. In 1861, with a clutch of daughters ready to be launched onto the London marriage market, they had rented a mansion in Pimlico, at 62 Warwick Square, a magnificent Cubitt-built property. Unfortunately, the census for 1861, which would have given a snapshot of the household, no longer survives. However, the census for 1871, by which time the property had passed to a clergyman of independent means, shows a governess, a butler, a cook, a parlourmaid, two housemaids, a nurse, a nursery maid and a kitchen maid, the kind of fantasy household that Mrs. Beeton nods towards in the *Book of Household Management.* Granny Jerrom, whose help was still required to look after the youngest tranche of Dorlings, seems to have remained mostly in Epsom. However, towards the end of her life she too was lodging in Pimlico, not amid the magnificence that was 62 Warwick Square, but just round the corner in the more workaday Rutland Street where she rubbed shoulders with laundresses, tailors, and the familiar livery men.

It was from stately Warwick Square that John Mayson, Isabella's only brother, launched himself into adult life. From the day he turned twenty-one in 1860 John's name starts to appear in documents relating to Dorling's expanding business and property empire. So it comes as no surprise that at the age of only twenty-five he is describing himself as "proprietor" of St. Katharine's Dock Hotel near the Tower of London, a handsome property consisting of thirteen bedrooms, four sitting rooms, a billiard room, "two elegant dining rooms" and a "splendid saloon" from where he also acted as the sole contractor for refreshments at the Epsom Grandstand. John's choice of bride, however, was rooted in earlier family history, long before Henry Dorling had swept him and his three sisters off to start a new life in Epsom. Emily Holt, whom he married in 1864, was the daughter of a publican who had kept house at Snow Hill, in Smithfield, near to where old Sam Beeton's Globe had stood. As a child she had lived at various addresses around Marylebone where she had been an early pupil at Queen's College, which trained girls for jobs as governesses. Unfortunately none of this meant that the marriage turned out to be particularly blessed. John almost certainly had syphilis, which he passed on to the unsuspecting Emily before dying, in a classic convulsion, at the age of only thirty-one. She, meanwhile, endured another agonizing ten years of creeping paralysis and insanity while working as a live-in companion to the future Duchess of Rutland before dying, exhausted and tellingly childless, at the age of forty-one.

There are scattered clues that by the time Isabella and Sam made the move from Pinner to the Strand in the spring of 1862 the second little Samuel Orchart was already beginning to fail. The Dorlings, naturally, made a connection between the baby's ailing and the move to the smoky city, and used this as another stick with which to beat Sam. Were it not for his financial messiness, they reckoned that Isabella would be leading the life of a middle-class matron at "Hotel Beeton, Woodridings" and her baby would be a fat, flourishing country child. It was in a desperate attempt to put some roses into the cheeks of little Samuel Orchart Beeton that Sam and Isabella decamped to Hove for Christmas that year. Letters from both sides of the family suggest that the baby was "very unwell" by the time they arrived at the Sussex Hotel, a medium-sized establishment from whose bedroom windows you could see and smell the sea. But the ozone didn't work, or didn't work fast enough. Three days after Christmas the child took a turn for the worse and on the very last day of the year Isabella and Sam watched helplessly as their only child died. He was three years old.

This was the second time that the Beetons had lost a baby while far from home. Five years earlier they had been staying with the Englishes in Newmarket when their three-month-old—another unlucky Samuel Orchart—slipped from the world. Now, as 1862 gave way to 1863, they found themselves in the even bleaker surroundings of a hotel room. Mrs. Beeton, the woman who advised other people on how to run a nurturing home, had failed once again to achieve such a thing for herself. Children died, everyone knew that. But they were not supposed to die in a rented bed, wrapped in strangers' sheets.

The first time the Beetons had lost a baby they had buried him where he had sputtered to a halt, in Newmarket. Now, they decided, it was the time to plan for all the deaths that were to come. On 2 January Sam's step-mother Eliza and his Uncle Tom went to Norwood Cemetery to purchase a family burial plot on his behalf. The plot, explained Eliza in a letter to her step-son, was "about 3 graves beyond Staggs [Sam's aunt

Thomasin Stagg and her baby Caroline] on the same line." Also nearby was an obelisk marking the place where Samuel Powell Beeton had been buried in 1854 and where, in only a year's time, Eliza would herself be laid to rest, alongside her daughter Helen and her brother, Edward Douse. This child, make no mistake, would be buried as a Beeton.

Eliza had made arrangements with undertakers to meet the bereaved parents at Norwood Junction with a hearse. She begged Sam not to return to the grim surroundings of the Strand straight after the funeral on Saturday, but to come instead to Milk Street, and stay at least until Monday. "Bring dear Bella here if you will come . . . we can be so quiet . . . I cannot express half I feel for you both," said Eliza, in a stream of hopeless suggestion. The Dorlings' reaction to the loss of their grandson is not recorded, but from this point they decided that everything bad that happened to Isabella was automatically Sam's fault. His business was haemorrhaging money, his name was becoming a regular fixture in *The Times*' law reports, he was unable to provide a home for his wife on whose professional services he depended in a manner that was less than manly, and now he had proved himself for the second time incapable of producing a healthy baby. For Henry Dorling, a man whose business affairs were peaking and who had fathered seventeen robust children, Sam's scantiness in all departments was starting to look suspicious.

The cause of death given on little Samuel Orchart's certificate was "suppressed scarlatina" and "laryngitis." Scarlatina was the term used for a mild form of scarlet fever, but the "suppressed" is hard to untangle. The point, really, is that a red, angry rash must have appeared somewhere on the baby in order to provoke the diagnosis. Syphilitic babies typically display a bright angry rash, and the "laryngitis" could well describe the chronic wheezy snuffles that were also characteristic of the disease. Babies born with syphilis who do not die within the first few months are prey to constant ill health, and we know from both Isabella's brother and Sam's half-sister that the child had been ill for some time before the final trip to Hove.

The question remains, of course, whether Isabella realized what was happening to her. Even if she never sought advice over her string of miscarriages, she must have consulted a doctor at some point about her baby's feebleness. And surely that doctor would have taken a thorough obstetric history of the worried young mother sitting in front of him, perhaps suggested an examination, or at least asked sharp questions about Mr. Beeton's own state of health? The answer, surprisingly, is probably not. Doctors who strongly suspected the reason why a particular married female patient was producing a string of scrunched and peeling foetuses or complaining of shooting pains down her legs and back were apt to keep the information to themselves. There was, after all, no real cure nor any good reason for adding to the lady's distress and shame. Even if it was decided to attempt treatment, the usual thinking was that the woman should be kept in ignorance of the real nature of her complaint. Her husband might be told, of course, but then the chances were that he already knew who was responsible for this whole waking nightmare. Discretion, wilful ignorance, misdirection and denial—these were the most common ways of dealing with this nastiest of diseases.

Isabella's return to London in January 1863 must have been desperately difficult. After seven years of marriage she had no baby and no magazine of her own. The *Queen*, a project dear to her heart, had been taken from her and she was left with only routine work on the *Englishwoman's Domestic Magazine*. It is true that the *Book of Household Management* was selling well, but the prospect of re-editing its unwieldy bulk into smaller and cheaper formats can hardly have fired her creative juices. Nor did she have the comfort of a home and, perhaps what was even more important to her, a garden. Instead she was obliged to camp out in rooms over her husband's office. If she felt like taking a walk, she would almost immediately find herself in some of the nastiest slums in London. And if she had hoped that living over the shop would mean more time with Sam, she was almost certainly disappointed. For S.O. Beeton was busier than ever, his days passing in a blur of frenzied activity as he juggled a publishing schedule that was always in danger of buckling under its own ambition.

But just when it seemed that things could not get any worse, the clouds parted. First, at the end of January 1863, the *Morning Herald* printed the article that fabulously puffed the publications of S. O. Beeton. And then, at the beginning of March, only eight weeks after the death of little Samuel Orchart, Isabella became pregnant again. Seven years after contracting syphilis, she was now, in a classic pattern, finally able to conceive and carry a healthy baby to term. Born in the unlikely surroundings of a publisher's office on 2 December this child, yet another boy, would thrive for eighty-three years, dying eventually in 1947. This time the baby was christened plain Orchart, perhaps to avoid the jinx that seemed to have settled on the name Samuel. This time, too, there would be no risks taken with the treacherous London air. Dorling disapproval and plain common sense suggested that an office building on one of the capital's busiest roads was no place to raise a child. A shift to country living was called for, and this time the Beetons chose to go south rather than north. In the spring of 1864 they moved to Greenhithe, a small village twenty miles out of London on the Kent side of the Thames estuary.

It was Sam's early training in paper that brought them there. Greenhithe was dotted with mills that turned old rags and the newer esparto grass into crisp, clean reams. Every day and at every hour boats shipped crates of paper up the river to the waiting printing sheds of Fleet Street and the Strand. Trade was brisk now that the irksome tax on paper had finally gone and the small place crackled with a renewed sense of purpose. Greenhithe had long been the residence of journalists, editors, and authors, who had followed their trade's raw materials to their source and decided to settle there. Their daily train journey may have taken a full sixty minutes, but it terminated at London Bridge, making it far more convenient than Pinner for the inky side of town. One of Sam's editors at the *Boy's Own Magazine,* John Tillotson, lived at Abbey Lodge which was a hop, skip and a jump from where the Beetons eventually made their new home. An architect friend called Vulliamy was living at Ingress Cottage in the adjoining village of Swanscombe. Meanwhile, a newspaper man called George Moss owned Mount Pleasant, a single-storey farmhouse that teetered on the edge of one of the many chalk quarries that pitted the area. This ubiquitous chalk formed the raw material for estuarine Kent's other great industry, cement, and in time Mount Pleasant would be pulled down to make way for a giant processing plant. In these more gentle times, though, the only drawback to living in Greenhithe was that everything and everyone was permanently coated with a fine layer of soft white dust.

In the spring of 1864 Sam rented Mount Pleasant from George Moss, who himself lived in a house in Swanscombe High Street. The only way of working out what Mount Pleasant looked like is to use early ordnance maps and aerial photography (viewed from the sky, the two acres of ground that comprised the small estate still show up as a wedge-shaped patch of lighter coloured earth). For the actual style of the place, we have reproductions of two photographs from a hot, dreamy family afternoon gathering that summer. The building appears oddly shaped, consisting of two distinct blocks situated at right angles. The outside walls are covered with creeper; there is a terraced arcade decorated with hanging flower baskets and a little thatched summerhouse. The garden is intersected with fussy box hedges and there is a croquet course laid out on the lawn. After nearly two years cooped up in a central London office, the Beetons were clearly keen to play at being country people. Sam kept a mare called Gertie who in time would share a field with a mule that M. Goubaud sent over from Paris. In the years to come there would also be a dog called Rough, a cat that went by the name of Puss, a flock of hens, two rabbits, and a canary.

Despite its average prettiness, the new residence naturally did not go down well with the Dorling clan. Charlotte, Isabella's eldest half-sister, remembered it later as "that nasty, damp house down by the river," which is odd, since it was a good half-mile from the Thames. Still, on that summer afternoon in 1864 when Charlotte's sister and half-sisters came to visit, they look pleased enough with the place. The family group sits in the garden, with the spire of St. Mary's parish church just visible in the background. Either Bessie or Esther Mayson is nursing six-month-old Orchart, while Isabella dandles her newest half-brother, Horace, who had been born when her mother Elizabeth was forty-seven. Sixteen-year-old Lucy Dorling, meanwhile, concentrates on the croquet.

The only verbal descriptions we have of Isabella from this time come from two pieces of sentimental journalism, dating from the 1930s when interest in "Mrs. Beeton" was beginning to swell. In 1938, having spent the last five years battling with Mayson Beeton over her attempts to write some kind of portrait of his increasingly illustrious mother, Joan Adeney Easdale decided to broadcast a talk on the Home Service entitled "In Pursuit of Mrs. Beeton." Much of Easdale's piece could just as easily have been written today, as she describes the familiar frustrations of the Beeton biographer, including all those research dead ends, vanishing witnesses, and muddled testimony. One of her rare sleuthing successes, however, was tracking down an elderly man called "Gentleman" Hoadley, who had been a tenor sax-horn in the Greenhithe band that played on the promenade. "Gentleman"—actually ninety-five-year-old John W. Hoadley—provides Easdale with his scanty recollections of Mrs. Beeton: "how pretty and kind she was" and "how she used to stop and speak to him sometimes as she passed down the road on her way to the station: that was when she went up to town almost every day to help her husband in his big publishing house in the Strand."

Hoadley's honeyed chat displays all the weaknesses of evidence recalled from a great distance. Isabella, in particular, has always been at the mercy of well-meaning anecdotalists who liked to emphasize her "prettiness," presumably as a way of offsetting the received notion of "Mrs. Beeton" as stout and middle-aged. In fact, a photograph from just about the time when Hoadley knew Isabella shows a woman who, while chic and even handsome, could by no stretch of the imagination be called "pretty." More solid altogether is Hoadley's evidence that Mrs. Beeton continued to commute almost daily to the Strand during 1864. This was despite having one baby at home and another on the way.

Isabella's working pattern is confirmed in another piece of journalism, this time from the *Portsmouth Evening News* of 5 February 1931. The article is written by "Bertha," the pseudonym of a woman journalist whose father had lived for a time at Greenhithe and who was herself a friend of the younger Dorlings. "Bertha" recalls in her "Ladies' Letter" how her father had told her that "Mrs. Beeton used to go up to town every day by the business train with her husband, a quite unusual thing for any woman of those times to do, and really more or less resented by the other travellers, who were mostly young men who all knew each other but had to curb their exuberant spirits when a lady was present."

As well as commuting daily to the Strand during this last hectic year of her life Isabella also continued to make annual visits to Paris to consult with the Goubauds, view the latest fashions for the magazine, and buy new dresses for herself (it was now that she began to get a reputation for stylishness among her sisters). Accompanied by Sam she had made the Paris trip in July 1863 and again in 1864, apparently unbothered by the fact that she was pregnant both times. The first trip was combined with a holiday to Germany, the first time Isabella had returned there since her honeymoon in 1856. For this second leg of the journey she kept a detailed diary. Unfortunately this has disappeared, and so we are dependent on the account that Nancy Spain, who did see the diary, published in her biography of 1948. From Paris it seems that the Beetons went directly to Berlin, where Sam had bookselling business. All the local talk at the time concerned Princess Vicky, Queen Victoria's eldest daughter, who had married the Prussian Crown Prince five years previously and become a social star in her adopted homeland.

Isabella was clearly thrilled that the ladies of Berlin shared her passion for Princess Vicky. With obvious satisfaction she noted how English rather than French was now the smart language to learn and how, every time Vicky went out in her carriage, "everybody takes off their hats and much more enthusiasm is displayed whenever she is seen in public than any other member of the Prussian Royal Family." At times Isabella's interest in Princess Vicky reaches a positive frenzy. In every royal building—and there were many—she insists on heading directly for Vicky's private apartments, and then recording what she found there in great detail. Thus we learn that the Princess's bedroom at Babelsberg was decorated with "Scotch plaid" while her private chambers in her own palace were hung with "Four splendid pictures in Gobelin tapestry given her as a wedding present by the Empress of the French." And then, in the voice that so exactly recalls that of the professional "Mrs. Beeton," Isabella concludes approvingly of the Empress's living arrangements: "A nice little palace, very nicely arranged."

The next trip to Paris, which took place a year later in that last summer of 1864, was, according to Nancy Spain, carefully documented by Isabella in that same paper refill diary. Recently, Nancy Spain's scrappy transcript of the 1864 diary has come to light in a cupboard in Exeter and from this, together with the more coherent account she published in 1948, it is possible to make a plausible narrative for one key afternoon that the Beetons spent at the Longchamps racetrack, just south of Paris. They were there to watch the second ever French Grand Prix, in which Derby-winner Blair Atholl was running. Immediately clear is the fact that both Isabella and Sam were expert spectators, casting knowledgeable eyes over the track's condition, the horses' form, the catering arrangements, and much more. Thus Isabella writes:

> Walked round the course. Much better condtn. than last year—although still covered with herbage. The ground is hard, but much has been done for it, much still remains to do. . . . Worst running ground in middle of course close to the Baron's (de Rothschild's) chateau, going down hill.

Her particular criticism was naturally reserved for the race cards, which were not only difficult to get hold of but "a muddle." On the page opposite this comment Sam has written, "Mr. Dorling and cardmakers might be advantageously imported," as well he might since he himself managed to get two similar-looking horses, Vermout and Bois Roussel, mixed up. Isabella, meanwhile, was shrewdly assessing two of the other runners.

"The horse (Blair A[tholl]) looked well, but the mare (Fille de l'Aire) seemed to be sweating a little under her cloth." By the end of the race, in which Blair Atholl unfortunately failed to perform, Isabella made some brisk calculations that, unsurprisingly, concluded with the suggestion that Epsom was distinctly superior to Longchamps: "The pace for the Grand Prix was not so great as in the Derby. We find on calculation that if the pace *had* been as fast, the race wd. have been run in 3m 25, whereas it occupied 3m 30 secs."

It looks from the diary as though both Sam and Isabella were planning to write articles on the French Grand Prix on their return to Britain. There are passages in Isabella's hand that read like a rough draft for an *EDM* article on "A Day at the French Races." Sam, meanwhile, seems to have decided on the spur of the moment that this would make excellent material for a piece in *Sporting Life*. At the front of the diary he has drafted a letter to the paper setting out why he thinks it should cover the race, citing the largeness of the pot, the number of spectators, the quality of the horseflesh and "the rank of the personages connected with the great French race" (no less a personage than Emperor Napoleon III had appeared that very afternoon).

Just why Sam should be writing to the *Sporting Life* at all is a puzzle. The previous twelve months had been dominated by a bad-tempered, expensive, and inconclusive court case in which Sam both sued and was sued over his involvement in the weekly racing newspaper. The associated cases of *Hutton v. Beeton* and *Beeton v. M'Murray* were so complex that on several occasions the judge and the barristers, including a couple of QCs and the Attorney General, admitted that the case was in a "state of confusion" and that "no one can understand anything without paying the utmost attention." What seems to have happened is that in March 1861 Sam agreed to buy the *Sporting Life* and two other similar titles from a paper merchant called M'Murray, as well as a half-share in the lease of 148 Fleet Street, together with fixtures and fittings for a total sum of over £8,000. He then installed Isabella's step-brother Edward J. Dorling, who was already printing the paper, as manager of all three titles. Eighteen months later it emerged that M'Murray had never been in a position to sell Beeton more than a half-interest in the papers, since the other half was still owned by a man called John Hutton. Hutton was now suing Sam for his presumption in taking all the profits and Sam was in turn cross-suing M'Murray for misleading him.

As the evidence unfurled interminably it became clear that there had been more than a little sleight of hand on Sam's part, with crucial letters being tampered with to suit his version of events. At one point, when it looked as if he was going to lose the newspaper altogether, Sam had even started to put out feelers about producing a "spoiler" publication, designed expressly to compete with the *Sporting Life*. By 6 May, when things had been going on like this for almost a year, Lord Justice Knight Bruce felt compelled to say, "There are three parties here engaged—Mr. Beeton, Mr. Hutton and Mr. M'Murray—and I must admit I have little or no admiration for either [sic] of them." On 9 July Beeton's case against M'Murray was finally dismissed and he was obliged to pay costs. His immediate response was to ask the judge to dissolve the partnership since, in the words of his barrister, Malins, "Mr. Beeton, on no account, will consent to remain joint proprietor with Mr. Hutton." Then, with typical bluster, he announced that he was going to appeal to the Lords.

So in these circumstances it is odd to find that only three weeks later Sam is writing to the *Sporting Life* suggesting that he cover the French Grand Prix for the newspaper. What the court case does explain, however, is just why the Dorlings were becoming implacably opposed to Sam in the years immediately before Isabella's death. Not only had he lost money and his good name in this ridiculously long-drawn-out case, which was reported in *The Times* on no fewer than thirty separate occasions, but he had dragged the name of Dorling into the sordid business too. Isabella's step-brother, the gentle Edward, was called as a witness on several occasions, and at one point was accused by the Attorney General, who was appearing for Hutton, of actively recruiting the *Sporting Life* workmen to work on a rival publication. The name of Dorling had long been associated with all that was orderly, progressive, and decent about the still suspect world of the racetrack. And here was Sam Beeton dragging it through the churned-up mud.

It was Sam's love of horseflesh that took him to Newmarket a few weeks later, in October, where he stayed with the now widowed Robert English at Warren Villa. Isabella stayed behind in Greenhithe, and it was on this occasion that Sam wrote the only letter to her that still survives from their marriage. Crucially, the letter contains important evidence that by late 1864 Sam was experiencing severe financial difficulties. It turns out that his trip to Newmarket has been undertaken to sell his beloved mare Gertie for 100 guineas. In his usual blustery way Sam crows to Isabella that he is on the point of closing a deal with the fishy-sounding Prince Soltikoff, and suggests jokingly, "I think I had better go into the horse-dealing line." (In the circumstances it is lucky that he did not: Gertie remained unsold and had to be ignominiously brought back to Greenhithe.) Next Sam gets down to business, which in this case means the prospective launch of a new magazine for teenage girls called the *Young Englishwoman.*

> I have asked Sidney [his half-brother Sidney Perkes Beeton] to get Young [Francis Young, one of his key employees] to write *his* notions on paper of what the Y E'woman shd be, irrespectively of mine, and if Y is there tomorrow, as I think he will be, ask Sidney to let you see him, and you can tell him what *you* think.
>
> Send the description of the 8 pages you have already got up for the YE'woman as soon as pos' with the cliché's [*sic*] to Cox and W[yman], and ask C W to let Poulter do the making up. These done, the next thing is the Sheet of Dble Demy with 2 sets of diagrams and Needlework patterns, giving us, that is to say, the Suppt for the Y E'woman for 2 weeks. These two sheets of Dble Demy (the pattern already pasted down and the diagrams as just mentioned) will set us right for 6 weeks. With No 1 I suppose we had better issue the Patterns and Diagrams 8 pp that is to say. N'est-ce-pas?

This letter shows convincingly that Isabella was much more than a lady editress who picked out her favourite fashions from home and commissioned pretty sketches of them. Nor was she simply a glorified secretary, carrying out routine tasks in the boss's absence (this had been one of the more persistent rumours floating around in the mid-twentieth century, partly as a consequence of Mayson Beeton's determination to reinsert his father back into the Beeton story). Instead, we see her here both supervising fiddly production processes and being consulted on important new projects. Conventional wisdom suggested that there was no point in producing a magazine directed at teenage girls since in this period they moved from childhood to adulthood without inhabiting any transitional stage. While Beeton had triumphantly shown that male adolescents were hungry for a literature of their own, it was far from clear that he could pull off the same trick with their sisters.

As it turned out, the decision to launch the *Young Englishwoman* two months later was one of the brighter moments in the sad months to come.

It became one of S. O. Beeton's most successful titles, lasting until the end of the century. In the Introduction to the first issue, anxious parents were assured that the magazine "may be placed without the slightest fear in the hands of girls of tender age." Even more than its elder sister, the *EDM,* the *Young Englishwoman* concentrated on domestic and practical topics. The fiction is anodyne and the articles steer clear of even the most coded references to "advanced" matters such as political and legal reform. There is a junior version of the "Conversazione," "Our Drawing Room," which leavens discussions about courtship with chats about bossy siblings. What *did* make the *Young Englishwoman* extraordinary, though, was that it sold for only 1d and, like its male equivalent, the *Boy's Penny Magazine,* contained material that had been exclusively commissioned. The days of doubling up and making do were well and truly over.

This may have been admirable but it was also extremely expensive. For several years now Sam had been borrowing heavily from the bank to meet his production costs. Things were getting desperate towards the close of 1864, when family rumour started to surface about how Sam was wearing Isabella out with his financial crises. For towards the end of that letter written from Newmarket he ponders their present happiness in finally producing a thriving child, before proceeding to an ominous hint that things are once again about to get worse, "Preserve to us our present joy, and we can bear a good deal of trouble, having that."

In her biography, written under strict terms of engagement with the Beeton family, Sarah Freeman is careful to leave out the reference to the "good deal of trouble," despite quoting heavily from the rest of the letter. Presumably she wanted to direct attention away from the fact that Sam was already deeply worried about his finances well before the infamous collapse of Overend and Gurney eighteen months later. For the fact that Sam went down with one of the most celebrated financial crashes of the nineteenth century was, in an odd way, the saving of his reputation. Instead of having failed by his own carelessness and bombast, sympathetic biographers like Hyde and Freeman could portray him as the victim of a financial scandal that had ruined thousands of honest, blameless Britons. All the same, Hyde was too scrupulous to let the misdirection pass entirely. At the end of a long paragraph explaining the catalogue of mistakes and mismanagement that led to the collapse of the wretched Overend and Gurney, he slips in a brief and oblique counterpoint: "Beeton himself had also over-traded in his business."

That first Christmas at Greenhithe must have been busy. There were now five magazines to get out, two of them weekly, and Isabella was already nearing the end of the *Dictionary of Everyday Cookery*. Yet in other, more important, ways the Beetons must have been hugging themselves with joy. In a few weeks' time Isabella was due to give birth, and for the first time in eight years of married life the Beetons were about to fulfil their dream of becoming a proper family. "They were so anxious to have two little boys playing together," remembered Matilda Browne, a Greenhithe neighbour whose life was about to become entwined with the Beetons' in ways that no one could possibly have imagined.

The Beetons got their wish of two little boys, but at a dreadful cost. The final sequence of events started on Sunday, 29 January. Family anecdote has Isabella busy correcting proofs of the *Dictionary of Everyday Cookery* when she went into labour. Things must have gone smoothly, because by the end of the day a healthy boy had been delivered. By Monday, however, Isabella was sick and shivery. Working backwards from an angry piece that Sam wrote six years later in the *Englishwoman's Domestic Magazine* about doctors' habitual slackness over hygiene being responsible for so many deaths from puerperal fever, it has always been assumed that this is what must have happened to Isabella. In fact there is no definite proof that Isabella was attended by a doctor, nor that he unwittingly transferred bacteria to her from attending a previous stillbirth (the commonest scenario in cases of puerperal fever). Certainly, though, by the time she died six days later on 6 February, the doctor in attendance was satisfied that the cause of death was "Peritonitis 2 days Puerperal Fever 6 days."

There was nothing easy about dying from puerperal fever, certainly none of the slipping away that you might expect from an Angel in the House. The fact that her symptoms came on so soon after the birth suggests that Isabella had contracted one of the more virulent strains. Streptococci would have passed from the doctor's hands, up the vaginal passage, through the uterine wall and into the bloodstream, sending her whole body into toxic shock. Her belly would have been rigid with pain and there was a particular terror associated with puerperal fever that even seasoned doctors found hard to watch.

But the angry family chatter that surrounded Isabella's death over the next fifty years was never really about whether she was or wasn't infected by a doctor who had not taken the precaution of washing his hands in a solution of chloride of lime. What the Dorlings and the Beetons debated, until well after the Second World War, was the extent to which Sam was guilty of burdening Isabella with too much work and worry, so that she became susceptible to opportunistic infection. Three quarters of women who caught puerperal fever in the 1860s survived, and the Dorlings wanted to know why Isabella, a young woman who on her German holiday just a few months before had thought nothing of climbing two mountains in one day while pregnant, should be one of the unlucky minority who succumbed.

The case for the prosecution, constructed over time by the Dorlings, goes like this. In the months leading up to her confinement, Sam expected far too much from Isabella in the way of work. Whenever they raised this with him his standard response was that childbirth was "a mere effort of nature," in other words not a medical condition or something to fuss about. While this sounds sensible to modern ears, to the Dorlings it seemed as if Sam was suggesting that there was absolutely no reason for Isabella to curtail her hectic schedule simply because she was expecting a baby. Caroline Baker, the maid at Greenhithe who is our chief witness for that last dreadful week, insisted later to both Matilda Browne and Bessie and Esther Mayson that "there is little doubt [Isabella] worked too long and too hard near her confinement" and that "on the day the baby was born she did too much work." The second plank of the prosecution is that, even once Isabella had been taken ill and was lying feverish in bed, Sam insisted on treating her as if she had a mild cold. His financial affairs were reaching a crisis point, and he was desperate to get her advice on what to do next. According to Caroline Baker, this time filtered through Bessie Mayson, "Sam Beeton was told not to worry her anymore, *by the doctor,* and he went into her room and told her all his latest troubles (as he always used)— something to do with banking—and she turned her face to the wall."

From here it was a short step to the conclusion, in the emphatic words of Charlotte Dorling, Isabella's half-sister, that "He killed her!" But all this proves, really, is that by the time of Isabella's death her band of sisters and half-sisters, taking the lead from their parents, had decided that Sam was a dreadful man who had married a clever, ladylike girl and reduced her to a drudge. Instead of the well-furnished and elegant lives enjoyed by the other Mayson and Dorling women, whether married or single,

Isabella had become a wage slave who was obliged to work up to the moment that she was about to give birth, like a peasant or a carthorse. The full extent of the pressure she was under was not apparent until the days and weeks following her death when brokers' men arrived at Mount Pleasant and started making off with the furniture. At least poor Bella had not had to watch while her home was dismantled and removed in a cart. This case for the prosecution was presented by Nancy Spain, Lucy Dorling's granddaughter, in her book *Mrs. Beeton and her Husband* in 1948 and again in a more damning new edition of 1956.

The case for the defence appears in books by H. Montgomery Hyde and Sarah Freeman, both of whom worked closely with the Beeton family in return for access to their papers. Montgomery Hyde argues in Sam's favour that Isabella was a healthy girl, and there is no reason to think that commuting to London or correcting proofs would have particularly tired her. Freeman adds the intriguing thought that, since Isabella was delirious during the week that she lingered, it made no difference what Sam did or said to her. In any case, says Freeman, the malignancy of puerperal fever depends entirely on which strain has been contracted. Environmental factors like noise and stress make very little difference to the outcome. Given that the doctor registered Isabella's cause of death as "peritonitis," which occurred only in the more virulent kind of postpartum infection, this part of Freeman's argument holds up. However, neither she nor Hyde mentions Mount Pleasant being broken up by duns, and both insist that Beeton never appeared in the bankruptcy court, which, in the contorted formula of Freeman, "would have added irretrievable disgrace to what was otherwise not dishonourable misfortune." So "not dishonourable misfortune," as far as the Beeton apologists were concerned, is what happened to Sam.

Whatever the Dorlings might have said in the difficult years that lay ahead, there is no doubting that Sam was flayed with grief at the sudden loss of Isabella. Her death came hard on the heels of two other unexpected bereavements. First, in September 1863, his twenty-three-year-old half-sister Nelly had died of consumption only a few months after her marriage to Thomas Lowden, yet another warehouseman. Then, just six months later, came the even worse blow of his step-mother's passing from heart disease at the age of fifty-four. After Samuel Powell Beeton's early death ten years earlier, it had been Eliza Beeton who had kept the Dolphin going single-handedly while managing to raise Sam's six half-siblings.

The bond between Sam and his step-mother was strong and spontaneous (he had never known his natural mother and Mrs. Beeton was always "mother" or "the missus"). He had lodged at the Dolphin throughout his adolescence and repaid Eliza's kindness after his father's death by helping out when he could, for instance by taking time off from his hectic work schedule to chaperone young Edward Albert out to his Parisian boarding school. And Eliza in return continued to be a tower of strength to the young man, even after her remarriage to Isaac Wyatt in 1857. Although already suffering from the heart disease that would eventually kill her, it was she and not the Dorlings who had taken charge in those dreadful days following the death of the second little Samuel Orchart in January 1863.

And now, on top of these devastating events, Sam had forfeited the person who meant more to him than anyone else. The energetic little man who had previously been able to rise above the loss of a fortune (in 1853) and two children (in 1857 and 1862) now found himself, finally, brought to his knees. Matilda Browne, the Greenhithe neighbour who was soon to become an integral part of his life, remembered what a frightful sight he made in the weeks following Isabella's death: "The first time I ever saw him was at Greenhithe station . . . and he avoided speaking or noticing any one. He looked very pale and thin . . . and hair and moustache neglected."

A week or so later Sam was pouring out his feelings in a black-bordered letter to William Stagg, his uncle by marriage and close friend of his late father's.

Greenhithe
Feb 18, '65

My Dear, Good Mr. Stagg,

I can hardly write a word to you that has reference to the great blow that it has pleased Heaven to strike me. I am able to attend to my business matters, and am, although exhausted in body, not worse in health than usual

. . .

To tell you all:—my agony is excessive, but I have hours of calm and quiet which refresh me and enable me to meet the dreadful grief that well nigh overpowers me, and renders me unable to move or stir. But I hope to conquer at last, and will strive, with all the courage I have and can receive by appeals to her good spirit, and to the All-Ruler, to live a good life, honest and pure, to hold the love and respect of good men, and not lose my own respect. In doing this, and in trying to bring up my two little ones, I shall obtain, I think, some comfort.

Tell me in a day or two how yr. darling wife is (oh! how Bella reverenced her!); and when she is able, she will write me a few of her kind lines. I have so yearned to see yr. face and press yr. hand, and was so glad to get yr. two notes.

All have been to me very good, here and in London, and one strain only can be heard of respect and love for her memory.

God bless you ever—and yours:

And Believe me Affny. Yr.

S.O.B.

Beneath the lachrymose puffery there is, surely, an overwhelming sense that Sam both loved and admired Isabella and thought it only natural that the rest of the world would feel exactly the same way. A few months earlier, in the letter Sam sent to Isabella from Newmarket, he had finished with a couple of paragraphs which come the closest to telling us what their relationship was like on the eve of its ending.

Goodbye, my girl, "Sweet kisses on thy fair-formed brow I'd give, but can't just now."

Receive, I pray you my good master, the assurance of my highest consideration, the intimation of my most considerable respect, and the expression of the warmest love from him who is, and ever shall be, paper without end, A man (qui est reussi)

S.O.B.

From the early days of their courtship a decade earlier Sam had inverted the usual gender codes, insisting, "I have no wish, I assure you, to have the 'management' of you," and instead was happy to acknowledge Isabella as his superior, his anchor, his "master mine." His pestering of her for financial advice during the last week of her life may have been selfish, but it shows just how much he valued her judgement. Expecting her to work nearly as hard as he when she had, for over half their time together, a child to look after was insensitive, but it was the opposite of condescending. Sam had the utmost respect for Isabella. Not the pretend, patronizing respect of, say, John Ruskin's hymn to lovely womanhood in *Sesame and Lilies* or Coventry Patmore's *Angel in the House,* but the real solid article. He valued Isabella for her education, her facility with languages, her unforced love of music. He admired her taste and trusted her judgement. He assumed that she would be as capable as he of managing the production side of the business, and was quite happy to admit that she had a firmer grasp of financial detail. Matilda Browne, who later worked with Sam, was clear that Isabella "ran everything at the Strand as well as at home." The Beetons, in short, had that rare thing, a companionate marriage based on respect, love, and an unspoken assumption of absolute equality.

Did Isabella love Sam? Undoubtedly. But nine years of marriage to him cannot have brought what she expected. The hard work she did not mind, since their rocky financial circumstances forced her to find a vocation that she might otherwise have missed. If Sam had been a more reliable provider she would have been at home all day, brooding over the empty nursery instead of bustling up to town to be useful. The problem was, of course, that the empty nursery was Sam's fault too. He had infected her with syphilis on her honeymoon and the result over the next six years was two dead babies and a series of miscarriages. It is impossible that Isabella did not begin to understand what was happening to her, especially since right from the start she had referred to her fiancé's "roving nature." She had grown up on a racetrack where prostitutes plied their trade. Walking in the streets around the Strand, the place where prostitutes habitually loitered and near which Sam had always worked, must have made her think, perhaps even have prompted that crucial conversation with him. Whatever the state of her understanding, there is a sad irony in the fact that just at the point where she was able to start bearing healthy children, an infection of another kind killed her. Isabella Beeton's life can truly be said to have been blighted by biology.

But just at the end, during that miserable last week of shivers and aches and delirium, there are signs that Isabella may finally have had enough of Sam. The crucial piece of evidence comes in that testimony from Caroline Baker, refracted through Bessie Mayson, which speaks of Sam pestering Isabella with "his latest troubles . . . something to do with banking," at which point, says Caroline/Bessie, "she turned her face to the wall." Throughout her relationship with Sam, which had lasted almost a decade, Isabella had never turned away from him. In those early courtship days she may occasionally have broken off communication, but that was a lover's strategy designed to get her stubborn fiancé to come running. Throughout their marriage, for much of which they lived and worked together twenty-four hours a day, there is not a single whisper of evidence that they were anything other than calm, loving companions. The Dorlings would surely have welcomed any little hint that they had been right all along about Sam's unsuitability as a husband, but Isabella never gave them the satisfaction. That last letter that Sam wrote to Isabella from Newmarket a mere six months before her death, when they both knew that the financial noose was tightening, is a lovely mix of productive shoptalk and romantic intimacy. And yet the fact remains that during the last few days of her life, as it became apparent that the house of S. O. Beeton really might be going under, which involved not just the Strand but Mount Pleasant being broken up, Isabella, for the only time on record, turned away from Sam in despair.

Isabella was buried at Norwood Cemetery at half past two on Saturday, 11 February 1865 in the grave that had been bought only two years earlier for the second little Samuel Orchart. No record of the funeral remains. Mrs. Beeton was a young married woman of no particular fame or social cachet who had written a cookery book for her husband that was said to be doing rather well. That was not enough, in the 1860s, to merit an obituary even in the local paper. Instead there was a curt notice in *The Times* which was repeated, with slightly different wording, in the local *Gravesend Journal:* "On the 6th inst., at Greenhithe, the wife of S. O. Beeton Esq., in the 29th year of her age. Friends will kindly accept this intimation."

But if there were no notices in the papers, or even in the magazines that she had done so much to shape, Mrs. Beeton would have one where she mattered most. In the days following her death the proof pages of the new *Dictionary of Everyday Cookery,* hewn from the *BOHM,* would have come back with her careful handwriting all over them. There was just time, before they went off to be printed and bound, to add a tribute. It is one of the finest things Sam ever wrote.

USQUE AD FINEM

Her hand has lost its cunning—the firm true hand that wrote these formulae and penned the information contained in this little book. Cold in the silent tomb lie the once nimble, useful fingers—now nerveless, unable for anything and ne'er to do work more in this world. Exquisite palate, unerring judgment, sound common sense, refined tastes—all these had this dear lady who has gone 'ere her youth had scarcely come. But four times seven years were all she passed in this world; and since the day she became wedded wife—now nearly nine years passed—her greatest, chiefest aims were to provide for the comfort and pleasure of those she loved and had around her, and to employ her best faculties for the use of her sisters, Englishwomen generally. Her surpassing affection and devotion led her to find happiness in aiding, with all her heart and soul, the Husband whom she richly blessed and honoured with her abounding love.

Her Works speak for themselves; and, although taken from this world in the very height of health and strength, and in the early days of womanhood, she felt that satisfaction—so great to all who strive with good intent and warm will—of knowing herself regarded with respect and gratitude.

Her labours are ended here; in purer atmosphere she dwells; and maybe in the land beyond the skies, she has a nobler work to accomplish. Her plans for the future cannot be wholly carried out; her husband knew them all, and will diligently devote himself to their execution, as far as may be. The remembrance of her wishes—always for the private and public welfare—and the companionship of her two little boys—too young to know the virtues of their good Mother—this memory, this presence, will nerve the Father, left alone, to continue to do his duty; in which he will follow the example of his Wife, for her duty no woman has ever better accomplished than the late

ISABELLA MARY BEETON

And that was the last time that the public had its attention drawn to the fact that Mrs. Beeton was dead. Once Sam's grief settled and his attention turned again to the desperate state of his business, it soon became clear that out of all his dwindling assets "Mrs. Beeton" was fast becoming the greatest. From the mouthful that was "The Book of Household Management edited by Mrs. Isabella Beeton" it was "Mrs. Beeton" that was beginning to emerge as the strongest selling point. This was the name that would appear in large letters on the *Dictionary of Everyday*

Cookery, this was the name that might just pull the firm of S. O. Beeton back from bankruptcy. To kill the goose that laid the golden eggs was madness. From now on the only sensible thing to do was pretend that Mrs. Beeton was alive, well, and looking forward to supplying the nation with yet more words of wisdom from her immaculately-run home.

INTERLUDE

The coloured plates are a novelty not without value.

ISABELLA BEETON,
Book of Household Management

BEETON'S BOOK OF HOUSEHOLD MANAGEMENT was the first British cookery book to use colour plates—ten of them, in fact—to show readers exactly how the food should look when it came to table. Right from the start, though, the Beetons realized that colour was about more than instruction, it was about pleasure. Until the mid-1850s colour reproduction was simply too expensive for mass-market publications which, as in the case of the first series of the *Englishwoman's Domestic Magazine*, used black and white woodcuts for the work that is today done by photographs. But once the pioneering (and insolvent) printer George Baxter sold licences for the use of his revolutionary technique of using both metal and wood blocks to produce the colour "separations" that resulted in a multi-tonal image, the way was clear to flood the previously monochromatic reading experience with jewel tones.

The Baxter licensee most associated with the Beetons is William Dickes of Old Fish Street and, while it is impossible to be certain, it looks as if it was he who enabled them to produce all those cod's heads and Christmas puddings in colour. Exciting though this might be, it was still the case that the plates from this first edition of the *Book of Household Management* are muted and restricted compared with the riot of colour and fine detail that appeared in later versions. None of Baxter's licensees had the time, patience, or funds to run to the twenty-seven separations that the master habitually used, with the result that their finished pieces during these early years were blunter and quieter than his exquisite signature pieces.

As for who drew all those Christmas puddings, boiled fowl with cauliflower, and boiled calf's head, it is impossible to be certain since there are no identifying signatures. In all their magazines the Beetons had used the best artists, that starry cohort that had first cut its teeth on the pioneeringly visual *Illustrated London News* and gone on to pursue successful careers as both painters and illustrators. Birket Foster and Harrison Weir are the two names most often associated with Beeton publications, and it certainly looks as if a high proportion of the animal drawings that appear at the head of the food chapters in the *Book of Household Management*—all those leaping deer and placid sheep—are the work of Harrison Weir, whose speciality was farmyard scenes.

However, while the subject of the Frontispiece—an idyllic farmyard scene—is exactly the sort of thing that Birket Foster liked to paint, it is another artist, Henry George Hine, who has signed the work. The fact that the title running under the picture reveals that it was originally commissioned to illustrate a line from a patriotic poem by Felicia Hemans, entitled *The Homes of England,* suggests that it was quite possibly left over from another Beeton publication and merely thrown in at the last minute to make up the pages (it did not appear in the part-work version). This scrabbling together of work by various anonymous artists exactly matches that sense of flux arising from Mrs. Beeton's own text, consisting as it does of other people's written bits and pieces.

Something remains to be said about the engraver, the often unsung hero who provided the skills that transferred the artist's original work into a format ready for the printers. His job was to cut into a block of fine-grained boxwood or metal, producing an exact reproduction of the original work (some artists were obliging enough to sketch their pictures directly onto the block). The work was fiddly and, in the wrong hands, could spoil an artist's reputation, which is why so many painters preferred to associate with one or two engravers whose touch they trusted. Birket Foster, for instance, was a confirmed fan of the engraver-turned-publisher Henry Vizetelly and it was due to the fact that the pair took off for Europe in the summer of 1852 to search for scenes for a new illustrated version of Longfellow's *Hyperion* that Vizetelly lost control of his investment in Sam Beeton's spectacularly profitable *Uncle Tom's Cabin* venture.

The Beetons, naturally enough in the circumstances, did not use Vizetelly as their engraver but instead stuck most often to H. Newsom Woods. Woods's work can be seen in the Frontispiece to the *Book of Household Management* and, in Sam's most ambitiously visual production, the *Illustrated Family Bible*, he is credited along with the artists such as Schnorer and Foster whose original work appears. It is "Mr. Woods," too, to whom Isabella mentions sending off the plate for *Management* during her Irish holiday in July 1860; and it is, once again, through Mr. Woods's contacts that the Beetons are able to do business with the right people during their trip to Paris three months earlier, when they are busy working out a way of getting the magnificent Jules David fashion plates into their newly visual *Englishwoman's Domestic Magazine*. For if the Beetons understood anything, it was that in the bright world of High Victorianism, the dominant sense was now sight.

CHAPTER ELEVEN

※

SPINNINGS ABOUT TOWN

PEOPLE, AS SAM SAID in his letter to William Stagg, had been very kind. In Greenhithe the Mosses, who owned Mount Pleasant and lived in nearby Swanscombe, rallied briskly round. Mrs. Moss found a wet-nurse for the baby. Help also came from the surprising source of Henry Mayson Dorling, Isabella's eldest step-brother. Dorling lived in Sydenham with his wife Annie and, despite their having been married five years, the nursery remained conspicuously bare. They offered to take in eighteen-month-old Orchy until his distraught father was well enough to cope. That Henry Mayson Dorling should reach out to Sam is surprising not simply because one might assume that he shared the family's implacable dislike of his disreputable brother-in-law, but also because he was known in later life as a particularly nasty man. By the 1890s, by which time he had long succeeded as head of his late father's business empire, the "Dictator of Epsom" was apt to say with grim satisfaction, "Everyone hates me—and I like it!" But that was certainly not the case in 1865 when Sam gratefully accepted his offer of a temporary home for his elder child, known as Orchy. The new baby, meanwhile, would be called Mayson Moss—Mayson after his mother and Moss after Sam's helpful Greenhithe friends. It made a conspicuous break from the various unlucky combinations of "Samuel" and "Orchart" that had been bestowed on the baby's three elder brothers.

That Mayson Moss would not actually be christened for another two years, along with the slightly older Orchy, in the parish church at the bottom of the garden, says a great deal about the chaos of Sam's life over the next few months. The bailiffs were continuing to press for payment, at least according to Nancy Spain, who maintains that one of them even moved into Mount Pleasant to stand guard over Sam's dwindling assets. Befuddled with grief, Sam made no attempt to face the situation. Instead, he saddled up Gertie and disappeared for hours on end.

Henry Mayson Dorling, who looked after Isabella's elder surviving baby, Orchart, in the weeks following her death.

One of his destinations was the nearby home of a young couple called the Brownes. And so starts the strangest part yet of the Beeton story. Twenty-eight-year-old Charles Rouse Browne worked at the Westminster Fire Office, the country's leading insurance agency which covered both commercial firms and private individuals against fire damage and had more recently added a life assurance service. Every day Charlie would commute from Greenhithe to the head office in King Street, a few hundred yards away from Beeton's office in the Strand. Since 1771 when Charlie's great-grandfather had been appointed chief clerk, the Westminster Fire Office operated as the effective fiefdom of the Browne family. However, it was not until 1879 that Charlie would finally succeed his own father to the top job of Secretary. Until that time he was obliged to work his way up the ranks and by 1865, around the time that he first met Sam, he had reached the dizzying heights of third assistant clerk on a very average £220 a year.

Still, Charlie was a young man with expectations and in 1860 he had married Matilda Walls, a clever, educated girl whose solicitor father served as one of the directors of the Westminster Fire Office. But for all that William Walls was liberal and progressive, he was still sufficiently a man of his class and time to dislike the idea of his daughter marrying into a "commercial" family. Matilda, though, was a determined young woman, and the marriage went ahead at Highgate parish church with her siblings, if not her father, in attendance. From here the young couple set up home in Kensington where they lived modestly, with just one maid.

It is not clear exactly when the Brownes moved to Greenhithe, nor how Matilda started to bring in extra money by working as a journalist. We know from her remark about setting eyes on a haggard-looking Sam for the first time at Greenhithe station, that she had not known him while Isabella was still alive. However, it appears that within a few weeks of her death Sam had co-opted Myra, as she was usually known, into taking his late wife's place at the *Englishwoman's Domestic Magazine*. The relentless production schedule at 248 Strand could not stop for grief, no matter how intense: according to a remark made in Sam's letter to William Stagg, he and Isabella had been due in Paris in only three weeks' time to make arrangements for the next batch of fashion plates. In fact it looks as if Sam never made the trip: the March and April issues are conspicuously lacking in colour illustration. All the same, the magazine still had to be got out in some shape or form, and the worried and clumsy tone of March's fashion notes suggests that this may well mark Myra's debut at the *Englishwoman's Domestic Magazine:* "Imagination is already fancying new fashions for spring, and our fair readers expect from us the most explicit statement on the subject; as yet, it is not easy to predict what changes may be adopted."

From these small beginnings grew an enduring *ménage à trois*. Or rather, *ménage à cinq*, since what drew Myra and Sam together initially, apart from the professional tie, was the two motherless boys. After five years of marriage Myra had yet to have a child, an absence that she felt deeply. The two little Beeton boys were to become her own sons, to the point where they themselves assumed that she was their real mother. From the start she was known as "Mama" and after their father's early death in 1877 she assumed sole moral and legal responsibility for Orchart and Mayson. The Dorlings, aghast at the way in which Sam had managed to replace Bella so quickly and completely, simply abandoned the boys to their Beeton-shaped fate.

Despite the fact that Charlie and Myra Browne had been warned by well-meaning gossips to avoid the debt-ridden Mount Pleasant, they soon made the decision to move in with Sam and the boys. The official reason was that the two little households were "putting their two poverties together," but what really seems to have happened is that Sam wanted to reproduce as exactly as possible the blended professional and domestic life that he had enjoyed with Isabella. Given that Sam was pretty much insolvent by this point, Charlie must have assumed the lion's share of the rent; certainly on the 1871 census it is he who is described as the head of the household at Mount Pleasant, with S. O. Beeton as his "boarder."

The question that immediately arises is whether Sam and Myra were lovers too. The issue goes straight to the heart of problems of historical interpretation in general and our attitudes towards the Victorians in particular. It would be easy to assume that Mr. Beeton and Mrs. Browne must have been partners in bed as well as everywhere else. However, the early- and mid-Victorians frequently found themselves having to replace missing family members, especially mothers who had died in childbirth. The resulting arrangements may seem odd to our eyes—spinster sisters-in-law and even paid companions taking up long-term residence in households headed by widowed men—but they made complete sense to the people involved.

On the other hand, it has to be admitted that the Beeton-Browne ménage was unusual, even by the standards of the day. Paradoxically, it was the presence of Charlie Browne at Mount Pleasant that made the situation both possible in the first place and mildly scandalous in the second. If Myra had not been married, it is unlikely that she could have moved in so swiftly to Mount Pleasant (spinster sisters-in-law or professional governesses were one thing, but the fact that Myra was simply a neighbour would have set tongues wagging). Yet the fact that Charlie continued to stand by while Myra stepped into the shoes of another man's wife made people wonder exactly what was going on. It was not even as though this were a stopgap arrangement, designed to be dissolved the moment a more permanent situation could be worked out. The Browne-Beeton ménage lasted for twelve years until Sam's death and even withstood a change of residence in 1876, when all three adults moved together up to London and took lodgings opposite their neighbouring business premises in Covent Garden. In her chatty incarnation as the editress of the *Englishwoman's Domestic Magazine* Myra was constantly sharing details about her home life—her children, her garden, her housemaids—with her readers. Only once, however, did she mention "the partner of my joys and sorrows," leaving it unclear as to whether it was Mr. Browne or Mr. Beeton to whom she was referring.

It is easy to see why Sam felt immediately at home with Myra. She was exactly the same age as Isabella and, like her, was petite and attractive, rather than merely pretty. Just like Isabella too, Myra had a passion for French fashion and, in time, a wardrobe full of the kinds of clothes that were not generally available to the wives of third assistant clerks, no matter how good their prospects. Surviving photographs from the 1880s show Myra Browne looking spectacularly chic, as befitted a woman who by that time was editing a fashion magazine that was built around her personality and preferences, *Myra's Journal of Dress and Fashion*. Both women, too, were sharp but not brilliant, educated but not intellectual, and with an above-average capacity for languages. But perhaps the most striking parallel was that both Isabella Beeton and Myra Browne had contrived to marry men of whom their families disapproved but whose modest finances allowed—compelled, even—them to pursue a productive life outside the home. By their late twenties both women had a reputation for being "managing"—that is organized, capable, keen to function in a role that went far beyond the genteel drawing room that their families had fondly hoped for them. It is a measure of how committed Myra was to a professional life that when the census enumerator came round to Mount Pleasant in 1871 she proudly declared herself to him as "Editress of a lady's magazine." Most middle-class married women who worked, Isabella included, were happy to be described simply as "wife."

None of this proves, of course, that Sam and Myra were lovers. It is quite conceivable that they were bound simply by a deep and fond friendship, centred on their joint endeavours as parents and business partners. In 1865 Sam was crazy with grief and his health was declining, hardly making him an obvious candidate for a new love affair. He was, however, a resolutely sexual man and while it seems quite likely that in those first desperate months Mrs. Browne was nothing but a staunch ally, it is hard to believe that she remained in that role for the twelve years remaining to him. Quite what Charlie Browne felt about it all must go unrecorded.

Myra Browne, née Walls, who became Sam's business partner, mother to his children and quite possibly his lover, too.

The Dorlings, certainly, thought that something odd was going on at Mount Pleasant. After that initial kindness on the part of Henry Mayson Dorling there are no references in letters to any contact between

314

the two families. The official records, however, do reveal an intriguing meeting that took place in the spring of 1871. According to the census for that year, taken on 2 April, Isabella's sisters Bessie and Esther were staying with the Mosses in their elegant house in Swanscombe High Street. The puzzle is why the Misses Mayson were not staying in Mount Pleasant two miles away with their brother-in-law and little nephews. Had they refused to stay under the same roof as the woman who had so aggressively taken poor Bella's place? More likely altogether is that it was Sam who refused to have them to stay at Mount Pleasant: in later life Bessie and Esther would repeatedly claim that they had been banished from the house. Either way, the upshot was that this was one of the very last times for decades that seven-year-old Orchart and his six-year-old brother Mayson would have any contact with their mother's family.

*Elizabeth Dorling, who seems to have made
no attempt to stay in touch with her
grandchildren following Isabella's death in 1865.*

In the archive of family papers that Mayson Beeton was busy gathering in the 1930s in preparation for the biography of his parents there is a letter from Charlotte McMahon, née Dorling, written in 1918 when she was seventy-five. Posted from her holiday home on the Isle of Wight the letter begins

Dear Mayson

You will wonder who is writing to you! So I must explain that I was your mother's half sister and was the eldest of the 2nd family *of Dorlings* when my Father married your Grandmother (Elizabeth Mayson).

From here the old lady wanders off into details of her own family—a dull listing of military men and their postings—before finishing with a postscript in which she turns back to the subject of Isabella and how pretty she looked on her wedding day. Across the top of the letter Mayson Moss has noted in pencil: "Written after Bessie Mayson made herself known to us." So it looks as if in 1918, perhaps mindful of all the young Dorling men who had recently been lost for ever on the fields of France, the eighty-one-year-old Bessie found herself thinking back deep into family history and wondering about the little boys, her nearest kin, whom she had last seen in Greenhithe nearly half a century ago. Just what she felt when she discovered from Mayson that, against all the odds, Matilda Browne, the woman who had played such a large part in the final estrangement, was also still going strong can only be imagined. The two determined old ladies marched on in parallel for at least another decade, Bessie dying in 1929 and Myra lasting until her hundredth year in 1936.

If Sam's living arrangements were irregular enough, his financial situation was even worse. The bailiffs who had circled Mount Pleasant in February 1865 seem somehow to have been paid off, but this was only the beginning of more severe troubles. In the summer of 1865, just a few weeks after Isabella's death, Sam was obliged to give the rival publisher Frederick Warne a financial interest in all his publications. Warne, an old friend, had recently left a partnership with Routledge and set up on his own. What better way could there be to begin than by taking over publication and distribution of S. O. Beeton's list? An advertisement inserted into *The Times* on 17 August explained how the new arrangement would work:

MESSRS FREDERICK WARNE and Co. (late of the firm of Routledge, Warne, and Routledge) have the pleasure to inform the trade and
the public that they had made such arrangements with Mr. S.O. Beeton
as give them the exclusive sale of all completed books, hitherto issued,
or to be hereafter published, by that enterprising house.

The popularity, always increasing, of Mr. Beeton's books is due—as far
as the large dictionaries and household works are concerned—to the
comprehensiveness of their scope, their easy intelligibility, and the conscientiousness with which their writing and editing have been performed . . .

It is proper to state that Mr. Beeton in no way lessens his rights in the
books hitherto published and to be hereafter issued, or loosens his connexion with them. The larger and smaller dictionaries will continue to
receive corrections and additions from time to time as heretofore; and
the works on home and household topics will have the like attention.
Many useful and important compilations now in the press will acquire
impetus in consequence of the present arrangement . . .

This arrangement held long enough for several new Beeton titles that
autumn and the following spring to be issued under the name of Frederick Warne of Bedford Street: *Beeton's Book of Chemistry, Beeton's Book
of Jokes and Jests* and *Beeton's Book of Football.* Readers would not
have noticed or cared, of course, but sharp-eyed professionals knew
exactly what it meant when a publisher started bringing out books from
someone else's press.

The final collapse came in May 1866. During that month Overend and
Gurney, the discount house that had spectacularly over-traded, went
down dragging thousands of businesses and individuals in its choppy
wake. Publishers were particularly badly hit, since they frequently relied
on bills of exchange to pay authors and suppliers when cash was short.
The unrealistically high interest rates offered by Overend and Gurney
might well have alerted the cautious Isabella had she been alive, but Sam
with his usual optimism had been happy to use them, both as lender and
creditor. "Black Friday" was a scene of apocalyptic chaos in the City, as
financial institutions that had once seemed safe started to tumble like
dominoes. Worried creditors and investors charged into Lombard Street,
Cornhill, and Bartholomew Lane in pursuit of their precious cash, turning
the normally sober streets into a grim carnival. In the weeks that followed

the catastrophe lunged out to engulf quiet market towns and well-behaved villages. Young men shot themselves and old ladies faded away with grief. Fathers vanished, leaving behind notes of apology to their ruined families. Even the kind of people who normally never got drawn into speculation and easy money—yeomen farmers, clergymen, peers—were bankrupted as over 250 companies went down. When the atmosphere eventually cleared the directors were put on trial but found, in the end, to be incompetent rather than criminal.

The distinction made no difference to Sam who, having lost all his money, was now unable to meet the heavy running costs of his business. Whether or not he was actually declared bankrupt has always been a dark question mark looming over the Beeton story. When Harford Montgomery Hyde went on "prospecting operations" for Mayson Moss Beeton (now Sir Mayson Beeton) in the 1930s one of his chief tasks was to look for evidence as to whether the terrible axe had actually fallen or merely threatened to fall. And it was with obvious relief that Hyde was able to report to Beeton in November 1935 that, despite exhaustive searches in Chancery records, he had been unable to find Sam's name on the list of bankrupts. By the time Hyde came to publish his biography in 1951 he had obviously done further research into how the bankruptcy laws worked in the 1860s. Now he was able to state with conviction that Samuel Beeton was "never adjudicated a bankrupt, since he entered into a composition with his creditors." From here the way was clear for Sarah Freeman to gloss the arrangement still further so that by the time she came to retell the story in 1977 there was no mention of creditors or compositions, but simply the explanation that Sam chose to stave off in solvency by selling his business to the rival publishers Ward, Lock and Tyler.

In fact the composition, or private arrangement, that Sam entered into with his creditors was a formal one, which had to be registered in the Bankruptcy Court to make it legal. Private arrangements of this kind were becoming increasingly popular in the difficult mid-1860s with creditors, who reckoned that they were more likely to recoup their money this way than if they relied on the court as debt collector. Sam's composition was duly filed on 8 September, and an assignee—a paper merchant called Venables—was appointed to contact all Beeton's creditors and invite them to send in their claims against his estate. Nearly two years later Venables placed a notice in *The Times*, headed "Bankruptcy Act of 1861

Estate of S. O. Beeton," informing creditors that they were about to be paid a dividend on the money still outstanding. So Hyde is right to say that Sam was never adjudicated a bankrupt but wrong to imply that this meant that he had dodged public disgrace. "S. O. Beeton, publisher of 248 The Strand" had been named and shamed as an insolvent debtor in no less an organ than *The Times*.

This point will not have been lost on Henry Dorling, who conspicuously failed to offer any financial help to his son-in-law. Sympathy for those who had suffered at the bungling hands of Overend and Gurney was high, especially in Epsom where several prominent citizens had been badly hit. But quite possibly Dorling considered that Sam's financial problems were of his own making and that the Overend and Gurney connection was merely a convenient fig leaf to cover years of recklessness and overspending. Even the thought of his grandsons, the children of his precious Isabella, going in need did not melt the old man's heart. Whether Sam applied to Dorling and was turned down is not clear, but by 1868, with his estate in the process of being publicly wound up, he was overflowing with bile.

The situation was made even more intense by the fact that Dorling had now reached his financial high-water mark, and was, for the first time in his careful life, happy to live like an officially wealthy man. In June 1868 he bought Stroud Green House, an imposing late-eighteenth-century stone house built in "the Italian style." Choosing to shift to Croydon might seem strange, until one learns that a few years earlier a new racecourse had been built adjacent to the property. But if Woodside Racetrack, at less than two miles, represented a scaling down for Dorling, Stroud Green House was itself an emphatic step up. The sale details show a reserved price of £20,000—a small fortune. The blurb proudly touts the property as "possessing extensive stabling, gardener's cottage, farmery, greenhouses, vineries with delightful pleasure grounds, gardens and park-like meadows, belted with thriving Timber, and an ornamental lake." There were ten bedrooms, six lavatories, four reception rooms and rudimentary central heating. On the ground floor alone there was a glass-domed roof, a "handsome marble fountain, ornamented with dolphins," "a Drawing Room decorated with Scagliola Pilasters," and a seemingly endless array of carved marble fireplaces. By the time the place was sold following the Dorlings' deaths in 1873, it was crammed with bad copies of Old Masters, chilly-looking nymphs and blood red drapes.

However it might strike us now, contemporary visitors to Stroud Green House thought it a palace. "Bertha," the female journalist writing in 1931 in the *Portsmouth Evening News,* recalled how "I often stayed there as a child, for the family was of all ages, the elder sisters friends of my mother, and the younger round about my age." In particular "Bertha" remembered the fun they had when all the children, mounted on horses and ponies, were led by the grooms through the imposing gates, "the strangers we passed no doubt taking us for a riding school."

As well as ponies for the little ones, there were parties and balls for the bigger children. "My first ball (except those at home, which didn't count)," remembered Bertha dreamily, "was in that house, and I felt frightfully grown-up, for I had not yet 'come out.'" An invitation from that time still survives: "Mrs. Dorling at Home on Thursday May 5th [1868]. Dancing at 9 O'clock, Stroud Green House, Croydon." It was a long way from the livery stables at Wyndham Mews.

Stories about all these ponies and parties must have got back to Sam, who would not have been able to help comparing the Dorlings' life of ease and pleasure with his own cramped and worried situation at Mount Pleasant. Maddened by the unfairness of it all, in that summer of 1868 he published a vicious attack on Henry Dorling that put an end to the hope of any rapprochement. The *Derby Carnival* cost 6d, was illustrated with tremendous dash by Phiz, and provided a commentary for anyone intending to follow the race, whether from Epsom or their armchair. The offending passage snarled as follows:

> There appears to be some idea in the public mind that there is some occult difficulty about getting into this charming enclosure [ie the Grandstand] . . . half a sovereign is the difficulty—that is all. Indeed, you may take it for a certainty that for money at Epsom all things are possible. The Clerk of the Course has studied too closely for one and twenty years the art of filling his pockets from every available source, and is too fond of the red gold, to have made everything that he had any control over quite easy to purchase. Ready, ay, ready to sell anybody or anything, that's the family motto.

Two years after this appeared Henry, now widowed and ailing, sat down to write his will. That Sam got nothing was only to be expected, but to punish Orchart and Mayson for their father's sins by refusing to leave them a penny seems hard indeed.

As part of the arrangement with his creditors Sam had agreed to liquidate his own company, sell off its physical assets such as printing presses, and transfer his copyrights together with his own labour and expertise to Ward, Lock and Tyler. Ward and Lock—Mr. Tyler came later—enjoyed a history that pretty much ran parallel to S. O. Beeton's various incarnations. Their list, like Beeton's, was rooted in the growing demand for instructive and informative texts from the new book-buying public of the 1850s. Like Beeton they combined these with reprints of American novels, together with original British fiction from popular authors. Among their periodicals was the sophisticated metropolitan magazine, *Temple Bar,* and the monthly *Ladies' Treasury,* which was a plodding copycat of the *Englishwoman's Domestic Magazine.* In 1865 Ward and Lock had been joined by Charles Tyler, who was a friend of Sam Beeton's. The fact that Tyler had previously been in partnership with Venables suggests that it was he who brokered the deal by which S. O. Beeton was able to become a "licensee in bankruptcy" to Ward, Lock and Tyler.

The terms under which Sam gave up control of his own firm have come down to us in detail. Ward, Lock and Tyler agreed to buy the whole of Beeton's copyrights, stock-in-trade, and business property, probably for the paltry sum of £1,900. In fact they quickly offloaded anything that they did not want, which led to the extra humiliation of a series of publicly advertised auctions in December 1866 when some of S. O. Beeton's less valuable titles, together with his printing presses and office furniture, were put up for sale to the highest bidder. What Ward, Lock and Tyler were after were Beeton's core assets—the *Englishwoman's Domestic Magazine,* the *Boy's Own Magazine* and, of course, that word-of-mouth bestseller *Mrs. Beeton's Book of Household Management.* Under the terms of the agreement Sam would continue to develop these titles while also working on new products under the "Beeton" brand. But he would be obliged to consult Ward, Lock and Tyler at every step of the way, something that naturally stuck in the craw of a thirty-five-year-old entrepreneur who had been his own boss since the age of twenty-one. The remuneration, though, was generous, especially considering that Sam was in no position to bargain. For the first year he got only £400 but from 1867 to 1869 he would get one sixth of all the firm's profits, rising by increments until 1871, by which time he would receive a quarter of all profit. The contract was clear, though, that this should not be taken to constitute a partnership of any kind. Beeton was to remain an employee of Ward, Lock and Tyler, who could be dismissed at any point with six months' notice, although in this case he would be entitled to £500 a year for life, on condition that he "should not directly or indirectly be engaged in or interested in, or permit his name to be used in connection with any other publishing or bookselling business, or any publication whatever."

Inevitably, Sam did not go easily into this new arrangement and his relationship with Ward, Lock and Tyler was fraught from the very start. "I'm not much of a bargainer, although you think I am," Beeton told Lock during the difficult weeks in September 1866 when the details were being hammered out. "I only want to be 'settled' and my future dependent on the moneys I aid in making, so I should be satisfied with one-third of the nett results as shown by the profits arising from the estate of S. O. Beeton." In other words, Sam wanted his financial fortunes to be pegged to his own titles, rather than to the performance of Ward, Lock and Tyler in general. Another man might have swallowed his pride and learned how to make the bastard arrangement work, not least for the sake of his two small sons. But Sam was not that man.

For the first few years things seem to have gone reasonably well. Ward, Lock and Tyler placed a series of prominent notices in *The Times* to advertise the fact that they were now the publishers of S. O. Beeton's publications. Sam, in turn, explained away the awkward situation with an announcement that "In consequence of MR. S. O. BEETON's premises being required by the New Courts of Law, he has arranged with MESSRS. WARD, LOCK, AND TYLER, of Warwick House, Paternoster Row, for the future publication of all his magazines and other works." And, in fact, there was truth in this face-saving formula: by the spring of 1867 Commissioners of Her Majesty's Works had indeed requisitioned 248 Strand in preparation for clearing eight acres of land and four thousand people in order to build that last great Gothic masterpiece of the Victorian age, the central Law Courts. The symbolism would not have been lost on Sam. Geographically, his had been a strange journey up and down London's print corridor. Starting in Fleet Street, the home of the publishing industry since its beginnings, Sam had moved westwards, culminating in 248 Strand, which stood on the hinge between the City and the West

End. Now he was to return to Paternoster Row, the crooked lane in the shadow of St. Paul's where printers, publishers, and booksellers had clustered for centuries.

Myra Browne made the transfer to Ward, Lock and Tyler along with Sam and settled in as his co-editor, or "Editress," at the *Englishwoman's Domestic Magazine*. From shaky beginnings, her increasingly distinctive voice came to be heard throughout the magazine, particularly in the guise of "The Silkworm," whose "Spinnings About Town" was a light, bright monthly column of shopping tips and careful product placement. Whereas Isabella had kept her personality out of her columns, appearing only as a nameless, disembodied expert voice giving authoritative advice on cooking and fashion, Myra developed a persona to which readers were invited to respond directly. The Silkworm's job was to be the readers' friend, possibly their guide, but emphatically not their teacher. She talked constantly about "her boys," otherwise known as "the wee Silkworms" or "those dear little ones in my nursery," keeping readers updated on the Beeton boys' toys, tantrums, sniffles, clothing, and trips to the pantomime. She also told readers about her holidays in Devon, the dreamy trips down the Thames in "our cosy cushioned boat," and her pride and pleasure at constructing a fernery in her own garden.

Mostly, though, the Silkworm's job was to go shopping, popping in and out of the haberdashers and perfumers of the City and the West End in search of the "prettiest" items for her discerning readers. Month after month she advises her "friends" on fans, scent, shoes, and handkerchiefs. She also follows her predecessor, whose authority she occasionally invokes as "the late Mrs. Beeton, in the well known Household Management," in puffing the new technology that will take some of the hard work out of small-scale living: imported American fridges, sewing machines, and even a prototype dishwasher. Where Myra departs radically from Mrs. Beeton, however, is in the ease with which she accommodates the idea of living on credit. In 1874, for instance, she suggests that young people setting up home for the first time should take advantage of hire purchase agreements from the likes of the General Furnishing Company, Southampton Street, the Strand. Although the dividing line between editorial and advertising copy had always been fuzzy in the *Englishwoman's Domestic Magazine,* by the late 1860s it was barely discernible. As a result, the Silkworm's column often sounds like one long puff for the goods and services of commercial companies who have almost certainly paid to be included in her "Spinnings."

Yet the Silkworm wasn't all gloss and sheen. While she might enjoy and celebrate the new consumer culture of the late 1860s, she always remained aware that there were some middle-class women who did not have the money for splashing out on American fridges or toilet water from M. Rimmel. In a blend that recalls the earliest days of the *English-woman's Domestic Magazine,* Silkworm/Myra is careful to endorse the woman who is obliged to do her own housework, insisting that "A lady is no less a lady because she is able to help herself and others, or because she not only knows what should be done but 'how to do it.' " What's more, with the call for reform in women's employment opportunities gathering pace in the 1860s, Myra is careful, too, to keep her readers up to date with the latest opportunities for independent living—training as a wood carver, taking out life assurance. Elsewhere in the magazine she and Sam continue to ensure that important new legislation, such as J. S. Mill's proposed amendment to the Suffrage Bill of 1866 and the Married Women's Property Act of 1870, is fully explained.

Yet while Myra was coming into her own as a writer, shaping the magazine around the new concerns and appetites of middle-class women in the late 1860s, she failed to develop the muscle a co-editor needed to save the magazine from the scandal that permanently engulfed its reputation and continues to haunt it to this day. In the years following Isabella's death, the "Conversazione"—the correspondence column that Sam had introduced in 1855 to replace "Cupid's Letter Bag"—was flourishing. Invited to "discuss any subject they please," readers sent in queries on anything from bottling gooseberries to the lives of Mormon women via that perennial favourite of how to get rid of freckles. Rather than simply receiving an answer from "Mr. Editor," contributors were encouraged to respond to each other's queries and, if the subject was sufficiently interesting, the discussion was allowed to run over several months.

The scandal started quietly enough, with a couple of letters that appeared in the spring issues of 1867. A mother wrote to say that she had returned from abroad to find that her daughter had been subjected to a "system of torture" at the hands of her headmistress designed to reduce the waists of her pupils by means of tight lacing. The poor girl's middle was now so small that it could be clasped with two hands and her muscles had atrophied to the point that she was obliged to wear a corset all the time. In the very next issue a correspondent called "Staylace" countered the worried mother's outrage by saying that she herself could think of nothing more delightful than the feeling of being constricted by a tight pair of stays:

> To me the sensation of being tight-laced in a pair of elegant, well-made tightly fitting corsets is superb, and I have never felt any evil to arise therefrom . . . [I] never feel prouder or happier than when I survey in myself the fascinating undulations of outline that art in this respect affords to nature.

From these harmless though slightly stagey beginnings the correspondence took flight into erotic fantasy. Each month there would be more letters, purporting to be from regular readers, which nudged the debate into distinctly sado-masochistic territory. Men joined in the conversation too, some claiming to enjoy wearing corsets themselves, while others recalled with pleasure the tiny female waists that they had known and loved. (The fact that these male correspondents tended to sign themselves "A Young Baronet" or "Medicus" makes one even more suspicious about their authenticity.) Sam was clearly transfixed by the letters pouring into his office at Warwick House, which tended to talk repeatedly about the pleasures of being squeezed ritually into your corset every morning by a governess or lady's maid. Although he claimed in November 1867 that he was ready to draw the correspondence to a close, he effectively sabotaged his position by simultaneously announcing the preparation of a book called *The Corset and the Crinoline* (later republished as *Freaks of Fashion*), which promised to contain a selection of letters from the correspondence. This exciting prospect naturally got the corset fetishists going again, and they resumed their correspondence with redoubled energy, this time verging into territory that was positively pornographic.

Just when it looked as if the tight-lacing correspondence was about to die down for good, an even more controversial conversational thread started up in the "Conversazione." This time the subject was that well-known staple of soft porn, the whipping of maidservants and young girls. Again, the debate started off harmlessly enough, with a discussion among harassed mothers as to whether smacking girls really did result in better behaviour. From here, the "Conversazione" soon roared off into a masturbatory free-for-all as "readers"—surely men and some women who enjoyed sharing their most private fantasies—eagerly sent in accounts of "real life" experiences of whipping which grew more preposterous by the month. Correspondents with pseudonyms such as "Etoniensis," "A Rejoicer in the Restoration of the Rod," "Miss Birch," and "R.O.D." told in immense and repetitive detail of ritualized floggings in ladies' boarding schools and in clergymen's studies. The virtues of the different implements were discussed with relish, as were the elaborate performances of removing clothing and strapping down the victims, the penitent tears and the urgent begging for mercy. Running in parallel was a second stream of letters purporting to be from women who had undergone such punishments and remembered them with gratitude, not to mention an enormous amount of detail. Frequently, correspondents wrote in and asked to be put in touch with each other, in order to continue the discussion in private.

Interspersed with these narratives—essentially erotic fiction masquerading as personal recollection—were letters from "Forbearance," "Truth (of Leicester)," or "Constance," genuinely horrified at the tone that had crept into their magazine. E. J., for instance, remarks, "I hope for the welfare of your Magazine that this correspondence (which has become quite indecent) will soon cease," while T. Miller asks whether the correspondence is "true or merely a fiction?" Sam always denied that there was any fabrication, and made a great point of insisting that correspondents supply him with a name and address, even if they wished to use a pseudonym. Yet although he periodically called a halt to the whipping correspondence, he seemed reluctant to let it drop completely.

Contemporaries struggled, just as critics still do today, to make sense of why Samuel Beeton nearly ruined his greatest magazine by using it as a vehicle for pornography. The *Telegraph* was the first paper to notice what was happening at Warwick House, but treated the letters as if they were quite genuine, concluding on 18 January 1869, "This correspondence is a serious thing; it reveals the existence of a whole world of unnatural and indefensibly private cruelty, of which the law ought to have cognisance." Ten days later the altogether more knowing *Saturday Review* suggested that the whole whipping correspondence was an elaborate hoax and that "Materfamilias," the "Marchioness," and other "Lovers of the Rod" were almost certainly the product of "the fertile brain of the conductor of the *Englishwoman's Domestic Magazine.*"

In Sam's defence, it has to be said that the *EDM* was not the only publication to run a highly eroticized readers' correspondence in the late 1860s, which expanded to cover such niche interests as nipple-piercing, the wearing of spurs, and cross-dressing. Even the *Queen,* long out of Beeton's control, pitched in enthusiastically to the corset controversy. Cultural historians have suggested that this odd trend may be part and parcel of the growing appetite for "Sensation" fiction, of which Miss Braddon's Gothic *Lady Audley's Secret* was the market leader. The second point is that Sam was not allowed to put out material unless sanctioned by his employers. Although there are no figures available, it looks as if folding pornography into the editorial mix substantially boosted the circulation of the *EDM.* What other reason could lie behind Ward, Lock and Tyler's decision in 1870 to let Sam produce a supplement dedicated to the whipping correspondence, on the grounds that it "appears to have aroused intense, not to say passionate, interest." In addition to the letters themselves, the tuppenny supplement carried advertisements for canes, whips, and birches, as well as *A History of the Rod* and *Flagellation and the Flagellants* by the Revd. W. Cooper. These supplements were, in turn, bound and sold in a 2s volume.

All the same, it is impossible to avoid the suspicion that Sam actively enjoyed receiving, reading, sifting, and publishing this sado-masochistic pornography. One of the characteristic symptoms of tertiary-stage syphilis is an indulgence in behaviour that is extravagantly antisocial and often obscenely sexual in nature. A decision to smuggle pornography into the pages of a supremely respectable women's magazine fits exactly with the sexual grandiloquence of the syphilitic who is entering the final stages of his horrible disease. And it is this symptomatic descent into dementia, rather than a pursuit of sales or even an active desire to hurt the reputation of Ward, Lock and Tyler, that most satisfactorily explains just why Samuel Beeton turned pornographer during the last decade of his life.

The whipping and tight-lacing episodes turned out to be just the beginning of Sam's capacity for spectacular offence. One of his great skills as the publisher of middle-brow magazines aimed at a broad swathe of the English reading public had always been his ability to touch on subjects close to his liberal heart without frightening his essentially conservative constituency. But from 1870 Sam lost all his former delicacy of touch, and simply stormed ahead, shouting views that were calculated to shock and annoy. The vehicle for the outrage this time was not the *Englishwoman's Domestic Magazine,* but the *Beeton Christmas Annual.* The *Annual* had been produced every December since 1859. Selling initially for 1s, its mix of sub-Dickensian fiction, jokes, games, and poems about robins had come to enjoy a modest stake in the nation's growing love affair with Christmas. But now Sam decided to ditch all that gentle good humour, and replace it with a sharp dose of social and political satire. In 1870 the pulse of public life in Britain quickened, especially among people like Sam Beeton and Myra Browne who conducted a significant part of their business life in Paris. In July of that year France had declared war on Prussia, but by December Paris was under siege. M. Goubaud had managed to send his old mule to Sam for safety before the cordon tightened, but smuggling out the *Englishwoman's Domestic Magazine*'s fashion copy and plates was quite another matter. In the end they went by pigeon post, with a series of pseudonymous women journalists contributing a "Paris Letter" which had less to do with frocks than with details about how dog tasted different from donkey, and the deliciousness of elephant's trunk, the result of the city's restaurants' raids on the Zoological Gardens.

Always a progressive in politics—from 1869 he had been, with Ward, Lock and Tyler's permission, editing the liberal *Weekly Dispatch*—the events of 1870–1 radicalized and galvanized Sam. Certainly by 1872 he was ready to go in a powerful new direction and that year the *Annual* was almost entirely given over to an extended spoof of Tennyson's poem about King Arthur, *Idylls of the King*. Taking off an illustrious writer was one thing, but what really shocked and titillated was the way in which *The Coming K—* satirized the Prince of Wales and, by implication, the whole principle of hereditary monarchy. The tone was smutty, disrespectful, and pointedly close to home. In the last section of the poem the Prince manages to lose the Derby, thanks to the fact that someone has dosed his horse with a big helping of Epsom salts (another pop at Henry Dorling who is now, implicitly, likened to a bucket of horse shit). Nothing about the Prince's dignity was spared, and for the price of a shilling readers could hear all about the ageing young man's vast sexual appetite and spicy goings-on at Marlborough House. Naturally enough, *The Coming K—* was a sensation.

The following year Beeton and his co-authors Dowty and Emerson cast their net wider. This time the *Annual* was written in the rhyming hexameters of Pope's translation of the *Iliad*. Its subject matter ranged over the corruption of Westminster politics, the doings of the royal family, and various social ills about which Sam felt particularly strongly. Cabinet ministers were portrayed lounging around brothels and scrapping with the police. The Queen, meanwhile, was pictured dancing about in front of the Albert Memorial waving a copy of *The Coming K—*. The most vicious vitriol of all, however, was reserved for a group of people with whom Sam was coming increasingly and unhappily into contact: "Since the first lawyer tempted mother Eve/ Has not their mission been to dupe, deceive."

The very next *Annual* plunged Sam into a catastrophic court battle from which he never really recovered. Although the *Siliad* had sold extremely well, Ward, Lock (Tyler, Sam's friend, had—significantly— gone by now) were increasingly perturbed as they watched the descent of *Beeton's Annual*, one of their expensively acquired assets, into scurrilous gutter journalism. So when, in 1874, highly personalized counterblasts started appearing in the press with denouncements such as "yet those who love him most confess at least/ That Beeton's animal's indeed a beast," Messrs. Ward and Lock knew that it was time to act. That summer they asked Sam to prepare something more suitable, in other words less controversial, for the next *Beeton Annual*.

But that summer, Sam had made an important new friend. Henri Rochefort was the sort of person who Sam would secretly have liked to have been. Born into a noble family, Rochefort had been sacked from the editorship of *Le Figaro* in 1863 and went on to start his own anti-imperial paper, *La Lanterne*. Several prosecutions, prison sentences, fines, and duels later, he fetched up as a member of the wartime National Assembly. However, siding with the revolutionary Communards after the war led to him being transported to New Caledonia. Nothing daunted, in 1874 Rochefort escaped on board an American vessel to San Francisco and eventually reached Europe, where he spent the summer hiding out in Greenhithe, ducking the police spies who were doing their best to stop him reviving *La Lanterne* by smuggling it back into France.

Faced with the spectacular political engagement of men like this, it is easy to see why Sam felt increasingly frustrated churning out anodyne material for the complacent British middle classes. The very people whom he had burned to educate and entertain with new kinds of reading matter in the 1850s were showing themselves to be disappointingly conservative now that they had got the things they wanted: the vote, money in their pockets, a sense of possibility. According to Ward, Lock's later testimony, Sam appeared not to respond that summer to their request that he come up with something uncontroversial for that year's *Annual*. So they commissioned Emerson, one of the co-authors of the *Siliad*, to produce the *Annual* instead. Sam was to protest later in court that he had shown himself willing and able in the summer to start work on the *Annual*, and that Ward, Lock had gone behind his back in commissioning Emerson. Whichever is true, both sides agreed that come November Sam inserted advertisements in the *Athenaeum* and elsewhere making it abundantly clear to both booksellers and the public that he had had nothing to do with the so-called 1874 *Beeton's Christmas Annual* published by Ward, Lock. Instead he had produced the genuine article independently, under the promising title of *Jon Duan*.

According to the terms of his contract with Ward, Lock, Sam should have shelved his own effort, a clever Byronic spoof, and bitten his tongue while the distinctly mediocre *Fijiad*—a weak prose satire on the damaging effects of civilization on a group of virtuous South Sea cannibals—was marketed under the Beeton banner. But by this point in his life, Sam's capacity for self-destruction knew no limits and he made a private arrangement with one of his former employees to go ahead with the printing of *Jon Duan*, clearly branding it as *Beeton's Christmas Annual for 1874, 15th Season*. And, just in case this weren't provocation enough, Sam and his co-writers Dowty and the new man Evelyn Jerrold inserted a snide description of Ward, Lock's rival publication as "vulgar" and "worn out."

In the weeks that followed Sam milked the rivalry between the two *Beeton Annuals* for all it was worth, inserting full-page announcements in the *Athenaeum* and the *Standard* proclaiming *Jon Duan* as the true article, and the *Fijiad* as a mere pretender. The fact that W. H. Smith refused to stock *Jon Duan*, fearing that it might provoke legal action from people who believed they had been libelled, only added to the growing buzz and sent sales soaring, so that within three weeks of publication a quarter of a million copies had been sold. Ward, Lock, by contrast, clung to their dignity, contenting themselves with a notice in the *Athenaeum* designed to clarify the situation for any reader who still felt confused:

> Mr. S. O. Beeton, as his advertisements proclaim, has been (notwithstanding our protest and legal agreement to the contrary) concerned in the publication of another Annual, which, for well-founded reasons, we have objected to publish, or be in any way concerned with. We have, in

consequence, made arrangements with an author of "The Siliad" [Emerson] for the production of Beeton's Annual in such an attractive form as to commend itself to popular favour and support.

Dignity aside, three days after this notice appeared Ward, Lock applied for an "injunction to restrain" Beeton from issuing advertisements under his own name. Sam, who at this point characteristically collapsed into ill health, did not attend the court, with the result that the injunction was served on him as he lay at home in Greenhithe. Ward, Lock allowed themselves one little gloating gesture and published news of their triumph in the very next *Athenaeum*. A fortnight later, however, Sam was up again and, just three weeks before Christmas, he applied to the courts to have the injunction lifted.

The case was heard in front of the Vice-Chancellor, Sir Richard Malins, who had been Sam's counsel in his 1862 case concerning the *Sporting Life*. From Malins's careful summing up, it is clear that he had long since got the measure of the man who had once paid his wages. He started by saying that "the case was a painful one in many respects . . . the defendant Beeton had long been known as a literary man, particularly in connexion with periodical publications," before going on to unpick Sam's case. It was quite obvious, said Malins, that when Ward, Lock and Tyler bought the rights to *Beeton's Annual* in 1866 they did so in perpetuity, regardless of whether S. O. Beeton himself was actively involved in the preparation of any particular edition. His Lordship took a particularly dim view of Beeton's blustery *Athenaeum* notice denouncing Ward, Lock's *Fijiad* and declared that this "was an advertisement issued by a servant calculated to injure his master, and was a clear breach of duty and improper conduct on the defendant's part." If Sam really felt that he had a case against Ward, Lock, said Malins, he should have taken legal action against them rather than indulge the "mere gratification of his own vanity" by issuing wild public statements. Nor was Malins going to allow Sam to hide behind his excuse of ill health as a reason for not coming to court sooner. He may have been ill when the original injunction was served, observed Malins, but he had been fit enough to instruct his solicitor to oppose it.

Throughout Malins's summing up, however, there are hints that he felt Ward, Lock were guilty of overplaying the shocked-moralist card (in the first hearing they had even claimed that they had published *The Coming*

K— without first reading the manuscript, which stretches credulity). Malins pointed out, for instance, that the 1873 *Annual,* the *Siliad,* had been extremely profitable for the firm, and "For some reasons not explained the plaintiffs became dissatisfied with the character of the Annual, but still continued to make a large sale of it." All the same, he felt he was left with no choice but to dismiss Sam's motion to lift the injunction and ordered him to pay all the costs.

Given Malins's ruling, it was clearly impossible for Sam to remain as an employee of Ward, Lock. He had broken one of the most important clauses of his contract—that of not allowing his name to be used for any publication not associated with Ward, Lock—and had contested another—the right of Ward, Lock to use the name of S. O. Beeton "for present and future publications." There was no alternative but to go their separate ways.

Sam doubtless represented his detour into political polemic as the response of a man who had, in a keener sense than most Englishmen, lived through the setting up of the Third French Republic and its near collapse in 1871. But the inconvenient fact remains that for the fifteen years during which he owned his magazines he managed to restrain his wilder enthusiasms and calibrate his political views so that they blended with the editorial content, content that was in the main conservative. He had even, in 1861, launched a magazine called the *Queen* which was pegged fulsomely to the identity of Victoria, and provided each purchaser of the first issue with a souvenir photograph of Her Majesty. It was not until Sam had nothing much to lose that he came out as a radical, ironically just at the moment when popular republicanism was becoming a spent force and the monarchy was edging back into favour. And it is hard not to wonder, too, about the extent to which he was propelled by a desire to provoke Ward and Lock, the men who had served him the ultimate insult of saving him from himself.

Just how irrational Sam's behaviour had become by the time of the split with Ward, Lock is apparent from a letter, or partial letter, that survives from April 1874 and which has never been quoted before, perhaps because it shows that by this point Sam was well on his way to derangement. It is written from Greenhithe, bordered in black, and is addressed to Lock, whom Sam always found the easier of the two original partners to deal with. Sam starts by complaining about some accounting inconsistencies he has uncovered which appear to show the firm siphoning off money owed to him: "I hope some one, I don't care who, will be a little more careful next time," he snaps, "for, as there are evidently a lot of blunders of all kinds, it makes one uncomfortable . . . when I see the errors all on one side, credits wh shd be put to me omitted, both in interest & drawings, and things & amounts charged w^h sh^d not be, I naturally wonder whether this is the first time this has occurred. This sort of blundering goes very badly with Mr. Ward's high moral pressure & gives me a greater distaste than ever for the rubbish I have had served up to me lately."

From here Sam spools back to the dark days of 1866 when all his troubles began and declares grandly, "I have forborne to take the simple measure w^h w^d set me right in fame and fortune before a certain portion of the world:—it is true I have been unable, from want of means, to attempt what w^d have ended in a real legal vindication of myself & my position, perhaps; and I know what justice is to the poor." Having failed to spell out exactly what it is he wants the world to know, as well as inserting himself into a grand political narrative, Sam's tone tips into self-aggrandizing pity: "Nobody knows what I have suffered in my mind; everybody knows what I have suffered in my pocket; everybody knows what Warwick House is built upon; & yet I am still suffering, in the minds of many, as a man who has, by recklessness & unreasonable expenditure &tc, been the cause of loss to his creditors to the extent of thousands." Clearly there was something about the way that the original bankruptcy arrangement had been handled in 1866 that still rankled with Sam, who felt that he had not been given sufficient time to put things right in his own way. "My creditors, if faith had been kept with me by my trustees, w^d have been paid to the uttermost farthing, and I shd have had a fortune—a nobleman's income. The income of two or three of my properties w^d have paid all I owed; and I know what I c^d have done, alone, in the last seven years." From here Sam launches into a flamboyantly one-sided account of all he has done for Ward, Lock which segues into the suggestion that they somehow actually engineered his original fall from grace: "You, the firm, have rec^d the principal advantage resulting from my misfortunes—both in stock, copy-rights, personal assistance, and increased knowledge." He then runs through all the new business he has brought to the firm: managing the takeover of the bankrupt publisher Moxon, introducing the work of Charles Reade, the profitable Lily Series and, of course, all Beeton's books. "Take all these away," Sam asks rhetorically, "& what remains?"

From the end of the 1860s Sam Beeton was spiralling out of control. Bereavement and bankruptcy must account for some of his wildness, but there were many men of the period who suffered both and managed to pull through somehow. The difference with Sam was that by now syphilis was eating into his brain, adding delusions of persecution and grandeur to ordinary unhappiness. In his own mind he was a martyred genius with enemies lying in wait everywhere. His extended legal battle with Ward, Lock represents only a fraction of the court cases that he charged into at this time. In 1869, for instance, he had tried to launch a penny weekly periodical called *Punch and Judy* and immediately found himself, as he must have known he would, brought to court by the long-established *Punch* magazine. Six years later, and having chosen to settle in chalky Greenhithe, he applied for an injunction to restrain the whiting works at the bottom of his garden from using the heavy machinery, which, he said, was spoiling his peace. The case ran for over three hours and in the end the Master of the Rolls decided in favour of Sam, but delayed granting the injunction so as to give the manager of the works the chance to put the situation right. In order to obtain this slight victory Sam had gone to the trouble and expense of hiring two QCs.

If Isabella had been alive she would surely have stopped all this non-sense before it had a chance to start. She knew the price of things, includ-ing all those lawsuits and barristers, and she would have urged caution before diving into yet another pointless struggle. She would also, surely, have found the whipping and tight-lacing material sufficiently odd not to have wanted to see it rubbing elbows in the magazine with her fashion copy and her letters from Paris. And, finally, given her instinctive interest in the monarchy—her devoted trailing round every single one of Princess Vicky's private apartments in Berlin—it seems likely she would have advised Sam to soft-pedal on some of the more offensive anti-monarchy buffoonery in the *Annuals*.

But Isabella was not there, and as a result of these latest actions by Sam she was about to be parted from him for a second and final time. For as Sam packed up his boxes in Warwick House following his loss of the court case to Ward, Lock, he was leaving behind not only the troubled *Englishwoman's Domestic Magazine* and the *Beeton Annuals* but what was fast becoming clear was the greatest prize of all, *Mrs. Beeton's Book of Household Management*. Sam had abandoned Mrs. Beeton to another, rival, publisher, where she remains to this day. She proved to be a fantastic acquisition for Ward, Lock, building them a multi-million-pound fortune over the next 150 years. The pity of it was that neither she, nor Sam, nor the thriving children they had both waited for for so long would see a penny of it.

INTERLUDE

Vegetables Reduced to Purée.—Persons in the flower of youth, having healthy stomachs, and leading active lives, may eat all sorts of vegetables, without inconvenience, save, of course, in excess . . . But for aged persons, the sedentary, or the delicate, it is quite otherwise. Those who generally digest vegetables with difficulty should eat them reduced to a pulp or a purée, that is to say, with their skins and tough fibres removed. Subjected to this process, vegetables which, when entire, would create flatulence and wind, are then comparatively harmless. Experience has established the rule, that nourishment is not complete without the alliance of meat with vegetables.

ISABELLA BEETON,
Book of Household Management

CONTRARY TO POPULAR BELIEF, Mrs. Beeton understood the link between health and diet and consistently urged her readers to think about the nutritional value of the food they put in their mouths. In order to help them she frequently provides bafflingly exact analyses, for instance reporting that the humble potato contains "75.52 per cent of water, 15.72 starch, 0.55 dextrine, 3.3 of impure saccharine matter, and 3.25 of fibre with coagulated albumen." However, just like those science-minded mid-Victorian couples who avoided sex during the wife's period on the grounds that she was then at her most fertile, Mrs. Beeton sometimes draws conclusions from her data which suggest that she only half understood their implications.

336

Vegetables and salads are a case in point. At one level Mrs. Beeton believes them to be a good thing, reporting with approval that the bad old days when Catherine of Aragon was unable to "procure a salad of English growth for her dinner" are long over, and that in this respect "England is now, perhaps, not behind any other country in Europe." However, she also believes that these foods represent a health risk to anyone but the young and fit. This is because, especially in their raw or lightly cooked form, vegetables and salads require the body to do extra digestive work before they can be converted into energy (one way of speeding this process is to douse them in vinegar first). "Remember," Beeton says, in her section on the "Sickroom," paraphrasing Florence Nightingale, "that sick cookery should do half the work of your poor patient's weak digestion." And again, "If the patient be allowed to eat vegetables, never send them up undercooked, or half raw." Instead the ailing and the elderly are to be presented with pap such as rice-milk, mutton broth, and invalid's jelly.

Thus the very people who might benefit from the extra roughage that comes with eating fruit and vegetables with their skins on are in fact deprived of them. Cauliflower, cucumber, carrot, and a score of others are all "difficult of digestion" and so best avoided. Yet at the same time Beeton conscientiously notes the many cases where the vegetable or fruit in question is known to have "a laxative effect." This, combined with the fact that advertisements for what William Kitchiner had originally designated as "peristaltic persuaders" appeared on the end pages of various Beeton part works, suggests that the Beeton reader was consistently steering a fine line between avoiding vegetables in order not to produce too much embarrassing wind, and consuming as many of them as possible to guard against seizing up completely.

This calculation was made even more difficult by the fact that Beeton recommends boiling vegetables so briskly that it is hard to see how any roughage—let alone vitamins or minerals—could be left by the time they came to table. This is despite the fact that she assumes vegetables go into the pot whole, rather than being first cut up into pieces. According to her instructions large carrots need up to two and a quarter hours, while large parsnips require one and a half hours. And yet, confusingly, in other cases, Beeton's boiling times seem closer to our own: twenty minutes for old potatoes sounds familiar, and twenty-five minutes for artichokes is entirely unremarkable.

What also stands out is Mrs. Beeton's assumption that a meal, in order to matter, must always contain meat. Salad or vegetables on their own will not give sufficient nutrition, while "the nutritive properties of fish are deemed inferior to those of what is called butchers' meat." For this reason Beeton dedicates three hundred pages to meat and only fifty pages to vegetables. Anyone following Mrs. Beeton's plan of "plain family dinners" would consume, on average, an extraordinary half a pound of beef, mutton or pork every day.

After following Mrs. Beeton's family menus for seven days, an average eater would have consumed 18,232 calories, which is slightly more than the current guideline of 17,850 for men and 13,580 for women. However, keeping warm and mobile in the days before central heating and lifts probably helped counter any tendency towards obesity. Anyone eating the Mrs. Beeton way would get twice as much Vitamin B_1 and significantly more Vitamin B_6 than today's guidelines suggest. They would be getting plenty of iron too, although the fact that there was so little Vitamin C in the Beeton diet (all that boiling) might well have hindered its uptake. Meanwhile zinc—crucial for immunity and fertility—was ample, and Vitamin D levels were far higher than today's recommended dose. Many more calories came from fat and protein than carbohydrate, which chimes surprisingly well with the current obsession with low-carb regimes. In short, the Mrs. Beeton diet was healthier than the food consumed in the average British family today.

✳

CHAPTER TWELVE

THE BEST COOKERY BOOK
IN THE WORLD

IT WOULD HAVE BEEN a miracle if Sam Beeton's split from Ward, Lock had gone smoothly. The problem was that Sam now did what he had threatened all along, and went back into business on his own account. *Jon Duan* had sold remarkably well, and while during the 1874 court case Sam had made a great deal of fuss about the fact that he had no financial interest in the product (for that would have meant admitting to an unambiguous flouting of his contract with Ward, Lock), the fact is that he had found a neat way of laundering his profit. While his co-authors Dowty and Jerrold got a cut, most of the money went to the publisher Charles Weldon, a former employee of S. O. Beeton. With these extra funds Weldon now financed Beeton and Mrs. Browne's new publishing venture, which was to be dedicated to producing a stable of publications similar to those they had left behind in Warwick House.

This posed a problem for Ward, Lock, who were faced with the likelihood that the value of their Beeton titles—the *Englishwoman's Domestic Magazine*, the *Young Englishwoman* and *Boy's Own Magazine*, not to mention the *Book of Household Management*—was now going to be decimated by a rival range of publications produced by the man himself, perhaps indeed even bearing his name. The two parties managed to last almost a year before they were again back in court. This time it was Sam who brought the case, his complaint being that Ward, Lock were putting the Beeton name to the kind of trash that he would never have countenanced and which might be "injurious" to his reputation. The case was once again heard before Sir Richard Malins who again found in favour of Ward, Lock, though not before declaring exasperatedly that both sides were "partly right and partly wrong."

At Malins's urging, it was clearly time to find a new way of going forward. In January 1876 Sam sat down and, on pages torn from an exercise book, drafted an arrangement that might actually have worked. The first and guiding principle is that Sam will continue to publish his own books, which will "be entirely within his control, both as to matter, manner, style & price." Once written they will be offered to Ward, Lock "to be published under the name of 'Beeton' or not, as SOB shall desire." Ward, Lock will have the right to refuse the books outright, or they may decide to produce them on the same terms as they currently follow with their bestselling author Miss Braddon. If Ward, Lock decide to have nothing to do with any particular title, then S. O. B. can publish it himself, choosing whether or not to brand it as one of "Beeton's Books." Sam will continue to be paid £500 a year and a quarter of all profits and, perhaps most surprising of all, he is to be provided with a suitable office at the new Warwick House, currently under construction in Salisbury Square. If the agreement is terminated, Sam will get £1,000 a year which, in the case of his death, will pass to his children for a period of ten years.

A covering letter that Sam has drafted below these jottings concludes: "I want my works to speak for me. . . . If I make mistakes, you will see that in every instance I have provided that I, & not you, shall smart for it." Here, in a nutshell, is Sam's philosophy. What he had always wanted, ever since he went into business at the age of twenty-one, was for "my works to speak for me." The idea of being muffled, muted or, worst of all, ventriloquized, was a kind of death. Whether this draft agreement was ever formalized looks unlikely. But what is clear is that despite Sam's oddness and difficult ways over the past few years, the Beeton name had still not become totally devalued in Ward, Lock's shrewd commercial eyes. The second important point is that while the document mentions generic publications—annuals, books, periodicals—there is no specific reference to *Mrs. Beeton's Book of Household Management.* Likewise, when Malins touched upon Beeton's business standing in his summing up of December 1875, he made only a fleeting reference to the fact that the "Beeton" brand name was in fact the work of two people: "Both the plaintiff and his late wife had acquired a high reputation in connexion with works for which the demand was great, and the use therefore of the plaintiff's name was of considerable value to the defendants." Fifteen years after the publication of the *Book of Household Management* the name "Mrs. Beeton" still had no particular pull.

While Sam may well have had a place in the new Warwick House in Salisbury Square, he spent most of his time in his new premises at 39 Bedford Street, Covent Garden, from where the Goubauds also ran their London office. Here he was joined by Myra Browne, who had become almost as annoying to Ward, Lock as Sam himself, not least because she had deliberately diluted the appeal of her popular Silkworm persona by using it for a prominent contribution to the *Jon Duan* annual. It was from Bedford Street in February 1875 that Myra and Sam launched a new magazine, *Myra's Journal of Dress and Fashion*, published initially by Charles Weldon from his nearby office.

By the last quarter of the century the women's magazine market was going through yet another shift, and there was a desire for a more democratic product at a cheaper price. *Myra's Journal,* at only 3d, with its textual illustrations rather than expensive fashion plates, exactly caught the mood. Weldon lost no time in posting advertisements in *The Times* explaining to readers the exact provenance of the new publication: "NEW Journal by Myra, late Editress of Beeton's Young Englishwoman"—which can hardly have thrilled Ward, Lock. Nor would they have been happy to read in an advertisement a few weeks later that a prominent feature of *Myra's Journal of Dress and Fashion* was "Spinnings in Town by Silkworm," not to mention "Dress and Fashion in Paris by Mme. Marie Goubaud," both names which had long been associated with the Beeton brand. Nor, surely, could they be anything but infuriated by the following open letter at the end of the first issue of *Myra's Journal:*

"THE SILKWORM" AND "MYRA"
TO THEIR OLD AND NEW FRIENDS.

It would be uninteresting at the present moment to explain the reasons of our retirement from the Editorship of Mr. Beeton's two Magazines "THE YOUNG ENGLISHWOMAN" and "THE ENGLISHWOMAN'S DOMESTIC MAGAZINE." Nevertheless, we think it proper, for many reasons, to state that Mr. Beeton must, in this connection, be entirely dissociated from his publishers, Messrs. Ward & Lock.

By way of response, Ward, Lock now introduced a new character to the *EDM*, the Hummingbird. Instead of producing "Spinnings" this new creature had a column called "Flittings." But without the flair of Sam and Myra, the heart had gone out of the magazine. The *EDM* limped on until 1877, at which point it was absorbed by the unenticing *Milliner and Dressmaker and Warehouseman's Gazette*.

Beeton family anecdote has always represented the arrangement with Weldon as a golden swansong for Sam, a taster of what the rest of his life might have been if it had not been cruelly terminated in the spring of 1877. In these accounts Weldon is also assumed to be younger than Sam and so, by implication, biddable. In fact Weldon was exactly the same age as Beeton and surviving evidence shows that, almost immediately, the two men were at each other's throats. There is a letter of 29 February 1876 in Sam's hand which begins ominously "Dear Sir" and which Mayson Beeton has duly noted as being directed to Weldon. The letter is a frosty complaint about sloppy book-keeping, which is making Beeton's job impossible. The letter continues tersely, "The results of your negligence are becoming more serious every day; & I beg you will post all a/cs immediately in both ledgers, so that the damage to my business may be lessened as much as possible." That this is no mere blustery play-acting is suggested by the fact that, just for once, Sam has not bothered to produce his elaborate swagger of a signature. Instead, his name is scarcely rendered as a dull, flat line.

Even if Mayson Beeton was mistaken, and this letter was not addressed to Weldon, there still remains a curious document in Sam's hand, again written on pages torn from an exercise book. The draft document is headed "Propositions, Made Without Prejudice by S. O. Beeton as between Mrs. Browne and Mr. Weldon, for the settlement of disputes sent for Mr. Levy's [the solicitor] amendments." The document is undated, but internal evidence suggests that it was written at the end of 1876. The story it tells is a grim one, of creditors, debtors, defamation of character, and threatened law suits. Sam and Myra's particular grievance appears to be the way that Weldon has been keeping back goods and money that do not belong to him. Even worse, from a business point of view, is the way that Weldon has been badmouthing Mrs. Browne to her creditors.

The relationship with Weldon cannot have been helped by the fact that for at least half of 1875 Sam was travelling in Italy for his health (ironically one of his main gripes against Ward and Lock had been that one or other of them was always away). There is a surviving letter from this time, written on 24 February, just after Sam had arrived in Naples. Even when he was out of the country Sam was still able and willing to make mischief for Ward, Lock. In the letter, Sam suggests to "Johnny" that he tries to get a man called Spice to work for him. Spice, who "can do pretty much everything, carpenter & paint & whitewash, & keep a/cs, & write & direct," has been working for ten years at Warwick House and is, apparently, miserable now that Sam has left. "He's much too good for the present company he is in," declares Sam and then lays out a detailed plan by which Spice can be lured away from his present employment.

Sam finishes the letter with a wry admission that he is not exactly flourishing under this new regime of forced idleness: "[I] can't get over the feeling that I'm shirking the hardships of life too much. I'm a bit of a Puritan, in that respect, & I'm not fond of myself unless I've got a crux or two on my shoulders." Here, in a rare moment of enforced stillness, Sam manages an insight that goes to the heart of his exasperating, exciting personality. He was a man who thrived on stimulus and, when it was lacking, immediately set about manufacturing it in order to feel properly alive. It did not matter that so many of the situations he unconsciously engineered for himself were painful—bankruptcy, court cases, illicit love, family feuds. He was addicted to trouble.

There was, though, one area of Sam Beeton's life that remained comparatively calm. The curious shadow marriage that he had made with Myra Browne seemed to suit and sustain both of them (whether it did the same for Mr. Browne is not quite so clear). In the letter from Naples Sam explains to Johnny that "Mama" is forwarding his mail regularly and that "Mama" is the person to contact for the address of Spice, the wonderful Renaissance man of Warwick House. The use of "Mama" to describe Myra Browne is intriguing. It is certainly what the Beeton boys called Mrs. Browne, but it seems strange, not to say creepy, to hear Sam following suit when communicating with another adult male. Perhaps, though, he had found a clever way to dodge drawing attention to the precise nature of his relationship with Myra Browne. To refer to her as "Mrs. Browne" would seem ridiculously stuffy, something of which you could never accuse Sam Beeton. But to mention her as "Myra" was to suggest an intimacy with her that would raise too many questions in the listener's mind. By calling her "Mama" Sam not only suggested to people that his primary relationship with Myra Browne was via his two motherless boys, he was also effectively desexualizing her. Interesting too is the way that Sam's letter takes it for granted that Myra is his business partner. He is confident about referring "Johnny" to her for Spice's details, knowing that she will be able to supply them with the minimum of fuss. Just like Isabella, she is his right hand, his better half.

Since the Beeton boys had never known their biological mother, as far as they were concerned Myra was indeed their "Mama." She, in turn, was delighted to have been presented with the family that she had given up hope of achieving for herself. In 1871, writing in her usual confiding style in the *EDM,* Myra had explained to her readers just how sad she had been before the boys had arrived (staying vague about the details, she was happy to let readers assume that they must be her own): "before children came to bless my home, what is now known as the 'children's hour' was then the 'dark hour' or 'blind man's holiday' to me. Very long and very dark it used to be." The anecdotes that have come down to us show Myra as an energetic, loving, and happy foster mother. She made clothes for the boys out of their father's cast-offs, romped around the floor pretending to be an elephant, told stories, listened to stories, made a toy garden, and supervised the making and sending of a Valentine card to herself. When the children were about eight (there was little more than a year between them) they were sent to a prep school in Exmouth run by the Revd. Carr (MA Oxon). During the bankruptcy arrangements of 1866 it had been agreed that the two houses in Wood Street that had passed to Sam from his mother, Helen Orchart, the prosperous baker's daughter, should be ring-fenced from Sam's estate so that they could be used to pay for his sons' upkeep. This is why, despite Sam's modest finances (he cannot have earned more than £500 in any year from 1866 to his death in 1877), he was able to give his sons a gentleman's education. After Exmouth both went to Marlborough, from where there was money enough to send Orchart, "Dorch," to Sandhurst and Mayson, "Dace," to Magdalen College, Oxford.

Letters written by Myra and Sam to the Beeton children while they were away at school in Exmouth still survive. They suggest a relationship steeped in unforced love and an instinctual understanding of what interests little boys. Myra's first surviving letter, from 13 June 1874, written from the office on *EDM*-headed letter paper, reads:

June 13 1874

My darling boys

Thank you for your kind nice letters . . .

The marrows are growing nicely in your gardens and Grant is now seeing about the bedding plants for you. Your peas are not yet ready. Shall I put them down to you? can you get them boiled?

. . .

I saw Jim on the pier on Wednesday; he looks pale, he was going on a steamer to see a yacht off Greenhithe; he wants some cricket to do him good, it is a glorious game. Mr. Carr must play well to carry his bat. How do you get on at swimming, I want to know this. Papa is much better, he sends his love to you both, and so do I. I have got a few coins collected but no good caterpillars; in your holidays you can get some hop-dogs, a very funny kind of caterpillar, but it only comes when the hops are ripe.

Your affec^ate Mother

MAMA

The next surviving letter in the sequence is written a fortnight later. This time Myra is in gently pedagogic mode, keen to extract moral lessons from every passing occurrence. Her letter starts:

My darling boys,

Thank you much for your kind letters. I had Dace's letter on Monday but he owes one still. Thank you much for your remembering my birthday which is next Monday, S^t. Peter's Day, when I was a little girl I could not bear St Peter, because I thought him so mean; now I am grown up I know that many people do mean things from want of courage and from getting frightened, but it is good to hear of brave men as we have this week, for Mon^s Rochefort [the radical Vicomte who had recently escaped with companions from prison] has been here and has told us all about his escape, how he swam away and how he waited for his friends and would not leave them. One, a Mon^s Pain, hurt his foot badly on the rocks and they all helped him and all six were saved. It is most interesting. I am so glad I know French or else I should not have understood a word. If Rochefort had not learnt to swim he could never have got away from the island, New Caledonia in the S. Pacific; you can look it out in your map, it lies Lat. 19° 37′, Long 163° 37′, a little to the right of Australia, if you can not find it, ask Mr. Dick.

Sam's letters to the boys show the same mixture of tenderness and high-minded exhortation, leavened with a fair dollop of sport, weather and wildlife. His first surviving letter, of 28 April, runs typically:

My dear boys,

I had your letters this afternoon, and I have sent them to Paris with my letter to Mama; she will be home, I expect, by Saturday or Sunday . . . Little Puss has had four kittens—two have been drowned; the others are beautifully marked, looking something like the lizard, wh, by the bye, Tommy caught and killed on the terrace. Your thrush sits closely to her nest, and does not move when I go to look at her. I have found outside the gate in the road opposite Breakneck Hill a tribe of Mason Bees, (not Mayson Beetons); they have hundreds of little holes into wh they are constantly carrying their honey, pollen etc. Rough [the terrier] is very funny; he cannot understand puss always keeping in the basket with her young ones; when you come home the kittens will be playing about, I have no doubt. You are very lucky in your cricket matches; bathing you won't begin, I suppose, till May. We have strong winds here to-day, but the weather is very fine; we want some rain, however, and the roads are very dusty. Poor Barrow, fifth! I am sorry to hear he is getting, as you say, worse and worse. Have you had any games at Chess?—it is hardly the weather for that, however, as it is better to be playing out of doors. Has Dace read The Watermatch and The Two Admirals? I can send him some more books to read, if he wishes. I hope he is keeping out of impots, and punishments; and if he can get to be Number Two instead of Three, and have a good character from Mr. Carr, it will delight me and all of us very much.

My love to both of you, my dear boys—

Your loving

FATHER

The letters that follow are in much the same vein, packed full of home news about dogs, cats, and rabbits and asking keen questions about cricket matches and exam results. There is certainly no hint that the man who is writing them has barely three years to live. For the trip to Italy the following year did little to restore Sam's health. Family anecdote maintains this was because Dowty, his loyal co-writer on *Jon Duan* and now his travelling companion, was taken seriously ill in Naples, putting Sam in the position of carer rather than patient. But in truth Sam's illness was now so advanced that nothing, certainly not a spell of mild weather, was going to halt it. The fact that he had been sent to the bright, light south by his doctors might seem to suggest that they were working to a diagnosis of TB. However, patients in the last stages of syphilis were also regularly sent to the sun. In only a few years' time Emily Mayson, the widow of Isabella's brother John, would go into an agonizing decline in a hotel room on the French Riviera, thoughtfully paid for by her aristocratic employers.

Highly significant, too, is the fact that Sam's doctor was none other than the celebrated Morell MacKenzie. MacKenzie's specialty was throats, not the consumptive lungs from which Sam was supposed to be suffering. Moreover MacKenzie's surviving case notes from 1885 show that many of the people who presented themselves at his Harley Street clinic were suffering from the dropped noses and ravaged throats of tertiary syphilis. This does not mean, of course, that patients found it easy to hear the truth about the origins of their ghastly pain (and, in the case of married women, it may well have been that MacKenzie followed the practice of many of his colleagues and simply did not enlighten them). When, in 1887, MacKenzie was famously called upon to treat Crown Prince Frederick of Germany—the very Crown Prince who had once been shown around the Grandstand—who was believed to be suffering from throat cancer, he found it impossible to get the court to contemplate his alternative diagnosis of syphilis. Whether or not it was cancer or syphilis that actually killed Frederick less than a year later, the point was that MacKenzie, as a throat man, was a specialist in both.

When Sam returned to Britain in the autumn of 1875 after several months' stay on the Continent he was as thin, ill, and jittery as ever (the bad-tempered court case he now brought against the whiting works at the bottom of the garden suggests that every little disturbance jangled him, body and soul). The best description of the dying man comes from T. P. O'Connor, at the time a young writer who would later become a distinguished politician and journalist. The two men had become friends when O'Connor had applied for a job as reader at the new Bedford Street premises (instead of offering him the job, Sam suggested that O'Connor should write a biography of Disraeli, which he duly did). O'Connor remembered:

> [Beeton] was almost a startling sight when first you met him. I have never seen so thin a man who yet was able to live. Indeed when first you saw him, you were only conscious of a pair of eyes—large, brilliant, burning, a beautiful and almost dazzling blue-grey in colour—they seemed to be the only living thing in the man to have alone survived the wreck of the rest of the frame. A ramrod with two shining little lamps near the top—that is something like what S. O. Beeton was in the days when I made his acquaintance.
>
> In some respects he might have stood for Don Quixote; for, in addition to this phenomenal thinness, he wore his beard in a peculiar style. It was a beautiful grey, like the eyes—and it was brought down to a point just as is the typical beard of the Spaniard. The intellect and the spirit of the man, however, shone as brightly as the eyes. He was a ferocious Radical; was a brilliant and fervent conversationalist; and often would talk to me for long hours together to the detriment of his health sometimes, and to the great alarm of those who were watching over the flickering candle of his existence.

Other reminiscences, unattributed but probably from Mrs. Browne, tell of Sam spiralling into self-neglect, taking no care of himself yet "frantic" if Orchart or Mayson should suffer from something as slight as a hurt finger. Each year the approach of two dates, 10 July and 6 February—the anniversaries of Sam and Isabella's wedding and Isabella's death respectively—was guaranteed to plunge him into even greater gloom. His very last surviving letter was written on 13 November 1876 to Mayson, or "Dace," who was still at school in Exmouth with his older brother "Dorch."

> My dear Dace,
> I have been expecting to see your "hand-write," as they say in Scotland, for many days. Mamma has written you and sent you things since her return; and I wrote you both in one letter just before we left [presumably for Paris]. Let me know how you are, and what's the last new

thing. I have just read a new book, intending to publish it next year for boys, "Captain Kyd, the Wizard of the Sea"—a wonderful catalogue of adventures. Ask me for it when you come home, with some others written by the same author Ingraham. As it is now almost certain that you will spend yr holidays in London, we are going to do the best we can to make you enjoy them . . . What's the game afoot now? Here, to-day, it is so dark that candles and gas alight everywhere in all the rooms—not like sunshiny Italy, nor, I hope, like Exmouth.

You will write me a few lines, between yr Meals and yr Mathematics, I hope.

Your loving Father,

With his kindest affection.

By this time, as the letter shows, the Beeton-Browne household had shifted up to London. At various points over the last few years Sam had stayed overnight in London to avoid the stress of the daily commute. Now his fragile health meant that it made sense for everyone to move permanently nearer their work. Accommodation was taken at Adelphi Terrace, a little nook just off the Strand, and it is here, presumably, that Dace and Dorch spent that last Christmas holiday with their father.

Any sense of diminishment or depression the boys may have felt at being cramped into an apartment when they were used to country living was offset by Sam's determination that they should have as good a time as possible. Sam's spirits were buoyant and so, unusually, were his finances. He had just published the most accomplished and successful of his Christmas annuals. *Edward VII: A Play on the Past and Present Times with a View to the Future* was a Shakespearean parody in seven acts which dealt with Beeton's favourite topic: "the vices and follies of the age." In the closing lines Sam—together with his co-authors Dowty and Jerrold—engineered a future for the British monarchy in which Queen Victoria abdicated in favour of Edward, a man for whom Sam had more sympathy than his fierce radicalism sometimes suggested. Despite the fact that republicanism was by now a spent political force, the knock-about rudeness of the *Annual* assured it a healthy sale and, what perhaps pleased Sam even more, plenty of huffing and puffing in the conservative press.

What also took everyone's minds off Sam's obvious decline during that last Christmas holiday was the curious fact that, at the age of forty, Myra Browne now found herself pregnant. One month after Sam's death she gave birth to a boy, who was duly christened Charles Gordon Meredith Browne. The earlier biographer Sarah Freeman put this late pregnancy down to that phenomenon by which women who adopt children after years of trying for their own find themselves pregnant, the happy result of dissolving psychological tension. Even if this is the case—and the fact that Myra had been fostering the Beeton boys for over a decade tends to put paid to the theory—the question remains, who was the father? The baby, always called Meredith, looked so startlingly like his mother that it is impossible to discern even the outlines of a likeness to either Sam or Charlie Browne. However, assuming that the pregnancy went to full term, then the baby would have been conceived in the first week of November. And it was just at that point, as the letter Sam wrote to Mayson on 13 November 1876 reveals, that Mr. Beeton and Mrs. Browne happened to be away together, most probably in Paris.

But if the Christmas school holiday passed off happily, by the time

Myra Browne, looking every inch the editor of a fashion magazine, with her son Meredith around 1885.

Easter came round it was another story. Sam went downhill fast from the beginning of April and was now so ill that all he could do was lie on a sofa, propped up by pillows. Around 1 June he was moved by Morell MacKenzie to a sanatorium just outside Richmond, in southwest London. Sudbrook Park was under the direction of Edward Lane, a doctor who believed in the healing powers of hydropathy. Accordingly, the Palladian mansion was fitted out with an imposing array of hot and cold baths and showers, designed to shock ailing systems into health. Controversially, patients might even be wrapped in wet bandages in an attempt to rouse their sluggish circulations. The regime was Spartan—no alcohol and emphatically no smoking and plain, regular meals. For those patients able to totter out, there were extensive pleasure grounds with fabulous views over Ham Common and a private gate into Richmond Royal Park. Sudbrook had always catered for the better class of invalid and potential clients were assured in the promotional blurb that there was plenty of stable room should they wish to bring their own horses.

Sam Beeton died at Sudbrook Park on 6 June at the age of forty-six. The death certificate says "phthisis" and it is impossible to say for certain that it was syphilis and not consumption that killed him. The obituaries were muted, the result of him having died in the middle of a career that might, in the next few years, have taken him soaring to dizzying new heights or back into bankruptcy. It was hard, at this midway point, for anyone to say whether S. O. Beeton's life had been one of glorious achievement or miserable failure. The *Athenaeum*, the magazine that had first noticed his publications in 1861 and in which he had subsequently spent hundreds of pounds on advertising, said: "We are sorry to hear of the death of Mr. S. O. Beeton, the publisher of many cheap and popular works. Although from an early age a sufferer from the disease from which he died, he displayed throughout his life immense energy and perseverance . . . In his literary labours he was much assisted by his wife, who died some years ago." *The Times* did not notice his death, but the *London Figaro* contained a long paeon probably written by his friend Dowty, which declared:

How energetic and how full of enterprise and spirits he was in spite of his ever present foes, those only who knew him well can appreciate. To the last his vitality was most extraordinary and his strength of mind never for a moment failed him, even when the fell disease was at its worst . . . He was courageous well nigh to temerity, and possessed the subtle power of inspiring all who worked with him with the most sanguine hopes of success; a power that is only given to the few, and is so largely developed in those who become leaders of men . . . An ardent lover of nature and a firm believer in the goodness of the Creator, Mr. Beeton hated with an intense abhorrence anything that smacked of bigotry or sectarian prejudice. In politics he held advanced views, being almost Quixotic in his well-meant efforts to do the masses good . . . As a friend Mr. Beeton was most constant and devoted, whilst those who have been unfortunate enough to be in a position antagonistic to him must admit the chivalrous nature of his opposition, even whilst suffering from its thoroughness and success . . . His funeral was a private one, but the few near friends who gathered round his grave could not but be sad when they thought what a real man, what a true and genial friend, what a fond father, and what a noble and gentle soul had been taken from their midst.

No matter how hard Dowty tried to say otherwise, there was a pall of frustration and unfinished business hanging over Sam's reputation at the time of his death. Everyone agreed that in the first few years of his working life he had been quite the marvellous boy. But from 1865, the year that Isabella died, it was hard to avoid the conclusion that he was periodically insane. The pornographic episodes of 1867–70 seem to be the action of a man who has lost touch with all sense of moral fitness and commercial soundness (although it has to be said that, since the *Englishwoman's Domestic Magazine* experienced increased circulation, there may have been method in his madness). The decision in 1868 to produce a publication dedicated to the Derby simply in order to accuse his father-in-law of meanness seems spiteful and undignified. The endless court cases, which meant hiring QCs at great expense to fight small battles about a single American copyright or some noisy machinery, seem positively destructive. And, finally, it has to be said that Sam's inability to work with anyone—his business relationships with Charles Clarke, Hutton, M'Murray, and Ward, Lock all ended in Chancery, and his arrangement with Weldon threatened to go that way too—does suggest that here was a man who was determined to have his own way.

Lucy Smiles, Isabella's half-sister, had declared in old age to Harford Montgomery Hyde that Sam Beeton "had the fate of all pioneers—he sowed and others reaped." And the old lady, who had not seen her brother-in-law since she was twenty, may well have had a point. As we have seen, Frederick Greenwood went on to become a venerated elder statesman of journalism. James Bowden, who had joined S. O. Beeton in 1865, moved to Ward, Lock in 1869 and was promoted to a partnership so that in July 1891 the firm became "Ward, Lock, Bowden & Co." Ward, Lock themselves made a spectacular fortune out of one particular Beeton publication, *Mrs. Beeton's Book of Household Management*, that pearl of great price that they had acquired without really knowing in 1866. All those publishers alongside whom Sam had laboured to produce good, cheap reading matter for the new middle classes—Warne, Macmillan, Cassell and Routledge—remain stalwarts in the book trade even to this day. Charles Weldon, Beeton's last associate, went on to found a periodical empire based around the integration of paper dressmaking patterns and popular women's magazines which Beeton and Goubaud had pioneered. Indeed, so powerful and enduring was the Weldon empire that even in the 1950s when Montgomery Hyde was writing his Beeton biography, he tactfully refrained from mentioning that the "associate" who had "defalcated" with so much of Sam's profits in 1876 was none other than Charles Weldon, for fear of embarrassing the still powerful family company.

All this was in the future, though, when Samuel Beeton was put into the ground alongside Isabella and the second little Samuel Orchart Beeton in Norwood Cemetery in June 1877. The following Christmas his old colleagues Dowty and Jerrold brought out an annual entitled *Finis,* from which all the profits went to the young Beeton boys. It included Sam's portrait and some memorial verses that echoed much of what had been said in Dowty's more formal appreciation in the *London Figaro.*

IN MEMORIAM

S. O. B.

We lack fit words to tell our grief,
For his great soul from earth removed;
A staunch companion, often proved,
His noble life was all too brief.

High-spirited, yet like a child
Though modest, yet as lion bold;

A man whom years could not make old.
Who through a life of torture smiled.

Who through a life of torture worked;
With busy brain and facile pen,
He wrought good for his fellow-men
No labour shunned, nor duty shirked . . .

There was, near the end of the poem, a brief reference to the fact that
S. O. Beeton had once been married:

A tender husband, jealous death
Begrudged his bliss, and 'twas o'ercast . . .

It was a nice thought, but more importantly it provides a vital snapshot of where Isabella's reputation lay in 1877. Even among professional
writers and editors, she was still essentially Sam's wife, a nice girl whose
personal and professional identity had been so absorbed into his that
there was no need to think of her as a separate person. The fact that
Isabella had written a book that, over the next twenty-five years, would
make her name live in history and eclipse that of Sam's would have
astounded everyone who gathered around the musty Norwood grave in
June 1877, including Jerrold and Dowty. But that transformation of
Isabella from "late wife" to cultural icon was about to begin.

Only six weeks after Sam's death, Myra gave birth to baby Meredith.
A few weeks later still, Orchart and Mayson arrived home from
Exmouth, desperately in need of reassurance, only to find their "Mama"
busy with the baby that she had waited for seventeen years to see. As if
that weren't enough disruption, both boys had left the relatively cosy
world of their prep school for the last time and were due in September to
start at Marlborough, one of Britain's toughest public schools. Still, Sam
had done all he could to ensure that their lives were disrupted as little as
possible. According to the terms of his will, "Matilda Eliza Browne, the
wife of Charles Rouse Browne" was appointed "the sole Guardian of my
two children who shall have the custody of their persons and sole control
of their education during their minorities." Under the guiding eye of
Sam's younger half-brother Sidney Perkes Beeton, Mrs. Browne was to
be given the entire proceeds of Sam's estate "for the support maintenance
education and clothing of my said two children." Making these arrange-

Charles, Meredith and Myra Browne in the late 1880s.

ments in 1869, when his disillusionment with his in-laws was at its height, Sam was determined that even once his own inconvenient presence had been removed, Isabella's family would not be given the chance of reclaiming Orchart and Mayson as their own.

If the arrangement meant raised eyebrows, it was nonetheless followed to the letter. The records from Marlborough, which Orchart and Mayson duly entered that autumn, show that their guardian was indeed "Mrs. Browne of 7 Adelphi Terrace." These school records also provide a glimpse of the two recently orphaned boys. Both were small, under five feet at the ages of fourteen and thirteen, respectively, and weighed scarcely six stones. Even by late adolescence they were only five feet six inches tall and about nine stones in weight, which suggests that, physically at least, they took after their father. Orchart had an undistinguished academic career, bumping along in the bottom half of the class before leaving in 1881 to go to Sandhurst. Mayson did slightly better and in 1879 was awarded a junior scholarship when he came top. By the time he was in the Upper Sixth, however, he could manage to be placed only seventeenth out of twenty students. This was still good enough to get him into Magdalen, Oxford, where he achieved the expected second-class degree in History.

School holidays were spent with the Brownes, who soon moved out of the cramped quarters in the Strand with their new baby and into a house in Kingston-upon-Thames. It was here that Myra lived until the end of her long life in 1936. Charlie by now had succeeded to the top job at the Westminster Fire Agency and the Brownes' style of living had taken a correspondingly smart step upwards from the riverine shabbiness of the Greenhithe days. They now employed a cook, housemaid, and nurse, placing them firmly in the upper half of the middle classes. It was from this substantial launch pad that Mayson was able to meet the equally well-set-up Louie Swinley Price Jones, who lived only a couple of streets away. Her father was a prosperous doctor, and the moment she came of age the young couple married at Surbiton parish church. Orchart, the elder boy who was somehow always the less promising and less important, made another south London suburban match. The year after Mayson's wedding, and now a lieutenant in the army, he married Janet Kennedy, a bank manager's daughter from Bromley.

During their growing years the boys seem to have had no contact with their mother's family. Quite possibly they were not told about the death of their only uncle John Mayson at the age of thirty-one in 1871, or the death of their grandmother Elizabeth Dorling that same year, nor that of their step-grandfather Henry Dorling just two years later amid the stately grandeur of Stroud Green House. They may not even have heard about the passing of their great-grandmother, Mary Jerrom, who finally died in the house in Rutland Street in 1874, just shy of eighty years old and no longer a crucial cog in the Dorling family enterprise. Granny Jerrom was buried with her sister Harriet Cates in Brompton Cemetery, in a grave arranged for by Edward Dorling, Isabella's gentle second step-brother. What a difference twenty years had made, for it was as recently as 1856 that Mrs. Jerrom had sat high up in the Epsom Grandstand gossiping with Isabella about her handsome, dashing fiancé, "dear Sam." But he had not been anyone's "dear Sam" for very long, and Mary Jerrom went to her grave quite possibly without ever having set eyes on the surviving children of her eldest and most precious granddaughter.

But while the people who had known Isabella Beeton began to die out in the 1870s, a strange thing happened. Instead of her memory dying with them, Mrs. Beeton began to be resurrected by a series of swaps and substitutions that gave the impression that the woman herself was still alive and well and busy in her increasingly iconic kitchen. The first and fullest impersonation was effected by Myra Browne who, as we have seen, stepped swiftly and completely into the gap left by Isabella Beeton. She raised Isabella's children, wrote her copy, edited her magazines, nursed her husband and, most importantly, in 1869 revised her famous *Book of Household Management.* She did, however, stop short of calling herself "Mrs. Beeton." This particular sleight of hand was left to Louie Swinley Price Jones, the doctor's daughter who had married Mayson Beeton in 1887. By the time he was twenty-three Mayson Beeton had set up "Beeton & Co.," a company producing a stable of women's magazines out of the old offices in Bedford Street, including the still very successful *Myra's Journal* and a new weekly magazine, *Hearth and Home.* It was to the second of these titles that Louie contributed a regular household column, under the by-line "Mrs. M. Beeton." The Beeton family might have long lost control of its most valuable asset, but it had the next best thing—a flesh-and-blood "Mrs. Beeton" to compete against Ward, Lock's spectral version.

Just how commercially important the name "Mrs. Beeton" was to the next generation of the family is shown in a letter that Mayson Beeton wrote in 1894, withdrawing from the management of *Hearth and Home.* Mayson Beeton turned out to be as hopeless a businessman as his father had ever been—disorganized, unpunctual, liable to lie under pressure, and dreadful with money. When the inevitable falling out came in 1894, Mayson's letter to his partner Colonel Talbot Coke declares, with an uncanny echo of his late father's bluster, "I have written to the office to say that my wife's connection with the papers can of course be no longer continued and should be glad if it were in my powers to do the same in connection with my own name." By some odd historical kink, the name of the woman who had died giving birth to Mayson Beeton had become so valuable that, thirty years on, he and his wife were able to use it as their strongest professional bargaining chip. The fact that no one quite knew how many Mrs. Beetons there were, and which was still alive, only helped the family to hang on to a small share of the cultural capital that it had let slip through its fingers in 1866.

Throughout the 1880s and 1890s these elisions of identity and relationship within the Beeton clan became even more dizzying. One of Mayson Beeton's first jobs on leaving Oxford was to set up a subsidiary publishing outfit to produce book spin-offs from the very successful "Myra" brand. This publishing company was called Myra and Son. Even more obfuscation arose when, in 1889, Myra and Son published *Myra's Cookbook* which was described as having been "enlarged and revised by Mrs. M. Beeton," who was, of course, Mayson's wife and not, as he doubtless hoped people might think, his mother. When in 1894 Mayson Beeton moved to work for Harmsworth he took *his* "Mrs. Beeton" with him. *Home Chat,* the phenomenally successful penny weekly which Harmsworth launched the following year, boasted a strong team of contributors, one of whom was "Mrs. M. Beeton." This substitution was effected so seamlessly that by 1925, when the rival publishing house of Cassell came to publish its own book-length history, they were happy to explain the failure of their own cheap magazine *Paris Mode* in the 1890s in terms of the fact that its main rival *Home Chat* had managed to bag Mrs. Beeton, "the author of the classic book on cookery." No one, surely, could be expected to compete with that.

Right from the start *Beeton's Book of Household Management* was a moveable feast, a shape-shifting entity that existed in a myriad of different forms. Barely had it appeared as a single volume in the winter of 1861 than Sam decided to reissue it from scratch, this time in twelve parts costing 6d each and with new, improved artwork. This second edition also appeared in due course as a single volume, again costing 7s 6d. So by the time Isabella died in February 1865 the *Book of Household Management* had all the makings of a bibliographic tangle, already consisting of two different part works and two distinct book-length editions.

As if that weren't enough, *Household Management* began to spawn infant versions of itself almost immediately. As we have seen, in January 1863 Isabella had produced *The Englishwoman's Cookery Book* at the cost of 1s, which consisted of a collection of the most economical recipes from the *BOHM* aimed "to help Plain Cooks and Maids of all Work." Two years later, on her deathbed, she was correcting proofs for another collection of alphabetically arranged recipes, this time entitled *Mrs. Beeton's Dictionary of Everyday Cookery* and selling for 3s 6d.

But just at the moment that Mrs. Beeton started to assume a greater prominence on the cover of her books, the outline of her actual life was beginning to smudge. After 1865 the "Usque Ad Finem" obituary was quietly dispensed with, never to appear again in any of the publications with which she had been associated. As late as 1889 you can spot the occasional reference to "the late" Mrs. Beeton in various Prefaces but this too was eventually dropped. An 1867 reissue of the *Englishwoman's Cookery Book,* for instance, carried the original Preface, initialled "I.B." and with nothing to suggest that Isabella Beeton had not personally supervised its release. Two years later Ward, Lock puffed its new series, "House and Home Books," as having been "prepared by Mrs. Beeton," fudging the fact that although volumes such as *How to Manage House and Servants* and *Diners and Dining* had indeed been hewn out of Mrs. Beeton's original text, the lady herself had been dead for four years. Sharp-eyed readers might have noticed that Mrs. Beeton now chose to bring out her books with Ward, Lock rather than S. O. Beeton but, really, all that mattered was that her increasingly reassuring name was somewhere prominent on the cover.

Over the next thirty years a whole range of titles appeared from Warwick House, all carved out of the *Book of Household Management* and targeted at those who had neither the need nor the cash to acquire the rapidly expanding master version. In fact, the full-length volume was increasingly becoming a symbolic item, something you gave as an important present to a bride or a young matron off to the colonies. The cut-down versions of *Mrs. Beeton* were, by contrast, working books that you might buy for yourself and refer to constantly with floury fingers. These included *Mrs. Beeton's Family Cookery, Mrs. Beeton's Penny Cookery, Mrs. Beeton's Sixpenny Cookery, Mrs. Beeton's Shilling Cookery* and *Mrs. Beeton's Cottage Cookery Book,* and were part of the trend for smaller, single-authored cookery books (as opposed to impersonal encyclopaedias) which marked the 1870s. An advertisement that Ward, Lock placed in 1880 runs through every kind of "Mrs. Beeton" available, matching them to a range of homes, from the masterwork, which is now "acknowledged as the First Cookery Book in the World," through *Mrs.*

Beeton's All About Cookery, designed "for households and families with more moderate means and requirements," right down to *Mrs. Beeton's Penny Cookery Book,* "for distribution in every cottage home as an incentive to improved domestic arrangement among the humbler classes, and as a gift in parish schools." Even once you had decided which version of Mrs. Beeton's wisdom you wanted, there were further choices to be made between part work and single volume, cloth or calf binding, colour plates or unillustrated.

After the Great War, Ward, Lock directed Mrs. Beeton—or at least the journalists employed to speak for her—away from "Plain Cooks and Maids of all Work" and towards the increasingly hard-pressed mistress who was having to make do with much-reduced staff. There now appeared a series called "Mrs. Beeton's Handy Reference Books" which included titles such as *Mrs. Beeton's Cake Making, Mrs. Beeton's Cold Sweets, Mrs. Beeton's Fish Cookery, Mrs. Beeton's Hors D'Oeuvres and Savouries* and several more. In the middle of the twentieth century there were fewer Beeton options (the curse of the unfashionable Victorians combined with a decade of food rationing) but by the 1960s Ward, Lock was busy once more thinking up new versions of Mrs. Beeton. In 1964 came the publication of *Continental Cookery (A Selection of Recipes from Mrs. Beeton's Cookery and Household Management),* while in 1973 there appeared *Mrs. Beeton's Easy to Cook Book* and three years later *Mrs. Beeton's Simple Cookery in Colour.* The 1980s were a slow time for Beeton, perhaps because it was now that Ward, Lock was in the process of being acquired by Cassell, another Victorian publisher dedicated to Universal Knowledge; but come the 1990s she was back again with *Mrs. Beeton's Traditional Housekeeping Today, A Gift From Mrs. Beeton, Mrs. Beeton's Traditional Christmas* and *Mrs. Beeton's Healthy Eating.*

Mrs. Beeton's bastard progeny are too many and too varied to look at in detail here. A more manageable task is to track the changes that crept into the master text until the point was reached, in 1906, where it became a swollen monument to Edwardian high living, barely recognizable as the work of the historical Mrs. Beeton. The first significant new edition appeared in 1869 and was undertaken by Sam at Warwick House, together with "feminine aid of the most valuable kind," in other words Myra Browne's. In his Preface Sam stresses that his "late wife's writing was clear and her instructions so practical" that the only changes he has had to make have been on account of "some new and modern information which, seven years ago, did not exist." This updating can be seen most clearly in the chapter on the kitchen. Here the original 1861 list of fifty items for the well-run household has been updated with some fancy new suggestions such as a chopping board, while more homely items like "a pair of bellows" are now only required for the unlucky minority who have not yet purchased a Leamington Kitchener. Potentially baffling new items, such as the table-top Mincing Machine, are helpfully described with a set of explanatory line drawings.

The fact that several of these illustrated items are clearly marked "R & J Slack, Strand" neatly demonstrates the way in which later editions of the *BOHM* continued to blur the boundaries between editorial and advertising copy. While in the 1861 edition Isabella Beeton had reproduced the contents of the kitchen catalogue from Slack's in the Strand, there had been no visual reinforcement of its provenance. But by 1869 the message that Slack's was the only place to buy your kitchen goods was getting louder and louder. To run a well-ordered home the Mrs. Beeton way no longer meant merely managing your time and space correctly, you also needed to know how to shop properly. To be a model provider you needed to become a model consumer too.

This emphasis is underlined by Sam's and Myra's other major innovation in the 1869 edition, the insertion of a whole new chapter on making ice cream. The mood here too is modern and technological, erasing any traces of wistfulness for a bucolic past discernible in Isabella's original text (that dairymaid making frothy syllabub straight from the cow's udder, for instance). Instead of the vanishing skills of the stillroom maid, all that the reader of the 1869 edition of the *Book of Household Management* need do in order to make her own ice cream is buy "Mr. Ash's Patent Piston Freezing Machine," which is available from 315c Oxford Street "where block-ice and freezing powders can also be procured." The mantra of the middle-class woman was increasingly "I shop, therefore I am," and Isabella Beeton's original text, with its emphasis on making do, was beginning to look dull and fusty.

The other noticeable change in the 1869 *BOHM* is the set of twelve entirely new colour plates. In the original 1861 edition the plates were there to describe and support the cooking process. They showed what a woodcock looks like when it is trussed, or how the sides of a Charlotte aux Pommes should be fluted. Sometimes, indeed, the detail could be off-putting in its literalness: the illustration of a "cod's head and shoulders" might be useful to the puzzled cook, but it could hardly have tempted the reluctant diner. The 1869 plates, by contrast, are all about pleasing the eye rather than providing instruction for uncertain fingers. Enormous care has been taken to use an effective colour palette of pinks, browns, and reds, but this often bears little relation to the desired appearance of the finished dish. Complex shapes have been smoothed and regularized to the point where the illustration of Calf's Ears à la Financière looks like a child's party hat while Pig's Feet with Truffles resembles a dish of muffins. The effect is visually charming, but quite baffling from an instructional point of view. (It is no surprise that it is plates from these later-nineteenth-century editions of *Mrs. Beeton* that tend to end up on the Christmas cards and tea towels.) Sam and Myra have made the decision, too, to illustrate the dishes that have French names in preference to the solid English dishes that featured in the original book. Thus Dish of Filleted Soles, Boiled Salmon, and good old Cod's Head and Shoulders have been replaced by pictures of Eel à la Tartare, Brochet of Smelts, and Mayonnaise of Filleted Soles.

In 1880 the *Book of Household Management* was again reissued in a new edition by Ward, Lock, who claimed that "this most successful work" had now sold 337,000 copies. This new edition consisted of the 1869 text supplemented with an appendix of 671 new recipes. Crude though this procedure might seem (it saved on the cost of resetting the bulk of the text), it actually differs little from that adopted in the apparently more sophisticated updates of 1888 and 1906. In other words, when the publishers boasted in their various Prefaces that Mrs. Beeton's original work was so excellent that it did not need changing so much as adding to, they were doing more than simply puffing the continuing viability of the Beeton brand. Beeton's original 1861 text survives surprisingly intact right up to the 1888 edition and remains a clear presence as late as 1906. It is, however, increasingly diluted by pages of new material, most frequently concerned with the kitchen and dining room. Information on the nutritional value of meats, the cost of ready-made sauces, new cooking equipment, fancy ways to fold a napkin, and, of course, hundreds of new recipes, bulk out the original text so that it swells first by a quarter (1869), then by a half (1888) until finally, in 1906, it ends up at twice the size of the original. Isabella Beeton's original text is not so much replaced by new editions of the *Book of Household Management* as swamped by them, with cookery taking up a larger and larger proportion. What had started out as a handbook for the home had become, according to the triumphant brag of the Preface to the 1888 edition, "The Best Cookery Book In the World."

It was with this 1888 *Mrs. Beeton* that, according to Elizabeth David, the rot really set in. David blames this 1,644-page volume for introducing "gentility and suburban refinement" into what had previously been a celebration of "sound, solid, sensible, middle-class Victorian food." She particularly dislikes the way in which virtually all the dishes have been given a French name in addition to their original British one—a practice which "must, I think, be held at least partly responsible for the muddled ideas about continental cookery held by generations of English housewives and their not very good plain cooks," wrote David crossly in 1961, as she searched for precedents for the equally bad kitchen French in evidence in the centennial edition of the *Book of Household Management*.

You can see David's point. Some of the French names in the 1888 edition seem schoolgirlishly literal—Mutton Cutlets with Mashed Potatoes becomes Côtelettes de Mouton à la Purée de Pommes de Terre, for instance, while others are just plain redundant, with Veal and Ham Pie rendered as Pâté de Veau à l'Anglaise (the recipes themselves, however, both remain quite unchanged from 1861). Still, this nod towards sophistication matches the increasingly luxurious mood of the book. Thanks to the increasing popularity of Service à la Russe, table-tops now groan with space-filling decoration. There are finger bowls floating with maidenhair, grape scissors, cherubs crouching by conch shells, and table napkins folded into the shape of mitres, stars, and roses. The crockery itself is a wonder to behold, and gets a colour plate all of its own. For, in David's acerbic words, *japonaiserie* runs "to raging chaos," with every conceivable surface covered with "octagonal teapots and porcelain sardine boxes encrusted with plum blossom, lovebirds and chrysanthemums." There are, finally, detailed instructions on how to fashion a Venetian chalet out of nougat and a swan out of Italian biscuit.

The advice in the 1888 edition to the mistress on social conduct likewise marks a move towards more formal and elaborate ways of living. She may, for instance, have a designated day on which she receives callers, and in this case she will have previously circulated a notice among her friends informing them of the hours during which they will be welcome. If she is the one making the call, then she may well have had her card printed on the reverse side with the words "Félicitation," "Adieu," and

"Visite" in the corners. Thus all she has to do is turn up the appropriate corner to convey the reason for her visit. Alternatively, she may find herself invited to a tennis or croquet party, or perhaps she has herself sent out invitations to a "Conversazione" or "Soirée." If she is holding a ball, then the programme for the evening will be headed with her monogram or, if she hasn't got one, the name of her house. Much of Mrs. Beeton's original advice still applies and has been repeated here—no children, no dogs and always keep the conversation light—but the contexts in which these golden rules apply have now proliferated into a dizzying number of settings.

The 1888 edition of the *Book of Household Management* also marks a distinct shift in its attitude towards servants. Whereas in 1869 Sam and Myra had repeated Isabella's benign advice about setting a good example and being present after breakfast to answer queries and dole out materials from the store cupboard, the 1888 edition adds a paragraph whose sharp tone changes everything:

> If a mistress observe slack or slovenly manners in her servant, she should call the attention of the servant to the unsatisfactory performance of her duties. Notice should be taken of the very first appearance of inattention or omission, so that the servant may know that her mistress's eye is quick to detect the least disorder, and be aware that the least falling off in properly doing her work will not be permitted. A small fault unnoticed will quickly grow, and what might have been easily remedied in the outset will become difficult to eradicate, if permitted to increase and strengthen.

From here the 1888 edition loses no chance to remind the reader that servants are, in some essential way, the enemy and want watching at all times. Thus the sensible mistress takes lunch in the nursery with her children, in order to guard against their picking up "many little vulgar habits" from their nurse. If lunch is to be served in the dining room, then the mistress needs to supervise closely since "A raw, ill-taught servant . . . coming for the first time into the dining room to get her first lesson in laying a cloth, will, if left to her own devices, lay that cloth, and the articles necessary to it, in a manner simply excruciating to witness." Should the mistress be unfortunate enough to be a memsahib then she will soon discover that "Indian servants . . . cannot be trusted implicitly, and *will* cheat if they have a chance." Mrs. Beeton, as always, needed to keep up with the times, and the times were permeated with a new moral panic known as "the servant problem." With well-paid jobs now available in offices and shops, the working classes were showing themselves less keen to sign up for the petty restrictions of a life of service in someone else's house. As a result, the voice of Mrs. Beeton becomes inflected with the frightened, resentful tone of the middle-class mistress who is obliged to accept, to an extent she has never quite known before, that her servants are now her masters.

Still, Elizabeth David is unfair to see the 1888 edition as unequivocally a Bad Thing, a bastard version (for no one knows who wrote it) poised midway between the Beeton-authored books of 1861 and the 1906 edition overseen by the renowned chef C. Herman Senn. The newly introduced sections in the 1888 edition on Australian, German, and Jewish cookery speak of a spirit of adventure and an unhindered appreciation for other people's cultures (how else can one take the blithe inclusion of recipes for Roasted Wallaby and Parrot Pie?). If the sections on French and Italian cookery seem grudging by comparison, notwithstanding the granting of French names to indigenous British dishes, they do no more than reflect popular prejudice of the time. The chapter on vegetarian cookery, meanwhile, opens with an enthusiastic appreciation of how good vegetables are for us, and what poor use we mostly make of them. Finally, the section on homeopathy could almost have been written today, with its wariness of the heavy drug dependency of allopathic medicine and its sensible suggestion that before one rejects alternative methods one might as well "give the system a fair trial."

The next edition of *Mrs. Beeton's Book of Household Management* appeared in 1906 and is the one that most casual readers think of as *the* Mrs. Beeton. If it never actually says "take two dozen eggs" it is nonetheless saturated with the kind of stately luxury that allowed a generation of music hall comics to set up Mrs. Beeton as a byword for culinary excess. This confusion about just what belongs to the "real" Mrs. Beeton and what belongs to those who have written in her name is, of course, a mark of Ward, Lock's ability to finesse the brand. And nowhere is this skill more apparent than in the Preface to the new 1906 edition. This new Preface is unsigned and impersonal, although the address at the end makes it clear that it has been issued from the publishers at Warwick House. So if Mrs. Beeton hasn't written her own new Preface, then no one else exactly has either.

The first paragraph of the Preface stresses Beeton's centrality in domestic history: "In every English-speaking country her 'Household Management' has appeared amongst the wedding presents of a bride as surely as the proverbial salt cellars." From here the speaker/writer is even happy to cannibalize the brand's status as a fictional trope. "Sir Arthur Conan Doyle, in his great study of married life, 'A Duet, with an occasional Chorus,' makes his heroine say 'Mrs. Beeton must have been the finest housekeeper in the world. Therefore, Mr. Beeton must have been the happiest and most comfortable man.' " What goes unspoken is the fact that Conan Doyle had a long association with the Beeton brand, with Sherlock Holmes making his first appearance in the short story "A Study in Scarlet" in the *Beeton's Christmas Annual* of 1888. This is yet another example of how the *Book of Household Management* was embedded in a dense network of print and publishing contacts rather than a unique product that popped out, fully formed, from Mrs. Beeton's increasingly mythological oven.

From here the Preface embarks on a contorted argument about how the original *Mrs. Beeton* was so perfect that "it stands practically unaltered to the present day" and yet how, simultaneously, it has been in need of so much updating that the current edition now stands at four times its 1861 size. The rationale for these additions is that good old one of modernity: "the world . . . has travelled of late at electric speed, and the far-reaching changes of time have touched household affairs from standpoints apparently far remote." It is in the cookery sections of the book, says the Preface, that the reader will notice the changes most. Developments in transport mean that the British kitchen now has access to fresh produce from around the world, while a new trend for middle-class girls to receive cookery lessons before marriage has resulted in a generation of mistresses who require "more variety and delicacy in their daily fare than the plain cook of old was wont to furnish."

So the expanded cookery section of the new edition will be a skilful blend of old and new. All the original recipes have been re-tested and "details altered wherever necessary." In addition there are now no fewer than two thousand new recipes "contributed by Mr. C. Herman Senn, the celebrated head of the National Training School of Cookery, assisted by some of the most famous chefs and teachers of the art that the world contains." Thus the centre of gravity of the *Book of Household Management* has shifted in two important ways. First, the expanded cookery section now completely dwarfs the book, whereas in the 1888 edition it only dominated. And second, the authority behind that section is no longer that of the British housewife, the imaginary Mrs. Beeton, but rather that of the professional male chef whose territory is nothing less than the world itself.

You can see this new sense of luxurious cosmopolitanism everywhere in Senn's vastly expanded recipe section. Most of the dishes continue to get a French as well as an English name, even when the results are absurdly literal: for instance Sheep's Tongues, Fried becomes Langues de Mouton Frites. This, says Senn, is so that the mistress can now construct a menu as easily in French as she can in English (the unanswered question, of course, is why assume that she would want to?). What is more, the shift in the recipes is towards elaborate dining, the kind of thing you might eat in the London restaurants which were now, for the first time, welcoming (accompanied) women patrons as well as their menfolk. If Mrs. Beeton had written her original book to show women how to run a household whose calm order would keep their husbands from spending too long at the club, the 1906 edition showed them how to turn their homes into something that resembled a good hotel. Before he had run the National Training School of Cookery, Herman Senn had been a chef at the Reform Club, the most celebrated incumbent since Alexis Soyer had walked out in a huff in 1852. Unlike Soyer, however, Senn seems to have had little knowledge or interest in the domestic kitchens of the British working or even middle classes. His contribution was to graft onto the original Mrs. Beeton an encyclopaedic knowledge of every dish that might be demanded of a professional cook working in a hotel, club, or mansion. What had started as a domestic bible aimed at housewives and their clumsy-fingered maids had morphed into a manual for professional caterers.

So while there had been eight recipes for sole in the 1861 edition and nine in 1888, by 1906 there were no fewer than twenty. Likewise the number of recipes for lobster doubled between 1861 and 1906. Here and there Mrs. Beeton's original cookery text can still be glimpsed—the instructions for boiling a tongue, for instance, remain exactly the same—but the vast majority of her recipes have been tweaked to make them suitable for modern tastes (no one in 1906 really wanted their buttered artichokes served with Brussels sprouts).

Above all what this new volume is concerned with is the idea of dining as spectacle and even theatre. The illustrative plates—more sophisticated than those of 1888—delight in showing various table settings, even including "the old fashioned" style (for despite Service à la Française being out of date, you had to admit that all those symmetrical dishes set off a table beautifully). There is a whole chapter on how to fold "serviettes" and an entire plate given over to showing the *dernier cri* in menu and guest cards, which include bits of paper fashioned into swans, ballet shoes, and even deckchairs. Finally the chapter on "Meals: Their Importance and Arrangement" includes sample menus of important dinners going back to 1561 and proceeding by way of a "menu of a royal city banquet served to his Majesty King George III." Just in case, presumably, you wanted to try it for yourself at home.

Thus the domestic sphere, according to the *Book of Household Management* of 1906, is now linked to the public world in new and important ways. Just as foodstuffs arrive regularly from South Africa, and exciting new cocktails from America, so the traffic between home and society is correspondingly brisk. Neatly entering into dialogue with Beeton's original 1861 text which quoted with approval the opinion of "the author of The Vicar of Wakefield" that a domestic woman is a good one, the 1906 edition declares: "Times have changed since 1766 when Goldsmith wrote extolling home virtues; and in few things is the change more marked than in woman's sphere; but a woman should not be less careful in her management or blameless in her life because the spirit of the age gives her greater scope for her activities." Again, Beeton's original strong warning about picking your friends with care and not gossiping, is neutralized by the 1906 advice that it is crucial not to become one of those people who is so starchy that no one feels comfortable: "One is apt to become narrow-minded by living too much in the home circle; it is not well to get out of the way of meeting fresh people."

And yet, when it comes to general principles you can still hear Beeton's original voice, stout and sensible, whispering through Senn's text. Throughout the 1906 volume the mistress is assured that "the lady who markets herself"—in other words does her own shopping—will end up with the best, that is the cheapest and most seasonal ingredients. For all Senn's fancy extra chapters, most of the "Introduction to Cookery" in the

1906 edition is taken directly from Beeton's 1861 original. Perhaps most tellingly of all, just before the 1906 edition embarks upon its huge swollen recipe section, it pauses to speak directly to the reader in a "Note," explaining why Mrs. Beeton's original layout of recipes, with ingredients at the beginning and timings at the end, still cannot be bettered: "By carefully reading the Recipes there should not be the slightest difficulty in arranging a repast for any number of persons, and an accurate notion will be gained of the Time required for the cooking of each dish, the periods when it is Seasonable, and its Average Cost." For all that Senn spoke to the professional chef, at home in a world of aspic and vegetables cut in the shape of a sailing bark, Mrs. Beeton's uncertain housewife, in need of a recipe book that would tell her how to get dinner on the table this evening, can still be dimly seen hovering in the background.

INTERLUDE

DID MRS. BEETON RUIN BRITISH COOKING?

ANYONE WHO HAS READ this far will know that the question is a tad beside the point. There is nothing in Mrs. Beeton's book that has not been taken from another source, and so to credit her with ruining anything would be to grant her powers that she neither desired nor claimed. Even so, by setting down in an accessible, organized and, as it turned out, popular way the best of British cookery writing available at mid-century, Beeton did help to entrench food practices, ambitions, and fears that might otherwise have stayed dispersed and fleeting.

Take the business of boiling vegetables. An inexperienced housewife in 1845 might have asked her mother or even her maid exactly how long you need to cook parsnips. The answer she got back would have been the result of years of trial and error. She, in turn, might tweak the timing until she got the result she wanted. In 1861, however, that same housewife, perhaps anxious not to display her ignorance, could simply consult *Mrs. Beeton* and find that the recommended time was one and a half hours. And such being the authority of the printed word, from now on parsnips in that household would come to the table pulped, a taste that might well be handed down through sons and daughters right into the twentieth century. The result was the casual, smirking conclusion of a much later generation of foreign-holidaying Britons that their countrymen couldn't "do" vegetables and that the person to blame was probably old Mother Beeton.

Yet it is hardly Mrs. Beeton's fault that the moment at which she attempted to codify the British eating experience was the point when both produce and practice went into sharp decline. As we have seen, Britain's move from an agrarian to an industrial culture had left the urban middle classes cut off from good food supplies in a way that was not the case in France, Germany or even America. Dependence on a whole chain of middlemen meant that by the time produce arrived on the urban table it tended to be far from fresh, while there was every chance that it had been adulterated in some way. Technologies for canning and, in time, freezing, which initially seemed to offer a neat way around the problem, would soon reveal themselves as simply a means for producers on the other side of the world to offload inferior stock. The scandals that had dogged home produce in the 1850s now threatened to engulf all food, whatever its provenance, that appeared on the British dinner table.

Where Beeton does perhaps bear some responsibility for the decline in British eating is in helping to turn formal dining into a competitive social sport, so diverting attention away from the quality of the food itself. From the 1860s how you ate became as important as what you ate. By incorporating several of the characteristics of Service à la Russe into her formal dinner plans, Beeton was gesturing towards the dinner party as a kind of social trial. Being aware of the rules of precedence for entering the dining room or knowing the proper use for each of the forks flanking your plate became the marker of a gentleman or lady (who your father was mattered less than it had ever done). In such tense circumstances, it is hardly any surprise that no one felt much like concentrating on the food.

Cut off from its own tradition of serving home-grown produce in relaxed and democratic conditions, the way was clear for the British middle class to adopt what it fondly imagined to be a high-tone French style of cookery. As food historians have been quick to point out, British cooking had actually been saturated with French influences from the time of the Norman Conquest. However, cultural memory being short, by the third quarter of the nineteenth century there seemed no option but to learn about French food all over again. The fact that it was now fifty years since we had been at war with our nearest neighbours eased any lingering worries felt by any die-hard John Bulls. And so, forgetting the robust vernacular tastes already within their reach, the British middle classes started straining after dishes with names like Liver and Bacon aux Fines Herbes, which Mrs. Beeton included in the original *BOHM*.

Yet to be fair to Beeton, when it came to those "plain family dinners" where there was no one to impress, she continued to suggest down-to-earth choices such as boiled leg of pork, stewed eels, and mutton cutlets.

Whether the mistress of the house and her staff put quite as much effort into these workaday dishes remains a moot point and it is here, believe some food historians, that a whole body of experience and knowledge about indigenous British cookery began to drain away. From this point it was a short hop to the rissoles and lumpy rice pudding that were popularly supposed to characterize British home and institutional cooking for most of the twentieth century.

But blaming all this on Mrs. Beeton is quite wrong. If she does anything it is to hold up a mirror to history, showing us what passed for common kitchen lore in the mid-nineteenth-century British kitchen. If we do not like what we see, insisting on identifying it as the precise moment when British cookery fell out of Eden and was damned for ever, then we need to think harder about how history happens and, more importantly, how it gets recorded. Confusing the messenger with the message really isn't fair.

CHAPTER THIRTEEN

A BEETONIAN REVERIE

BY THE TIME THE SIXTH major new edition of the *Book of Household Management* appeared in 1923 (there had been none during the Great War), Isabella Beeton's original voice was barely more than a whisper. And yet, just at the moment when the book seemed finally to have slipped completely free of its original author, the lady herself started to move back into focus. This interest in Mrs. Beeton's identity began in the 1920s as part of a more general urge among intellectuals to sort, sift, and weigh just what they had inherited from their parents' generation. The cleverest writers got there first. Lytton Strachey's plans to write a biography of Mrs. Beeton are undated but, assuming he was considering her for a role as one of his *Eminent Victorians,* then he would have been casting around for material from 1912. Wyndham Lewis, meanwhile, produced an eight-line humorous playlet on Mrs. Beeton for the *Daily Mail* in 1924 and J. B. Priestley published his essay "A Beetonian Reverie" in 1923. Writing well before the National Portrait Gallery photograph provoked a national conversation about the real identity of Mrs. Beeton, Strachey and Priestley were more interested in what she might be made to say about their own relationship with Victorianism. Priestley, indeed, admitted that he was far too lazy to find out whether there actually had ever been such a person as "Mrs. Beeton." Instead he was happy to imagine her as a "grand old lady," just as Strachey had been keen to picture "a small tub-like lady in black."

Priestley starts his essay with a meditation on how much he dislikes the modern cut-down *Mrs. Beeton* of 1909 that he currently has before him. It is designed for smaller households, and seems a mean and shabby thing compared with the lustrous first edition that he remembers from his childhood (although one wonders from Priestley's description whether it wasn't actually the 1888 edition that he was recalling). Particularly funny is Priestley's speculation on what Mrs. Beeton's husband must have been like. He imagines him playing G. H. Lewes to Mrs. Beeton's George Eliot, in other words "he would look after her affairs, arrange her *salon,* and shield her from adverse criticism." However, Priestley also floats the possibility that Mr. Beeton was neglected by his wife since, as he perceptively points out, "you cannot compile a gigantic volume on housekeeping and keep house at the same time." So in Priestley's imagination, Mr. Beeton becomes "a little wistful man, with something of the visionary's look stamped upon his partially emaciated features, rising, with a half-suppressed sigh, from his cold mutton and lumpy potatoes to visit his wife in her study and to inquire, a little timidly, how she is progressing . . . And as he goes tiptoeing away, perhaps to finish up the cold rice pudding, little Beeton seems to me at once a touching and noble figure, to be honoured by posterity."

With the public presentation of the National Portrait Gallery photograph seven years later, the whole business of Mrs. Beeton's identity now came before a much more general public. Correspondingly the writers who now came forward wanting to write about her were noticeably middle-brow and female (indeed these two identities were, in a fundamental way, interlinked). The vast majority of journalists who wrote to Mayson Beeton asking to be allowed to undertake a biography of his mother were women who made a living writing for the magazines that were directly descended from those founded by Sam and Isabella in the 1860s and by Mayson Beeton himself in the 1890s.

To all these requests Mayson Beeton said no, explaining that "he reserved the right to produce any memoir of his parents to himself." This wasn't legally enforceable, but by withholding access to his cache of family material, Beeton made sure that it was practically so. He was, as always, torn between the desire to set his parents before the world and an equal need to keep tight control over how they were perceived. Yet while he could effectively stop someone writing a book-length biography of his mother, there was not much he could do about imaginative interpretations based on material that was already in the public domain. Much to his fury, in the mid-1930s the BBC broadcast two radio plays about Mrs. Beeton. The first took him entirely by surprise, for he only heard about *Meet Mrs. Beeton* a fortnight before it was due to be performed on the Home Service on 4 January 1934. The hour-long piece "specially written for the microphone" was the work of L. Du Garde Peach, an established author and playwright who specialized in giving historical subjects a light, commercial twist. Du Garde Peach's "culinary comedy" concerns a young married couple, the Beetons, and their two sets of older married friends, the Jenningses and the Rombases. Mrs. Beeton has given her middle-aged women friends advice on improving their cooking and, as a result, their husbands have managed to fall hopelessly in love with the young housewife and her veal patties and stewed rabbit. Both men urge Mrs. Beeton to elope with them, a request that she finds quite ridiculous since, as she explains, she is utterly in love with her "dear Sam." Instead she invites both couples to dinner and serves up a meal heavily tinctured with shoe polish and other foul-tasting household ingredients. Mr. Rombas and Mr. Jennings leave the Beetons' house once again happy with their wives.

The story sounds suspiciously similar to the anecdote told by Frederick Greenwood's centenarian niece to J. W. Robertson Scott, his biographer, about how Mrs. Beeton had once served up a shocking meal "in order to teach men not to criticize their wives." The problem is that Scott's book was not published until 1950, which means Du Garde Peach was highly unlikely to have got his information directly from this source. Indeed, what starts to look more possible is that the elderly Mrs. Robinson, in her desire to be helpful and recall something—anything—about the increasingly legendary Mrs. Beeton, had managed to turn a half-remembered radio play from almost twenty years earlier into a bona fide personal memory.

There is, though, a further twist. At some point soon after the broadcast in the first week of 1934, Du Garde Peach completely rewrote *Meet Mrs. Beeton* as a stage play, in the process organizing it around another Beeton anecdote entirely. This time Mrs. Beeton is an aspiring novelist who, together with her husband, is invited to dinner by Mr. Jennings, the publisher to whom she has recently sent a manuscript. As Jennings explains to his wife before the young couple arrive, "Mrs. Beeton is an elegant female but a poor authoress. Only last week she brought me a novel with a view to publication. It is to soften the blow of refusal that I have invited her and her spouse to dine here this evening." In the course of what turns out to be a foul-tasting dinner, the young Mrs. Beeton intervenes tactfully with a few suggestions to rescue mulligatawny soup that tastes of blacking and fish that resembles cotton wool. So delighted is Mr. Jennings with his young guest's accomplishments that he announces, "As a novelist, my dear Mrs. Beeton, you would be forgotten in a month. But if you will agree to write for me a book of *another* kind, your name will live for ever!"

It is this second version of *Meet Mrs. Beeton* that was published and circulated widely among amateur dramatic companies right through the 1940s and beyond. Mayson Beeton loathed it almost as much as the original radio version, writing to the publishers in 1941: "the plot is as untrue to the facts of the case as it is in the characterisation. Miss Acton the authoress of a Cookery Book published many years previously was the lady to whom according to the literary gossip of the day the Longman of the period gave the advice to win fame by ceasing to write novels and turn to Cookery." Beeton finished this particular letter by asking the publisher to take the play out of circulation and offering "to contribute any reasonable sum to compensate the financial interests involved." That he regularly offered to pay people to stop them writing about his parents suggests how fiercely Beeton felt the need to exert control over the way they were perceived. In this case, as in every other on record, the offer seems to have been declined.

What Mayson Beeton particularly loathed in both versions of *Meet Mrs. Beeton* was the characterization of his father as a vain, stuffy man obsessed with drains. None of this seems terribly offensive unless, of course, it is your own late father who is being made to look silly, in which case it becomes deeply upsetting. In the case of the first version, Beeton managed to insist on some last-minute changes, including turning all the "Samuels" to "Sams" before the broadcast. The BBC also sportingly invited the elderly Sir Mayson along to a rehearsal "which would give you plenty of time to make any further alterations you might desire." Beeton evidently accepted, and so he must have seen actors of the calibre of George Sanders (Mr. Beeton), Richard Goolden (Mr. Rombas), and Norman Shelley (Mr. Jennings) bring his parents' dining room to life. But although he loved a smart name—and surely having George Sanders play your father was something to feel pleased about—Beeton was still not satisfied. Seven years later, and learning that the second version of the play was still in circulation, he was quick to speak of the "worry," "annoyance" and "natural indignation" that the wretched "Mr. Peach" (as he insisted on styling Dr. L. Du Garde Peach) had caused him.

The *Meet Mrs. Beeton* episode left Mayson Beeton in such a state of high alert that when, four years later, he received a letter from the BBC informing him that it was shortly to broadcast a biographical play about his mother, he immediately panicked. Even Mr. C. A. Cliffe's pre-emptive assurance that "the programme is an attempt at a serious biography, and has no connection with the programme by Mr. L. du Garde Peach which was broadcast in 1934" was not enough to soothe him. Especially when he heard that the author of the script was none other than Joan Adeney Easdale, a pushy young woman who had been pestering him for information about his mother over the previous five years. Having read the proffered script, Beeton immediately wrote back to Cliffe expressing his outrage. The play was full of factual errors and Miss Easdale had been dishonest to represent herself to the Corporation as someone qualified to write about his parents. The letter ended with a threat to take legal action if the play was not withdrawn. The very next day Mr. Cliffe received a letter from the Revd. E. E. Dorling of Epsom, writing as "head of the Dorling family," and explaining, "I have read this astonishing production, which reflects so seriously on some of my relations, and with Sir Mayson, I feel it my duty to protest against the production of Miss Easdale's play." Dorling followed this up by attending a summit at Broadcasting House at which Cliffe, Easdale, as well as John Richmond, the producer, were all present.

By dint of several emollient letters and an invitation to come and hear a recording of the rather innocuous broadcast, the BBC eventually managed to appease Sir Mayson Beeton. To his face they doubtless apologized for any offence or distress they had caused, although it is clear that behind the scenes they felt rather differently. In an internal memo of 17 November 1937 the executive producer D. H. Rose said: "It seemed to me that Miss Easdale had done a very great deal of research and the only points she could not be accurate about were covered by documents in Sir Mayson Beeton's possession which he would not allow her to see as he obviously wished to use the material himself. This last fact is the heart of the matter I fancy." As if to confirm—perhaps send a message—that the BBC was basically happy with Miss Easdale's work, it allowed her just four months later to broadcast a Home Service "Teatime Talk" entitled

In Search of Mrs. Beeton in which she described her four years of foot-slogging fieldwork. During that time she had managed to come up with some genuinely new leads, which included tracking down the woman who did Mrs. Beeton's household washing in Pinner, the boy who let out her chickens and, as we have seen, the young saxophone player who had often seen her on the Promenade at Greenhithe during that last summer of 1864.

Pointedly, none of these findings was ever followed up by Mayson Beeton, who was now busy working with Harford Montgomery Hyde on his own biographical portrait of his parents. And it is now that Beeton's reasons for picking the young Montgomery Hyde as his trusted adjutant become fully clear. Hyde was not simply a promising young sprig of the family who had happened to attend the same Oxford college as Beeton. He was also a sophisticate in sexual matters. Highlights of his post-war career would include writing *The Trial of Oscar Wilde,* appearing as a witness in the *Lady Chatterley* trial and, in his job as a Northern Irish MP, championing the recommendations of the Wolfenden Report. Whatever "Montgomery the Mole" was likely to trip over during his various "prospecting operations" on behalf of Sir Mayson, the chances are that the young man could be counted on to behave with sympathy and, above all, tact.

The outbreak of the Second World War created a hiatus in new versions of *Mrs. Beeton,* perhaps because the old ones seemed quite powerful enough. There is an apocryphal story that British POWs in Singapore used her as the basis for their fond fantasies of home (although when a portion of them did eventually return, they must have found strictly rationed Britain a huge disappointment). With Montgomery Hyde away on war duties, Beeton had no stomach to continue with the long-planned "memoir" on his own. Instead, as we have seen, in 1945 he handed over the task to Nancy Spain, a young cousin on the Dorling side.

If Spain's first edition of *Mrs. Beeton and her Husband by her great-niece Nancy Spain,* published in August 1948, disappointed the Beeton family with its subtle but insistent slant against Sam, it was nothing compared with what was to come. By 1956 Spain was a big star, with a high profile in print, wireless, and the new medium of television. She was about to publish her autobiography, the chatty, candid-seeming but utterly discreet *Why I'm Not A Millionaire* in which she told larky tales about her life on Fleet Street in which she figures as an incorrigible tomboy rather than as a sexually active lesbian (although the Preface written by Noël Coward must surely have made alert readers wonder). The time seemed right for a reprint of her 1948 Beeton book which, while modestly successful, had suffered at the time from being written by a complete unknown. Apart from some good reviews by Dingle Foot and Elizabeth Bowen, the only publicity the book had generated was an odd little *Desert Island Discs*-type programme that Spain broadcast on the Home Service on 23 November 1948 in which key moments in Isabella's life were punctuated by recordings such as Offenbach's "Cancan" (to illustrate the Paris leg of the honeymoon) and the "Eton Boating Song" (to accompany an anecdote about little Edith Dorling falling into the Epsom pond and being saved by her crinoline).

Even better as far as the relaunch of her Beeton biography was concerned, Spain now had some new sensational material with which to make a splash. In the Preface to the 1956 edition of her book, retitled *The Beeton Story*, Spain declares that she was tipped off about the corset and whipping pornography by Doris Langley Moore, the costume historian whose interest in Victorian women's waist size had led her to the *Englishwoman's Domestic Magazine* correspondences in the British Library. This, in turn, had alerted Spain to "all the new and alarming material about Sam Beeton which has never been published before." Naturally she lost no time in including all this "new and alarming material" in the revised edition of the book—published, ironically, by Ward, Lock. As well as including the pornography scandal, she also firmed up her previous hint that Sam had contracted venereal disease as a young man. Whereas in her first version, published in 1948, Spain vaguely suggests that Sam "appeared to have lived the usual life of a would-be sophisticated young man about Fleet St.," in her 1956 edition Sam now dropped "hints about the depravity of his early years, [and] it is fair to assume that . . . [his] illness was contracted as a result of licentious London life." No longer needing to worry about Mayson Beeton, who had died nearly ten years earlier, Spain provided a pious prefatory note explaining why she had now decided to spill the beans about what had really gone on during the Beeton marriage. Apparently as her research progressed she "had the oddest feeling about Sam. His was an attractive personality, a weak and fascinating character, a dangerous man to know, to marry, to write about . . . And though the discovery that their Grandfather was a bit of a villain may distress Mayson Beeton's children—as it might have distressed my Grandmother, Isabella Beeton's little sister—I know I am right to have made the truth known."

There was no stopping Nancy Spain now. Four years later, to mark the publication of the new centennial edition of the *Book of Household Management,* she wrote a series of three pieces for the women's magazine *Ideal Home,* retelling the story of Mrs. Beeton. In the course of these pieces she reveals (or invents) some entirely new bits of information for the occasion. The first is that Isabella Beeton was only five feet one inch tall and had a much-hated mole on the side of her nose (by the time Spain was writing the introduction to *The Nancy Spain Colour Cookery Book* two years later, Bella had stretched an extra inch to five feet two inches). The second is a full direct quotation from Spain's late grandmother Lucy Smiles, Isabella's half-sister, containing information that had previously only been hinted at. " 'Goodness knows how many [of Isabella's babies] were stillborn, or how many times she miscarried, my dear,' Granny used to say, shaking a melancholy head." That Spain, a lesbian who was sexually and socially active first in the navy and then in post-war London, did not understand exactly what she was implying—that Isabella had contracted syphilis from Sam and that, what's more, the Dorlings were quite aware of this fact—is hard to believe.

Developing her theme of Sam as a libertine and scoundrel, Spain's *Ideal Home* articles let rip in a way that she had never allowed herself in her books. In this new version, "Sam lived like a lord, travelling abroad, dining in the best restaurants, buying the latest fashions, smoking the most expensive cigars, dealing in horses, losing money at the races." The pornography episode, naturally, gets another scandalized airing: "In the Conversazione of the Englishwoman's Domestic Magazine there appeared startling paragraphs about Tight Lacing, High Heels, Whipping and all the other subjects beloved of the amateur and professional pornographer. (For years these volumes of the Englishwoman's Domestic Magazine have been kept under lock and key at the British Museum and can only be consulted by special permission. They are notorious. I assure you I am not exaggerating.)"

The implication, never far from the surface of Nancy Spain's various versions of the Beeton story, was that if Sam liked reading about flagellation, tight lacing, high heels and spurs, then he must surely have insisted on exploring them with poor Isabella in the marital bed. And so, by a series of slides and elisions, the "worries" that Sam is repeatedly blamed for burdening Isabella with become not just those of financial ruin, but the pain and humiliation of being laced into a tiny corset or strapped to the bed and whipped. What Spain seems never to have grasped is that the nature of fantasy is that it is just that—a fantasy that would lose appeal if acted out literally. Neither does Sarah Freeman. Writing in the 1970s, and with strict instructions from Audrey Beeton, Mayson's daughter, that she is to skate lightly over the whole scandal, Freeman chooses to believe that all those pornographic letters were literal accounts of nursery and school-room cruelty. Her line is that both the whipping and the corset correspondences performed an important task "of revealing . . . custom[s] which stood in urgent need of examination and appraisal." To counteract Spain's version of Sam as a private pervert, Freeman insists on his status as a public servant.

Particularly hurtful—"nauseating" was actually the word they used—as far as Mayson Beeton's daughters were concerned, was the way in which Nancy Spain insisted on corralling their late father into this newly sensationalized version of the Beeton tragedy. "In 1865 Mayson, later to be knighted for his services to British commerce, was born into a bankrupt home," intoned Spain, milking the drama for all it was worth. And, again, "It took Mayson's lifetime of devoted work for Empire trade to wipe out his father's villainies." Spain even has her grandmother Lucy eventually consenting to meet the adult Mayson and pronouncing him "a charming man." This was too much for the Beeton girls. "Dad did not meet Lucy Smiles, but *I did*," spluttered Isabel in a letter to her eldest sister Marjorie as they pored over the "mixture of half truths & downright lies" peddled by their ghastly second cousin.

There was, though, an even worse affront waiting in the wings, one that has the fingerprints of Nancy Spain all over it. The offending article appeared in the *Daily Express* on 20 October 1960 under the picture by-line of the book critic Peter Forster, who "exposes The Man Behind Mrs. Beeton: His was the big idea—she merely slaved to put this mammoth book together." Forster wastes no time on subtlety: "Sam Beeton was, for one thing, a very remarkable rogue . . . an artful dodger who also put out scurrilous doggerels against Queen Victoria, and who specialised in pornography." Having married "the beautiful, extremely capable, young Isabella Mayson" he managed to kill her "due to exhaustion and worry over a business crash." Up until this point there is nothing in Forster's highly coloured piece to suggest that he had done anything more than skim and regurgitate Nancy Spain's *The Beeton Story*. It is the next paragraph, however, that really makes one jump. According to Forster, after Isabella's death Sam formed "a liaison with a widow named Mrs. Brown in the Isle of Dogs, to which he walked every night after finishing work in Fleet-street."

Here is the first and only statement, albeit madly garbled, in all the earlier biographical writing on the Beetons to suggest that Myra Browne and Sam Beeton were lovers. In a few paragraphs Peter Forster had managed to say in print exactly those things about Sam Beeton that Nancy Spain had been hinting at over the past four years, ever since the publication of her spiced-up version of the Beeton biography. One possibility is that Forster, who was writing for the very book pages that had been edited by Spain herself a few years earlier, was simply repeating a version of the Beeton story that he had heard from her one night in a Fleet Street pub. Alternatively, Spain may have used Forster as a convenient cover to print what she really felt about the Beetons without attracting even more loathing from Mayson Beeton's daughters. Spain liked the opacity that came with pseudonyms and, indeed, she used the name "Jane Dorling," that of Isabella's eldest step-sister, whenever she was asked to write an article that was too "soppy" for Nancy Spain. (What Spain had missed was that the historical Jane Dorling, with her "little sharp ways," was hardly the kind of woman to be paired with soppiness in any shape or form.) Whatever the exact pathway by which the information came to be transmitted, the result was that, for the first and only time, the possibility that Mr. Beeton and Mrs. Browne had been lovers was put before the public. The reaction of the Beeton daughters was predictable: "foul."

The 1960 publication of the centenary edition of the *BOHM*, which had sparked the *Express* article as well as Nancy Spain's *Ideal Home* contributions, also produced an important intervention from Elizabeth David. From the publication of *A Book of Mediterranean Food* in 1949 and *French Country Cooking* a year later, David gradually established herself not simply as a great food writer but a great writer full stop. Her lyrical evocations of impeccably fresh ingredients simply cooked have all the skill of a first-rate novelist or painter and by 1960 her word was pretty much law in the well-heeled British kitchen. So when, in an article written for the spring 1961 issue of *Wine and Food*, she explained how superior she thought the modestly obscure Eliza Acton was to the swollen importance of Mrs. Beeton, people naturally took notice. For David, the reason that Acton's work had been so completely consigned to oblivion was because she was

> living the manner and writing of a style of English domestic life already doomed. Her book was the final expression, the crystallization, of pre-Industrial England's taste in food and attitude to cookery. The dishes she describes and the ingredients that went into them would have been familiar to Jane Austen and Lord Byron, to Fanny Burney and Tobias Smollett. They would have been served at the tables of great political hostesses such as Lady Melbourne, and of convivial country gentlemen like Parson Woodforde.

Whether David is strictly correct about the provenance of Acton's recipes, her championing of the Georgians as living in a prelapsarian world of unforced sociability and natural ingredients has been extremely influential. Never more so than over the past few years when, once again, the long eighteenth century has been reinvented as an era of sexual, social, and "modern" freedoms, scandalously stamped upon by the bad-tempered, repressive, and philistine Victorians. The most forceful rearticulation of this position with regard to cookery writing comes from Clarissa Dickson Wright, a protégée and friend of David's who made her name as one of the *Two Fat Ladies* television cooks in the mid-1990s. In 1999, speaking to Sue Lawley on *Desert Island Discs,* Dickson Wright maintained that "[in] Georgian books . . . even the very early Victorian books, the first editions, for instance, of Eliza Acton, there are enormous swathes of literature about not overcooking your vegetables." Mrs. Beeton, by contrast, is responsible for the Victorians forgetting that they ever knew how to cook, so tipping British cuisine into a century of decline and watery cabbage. Not that Beeton ever went near the kitchen, according to Dickson Wright. Instead her husband, "Tom Beeton [*sic*] . . . the Robert Maxwell of his day," simply compiled the book from readers' recipes and "put her name on it, put her picture on it. She had a good face for it." (The fact that Isabella Beeton's image was quite unknown until the last few days of 1932 seems quite to have passed Dickson Wright by.)

As if to underline her allegiance with David's developmental map of British cookery, in 2000 Dickson Wright followed her example by writing an article on the occasion of a new edition of the *Book of Household Management.* In this case it was Oxford University Press that was bringing out an abridged version of the original 1861 edition and, rather than appearing in the *Spectator* as David's piece had done, Dickson Wright's was published in the *Mail on Sunday*'s supplement "Night and Day." It is an extraordinary parade of inventive invective. Underlying Dickson Wright's loathing of the Beetons is her palpable distaste for the way they were catering for a new generation of lower-middle-class people hungry to ape a lifestyle that they fondly imagined to be genteel. The Beetons, in short, were common and they encouraged other common people to get ideas above their station. Most damaging of all is Dickson Wright's account of how Mrs. Beeton gathered her material. "The recipes were supplied by cooks from other households, who submitted them in answer to an advertisement offering generous payment, which most of them never received. These recipes were not tested and, in many cases, didn't work. But they were received with enthusiasm by the yuppie population, who scorned the better, more prudent works of Eliza Acton and Mrs. Raafald [*sic*]."

Elizabeth David's 1961 article was the first time that most British people would have had any inkling that Mrs. Beeton leaned heavily on earlier texts, especially Acton's *Modern Cookery*. But once this information started filtering down from the relatively elite readership of *Wine and Food*, it became impossible for anyone attempting a serious biographical treatment of Mrs. Beeton to ignore the issue. And yet to expose Beeton as a plagiarist, while it offered sensational dramatic possibilities, left the narrative arc with nowhere much to go (what, for instance, would be the point in pursuing the course of her post-book life?). Perhaps this is why there were no significant documentary treatments of the Beeton story until the turn of the millennium when two radio plays, both broadcast by Radio 4, dealt with the issue in different ways. *Before Beeton—The Eliza Acton Story* put the plagiarism issue at the centre of the drama, while *Isabella—The Real Mrs. Beeton* used it to add texture to a reconstruction of Sam and Isabella's working partnership.

Before Beeton—The Eliza Acton Story by Jyll Bradley is that curious hybrid, a docudrama. Scenes played by actors are intercut with interviews, principally with Sarah Freeman and Clarissa Dickson Wright. The story opens with Sam and Isabella having dinner in Pinner. Isabella is busy sorting through the avalanche of letters that has recently descended in response to the *EDM*'s request for tried and tested recipes. A reader from Glossop has sent in a formula for Portable Giblet Soup, while

Stewed Ox-tongue in Tapioca comes from a lady temporarily residing in Weston-super-Mare. Isabella is so overwhelmed by the volume of recipes that she suggests that she and Sam should incorporate them into their daily menu. Sam, more interested in the bigger picture, makes excited plans for his various freelancers to provide Isabella with the technical copy that she will need for her projected *Book of Household Management:* "Miss Dillinger can do you Natural History by the hundredweight!"

Some days later Mrs. Beeton is watching in the kitchen while her maid Aggie tests a recipe for greengage jam. Just as the whole thing is about to descend into disaster, a stranger appears at the door. The middle-aged woman refuses to divulge her identity, "my name is of no importance—regrettably," but simply bustles in and starts instructing Mrs. Beeton and Aggie on how to rescue the jam. From here she proceeds to produce from her large bag a fresh mackerel and some Dover soles (she explains that she has travelled this morning from Hastings), and embarks upon a running commentary on how to choose and cook these different fish to perfection (the mackerel should be fresh, but the sole "a little aged"). Overwhelmed by the Visitor's obvious authority, Mrs. Beeton and Aggie can only stand and watch. These scenes are intercut with voice-overs from Freeman and Dickson Wright, identifying Acton (clearly the Visitor) as an instinctual artist-cook as opposed to Beeton who is simply a promiscuous copyist of other people's work.

A short while later—it is not clear whether it is days or weeks—the Visitor again appears at Mrs. Beeton's kitchen door, this time announcing that she intends to teach her all about puddings. It is not, however, until her third appearance that the Visitor reveals her true passion. It is now that she arrives to teach Mrs. Beeton and Aggie about making bread. In her lyrical account of how humble flour, yeast, and water are all that is required to make the staff of life, and how adulteration is a kind of moral as well as social crime, we hear the engagement of the poet-artist-cook, beside whom the note-taking Mrs. Beeton looks increasingly sham. "I don't cook. Aggie cooks and I . . . observe," announces Mrs. Beeton apologetically to the Visitor's suggestion that she begin to knead the dough herself. It is now that the Visitor is heard to mutter about "Strangers taking the credit and profits of my toil."

The dough mixed, the Visitor suggests that it be taken into the north-facing library to rest (the idea of 2 Chandos Villas having any sort of library, let alone a north-facing one, is intriguing). Once surrounded by books, the stranger's identity is coaxed into the open. She is none other than Eliza Acton, author of *Modern Cookery for Private Families*. "I knew you would steal from me like all the others," declares an agitated Miss Acton. "Read me, eat my words!" To which a genuinely humble Mrs. Beeton replies, "I'm an editor, Miss Acton; my work is composed with scissors and paste, yours with pen and ink." "Well, granted at least you recognize it," retorts Acton and, having secured from Beeton the promise that she will at least credit her in the *Book of Household Management* with this recipe for bread, she disappears down the hall, unseen by Sam who arrives home at that very moment.

The dramatic sequences in *Before Beeton—The Eliza Acton Story* use the device of haunting—Miss Acton is clearly a ghost—to express the way in which the cookery section of the *Book of Household Management* is inflected by her intellectual presence. It manages, cleverly, both to bring the issue of plagiarism out into the open and, at the same time, to absolve Mrs. Beeton of any blame. Miss Acton, after all, has been a willing if tetchy presence in the Beeton kitchen, and she is only too keen to impart her practical knowledge as both cook and writer to the younger woman who, by her own admission, will never be more than a scissors-and-paste hack. The commentary from Freeman and Dickson Wright, meanwhile, firms up the distinctions between the two women. Acton is the "true" cook, Beeton the ploddy journeyman. And, to finish, a short contribution from Delia Smith underscores that customary coupling of Acton and Elizabeth David as true artists, leaving Beeton as the person with whom no one wants to be compared. (It is, of course, ironic that it is Smith, with her comprehensive, ungimmicky approach, who most often gets saddled with the "modern Mrs. Beeton" tag.)

The following year, in 2001, Radio 4 broadcast another play about Beeton. *Isabella—The Real Mrs. Beeton* by Tony Coult is a straightforward attempt at documentary drama and draws heavily on Sarah Freeman's 1977 *Isabella and Sam*. The action is framed by Sam's last few sweat-drenched days in the sanatorium at Petersham in the spring of 1877 as he pores over his cache of love letters exchanged with Isabella during their courtship year. Coaxing him into conversation, the young nurse Annie Barnfield is tickled to learn that her patient is the husband of none other than the great Mrs. Beeton. Annie's mother has always maintained that a young woman's education need consist of no more than "the Bible, the works of Shakespeare, and *Mrs. Beeton*." This elevating of Mrs.

Beeton to iconic status thirty years too soon is again repeated in the final flashback scene, where the doctor arrives at Greenhithe to deliver Isabella's last baby and pronounces himself honoured to be attending such a "distinguished patient." Historically, of course, Mrs. Beeton was no one until at least twenty years after her death.

The first flashback scene in Coult's script is a faithful rendering of Sarah Freeman's suggestion that Sam and Isabella met for the first time as adults at the Dolphin. In Coult's version Isabella bangs out Beethoven and Chopin on "the old tavern piano," while Sam alternately moons and asks her for advice on various "marketing opportunities" for his magazines. From the other side of the pub the young couple is watched by Eliza Beeton and Elizabeth Dorling, who speculate on a possible romance between the young couple. Almost immediately it becomes clear that there is a big obstacle to the courtship. As Eliza Beeton tells the distinctly snooty Elizabeth Dorling, "I have done little to encourage Sam, I can promise you that. He knows well enough that you and Mr. Dorling didn't send . . . [Isabella] to Ladies' School in Germany to fall into the arms of a tavern-owner's grandson!"

With the problem of class discrepancy quickly surmounted by true love, *Isabella—The Real Mrs. Beeton* then turns its attention to Beeton's plagiarism. Since the play's source is Freeman's 1977 biography, the focus remains exclusively on borrowings from Eliza Acton, with no mention made of the huge number of lifts from elsewhere. In an early flashback scene Sam advises Isabella to go prospecting for her material in texts that are already on the market, to which she responds incredulously, "You want me to steal other cooks' recipes?" Sam's soothing response is that all he is asking her to do is "discover, excavate and polish up" existing material using her "delightful economy of language and attention to detail." The scene ends with Bella's rueful soliloquy: "What have I let myself in for? I know nothing about cookery. Except . . . Except Miss Acton's book. Where is it?"

Mrs. English makes an appearance in *Isabella—The Real Mrs. Beeton*, reading out A Suffolk Recipe for Pickling Hams in a very strong regional accent which, suffice it to say, does not sound much like Mrs. English's native French. Still, there would be little point in looking at imaginative reconstructions of Mrs. Beeton's life if it were only to point out those places where the creative text deviates from the documentary record (which, in the case of Beeton, is itself heavily spotted with bits of fiction).

What makes Coult's script valuable is the way that, by amplifying a thread of feeling barely visible in the original material, a whole new aspect of biographical interpretation is thrown into high relief. For instance, the honeymoon bedroom scene in *The Real Mrs. Beeton* has Isabella, played by Natasha Little, intoxicated by her introduction to sex, and asking eagerly for Sam, played by Michael Maloney, to "love me again," to which he is obliged to explain sheepishly, "there needs to be a period of . . . recuperation, dearest. For vigour to return." So intrigued is Isabella by this piece of information that she suggests, only half joking, that they should run a regular sex column in the *Englishwoman's Domestic Magazine.* "We'd be closed down within the week," is Sam's swift professional response.

This scene is, of course, fictional. Or, at least, we can say it is not factual. But it still manages to add to our understanding of Isabella's character and Sam's passion for "the widest possible dissemination of the greatest possible amount of useful and practical knowledge." It would make sense for Isabella, in that same spirit of helpful endeavour, to suggest that just such a bride's handbook should include an informative section on sex, including her own newly made discovery that "it is not possible [for gentlemen] to function at will." Coult's fictional intervention catches both the engaging optimism and the aggrandizing daftness of the mid-Victorians' ambition to slap Universal Information between the covers of a book, and also neatly points out that firm rules remained in place about just who was allowed to know what and when (sexual knowledge, for instance, being appropriate only for married women).

Coult's play was based on Alison Neil's *Bella—The Story of Mrs. Beeton,* a one-woman show written by Neil in 1988 and performed by her until 2002 (she gave up at the point where she believed she could no longer pass as a twenty-one-year-old). Neil's appearance meticulously reproduces that of Beeton in the two known surviving photographs (plump and stripey, slim and chic) as she tells the story of her life to the audience, occasionally slipping into the character of her mother (usually disapproving), or a housemaid (always flustered). Neil's script sticks closely to Freeman, but chooses to develop points towards which Freeman has only gestured. Thus Neil's Mrs. Dorling manages to be "queenly" (arising from that childhood recollection from her grandson E. E. Dorling) throughout, arriving at the Grandstand for an inspection as if she were indeed Her Majesty Queen Victoria. Henry Dorling, by contrast, is a kindly and loving step-papa who favours Isabella and Bessie over his own girls by sending only them to Heidelberg. One of the most strikingly effective passages in Neil's sympathetic ventriloquizing of Isabella Beeton is when she asks the audience rhetorically, "What can I tell you about Sam?" and then proceeds to answer her own question.

> He was like no one else I had ever met. He spoke like a poet. His words melted my heart right from the beginning, although I hope I did not let it show. He was impulsively enthusiastic; his eyes blazed with excitement at his own plans. He was quite brilliant in his field—affordable books and magazines for the middle-classes . . . he was so sure of his own talents, I believed he could achieve anything. He was fun! Charming, handsome, although pale with ill-health, he liked working into the night, prize fights, ratting,—and me! So flattering! He thought me a catch, with my fine manners, and foreign education. I thought him . . . more than I ever dreamed of.

Alison Neil, however, was not the first person to think of putting Mrs. Beeton on the stage, even if you discount the several am-dram and schools productions of Du Garde Peach's published version of *Meet Mrs. Beeton*. Tucked away in the papers of the director Frith Banbury, which are now lodged at the University of Texas, is a reference to *Sam and Bella*, a musical Banbury was planning to direct between 1961 and 1963. Undertaken at Nancy Spain's suggestion, the musical was never performed, and may not even have been completed, although a detailed synopsis by the scriptwriter William Sansom does survive. In Sansom's rendering young Sam Beeton is a sexual dilettante, who likes to frequent Kate Hamilton's infamous whorehouse where he has been having a long-running affair with one of her girls, called Adèle. Sam has pledged, however, to give up whoring on his marriage to Isabella, the only girl he really loves. However, before the reluctant Dorlings will grant Sam their eldest daughter's hand, he has to prove that he has £10,000 in the bank. To raise this vast sum Sam has been obliged to borrow from a sinister financier called Tallow who, in return for the favour, insists on being introduced to the lovely Adèle whom he proceeds to make his mistress.

Written in 1963, on the cusp of women's lib, *Sam and Bella* is interesting particularly for the way it feels about women's roles. Percy Pratt, Beeton's clerk, is disapproving of the fact that Bella starts to work in her husband's business, although it eventually becomes clear that this is because he is infatuated with her. Beeton's most sinister employee is a woman called Myra, or the Silkworm, who is strange and cold and wears trousers ("spinsterish and feminist," say Banbury's background notes). To complicate things, however, there is another journalist working at the Strand called "Mrs. Browne," who also happens to be the Beetons' neighbour in Pinner (and, as Spain noted in her book, there was indeed a "Mrs. Browne" living at 1 Chandos Villas). In contrast to the sinister Myra, Mrs. Browne is warm, cosy, and a particular friend to Isabella.

From here the stage is set for a hurtling story in which Sam goes back to his wicked ways at Kate Hamilton's. Tallow, jealous that Adèle still clearly loves Sam, calls in the loan. The only way Sam is able to repay Tallow is by borrowing the sum from Adèle, who hopes that by handing over her savings she will resume her role as Sam's mistress. During two of Sam's trips to Kate Hamilton's he manages to bump into Henry Dorling, who is clearly a habitué of the brothel. Isabella, meanwhile, realizes that she is hopeless at keeping house—there is the mandatory failed dinner party scene—and, in order to educate herself, writes the *Book of Household Management*. Increasingly aware that Sam is an inept businessman, Isabella also takes over control of the office at the Strand and, to symbolize that she means business, takes to wearing trousers instead of her usual crinoline. Always aware of Sam's roaming eye, it is not until she hears, erroneously, that Adèle now wants her £10,000 back, that Isabella storms off to confront the girl as she plies her business in the street. It turns out that the evildoer is not Adèle but Tallow, who is trying to close down Sam in order to gain control of *Mrs. Beeton's Household Management*: "I've always loved that cookery book. It's a goldmine. And I love gold!"

Having taken a lease of her own accord on the Greenhithe property, Isabella moves down to Kent to await the birth of her baby. Sam, meanwhile, stays mostly in town, trying to find ways to rescue his still ailing business. Despite the best endeavours of Mrs. Browne, who seems also to have moved to Greenhithe, Isabella catches a serious infection after the birth of the baby. Just as she is on the point of death, Sam bursts in with the news that the *Book of Household Management* has sold an incredible hundred thousand copies, so saving the firm of S. O. Beeton from certain ruin. As a grand finale a cavalcade of women dressed in everything from crinolines through flappers' dresses to mini-skirts passes over the stage, signalling their indebtedness to *Mrs. Beeton's Book of Household Management.*

Most musicals sound silly when described in outline and *Sam and Bella* is no exception. However, it is worth bearing in mind that the vastly experienced Frith Banbury was keen to make it work, that Hal Prince was said to be interested, and that outlines were sent to Julie Andrews in Hollywood in the hope that she would play the main role. Yet even with omens as good as these, *Sam and Bella* failed to take to the stage. The problem, according to the letters that flew between various interested parties who read the synopsis, was that Bella's story refused, dramatically, to catch fire. "I think," wrote Banbury in an undated letter to Sansom, "that there is a seductive danger of the musical becoming the chronicle of a rake's progress along a rather specially peculiar primrose path, with relatively minor interest lent to the tale through the fact that the rake's wife wrote a famous book of recipes." And despite months' worth of meetings, conversations, and script tinkering, the rake's progress never really did progress.

One musical that did, however, manage to get to performance was *The Way To A Man's Heart.* It, too, was based on Nancy Spain's book, which had been taken out of Hendon library in the 1960s by a journalist and semi-professional lyricist called Irwin Ferry. Ferry, however, softens Spain's insistent slant against Sam and instead devolves the role of sexual aggressor onto Jane Dorling, Isabella's step-sister. Jane is an incorrigible flirt who manages to induce two suitors—Mr. Wood and Mr. White—to fight a duel over her. (The idea of George White, the middle-aged, widowed, and highly pedantic Epsom solicitor whom the real Jane Dorling eventually married fighting a duel with anyone is one of the more enchanting possibilities the musical offers.) Bella, meanwhile, is taking her interest in pastry-making so seriously that she actually stands behind a counter and serves afternoon tea in the Epsom bakery shop. Sam's nemesis is none other than the rival publisher Vizetelly who is determined to get control of Sam's business through steep loans, just as the evil Tallow did in *Sam and Bella.* "Fred" Greenwood, meanwhile, has been turned into a faithful assistant, who is nonetheless resentful of the way that Mrs. Beeton is trying to assert her authority in the office (shades of Percy Pratt in the earlier musical). The score includes a rousing song for Granny Jerrom called "On the Portsmouth Road" (a reference to an unproven suggestion in Spain's book that Mary and Isaac Jerrom's livery stable was on the main London to Portsmouth road), a tender duet for Henry and Elizabeth entitled "My Once Upon A Time Girl" which recalls their early, abortive love affair, and a rousingly bitter choral piece, "Nice Behaviour I Must Say!," in which the Epsom ladies express their disapproval at Bella turning shopgirl. The musical ran for five nights at the Epsom Playhouse in 1991 and, apart from the very occasional schools' production, has never been seen since.

Musicals, of course, are not the only way of setting a subject to music. In 1983 the composer Michael Hurd was commissioned to write *Mrs. Beeton's Book: a Music-Hall Guide to Victorian Living* for "the combined Ladies Choir" of the Petersfield Music Festival. The piece consists of a sequence of songs and spoken narration that lasts about thirty minutes. Hurd's narrator quotes directly from the opening section of the original 1861 text of *Household Management*, advising the audience on the "Duties of the Mistress," "Early Rising," "Frugality and Economy," "Conversational Topics," and "Good Temper." These excerpts are interspersed with songs that comment on or amplify Beeton's formulae. For instance, her advice that "trifling occurrences, such as small disappointments, petty annoyances, and other every day incidents should never be mentioned to your friends," is followed by a song which begins, "The other day, To my dismay, An awful thing occurred, And promise if I tell you You will never breathe a word! Well, first I broke my looking-glass My mother gave to me! And then, my dear, I rather fear I spilt a cup of tea!" Likewise, the narrator's reassurance that everyone gets nervous before a dinner party is followed by the lyric, "Now the moment is approaching Friends are coming here to dine. Minute on the hour encroaching! Will they be on time? Cook has been a trifle awkward, And her language was appalling, Said she'd half a mind to go And find another place!"

Hurd's score, then, uses spoken snatches from the *Book of Household Management* as a jumping-off point for his own lyrics. Other dramatists have been content to let Mrs. Beeton write the entire script. The BBC2 play *Mrs. Beeton* which was broadcast in 1970 consists simply of Margaret Tyzack, dressed as the lady herself, pottering in her kitchen and delivering sections of the *Book of Household Management* straight to camera. Significantly, when Tyzack's Mrs. Beeton announces that she is going to present her readers/viewers with a recipe, she chooses one for

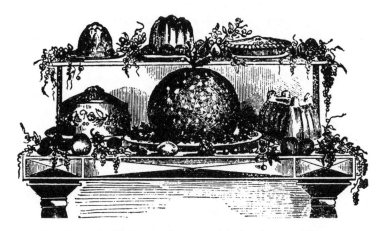

Mrs. Beeton's Christmas desserts, with the plum pudding taking its customary central place.

Plum Pudding. For puddings, and plum puddings in particular, have become a symbolic stand-in for Mrs. Beeton.

Certainly when, thirty years later, the composer John Harle decided to set a recipe of Mrs. Beeton's to music, he chose her "Christmas Plum-Pudding (price 3s 6d)." The score is designed for four unaccompanied voices singing in barbershop style. The lyrics, which have been written by the novelist Charlotte Cory, stick close to Beeton's original formula (paragraph 1328 in the 1861 edition). Periodically alongside and underneath the singers can be heard two brittle voices apparently from the 1940s discussing their making of "Mrs. Beeton's famous Christmas Pudding," which, thanks to slightly over-enthusiastic flambéing, has required the attendance of the fire brigade. The piece was written for the BBC singers to perform on *Illuminare, Carols for a New Millennium*.

In interview Harle explained the choices he made in the course of setting Mrs. Beeton to music.

> So we thought, OK, if we are going to set Mrs. Beeton then let's look at
> the period of Mrs. Beeton, let's look at the old BBC and the old ribbon
> microphone and "Uncle Mac," and of course the musical genre we came
> up with was barber shop . . . Then of course the idea of spoken interjec-
> tions seemed a good idea, and thinking back to the "Uncle Mac" pro-
> grammes on the BBC it seemed a good idea to get some old English
> voices, so we got Eleanor Bron, who's one of my favourite actresses of

all time, and Charles Collingwood who plays Brian Aldridge in *The Archers* . . . We then had to take away all that recorded material and treat it so that we could add some crackly old '78 sounds and the scratching of the needle and other novelty sounds.

What immediately leaps out is Harle's assumption that Mrs. Beeton belongs to the period of "the old ribbon microphone and 'Uncle Mac' " and crackly old '78s, by which he presumably means the 1940s. Also striking is his description of Bron's and Collingwood's delivery as that belonging to "old English voices," by which he implies Received Pronunciation of the same period. (And, indeed, according to directions accompanying the score, the male speaker should use "the plummy tones of Lord Reith.") For Harle, born in 1956, the past from which Mrs. Beeton hails is that of the time just before his own, the 1930s and 1940s. If he had been born in 1936, then the chances are that his Mrs. Beeton would have been an Edwardian, and Eleanor Bron, rather than being a harassed 1940s housewife obliged to rub along with a grumpy cook, would have been asked to drawl like a duchess giving instructions to her housekeeper. Just as Mrs. Beeton represented the idea of Victorianism to a generation of authors writing in the opening decades of the twentieth century, for John Harle and many of his peers Mrs. Beeton represents simply "the olden days." It says much for the success of Ward, Lock's strategy of liberating Mrs. Beeton from the constraints of earthly time, that plenty of otherwise well-informed people are obliged to admit that they are not really sure when Beeton was living and working. If plum pudding has come to stand for Mrs. Beeton, then Mrs. Beeton has come to stand for the ageless past.

THE POINT, REALLY, is that, just as the first viewers of the National Portrait Gallery portrait could not agree on whether the young woman in front of them was plump or slim, strict or gentle, so the protean Mrs. Beeton has found herself over the last seventy years cast as a governessy scold, sneaky plagiarist, co-dependent submissive, sexual emancipator, and much more. The small stock of sources, codified in the three mid-century biographies, has been combed to provide authority for just about any kind of Mrs. Beeton the moment requires. And now, at the beginning of a new century, Mrs. Beeton finds herself once again a vital figure, drawn into the heart of two especially urgent conversations about the safety of our food and the business of being a woman.

To take food first. Anxieties about the provenance and safety of our diet are currently at fever pitch. Worries about genetically modified crops and intrusive agri-business have led to a huge expansion in the commercial provision of "organic" food, that is food that is certifiably free of unnecessary interventions at all stages of growth and harvest. If the customers who flock to Fresh & Wild and Planet Organic have a fantasy about where the rather expensive food in their shopping trolley has come from, it would perhaps resemble an updated version of the *Book of Household Management*'s Frontispiece: a happy farmstead where the cows look as if they are having a nice time and the chickens have been allowed to roam at will.

Even those people who do not buy from specialist organic stores are increasingly expressing concerns about the quality of the food they put into their bodies. In response all the major supermarkets now produce their own organic lines, and several recent advertising campaigns have concentrated on showing consumers the attention, care (love, even?) that are devoted to sourcing their ranges. But for those manufacturers that have been producing processed foodstuffs for decades this growing demand of the public to know—and celebrate—the origins of their food has been harder to meet. It is not feasible for companies such as these to "go organic," yet mass-produced bread, pasties, sausages, and pies look not only unappetizing but old-fashioned (and not in a good way) as they compete with products able to boast loudly about their point of origin.

For this reason Ward, Lock, and then Cassell, who acquired the firm in 1989, have found themselves over the last few years able to pursue a very lucrative sideline licensing Mrs. Beeton's name to food manufacturers who wish to harness her "brand qualities" to their own. Internal market research carried out by various licensees reveals that "Mrs. Beeton" plays well to the target audience of women between the ages of twenty-five and forty-five from the B to C2 social categories who are in charge of the weekly shop. From one piece of research it emerged that Mrs. Beeton represented "homeliness and economy, traditional values ie all the benefits of the family occasion," even though "those questioned weren't sure whether Mrs. Beeton really lived, how old she was when she wrote the book or whether she was a myth." Another piece of research showed that, in blind trials, when a product was branded "Mrs. Beeton" it scored ten percentage points higher than if it was presented to the taster as a generic product. So it is hardly surprising that manufacturers have been happy to pay large fees to Ward, Lock in order to be able to use the name "Mrs. Beeton" to promote savoury pies, Bakewell slices, trifle sponge slices, lasagne, tea buns, yeast-raised doughnuts, baps, chutneys, sausages, wholemeal loaves, malt loaves, crusty bloomers, and much much more.

Indeed, in 1995 one company, Ginster's, decided that the "Mrs. Beeton" name was so valuable that it paid Ward, Lock £1 million to use it in perpetuity on its range of pasties and meat products. (There is a strange irony, of course, that 130 years earlier Ward, Lock itself paid Sam a sum of money, quite possibly £1,900, for the use of the name "Beeton" in perpetuity.) Mrs. Beeton stands for quality and wholesomeness (and, subliminally, perhaps, the perfect nurturing mother whom we both long to be and long to have). She is, in short, a premium product whose cultural clout is so great that any lingering curiosity about the constitution of a particular sausage or a certain pasty fades into insignificance.

What all this suggests is that, as far as Mrs. Beeton's status as an intellectual adulterer goes, she is actually more sinned against than sinning. Quite aside from the modern licensing arrangements from which Ward, Lock and Cassell have been able to profit, there is the fact that from the moment of Beeton's death her text was hacked about, diminished, supplemented, and, eventually, rewritten, so that by the 1930s not a single word of her original voice remained. By the 1990s, as we have seen, "Mrs. Beeton" was being used to sell a bewildering array of titles including *A Picnic with Mrs. Beeton, Mrs. Beeton's Christmas Book, Breakfast with Mrs. Beeton, Mrs. Beeton's Simple Cake Decorating, Mrs. Beeton's Pantry* and *Mrs. Beeton's Hand-Made Gifts,* none of which she would have recognized as her own work. It is exactly the kind of aggressive franchising operation that any Victorian publisher, and especially S. O. Beeton, would have been proud of.

The second point about Beeton's intellectual adultery is that, since our own "post-modern" culture claims to be comfortable with the concept of intellectual borrowing (all those pastiches, remakes and cultural "quotations"), it is odd that we remain so unsettled by the revelation that her book is made up of printed bits and pieces already circulating in the late 1850s. The early- and mid-Victorians, by contrast, really did appreciate the way in which texts emerge from a whole network of material and social processes rather than out of the unique vision of a single author. In the hectic context of the mid-nineteenth-century book trade, when texts were constantly being re-presented in different formats and bindings, not to mention editions, men like Samuel Beeton realized that the business of copyright was slippery in the extreme. Sometimes this worked in your favour (as with *Uncle Tom's Cabin*) and sometimes it did not (by 1870 Ward, Lock were complaining that purloined versions of *Mrs. Beeton* were appearing all over town). With this in mind, Elizabeth David's emphatic identification of Acton as a pre-Victorian writer may well have had something to do with a desire to see her as coming from the Romantic period, when genius was situated in the souls of a few unique individuals such as Byron and Shelley and, by implication, Acton herself. David's Beeton, by contrast, hails from the age of mechanical reproduction.

The second contemporary conversation in which Mrs. Beeton figures prominently concerns what women are and what they should be. Until the 1970s Mrs. Beeton appeared to exist almost independently of the wider political, social, and economic contexts that had seen women's lives transformed in the hundred years since she had died. Hyde and Spain, both writing in the immediate post-war period when British women were returning to full-time domestic duties, managed to tell the Beeton story with only a glancing reference to the way that the *Book of Household Management* informed married women of their legal rights and the *Englishwoman's Domestic Magazine* discreetly championed advances in female education and employment. By contrast, Sarah Freeman writing in the mid-1970s could hardly avoid placing Mrs. Beeton more directly in terms of the two waves of feminism that had occurred in the 1860s and again in the late 1960s. Freeman's offence-avoiding strategy—no one wanted a bra-burning Mrs. Beeton, least of all her granddaughter and great-grandson who still controlled the archive—was to position Beeton as an instinctive gradualist who, while interested in the improvement of women's lives, managed never to "forget" her femininity. Freeman's Beeton was a homemaker first and a working woman only by default.

Another commentator in the 1970s, however, took a different view entirely. For Patricia Fisher, a great-niece on the Dorling side and a first cousin of Nancy Spain, Mrs. Beeton was "a career woman—and, as such, much in advance of her time." Lady Fisher was a Northern Irish MP who had taken over the parliamentary seat of her father, Sir Walter Smiles, after his accidental death in 1953. Fisher, the tallest woman at Westminster and a powerhouse of energy, frequently gave talks on her great-aunt to women's groups, out of which evolved a recipe book called *On the Beeton Track* to raise money for her reconciliation Belfast charity. In all the versions of her standard twenty-minute presentation Fisher always liked to emphasize Beeton's brisk modernity, her refusal to conform to stereotypical ideas about what a wife and mother should be (all the while, of course, being devoted to her husband and children). It was this view that fed straight into a 1990 Radio 4 documentary called *The Making of Mrs. Beeton* for which Fisher was the main source. A couple of years earlier, and writing her one-woman theatre play *Bella—The Story of Mrs. Beeton,* Alison Neil also chose to position Mrs. Beeton as a thoroughly modern working wife juggling her responsibilities who, much to her mother's disapproval, managed to see her baby for only half an hour after tea. Ten years later, and nudging into the millennium, Tony Coult developed this reading of the Beetons' marriage as a modern partnership even further. In his radio play the first little Samuel Orchart is taken ill with croup at Newmarket while in his father's care, Isabella being busy working on her book with Mrs. English.

What is striking about all these attempts to read Isabella's particular brand of womanhood is that they fail to take account of its original context. As we have seen, when she decided to work after marriage, Isabella was doing something old-fashioned rather than new-fangled. Her mother, mother-in-law, and grandmother had all combined domestic duties with being, at times, virtual co-partners in their husbands' businesses. It was Isabella's insistence on continuing this tradition, rather than observing the new codes of gentility which demanded that middle-class women should not engage in productive labour, that made the Dorlings grumble. Not that it was exactly the old-fashionedness that bothered them, so much as the fact that Isabella appeared to be living the life of a woman several notches beneath her in the social scale.

It is this dissonance, this sense of Mrs. Beeton as being out of step with her own times, whether striding out in front or lagging behind, that explains why she is most frequently drafted in to the current conversation about the "new domesticity." This is the "trend" by which highly educated women with a wide range of career possibilities choose to concentrate their energies and identity on activities associated with home-making. The most obvious British example is Nigella Lawson and her bestselling *How to Be A Domestic Goddess*. Written by a strikingly good-looking, well-connected journalist, the book, whose subtitle is *The Art of Baking and Comfort Cooking*, is predicated on the idea that beneath the shiny surface of the modern "career woman" is a cosy housewife longing to get out. Now that feminism has—allegedly—delivered equal pay and equal opportunities, it is safe to go back in the kitchen and enjoy recreating those cosy Saturday afternoons spent there with mother. Similarly in the United States Harvard-educated lawyer Cheryl Mendelson has written *Home Comforts*, in which she describes the joy she gets from sheet folding and tackling stubborn stains. In an explanatory Preface Mendelson explains how one day she came home from her high-powered job to an ill-kempt flat and suddenly realized that she would be far happier keeping house along the lines that she had witnessed during her 1950s childhood.

In the endless newspaper columns that have been dedicated to pondering just what the new domesticity of Lawson and Mendelson "means," Mrs. Beeton's name is nearly always invoked. Often referred to as "the first domestic Goddess" she is frequently drafted in to represent the golden age of housekeeping—knowledgeable, nurturing—to which Lawson, Mendelson, and their post-modern sisters gesture. The confusions at the heart of this thesis are telling. The first, of course, is that Isabella Beeton was never an instinctual or experienced housekeeper-cook. Instead, just like Lawson, she was a journalist who alighted on domestic science as a good subject ripe for repackaging. Second is the fact that Beeton and Lawson are performing their literary housekeeping in very different social and political contexts. The appeal of baking to Lawson or housekeeping to Cheryl Mendelson is entirely dependent on its voluntary status. Highly educated and well paid even before they became media figures, Lawson could well afford to buy her cakes from a pâtisserie while Mendelson was easily able to pay for a daily cleaner. It is the fact that the domesticity is chosen that makes it desirable (and, judging from press coverage, wildly erotic to male spectators). When it all gets too much, or when the camera or tape recorder is turned off, these domestic goddesses can simply stop and pay someone else to take over.

Isabella Beeton, by contrast, was writing at a time when active housekeeping was increasingly looked upon as a dreary chore by many middle-class women who fantasized about the day when they would be able to buy their way out of its daily disciplines and escape into ladyland. The Beetons' achievement—first Sam with the *Englishwoman's Domestic Magazine* and then Isabella with the *Book of Household Management*—was to elevate domestic duties so that they became something you could be proud of doing well. After reading the *Book of Household Management* the middle-class housewife who was unlucky enough not to have a full complement of housemaids and footmen no longer felt herself a drudge. She was, rather, the Commander of an Army, albeit an army that consisted of a teenage girl and a boy who came in once a week. By attempting to master science, natural history, mathematics, and all the other allied disciplines that Mrs. Beeton laid out as vital to the well-run home, the middle-class woman could start to take pride in her labour. Nor was this simply satisfaction in sparkling windows, a light sponge cake, and healthy children, but a genuine sense of competence that came from doing the whole thing on a budget. Just as her husband kept order in the workshop, classroom, or bank, so the reader of the *Book of Household Management* presided over a home that ran like clockwork.

But that was not all. In the decades that followed the publication of the original *Book of Household Management,* as women from middle-class homes started to make their living in the marketplace, they drew upon the very skills that Mrs. Beeton had taught their mothers and, by a process of osmosis, had continued to teach them. Primary school teaching, nursing, and, in time, secretarial work and bank clerking all required the ability to organize one's immediate environment and work in a systematic, productive and energy-saving way. While many of these new jobs built on women's perceived innate qualities—kindness, neatness, honesty—they also required the kind of rigour and energy that Mrs. Beeton had worked so hard to inculcate in "the mistress of the house." As the years went by and tattered volumes of the original *Book of Household Management* were passed from mother to daughter and sister to cousin, it became increasingly clear that Mrs. Beeton's masterwork was much more than an instruction manual for the home. It was, in fact, a primer for Everywoman as she stepped out to meet the huge social, economic, and political challenges that lay just beyond the front door.

NOTES AND SOURCES

All letters cited are in the Mayson Moss Beeton Archive, unless otherwise indicated. Speculative information, e.g. where a letter's date of composition has been identified by postmark or by its apparent place in a correspondence, is indicated by [?].

All parish records were viewed on microfilm at the designated record office.

MANUSCRIPT LOCATIONS

BBC	BBC Written Archives Centre, Caversham.
Brompton	Brompton Cemetery Records, London.
CKS	Centre for Kentish Studies, Maidstone.
Coke Mss	Coke-Steel Family Papers, Trusley.
Croydon	Croydon Local Studies Library and Archives, Croydon.
Cumbria	Cumbria Record Office, Carlisle.
East Sussex	East Sussex Record Office, Lewes.
Essex	Essex Record Office, Chelmsford.
FRC	Family Records Centre, London.
Frith Banbury	Frith Banbury Papers, held at Harry Ransom Research Center, University of Texas at Austin.
Guildhall	Guildhall Library, London.
Lambeth	Lambeth Archives Department, London.
Licensed Victuallers	Licensed Victuallers' School, Ascot.
LMA	London Metropolitan Archives, London.
MMB Archive	Mayson Moss Beeton Archive, currently owned by Kathryn Hughes.
MMB Archive, family	Individual items once in the MMB Archive, now in the possession of the Beeton and Dorling families.
NPG	Heinz Archive & Library, National Portrait Gallery, London.
PRONI	Public Record Office of Northern Ireland, Belfast.

Richmond   Richmond Golf Club Archive, Petersham.
Suffolk   Suffolk Record Office, Bury St. Edmunds.
Surrey   Surrey History Service, Woking.
Tree Collection   Herbert Beerbohm Tree Collection, University of
         Bristol Theatre Collection, Bristol.
Wellcome   Wellcome Library for the History and Understanding of
         Medicine, London.
Westminster   Westminster Record Office, London.
West Sussex   West Sussex Record Office, Chichester.

EPIGRAPHS

2   "Henrietta English." Letter, Henrietta English to Isabella Beeton (hereafter IMB), July 21, 1857.
"She is a goose." James Lees-Milne, *A Mingled Measure,* London, 1994, p. 259.

PROLOGUE

3   "the famous *Book of Household Management.*" Acquisition file for NPG P3, NPG.
4   " 'any writing at all.' " Memo, G. K. Adams to H.M. Hake, January 4, 1933, acquisition file NPG P3.
"slightly earlier period." *Manchester Guardian,* June 19, 1931.
7   "after all." [Florence White], "The Real Mrs. Beeton," *The Times,* February 3, 1932.
"when she was nineteen years old." The NPG dated the photograph 1860–5, a fact that has subsequently slipped into the public record. However, since Isabella is not wearing an engagement or wedding ring and her dress is made from material given to her just after the Derby of 1855, it is most likely that the photograph was taken around June 1855.
8   " 'dismally frumpish.' " [Florence White], "The Real Mrs. Beeton."
" 'at least a parallel case.' " Letter, H. M. Hake to R. M. Barrington Ward, February 25, 1932, acquisition file NPG P3.
"*Eminent Victorians* of 1918." "Portraits for the Nation By Our Art Critic," transcript, unattributed cutting, MMB Archive. In the MMB Archive is a clutch of carefully transcribed newspaper cuttings from December 1932. However, the transcriber—in fact MMB's daughter Isabel—has failed to note where the articles first appeared. I have been able to locate most of the source material, but this article, in which the writer refers to being a personal acquaintance of Lytton Strachey, remains unidentified.
9   " 'circulation of a best-seller.' " "Has Mrs. Beeton Failed?," transcript, unattributed cutting, MMB Archive.

" 'a million homes.' " Transcript, unattributed cutting, MMB Archive.

10 " 'long-distance flyer.' " *Daily Mirror,* December 28, 1932.

"Emma Hamilton." *Star,* November 1935.

"was not." *Daily Express,* December 28, 1932. *Evening News,* December 28, 1932.

" 'gentle' face." *Daily Express,* December 28, 1932. "Mrs. Beeton's Portrait for the Nation," transcript, unattributed cutting, MMB Archive.

"elegant slenderness." *Guardian,* December 28, 1932. "Portraits for the Nation," transcript, unattributed cutting.

" 'on the wings of a contract.' " *Daily Mail,* December 28, 1932.

11 "handsome calf binding." Letter, R. K. Cardew to MMB, April 1, 1936.

"in the '60s." Letter, S. B. McCallum to MMB, July 6, 1936.

"lonely sheep station." Letter, Elizabeth Blair Hales to MMB, April 21, 1936.

"the top of incoming mail." For example, see MMB's note on outside of envelope received from S. B. McCallum, July 6, 1936.

" 'Victorian' face." Selection of letters written to MMB between 1932 and 1936.

"for a visit." Letter, W. F. Downing to MMB, April 20, 1936.

"at least a small book." MMB always used the term "memoir" to describe what he had in mind, by which he seems to have meant a joint biography of his parents.

12 "uncomprehending gaze of strangers." Letters, MMB to C. A. C. Cliffe, November 1; November 10, BBC.

"material over to them." For example, the note scribbled at the top of letter from M. Sherriff Holt to MMB, April 20, 1936.

"proof to him first." See notes written by MMB on letters received from Joan Hunter, September 18, 1936; Mary Stollard, July 2, 1936.

"carefully dated for posterity." For example, note scribbled at the top of M. L. Stollard, "A Famous Victorian," *Lady,* July 16, 1936, MMB Archive.

"using a collaborator." Letter, Osbert Burdett to MMB, April 13, 1936.

13 " 'discovering other people's secrets.' " H. Montgomery Hyde, manuscript autobiography, "Leaves of Memory," p. 181, Montgomery Hyde Papers, PRONI.

"at 'High Lands.' " Nancy Spain, *Why I'm Not A Millionaire,* London, 1956, p. 86.

"netting him a knighthood in 1920." The citation is actually "for services in connexion with the Newfoundland Forestry Corps," which Beeton ran from the Finance Department of the Ministry of Munitions.

"for the capital's rebuilding." Sally England, "Saving Mayson Beeton: a neglected discrete collection within the English Heritage Library," unpublished MA dissertation, University of London, 2002.

14 *"Thank You Nelson."* Nancy Spain, *Why I'm Not A Millionaire,* p. 85.

" 'me out of all the world.' " Ibid., p. 86.

"benign to the Beetons." Lucy Smiles, letter, *The Times,* February 6, 1932; Lucy Smiles, "The Great Mrs. Beeton By Her Sister," *Star,* February 17, 1932.

15 "the nation fondly imagined." Nancy Spain's *Mrs. Beeton and her Husband*

was published by Collins in August 1948, with a second edition following in October. In 1956 it was revised and issued by Ward, Lock as *The Beeton Story*.

"run out of time." H. Montgomery Hyde's *Mr. and Mrs. Beeton* was published by Harrap in 1951. In his Preface to Sarah Freeman's biography of 1977, Hyde claims that "it was to avoid conflicting with Miss Spain's book that I further postponed the publication of my own."

16 "Beeton family name into his." MMB, Will, May 26, 1937, Administration, November 6, 1947.

"by an invoice." Examples of Levick's eccentricities drawn from conversation and correspondence with those who met him, including Sarah Freeman, Lucy Lunt, Mary Rose Myrtle, Mary Geneste Holliday, J. Keith Killby.

"about the Beeton archive." *The Times*, February 11, 1974.

17 "book published in 1956." The terms under which Sarah Freeman was granted access to the MMB Archive were explained in conversation with the present author in 2001.

"expensive residential accommodation." Conversation with Sarah Freeman, 2001.

CHAPTER ONE

21 "two to twenty men." Mannix and Whellan, *History, Gazeteer and Directory of Cumberland*, Beverley, 1847, p. 479.

"the future Mrs. Beeton." Bishop's Register, August 7, 1785, Cumbria.

22 "shoe-horned into the brief notice." *The Times*, July 14, 1856.

"a man of the cloth." Letter, MMB to H. M. Hake, July 9, 1932, acquisition file NPG P3.

"from another man." Land Tax, Threlkeld Return, 1780, Cumbria.

"to be taken care of." Wreay Chapel Register, 1761–70, Cumbria.

"St. Andrew's, Thursby." Bishop's Register, July 30, 1786.

"the care of two hundred souls." Ibid., December 14, 1825. There is, though, uncertainty about how much the living was worth. In 1795 it was valued at £140 but by 1845, the year Mayson died, it had leapt to £370.

23 "wheat and cash." George Tremel, Will, February 17, 1784, Administration, August 19, 1785, Cumbria.

"just enough to marry on." John Mayson, Will, September 12, 1782, Administration, May 28, 1783, Cumbria.

"mother's youngest brother." Ibid.: Esther was born on November 30, 1793; John on January 11, 1796; Benjamin on July 24, 1801.

"buried at Thursby." *Carlisle Journal*, October 14, 1820. Thursby Parish Register, October 10, 1820.

" 'aged 39 years.' " *Carlisle Journal*, August 1, 1840.

24 "cost of 11d a letter." William Tennant Trimble, *The Trimbles & Cowens of Dalston, Cumberland*, Carlisle, 1935, p. 18.

25 "serve his apprenticeship." For more information on the Cowens' business activities see ibid., pp. 30–8.

"the shadow of St. Paul's." Marylebone Rate Books, 1834–8, Westminster. *Robson's Directory,* London, 1831, p. 264.

26 "for the record." St. Martin-in-the-Fields Parish Register, July 24, 1814, Westminster.

"for clothing and travel." Goodwood, Stable Accounts, 1792–1809, West Sussex.

"from 1802 racers too." Giles Worsley, "A Kingdom for the Horse," *Country Life,* September 25, 1997, pp. 90–4.

"and then Harriet." Westhampnett Parish Register, West Sussex, shows the following baptisms: February 9, 1794, Mary, daughter of William and Elizabeth "Standing"; March 20, 1796, Sarah, daughter of William and Elizabeth "Standen." No entry for Harriet has been found, although it is clear from later census and burial records that she was indeed a younger sister of Mary Standage and that she, Sarah and Mary spent their adult lives in London.

"who worked with horses." Harriet married George Cates, while Sarah married William Fenton, both coachmen.

27 "social beast trundling forward." St. Mary-le-Bone Parish Register, June 4, 1815, LMA; ibid., March 3, 1817.

"ran a livery stables in Marylebone." It seems likely that John Jerrom originally came from Hartley Wespall in Hampshire.

"the only resident male servant." William Tayler, *Diary of William Tayler, Footman, 1837* (London, 1962), London, 1998, p. 12.

28 "numbers 1, 4, 5, and 10." Marylebone Rate Books, 1820–35.

"death from consumption." Isaac Jerrom died on April 19, 1839, at 1 Wyndham Mews. James Mitchell and his son were still running the livery business out of Marylebone, and quite possibly Kensington too, as late as the 1880s.

"a hundred years later." "Bertha," "Our Ladies' Letter," *Portsmouth Evening News,* February 25, 1931.

29 "London girl called Emily Clarke." Henry Dorling married Emily Clarke at Epsom on September 20, 1834.

30 "with Benjamin Mayson." St. Mary Bryanston Square Parish Register, May 2, 1835, LMA.

"anyone could remember." Isabella was baptized on April 20 at the same church where her parents had married a year earlier. Her father, significantly, describes himself in the register as "Gent[leman]."

31 "and then again in September." [Anon.], "Merchant Princes, A Walk Through A London Warehouse," in *The Busy Hives Around Us,* London, 1861.

" 'with black velvet.' " *Englishwoman's Domestic Magazine* (hereafter *EDM*), New Series (hereafter NS), vol. 1, July 1860.

"northwest England." *EDM,* NS, vol. 6, November 1862.

"the right to vote." Electoral Register, City of London, 1836–9, Guildhall.

32 "seventy years later." Nancy Spain, *Mrs. Beeton and her Husband,* p. 26.

"in February 1841." Bessie was born March 1, 1838; John on September 2, 1839; Esther on February 17, 1841.

33   "a strawberry blonde." Letter, Marjorie Killby to NPG, November 13, 1968, acquisition file for NPG 32791, NPG.

"fairer than the rest." Watercolour ascribed to Henry Dorling, NPG 5473, NPG. Whether or not the painting actually was executed by Dorling, three companion portraits consisting of more disembodied cherubs are in the possession of the family. These cherubs, presumably, are young Dorlings, although their individual identities remain a mystery.

34   "from their youth." "Their speech used to puzzle me, as they always said 'Ain't' and dropped their aitches. This was the fashion in their youth apparently. They referred to the 'laylock' tree in the garden, and yellow was always 'yaller.' " Rosemary Fellowes quoted in Sarah Freeman, *Isabella and Sam,* London, 1977, pp. 50–1.

"says 'Apoplexy.' " Death certificate, Benjamin Mayson, 27 July 1840.

"only thirty years later." Death certificate, John Mayson, 2 June 1871 .

"buckled under her burden." On Benjamin's death certificate the informant, "her widowed mother Mary Jerrom," gives her address as 24 Milk Street.

"Sarah Robinson." Census, 1841, Parish of Orton.

35   "tasted different." William Parson and William White, *A History, Directory and Gazetteer of Cumberland and Westmorland,* Leeds and Newcastle, 1829, p. 377.

"twenty years later in the *Book of Household Management*." IMB, ed., *Book of Household Management* (hereafter *BOHM*), London, 1861, p. 830.

"burn in your mouth." Thanks to John Crouch for expert briefing on the way that domestic and international trade patterns impacted upon domestic diet in early-nineteenth-century Cumberland.

"describe her as a 'warehouseman.' " *Kelly's Post Office Directory,* London, 1841, p. 169.

"originally from Sussex." Petworth Parish Register, August 24, 1806, West Sussex. Census, 1841, Parish of Saint Mary Magdalen Milk Street.

"a small fortune." Administration of Benjamin Mayson's estate granted to Elizabeth Mayson, "the relict of the said Deceased," August 10, 1840, FRC.

36   "Revd. Mayson's reply." Mayson's reply has also been lost, but evidently at a much later date since Sarah Freeman saw the original document in the early 1970s.

" 'engage a curate.' " This was John Aldersey, Bishop's Register, July 27, 1842.

37   "prosperous farmer's wife." Administration of Revd. John Mayson's estate granted to Esther Burtholme, September 19, 1845, Cumbria.

"her own Benjamin." Twenty-nine-year-old Emily Dorling died on February 27, 1840, following "debility twelve days after her confinement," very probably caused by puerperal fever. Death registered March 6, 1840.

"sweetly romantic business." Copy of Gretna marriage certificate, MMB Archive.

38   "whisky, and gin." The itemized bill for the festivities was seen by both Nancy Spain and H. Montgomery Hyde, although they transcribed it slightly

differently. However, it seems to have disappeared by the time Sarah Freeman was researching her book in the early 1970s.

"seven and a half months later." Charlotte Emily Dorling was born on November 11, 1843.

"old-fashioned way." Marriage Licence Allegation, March 25, 1843.

"was temporarily living." St. Mary Islington Parish Register, March 27, 1843, LMA. The bride's father's name is incorrectly given as "William Jerram."

INTERLUDE

39 " 'The Free, Fair Homes of England.' " Felicia Hemans, *The Homes of England*, London, 1827.

41 "the required froth." IMB, ed., *BOHM*, 1861, p. 749.

  " 'task of rumination.' " Ibid., p. 320.

  "Harvest Festival supper." Ibid., p. 361; p. 523; p. 507; p. 543.

  "boilerman on a steamship." Ibid., p. 988; p. 1008.

42 "to the nation." Ibid., p. 830; p. 833.

CHAPTER TWO

43 " 'that may be counted in millions.' " Charles Dickens, "Epsom," *Household Words*, June 7, 1851. However, David Pascoe notes that W. H. Wills may have been responsible for some of the article, including this opening paragraph. David Pascoe, ed., *Charles Dickens, Selected Journalism, 1850–70*, London, 1997, p. 534.

44 " 'just throw them back.' " David Hunn, *Epsom Racecourse*, London, 1973, pp. 30–1, pp. 53–8; *Derby Day 200*, London, 1979, pp. 11–12, p. 71.

  "all the way to Epsom." E. E. Dorling, *Epsom and the Dorlings*, p. 61; James Andrews, *Reminiscences of Epsom*, Epsom, 1904, p. 32; *Derby Day 200*, p. 16.

  "spirit stalls." James Andrews, *Reminiscences*, p. 17.

46 "on his cob." Michael Seth-Smith and Roger Mortimer, *Derby 200*, Enfield, 1979, p. 28.

  "satisfactorily explain." *Derby Day 200*, p. 112.

  "that year's Derby." E. E. Dorling, *Epsom and the Dorlings*, p. 62.

  "protection for his family." James Andrews, *Reminiscences*, p. 30; David Hunn, *Epsom Racecourse*, p. 96.

  "down from London." For a selection of paintings showing the crowds on the road to the Derby, see *Derby Day 200*, pp. 13–16.

  "ninety distinct figures." H. Montgomery Hyde, *Mr. and Mrs. Beeton*, p. 27. I have not been able to locate this correspondence and it was never part of the MMB Archive.

47 "about their posh manners." W. P. Frith, *My Autobiography and Reminiscences*, London, 1890, p. 184.

  "wherever it went." *Derby Day 200*, p. 72. The painting has now come to rest in Tate Britain, London.

" 'all classes of society.' " *Illustrated London News* (hereafter *ILN*), June 3, 1843.

48 "to the Jockey Club." David Hunn, *Epsom Racecourse*, pp. 64–5.

"the fulsome tone." *Sporting Life*, March 29, 1873.

"quite have liked." David Hunn, *Epsom Racecourse*, p. 62.

49 "the Promised Land." E. E. Dorling, *Epsom and the Dorlings*, p. 27.

"and general store." Mrs. Brook's Account with L. Dorling, 1819, Brook Collection, Bexhill Museum. I take "L Dorling" to be William's wife, Lucy. Bexhill Poor Rate Book, 1810–21, East Sussex.

50 "Kent Fire Office." Advertisements for William Dorling's Library and Stationers, in the possession of Richard Dorling; *Pigot's Directory*, Surrey, 1828, p. 671.

" 'every likely point.' " *ILN*, June 4, 1859.

51 " 'shall be preserved.' " *Morning Chronicle*, April 12, 1830.

"paid off after all." David Hunn, *Epsom Racecourse*, p. 57.

52 "to see the race." Charles Dickens, "Epsom," p. 542.

"watchers in the Grandstand." Quoted in David Hunn, *Epsom Racecourse*, pp. 66–71; E. E. Dorling, *Epsom and the Dorlings*, pp. 82–7.

53 " 'convenient edifice.' " Quoted in David Hunn, *Epsom Racecourse*, p. 71.

"siphon off extra income." *Sporting Life*, March 29, 1873.

"pie on the Downs." The Grandstand and racecourse records are archived at Surrey History Service, Woking. Henry Dorling's personal and business papers have yet to come to light.

54 " 'colours of the riders!' " Charles Dickens, "Epsom," pp. 535–40.

"Jockey Club were concerned." William George Bentinck Dorling came into the world on January 27, 1846, just months after Dorling took over the running of the Grandstand. He died in 1880 in New Orleans, having emigrated to work in the American horse-racing industry.

" 'you have made it so.' " Nancy Spain, *Mrs. Beeton and her Husband*, p. 34.

55 "motherless Dorling children." Census, 1841, Parish of Epsom.

"a coach proprietor." Census, 1851, Parish of Epsom. Evidence from a letter written by Isabella in April 1856 suggests that "Mr. Woodruff" was a permanent paying guest rather than a chance visitor on the night of the 1851 census.

"been the case." Nancy Spain, *Mrs. Beeton and her Husband*, p. 35. Spain, armed with information from her grandmother Lucy and great-aunt Amy, hints that Henry Mayson, Edward, Jane and Mary Dorling resented the fact that their father treated his step-children on equal terms. Splitting the Dorling fortune seventeen ways was bad enough, but dividing it into twenty-one portions may have seemed over-generous.

56 "very long lives." Henry Dorling, Will, July 3, 1871, Administration, April 3, 1873.

"his teenage son." While Nancy Spain refers to Alfred being sent away to sea at the age of thirteen, it is Sarah Freeman who supplies the reason, Isabella and Sam, p. 38.

58 " 'fighting our children.' " David Hunn, *Epsom Racecourse*, p. 78.

59 " 'a parent can bestow.' " IMB, ed., *BOHM*, 1861, p. 17.

"portable than buildings." The 1851 census shows William living at the post office in the High Street with daughter Lucy, son-in-law William Andrews, their two children and a single servant.

" 'to gossip with her.' " Letter, IMB to Samuel Beeton (hereafter SOB) [February? 22, 1856].

"calm of Ormond House." Letter, IMB to SOB, May 26, 1856.

"the position of clerk." Letter, IMB to SOB [April? 4, 1856]. Henry Dorling took up the position of clerk to Brighton racecourse in 1851. This was the only clerkship he held alongside that of Epsom.

60   "during the holidays." Sarah Freeman, *Isabella and Sam*, p. 36.

" 'Mr. Dorling to the Derby.' " *ILN*, June 4, 1859.

" 'could have it to *Herself*.' " David Hunn, *Epsom Racecourse*, p. 100.

" 'the Misses Dorling.' " Ibid., pp. 83–4.

62   " 'mixing the salad!' " Charles Dickens, "Epsom," p. 540.

"and shrill screams." Nancy Spain, *Why I'm Not a Millionaire*, p. 87.

63   "knitting furiously." Nancy Spain, *Mrs. Beeton and her Husband*, p. 40.

"Cuthbert John Hopkins." Thanks to Jeremy Harte, curator of Bourne Hall Museum, Ewell.

64   "in her eighties." "Bertha," "Our Ladies' Letter."

"move to Epsom." This is the address Elizabeth gave to the parish clerk when she married Henry Dorling in March 1843.

65   "Miss Mary Richardson." From 1828 to 1844 Revd. Robert Simson ran Colebrooke House Academy out of 1 Colebrooke Row, a property that he owned outright. The Misses Richardson seem to have been family friends who originally lodged with Simson and his wife before setting up a girls' school at the same address. By 1851 the school was being run by the Woodhouse sisters, although the property still belonged to Revd. Simson. *Post Office Directories*, London, 1843–51; Census, 1841, Parish of Islington. Land Tax Assessment, Parish of Islington, 1843; Church Rates, Parish of Islington, 1840, 1843; Electoral Register, King's Cross Polling District, 1852, all LMA.

"Mary and Charlotte." Census, 1851, Parish of Islington.

"the same address." *Post Office Directories*, London, 1845–9.

66   " 'laughing about nothing.' " *EDM*, vol. 1, June 1852.

" 'Mr. Young's, Walbrook.' " *The Times*, September 28, 1850.

"finish until 5 p.m." Information supplied by Petra Nellen, whose chapter "Der lange Weg von der Magdleinschule zur Universität" in *Die Vergangenheit ist die Schwester der Zukunft*, Heidelberg, 1996, draws on the information Miss Heidel gave when she applied to the city for official status in 1837. Thanks to Stephen Smithson for translation.

"fifteen and a half." Since the register has not survived, it is impossible to be certain about when and for how long Isabella attended school in Heidelberg. Summer 1851 to summer 1854 remains the best guess.

67   "time and money." From Sam and Isabella's letters for the first half of 1856 it is clear that chaperoning British boys and girls to their schools in continental Europe put a strain on middle-class British families of modest means.

" 'best love' to Isabella." Letter, Esther Mayson to IMB, March 8, 1857.

"honey and chocolate." Letter, SOB to IMB, [February? 1856].

68 "paid the rent." Clive Brown, "Julius Benedict 1804–1855," *Oxford Dictionary of National Biography* (hereafter *DNB*), Oxford, 2004.

69 "virtually in parallel." George Eliot, *Middlemarch* (London 1871–2), London, 2003, p. 243, pp. 832–4.

70 " 'not quite nice.' " Lucy Smiles, "The Great Mrs. Beeton By Her Sister."

INTERLUDE

71 " 'of its management.' " IMB, ed., *BOHM,* 1861, p. 19.
    "will give you." Ibid., p. 8.

72 "iconic *Self-Help.*" Samuel Smiles, *Self-Help: with illustrations of Character and Conduct*, London, 1859.
    " 'every station in life.' " Ibid., Oxford, 2002, p. 10.

73 "went hungry." Sarah Freeman, *Isabella and Sam,* p. 49.

CHAPTER THREE

74 "went to get their mead." Caroline Gordon and Wilfrid Dewhirst, *The Ward of Cripplegate in the City of London,* London, 1985, p. 29.
    "as any village." David Kynaston, *The City of London,* 2 vols., London, 1994, vol. 1, p. 29.

75 "cheap and easy kindling." Caroline Gordon and Wilfrid Dewhirst, *The Ward of Cripplegate,* p. 29.
    "West End." David Kynaston, *The City of London,* vol. 1, p. 25.
    "live and trade." Francis Sheppard, *London 1808–1870: The Infernal Wen,* London, 1971, p. 85.
    "a pre-industrial age." Roy Porter, *London: A Social History,* London, 1994, ch. 8.
    "private bankers." Martin Daunton, "London and the World," in Celina Fox, ed., *London, World City, 1800–1840,* London, 1992, p. 21.

76 "waitresses and potboys." Brian Harrison, "London Pubs" in H. J. Dyos and M. Wolff, eds., *The Victorian City,* 2 vols., London, 1973, vol. 1, p. 161. For more on the subject, see Mark Girouard, *Victorian Pubs,* London, 1975.

77 "the afternoon's work." J. L. Garvin and Julian Amery, *The Life of Joseph Chamberlain,* 6 vols., London, 1932–69, vol. 1, p. 39.
    "cobbling and clothing trades." In the autumn of 1803 the Beetons were living in Cow Lane, Company of Patten-makers, Entry of Freedom Commencing 1801, October 12, 1803, Guildhall. By the summer of 1807 they had shifted a few hundred yards to Copice Row, St. Sepulchre Parish Register, May 19, 1807, Guildhall.

78 " 'confounded the senses.' " Charles Dickens, *Oliver Twist* (London, 1837–9), London, 2002, p. 203.
    "the tailors." Company of Patten-makers, Entry of Freedom Commencing 1801, October 12, 1803.

"at adjoining Newgate." G. H. Salter, *A Watcher at the City Gate,* London, 1956, p. 42.

"left it soon afterwards." There is no further trace of Ann Thomason after her baptism at St. Sepulchre on May 19, 1807.

"rich for their pockets." Charles Fitch, *History of the Pattenmakers' Company,* Bungay, 1926, pp. 95–6.

79 "Dolphin in Milk Street." The Beetons baptized Lucy at St. Sepulchre, even though they were now living at "39, Milk Street." St. Sepulchre Parish Register, May 13, 1808.

"it so desperately needed." Roy Porter, *London,* p. 243.

"to His Majesty." Minutes of the Proceedings of the Ward of Cripplegate Within, Court of Common Council of the City of London, 1813–28, Guildhall.

" 'Edward Albert.' " Victoria Beeton was born in 1838, followed by Edward Albert Beeton in 1842.

" 'unceasing perseverance.' " Nancy Spain, *Mrs. Beeton and her Husband,* p. 48. This snuffbox was last seen in 1990 when it was in the possession of Rodney Levick. It has since disappeared. Information from Lucy Lunt.

80 "the substantial Yorkshire Grey." Letter from H. R. Beeton to MMB, April 12, 1920. See also notes summarizing correspondence between H. C. Beeton and H. R. Beeton which confirm that the Yorkshire Grey was bought with money lent to Robert Beeton by his uncle Samuel, both MMB Archive, family.

"Robert Francis." Samuel Powell was a strapping eight and a half years when he was baptized, while Robert Francis was a mere eight and a half months.

"Cripplegate Ward." Company of Patten-makers, Entry of Freedom Commencing 1801, January 30, 1827; Minutes of Ward of Cripplegate Within, 1838.

"(his affiliation was Liberal)." *The Times,* January 3, 1835.

"Wood Street." All Hallows Bread Street Parish Register, April 21, 1830, Guildhall.

"the brewing trade." Ibid., April 5, 1831.

81 "very ill indeed." Roy Porter, *London,* p. 260.

"sleeping peacefully." L. C. B. Seaman, *Life in Victorian London,* 1973, p. 36.

"still passed for country." The Chamberlains at 36 would make the same shift to Camberwell in a few years' time.

"and his wife 'Eleanor.' " Camberwell Parish Register, September 14, 1834, LMA.

"only eight weeks later." St. Alban Wood Street Parish Register, December 5, 1832, Guildhall.

"her firstborn, Samuel Orchart." This insistence that Samuel Beeton inherited TB from his mother was woven so strongly into his personal mythology that it even cropped up in the obituaries that followed his death in 1877. See, for instance, that which appeared in the *London Figaro,* June 16, 1877, written by someone who identified himself as a close friend of Beeton, probably A. A. Dowty.

"in 1834." Marriage Licence Allegation, September 22, 1834.

"in the pub." Both women are described as "FS" or "female servant" rather than "sister-in-law." Census, 1841, Parish of St. Mary Magdalen Milk Street.

82   "lodged at the Dolphin." Maria Brown married Thomas Beeton on April 2, 1858, a good seven years after she had first lodged alongside him at the Dolphin.

"as a bell." Census, 1841, Parish of Hadleigh. The household consisted of Lucy, her youngest daughter Caroline, five-year-old Eliza and one servant. Sam must have been away at school on the night the census was taken.

83   "for extra policing." W. A. B. Jones, *Hadleigh through the Ages*, Ipswich, 1977, ch. 9.

"had pull." Samuel Beeton, Will, February 15, 1834, Administration, March 17, 1836.

"farmer called Robert Kersey." Aunt Carrie married Mr. Kersey in 1848 and became, for a while at least, "Aunt Kersey."

"make it into the Guards." *ILN*, December 30, 1843.

"over the age of fifteen." Census, 1841, Parish of South Weald.

84   "dead languages." *Chelmsford Chronicle*, January 19, 1838; Census, 1841, Parish of South Weald.

"Louis Morell." Census, 1851, Parish of South Weald, Essex.

"every Sunday morning." Diocesan Board of Education Returns, 1839, Parish of South Weald.

"work in French." Everything about Samuel Beeton's adult life and career suggests that he was at ease in French. However, it has not been possible to verify Nancy Spain's anecdote about this book prize. Nancy Spain, *Mrs. Beeton and her Husband*, p. 49.

"clever chess games." Letters, SOB to Orchart Beeton and MMB, April 28 to July 17, 1874.

"going on to university." It has not been possible to verify the gift of a *Complete Shakespeare*, which is reported by Nancy Spain in *Mrs. Beeton and her Husband*, p. 49. Even if, by some odd fluke, Sam had made it to Oxford or Cambridge he would not of course have been able to read for an English degree since no such thing existed.

85   "gulping down a chop." For a vivid, first-person account of London's burgeoning print industry in the early Victorian period see David Masson, *Memories of London in the Forties*, London, 1908.

"Victuallers' committee meetings." Society of Licensed Victuallers Minute Book, 1821.

"bowels of the City." For more on the paper, print and publishing industry of the early nineteenth century see: Ellic Howe, *From Craft to Industry*, London, 1946; D. C. Coleman, *The British Paper Industry 1495–1860*, Oxford, 1958; David Platzker and Elizabeth Wyckoff, *Hard Pressed: 600 Years of Print and Process*, New York, 2000; Andrew King and John Plunkett, eds., *Popular Print Media, 1820–1900*, London, 2004; Ian Haywood, *The Revolution in Popular Literature: Print, Politics and the Press*, Cambridge, 2004.

86   "in a wholesale stationery firm." Census, 1851, Parish of Hackney.

" 'paper without end.' " Letter, SOB to IMB, October 11, [18]64.

"a publisher's reader." A. J. A. Morris, "Frederick Greenwood 1830–1909," *Oxford DNB.*

"imprint of S. O. Beeton." The work for which James Greenwood is best known is "The Amateur Casual," an essay in which he described the experience of spending the night in a Lambeth workhouse.

87   " 'to the good.' " Quoted in J. W. Robertson Scott, *The Story of the Pall Mall Gazette,* London, 1950, pp. 113–14.

"around the village pump." Ibid., p. 114.

" 'read books enough.' " Letter, SOB to Orchart Beeton, July 9, 1874.

88   "didn't want company." J. W. Robertson Scott, *The Story of the Pall Mall Gazette,* p. 116.

" 'began life too soon.' " Nancy Spain, *Mrs. Beeton and her Husband,* p. 50.

"the infamous window." H. Montgomery Hyde, *Mr. and Mrs. Beeton,* p. 30.

89   "freelance operators." For more on Victorian prostitution, see Judith Walkowitz, *Prostitution and Victorian Society: Women, Class and the State,* Cambridge, 1980.

"their vital teens and twenties." E. M. Sigsworth and T. J. Wyke, "A Study of Victorian Prostitution and Venereal Disease," in Martha Vicinus, ed., *Suffer and Be Still,* Indiana, 1972, pp. 85–6.

"he had sprung." It is impossible to trace exactly how money from Helen Orchart Beeton would have passed to her son. Her wealthy father predeceased her by six months, and his will leaves everything to her only brother, Thomas Davidson Orchart. However, the fact that Samuel Beeton and Samuel Powell Beeton are two of Orchart's executors in July 1832 suggests that they were integrated into his business affairs (Orchart had, after all, had an earlier financial interest in the Dolphin). When Samuel Powell Beeton died in 1854 he left two houses in Wood Street to Samuel Orchart Beeton, while the children of his second marriage received only £500 each in cash. This suggests that Helen Orchart brought the Wood Street houses with her as part of her marriage settlement in 1830. Did she also bring some capital, and was it this money that was used to set up Samuel Orchart's partnership with Charles H. Clarke?

90   "to sell at 2s 6d." Henry Vizetelly, *Glances Back through Seventy Years,* 2 vols., London, 1893, vol. 1, p. 359.

"a thousand copies a week." There are four distinct versions of what happened when *Uncle Tom* was first published in Britain. Vizetelly's version can be found in his autobiography, *Glances Back,* which is itself a repeat of an earlier essay. Clarke and Co. and Sampson Low both provided Charles Edward Stowe, Harriet's son, with slightly variant versions which he reproduced in his biography of his mother, *Life of Harriet Beecher Stowe,* London, 1889, pp. 189–92. Frederick Greenwood, meanwhile, gave a fourth version of events in a piece he wrote for the *Tatler,* December 4, 1901. The print runs, costings and consequences vary significantly depending on who is telling the story.

"7s 6d." I am indebted to the expert help of Major Christopher Beeton, who holds what must be the largest indexed archive of books published by S. O. Beeton in the world.

"British copyright." Henry Vizetelly, *Glances Back,* vol. 1, pp. 189–91; Frederick Greenwood, "Uncle Tom's Cabin: Its First Appearance in England," *Tatler,* December 4, 1901.

91 "point of her work at all." Transcript of letter, Harriet Beecher Stowe to "Mr. Beaton," September 27, [1852]. Two letters from Harriet Beecher Stowe were originally in the MMB Archive, along with a later letter from Harriet Martineau. However, these three originals have disappeared, leaving only the transcripts. In view of the celebrity of the authors, it seems likely that these were sold off separately at some point to raise cash.

"promise, or obligation." Ibid.

"sequel to *Uncle Tom.*" Edward Marston, *After Work: Fragments from the Workshop of an Old Publisher,* London, 1904, p. 60.

92 "phenomenal popular success." Charles Edward Stowe, *Harriet Beecher Stowe,* p. 188.

"abiding dislike of the cocky upstart." Vizetelly claimed that he had scared Sam into giving him a payment of £500 in order to avoid further legal complications. Henry Vizetelly, *Glances Back,* vol. 1, p. 360.

" 'into speedy liquidation.' " Henry Vizetelly, *Glances Back,* vol. 1, p. 361. That Vizetelly was truly bitter about his near miss with *Uncle Tom* is suggested by the fact that he took exception to the claim made in an obituary of S. O. Beeton that it was young Beeton who had been the first person to spot the book's potential for the British market. "Permit me to inform you that Mr. Beeton had no connection with the repeating of that work in England until some hundreds of thousands of copies of it had been sold, and its success was a matter of public notoriety," explained Vizetelly tartly in a letter to the *London Figaro,* June 17, 1877.

93 "would emerge vindicated." *The Times,* February 6, 1857.

"Wendell Holmes, and Longfellow." Letter, Harriet Beecher Stowe to SOB, undated, transcript. *London Figaro,* June 16, 1877.

" 'receipts in America.' " Harriet Beecher Stowe, *Uncle Tom's Cabin* (London, 1852), London, 1853, Preface.

"payment of £500." *Beeton's Dictionary of Universal Information,* 2 vols., London, 1861, vol. 1, p. 118. This anecdote was then repeated by Frederic Boase in his influential *Modern English Biography,* 6 vols., Truro, 1892–1921, vol. 1, p. 222. Much was also made of it in Sam's obituary, probably written by A. A. Dowty, which appeared in the *London Figaro,* June 16, 1877.

INTERLUDE

94 " 'sometimes adulterated.' " IMB, ed., *BOHM,* 1861, p. 299.

95 "40 per cent extra profit." For a classic account of food adulteration in the 1850s see John Burnett, *Plenty and Want,* London, 1966, ch. 10.

" 'impregnated with poisonous particles.' " IMB, ed., *BOHM,* 1861, p. 32.

" 'too severely reprobated.' " Ibid.

96 " 'their freshness for years.' " Ibid., p. 299.

CHAPTER FOUR

98   "the Licensed Victuallers' School." H. Montgomery Hyde, *Mr. and Mrs. Beeton,* pp. 16–17. Thoroughbred Heritage website, *www.tbheritage.com. News of the World,* April 5, 1851.

"lesser Epsom meetings." Ibid., April 5; November 9, 1851.

"other in Suffolk." William Dorling, son of Jonathan and Elizabeth, was born in Ipswich in 1775. Even today Cambridgeshire and Suffolk are richly stocked with Beetons and Dorlings.

"his habitual cigars." On April? 16, 1856, Isabella refers to Sam's "resolution of not smoking." A letter from his half-sister Nelly a year later, however, suggests that on that occasion he failed. Helen Beeton to IMB, March 8, 1857.

99   "what she meant by it." Letter, SOB to IMB [February? 1856].

" 'BELLA MAYSON.' " Letters, IMB to SOB, December 26, 1855; IMB to SOB, June 22, 1856.

" 'my own precious one.' " Letter, IMB to SOB, June 1, 1856.

100   " 'feel very jolly.' " Letter, SOB to IMB [April? 12, 1856].

" 'my own Bella!' " Letter, SOB to IMB [June? 6, 1856].

" 'most excellent abilities.' " Letter, SOB to IMB [May? 2, 1856].

"a happy distraction." Samuel Powell Beeton had died unexpectedly in the summer of 1854, thus rendering Samuel Orchart an orphan at the age of twenty-three. Might a sense of sudden vulnerability have pushed Sam into making what was, by the standards of the day, an early marriage?

101   " *'sister-in-law.'* " Letter, Helen Beeton to IMB, March 8, 1857.

"solemn joy." James Hayllar, *The Only Daughter,* undated, now hanging in the Forbes Collection, Old Battersea House, London.

"been barely twenty." Isaac Jerrom, "the natural and lawful father of the said minor," had been required to give his consent before the marriage licence could be granted. Marriage Licence Allegation, April 30, 1835.

"their wedding plans." Letter, IMB to SOB, June 13, 1856.

" 'wondrous kind.' " Letter, SOB to IMB [June? 17, 1856].

" 'dear Sam.' " Letter, IMB to SOB [February? 22, 1856].

102   "lawyer and doctor respectively." Jane Dorling married the solicitor George White, while her sister Mary married Dr. Edmund Willett.

"women in the street." *The Times,* May 31, 1842.

"hard labour." I am indebted to Isobel Sutton for details about her great-grandfather Edward Albert and, indeed, for her path-finding research into Beeton family history.

"typically, in court." See pp. 315–16.

103   " 'those stamped affairs.' " Letter, IMB to SOB, January 3, 1856.

" 'approbation or thunders.' " Letter, SOB to IMB [June 1856].

"Great Man of Epsom." Letter, SOB to IMB [April? 6, 1856].

" 'care about racing.' " Letter, IMB to SOB [April? 10, 1856].

104   "vote of confidence." Letter, IMB to SOB [February? 22, 1856].

107   "nervously in late April." Letter, SOB to IMB [April? 23, 1856].

" 'on my poor account.' " Letter, SOB to IMB [May? 27, 1856].

"bound to hurt." Letter, SOB to IMB [April? 6, 1856]. Letter, IMB to SOB [April? 16, 1856].

"went on holiday." Letters, IMB to SOB, January 12, 1856 [misdated 1855]; IMB to SOB, January 3, 1856.

"kind of purgatory." Internal evidence from the letters and postmarks suggests that Sam spent some time in Soham, Cambridgeshire, as well as visiting his grandmother and Aunt Kersey in Hadleigh and possibly Isabella's Uncle Edward (Henry Dorling's younger brother) and wife Elizabeth in Ipswich too.

" 'to enjoy ourselves.' " Letter, IMB to SOB, December 26, 1855.

108   " 'because so unexpected.' " Ibid.

" 'agreeable to me before.' " Letter, IMB to SOB, December 31, 1855.

" 'which exactly suited me.' " Ibid.; letter, IMB to SOB, December 31, 1855; January 3, 1856.

"Beetons in Mile End." Letter, IMB to SOB, December 31, 1855.

" 'what you are doing.' " Ibid.

109   "young man about town." Letter, IMB to SOB, January 3, 1856.

" 'I for one have.' " Ibid.

"unlikely this was." Letter, IMB to SOB, January 8, 1856.

" 'Tuesday, Jan[uar]y 15th.' " Ibid.

110   " 'refuse to come.' " Letter, IMB to SOB, January 12, 1856.

"both visited regularly." Letter, IMB to SOB, May 8, 1856.

111   "knowing their business." Letter, IMB to SOB, December 31, 1855.

" 'account for it?' " Letter, IMB to SOB [April? 25, 1856].

" 'Manor House.' " Letter, SOB to IMB, December 31, 1855.

112   "down to Brighton." The Dorlings had a house at 72 Marine Parade, Brighton, near to the racecourse.

"domestic duties intervened." On February 4, 1932, Lucy Dorling (now Smiles) dashed off a letter to *The Times* in response to Florence White's piece on "The Real Mrs. Beeton": "Sir,-I feel compelled to add to your notice of my sister, Mrs. Beeton in *The Times* of February 3 that she was an accomplished pianist, educated in Heidelberg, and later was a pupil of Sir Julius Benedict." *Times*, February 6, 1932.

" 'to come up.' " Letter, IMB to SOB, December 31, 1857.

"fiddle with embroidery." Letters, IMB to SOB, January 12, 1856; IMB to SOB, May 8, 1856; IMB to SOB [January? 20, 1856].

" 'rather hard lines.' " Letters, IMB to SOB [April? 16, 1856]; IMB to SOB, May 3, 1856.

" 'so much about me.' " Letter, IMB to SOB, June 22, 1856.

113   "dated in full." Letter, IMB to SOB, May 8, 1856.

"by their neediness." Letters, IMB to SOB, May 3, 1856; IMB to SOB [April? 10, 1856].

"that she is 'soft.' " Letters, IMB to SOB, June 13, 1856; IMB to SOB, January 3, 1856; IMB to SOB, May 26, 1856; IMB to SOB, December 31, 1855.

" 'next Sabbath Day.' " Letter, SOB to IMB [April? 23, 1856].

" 'this morning.' " Letter, SOB to IMB [April? 12, 1856].

" 'disagreeably desolate.' " Ibid.

" 'namby pamby nonsense.' " Letters, IMB to SOB [April? 4]; SOB to IMB, January 31, 1856.

114 " 'please don't disappoint.' " Letter, IMB to SOB [January? 20, 1856].

" 'before this.' " Letter, SOB to IMB, January 31, 1856.

"love with her." Ibid.

" 'very glad.' " Ibid.

115 " 'so very formidable.' " Letter, IMB to SOB [February? 22, 1856].

" 'stubborn things.' " Letter, IMB to SOB [April? 4, 1856].

" 'or even one?' " Letter, SOB to IMB [April? 6, 1856].

" 'arrangements for Sunday.' " Letter, IMB to SOB [April? 10, 1856].

" 'pleasure of your company.' " Letter, IMB to SOB [April? 12, 1856].

116 " 'by annoying you.' " Letter, SOB to IMB [April? 12, 1856].

" 'sparing of your company.' " Letter, IMB to SOB [April? 16, 1856].

117 "visit it with him?" Letter, SOB to IMB [April? 23, 1856].

" 'for the train to-morrow.' " Letter, IMB to SOB [April? 25, 1856].

" 'disappointed in *me*.' " Ibid.

" 'and many kisses.' " Letter, IMB to SOB, May 2, 1856.

118 " 'affectionately S. O. Beeton.' " This crucial letter remains undated, but it seems most likely that it was written around May 1, 1856. Working out an exact sequence is made more complicated by the fact that on occasions when feelings ran high Isabella's and Sam's letters overlapped.

" 'will be the consequence.' " Letter, IMB to SOB, May 3, 1856.

119 " 'as soon as perused.' " Letter, IMB to SOB, May 26, 1856.

120 " 'consider it not there.' " Letter, SOB to IMB [May? 2, 1856].

" 'do on Sunday alone.' " Letter, SOB to IMB [June? 14, 1856].

121 " 'Adieu.' " Letter, IMB to SOB, June 16, 1856.

" 'at his stepping?' " Letter, SOB to IMB [June? 17, 1856].

122 "he truly loves." Ibid.

" 'S. O. Beeton.' " Ibid.

INTERLUDE

123 " 'substantial kind.' " IMB, ed., *BOHM*, 1861, p. 959.

124 "saved on servants." Ibid., p. 956.

"marmalade and butter." Ibid., p. 959.

125 " 'for luncheon.' " Ibid.

"finished her 'lunch.' " For more information on this whole topic see C. Anne Wilson, ed., *Luncheon, Nuncheon and Other Meals*, Stroud, 1994.

CHAPTER FIVE

126 "from Ormond House." Letter, SOB to IMB [May? 2, 1856].

" 'not at home.' " Letter, IMB to SOB, June 3, 1856.

127 " 'affecting a combat.' " Letter, SOB to IMB [June? 1856].
"physical convulsion." Quoted in Sarah Freeman, *Isabella and Sam*, p. 125.
" 'your dear welfare.' " Letter, SOB to IMB [May? 27, 1856].
" 'maiden of twenty.' " Letter, IMB to SOB, June 1, 1856.
" 'very rude girl.' " Letter, IMB to SOB, May 3, 1856.
" 'for our affair.' " Letter, IMB to SOB, June 22, 1856.
" 'hug you to pieces.' " Letter, IMB to SOB, June 13, 1856.

128 " 'am I not, darling?' " Letter, SOB to IMB [June 17, ?1856].
" 'excitement of the dancers.' " Letter, SOB to IMB [February? 1856].
" 'I yearn immensely.' " Letter, SOB to IMB [June? 1856].
" 'boy for going.' " Letter, SOB to IMB [February? 1856].
" 'on this point.' " Letter, SOB to IMB [May? 27, 1856].

129 " 'case may be.' " Letter, IMB to SOB, June 3, 1856.

130 " 'wish for recovery.' " Letter, IMB to SOB [June 20, 1856].
"been sent out." Letter, IMB to SOB, June 17, 1856.
"the Crimean fireworks." Letter, IMB to SOB, May 28, 1856.
" 'less of self.' " Letter, SOB to IMB [May? 27, 1856].

131 " 'I see you.' " Letter, IMB to SOB, June 3, 1856.
"than the 10th." Letter, IMB to SOB, June 20, 1856.
" 'to be very strong.' " Letter, IMB to SOB, June 22, 1856.
" 'most delicate nature.' " Letter, IMB to SOB, May 8, 1856.
"and so forth." Phillis Cunnington and Catherine Lucas, *Costumes for Births, Marriages and Deaths*, London, 1972, pp. 280–1.
"the dress itself." Letter, Charlotte MacMahon to MMB, 1918.
"own unique design." Lucy Smiles, "The Great Mrs. Beeton."

132 "look suitably smart." Letter, IMB to SOB, June 16, 1856.
" 'for the occasion.' " Letter, SOB to IMB [May? 27, 1856].
" 'what he is thinking about, &c. &c. &c.' " Letter, IMB to SOB, June 22, 1856.
"new-fangled veil." Lucy Smiles, "The Great Mrs. Beeton"; letter, Charlotte MacMahon to MMB, 1918.
"with three tiered skirts." There is some confusion over which bridesmaids wore mauve and which wore green. Lucy says that there were three of each; a late May letter from Sam suggests that his sisters (how many is not clear) wore green. However, it looks as though there were four Mayson-Dorling senior bridesmaids and only two Beetons. This suggests that seventy-four-year-old Lucy's memory may have been blurred, and that there were four bridesmaids in mauve and two in green.

133 "her first corn." Lucy Smiles, "The Great Mrs. Beeton."
"lavender doeskin." Ann Monsarrat, *And the Bride Wore*, London, 1973, p. 206.
" 'fringed parasols.' " Lucy Smiles, "The Great Mrs. Beeton."
"at the Grandstand." John Mayson, letter, *The Times*, December 15, 1864.
"enthused to Sam." Letter, IMB to SOB, May 8, 1856.

135 " 'Step-Grandfather W. Dorling.' " Letter, William Dorling to IMB, July 1856.

"married life together." Lucy Smiles, "The Great Mrs. Beeton."

"little more than slums." For more on the Victorian suburb see H. J. Dyos and D. A. Reader, "Slums and Suburbs," in H. J. Dyos and M. Wolff, eds., *The Victorian City*, vol. 1, ch. 15; F. M. L. Thompson, "The Rise of Suburbia," in R. J. Morris and Richard Rodger, eds., *The Victorian City: A Reader in British Urban History 1820–1914*, London, 1993; Richard Rodger, *Housing in Urban Britain 1780–1914: Class, Capitalism and Construction*, Basingstoke, 1989.

136 " 'that smoky London.' " Letter, Helen Beeton to IMB, March 8, 1857.

"called Hatch End." See Patricia Clarke, "The Lost Suburb of Woodridings," *Pinner Local History Newsletter*, August 1982.

" 'a rural district.' " Richard Field, *Country Advantages, or, Pinner, within Harrow, Middlesex: Woodriding's Estate*, London, 1855.

"a stinking business." Vestry Minutes for Pinner, 1871, LMA.

" 'and knows nothing.' " Richard Field, *Country Advantages*.

"season ticket to London." There remains a mystery over the length of time of Sam's free rail travel. In general, developers matched miles from London with length of season ticket, which would mean that those living at Woodridings should have enjoyed thirteen free years. However, it is clear from a letter Sam wrote to Isabella, probably on April 6, 1856, that his ticket was valid for only seven, which was also the standard length of a lease on a domestic property.

"£200 a year." Richard Field, *Country Advantages*.

137 "closed for good." Thanks to Dr. Christopher Tyerman, archivist of Harrow School, for an expert briefing on the Lyon Statutes.

138 "water and oil lighting." Information from Patricia Clarke of the Pinner Local History Society.

"War Office." Census, 1861, Parish of Harrow.

"family's annual income." IMB, ed., *BOHM*, 1861, p. 20.

" 'as a fire.' " Ibid., p. 19.

139 " 'up to the mark.' " Letter, SOB to IMB [April? 12, 1856].

" 'breakfast this morning.' " Ibid.

"digging the borders." Letter, SOB to IMB [April? 4, 1856].

140 " 'very desirable at Pinner.' " Letter, IMB to SOB [April? 12, 1856].

" 'vegetable Marrow plant.' " Letter, SOB to IMB [June? 6, 1856].

"show the carpenter." Letter, SOB to IMB [April? 23, 1856].

" 'with me to-morrow.' " Letter, IMB to SOB [April? 25, 1856].

" 'petit dinners.' " Letter, SOB to IMB [June? 1856].

" 'and other matters.' " Letter, SOB to IMB [April? 12, 1856].

" 'hard up for beds.' " Letter, SOB to IMB [June? 6, 1856].

"hanging on the walls." Letter, SOB to IMB [May? 27, 1856].

" 'all wide open.' " Letter, SOB to IMB [June? 6, 1856].

" 'chimney will smoke.' " IMB, ed., *BOHM*, 1861, p. 20.

141 " 'legs of the inmates.' " Ibid.

" 'cannot be over-rated.' " Ibid., pp. 19–20.

" 'be deemed objectionable.' " Ibid., p. 2.

" 'on 1st floor.' " Letter, SOB to IMB [June? 6, 1856].

" *'very reasonable.'* " Letter, IMB to SOB [April? 16, 1856].

" 'actually no.' " Letter, SOB to IMB [April? 23, 1856].

142 " 'Milk St. division.' " Letter, SOB to IMB [May? 27, 1856].

"in early August." Letter, SOB to IMB [June? 17, 1856].

" 'speaks from experience.' " Letter, IMB to SOB [April? 16, 1856].

" 'in the winter.' " Ibid.

" 'for the country.' " Letter, IMB to SOB, June 17, 1856.

" 'with them at all.' " Letter, SOB to IMB [June? 17, 1856].

143 " 'suit you best.' " Letter, IMB to SOB, June 22, 1856.

" 'peace and quietude!' " Letter, SOB to IMB [April? 23, 1856].

" 'for a continuance.' " Letter, SOB to IMB [April? 12, 1856].

"housemaid, and nursemaid." IMB, ed., *BOHM*, 1861, p. 8.

"possibly Mr. Scott." Lucy Smiles, "The Great Mrs. Beeton."

"Anne Green." Census, 1861, Parish of Harrow.

144 "fuel supplies." IMB, ed., *BOHM*, 1861, p. 23.

" 'plate-warmer attached.' " Ibid., p. 27.

145 " 'price £1 1s?' " *Boy's Own Magazine* (hereafter *BOM*), June 1856.

146 "on the Continent." Letter, SOB to IMB [June? 1856].

" 'at Heidelberg.' " Letter, SOB to Frederick Weaklin, July 25, 1856.

147 " 'Fredk Weaklin.' " Letter, Frederick Weaklin to Thomas Beeton, October 10, 1881.

INTERLUDE

148 " 'carving it well.' " IMB, ed., *BOHM*, 1861, p. 506.

149 "colour illustration." Ibid., p. 667.

" 'found the best.' " Ibid., p. 506.

" 'liked and relished.' " Ibid.

CHAPTER SIX

151 "casualty of childbirth." Anne Addison died on July 13, 1856, at the age of thirty-two, just two days after giving birth to her second son Jeremiah.

"hope of marriage." The classic and alarming articulation of this phenomenon came from William Rathbone Greg, "Why are women redundant?," *National Review,* April 1862.

152 "on the eccentric." Aileen Smiles, *Samuel Smiles and His Surroundings,* London, 1956, p. 129.

" 'grandchildren and all.' " Letter, Jane White to Lucy Smiles, October 21, 1928.

"before the wedding." Letter, IMB to SOB, June 22, 1856.

153 "the wanderer's return." Lucy Smiles, "The Great Mrs. Beeton."

"poor Bella." Ibid.

"angry chatter." Nancy Spain's account, which appears in *Mrs. Beeton and her Husband*, pp. 121–2, is clearly based on Lucy's piece in the *Star*, but was presumably supplemented by subsequent conversations with her late grandmother.

154 *"How to Get Money."* The original title of this classic by the American Edwin Troxell Freedly had been *A practical treatise on Business: or, how to get, save, give, lend and bequeath money*, Philadelphia, 1852.

155 " 'S. O. Beeton.' " *BOM*, January to March, 1856.
"people he employed." Despite the careful archiving of so many British publishers' records over the past ten years, no trace has yet been found of Beeton's operations before 1874.

156 " 'how could I do it better?' " This is the question that continues to stand at the heart of "Femail," the highly successful women's section of the *Daily Mail* and the *Mail on Sunday*. So it is a nice coincidence that Bouverie Street would actually become the home of the *Daily Mail* for a lengthy stretch of the twentieth century. Telling, too, is the fact that Sam and Isabella's younger son Mayson Beeton forged his career and reputation at the *Daily Mail* under the guidance of his great friend Lord Northcliffe, for whom he went scouting in Canada for, of all things, paper. There was no escaping the Beeton inheritance.
"Ladies' Companion." My discussion of these early ladies' journals is indebted to the following classic sources: Margaret Beetham, *A Magazine of her Own?*, London, 1996; Alison Adburgham, *Women in Print, Writing Women and Women's Magazines from the Restoration to the Accession of Queen Victoria*, London, 1972; Cynthia L. White, *Women's Magazines, 1693–1968*, London, 1970.

157 " 'management of the family.' " Margaret Beetham, *A Magazine of her Own?*, p. 27.
" 'a young French nobleman.' " *La Belle Assemblée*, Second Series, vol. 27, March 1823.

158 " 'Education for Females.' " *Ladies' Monthly Museum*, vol. 23, April 1826.
"more fantastic fiction." See Sally Mitchell, "The Forgotten Woman of the Period: Penny Weekly Family Magazines of the 1840s and 1850s," in Martha Vicinus, ed., *A Widening Sphere: Changing Roles of Victorian Women*, Indiana, 1977.

159 " 'concisely as possible.' " [R. K. Philp], *Family Friend*, 1852, Preface.

160 "falls from grace." [Bessie Rayner Parkes], "The Profession of the Teacher. The Annual Reports of the Governesses' Benevolent Institution, from 1843 to 1856," *English Woman's Journal*, vol. 1, March 1858.

161 " 'their homes attractive.' " *EDM*, vol. 1, May 1852.

164 " 'in these qualities.' " Ibid.
" 'in perpetual brawls.' " Ibid., vol. 2, June 1853.

165 " 'a second consideration.' " Ibid., vol. 4, December 1855; ibid., vol. 5, July 1856.
"before her marriage." Ibid., vol. 5, December 1856.
" 'the hands of men.' " Ibid., vol. 6, May 1857.

166 " 'don't write at all.' " Ibid., vol. 1, June 1852.

" 'Customs in England.' " Ibid., vol. 1, December 1852.

" 'Make the Best Husbands?' " Ibid., vol. 2, April 1854.

167 "his dizzy correspondents." Ibid., vol. 1, July 1852.

" 'as soon as possible.' " Ibid., vol. 1, August 1852.

"to companionate marriage." Ibid., vol. 1, May 1852.

168 "sugar out of sawdust." Ibid., vol. 1, December 1852.

" 'supple-endid' isn't it?" Letter, SOB to IMB [April? 23, 1856].

" 'he drinks his.' " *EDM,* vol. 2, December 1853.

" 'calling with you.' " Ibid., vol. 2, July 1853.

169 "the final page." Ibid., vol. 1, September 1852.

170 "better her chances." Letter, IMB to SOB [April? 4, 1856].

"viewed on demand at the office." *EDM,* vol. 3, December 1854.

"free editorial support." Letter, IMB to SOB [February? 22, 1856].

"bit of business." See, for example, *EDM,* vol. 5, August 1856.

"to 50,000." Ibid., vol. 3, May 1854; ibid., vol. 6, May 1857.

171 *"Ladies' Treasury."* Ironically this was published by Ward and Lock, the company that eventually acquired the *EDM* and the *BOHM.*

" 'domestic information.' " Sam incorporated these endorsements into the advertisements for the *EDM* with which he saturated the endpapers of his other partwork publications including, incongruously, *The Illustrated Family Bible,* London, 1861–3.

" 'of fish used.' " Ibid., vol. 5, August 1856.

"months at a time." For instance, it failed to appear for a long stretch at the beginning of 1857. Could the growing rift with Clarke, culminating in the acrimonious court case of January 1857, lie behind the *EDM*'s cookery writer deciding that she no longer wanted to contribute to the magazine?

172 "it was a boy." A large envelope containing these letters was originally part of the MMB Archive, but seems to have disappeared sometime after 1945 when its contents were viewed by Nancy Spain, from whose book these details are taken. Nancy Spain, *Mrs. Beeton and her Husband,* p. 114.

" 'beneficial to you.' " All Mrs. English's correspondence with Sam and Isabella has disappeared from the MMB Archive. I have used Nancy Spain's transcript here, and it is interesting to note how it differs from that offered by H. Montgomery Hyde. Nancy Spain, *Mrs. Beeton and her Husband,* pp. 117–18; H. Montgomery Hyde, *Mr. and Mrs. Beeton,* p. 82.

173 " '12 Hours certified.' " The death was registered the very next day by Sam. It is not known whether a doctor was called, and thus whether the diagnosis of "cholera" comes from Sam or from a professional medical man.

"he left Pinner." H. Montgomery Hyde, *Mr. and Mrs. Beeton,* p. 83.

"letter of condolence." Nancy Spain, *Mrs. Beeton and her Husband,* p. 114.

"the infant suffocates." Sarah Freeman, *Isabella and Sam,* p. 140.

"his first illness.' " Nancy Spain, *Mrs. Beeton and her Husband,* p. 50.

174 "has been contracted." For a clear account of the progression of untreated syphilis, see Derek Llewellyn-Jones, *Sexually Transmitted Diseases,* London, 1990, ch. 8.

"became too intense." Judith R. Walkowitz, *Prostitution and Victorian Society*, pp. 49–50.

"the tertiary stage." Derek Llewellyn-Jones, *Sexually Transmitted Diseases*, p. 90.

"up to five years." Mary Spongberg, *Feminizing Venereal Disease: The Body of the Prostitute in Nineteenth Century Medical Discourse*, London, 1997, p. 85.

"even worth it." J. D. Oriel, *The Scars of Venus*, London, 1994, p. 85.

175   "quite account for." Ibid., p. 69.

"essay competition." The August 1857 issue of the *EDM* is conspicuously thin, bearing signs of being thrown together with whatever recycled material was closest to hand.

"from Mrs. English." Of course we will never know for certain that Isabella and Sam had syphilis. In *Pox: Genius, Madness, and the Mysteries of Syphilis*, New York, 2003, Deborah Hayden warningly subtitles one of her key chapters, "The Fragile Art of Retrospective Diagnosis." Before the arrival of the Wassermann test at the beginning of the twentieth century, it was impossible to prove whether an individual had contracted the disease. The fact that its symptomology was so varied—encompassing everything from paralysis to insanity, rashes to breathing difficulties—means that syphilis was dubbed during the Beetons' day "The Great Imitator," thanks to the way it mimicked other illnesses.

176   "extended family." These notes of condolence were in the envelope that has gone missing.

" 'went away from us.' " Letter, SOB to IMB, October 11, [18]64.

INTERLUDE

177   " 'climate it inhabits.' " IMB, ed., *BOHM*, 1861, p. 269.

178   " 'of their existence.' " Ibid., p. 105.

179   "ginger, and raisins." Ibid., p. 691.

" 'in the Creation.' " Ibid., p. 110.

CHAPTER SEVEN

181   "exploit so successfully." *Beeton's Book of Birds*, 1862; *Beeton's Historian*, 1860; *Beeton's Book of Songs*, 1865.

"homes of England." For the anecdote about the rats I am indebted to Peter Giles, the godson of the late Lady (Constance) Fretwell, widow of the Englishes' great-grandson.

"kitchen in the country." Henrietta English's letters have all disappeared from the MMB Archive and I have been obliged to use the transcripts of Spain, Hyde and Freeman.

" 'Best Woman Cooks.' " Mrs. English doesn't mention Rotival by name, but he was still working for Lord Wilton in 1857.

182 "H English." I have used Nancy Spain's transcript, correcting "V English" to "H English." Nancy Spain, *Mrs. Beeton and her Husband,* p. 116.

183 "than above stairs." IMB, ed., *BOHM,* 1861, Preface.
"a prosperous farmer." Census, 1871, Parish of Fordham. Painting of Vale Lodge, Fordham, by Caroline Emma English, in the possession of Peter Giles.
" 'gentleman.' " Robert English, Will, January 19, 1874, Administration, October 24, 1874.

184 "Thirty-eight separate dishes." John Simpson, *A Complete System of Cookery,* London, 1806, p. 407.
"semi-detached in Didsbury." Quoted in Nancy Spain, *Mrs. Beeton and her Husband,* p. 116.
" 'can be done.' " Nancy Spain, *Mrs. Beeton and her Husband,* p. 117.
" 'much as possible.' " Letter, IMB to SOB [February? 22, 1856].

186 " 'to meet emergencies.' " Ibid.
" 'four or five eggs.' " Ibid., vol. 6, May 1857.

187 "had been born." The original twenty-four parts may still be seen at the British Library.
"Wine and Plum Cake." *EDM,* vol. 8, April 1860.
" 'criticize their wives.' " J. W. Robertson Scott, *The Story of the Pall Mall Gazette,* p. 115.

189 "had in mind." Elizabeth David, "The Excellence of Eliza Acton," in Elizabeth Ray, ed., *The Best of Eliza Acton* (London, 1968), reprinted in Alan Davidson, ed., *On Fasting and Feasting,* London, 1988, p. 33.
" 'incessant labour.' " IMB, ed., *BOHM,* 1861, Preface.

190 *"haute cuisine."* For more on Carême see Ian Kelly, *Cooking for Kings,* London, 2003.
"elegant luxury." IMB, ed., *BOHM,* 1861, p. 659.
"without comment." Ibid., p. 471; ibid., pp. 613–14; ibid., p. 821.

191 " 'maître d'hôtel' might be." Charles Francatelli, *The Modern Cook* (London, 1846), London, 1888, pp. 137–8; IMB, ed., *BOHM,* 1861, p. 168. Charles Francatelli, *The Modern Cook,* p. 360; IMB, ed., *BOHM,* 1861, p. 572.
" 'into hot water.' " IMB, ed., *BOHM,* 1861, p. 95; John Simpson, *A Complete System of Cookery,* p. 2.
"avoid over-boiling." IMB, ed., *BOHM,* 1861, p. 144; John Simpson, *A Complete System of Cookery,* p. 185.

192 "appearing in monthly parts." For more on Soyer, see Elizabeth Ray, *Alexis Soyer, Cook Extraordinary,* Lewes, 1991; Helen Morris, *Portrait of a Chef,* Cambridge, 1938.
"improves their presentation." IMB, ed., *BOHM,* 1861, pp. 614–15; ibid., p. 897.
"Alexis Soyer." I am particularly indebted to Ruth Cowen, author of a forthcoming major biography of Soyer, for sharing her research with me.

193 " 'country? &c.' " *BOHM,* 24 parts, 1859–61, part 2, December 1859, advertisement.

194 " 'the same manner.' " Alexis Soyer, *The Pantropheon* (London, 1853), London, 1977, p. 278.

" 'the same manner.' " IMB, ed., *BOHM*, 1861, p. 218.

" 'on his fish.' " Alexis Soyer, *The Pantropheon*, p. 214.

195 " 'companionship of rats!' " IMB, ed., *BOHM*, 1861, pp. 111–12.

"manual of instruction." Ibid., p. 55.

196 "designed to make money." Gilly Lehmann, *The British Housewife*, Totnes, 2003, pp. 108–11.

"by Hannah Woolley." Ibid., p. 10.

197 " 'very good ones.' " Hannah Glasse, *The Art of Cookery* (London, 1747), Totnes, 1983, pp. i–ii.

" 'the meanest capacity.' " Elizabeth Raffald, *The Experienced English Housekeeper* (Manchester, 1769), Lewes, 1997, p. 1.

198 "thirty-three in all." Biographical details taken from Roy Shipperbottom's Introduction to the 1997 facsimile edition of *The Experienced English Housekeeper*, published by Southover Press, Lewes.

"made-up goods." Elizabeth Raffald, *The Experienced English Housekeeper*, p. 2.

" 'to improve themselves.' " Ibid., p. 1.

" 'Roasting' and 'Boiling.' " Ibid., pp. 2–3.

199 "a Second Way." IMB, ed., *BOHM*, 1861, p. 192; Elizabeth Raffald, *The Experienced English Housekeeper*, p. 178.

"this particular ingredient." IMB, ed., *BOHM*, 1861, p. 192.

"families of Manchester." Ibid., pp. 854–5; Elizabeth Raffald, *The Experienced English Housekeeper*, p. 134.

" 'a good confectioner's.' " IMB, ed., *BOHM*, 1861, p. 851.

"keeping house." Maria Rundell, *Domestic Cookery by a Lady* (London, 1806), London, 1843, "Advertisement."

200 "of their households." Ibid., pp. 1–21.

"introductory remarks." Ibid., "Advertisement"; ibid., p. 107; ibid., p. 281.

" 'he praiseth her.' " Ibid., p. 4; IMB, ed., *BOHM*, 1861, p. 1.

" 'to be heavy.' " Maria Rundell, *Domestic Cookery*, p. 253; IMB, ed., *BOHM*, 1861, p. 836.

201 "a collection of recipes." Elizabeth Ray, Introduction to Eliza Acton, *Modern Cookery for Private Families* (London, 1845), Lewes, 1993, p. vi.

"thin suet." Eliza Acton, *Modern Cookery*, p. 356; ibid., p. 369.

" 'to find a name . . .' " Ibid., p. 426.

202 "through the recipe." This is exactly what Beeton recommends inexperienced cooks to do. IMB, ed., *BOHM*, 1861, p. 55.

" 'should be *studied*.' " Elizabeth Ray, Introduction to Eliza Acton, *Modern Cookery*, p. vii.

" 'have been appropriated.' " Eliza Acton, *Modern Cookery*, p. 2.

"other preparations besides." IMB, ed., *BOHM*, 1861, pp. 498–9; ibid., pp. 839–40.

"with medical books." Anita McConnell, "William Kitchiner 1778–1827," *Oxford DNB*.

203 " 'whether we drink.' " William Kitchiner, *The Cook's Oracle* (London, 1817), London, 1821, p. 9.

"its usual span." There is, however, an interesting hint that Kitchiner may not have died of natural causes, Anita McConnell, "William Kitchiner."

"Stewed Oysters." IMB, ed., *BOHM*, 1861, pp. 826–7; pp. 380–1; p. 589; p. 144. William Kitchiner, *The Cook's Oracle*, pp. 421–2; pp. 155–6; p. 207, p. 241.

204 "wild pigeons." IMB, ed., *BOHM*, 1861, pp. 441–6.

" 'the Dining Room.' " William Kitchiner, *The Cook's Oracle*, p. vi.

" 'to *cure* them.' " Ibid., p. ix.

" 'and the Economist.' " Ibid., p. xiii.

"and eager lovers." Jean-Anthelme Brillat-Savarin, *The Physiology of Taste* (Paris, 1825), London, 1994, pp. 143–5.

205 "from Brillat-Savarin." Ibid., pp. 222–3; IMB, ed., *BOHM*, 1861, p. 258. In fact Beeton liked the anecdote about the Croat soldiers so much that she used it again, at the end of her book, p. 905, suggesting once again how barely the text was edited.

"her own experience." IMB, ed., *BOHM*, 1861, pp. 527–8.

"referred to at all." Ibid., p. 917; pp. 615–16.

"other people's recipes." Ibid., p. 905.

" 'well as wholesomely.' " Ibid., p. 205, p. 207.

206 "University College, London." Nicholas Edwards, "Thomas Webster 1772–1844," *Oxford DNB*.

"sharply into focus." As this book was going to press I was alerted to the existence of Rachel Goodyear's unpublished MA dissertation, "Tradition, Innovation and Borrowing in Nineteenth-Century Household Books: *An Encyclopaedia of Domestic Economy* and *Beeton's Book of Household Management*," Leeds University, 1975, which I have not been able to view.

207 "various stoves." IMB, ed., *BOHM*, 1861, pp. 25–7.

" 'deservedly celebrated.' " Thomas Webster, *An Encyclopaedia of Domestic Economy*, London, 1844, p. v.

"as Beeton does." Ibid., pp. 940–1.

" 'original preparations.' " IMB, ed., *BOHM*, 1861, Preface.

"into the *BOHM*." See, e.g., "Aunt Nellie's Pudding."

208 "handwritten text." *EDM*, vol. 1, June 1852.

"her with recipes." IMB, ed., *BOHM*, 1861, Preface.

"transferring to the *BOHM*." IMB, ed., *BOHM*, 1861, Preface.

"à la Solferino." Ibid., p. 80.

"scrappy handwritten notes." Letter, Louisa and Auguste Heidel to IMB, September 3, 1860.

"damning verdict." Lucy Smiles, "The Great Mrs. Beeton."

209 "weekend house party." Eliza Acton, *Modern Cookery*, p. 252.

"text without comment." IMB, ed., *BOHM*, 1861, p. 659.

"it must be fine." Eliza Acton, *Modern Cookery*, pp. 408–9.

"from Carême." IMB, ed., *BOHM*, 1861, p. 659.

INTERLUDE

210   " 'which she lives.' " IMB, ed., *BOHM*, 1861, pp. 84–5.
211   "same volume." Quoted in Sarah Freeman, *Mutton and Oysters*, London, 1989, p. 126.
      "454 calories." Thanks to Jane Frank for nutritional analysis.
      "general principles." IMB, ed., *BOHM*, 1861, pp. 49–54.
212   " 'M. Ude's recipe.' " Ibid., pp. 97–100.

CHAPTER EIGHT

213   *"Household Management."* This work has already been done for Robert Chamber's *Vestiges of Natural Creation: James A. Secord, Victorian Sensation*, Chicago, 2000.
214   " 'sifted loaf sugar.' " IMB, ed., *BOHM*, 24 parts, 1859–61, part 13, December 1860.
      "an imaginary reader." This fictional account is based on the following sources: Leonore Davidoff and Catherine Hall, *Family Fortunes: Men and Women of the English Middle Class 1780–1850*, London, 1987; Leonore Davidoff and Ruth Hawthorn, *A Day in the Life of A Victorian Domestic Servant*, London, 1976; "Whatever Shall I Do?," *EDM*, vol. 8, September 1859, in addition to IMB, ed., *BOHM*, 1861, pp. 1–44.
224   " 'Dessert.' " IMB, ed., *BOHM*, 1861, p. 916.
228   "routine accordingly." IMB, ed., *BOHM*, 1861, p. 988, p. 992, p. 995.
      " 'the footman's share.' " IMB, ed., *BOHM*, 1861, p. 43, p. 966.
229   "go one better." R. K. Philp, *The Practical Housewife*, London, 1855.
230   " 'Physick and Chyrurgery.' " Hannah Woolley, *The Gentlewoman's Companion* (London, 1673/75), Totnes, 2001, p. 104; p. 115; p. 173.
      " 'Cherries Preserved.' " Ibid., p. 185, p. 191.
      " 'Mad Dog.' " Hannah Glasse, *The Art of Cookery*, p. 166.
231   "jelly and sago." Elizabeth Raffald, *The Experienced English Housekeeper*, ch. 7.
      " 'of a duchess.' " William Cobbett, *Cottage Economy*, London, 1823, par. 107.
      "conversational Italian." Esther Hewlett Copley, *Cottage Comforts*, London, 1825; *The Housekeeper's Guide: or, A plain and practical system of domestic cookery*, Manchester, 1834.
232   "possible location." Sarah Stickney Ellis, *The Daughters of England, their Position in Society, Character and Responsibilities*, London, 1842; *The Wives of England, their Relative Duties, Domestic Influence, and Social Obligations*, London, 1843.
      " 'vulgar the next.' " Agogos, pseud. [Charles Day], *Hints on Etiquette and the Usages of Society, with a glance at bad habits*, London, 1834, p. 13.
      "anywhere near mouths." Ibid., p. 16.

232–233 "to court circles." J. H. Walsh, *A Manual of Domestic Economy*, London, 1856.

"of the evening." IMB, ed., *BOHM*, 1861, pp. 10–11, p. 12, p. 13.

" 'the feminine gender.' " Ibid., p. 1001.

234 "the open market." For more on this complex and ongoing debate, see Robert B. Shoemaker, *Gender in English Society, 1650–1850: The Emergence of Separate Spheres?*, London, 1998; Amanda Vickery, "Golden Age to Separate Spheres? A Review of the Categories and Chronology of English Women's History," *Historical Journal*, 36, 1993.

"fuzzier way." See, for instance, Catherine Hall, "The Early Formation of Victorian Domestic Ideology" in her *White, Male and Middle Class, Explorations in Feminism and History*, London, 1992; A. James Hammerton, *Cruelty and Companionship: Conflict in Nineteenth-Century Married Life*, London, 1992.

235 "*She Taught Me.*" Mrs. [Eliza] Warren, *How I Managed my House on Two Hundred Pounds a Year*, London, 1864; *My Lady-help, and What She Taught Me*, London, 1877.

236 " 'to commence it.' " IMB, ed., *BOHM*, 1861, Preface.

237 "do so herself." Nancy Spain, *Mrs. Beeton and her Husband*, p. 62.

" 'mid-Victorian life.' " Nicola Humble, ed., *Mrs. Beeton's Book of Household Management*, Oxford, 2000, p. xii.

" 'find at home.' " Hannah Woolley, *The Gentlewoman's Companion*, p. 136.

238 "bark orders." Coventry Patmore, *The Angel in the House*, 1854.

" 'of a family.' " IMB, ed., *BOHM*, 1861, p. 1.

" 'or virago queens.' " Ibid.

239 " 'thinks she is.' " Ibid., p. 18.

" 'his safest steward.' " Ibid., pp. 18–19.

240 " 'contrasted with another.' " Ibid., p. 6.

" 'provisions to buy.' " Ibid.

"domestic environment." Samuel and Sarah Adams, *The Complete Servant*, London, 1825.

241 "may not know.)" IMB, ed., *BOHM*, 1861, p. 12.

" 'easily terminated.' " Mrs. [Frances] Parkes, *Domestic Duties*, London, 1825, p. 42.

" 'readily terminated.' " IMB, ed., *BOHM*, 1861, p. 10.

" 'be gentlemen.' " Mrs. Parkes, *Domestic Duties*, p. 51.

242 " 'be gentlemen.' " IMB, ed., *BOHM*, 1861, p. 11.

" 'beside her.' " Mrs. Parkes, *Domestic Duties*, p. 64.

" 'right hand.' " IMB, ed., *BOHM*, 1861, p. 13.

" 'of the company.' " Ibid., p. 12.

243 "virtually self-sufficient." Ibid., p. 22.

244 " 'and her maid.' " Ibid., p. 961.

"loyal service." Ibid., p. 962.

" 'spirits of wine.' " Ibid., p. 969; p. 995.

245 "speaker is male." Ibid., p. 976.

"currently involved." Ibid., p. 970.

"concern the recipes." Ibid., p. vi.

"rabbits in milk." Ibid., ch. 38.

246 "with the nursemaid." Ibid., p. 1016.

" 'by a solicitor.' " Ibid., Preface.

" 'health and life.' " Ibid., p. 1026.

INTERLUDE

248 " 'large establishment.' " IMB, ed., *BOHM*, 1861, p. 955.

" 'come together.' " Ibid., p. 958.

250 " 'down the middle.' " Ibid., p. 954.

"Service à la Russe." Ibid. p. 955.

"let real life win." For more on this see Peter Brears, "*A La Française*, the Waning of a Long Dining Tradition," in C. Anne Wilson, ed., *Luncheon, Nuncheon and Other Meals*, ch. 5 and, in the same book, Valerie Mars, "*A La Russe*: the New Way of Dining," ch. 6.

CHAPTER NINE

251 "another Samuel Orchart." The baby was born at "Woodridings, Pinner" on June 3, 1859.

252 " 'A Beautiful Steel Engraving.' " *EDM*, vol. 8, December 1859.

"eleven strapping children." Jane married George White at Epsom on October 4, 1860.

253 "Bouverie Street." See IMB, *BOHM*, 24 parts, 1859–61, parts 5–8, May–July 1860.

255 "or private thoughts." The diary, however, is not pre-printed with dates. Isabella simply makes a note when she is about to begin a new entry, MMB Archive, family.

257 "three hours' sleep." IMB, Diary, March 7, [1860].

258 " 'tolerably nice.' " Ibid., March 9, [1860]. The diary entries appear to jump from March 7 to 9.

"other than his mother." Isabella never refers to her baby once during the course of this trip, nor during one made later in the year to Ireland.

259 " 'a bad character.' " IMB, Diary, March 10 [1860].

" 'represented to me.' " Ibid, March 12 [1860].

"luxury *Englishwoman's Domestic Magazine*." Ibid., March 11 [1860].

260 " 'wine included.' " Ibid., March 12 [1860].

" '12000 just pays.' " Ibid, undated page.

"done for Sam." Ibid., March 13 [1860].

"he appears." Ibid.

261 "heavy paper duty." In fact, the legislation had got tangled up in the Lords and it was not for another year that the tax was finally repealed. The Beetons' decision to go ahead lost them £1,000 in extra production costs.

"*Household Management.*" *EDM,* NS, vol. 2, December 1860.

262 " 'muslin under-sleeves.' " *EDM,* NS, vol. 1, May 1860.

" 'size for working.' " *Boy's Own Journal,* vol. 8, December 1862. These pattern sheets have tended not to survive, unlike the magazines themselves.

" 'morning cap.' " *EDM,* NS, vol. 3, May 1861. This largesse was picked up by the press, just as Isabella and Sam doubtless hoped: see the endpage of Beeton's *Illustrated Family Bible,* vol. 1, August 12, 1861.

263 " 'inside to match.' " *EDM,* NS, vol. 1, October 1860.

" 'can be made.' " *EDM,* NS, vol. 7, October 1863.

" 'transparent fabric.' " *EDM,* NS, vol. 6, April 1863.

"bought for 6d." *EDM,* NS, vol. 5, July 1862.

264 " 'walk westward.' " *EDM,* NS, vol. 5, June 1862.

"presents too." *EDM,* NS, vol. 6, December 1862; ibid., January 1863.

"fashionable, international." Margaret Beetham, *A Magazine of Her Own?,* p. 78.

"shoulder size." *EDM,* NS, vol. 6, November 1862.

265 "as the manageress." Census, 1881, Parish of St. Paul Covent Garden.

"Charles Weldon." Letters, MMB to Charlotte Talbot Coke, Coke Mss.

" 'to write.' " *EDM,* NS, vol. 3, July 1861.

"puffs and notices." See the endpages of each part work of Beeton's *Illuminated Family Bible.*

266 "the first issue." *Queen,* September 7, 1861.

" 'post free.' " *Boy's Own Magazine* (hereafter *BOM*), vol. 7, September 1861.

267 " 'few misgivings.' " *Saturday Review,* March 1, 1862.

268 " 'he addresses.' " [Geraldine Jewsbury], *Athenaeum,* July 19, 1862.

" 'the joy of it.' " Letter, Harriet Martineau to IMB, March 4, 1862. Along with those from Harriet Beecher Stowe, the original letter from Harriet Martineau has also disappeared from the MMB Archive, leaving only this transcript.

269 " 'January 1863.' " IMB, *The Englishwoman's Cookery Book,* London, 1863, Preface.

" 'Three Shillings and Sixpence.' " IMB, *Mrs. Beeton's Dictionary of Everyday Cookery,* London, 1865, Preface.

270 "from Dublin." Donal Horgan, *Echo After Echo, Killarney and Its History,* Cork, 1988, pp. 63–5.

" 'coffee room.' " IMB, Diary, July 9, [1860]. As with her Paris trip, Isabella seems to have skipped an initial day of diary-keeping, perhaps as a result of the disruption caused by travelling overnight.

271 "tourists coming back." See Donal Horgan, *The Victorian Visitor in Ireland, Irish Tourism 1840–1910,* Cork, 2002.

"four day stay." The Beetons enthusiastically recycled their Killarney experiences to provide a detailed account of the Queen's Irish holiday in the very first issue of *Queen.*

" 'surrounding country.' " IMB, Diary, July 9, [1860].

"garrulous boatmen." Ibid., July 10, [1860].

272 " 'fashions, &c.' " Ibid., July 13, [1860].
     " 'shade of glacé.' " *EDM*, NS, vol. 1, August 1860.
     "back in London." Ibid., July 17, [1860].
273 "cooked the fish." Ibid., July 18, [1860].
     "sounding nostalgic." Ibid., July 19, [1860].
     "businesslike mind." IMB, Diary, undated pages.
274 "40,000 copies." *BOM*, vol. 4, October 1858, Preface. *BOM*, vol. 8, 1862, Preface.
     " 'a great number of Boys.' " *Boy's Penny Magazine*, vol. 1, January 1863.
275 " 'degree of popularity.' " *BOM*, vol. 8, November 1862.
     "cusp of empire." Louis James, "Tom Brown's Imperialist Sons," *Victorian Studies,* vol. 17, 1973. See also Kirsten Drotner, *English Children and Their Magazines, 1751–1945,* London, 1988.
     "have thrilled him." *Morning Herald,* January 26, 1863.
276 "a great debt." For more on the family connections between this branch of the Beetons and H. Montgomery Hyde, see Hyde's Foreword to Sarah Freeman, *Isabella and Sam.*
     " 'mere money-making.' " *BOM*, NS, vol. 2, July 1863, endpapers.
     " 'memoir was born.' " *The Times,* March 13, 1862.
277 " 'unfortunately, prevailing.' " [Samuel Davidson], *Athenaeum,* November 14, 1863.
278 "*How I Managed My House.*" For more details see Dena Attar's monumental *A Bibliography of Household Books Published in Britain 1800–1914,* London, 1987.
     "178,000 copies." IMB, *BOHM*, London, 1869, title page. Significantly, the book is no longer described as being "edited" by Mrs. Isabella Beeton. Now it is simply "By Mrs. Isabella Beeton."

INTERLUDE

279 " 'into vermin.' " IMB, ed., *BOHM*, 1861, pp. 362–3. See also James Buzard, "Home Ec with Mrs. Beeton," *Raritan,* vol. 17, Fall 1977.
     "shoal of mackerel." IMB, ed., *BOHM*, 1861, p. 141.
280 " 'human existence.' " Ibid., p. 905.
281 "the green dress." Ibid., p. 970, p. 968.
     "murdering their laird." Ibid., p. 383.
     "urban middle class." Ibid., p. 969.

CHAPTER TEN

282 "production costs." Typically, Sam turned this into a marketing puff. *EDM*, NS, vol. 3, May 1861.
283 "without a job." Greenwood's replacement Helen Lowe would become, in time, legendary among magazine editors. Recalling her in the 1890s the jour-

nalist Dorothy Peel described "dear old Miss Lowe who wore a mushroom hat tied under her chin and looked like Queen Victoria."

"its prestigious pages." Bill Bell, "George Smith 1824–1901," *Oxford DNB*.

"a biography." *The Times,* December 17, 1909; J. W. Robertson Scott, *The Story of the Pall Mall Gazette,* London, 1950.

"found for Meason." *The Times,* June 5, 1862.

284   "over the shop." Sarah Freeman, *Isabella and Sam,* p. 220.

285   "H. Montgomery Hyde." Freeman has the Beetons at the Strand for six months; Spain is contradictory, suggesting one minute that the Beetons were living in London in the winter of 1862, and the next that they moved to Greenhithe in either 1861 or 1862; Hyde, meanwhile, has them living at the Strand for "inside a month or so." Since the 1861 census shows the Beetons in Pinner on April 8, this suggests that they gave up their lease at the end of that rental year, that is April 1862. When their third baby was born on December 31, 1863, they were still living at 248 Strand. Housewarming photographs—too poor to be reproduced here—suggest that by the time the child was a few months old the Beetons had moved to Greenhithe. Thus the best estimate is that the Beetons lived at the Strand between April 1862 and early summer 1864.

" 'cookery etc ditto.' " Ephemera, MMB Archive.

286   "in the world." Eliza Beeton had married Isaac Wyatt in 1857 and now ran the Dolphin jointly with her younger husband. Four of her daughters married warehousemen while the fifth, Mary Ann, stayed single.

"Book of Household Management." Census, 1871, Parish of St. George Hanover Square.

"mostly in Epsom." Census, 1871, Parish of Epsom.

"familiar livery men." Death certificate, Mary Jerrom, August 11, 1873.

"Epsom Grandstand." *The Times,* January 9, 1845; *The Times,* December 15, 1864.

"as governesses." I am indebted to Anna Greening, archivist at Queen's College, London, for providing me with details of Emily's career there.

287   "only thirty-one." Death certificate, John Mayson, May 29, 1871.

"at the age of forty-one." Emily's much younger sister Maud married the actor-manager Herbert Beerbohm Tree. It is for this lucky reason that Emily's dying correspondence has been preserved and can be read in the Tree Collection, University of Bristol Theatre Collection. She died on January 10, 1883, the cause of death given as "Paraplegia, Bed sores, Exhaustion." For the past few years she had been companion to Marion Margaret Violet Lindsay, daughter of the Earl of Crawford and Balcarres, who became the wife of the 8th Duke of Rutland and mother of Lady Diana Cooper.

"smell the sea." These letters of condolence belong to the envelope of correspondence missing from the MMB Archive. I have therefore been obliged to use Nancy Spain's transcriptions. According to these, in his letter of January 5, 1863, John Mayson mentions the boy's poor health as being the reason for the trip to Brighton, while Sam's half-sister Eliza refers to the child as being "very unwell" prior to the holiday. Nancy Spain, *Mrs. Beeton and her Husband*, p. 170; p. 172.

"in Newmarket." Samuel Orchart Beeton was buried on August 27, 1857. All Saints Parish Register, Suffolk.

"on his behalf." Sexton's Book, Norwood Cemetery, January 2, 1863, Lambeth.

288 " 'the same line.' " This letter has been lost, and I am dependent on Nancy Spain's transcription. Nancy Spain, *Mrs. Beeton and her Husband*, p. 172.

"hopeless suggestion." I have reconstructed this letter as far as I am able using Nancy Spain's partial transcription, together with that of Sarah Freeman, *Isabella and Sam*, p. 222.

289 "nastiest of diseases." "Given the almost complete ignorance of women on such matters at this time, it is very likely that many suffered from syphilis without being aware of it and also that many consulted doctors but were not treated in order to prevent them from knowing the real cause of their affliction," Mary Spongberg, *The Feminization of Venereal Disease*, p. 152. See also Kate Taylor, "Syphilis and Marriage during the *Fin de Siècle:* Doctors, Society and Women Novelists," unpublished MA dissertation, University of London, 1977.

"healthy baby to term." One of the most baffling characteristics of syphilis is the way it affects the pattern of pregnancy. As a general rule the longer the time that has elapsed since a woman's initial infection the more likely she is to produce a non-syphilitic baby. However, it is not impossible for a healthy baby to be sandwiched between two syphilitic siblings, and doctors, then as now, have noted an almost infinite number of variations on miscarriage, stillbirth, syphilitic baby and healthy baby.

"dying eventually in 1947." Major Orchart Beeton died on January 18 in the same year as his slightly younger brother Mayson.

290 "to settle there." See J. A. Sparvel-Bayley, *Swanscombe Local History*, Gravesend, 1875.

"made their new home." Death certificate, John Tillotson, May 13, 1871.

"village of Swanscombe." There is some confusion about the relationship between the Beetons and the Vulliamies. H. Montgomery Hyde claimed that there was a journalist living in Greenhithe called Benjamin Vulliamy who gave Isabella the recipe for Soup à la Solferino and later became Mayson's godfather. However, the only Vulliamy who shows up on the records is George. As the architect of the new parish church and its first churchwarden, he nonetheless remains a likely candidate for being Mayson's godfather. H. Montgomery Hyde, *Mr. and Mrs. Beeton*, p. 103 and n.

"pitted the area." Voting Register, 1870, CKS; *Post Office Directory*, Kent, 1862.

"soft white dust." See J. A. Sparvel-Bayley, *Swanscombe Local History*.

"gathering that summer." These photographs seem to have come to light sometime between 1952 and 1956. They are so indistinct that it is impossible to be certain about the identity of individual members of the group. Nancy

Spain maintains that the shadowy figures are Sam's half-brothers and -sisters; Nancy Spain, *The Beeton Story*, 1956, p. 169. Sarah Freeman, more convincingly, maintains that they are Maysons and Dorlings; Sarah Freeman, *Isabella and Sam*, p. 228.

291   "from the Thames." Nancy Spain, *Mrs. Beeton and her Husband*, p. 225.
"'publishing house in the Strand.'" Joan Easdale, "In Pursuit of Mrs. Beeton," broadcast BBC Home Service, April 21, 1938, transcript, BBC.

292   "'a lady was present.'" "Bertha," "Our Ladies' Letter."

293   "just south of Paris." Thanks to Tom West, who discovered and gave me Spain's transcripts which he had found among the effects of his late brother, the antiquarian book dealer W. J. West.

294   "that very afternoon." Nancy Spain, *Mrs. Beeton and her Husband*, pp. 209–19. Nancy Spain, partial transcript of IMB's Diary 1863–4, MMB Archive.

295   "'either [*sic*] of them.'" *The Times*, May 6, 1864.
"'with Mr. Hutton.'" Ibid., July 11, 1864.

296   "'N'est-ce-pas?'" Letter, SOB to IMB, October 11, [18]64.

297   "'tender age.'" Cynthia White, *Women's Magazines, 1693–1968*, p. 71.

298   "'in his business.'" H. Montgomery Hyde, *Mr. and Mrs. Beeton*, p. 134.
"possibly have imagined." Nancy Spain, *Mrs. Beeton and her Husband*, p. 242.
"had been delivered." Birth certificate, Mayson Moss Beeton, February 27, 1865.
"'6 days.'" Death Certificate, Isabella Beeton, February 9, 1865.

299   "minority who succumbed." Ibid., p. 7.
"to fuss about." Nancy Spain, *Mrs. Beeton and her Husband*, p. 173.
"'did too much work.'" Ibid., p. 246; Nancy Spain, *The Beeton Story*, p. 172.
"'face to the wall.'" Nancy Spain, *Mrs. Beeton and her Husband*, pp. 246–7. What may also have annoyed the sharp-eyed Dorlings is that while Isabella lay dying Sam still found time to insert the following self-absorbed announcement in the Births column of *The Times*: "On January 29th, at Mount Pleasant, Greenhithe, the wife of S. O. Beeton, Esq., FRGS, FSA, of a son," *The Times*, February 1, 1865.
"'He killed her!'" Nancy Spain, *Mrs. Beeton and her Husband*, p. 246.

300   "making off with the furniture." Ibid., p. 247.
"particularly tired her." H. Montgomery Hyde, *Mr. and Mrs. Beeton*, p. 128.
"difference to the outcome." Sarah Freeman, *Isabella and Sam*, p. 238, p. 234. Interestingly, one dominant strand in the debate about the causes of puerperal fever among doctors in the pre-Semmelweiss era was whether or not environmental factors predisposed a woman to vaginal/uterine streptococcal infection. Irvine Loudon, *The Tragedy of Childbed Fever*, pp. 81–2.
"'not dishonourable misfortune.'" Sarah Freeman, *Isabella and Sam*, p. 248.
"another warehouseman." Death Certificate, Helen Lowden, September 29, 1863.
"the age of fifty-four." Eliza died at the Dolphin on April 12, 1864.

301   "Isaac Wyatt in 1857." Wyatt continued to run the pub solo and died in 1888 a comparatively wealthy man, looked after by his niece, who doubled as his housekeeper.

" 'moustache neglected.' " Nancy Spain, *Mrs. Beeton and her Husband*, p. 231.

302   " 'S. O. B.' " Letter, SOB to William Stagg, February 18, 1865.

" 'S. O. B.' " Letter, SOB to IMB, October 11, [18]64.

" 'master mine.' " Letter, SOB to IMB [February? 1856].

303   " 'as at home.' " Nancy Spain, *Mrs. Beeton and her Husband*, p. 161.

304   "the second little Samuel Orchart." Sexton's Book, Norwood Cemetery, February 11, 1865, Lambeth.

" 'accept this intimation.' " *The Times*, February 9, 1865; *Gravesend Journal*, February 15, 1865.

305   " 'ISABELLA MARY BEETON,' " IMB, *Dictionary of Everyday Cookery*, unnumbered page.

INTERLUDE

307   " 'without value.' " IMB, ed., *BOHM*, 1861, Preface.

"jewel tones." I am indebted to Ann Bagnall of Southover Press, Lewes, for guiding me through the complex history of mid-nineteenth-century colour printing. See also Max E. Mitzman, *George Baxter and the Baxter Prints*, Newton Abbot, 1978; Charles Thomas Courtney Lewis, *The Picture Printer of the Nineteenth Century: George Baxter 1804–67*, London, 1911.

"was farmyard scenes." For an example of Harrison Weir's work, see Harrison Weir, *The Poetry of Nature*, London, 1861.

"signed the work." For more on Birket Foster's career see Jan Reynolds, *Birket Foster*, London, 1984.

309   "newly visual *Englishwoman's Domestic Magazine*." IMB, Diary, March 9, [1860]; IMB, Diary, July 25, [1860].

CHAPTER ELEVEN

310   "remained conspicuously bare." Henry Mayson Dorling, whose status at this point veered between "Gentleman" and "Wholesale Stationer," had married Anne Fielder on September 1, 1860. Census, 1871, Parish of Lewisham.

" 'and I like it!' " E. E. Dorling, *Epsom and the Dorlings*, p. 104.

311   "hours on end." Nancy Spain, *Mrs. Beeton and her Husband*, pp. 247–8.

"average £220 a year." Records of the Westminster Fire Office, Westminster.

"into a 'commercial' family." Information from Mrs. Joan Browne.

"just one maid." The 1861 census shows them at 14 Victoria Road, employing twenty-four-year-old Eliza James.

312   "she felt deeply." *EDM*, NS2, vol. 11, November 1870.

"real mother." H. Montgomery Hyde, *Mr. and Mrs. Beeton*, p. 158.

"with Isabella." Ibid., p. 136. It is not clear whom Montgomery Hyde is quoting in the phrase "put their two poverties together." An even greater mystery is Hyde's insistence that the Browne-Beeton household soon left Mount Pleasant and moved into an old coastguard cottage, a fact which Sarah Freeman repeats. The 1871 census clearly shows the Beetons and the Brownes still living at Mount Pleasant, and it has proved impossible to identify any such cottage.

313 "as his 'boarder.' " Census, 1871, Parish of Swanscombe.
"she was referring." *EDM*, NS2, vol. 16, May 1874.

314 " 'lady's magazine.' " Census, 1871, Parish of Swanscombe.
" 'wife.' " Census, 1861, Parish of Harrow.

315 "Swanscombe High Street." Census, 1871, Parish of Swanscombe.
"banished from the house." Nancy Spain, *Mrs. Beeton and her Husband*, p. 244.

316 " 'known to us.' " Letter, Charlotte McMahon to MMB, 1918.

317 " 'of the present arrangement.' " *The Times*, August 17, 1865.
"cash was short." Alexis Weedon, *Victorian Publishing: The Economics of Book Production for a Mass Market 1836–1916*, Aldershot, 2003, pp. 47–8.

318 "list of bankrupts." Letter, H. Montgomery Hyde to MMB, November 19, 1935.
" 'with his creditors.' " H. Montgomery Hyde, *Mr. and Mrs. Beeton*, p. 134.
"Ward, Lock and Tyler." Sarah Freeman, *Isabella and Sam*, p. 248.
"as debt collector." For more information about how the insolvency laws worked in the nineteenth century see V. Markham Lester, *Victorian Insolvency: Bankruptcy, Imprisonment for Debt and Winding-up in Nineteenth-century England*, Oxford, 1995.

319 "still outstanding." *The Times*, July 3, 1868.
"been badly hit." James Andrews, *Reminiscences*, p. 30.
"blood red drapes." Sales Particulars, Stroud Green House, 1868, 1873. Croydon.

320 " 'come out.' " "Bertha," "Our Ladies' Letter."
"at Wyndham Mews." Ephemera, MMB Archive.
" 'the family motto.' " [S. O. Beeton], *London's Great Outing: the Derby Carnival*, London, 1868, p. 6.

321 "various incarnations." For the history of Ward, Lock, see Edward Liveing, *Adventure in Publishing: The House of Ward, Lock, 1854–1954*, London, 1954.
"Ward, Lock and Tyler." "Venables & Tyler," paper merchants of Queenhithe, appear in various trade directories throughout the first half of the 1860s.
"highest bidder." *The Times*, December 4, 1866.

322 " 'publication whatever.' " Notes by H. Montgomery Hyde summarizing L.R. 19 Equity Cases 207 [1874], MMB Archive.
" 'S. O. Beeton.' " This quotation appears in H. Montgomery Hyde, *Mr. and Mrs. Beeton*, p. 135, but remains unsourced.
" 'and other works.' " *Boy's Own Magazine*, vol. 8, November 1866.

323   "in her own garden." *EDM,* NS2, vol. 17, July 1874; *EDM,* NS2, vol. 11, August 1871; *EDM,* NS2, vol. 10, June 1871.

"prototype dishwasher." *EDM,* NS2, vol. 7, July 1869; *EDM,* NS2, vol. 9, July 1870; *EDM,* NS2, vol. 6, March 1869; *EDM,* NS2, vol. 10, May 1871.

"the Strand." *EDM,* NS2, vol. 15, November 1873.

324   " 'how to do it.' " *EDM,* NS2, vol. 16, April 1874.

"life assurance." *EDM,* NS2, vol. 6, February 1869; *EDM,* NS2, vol. 10, February 1871.

"all the time." *EDM,* NS2, vol. 3, March 1867.

325   " 'affords to nature.' " *EDM,* NS2, vol. 3, April 1867.

"positively pornographic." For a much fuller discussion of this infamous "corset controversy," see Valerie Steele, *The Corset,* London, 2001; David Kunzle, *Fashion and Fetishism: A Social History of the Corset, Tight-lacing and Other Forms of Body Sculpture,* New Jersey, 1980.

"from the correspondence." *EDM,* NS2, vol. 4, November 1867.

326   "clergymen's studies." *EDM,* Supplement, 1870, April, May, June.

"in private." These correspondents asked to receive prospectuses from those writers who claimed to run boarding schools where corporal discipline was enthusiastically pursued—presumably brothels by another name.

" 'merely a fiction?' " *EDM,* Supplement, 1870, May, July, September.

"let it drop completely." *EDM,* NS2, vol. 7, December 1869.

" 'to have cognisance.' " *Daily Telegraph,* January 18, 1869.

"Englishwoman's Domestic Magazine." Saturday Review, January 30, 1869.

327   "market leader." Margaret Beetham, *A Magazine of Her Own?,* p. 71, p. 74.

" 'passionate, interest.' " *EDM,* Supplement, 1870, November.

"2s volume." The 1870 Supplement may be read in the British Library, but only at a special desk under the watchful eye of a librarian.

328   "Zoological Gardens." *EDM,* NS2, vol. 10, January 1871; ibid., February 1871.

"galvanized Sam." A letter in the MMB Archive shows Sam busy lobbying his old friend Frederick Weaklin to try to help him get permission to print the paper on a Sunday, ready for distribution on Monday.

"bucket of horse shit)." *The Coming K—,* London, 1872, p. 45.

329   " 'to dupe, deceive.' " *The Siliad,* London, 1873, p. 37.

"time to act." "An Outsider," *The Blatant Beast Loose Again!,* Bury St. Edmunds, 1874, p. 2.

"La Lanterne." For more on Rochefort's life, see Roger L. Williams, *Henri Rochefort: Prince of the Gutter Press,* New York, 1966.

"that year's *Annual." The Times,* November 26, 1874.

330   " 'worn out.' " *Jon Duan,* London, 1874, p. 87.

331   " 'and support.' " *Athenaeum,* November 21, 1874.

"in Greenhithe." *The Times,* November 26, 1874.

"very next *Athenaeum." Athenaeum,* December 5, 1874.

"the injunction lifted." *The Times,* December 22, 1874.

"to oppose it." Ibid.

332 "stretches credulity)." Ibid., November 26, 1874.

" 'of it.' " Ibid., December 22, 1874.

"back into favour." Republicanism was pretty much a spent force by 1872. In that year the nation celebrated the recovery of the Prince of Wales from typhoid fever with a service of thanksgiving in St. Paul's. Two days later, a failed attempt to assassinate the Queen provoked another wave of loyalty to the Crown. Thus Beeton's republican *Annuals* of 1872, 1873, 1874 and 1876 (there was none in 1875) had somewhat misjudged the mood.

334 " '& what remains?' " Letter, SOB to George Lock, April 28, 1874. Just whose death the black-bordered letter was marking remains a mystery. Henry Dorling had died exactly a year previously, but it seems unlikely that Sam would display such conventional courtesy for a man he had come to loathe.

"*Punch* magazine." *The Times*, November 4, 1869.

"hiring two QCs." Ibid., November 17, 1875.

335 "remains to this day." There is some irony in the fact that Cassell, who eventually took over Ward, Lock in the 1980s, had originally been one of S. O. Beeton's chief rivals.

INTERLUDE

336 " 'meat with vegetables.' " IMB, ed., *BOHM*, 1861, p. 600.

" 'coagulated albumen.' " Ibid., p. 584.

337 " 'country in Europe.' " Ibid., p. 212.

"invalid's jelly." Ibid., p. 893.

" 'a laxative effect.' " Ibid., p. 569.

"seizing up completely." See, for instance, the many advertisements across Beeton publications in the late 1850s for "Norton's Camomile Pills," "Frampton's Pill of Health" and "Holloway's Pills," all of which claim to help constipation and indigestion.

"one-and-a-half hours." IMB, ed., *BOHM*, 1861, p. 562; p. 579.

"entirely unremarkable." Ibid., p. 583; p. 551.

338 " 'butchers' meat.' " Ibid., p. 110.

"low-carb regimes." Thanks to nutritionist Jane Frank for analysing one week's worth of Mrs. Beeton's "Plain Family Dinners" for February.

CHAPTER TWELVE

339 "laundering his profit." *The Times*, December 22, 1874.

"to his reputation." Ibid., December 22, 1875.

340 " 'partly right and partly wrong.' " Ibid.

"of ten years." Draft legal agreement, January 14, 1876, MMB Archive.

" 'smart for it.' " Ibid.

341 " 'value to the defendants.' " *The Times*, December 22, 1875.

"caught the mood." The "Myra" brand would become enormously successful, spawning such offshoots as *Myra's Threepenny Journal, Myra's Journal of Dress and Needlework, Myra's Mid-Monthly Journal and Children's Dress.*

"the Beeton brand." *The Times,* February 26, 1875.

"Ward & Lock." *Myra's Journal of Dress and Fashion,* vol. 1, February 1875.

342 "dull, flat line." Letter, SOB to Charles Weldon?, February 29, 1876.

"to her creditors." Propositions Made Without Prejudice by S. O. Beeton between Mrs. Browne and Mr. Weldon [1876?], MMB Archive.

"Ward, Lock." There is some mystery as to whom the letter is addressed. It begins "Dear Johnny" but MMB has written on the envelope that the recipient is Sam's old friend William Gard, the manufacturer of an impregnated plate cloth called "Sapoline," who at the time was in partnership with Charles Tyler.

343 " 'on my shoulders.' " Letter, SOB to "Johnny," February 24, 1875.

344 "his better half." Mrs. Joan Browne reports that family anecdote records Myra as extremely "managing."

" 'Mama.' " H. Montgomery Hyde, *Mr. and Mrs. Beeton,* p. 137, p. 159.

" 'used to be.' " *EDM,* NS2, vol. 11, January 1871.

"to herself." Selection of "Spinnings," *EDM,* NS2, 1867–74.

345 " 'your affecate Mother/Mama.' " Letter, Myra Browne to Orchart Beeton and MMB, June 13, 1874.

" 'ask Mr. Dick.' " Letter, Myra Browne to Orchart Beeton and MMB, June 27, 1874.

346 " 'Your loving Father.' " Letter, SOB to Orchart Beeton and MMB, April 28, 1874.

347 "aristocratic employers." Letters between Emily Holt and Maud Tree, Tree Collection, Theatre Archive, Bristol University.

"tertiary syphilis." Morell MacKenzie, Case Notes 1885, Wellcome.

"specialist in both." More work needs to be done on the whole unfortunate episode of MacKenzie's involvement with the Crown Prince's final illness, which effectively blighted the tail end of his career. P. A. Grace, "Doctors Differ over the German Crown Prince," *British Medical Journal,* December 19, 1992. For older accounts see R. S. Stevenson, *Morell MacKenzie: The Story of a Victorian Tragedy,* London, 1946, as well as MacKenzie's own ill-advised and less than candid *The Fatal Illness of Frederick the Noble,* London, 1888.

348 " 'his existence.' " H. Montgomery Hyde notes this quotation as coming from O'Connor's autobiography. However, no such passage appears in *Memoirs of an Old Parliamentarian,* 2 vols., London, 1929, and, from an entry in the MMB Archive index, it seems that this passage appeared in the press in 1927, under the title "Mrs. Beeton's Husband." I have not, however, been able to locate the piece.

"into even greater gloom." Unsourced quotation, Nancy Spain, *Mrs. Beeton and her Husband,* p. 250.

349 " 'his kindest affection.' " Letter, SOB to MMB, November 13, 1876.

"psychological tension." Sarah Freeman, *Isabella and Sam,* p. 253.

351 "their own horses." Advertisement for Sudbrook Park, Richmond.

" 'some years ago.' " *Athenaeum,* June 9, 1877.

352   " 'from their midst.' " [A. A. Dowty], *London Figaro,* June 21, 1877.

" 'others reaped.' " H. Montgomery Hyde, *Mr. and Mrs. Beeton,* p. 178.

353   " 'Ward, Lock, Bowden & Co.' " Edward Liveing, *Adventure in Publishing,* pp. 53–4.

"family company." H. Montgomery Hyde, *Mr. and Mrs. Beeton,* p. 173.

354   " ' 'twas o'ercast,' " [A. A. Dowty and E. D. Jerrold], *Finis,* London, 1877.

"to baby Meredith." Charles Gordon Meredith Browne was born on July 20, 1877, at 7 Adelphi Terrace.

" 'said two children.' " S. O. Beeton, Will, November 30, 1869, Administration, November 17, 1877.

355   "of twenty students." Thanks to Dr. Terry Rogers, Honorary Archivist of Marlborough College, for extracting these details from the school's records.

356   "middle classes." Census, 1881, Parish of Kingston.

"from Bromley." Mayson Moss Beeton married Louie Swinley Price Jones on March 21, 1888. Orchart Beeton married Janet Kennedy on February 23, 1889.

"Stroud Green House." Elizabeth Dorling died on June 10, 1871, at the age of fifty-six from "obstruction of the Bowel 3 years." Henry Dorling died a bare two years later, on March 20, 1873, apparently desolate at the loss of his second wife.

"second step-brother." Mary Jerrom was buried on August 12, 1873; Harriet Cates on June 7, 1875. E. J. Dorling made the arrangements in both cases, a particular kindness since neither woman was his blood relation. Sexton's Book, Brompton.

357   *"Household Management."* IMB, *BOHM,* 1869, p. iv.

" 'Mrs. M. Beeton.' " *Hearth and Home* started publishing in May 1891 and went on to be one of the most successful magazines of the late nineteenth/early twentieth-century period.

" 'my own name.' " Letter, MMB to Colonel Talbot Coke, February 9, 1894, Coke Mss.

358   "his mother." *Myra's Cookery Book, Enlarged and Revised by Mrs. M. Beeton,* London, n.d.

" 'book on cookery.' " Simon Nowell-Smith, *The House of Cassell, 1848–1858,* London, 1958, p. 181 n. However, having pointed out George Dilnot's error in confusing "Mrs. M. Beeton" with Isabella in his *The Romance of the Amalgamated Press,* London, 1925, Nowell-Smith then proceeds to index "Mrs. M. Beeton" as "Mrs. Myra Beeton," p. 281 in his own book.

"new, improved artwork." As well as the different plates, this edition is also distinguished from the first by the fact that the address of S. O. Beeton is given as "248 the Strand" rather than "18 Bouverie Street."

359   "which marked the 1870s." For a detailed listing of these titles together with a developmental map of cookery book publishing during this later period see Elizabeth Driver, *Cookery Books Published in Britain 1875–1914,* London, 1989.

360   "colour plates or unillustrated." Information about the various versions of

Mrs. Beeton on offer from Ward, Lock come from the advertisements which appeared on the endpapers of their countless publications.

"Myra Browne's." IMB, *Book of Household Management,* 1869, p. iv.

" 'did not exist.' " Ibid.

361   "line drawings." Ibid., pp. 33–7.

" 'also be procured.' " Ibid., p. 824.

362   "dish of muffins." Ibid., plate opposite p. 337.

"Filleted Soles." Ibid., p. xli.

"337,000 copies." IMB, *BOHM,* London, 1880, p. iv.

" 'In the World.' " Ibid., p. viii.

363   *"Book of Household Management."* Elizabeth David, "Isabella Beeton and Her Book," *Wine and Food,* Spring 1961, reprinted in *An Omelette and a Glass of Wine,* pp. 305–6.

" 'lovebirds and chrysanthemums.' " Ibid., p. 306.

"Italian biscuit." IMB, *BOHM,* London, 1888, pp. 1073–9.

"will be welcome." Ibid., p. 10.

"the name of her house." Ibid., pp. 10–11.

364   "number of settings." Ibid., p. 10.

" 'increase and strengthen.' " Ibid., p. 8.

"from their nurse." Ibid., p. 11.

" 'excruciating to witness.' " Ibid., p. 1326.

" 'have a chance.' " Ibid., p. 1263.

365   "Parrot Pie?)" Ibid., pp. 1259–60.

"make of them." Ibid., p. 704.

" 'a fair trial.' " Ibid., p. 1617.

"Warwick House." IMB, *BOHM,* London, 1906, vol. 1, p. vii.

366   " 'comfortable man.' " Ibid., pp. v–vi.

" 'wont to furnish.' " Ibid.

" 'wherever necessary.' " Ibid., p. 106.

" 'world contains.' " Ibid., pp. vi–vii.

367   "she would want to?)" Ibid., p. 106.

"twenty." Ibid., pp. 383–91.

"and 1906." Ibid., pp. 342–9.

368   "even deckchairs." Ibid., ch. lxvi.

" 'King George III.' " Ibid., pp. 1687–8.

" 'for her activities.' " Ibid., p. 9.

" 'meeting fresh people.' " Ibid., p. 11.

"most seasonal ingredients." Ibid., p. 85.

369   " 'Average Cost.' " Ibid., p. 128.

INTERLUDE

370   "into the twentieth century." Of course, there is nothing to stop someone adjusting information from a cookery book, but such is the authority of the printed word that it seems less likely.

373 "more than a whisper." The final pre-war edition was actually published in
1915.

" 'A Beetonian Reverie' in 1923." The essay was first published in *I for One*,
London, 1923, and reprinted in J. B. Priestley, *Essays of To-Day and Yesterday*, London, 1926.

"as 'Mrs. Beeton.' " Ibid., p. 56.

374 " 'the same time.' " Ibid.

" 'honoured by posterity.' " Ibid., pp. 56–7.

" 'parents to himself.' " Letter, MMB to C. A. Cliffe, November 1, 1937, BBC.
MMB is quoting the response he had given to Joan Easdale in 1933.

375 "with their wives." L. Du Garde Peach, *Meet Mrs. Beeton, A Culinary Comedy
Specially Written for the Microphone*, 1934, original script, MMB Archive.

" 'their wives.' " See p. 197.

376 " 'here this evening.' " L. Du Garde Peach, *Meet Mrs. Beeton, A Culinary
Comedy in One Act*, London, 1934.

" 'will live for ever!' " Ibid.

" 'turn to Cookery.' " It was, of course, poetry and not fiction which Miss
Acton hoped to publish with Longman.

" 'financial interests involved.' " Letter, MMB to Colin H. Deane, January
25, 1941.

" 'you might desire.' " Letter, R. Burns to MMB, January 1, 1934.

"to life." *Radio Times*, December 29, 1933.

377 "had caused him." Letter, MMB to Colin H. Deane, January 25, 1941.

"to soothe him." Letter, C. A. Cliffe to MMB, November 1, 1937.

"was not withdrawn." Letter, MMB to C. A. Cliffe, November 1, 1937, BBC.

" 'Miss Easdale's play.' " Letter, E. E. Dorling to C. A. Cliffe, November 3,
1937, BBC.

"were all present." "Meeting with Revd. E. E. Dorling on 4th Nov. 1937,"
Memo, BBC.

" 'matter I fancy.' " Memo from D. H. Rose, November 17, 1937, BBC.

378 "foot-slogging fieldwork." Joan Easdale, In Search of Mrs. Beeton, broadcast
BBC Home Service, April 21, 1938, transcript, BBC.

"summer of 1864." See pp. 311–12.

379 "alert readers wonder." Noël Coward, "Copy of a Letter From Noël Coward," Nancy Spain, *Why I'm Not a Millionaire*.

"by her crinoline)." Nancy Spain, "In Search of A Great Aunt," broadcast
Northern Ireland Home Service, November 23, 1948, transcript, BBC.

" 'been published before.' " Author's Note, Nancy Spain, *The Beeton Story*.

" 'licentious London life.' " Nancy Spain, *Mrs. Beeton and her Husband*,
p. 50. Nancy Spain, *The Beeton Story*, p. 42.

380 " 'the truth known.' " Ibid., Author's Note.

"five feet two inches." Nancy Spain, "The Real Mrs. Beeton," *Ideal Home*,
November 1960. Nancy Spain, *The Nancy Spain Colour Cookery Book*, London, 1963, unnumbered page.

" 'melancholy head.' " Ibid.

" 'money at the races.' " Ibid., December 1960.

" 'I am not exaggerating.' " Ibid.

381   " 'and appraisal.' " Sarah Freeman, *Isabella and Sam*, p. 272.

" 'a charming man.' " Nancy Spain, "The Real Mrs. Beeton," *Ideal Home*, October 1960.

"ghastly second cousin." Letter, Isabel Farebrother to Marjorie Killby, December 2, 1960.

382   " 'work in Fleet-street.' " Peter Forster, *Daily Express*, October 20, 1960.

"for Nancy Spain." Nancy Spain, *Why I'm Not a Millionaire*, p. 142.

" 'foul.' " Letter, Isabel Farebrother to Patricia Fisher, October 26, 1960.

" 'people naturally took notice.' " Elizabeth David, "Isabella Beeton and her Book," p. 302.

383   " 'like Parson Woodforde.' " Elizabeth David, *The Best of Eliza Acton*, pp. 33–4.

"philistine Victorians." Anyone who follows trends in popular history, whether on the television screen or in publishing, will have noticed that the past five years have been all about re-imaging the Georgians as people who spent their time shopping, eating and having sex—as thoroughly modern, in fact.

" 'face for it.' " Clarissa Dickson Wright interviewed by Sue Lawley, *Desert Island Discs,* broadcast BBC Radio 4, September 3, 1999.

384   " 'Mrs. Raafald [*sic*].' " Clarissa Dickson Wright, "Did Mrs. Beeton Cook the Books?" "Night and Day," *Mail on Sunday,* May 7, 2000.

386   "that very moment." Jyll Bradley, *Before Beeton—The Eliza Acton Story,* broadcast BBC Radio 4, December 11, 2001. Transcribed by Kathryn Hughes. Reprinted by permission of PFD on behalf of Jyll Bradley © Jyll Bradley 2000.

"Isabella and Sam." Tony Coult, *Isabella—The Real Mrs. Beeton,* broadcast BBC Radio 4, January 27, 2001.

387   " 'tavern-owner's grandson!' " Ibid., unpublished script, titled "Bella, the Story of Mrs. Beeton," Scene 2a.

" 'Where is it?' " Ibid., Scene 10a.

388   " 'function at will.' " Ibid., Scene 9.

389   " 'ever dreamed of.' " Alison Neil, *Bella—The Story of Mrs. Beeton,* 1988.

"does survive." William Sansom, synopsis, *Sam and Bella,* 1962–3, Frith Banbury.

391   "play the main role." Information supplied in conversation with Frith Banbury, 2005.

" 'book of recipes.' " Letter, Frith Banbury to William Sansom, undated, Frith Banbury.

"Irwin Ferry." I am grateful to Irwin Ferry for letting me view the video of the 1991 Epsom Playhouse performances.

392   " 'find another place!' " Michael Hurd, *Mrs. Beeton's Book: a Music-Hall Guide to Victorian Living,* London, 1983.

"for Mrs. Beeton." Rosemary Hill, *Mrs. Beeton,* broadcast BBC 2, January 12, 1970, transcript, BBC.

393   *"New Millennium."* John Harle (with Charlotte Cory), *Mrs. Beeton's Christmas Plum Pudding,* London 2000.

394   " 'novelty sounds.' " John Harle in interview with Michael Stewart, 2000, *www.imageandmusic.com*

      " 'of Lord Reith.' " John Harle, *Mrs. Beeton's Christmas Plum Pudding,* inside front cover.

395   "at fever pitch." This book is going to press in the wake of Jamie Oliver's campaign to improve school dinners.

      "roam at will." Indeed, the promotional photographs with which Fresh & Wild decorates its walls are, in many ways, simply modern versions of the Frontispiece of *BOHM,* 1861.

      "generic product." I have been lucky enough to acquire much market research material conducted by various agencies around the Mrs. Beeton brand. I have, however, been asked not to identify the companies concerned.

398   "reconciliation Belfast charity." After Lady Fisher's early death, the book was published by her daughter, Sally Grylls, *On the Beeton Track, Delicious Recipes from the Family Home of Mrs. Beeton's Great-Niece,* in aid of the "Women Caring Trust," London, 1998.

      "husband and children." Patricia Fisher, "Great-Aunt Isabella," many draft versions, MMB Archive, family.

      "the main source." *The Making of Mrs. Beeton,* broadcast Radio 4, 1990.

      "after tea." Alison Neil, *Bella—The Story of Mrs. Beeton,* unpublished script.

      "Mrs. English." Tony Coult, *Isabella—The Real Mrs. Beeton,* Scene 15.

      "A Domestic Goddess." Nigella Lawson, *How to Be A Domestic Goddess,* London, 2000.

399   "1950s childhood." Cheryl Mendelson, *Home Comforts: The Art & Science of Keeping House,* New York, 1999, p. 5.

SELECT BIBLIOGRAPHY

Primary Sources

MANUSCRIPT SOURCES

ARCHIVES

Personal and Institutional Records

Frith Banbury Papers, Harry Ransom Research Center, University of Texas at Austin.

BBC Written Archives, BBC Written Archives Centre, Caversham.

Mayson Moss Beeton Archive, currently in the possession of Kathryn Hughes.

Mayson Moss Beeton Archive, family, held by various Beeton and Dorling descendants.

Brompton Cemetery Records, Brompton, London.

Brook Collection, Bexhill Museum.

Coke-Steel Family Papers, Trusley.

Heinz Archive & Library, National Portrait Gallery, London.

H. Montgomery Hyde Papers, Public Record Office of Northern Ireland, Belfast.

Society of Licensed Victuallers Records, Licensed Victuallers' School, Ascot.

Morell MacKenzie Papers, Wellcome Library for the History and Understanding of Medicine, London.

Norwood Cemetery Records, Lambeth Archives Department, London.

Portraits of the Residents of Epsom, Ashtead and Elsewhere, Surrey History Service, Woking.

Richmond Golf Club Archive, Petersham.

Herbert Beerbohm Tree Collection, University of Bristol Theatre Collection, Bristol.

United Race Course Ltd. Records, Surrey History Service, Woking.

Westminster Fire Office Records, Westminster.

PARISH AND OTHER LOCAL RECORDS

Parish, electoral, guild, council and estate records were consulted at the following
Record Offices:
Centre for Kentish Studies, Maidstone.
Croydon Local Studies and Archive.
Cumbria Record Office, Carlisle.
East Sussex Record Office, Lewes.
Essex Record Office, Chelmsford.
Family Records Centre, London.
Guildhall Library, London.
London Metropolitan Archives, London.
Medway Archives, Strood.
Suffolk Record Office, Bury St. Edmunds.
Surrey History Service, Woking.
Westminster Record Office, London.
West Sussex Record Office, Chichester.

PRINTED SOURCES

Magazines published by S. O. Beeton
Boy's Own Journal
Boy's Own Magazine
Boy's Penny Paper
Englishwoman's Domestic Magazine
The Queen
Sporting Life
The Weekly Dispatch
The Young Englishwoman

Magazines published by S. O. Beeton for Weldon & Co.
Myra's Journal of Dress and Fashion
Myra's Mid-Monthly Journal and Children's Dress

**Editions and Derivations of the *Book of Household Management*, prepared by
Isabella Beeton and published by S. O. Beeton**
Beeton, Isabella, ed., *Beeton's Book of Household Management*, 24 parts, London,
    1859–1861.
Beeton, Isabella, (ed.), *Beeton's Book of Household Management*, London, 1861.
Beeton, Isabella, (ed.), *Beeton's Book of Household Management*, London, 1863.
Beeton, Isabella, *The Englishwoman's Cookery Book*, London, 1863.
Beeton, Isabella, *Mrs. Beeton's Dictionary of Everyday Cookery*, London, 1865.

Editions and derivations of the *Book of Household Management* prepared after Isabella Beeton's death and published by Ward, Lock and Cassell in chronological order (represents a tiny fraction of total)

Beeton, Isabella, *Book of Household Management*, London, 1869.

Beeton, Mrs., *All About Cookery: a collection of practical recipes*, London, 1871.

Beeton, S. O., *Beeton's Book of the Laundry: or, The Art of Washing, Bleaching and Cleansing*, London, 1871.

Beeton's Book of Cottage Management, London, 1873.

Beeton, Isabella, *Book of Household Management*, London, 1880.

Ward and Lock's Home Book: a Domestic Cyclopaedia, being a companion volume to "Mrs. Beeton's Book of Household Management," London, 1881.

Beeton's Cookery Book for the People, and Housekeeper's Guide to Comfort, Economy and Health, London, 1886.

Beeton, Isabella, *Book of Household Management*, London, 1888.

Beeton, Isabella, *Book of Household Management*, London, 1892.

Beeton, Mrs., *The Best of Household Management*, London, 1895.

Beeton, Isabella, *Book of Household Management*, London, 1906.

Mrs. Beeton's Penny Cookery Book, London, 1908.

Mrs. Beeton's Sixpenny Cookery, London, 1910.

Beeton, Isabella, *Mrs. Beeton's Book of Household Management*, London, 1915.

Beeton, Isabella, *Mrs. Beeton's Book of Household Management*, London, 1923.

Mrs. Beeton's Family Cookery Book, London, 1923.

Beeton, Mrs., *Mrs. Beeton's Jam-making, including preserves, marmalades, pickles and home-made wines*, London, 1924.

Beeton, Mrs., *Mrs. Beeton's Hors d'Oeuvres and Savouries, including cheese and egg dishes, sandwiches, salads and dressings*, London, 1925.

Beeton, Isabella, *Mrs. Beeton's Household Management*, London, 1936.

Beeton, Mrs., *Mrs. Beeton's Household Management*, London, 1950.

Beeton's Dictionary of Practical Recipes and Everyday Information, London, 1971.

Mrs. Beeton's Easy-to-Cook Book, London, 1973.

Mrs. Beeton's Favourite Party Dishes, London, 1973.

Mrs. Beeton's Favourite Recipes—Specially Selected for Damart Customers, London, 1985.

Mrs. Beeton's Favourite Recipes, London, 1985.

Breakfast With Mrs. Beeton: Hearty Fare, London, 1990.

Sunday Lunch With Mrs. Beeton: Traditional Classics, London, 1990.

Mrs. Beeton's Complete Book of Puddings & Desserts, London, 1990.

A Gift from Mrs. Beeton: Edible Delights, London, 1991.

Supper With Mrs. Beeton, Delicious Spreads, London, 1991.

Mrs. Beeton Traditional Housekeeping Today, partwork, London, 1990–1993.

Mrs. Beeton's Traditional Christmas, London, 1993.

Beeton, Mrs., *A Victorian Alphabet of Every Day Recipes*, London, 1993.

Supper With Mrs. Beeton, London, 1991.

A Picnic With Mrs. Beeton, London, 1991.

Mrs. Beeton's Healthy Eating, London, 1994.

Mrs. Beeton's Christmas Menus: Creative Ideas For Festive Entertaining, London, 1996.

Essential Beeton: Recipes and Tips From The Original Domestic Goddess, London, 2004.

Books published by S. O. Beeton—both as Clarke & Beeton and S. O. Beeton—in chronological order (represents a tiny fraction of total)

Mackenzie, Eneas, *The Emigrant's Guide to Australia,* London, 1853.

Strickland, Jane Margaret, *Adonijah, a tale of the Jewish Dispersion,* London, 1856.

Motley, John Lothrop, *The Rise of the Dutch Republic,* London, 1859.

Beeton's Historian, London, 1860.

The Book of Garden Management and Rural Economy, London, 1861.

Beeton, S. O., and Sherer, John, *Beeton's Dictionary of Universal Information,* London, 1862.

Beeton's Book of Birds, London, 1862.

Beeton's Book of Poultry and Domestic Animals: showing how to rear and manage them, in sickness and in health, London, 1862.

Edgar, John G., *How I Won My Spurs,* London, 1863.

Illustrated Family Bible, London, 1863.

Edgar, John G., *Cressy and Poitiers,* London, 1865.

Greenwood, James, *Curiosities of Savage Life,* London, 1865.

Wood, Frederick, *Beeton's Cricket Book,* London, 1866.

Books written or edited by S. O. Beeton but published by Ward, Lock [& Tyler] in chronological order (represents a tiny fraction of total)

[Beeton, S. O.], *London's Great Outing: the Derby Carnival,* London, 1868.

Beeton's Dictionary of Universal Biography, London, 1869.

Beeton's Book of Needlework, London, 1870.

Beeton's Guide Book to the Stock Exchange and Money Markets, London, 1870.

Beeton's Medical Dictionary, London, 1871.

Beeton's Hand-Book of the Law Relating to Divorce and Matrimonial Causes, London, 1871.

[Beeton, S. O., Dowty, A. A., and Emerson, S. R.], *The Coming K—,* London, 1872.

[Beeton, S. O., Dowty, A. A., and Emerson, S. R.], *The Siliad or The Siege of the Seats,* London, 1873.

Beeton's Complete Letter-Writer For Ladies, London, 1873.

Books written or edited by S. O. Beeton but published by Weldon & Co.

[Beeton, S. O., Dowty, A. A., and Jerrold, E. D.], *Jon Duan. A Twofold Journey with Manifold Purposes,* London, 1874.

[Beeton, S. O., Dowty, A. A., and Jerrold, E. D.], *Edward VII. A Play on the Past and Present Times with a View to the Future,* London, 1876.

Critical and Creative Interpretations of Mrs. Beeton's life

Aldridge, Ron, *Me and Mrs. Beeton,* London, 2000.

Bradley, Jyll, *Before Beeton: The Eliza Acton Story,* London, 2001.

Coult, Tony, *Isabella—The Real Mrs. Beeton,* London, 2001.

Du Garde Peach, L., *Meet Mrs. Beeton, A Culinary Comedy Specially Written for the Microphone,* London, 1934.

———. *Meet Mrs. Beeton, A Culinary Comedy in One Act,* London, 1934.

Easdale, Joan, "In Search of Mrs. Beeton," London, 1938.

Ferry, Irwin, Russell, Brian, and Bird, Clifford, *The Way To A Man's Heart,* London, c.1963.

Fisher, Patricia, "Great Aunt Isabella," many versions, 1960–1990?

Freeman, Sarah, *Isabella and Sam,* London, 1977.

Harle, John (with Cory, Charlotte), *Mrs. Beeton's Christmas Plum Pudding,* London, 2000.

Hill, Rosemary, *Mrs. Beeton,* London, 1970.

Hurd, Michael, *Mrs. Beeton's Book, a Music-Hall Guide to Victorian Living,* London, 1984.

Hyde, H. Montgomery, *Mr. and Mrs. Beeton,* London, 1951.

Lunt, Lucy (producer), "The Making of Mrs. Beeton," London, 1990.

Neil, Alison, *Bella—The Story of Mrs. Beeton,* London, 1988.

Priestly, J. B., "A Beetonian Reverie," in *Essays of To-Day and Yesterday,* London, 1926.

Sansom, William, with Banbury, Frith, *Sam and Bella,* synopsis, London, 1962–3.

Spain, Nancy, *Mrs. Beeton and Her Husband,* London, 1948.

———. *The Beeton Story,* London, 1956.

NEWSPAPERS

Carlisle Journal
Chelmsford Chronicle
Daily Express
Daily Mail
Daily Mirror
Evening News
Evening Standard
Figaro
London Figaro
Mail on Sunday
Manchester Guardian
Morning Advertiser
Morning Chronicle
Morning Herald
Portsmouth Evening News
The Sporting Life
The Star
The Telegraph
The Times

MAGAZINES

La Belle Assemblée
Country Life
English Woman's Journal
The Family Friend
Hearth and Home
Ideal Home
Illustrated London News
The Ladies' Cabinet
The Ladies' Companion
Lady's Monthly Museum
The Ladies' Treasury
La Lanterne
Le Moniteur de la Mode
Myra's Threepenny Journal
Myra's Journal of Dress and Needlework
Myra's Mid-Monthly Journal and Children's Dress
National Review
Radio Times
Saturday Review
Tatler

DIRECTORIES

Kelly's Post Office Directory
Pigot's Directory
Post Office Directory
Robson's Directory

BOOKS

Acton, Eliza, *Modern Cookery for Private Families,* London, 1845.

Adams, Samuel, and Sarah, *The Complete Servant,* London, 1825.

Agogos, pseud. [Charles Day], *Hints on Etiquette and the Usages of Society, with a glance at bad habits,* London, 1834.

Anon., *Can This Be Beeton? A Guinness Gallimaufry,* London, 1956.

Anon., *The Busy Hives Around Us,* London, 1861.

Beeton, M., *Myra's Cookery Book, Enlarged and Revised by Mrs. M. Beeton,* London, n.d.

Boase, Frederic, *Modern English Biography,* 6 vols., Truro, 1892–1921.

Brillat-Savarin, Jean-Anthelme, *The Physiology of Taste,* Paris, 1825, trans. Anne Drayton, as *The Philosopher in the Kitchen,* London, 1988, 1994.

Cobbett, William, *Cottage Economy,* London, 1823.

Copley, Esther Hewlett, *Cottage Comforts,* London, 1825.

———, *The Housekeeper's Guide: or, a plain and practical system of cookery,* Manchester, 1834.

Dickens, Charles, *Oliver Twist,* London, 1837–39.

[Dowty, A. A., and Jerrold, E. D.], *Finis,* London, 1877.

Ellis, Sarah Stickney, *The Daughters of England, their Position in Society, Character and Responsibilities,* London, 1842.

———, *The Wives of England, their Relative Duties, Domestic Influence, and Social Obligations,* London, 1843.

Field, Richard, *Country Advantages, or, Pinner, within Harrow, Middlesex: Woodriding's Estate,* London, 1855.

Francatelli, Charles Elmé, *The Modern Cook,* London, 1846.

———, *Plain Cookery for the Working Classes,* London, 1861.

Frith, W. P., *My Autobiography and Reminiscences,* London, 1890.

Glasse, Hannah, *The Art of Cookery Made Plain and Easy,* London, 1747.

Hemans, Felicia, *The Homes of England,* London, 1827.

Hill Hassell, Arthur, *Food and Its Adulterations,* London, 1855.

Hyde, H. Montgomery, *Mr. and Mrs. Beeton,* London, 1951.

Kitchiner, William, *The Cook's Oracle,* London, 1817.

———, *The Housekeeper's Oracle,* London, 1829.

MacKenzie, Morell, *The Fatal Illness of Frederick the Noble,* London, 1888.

Marshall, Mrs., *Mrs. A. B. Marshall's Cookery Book,* London, n.d.

Marston, Edward, *After Work: Fragments from the Workshop of an Old Publisher,* London, 1904.

Pascoe, David (ed.), *Charles Dickens, Selected Journalism,* 1850–70, London, 1997.

"An Outsider," *The Blatant Beast Loose Again!, Thoughts (in verse) on the 14th Beeton's Animal (ie Beeton's Christmas Annual), in the year 1874,* Bury St. Edmunds, 1874.

Philp, R. K., *The Practical Housewife,* London, 1855.

Parkes, Mrs. [Frances], *Domestic Duties,* London, 1825.

Patmore, Coventry, *The Angel in the House,* London, 1854.

Raffald, Elizabeth, *The Experienced English Housekeeper,* Manchester, 1769.

[Rundell, Maria], *Domestic Cookery by a Lady,* London, 1806.

Simpson, John, *A Complete System of Cookery,* London, 1806.

Smiles, Samuel, *Self-Help: with illustrations of Character and Conduct,* London, 1859.

Ruskin, John, *Sesame and Lilies,* London, 1865.

Soyer, Alexis, *Gastronomic Regenerator,* London, 1846.

———, *Modern Housewife,* London, 1851.

———, *The Pantropheon,* London, 1853.

———, *A Shilling Cookery for the People,* London, 1854.

Spain, Nancy, *Why I'm Not a Millionaire,* London, 1956.

————, *The Nancy Spain Colour Cookery Book*, London, 1963.

Stowe, Charles Edward, *Harriet Beecher Stowe*, London, 1889.

Stowe, Harriet Beecher, *Uncle Tom's Cabin*, London, 1852.

————, *The Key to Uncle Tom's Cabin*, London, 1853.

Tayler, William, *Diary of William Tayler, Footman, 1837*, London, 1998.

Ude, Louis Eustache, *The French Cook*, London, 1827.

Vizetelly, Henry, *Glances Back Through Seventy Years*, 2 vols., London, 1893.

Walsh, J. H., *A Manual of Domestic Economy*, London, 1856.

Warren, Mrs. [Eliza], *How I Managed My Household On Two Hundred Pounds A Year*, London, 1864.

————, *My Lady-help, and What She Taught Me*, London, 1877.

Webster, Thomas, *An Encyclopaedia of Domestic Economy*, London, 1844.

Woolley, Hannah, *The Gentlewoman's Companion*, London, 1673.

Secondary Sources

BOOKS

Adburgham, Alison, *Women in Print, Writing Women and Women's Magazines from the Restoration to the Accession of Queen Victoria*, London, 1972.

Ames, Kenneth L., *Death In the Dining Room and Other Tales of Victorian Culture*, Philadelphia, 1992.

Andrews, James, *Reminiscences of Epsom*, Epsom, 1904.

Anon., *Derby Day 200*, London, 1979.

Attar, Dena, *A Bibliography of Household Books Published in Britain 1800–1914*, London, 1987.

Aylett, Mary, and Ordish, Olive, *First Catch Your Hare*, London, 1965.

Barnes, Julian, *The Pedant In The Kitchen*, London, 2004.

Beetham, Margaret, *A Magazine of Her Own? Domesticity and Desire in the Woman's Magazine 1800–1914*, London, 1996.

Ballaster, Ros, Beetham, Margaret, Frazer, Elizabeth, and Hebron, Sandra, *Women's Worlds: Ideology, Femininity and the Woman's Magazine*, Basingstoke, 1991.

Branca, Patricia, *Silent Sisterhood*, London, 1975.

Briggs, Asa, *Victorian Things*, London, 1988.

Burnett, John, *Plenty and Want*, London, 1966.

Caine, Barbara, *Victorian Feminists*, Oxford, 1992.

Coleman, D. C., *The British Paper Industry 1495–1860*, Oxford, 1958.

Cowan, Ruth Schwartz, *More Work for Mother: the Ironies of Household Technology from the Open Hearth to the Microwave*, London, 1983.

Cunnington, Phillis, and Lucas, Catherine, *Costumes for Births, Marriages and Deaths*, London, 1972.

David, Elizabeth, *A Book of Mediterranean Food*, London, 1950.

————, *French Provincial Cooking*, London, 1960.

————, Elizabeth, *An Omelette and a Glass of Wine*, London, 1986.

Davidoff, Leonore, and Hawthorn, Ruth, *A Day in the Life of A Victorian Domestic Servant*, London, 1976.

Davidoff, Leonore, and Hall, Catherine, *Family Fortunes: Men and Women of the English Middle Classes: 1780–1950*, London, 1987.

Davidoff, Leonore, *Worlds Between: Historical Perspectives on Gender and Class*, Oxford, 1995.

Davidson, Alan (ed.), *On Fasting and Feasting*, London, 1988.

Davidson, Caroline, *A Woman's Work is Never Done: a History of Housework in the British Isles, 1650–1950*, London, 1982.

Davies, Jennifer, *The Victorian Kitchen*, London, 1989.

Dilnot, George, *The Romance of the Amalgamated Press*, London, 1925.

Dorling E. E., *Epsom and the Dorlings*, London, 1939.

Driver, Elizabeth, *A Bibliography of Cookery Books Published In Britain, 1875–1914*, London, 1989.

Drotner, Kirsten, *English Children and Their Magazines, 1751–1945*, London, 1988.

Druett, Walter W., *Pinner Through the Ages*, London, 1937.

Dyos, H. J., and Wolff, M. (eds.), *The Victorian City*, 2 vols., London, 1973.

Eliot, George, *Middlemarch*, London, 1871–72.

Ferguson, Marjorie, *Forever Feminine: Women's Magazines and the Cult of Femininity*, Aldershot, 1985.

Fernandez-Armesto, Felipe, *Food: A History*, London, 2001.

Fitch, Charles, *History of the Pattenmakers' Company*, Bungay, 1926.

Flint, Kate, *The Woman Reader, 1837–1914*, Oxford, 1993.

Fox, Celina (ed.), *London, World City, 1800–1840*, London, 1992.

Freeman, Sarah, *Mutton and Oysters: The Victorians and Their Food*, London, 1989.

Garvin, J. L., with Julian Amery, *The Life of Joseph Chamberlain*, 6 vols., London, 1932–69.

Gerard, Jessica, *Country House Life: Family and Servants, 1815–1914*, Oxford, 1994.

Girouard, Mark, *Victorian Pubs*, London, 1975.

Gordon, Caroline, and Dewhirst, Wilfrid, *The Ward of Cripplegate in the City of London*, London, 1985.

Grigson, Jane, *English Food*, London, 1974.

Grylls, Sally, *On the Beeton Track, Delicious Recipes from the Family Home of Mrs. Beeton's Great Niece*, in aid of the "Women Caring Trust," London, 1998.

Hammerton, James, *Cruelty and Companionship: Conflict in Nineteenth-Century Married Life*, London, 1992.

Hardyment, Christina, *Behind The Scenes: Domestic Arrangements in Historic Houses*, London, 1992.

Hartley, Dorothy, *Food in England*, London, 1954.

Hayden, Deborah, *Pox: Genius, Madness, and the Mysteries of Syphilis*, New York, 2003.

Haywood, Ian, *The Revolution in Popular Literature: Print, Politics and the Press*, Cambridge, 2004.

Hermes, Joke, *Reading Women's Magazines: An Analysis of Everyday Media Use,* Cambridge, 1995.

Horgan, Donal, *Echo After Echo, Killarney and Its History,* Cork, 1988.

———, *The Victorian Visitor in Ireland, Irish Tourism 1840–1910,* Cork, 2002.

Horn, Pamela, *The Rise and Fall of the Victorian Servant,* Stroud, 1975.

Horsefield, Margaret, *Biting The Dust: The Joys of Housework,* London, 1997.

Howe, Ellic, *From Craft to Industry,* London, 1946.

Hughes, Kathryn, *The Victorian Governess,* London, 1993.

———, *George Eliot: The Last Victorian,* London, 1998.

Hunn, David, *Epsom Racecourse,* London, 1973.

Jones, W. A. B., *Hadleigh Through The Ages,* Ipswich, 1977.

Kelly, Ian, *Cooking for Kings,* London, 2003.

Kent, Robin, *Aunt Agony Advises: Problem Pages through the Ages,* London, 1979.

King, Andrew, and Plunkett, John (eds.), *Popular Print Media, 1820–1900,* London, 2004.

Kunzle, David, *Fashion and Fetishism: A Social History of the Corset, Tight-lacing and Other Forms of Body Sculpture,* New Jersey, 1980.

Kynaston, David, *The City of London,* 2 vols., London, 1994.

Langland, Elizabeth, *Nobody's Angels: Middle-Class Women and Domestic Ideology in Victorian Culture,* Ithaca, 1995.

Lawson, Nigella, *How To Be A Domestic Goddess,* London, 2000.

Leavitt, Sarah A., *From Catherine Beecher to Martha Stewart: A Cultural History of Domestic Advice,* London, 2002.

Lees-Milne, James, *A Mingled Measure,* London, 1994.

Lehmann, Gilly, *The British Housewife,* Totnes, 2003.

Levine, Phillipa, *Victorian Feminism,* London, 1987.

Lewis, Charles Thomas Courtney, *The Picture Printer of the Nineteenth Century: George Baxter 1804–67,* London, 1911.

Lewis, Lesley, *The Private Life of a Country House,* Newton Abbot, 1980.

Liveing, Edward, *Adventure in Publishing: The House of Ward, Lock, 1854–1954,* London, 1954.

Llewellyn-Jones, Derek, *Sexually Transmitted Diseases,* London, 1990.

Loudon, Irvine, *The Tragedy of Childbed Fever,* London, 2000.

Luard, Elizabeth, *Still Life,* London, 1998.

McBride, Theresa, *The Domestic Revolution: the Modernisation of Household Service in England and France, 1820–1920,* London, 1976.

MacDonough, Giles, *Brillat-Savarin: The Judge and His Stomach,* London, 1992.

Maclean, Virginia, *A Short-Title Catalogue of Household and Cookery Books Published in the English Tongue, 1701–1800,* London, 1981.

Mannix & Whellan, *History, Gazeteer and Directory of Cumberland,* Beverley, 1847.

Markham, Lester V., *Victorian Insolvency: Bankruptcy, Imprisonment for Debt and Winding-up in Nineteenth-century England,* Oxford, 1995.

Mason, Laura, with Brown, Catherine, *Traditional Foods of Britain: A Regional Inventory,* Totnes, 1999.

Masson, David, *Memories of London in the Forties,* London, 1908.

Mendelson, Cheryl, *Home Comforts: The Art & Science of Keeping House*, New York, 1999.

Mennell, Stephen, *All Manners of Food, Eating and Taste in England and France from the Middle Ages to the Present*, Oxford, 1985.

Mitzman, Max E., *George Baxter and the Baxter Prints*, Newton Abbot, 1978.

Monsarrat, Ann, *And The Bride Wore*, London, 1973.

Morris, Helen, *Portrait of a Chef: Alexis Soyer*, Cambridge, 1938.

Morris, R. J., and Rodger, Richard (eds.), *The Victorian City: A Reader in British Urban History 1820–1914*, London, 1993.

Nellen, Petra (ed.), *Die Vergangenheit ist die Schwester der Zukunft*, Heidelberg, 1996.

Oxford Dictionary of National Biography, Oxford, 2004.

Nowell-Smith, Simon, *The House of Cassell, 1848–1858*, London, 1958.

Nown, Graham, *Mrs. Beeton: 150 Years of Cookery and Household Management*, London, 1986.

Oriel, J. D., *The Scars of Venus*, London, 1994.

Pacher, Maurice, *Bookbinders of Victorian London*, London, 1991.

Palmer, Arnold, *Movable Feasts: Changes in English Eating Habits*, London, 1952.

Parson, William, and White, William, *A History, Directory and Gazetteer of Cumberland and Westmorland*, Leeds and Newcastle, 1829.

Paston-Williams, Sara, *The Art of Dining, A History of Cooking and Eating*, London, 1993.

Pirbright, Peter, pseud., *Off the Beeton Track*, London, 1943.

Platzker, David, and Wyckoff, Elizabeth, *Hard Pressed: 600 Years of Print and Process*, New York, 2000.

Porter, Roy, *London: A Social History*, London, 1994.

Quayle, Eric, *Old Cookery Books*, London, 1978.

Ray, Elizabeth, *Alexis Soyer, Cook Extraordinary*, Lewes, 1991.

Reynolds, Jan, *Birket Foster*, London, 1984.

Richards, Thomas, *The Commodity Culture of Victorian England: Advertising and Spectacle, 1851–1914*, Stanford, 1990.

Robertson Scott, J. W., *The Story of the Pall Mall Gazette*, London, 1950.

Rodger, Richard, *Housing in Urban Britain 1780–1914: Class, Capitalism and Construction*, Basingstoke, 1989.

Russell, Leonard (ed.), *The Saturday Book*, London, 1945.

Salter, G. H., *A Watcher At The City Gate*, London, 1956.

Sambrook, Pamela A., *The Country House Servant*, London, 1999.

Sambrook, Pamela, and Brears, Peter (eds.), *The Country House Kitchen, 1650–1900: Skills and Equipment for Food Provisioning*, Stroud, 1996.

Seaman, L. C. B., *Life in Victorian London*, London, 1973.

Secord, James A., *Victorian Sensation*, Chicago, 2000.

Seth-Smith, Michael, *Lord Paramount of the Turf*, London, 1971.

Seth-Smith, Michael, and Mortimer, Roger, *Derby 200*, Enfield, 1979.

Sheppard, Francis, *London 1808–1870: The Infernal Wen*, London, 1971.

Shoemaker, Robert B., *Gender in English Society, 1650–1850: The Emergence of Separate Spheres?*, London, 1998.

Smiles, Aileen, *Samuel Smiles and His Surroundings,* London, 1956.

Sparvel-Bayley, J. A., *Swanscombe Local History,* Gravesend, 1875.

Spongberg, Mary, *Feminizing Venereal Disease: The Body of the Prostitute in Nineteenth Century Medical Discourse,* London, 1997.

Steele, Valerie, *The Corset,* London, 2001.

Tannahill, Reay, *Food In History,* London, 1973.

Theophano, Janet, *Eat My Words,* Basingstoke, 2002.

Stevenson, R. S., *Morell Mackenzie: The Story of a Victorian Tragedy,* London, 1946.

Trimble, William Tennant, *The Trimbles & Cowens of Dalston Cumberland,* Carlisle, 1935.

Vicinus, Martha (ed.), *Suffer and Be Still,* Indiana, 1972.

——— (ed.), *A Widening Sphere: Changing Roles of Victorian Women,* Indiana, 1977.

Visser, Margaret, *Much Depends on Dinner: The Extraordinary History, Mythology, Allure and Obsessions, Perils and Taboos, of an Ordinary Meal,* London, 1986.

———, *The Rituals of Dinner,* Toronto, 1991.

Walkowitz, Judith, *Prostitution and Victorian Society: Women, Class and the State,* Cambridge, 1980.

Weedon, Alexis, *Victorian Publishing: The Economics of Book Production for a Mass Market 1836–1916,* Aldershot, 2003.

Weir, Harrison, *The Poetry of Nature,* London, 1861.

Williams, Roger L., *Henri Rochefort: Prince of the Gutter Press,* New York, 1966.

White, Cynthia L., *Women's Magazines, 1693–1968,* London, 1970.

White, Florence, *Good Things in England,* London, 1932.

Wilson, C. Anne, (ed.), *Luncheon, Nuncheon and Other Meals: Eating With The Victorians,* Stroud, 1994.

ARTICLES AND CHAPTERS IN BOOKS

Beetham, Margaret, "Women and the Consumption of Print," in Shattock, J. (ed.), *Women and Literature 1800–1900,* Cambridge, 2001.

Brears, Peter, "A La Française, the Waning of a Long Dining Tradition," in Wilson, C. Anne (ed.), *Luncheon, Nuncheon and Other Meals: Eating with the Victorians,* Stroud, 1994.

Burchill, Julie, "The New Domesticity," *Guardian,* November 4, 2000.

Buzard, James, "Home Ec With Mrs. Beeton," *Raritan* 17, Fall 1997.

Clarke, Patricia, "The Lost Suburb of Woodridings," *Pinner Local History Society Newsletter,* August 1982.

Daunton, Martin, "London and the World," in Celina Fox (ed.), *London, World City, 1800–1840,* London, 1992.

David, Elizabeth, "The Excellence of Eliza Acton," in Elizabeth Ray (ed.), *The Best* of *Eliza Acton*, London, 1968, reprinted in Alan Davidson (ed.), *On Fasting and Feasting*, London, 1988.

————, "Isabella Beeton and Her Book," *Wine and Food*, Spring 1961, reprinted in *An Omelette and a Glass of Wine*, London, 1986.

Grace, P. A., "Doctors Differ over the German Crown Prince," *BMJ*, December 19, 1992.

Hall, Catherine, "The Early Formation of Victorian Domestic Ideology," in *White, Male and Middle Class, Explorations in Feminism and History*, London, 1992.

Howsam, Leslie, "Women's History/Women's Books: Recovering the Nineteenth-Century Mrs. Beeton," unpublished paper, University of Windsor.

Humble, Nicola, Introduction, *Mrs. Beeton's Book of Household Management*, Oxford, 2000.

Hunter, Lynette, "Proliferating Publications: The Progress of Victorian Cookery Literature," in Wilson, C. Anne (ed.), *Luncheon, Nuncheon and Other Meals: Eating with the Victorians*, Stroud, 1994.

James, Louis, "Tom Brown's Imperialist Sons," *Victorian Studies*, vol. 17, 1973.

Lane, Harriet, "Twenty Years On, We're Still in Love with Delia," *Observer*, December 12, 1999.

Mars, Valerie, "A La Russe: The New Way of Dining," in Wilson, C. Anne (ed.), *Luncheon, Nuncheon and Other Meals: Eating with the Victorians*, Stroud, 1994.

McKirdy, Michael, "Who Wrote Soyer's Pantropheon?," *Petit Propros Culinaire* 29, 1988.

Vickery, Amanda, "Golden Age to Separate Spheres? A Review of the Categories and Chronology of English Women's History," *Historical Journal* 36, 1993.

Wilson, C. Anne, "Meal Supply and Food Patterns in Victorian England," in Wilson, C. Anne (ed.), *Luncheon, Nuncheon and Other Meals: Eating With the Victorians*, Stroud, 1994.

UNPUBLISHED THESES

England, Sally, "Saving Mayson Beeton: a neglected discrete collection within the English Heritage Library," unpublished MA dissertation, University of London, 2002.

Taylor, Kate, "Syphilis and Marriage during the Fin de Siècle: Doctors, Society and Women Novelists," unpublished MA dissertation, University of London, 1977.

ACKNOWLEDGEMENTS

If this book has taught me anything, it is about the kindness of strangers. Over the past five years I have been consistently touched by the way that people who do not know me have allowed me to invade their lives in my search for Mrs. Beeton. I have lost count of the times that I have been picked up from stations, given lunch, allowed to search through attics and photographs, shown around parish churches, and listened to politely as I droned and drooled about the woman—and her husband—who had become pretty much my only topic of conversation.

In the certain knowledge that I am forgetting people whose help was invaluable, I would particularly like to thank the following.

Mary Rose Myrtle and her husband Brigadier Andrew Myrtle for welcoming me into their lives and allowing me to poke about under their sofa and in their lumber room in the pursuit of more clues about Mary Rose's great-great-aunt. I am particularly grateful for the extended loan of Isabella Beeton's diary for 1860. From the other side of the family, Major Christopher Beeton, MBE, was an exemplary host and shared with me his encyclopaedic knowledge of S. O. Beeton's publications. I am indebted too to Isobel Sutton, née Beeton, whose genealogical skills allowed me to get to grips with the complicated Beeton family tree much faster than I would otherwise have done and whose generosity and enthusiasm were inspiring.

Other members of the extended Dorling and Beeton families who were kind beyond the call of duty include Neil and Rosemary Roberton, Richard Dorling, Anthony Dorling, Philippa Dorling, Lady (Sally) Grylls, Mary Geneste Holliday, Suzanne Ivey. I am also most grateful to Joan Browne, Peter Giles, and J. Keith Killby for sharing with me their family connections to the Beeton story.

The following people helped me hugely with their Beeton-related expertise and, in some cases, access to archives and artefacts too: Ann Bagnall of the Southover Press, Bill Beeton, Doug Brown, John Crouch, David and Jane Coke-Steel, Susan Dixon, Sally England, Jeremy Harte of Bourne Hall Museum, Frank Hermann, Dr. Leslie Howsam of the University of Windsor, Canada, Bridget Jones, Rupert Shortt, Ion Trewin of the Orion Group, Hon. Georgina Stonor, John Wilson, Julia Woolger.

Others who kindly answered my queries include Penny Aldred, Kathryn Bellamy of Goodwood, John Coles of Richmond Golf Club, Ian Crump of the Licensed Victuallers' School, Irwin Ferry, Anna Greening of Queen's College, Sarah Freeman, Dr. Terry Rogers of Marlborough College, Celia Robertson, Kate Thirkell, Dr. Christopher Tyler of Harrow School. Thank you to Dr. Peter Franklin for his immaculate work transcribing assorted documents, and to Jane Frank for bringing her nutritional expertise to bear on Mrs. Beeton's menu plans.

I would probably not have been able to purchase all the Beetons' extant letters, together with a great deal of associated material, had it not been for the generous brokering of Elizabeth Drury, who had planned to write a book about the Beetons herself together with Philippa Lewis. I am more grateful to her than I can say. Thanks, too, to Nicola Beauman and Mr. N for agreeing to sell me their individual caches of material.

Isabella Beeton's German schooldays posed a problem to someone as insular as me, so I am very grateful to Esther Galan for accompanying me to Heidelberg, the city where both she and Isabella went to school, and to Stephen Smithson for translating academic texts and letters, often at a moment's notice. Thanks too to Dorothee Sadgrove for re-visiting her childhood tongue to help me with colloquial German.

At the University of East Anglia I am indebted to Colleen Clayton, Aileen Davies, Professor Richard Holmes, Professor Vic Sage and Professor Clive Scott, in addition to all the "Lifers" who have passed through the MA in Lifewriting over the past five years. I am delighted to be able to prove to them that—look, really—I was making progress with Mrs. B. all along.

As far as more material help goes, I am grateful to the Arts Council of England for giving me a Writers' Award and to the Society of Authors for granting me funds from The Authors' Foundation.

Thank you to the staff of the following record offices, libraries and museums: BBC Written Archives Centre, Brompton Cemetery, the National Portrait Gallery, the Public Record Office of Northern Ireland, the Wellcome Library for the History and Understanding of Medicine, Lambeth Archives Department, Surrey History Service, the Theatre Collection, Bristol University, Westminster Record Office, Centre for Kentish Studies, Cumbria Record Office, East Sussex Record Office, Essex Record Office, Family Records Centre, Guildhall Library, Medway Archives, London Metropolitan Archives, Suffolk Record Office, West Sussex Record Office, the Bodleian, the British Library, the London Library. For permission to quote from their copyrighted work I am grateful to Jyll Bradley, Frith Banbury, Tony Coult, Michael Hurd, Alison Neill and Michael Stewart. Thank you to David Higham Associates and John Murray for permission to quote from the work of the late James Lees-Milne. Thanks go too to Nick Werner Laurie for allowing me to quote from the work of Nancy Spain. Despite strenuous efforts, it may be that I have failed to locate and acknowledge a particular copyright holder. If anyone believes this to be the case, I would be delighted to put this right in any subsequent edition.

Writing is an intensely solitary process, but producing this book has turned out to be a joyously collaborative one. I am, as always, very grateful to my agent Rachel Calder of the Tessa Sayle Literary Agency, for not minding when I don't speak to her for years and then demand her attention on a daily basis. Thanks go too to Julia Kreitman at The Agency for easing Mrs. Beeton towards the screen. At Fourth Estate, Mitzi Angel has been a wonderfully astute editor while Catherine Heaney has been an extraordinarily unflappable one. For giving my commas and endless parentheses more expert care than Samuel Beeton ever lavished on Isabella's in the *Book of Household Management,* I am very grateful to Morag Lyall, Sue Phillpott and Patricia Hymans. For making the book look so beautiful, thank you Rachel Smyth and Rose Cooper. And my gratitude also goes to Robin Harvie for handling publicity for the book so deftly.

Last of all, my thanks are due to the following additional friends who have taken what has felt like a genuine interest in the book's progress: Richard Adams, Midge Gillies, Amanda Lambert, Jo Mears, Karen Merrin and Judy Sadgrove. I am sorry to have been such an absent presence for quite so long.

June 2005

INDEX

Page references in *italic* refer to illustrations.

Kathryn Hughes is the author of *George Eliot: The Last Victorian,* which won the James Tait Black Memorial Prize for Biography, and *The Victorian Governess,* which remains the standard text on the subject. Educated at Oxford University, she holds a Ph.D. in Victorian studies and now teaches biographical studies at the University of East Anglia. She is a *Guardian* book critic.

A NOTE ON THE TYPE

The text of this book was set in Sabon, a typeface designed by Jan Tschi-
chold (1902–1974), the well known German typographer. Based loosely on
the original designs by Claude Garamond (c. 1480–1561), Sabon is unique
in that it was explicitly designed for hotmetal composition on both the
Monotype and Linotype machines as well as for filmsetting. Designed in
1966 in Frankfurt, Sabon was named for the famous Lyons punch cutter
Jacques Sabon, who is thought to have bought some of Garamond's matrices
to Frankfurt.

Composed by North Market Street Graphics,
Lancaster, Pennsylvania
Printed and bound by Berryville Graphics,
Berryville, Virginia
Designed by M. Kristen Bearse